THE LYRIC AGE OF GREECE

To
MARY
in memory of all our journeys

THE
LYRIC AGE
OF GREECE

ANDREW ROBERT BURN

Reader in Ancient History
at the University of Glasgow

MINERVA PRESS

Contents

PART I
GREECE AT THE DAWN OF HISTORY

PART II
THE EXPANSION OF GREECE

PART III
THE REVOLUTION IN GREEK SOCIETY

Contents

PART IV

THE REVOLUTION IN GREEK THOUGHT

Maps

Foreword to Second Impression

THE welcome call for a second impression has given me the opportunity to introduce a number of corrections, for most of which I thank Mr D. M. Lewis. I have also taken the opportunity to introduce references to a number of recent publications, especially the valuable annotated bibliography of Soviet archaeological work on the Black Sea colonies by E. Belin de Ballu (1965; see p. 127), and the publication of *Chronicles of Chaldaean Kings* in the British Museum by D. J. Wiseman (1956; see pp. 130, 244).

Glasgow, 1967.   A. R. BURN

Foreword

THE attempt to produce an account of the Greek world in the seventh and sixth centuries B.C. requires no apology. These centuries were the time of the revolution in Greek civilisation, from which classical Greece, the first Europe, emerged to play a unique part in the human enterprise. To understand this age is of importance for the understanding of human history in general.

The age is also that of the first historical Europeans known to us as characters: the early lyric poets, known to us from their own words, partly from papyrus fragments but still chiefly in quotation by later Greek scholars. To present these colourful characters in their historical context is also an objective worth while for its own sake. Papyri have increased what we know of them; and archaeology, the chief growing-point of classical studies today, has vastly increased what we know of their world. Archaeology has confirmed in general the picture of Greek colonial expansion given by our scanty remains of the ancient literature; it confirms even scraps of information given by an Avienus or a John Malalas, and we are able to put back into our histories some details rejected out of hand by nineteenth-century criticism.

I have tried to produce a picture of the expansion and transformation of the Greek world, as one process, in one volume of moderate size. (It would have taken less time to produce a much longer book.) This is a difficult task. The history, being, like that of the modern west on a vaster scale, that of many states and their colonies, imposes to some extent the necessity of presenting the material in a geographical order, region by region. I have tried to bring out the close connection between the oversea activity of the chief colonising cities and their fortunes at home (pp. 85ff, 218ff, etc.), and would gladly have kept the accounts of Greek culture in Western Sicily or the Black Sea for treatment later in the book, in a more chronological order; but this seemed, when attempted, to involve breaking the history into too many and too short sections, making troublesome demands upon the mental agility of the reader. The problem, insoluble in the last analysis, is presented by the fact that the historical process, taking place in all the dimensions of space and time, has to be presented in the one dimension of a single 'thread of narrative'. Some repetitions will be found which, after reflection, I have allowed to stand.

The notes, it is hoped, will provide a sufficient guide to the ancient sources and to the chief recent contributions to the subject, especially in English. In them I have departed, in some matters, from current practice. I have restricted the use of the abbreviation *op. cit.*, having found it sometimes to require troublesome page-turning by the reader who wishes to look up a reference; and I have often referred to the works of lost historians or poets by reference to the later authors who quote them, rather than to their Collected Fragments. Much more than half of all our evidence, outside of Herodotos, is preserved by a mere handful of late Greek writers; and it is not only instructive but positively a saving of trouble to refer to such passages as those of Clement of Alexandria on Plagiarism in the Classics, Diogenes on the Seven Sages, Athenaios on Ancient Luxury or on Slavery, where passages from earlier writers are so learnedly collected, to be 'fragmented' with equal assiduity by modern scholarship. The more widely scattered fragments can still be traced most conveniently in the collections, especially the great and indispensable work of Jacoby. For poets of whom little is preserved, such as Kallinos or Phokylides, I have not always thought it necessary to give references; any fragment can be quickly found in the Loeb edition (Edmonds) or that of Diehl; for the philosophers, I have given references to Kranz' edition of Diels' *Vorsokratiker* ('DK').

Greek names have as a rule been transliterated, not Latinised; it seems a pity to change the euphonious endings -os, -on into -us, -um, etc.; no one uses a completely consistent Latin system, which would include such forms as Solo, Cimo, Clisthenes, Lesbus; nor does consistency appear to be a cardinal virtue in dealing with names which, in any case, we Anglicise in pronunciation. I have used, however, the familiar forms of some of the most familiar names, such as Corinth, Cyrene, Aeschylus, Thucydides (but Thk. in abbreviation), and, after some hesitation, Delphi. Long vowels are indicated (by ^) in the Index. And traditional early dates, of whose accuracy I have grave doubts, have been given with the warning note 'tr.'; see further pp. 403-8.

This book has been long in gestation. Germs of it exist in essays awarded the Charles Oldham Prize (1924) and Arnold Historical Essay Prize (1927) at Oxford, and the Cromer Greek Prize for 1926 (this last published in *JHS* XLVII and XLIX). The conception of it goes back to the reading of Herodotos and the lyric poets (subject of my Charles Oldham essay), the teaching of R. H. Dundas and J. L. Myres, and much undergraduate conversation with my senior contemporary, the late and greatly to be lamented Alan Blakeway. Its appearance, optimistically foreshadowed in the Preface to my *World of Hesiod* (1936), has been delayed by the production of other books and articles, published and unpublished, teaching and other work, World War II, etc.; but the delay has probably been for the best. The intervening years have been rich in the publication of many distinguished works from which I have, I hope, profited; they have brought opportunities or, sometimes, the necessity, of wider travel, with visits to sites and museums ranging from Ensérune and Ampurias to Beirut and Odessa, and wider experience, including that of the years 1940-46 in Greece and the Near East, which was extremely educative. When Messrs Edward Arnold commissioned the present work, the text which had been half-finished in 1939 no longer satisfied me, and the book as it stands dates from the years 1954 to 1959. I have made great efforts to bring it up to date. I hope that it may be found useful by many Greek-less readers, and have kept their needs consistently in view.

I am deeply indebted to scholars who, amid the considerable pressure of their own work, have found time to read the whole of this book in proof and suggested many improvements in detail: to Professor A. Andrewes, Mr R. H. Dundas, Mr Russell Meiggs and Mr W. G. Forrest; to Dr M. Miller, whose own work on the methods of early Greek chronographers is in preparation for publication; also to Professor E. R. Dodds, who kindly read the chapters on religious developments. A few points made by them are distinguished, in the footnotes, by initials, but more have been tacitly adopted by modification of the notes or text. For any blemishes that remain, it is no mere convention to say that they have no responsibility.

Abbreviations

acc.	*accessit*
Aelian, *VH*	*Varia Historia*
AJ	*Antiquaries' Journal*
AJA	*American Journal of Archaeology*
Anakr.	Anakreon
A.P.	*Anthologia Palatina*
Apollod.	Apollodoros
Ap. Rhod.	Apollonios Rhodios
Ar.	Aristotle
Arch. Anz.	*Archaeologische Anzeiger*
Arrian, *P.P.E.*	*Periplous Pontou Euxeinou*
Ath.	Athenaios
Ath. P.	*Athenaion Politeia*
ATL	*Athenian Tribute Lists*, ed. Merrit, Wade-Gery and McGregor
BCH	*Bulletin de Correspondance Hellénique*
Bilabel, *Ion. Kol.*	*Die Ionische Kolonisation*
BM	British Museum
BSA	*Annual of the British School at Athens*
Burnet, *EGP*	*Early Greek Philosophers*
Buschor, *Gr. Vm.*	*Griechische Vasenmalerei*
CAH	*Cambridge Ancient History*
CIG	*Corpus Inscriptionum Graecarum*
Clem. Alex. *Strom.*	Clement of Alexandria: *Stromateis*
CQ	*Classical Quarterly*
CR	*Classical Review*
D.H.	Dionysios of Halikarnassos
Dion. Byz.	Dionysios of Byzantion
Ditt. Syll³ (or SIG³)	Dittenberger: *Sylloge Inscriptionum Graecarum*, edn. 3.
DK	Diels-Kranz: *Fragmente der Vorsokratiker*
D.L.	Diogenes Laertius
D.S.	Diodorus Siculus
*EB*¹¹	*Encyclopaedia Britannica*, 11th edn.
Edmonds, *E & I*	*Elegy and Iambus* (Loeb series)
Edmonds, *LG*	*Lyra Graeca* (Loeb series)
Eus. Arm.	Eusebios, Armenian Version
Euseb., *Praep. Ev.*	Eusebios: *Praeparatio Evangelica*
FGH	(Jacoby) *Fragmente der Griechische Historiker*
FH	F. Clinton, *Fasti Hellenici*
FHG	(Müller) *Fragmenta Historicorum Graecorum*
fl.	*floruit*
fr.	fragment(s)
Frazer, *GB*	*Golden Bough*

GG	(Beloch, Busolt) *Griechische Geschichte*
GGM	*Geographici Graeci Minores*
GQ	see Plutarch
Harpokr.	Harpokration
Hdt.	Herodotos
Head, *HN*	*Historia Nummorum*
Herakl. Pont.	Herakleides Pontikos
Hesp.	*Hesperia*
H.H.	Homeric Hymn(s)
Iamb.	Iamblichos
IG	*Inscriptiones Graeci*
Il.	(Homer) *Iliad*
ILN	*Illustrated London News*
Jacoby, *FGH*	*Fragmente der Griechische Historiker*
JHS	*Journal of Hellenic Studies*
JNES	*Journal of Near Eastern Studies*
Jos.	Josephus
JRS	*Journal of Roman Studies*
Kyr. Pol.	*Kyrenaion Politeia*
LAAA	*Liverpool Annals of Archaeology and Anthropology*
LP	*Lakedaimonion Politeia*
Meyer, *GdA*	*Geschichte des Altertums*
Müller *FHG*	*Fragmenta Historicorum Graecorum*
Nat. Hist. ⎱ N.H. ⎰	(Pliny) *Natural History*
Nik. Dam. ⎱ N.D. ⎰	Nikolaos Damaskenos
Not. d. Scavi	*Notizie degli Scavi*
N.S.	New Series
Od.	(Homer) *Odyssey*
O.P.	Oxyrhynchus Papyrus
Paus.	Pausanias
Phot. *Lex.*	Photius: *Lexicon*
Pl.	Plato
Plut., GQ	Plutarch: *Greek Questions*
Plut., Mor.	Plutarch: *Moralia*
Polyain.	Polyainos
Polyb.	Polybios
PW	Pauly-Wissowa: *Realencyclopädie*
q.	quoting or quoted (according to context)
Revue des Et. Gr.	*Revue des Etudes Grecques*
Rostovtzeff, *IGSR*	*Iranians and Greeks in S. Russia*
s.a.	*sub anno*
Sall.	Sallust
S.B. ⎱ Steph. Byz. ⎰	Stephanos Byzantinos
SEG	*Supplementum Epigraphicum Graecum*
SIG³	see Dittenberger
Soph. O.C.	Sophokles: *Oedipus Coloneus*
Stob., Fl.	Stobaeus: *Florilegium*
Str.	Strabo

s.v.	*sub voce*
Tac. *Ann.*	Tacitus: *Annals*
TAPA	*Transactions of the American Philological Association*
Thk.	Thukydides
Tod, *GHI*	Tod: *Greek Historical Inscriptions*
tr.	traditional(ly)
Tyrt.	Tyrtaios
v.l.	varia lectio
WD	(Hesiod) *Works and Days*
WG	(Dunbabin) *Western Greeks*
Xen. *Anab.*	Xenophon: *Anabasis*
Xen. *Hell.*	Xenophon: *Hellenika*

PART I

Greece at the Dawn of History

CHAPTER I

The Legacy of the Bronze Age

WHEN Sophocles was born, about 495, Hesiod was perhaps not yet two hundred years dead. So little time separates classical Athens, whose 'modernity' is a commonplace, from the poet of the Early Iron Age, the only early Greek writer to commend to us a number of odd but world-wide superstitions, and the poet whose advice on sea-faring starts from the premise that the best thing is not to do it at all.[1] The object of this book is, while describing the culture of Greece in this age of swift change, and relating it to its political and economic environment, to try also to account for the unique course which Greek development took.

The period is that which Karl Jaspers has called the *Achsenzeit*, the age which, not only in Greece but in Judaea, China, India and almost certainly Persia, where chronological evidence is scanty, witnessed the rise of the first philosophies and the first higher religions (religions with predominantly ethical content, and of potentially universal application). I have suggested elsewhere that, rather than attribute this astonishing coincidence to chance, we might tentatively account for it by the fact, itself remarkable, that in all these areas it took about the same time for the first human civilisations to work themselves out, for the precocious bronze-age cultures to decline and fall, and for cultures of a new 'second generation' to arise from their ruins.[2]

The discovery of copper and then of bronze did not greatly increase the potentialities of neolithic agriculture; for centuries the metals were too scarce and costly to be within the reach of peasants. But they did provide those who were able to get them with superior weapons.[3] Also, since the chief centres of population were on the alluvial soil of

---

[1] WD 746ff, 646ff; cf. Burn, *World of Hesiod*, 45ff.

[2] In *History*, N.S. XLI (1956), pp. 1-15 (review of Toynbee's *Study of History*); esp. pp. 9ff.

[3] See V. Gordon Childe, *What Happened in History*, and now his *Prehistory of European Society* (Penguin Books, 1958).

the great rivers, while the nearest mines were at a distance (e.g. in Sinai or the Taurus mountains), a premium was placed, for the first time in human history, on the development of long-distance trade. Those potentates who were able to organise and protect the trade in metals between Sinai and the Nile or on the much longer route from Meso-potamia to the Taurus were in a position to dominate large populations, to exercise unprecedented power, and to have the first draft on the luxury materials, gold, silver, lapis lazuli and jewels, which came from the mining areas.

The decline of the bronze-age empires set in when power corrupted its holders, when monarchies became oppressive, when class-divisions appeared and widened, and when the kingdoms, which probably dared not arm their proletariats, fell, some of them more than once, before barbarian tribes in which every man was still a warrior: Kassites and Chaldaeans, Hyksos and Ethiopians, Achaians and Dorians. The dis-covery of iron-working was not, as was once believed, the *cause* of the decline; it was made, probably in eastern Asia Minor, when the decay was already far advanced; but the availability of iron, a metal whose ores are far more plentiful than those of copper (let alone tin), meant the availability of swords or spears for all; and that meant that, when at last the great wars and the great migrations ended in exhaustion, giving place to petty bickerings between neighbouring states, and when (given the virtual impregnability of walled towns except to overwhelm-ing force) security and prosperity began to increase again, the basic preconditions of power were more widely distributed.

The new, early iron-age world had also a firm basis in the arts and crafts of peace. The continuity of the old traditions of fine art, which had ministered to the luxury of princes, had almost everywhere been broken; only in Egypt were they preserved by slavish imitation, where-as in Syria and Assyria, Asia Minor and the Aegean entirely new styles arise. But of the arts of daily life, little was lost; in house-building and fortification, metalwork, ship-building and farming, and in star-lore, important to the farmer and the sailor, accumulated by priests and known also to sages like Hesiod (a seafarer's son), the new settled societies began not where the Bronze Age had begun, but where it left off.

In thought also there was an opportunity for a new beginning. In the close-knit society of a barbarian tribe or a peasant community there was no room for thought on other than traditional lines. On the basis of prehistoric religion and magic (the traditions and practice of which, the world over, have much in common; the natural expression of man's untutored thought[4]) the Bronze Age had evolved the idea of personal gods, conceived as living in heaven the same kind of life as kings and queens and their families, who were their favourites on earth. But these high gods perhaps nowhere, and certainly not in Greece, commanded quite the affection with which peasants continued to worship, with prayer and magical rites, their local and earth-bound powers. While the great kingdoms stood, they kept their prestige; even an Akhnaton, Pharaoh of Egypt, could gain no effective support for a higher religion of his own invention. But when the old monarchies fell on evil days, there was a 'crisis of faith' for those thousands whom city life had de-tribalised – a crisis of which we have the evidence in pessimistic litera-ture, both from Mesopotamia and from Egypt; and when times became a little better again, there was an audience for those prophets and sages who, in a world still full of trouble, thought out or felt themselves inspired to declare the will of a righteous and merciful God; such thoughts as, according to the Hebrew tradition, had already inspired the bronze-age heroes Moses in Egypt and, still earlier, Abraham in Ur.[5]

In Greece, the Minoan civilisation had grown rich partly, it seems, by supplying metals from the west to Egypt and Syria. Pottery from the Lipari Islands shows Aegean sailors establishing a post there (hardly for the sake of land!); an Egyptian bead or two, and the relief-carvings of a Mycenaean axe and dagger at Stonehenge, show the remote radiation of Mediterranean culture affecting the rich Bronze Age of Wessex.[6] Thereafter, things took much the same course there as further east. The legends tell of Minos the great sea-king and law-giver, the personifica-tion of his age, but also a tyrant; the great sea-raids on Egypt, the epic tradition of the sacking of Thebes and Troy, and late bronze-age im-provements in weapons and in fortification tell of an age of increasing war and insecurity. Already far back in the Bronze Age, Greek Achaians had taken over the chief centres of a civilisation founded by southern people, speaking, as place-names show, a language akin to one spoken in

---

[4] Argued in *World of Hesiod*, chap. III.
[5] On Egypt and Mesopotamia, cf. Frankfort, Wilson and Jacobsen, *Before Philosophy*, esp. chaps. III, IV, VII.
[6] Cf. Bernabo Brea, *Sicily before the Greeks*; Childe, *Preh. of European Society*, 159f; cf. 105, 116, etc.

southern Asia Minor[7]; at the end of that age the Dorians overwhelmed their aristocratic culture, warlike indeed, but grown rich and flimsy in turn. Crete, Rhodes, the southern islands and the coasts of the Peloponnese fell under the dominion of the newcomers, with their dialects of north-western antecedents; Greek of the most ancient type survived only in inland, mountainous Arcadia, cut off from the sea except in the south-west, and in distant Cyprus, where the Dorians, arriving in an age when trade with the east no longer offered rich prizes, did not follow them.

Further north, Athens, with her Acropolis heavily fortified and equipped with a secret stairway down to a spring,[8] outrode the storms both of an attack by the Dorians of the Peloponnese and, earlier, of the coming of the Boiotoi, the northern people who, when the Achaians sacked Kadmeian Thebes, moved in to occupy the lands of the vanquished.[9] It may well have been the prestige of this resistance that led to Athens, before the beginning of her documented history, becoming the acknowledged capital of Attica, a 'country' of 1000 square miles, in which local legends, citadels and royal tombs indicate that there had been local princes, in the Tetrapolis of Marathon, at Thorikos down the peninsula and at Eleusis.[10] While elsewhere almost every known Mycenaean palace perished by fire, and many of their sites were deserted – survivors having taken to the hills, and invaders settling outside the ruins – and while the pottery-series at many sites shows a clear break, at Athens there was continuity and some shadow of surviving culture. At Athens, later tradition claimed, refugees from the Peloponnese found shelter, and were presently organised into expeditions that sailed to conquer new homes in Ionia; and at Athens there appeared, perhaps in the eleventh century (dating is difficult, in the absence of contact with Egypt) the first trace of a new culture, capable of bold innovations: the practice of cremation (which Homer anachronistically ascribes to the heroes of the Trojan War), and the beginning of

[7] Centuries before 1400 B.C., certainly if the Ventris decipherment of the Mycenaean Linear B documents is substantiated, and almost certainly on the archaeological evidence alone.

[8] Broneer in *Hesperia*, VIII (1939); Mrs Hill, *The Ancient City of Athens*, 12f.

[9] Thus the *Iliad* consistently speaks of Kadmeioi in Boiotia at the time of the Theban Wars, Boiotoi at the time of the Trojan War: cf. iv, 385, 388, 391, v, 804, 808, with ii, 494, 510, xvii, 597, etc.

[10] Cf. Thk. ii, 15 (Eleusis); Philochoros in schol. on Euripides, *Hippolytos*, 35; Plut. *Theseus*, ch. 13 (Pallene); Apollod. i, 9, 4, ii, 4, 7, iii, 15, 1 (Thorikos); Str. viii, 338 (Marathon).

a new art-style in the satisfactory shapes and chaste, confident decoration, with much use of concentric circles, of Protogeometric pottery.[11]

In Ionia, as the refugee settlements consolidated into strong, walled cities, enslaving or pushing back the native inhabitants, there was another achievement: the development of epic poetry. Epic developed, as the Greeks believed, and as we may believe on the analogy of other 'heroic ages', from ballads such as Homer represents being sung by Achilles himself in his hut before Troy, and by bards in kings' palaces in the *Odyssey*, celebrating the stirring events of recent times as Greek countrymen have continued to do, even down to the Second World War. That the Ionian states, as well as the probably earlier Aiolic cities to the north of them, started as refugee settlements, as a direct consequence of the Dorian drive into the Peloponnese, there has never been any very strong reason to disbelieve, though archaeological evidence from Ionia proper is still lacking; the discovery of protogeometric pottery at Smyrna confirms the early date of that city, at least in its earliest phase, before it was captured from the Aiolians by the Ionians of Kolophon.[12] In Ionia a new class of *rhapsôdoi* grew up, probably after the whittling away of the kingly power by the groups of noble families of royal descent: a class of reciters, declaiming now in market-places and at festivals, where men of several cities might compete in music and athletics, and no longer accompanying themselves on the lyre, but leaning on the staff which supported them also on their professional wanderings.

Probably late in the Dark Age, though for lack of evidence the Greeks themselves estimated his age most variously, appears the great genius, Homer, who superseded and ultimately caused the loss of all earlier chronicle-epics or ballad sequences, by his invention of the great epic with a plot; preserving a literary unity, even while painting on a wide canvas a vivid picture of the scene (not a chronicle) of the whole Trojan War and of the society that waged it.[13]

[11] V. R. d'A. Desborough, *Proto-Geometric Pottery* (Oxford, 1952), esp. pp. 296-303.

[12] J. M. Cook, 'Archaeology in Greece', *JHS* LXXII and in BSA Report, 1950-51, pp. 40-41 and figs. 9, 10: The deposit 'proved to be a rich one, consisting of more than one stratum, and seems to have covered a considerable span of time; . . . the pottery corresponds closely to Attic Protogeometric . . . A few scraps of Mycenaean vases came to light as strays in Protogeometric and latest prehistoric levels.' Ionian conquest, from Ephesos and Kolophon, Str. xiv, 634, q. Mimnermos (fr. 12 Diehl). Early geom. near Ephesos, Cook, 'Arch. in Greece', *JHS* LXXIII and BSA Report, 1951-52, p. 39.

[13] Amid the enormous literature, cf. esp. Wade-Gery, *The Poet of the Iliad*, Lecture III; Bowra, *Homer and his Forerunners* (Andrew Lang Lecture, Nelson, Edinburgh, 1955).

The importance of Homer can hardly be exaggerated. It is not only that, as a story-teller, he has been loved and imitated to this day; not only that his style influenced all later Greek poetry. Homer and his age also gave to Greece a pattern of conduct: the conception of the Hero. In a sense it is the discovery, often in part lost and made again, of the dignity of the individual.

Homer's heroes are in a predicament typical, we may suppose, of the end of the Bronze Age. Their society is insecure. Homer himself, for all his enjoyment of the beauty and good things of life, is deeply pessimistic. Life and its glory are fleeting; and the ghost-life to which he looks on in the House of Hades is that of a gloomy limbo, whose only pleasure is the remembrance of earth; a life, to disbelieve in which was, to later Epicureans, a liberation. Even on earth, the fortunate man is one who has some good fortune mixed with ill; the unfortunate man has trouble only: 'Hunger drives him wandering over the earth.' 'There is no creature more miserable than a man,' says the Father of Gods and Men himself. Nor is religion a consolation. Homer's religion is not wholly amoral; Zeus may send disasters, such as rain at harvest-time, upon men who 'with violence give crooked judgments'. But as they are generally represented, the gods merely favour their favourites and take revenge on those who have forgotten to sacrifice to them.[14] As Xenophanes of Kolophon was to say, 'Homer and Hesiod have ascribed to the gods all deeds that are shameful and dishonourable among men: theft and adultery and deceiving one another' (p. 343). Indeed, it is to the credit of Homer and his patrons that they do not take such gods as these very seriously. The gods are stage machinery in the traditional stories; but when the scene is set in Olympos itself, more often than not the object is comic relief of a crude kind. The poet who, in the *Odyssey*,[15] gives the tale of Ares and Aphrodite caught in a net in their adulterous embrace, and laughed at merrily by the other gods, invited in by Hephaistos the outraged husband, cannot have been in any very grave fear of divine vengeance. There is likeness as well as contrast in the attitude of Elijah, when he suggests that, if Baal is not answering callers, he is probably asleep, or away, or out hunting. The fact is that the gods of the Bronze Age, conceived in the likeness of earthly rulers, became less worshipful the more they became the heroes of stories; and

[14] *Od.* xi, 488ff; *Il.* xxiv, 525ff; xvi, 385ff (and cf. *Od.* ix, 269ff); *Il.* ix, 533ff; Burn, *Minoans, Philistines and Greeks*, pp. 202f, 245ff. [15] viii, 266ff.

the legends themselves, originally in some cases religious myths, developing out of agrarian or other ritual, became, especially when transported by migrants away from their original homes, more and more *merely* themes for poets to embroider; in effect, fairy-tales. The gods had been detribalised along with their worshippers.

Ultimately, Greeks began to attempt to fill the gap thus left, by means of new religious cults, as well as by science and religious or irreligious philosophy. In religion they achieved less than the peoples of some other regions; in philosophy, as much as any; and in laying the foundations of a scientific view of the world their contribution was unique. But for any of these activities the state of society was not yet ready in Homer's time; and meanwhile, indeed through all the years since the fall of the great palaces, men had to confront the realities of a dangerous life and a probably early death without spiritual comfort either from priest or philosopher, god or man; but alone, like Homer's Hector, the most sympathetic of his creations, between the city wall and the advancing foe. Like other peoples in a similar spiritual vacuum, the pagan Northmen, for example, or the makers of the Border Ballads, the migrant Ionians faced the worst, and survived. It is reasonable to suppose that their pre-Homeric poetry was as fierce, tragic and stoical as the ballads or the sagas. But it meant much to Greece that late in the Dark Age a poet of transcendent genius summed up the heroic code. Achilles, choosing to carry out his duty under the code by avenging his friend, though he knows that his own death must follow; Hector, determined to fall 'not without effort and not without honour', since fall he must; the resource and the determination of Odysseus to live and reach home, remained as an inspiration. Hector's famous repudiation of gloomy oracles: 'One omen is best – to fight for your country' is learned by every Greek school child at the present day. Plato's Socrates, quoting, when he might have escaped death, the example of Achilles as scriptural justification for 'remaining in the position where God has placed me', as he stood where he was stationed by a human general, is the outstanding example of what the moral code of Homer meant to classical Greece.[16]

Homer's and Hesiod's works were also 'the Bible of the Greeks' in that they systematised and codified the relationships of the dozen great

---

[16] *Il.* xviii, 80-129; xxii, 304f; xii, 243. Plato, *Apology*, 28 (Socrates quotes *Il.* xviii, 95ff). Cf. Bowra, *Heroic Poetry*, chaps. iii, xiii.

gods and innumerable local deities of the classical pantheon. After the chaos of the great migrations, there must have been many identifications of gods familiar to men in their old homes with those found in the new; sometimes with odd results, as when the name of Zeus, the Indo-European sky-god, was given to the dying god of Crete, or that of Artemis, the Mistress of Beasts and virgin huntress of Arcadia, to the many-breasted, Asian mother-goddess (because she also was a mistress of beasts), 'great Artemis of the Ephesians'. The epic poets are rightly credited by Herodotos with having given order and system to the resulting extremely complex polytheism.[17] But their code of ethics, limited and even barbarous as it is, was a nobler work.

A whole civilisation had risen and fallen to produce Homer. Without the splendours and the social disintegration of the Bronze Age, and without its fall, the individualist and humanist code of the Hero could not have come into being. *Tantae molis erat.*

[17] ii, 53.

CHAPTER II

The Cities

THE early Greeks of whom history has most to say, that is the aristocratic leaders in the city-states, are therefore in no proper sense 'primitive'. If the word is to be used of them at all, it is in the strictly *im*proper sense, applied to Italian art, heir to the Byzantine tradition, just before the renaissance of humanism. That a similar movement from traditionalism and convention in art to freedom and humanism took place in Greece, between 700 and 400, in similar external circumstances, but *without* any rediscovery of the older Aegean art, is a fact on which it is stimulating to meditate. Primitive in a stricter sense were the peasants, the agrarian foundation of society; many classical religious rituals, especially in the worship of Demeter, Persephone and Dionysos, are based on magic, of kinds widely paralleled among savages and modern peasants and probably as old as the neolithic age.[1] But the aristocrats, who claimed descent from the Homeric heroes, worshipped rather the Homeric gods, to whom the chief temples of the cities were dedicated; and it is reasonable to suppose that, where Homer's poetry was recited, many of them shared also Homer's life-loving but sombre views.

Prudent men kept on good terms with the gods, with periodic sacrifice and outward respect; Homer himself indicated that it was dangerous to do otherwise. Xenophon, the disciple of Socrates, shows much simple piety, especially in hours of danger. Nobody disbelieved in the existence and power of the Olympians. It was scandalous and socially unsafe to be a declared atheist, even in Athens in the late fifth century; though Homer's ribald stories of the gods had their counterparts in comedy. And the festivals of the gods were the occasions of all those rejoicings which marked the high tides of Greek life: the choral dancing and singing, the athletics, the new poems (and old), the dedication of works of art: great bronze caldrons on their three-legged stands, for

[1] Cf. my *World of Hesiod*, chaps. II, III, for refs. and full discussion.

use in the sacrificial feasts; brightly painted terracotta images, ranging from great cult-statues of the god himself to the innumerable small figures of his (or her) sacred animal, or votives of the worshipper, vowed to do him honour in his courts for ever; the annual new frock for the city's goddess, embroidered with tender care and with pride in their skill, by the daughters of the noblest families. Greek poetry depicts the scene, above all the early hexameter 'Homeric' *Hymn to Apollo*:

> Lord of the Silver Bow, Far-Shooting Apollo. . . . Many are thy temples and shady groves; and dear to thee are all the peaks and jutting crags of the high hills, and rivers that flow to the sea. But in Delos, O Phoibos, dost thou most delight, where the long-robed Ionians gather with their children and their wedded wives. With boxing and dancing and song they make thee glad, contesting. A man would say that they were deathless and ageless for ever, if he should come upon them then, when the Ionians are assembled; for he would see the beauty of all of them, and be glad at heart, at sight of the men and the women's beautiful figures and their swift ships and their wealth.

And the poet goes on in conclusion, in a manner quite alien to the self-effacement of the poet of the *Iliad*, to address his girl-choristers or dancers and remind them of what to say if any man asks them who is their favourite poet: 'He is a blind man, and he lives in rugged Chios; and all his songs are the best, both now and hereafter. And I will carry your praises wherever I go among fair cities of men; and men will believe me, for it is the truth.

'And I will never cease to praise the Far-Shooter Apollo, Lord of the Silver Bow, whom long-haired Leto bore.'[2]

The frank and confident self-advertisement is characteristic of that new age, when social vitality and confidence were increasing again. Thucydides, who quotes the lines on the Delian festival,[3] with many verbal differences from our manuscripts of the Hymns – characteristically of an age in which much poetry was repeated orally – calls the Blind Man of Chios, without hesitation, Homer. There was still in Plato's time a clan or guild of poets in Chios called the Homeridai[4]; and if many other cities also laid claim to so great a figure, that would

---

[2] 143ff.   [3] iii, 104.
[4] Pl. *Ion*, 530; Wade-Gery, *Poet of the Iliad*, 29ff.

be the more possible if he was indeed a wandering rhapsodist. It has been universal practice among scholars since the nineteenth century to date the Hymns much later than the *Iliad*. But now that it is generally recognised that the *Iliad* is an artistic unity (in spite of some internal inconsistencies) such as might well have been composed by a poet of genius, working on a great mass of traditional material; now, too, that we have reason to scale down many traditional early Greek dates, including the widely varying dates for Homer, it would be difficult, at least, to *dis*prove the hypothesis that the poet at Delos, who is so sure of his fame, might be an eighth-century Homer himself; the reference to his own personality, in contrast to epic practice, might be permissible in the quite different circumstances of the festival hymn.[5]

In any case, the Blind Man of Chios lives in his own right, with the scene that he preserves for us: the circle of young faces, flushed from the dancing, and all the crowds and the wealth and gaiety that he can no longer see, except with the inward vision, as he sees the gods too; and the blind, old man, still vigorous and looking forward to many more professional journeys and such scenes of festival.

It requires some effort to imagine the Greek cities as they were on the eve of the great colonial expansion. They were not yet the cities of later antiquity, with their marble temples and colonnades; and the hills around them were not the bare hills of modern Greece. Almost all buildings were still of timber, or timber and mud brick, sometimes on a stone foundation, like the early temple of Hera at Olympia. A porch outside a door set in the end wall, as in the Mycenaean palaces, might be a feature even of unpretentious dwellings; such a place is a welcome amenity, giving fresh air with shade and a view of what the neighbours may be doing on *their* porches, all things to value in a hot climate and among a people so sociable as the Greeks. Roofs, on the mainland, were gabled and high-pitched against the heavy winter rains, as in the porched terracotta models of houses (or temples) of Geometric date found at Argos and Perachora. In the islands, where it is drier, they may have been flat, as they often still are, like the roof from which Elpenor in the *Odyssey* fell, when 'heavy with wine', to break his neck.[6] A regular Place of Gathering, *agora*, was a social necessity: a place where all free men assembled when called by the Herald, to hear important

[5] Cf. Wade-Gery, *op. cit.* 16ff, 27f.   [6] *Od.* x, 552ff.

decisions of the Kings (sometimes plural, as in Alkinöos' kingdom or in Hesiod's time at Thespiai[7]) or of a ruling Council; or with their arms, to repel a raid, when the emergency signal was given by a beacon.[8] The general use of the *agora* as a market was later; a feature of a more developed economy than that of Hesiod's society, in which nearly everyone who was anybody owned some land and lived on the proceeds; but from time to time there would be pedlars or merchants there, from a ship in the harbour a few miles away (few cities were right on the sea, for fear of sea-raids[9]), or arriving with a caravan of mules, like the islanders of Aigina in the interior of the Peloponnese.[10] Merchants, like travelling rhapsodists and other entertainers, naturally came especially at the times of the most frequented religious festivals. Only bad men would rob a stranger, once he was within your own territory; strangers were under the protection of Zeus Xenios and, if they were merchants, also of the king or chief men, to whom, at the first opportunity, they would give presents[11]; but well into classical times, in the wilder parts of Greece, it remained entirely honourable to hold up or cut out a merchant ship or caravan bound for somewhere else.[12]

The market-place was usually at the foot of the citadel, where the tracks and paths converging towards the gate formed the 'broad ways' that gave the city one of its Homeric epithets. There would be no broad streets inside the gate, at least as a rule, but only winding and rocky alleys between the houses, which huddled close against the citadel rock and inside the wall for protection. When times grew better, or population increased, the Agora became surrounded by the houses of the new lower town or 'great' *asty*, itself in due course surrounded by a later wall, like that of Themistocles at Athens; and it might become necessary to put up boundary-stones, inscribed, as at Athens in the sixth century, 'I am the boundary-marker of the Agora'[13]; a warning to market-people not to replace their stalls by permanent structures, and

---

[7] *Od.* viii, 40f; Hes. *WD* 38f, 248.   [8] For beacons, cf. Theognis, 549f.

[9] Cf. the positions of ancient Athens, Megara, Corinth, Knossos; still in the smaller islands the chief village, Khora, often stands back from the harbour, Skala, where more people come to live when conditions are secure. Phaleron burnt by a raid from Aigina, Hdt. v, 81; cf. Thk. ii, 93, Xen. *Hell.* v, 1, 18ff, for 'smash and grab' raids even against classical Athens, upon Salamis and Peiraieus.

[10] Paus. viii, 5, 5.   [11] *Od.* ix, 270f; *Il.* vii, 467ff.

[12] Cf. the treaty between Oiantheia and Chaleion on the Corinthian Gulf, agreeing not to cut out ships inside each other's harbours (Tod, *GHI* no. 34); the high seas are not mentioned! Cf. p. 32, below.

[13] I. T. Hill, *Ancient City of Athens*, 61; *Hesperia*, Suppl. iv, 107ff.

to those under a cloud, e.g. of homicide with extenuating circumstances, to Keep Out.

The City proper was originally the Citadel; the Acropolis always
remained simply 'Polis' in Athenian official language: a defensible hill,
sufficiently steep-sided and flat-topped, with water-supply, the best
available as a refuge and secure dwelling for the people who cultivated
the adjacent plain. And this brings us to the factor determining the
whole character of early historic Greece.

Defensible rocks were to be found anywhere; but fertile plains occurred only at intervals. Where they do occur, the soil is good, creating
a wide economic division, as we shall see, between the 'lowland lairds'
who occupied it and the 'crofters' or hill-farmers who, like Hesiod's
father, when the plain was full up, had cleared and stubbed their pieces
of the inferior, stony land of the hill-foot. The size, wealth, population,
power and importance of every early Greek city depend on the size and
fertility of its plain. Big cities have big plains, small cities have small
plains or shares of a plain. No city has no plain, and no plain has no
city, unless too small to support a viable unit in a warlike world; in
which case, its inhabitants constitute a 'village' or 'township', politically
dependent, whether as serfs or subordinate 'allies', on whatever larger
neighbour proved mightiest locally.

The plains, it must be repeated (since what is meant by the poverty
of Greece is often misunderstood) are often of good, rich soil. The
populations which they support at this day are thick: Attica and Boiotia,
exclusive of Athens and Peiraieus, had 280,000 inhabitants in 1940;
Lakonia 172,000; Messenia, exclusive of the port of Kalamata, 250,000;
Achaia, exclusive of Patras, 161,000; Elis 151,000. Of the islands Corfu
(Kerkyra) had 114,000 inhabitants, including some 30,000 in the town;
Kephallenia with Ithaca, 76,000; Zakynthos 45,000; Samos 75,000
(about 25,000 in the three chief townships); Chios 80,000 (25,000 in the
capital); Lesbos 140,000 (30,000 in Mytilene).[14] These rural populations
include the cultivators of much terraced hillside country which in early
historic times was wild, in many places dense, deciduous forest.[15] (The

[14] Greek Census, 1940.
[15] Dense oak-forest on the hills behind Thermopylai (where there are still some remains
of it), Hdt. vii, 218; woods on Mykonos, now one of the barest of islands, Ephoros,
fr. 107 Müller (in Steph. Byz. *s.v.* Paros); trees on Cape Sunium, Soph. *Ajax*, 1217.
Remains of oak forest in Arcadia, beech forest on Mt Pelion, etc., contribute to form my
opinion that even good historical geographers have often exaggerated the bareness and
dryness of ancient Greece.

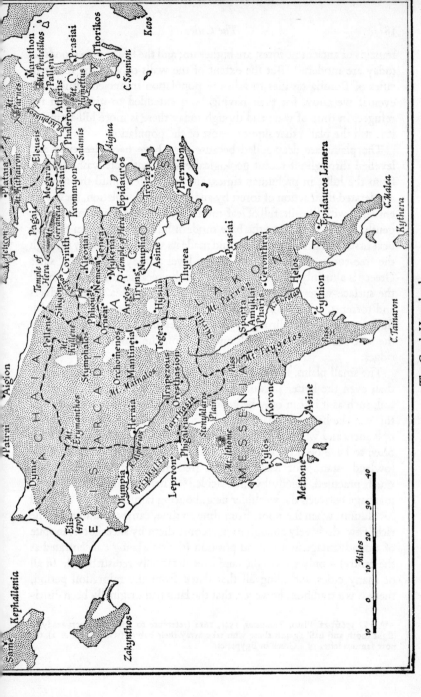

The Greek Homeland
(The unshaded land areas represent plains)

remains of ancient fir forest are higher up; and the lower pine woods of today are modern.) But the extent of the walls of, say, the fourteen cities of Boiotia testifies to a heavy population in ancient times too, even if we allow for their having been extended to give room for refugees in time of war; and though today there is more hill-farming, it is still the plains that support most of the population.

The plains are deep-soiled because they have been deepened and levelled throughout recent geological epochs with silt washed down from the hills; in prehuman times, and still largely until the modern accelerated destruction of forest by an increasing population, they were enriched with fine silt, full of leaf-mould, percolating down much more gently than it does from the bare modern hills, in days when the rain beat first upon growing foliage, and made its way down slowly through the tree-roots. And the plains are so level as they are because, since Greece is a mainly limestone country (with volcanic intrusions), not all the surface-water either evaporates or reaches the sea through rivers and torrents, which when in flood carry some soil away. Much also finds its way down through swallow-holes and cracks, concealed by the soil, leaving its silt to fill and level off the basins between rock ridges.

The small plains, therefore, are not only richer but *very much* richer than even the better portions of the hill-foot and hillside, where the soil, such as it is, can only be kept in position by terrace-walling; and this was the basis of a sharp class-division between poor and primitive uplanders and well-to-do plainsmen. The class-division does not seem often to have been broken down through excessive subdivision of the lowland estates; for Malthusianism (recommended by Hesiod) was much practised, chiefly by infanticide.[16] There was also much inter-marriage between the wealthier neighbouring families. Only by social revolution, when the poor, from time to time, came to outnumber the rich 'Few' decisively enough to overcome them by sheer force, in spite of a disadvantage in arms and position (the rich being concentrated at the centre) – only so was the land ever drastically redistributed. In all or many cities, including all that dated from the migration period, there was a tradition, however, that the land had originally been distri-

---

[16] *WD* 376ff; cf. Plato, *Theaitetos*, 151c, 161a (reference to young mothers ready to 'fight tooth and nail' against those who take away their babies); *O.P.* 744 (B.C.1), the now famous letter of a Greek in Egypt; etc.

buted in lots, as equally as possible, by the hero-founder; and accordingly, when great inequalities developed, not least through concentration by inheritance in relatively infertile families, the cry for a redistribution (*ges anadasmos*) regularly became the slogan of revolutionary parties.[17]

A social and political division between Plain-dwellers, Uplanders and, where they existed, Coast-dwellers, such as we hear of later in Athens (pp. 304ff), must almost certainly have been characteristic also of many other cities. In every way the Plainsmen had great advantages. Their land was not only richer; it was more defensible. Upland farms and outlying villages were more liable to be devastated in border raids; whereas marauders who descended into the central plain, unless in great strength, were liable to a counter-attack by the full force of the city, including charioteers and, with the coming of the thoroughbred horse in post-Homeric times, mounted men. These latter, like Homeric heroes, probably dismounted to fight; but their advantage was that their mounts could carry them and their heavy armour 'swiftly over the plain', to arrive unexhausted. Even to afford the best armour, let alone a horse, was beyond the means of the less well-to-do, whether they lived in plain or upland, and the equestrian classes often asserted a claim to political privileges in accordance with their power.

With their greater and more secure wealth, the Plain-dwellers were also able to advance more rapidly in civilisation. It was they who could afford slaves, male and female, to do the rough work in the fields and about the house; it was their wives and daughters who could thus devote the best of their energies to fine weaving and needlework, and they themselves who were thus conspicuously the best dressed when they went out, like the husband of the Good Woman in *Ecclesiasticus*, to sit with the other city elders 'in the gate'. It was they who were on the spot, and could best afford time to listen, when a rhapsodist or stranger with news of foreign parts was in town; they who could afford the foreign luxury-goods brought in by pedlars; they who could best entertain the stranger; they who could afford the time to go abroad to the 'general gatherings' (*panegyreis* – still a current word in the Greek countryside) at religious festivals, especially some which acquired 'international' celebrity *because* they were held at sanctuaries not dominated by a great city: Olympia in the Peloponnese, Delphi, or the tiny but

[17] *Ath. P.* 11, 2; Plato, *Republic*, 566a; cf. Hdt. iv, 163; etc.

centrally-placed isle of Delos. While they, like the later rich man in Palestine, dressed in fine linen and ate well every day, the poorer countrymen still dressed in rough woollen tunics, with skin cloaks, like the 'shaggy capote' of the modern Greek shepherd; serviceable, immensely hard-wearing, and good against the colder nights of the upland; but difficult to keep clean, seldom changed, and conspicuous and despised by the elegant city noble (*gnorimos*, 'well-known man') when the countryman, nicknamed 'sheepskin-wearer' or 'dusty-feet', had occasion to come to town.[18]

Government was still in many cities headed by a King; but such an official was far from being a despot. 'Hereditary (*patrikai*) monarchies with defined prerogatives' is Thucydides' summary.[19] The king was bound by laws, that is the unwritten customs of his community, and knew he would be eliminated if he flagrantly offended against the interest or prejudices of influential people. Many ancient sagas told how pride and lawlessness, even in a king, constituted a sin against the gods, brought plagues upon the people, divided royal families and led to a fall.

The particular influential people, whose power limited the authority of the king, and who would act against him in the name of divine law if he gravely offended them, were first and foremost his own relatives, descended like him from the Conqueror or a hero-king. Of these, in the course of nature, unless internal feuds kept their numbers down, there would after several generations be a considerable clan, like the governing groups of Basilidai of whom we hear at Ephesos and Erythrai,[20] or the children of Penthilos (son of Orestes) at Mytilene.[21] At Corinth, an annotated list of early kings informs us, the 'senior descendant' of Aletes, the Herakleid Conqueror, reigned in succession for nine generations[22]; *not* necessarily, it seems, the son of the late king; a type of succession of which there are traces also in western Europe, e.g. in the Wessex of Alfred and in the *tanistry* of pre-Norman Scotland.

After the reign of Bakchis, the fifth king, the Corinthian dynasty came to be known not as Herakleidai or Aletidai but as Bakchiadai. This is explained by later writers as due to Bakchis (of whom nothing else is known) having been particularly distinguished; but an attractive

---

[18] Theognis, 55; *katonakophoroi* (at Sikyon), Moiris, *s.v.*, q. Theopompos; *konipodes* (at Epidauros), Plut. GQ 1.
[19] i, 13.   [20] *Suda*, *s.v.* Pythagoras; Ar. *Politics*, 1305b.
[21] Ar. *Politics*, 1311b; cf. Alkaios, fr. 43 Diehl.
[22] D.S. vii, fr. 9, in Synkellos, *Chron.* p. 179.

theory has been suggested, that the clan operated like the group of kinsmen called, in classical Athens, the *anchisteia*, who inherited the property of an intestate without near relatives.[23] This group, *hoi kat' anchisteian* or 'the nearest', included relatives as far as second cousins,[24] that is descendants of a common great-grandfather, the remotest ancestor of whom a living memory might be expected to be preserved. Perhaps there was – and if so, doubtless not without trouble – a kind of *serrata del consiglio*, in which the descendants of Bakchis excluded from consideration their remoter kinsmen, descended from the earlier kings. In the fourth reign after Bakchis, there is again a crisis: Aristomedes, the eighth king, left the throne to his young son Telestes; that is to say, he bequeathed it, like property. After so many generations of settled life, the feeling was certainly gaining ground that land could be owned, rather than that, as in the recently migrant tribe, all the lands of the people or clan belonged, in the last resort, to the people or the clan jointly. (Hesiod, whose father had probably cleared his own farm out of the waste, refers to buying or selling land as something quite usual.[25]) But Telestes, the inheritor from his father, was dispossessed by his uncle and guardian Agemon (who could claim that he was a generation *nearer to Bakchis*; one is reminded of the elder Bruce's claim against John Balliol). Agemon was succeeded by Alexandros, whose relationship is not stated; and then at last the dispossessed Telestes, now a middle-aged man, murdered Alexandros, reigned, it is said, for twelve years, and was succeeded by one Automenes. The point had been reached, five generations after Bakchis, at which an attempt might have been made to limit eligibility *kat' anchisteian*, even if the kings did not succeed in establishing the new rule of succession in the male line. But this time the result was different. The Bakchiads, a clan ultimately over 200 in number, stood together, deposed Automenes within the year, and took sovereign power into their own hands, functioning as a Senate and appointing an annual President (Prytanis) as chief executive. This consummation was reached, according to Diodoros, in 747. It was thus probably the new régime, in its earliest years, which embarked on the great enterprise of Corinthian colonisation in the west.[26]

---

[23] Dr M. Miller, in her learned Glasgow University doctoral dissertation, *Prolegomena to the Study of Greek Chronography*, typescript, pp. 26ff; cf. her *Genealogical Studies* (publication pending).

[24] Isaios, *On the Property of Apollodoros*, p. 65.

[25] *WD* 341.   [26] Cf. p. 72 below.

The Corinthian tradition enables us to guess something of the process
by which an oligarchy could replace a monarchy, seen in terms of the
tensions within an increasingly numerous royal clan. Athenian scholars, supplementing traditions with inferences from the facts of legal
history and religious organisation, picture the same process from a legal
point of view, which, even if there were struggle, would not be likely
to show us anything of it. That the kingship was abolished because the
sainted memory of King Kodros, who gave his life to save the city
from the Dorians, was so revered that no man was deemed worthy to
succeed him, has long been recognised as a seemly mask to cover the
brute fact that the abolition took place to the advantage of the nobility.
But the story worked out by Athenian antiquaries gives a not improbable picture of a gradual process, in which the *name* of King never
disappeared at all.

At a time when war threatened and the reigning King was not much
of a fighting man, it was agreed that a separate War-Leader, *Polemarchos*,
should be appointed.[27] The choice would naturally be made by the
Elders or 'best men' in council; it was a decisive step. Naturally the
tradition finds a precedent for it in, or even reflects the reform back
into, the Heroic Age, unhistorically. In those rough days, if the King
was not a fighting man, he would in the course of nature have been
replaced by someone who was; but in the more stable conditions of the
Geometric period, things could be done more gently.

After the King had thus become a *fainéant* in war, his loss of the
headship of state was only a matter of time. The decisive step was the
appointment of the *Archon* ('Regent'), holding office, at first, for life,
but never by hereditary succession, and taking over the King's civil
duties: that is to say, judicial work, except such of it as was too intimately linked with sacred matters to be taken out of the sacred hands of
the King. Thus, still in classical Athens, when both Regent and King
were annual, routine officials, the 'King', in his colonnade in the corner
of the Agora, dealt with accusations of 'impiety', including the case of
Socrates.[28] In greater state, up at the Hill of Ares, he still presided over
the ancient Council of Areopagus, when it sat to try charges of murder;
fulfilling the function allotted to it, as legend said, by Athena herself,
of seeing justice done, but also of making peace between families and

[27] *Ath. P.* 3, 2-3.
[28] *id.* 57; Plato, *Euthyphron*, 1.

within families, bringing to an end the otherwise interminable operations of the vendetta.[29]

The King also remained for many other purposes the head of the state religion. (Even at Rome, where the rule of a foreign dynasty had brought the name of king into execration, still a priest-king, *rex sacrorum*, was felt to be necessary for some rites.) In classical Athens still, in the worship of Dionysos the wine-god and vegetation-spirit, a Sacred Marriage of the Queen, the wife of the annual Basileus, consummated in the sacred building called the Hall of the Cowherd, formed an essential part of the rites celebrated since prehistoric times for the fertility of the land and of the people.[30] The language of the Aristotelian *Constitution of Athens* is explicit; probably the Basileus was held to be 'possessed' by the god on this occasion, and he and his wife performed for the welfare of the people this sacred sexual act.

Hence the *Constitution* notes that the Regent did *not* perform any of the 'ancestral' religious functions, as did the King and the Polemarch (who sacrificed to the War-God and to Artemis of the Wild, the rough frontier country[31]). What he was, from the first, was the guardian of property. His appearance belongs exactly to the age when personal property in land was becoming established, and the oath which he swore on taking office was that he would do his duties 'as in the time of Akastos' (the son of Medon the son of Kodros), and that 'every man should hold and possess to the end of his Regency that which he held at its beginning'.[32] Among his duties, accordingly, was the supervision of the property of orphans, and particularly of heiresses until they reached the age of fourteen[33] – when, by Athenian law, an heiress must marry her nearest male kinsman, who for his part had to divorce his wife if already married[34]; all this, that the property might not pass out of the family. As public affairs became more complex, all the most important new business was also referred to the Archon, including even the administration of religious festivals newly introduced, like the 'great' Dionysia in the sixth century, and the Ionian scape-goat ritual of the Thargelia.[35]

Eligibility to the Archonship was at first confined to the descendants of Medon: the senior branch of the old royal family, putting the royal

[29] *Ath. P. ib.*; Aeschylus, *Eumenides*, esp. 483f.
[30] *Ath. P.* 3, 5.   [31] *ib.* and *id.* 58, 1.   [32] *id.* 3, 2 and 56, 2.   [33] *id.* 56, 7.
[34] Isaios, *Property of Pyrrhos*, p. 44.   [35] *Ath. P.* 56, 5.

power into commission indeed, an oligarchic move, but keeping it to themselves, it seems, *kat' anchisteian*, like the Bakchiadai.[36] Later, again as at Corinth, the whole body of the Eupatridai or 'patricians' asserted the principle that anyone of their number was eligible. Tenure for life was abolished in favour first, according to our late authorities, of tenure for ten years,[37] and finally for one year; this consummation may have taken place in 683, from which time a list of annual archons (by whose names the years were distinguished) *may* have been kept. At an unknown date, as population and business increased, six junior archons were also appointed, making up the classic *collegium* of the Nine Archons; the judicial function of the six is indicated by their title of *Thesmothetai*, Givers of Decisions or Layers Down of the (case-) Law, by which the traditional *Nomos* (Custom) or *Dike* (Division, Sharing, Decision, and so Right) was applied in practice. As writing came into use, one of their duties came to be to record the decisions (*Thesmia*) and preserve them for reference.[38] The emphasis on case-law and precedent thus appears to be primitive; it is reminiscent of the pre-literate Greece described by Homer; also of classical Rome, where the primitive simplicity of the Code of the Twelve Tables made the continuance of case-law necessary, at a time when the Greek world had gone over to the general use of comprehensive, written codes. Meanwhile the chief or Eponymous Archon, who gave his name to the year, remained head of the state, and the position, even when made annual, long continued to be, like the Roman consulship, the object of intense competition.[39]

The composition of the primitive Athenian Council is unknown; in some early Greek states, the Council consisted of the heads of the chief families only, a 'House of Lords' principle, under which no man with a father or elder brother living could be a member, which seemed to later Greeks extraordinary.[40] Under the mature Athenian oligarchy, however, all ex-archons probably became members, while the Council itself appointed the archons. The Council appointed 'whom it thought

[36] Eusebios' Chronology makes the Life-Archons a hereditary line, son succeeding father; though it is unlikely that the original compilers had evidence of this.

[37] Paus. iv, 5, 10; that the fall of the Medontids was connected with the legendary scandal of the ten-year archon Hippomenes (*accessit* 722 tr.), related by Herakleides (i, 3) and Nikolaos (fr. 51 Müller) seems to be only a 19th-century theory. Most modern scholars disbelieve that there ever was a ten-year archonship; but cf. Ar. *Politics*, 1310b, on long-term magistracies in early times.

[38] *Ath. P.* 3, 4.   [39] *id.* 13, 2.

[40] Cf. Ar. *Politics*, 1305b (Knidos and, as late as the 6th century, Massalia, Istros, Herakleia (probably Bithynia)).

fit' to each post[41]; and presumably family influence and the expectation of a *quid pro quo* when one supported another aristocrat's son or nephew played a major part in selection. As a body of men, recruited from a close circle of families, and all of them with judicial and administrative experience, this early Council reminds one of the Roman Senate; once more we find that early Greece, but not classical Greece, shows features reminiscent of republican Rome. Meanwhile, in a period of stability, in which Athens fought no life-and-death wars and sent out no colonies, occasions necessitating the convening of the Assembly must be presumed to have become few; in any case, most of the people lived at a distance, many even at a distance that could not possibly be covered twice in a day. Thus the Council, filling up its own ranks through the archonships, governed Athens as a close oligarchy until after 600.

On no other early Greek city have we even as much evidence as this. In some, a kingship with limited prerogatives but not without importance survived, as at Argos[42] and, anomalously, in the two royal families at Sparta. In many cities we hear of ancient councils with limited numbers, sometimes surviving anomalously within a reformed constitution: 180 at Epidauros, 90 in Elis, 80 at Argos, 60 at Knidos, and so few as 30, including the two kings, at Sparta.[43] These states, one notices, are all Dorian, except Elis; and Elis also was a 'conquest' state. In other regions we hear of councils with fixed numbers (always larger numbers[44]) only as part of more liberal constitutions; but in early times, governing bodies entirely composed of those claiming royal descent appear, as we have seen, also at Mytilene and Erythrai.[45]

In the Peloponnese outside Argolis and the Isthmus region, as well as in the whole north-west of Greece, where Mycenaean civilisation had not penetrated, the walled city was slow to develop. Leagues of neighbours existed, often with sufficient unity for effective defence and with annual *panegyreis* at a common shrine (as in Elis, at Olympia, and even in city-strewn Boiotia, near Koroneia and at Onchestos[46]); but many

[41] *Ath. P.* 8, 2, cf. 3, 6.
[42] Hdt. vii, 149, 2, and, even later, Tod, *GHI* no. 33; but by then the King, as his name is used for dating a treaty, is probably an annual magistrate.
[43] Respectively, Plut. *GQ* 1; Ar. *Politics*, 1306a; Thk. v, 47, 9; Plut. *GQ* 4; the Spartan Rhetra in Plut. *Lykourgos*, 6, cf. Hdt. vi, 57.
[44] 400, later 500 at Athens, *Ath. P.* 8, 4; 21, 3; 600 in Elis, Thk. v, 47, 10, Massalia, Str. iv, 179, Herakleia, Ar. 1305a; 1000 at Kyme (an aristocratic assembly rather than a deliberative council), Herakleides, *Kym. Pol.* (fr. 11) and perhaps Kolophon, Ath. xii, 526c, q. Theopompos (fr. 129 Müller) and Xenophanes.
[45] p. 20, nn.
[46] Str. ix, 412.

peoples were slow to effect the transition to such centralised city life as
Attica, under threat of invasion, had achieved at the end of the Bronze
Age, and as the cities of Asia, in face of dispossessed natives, adopted
from the first. Strabo the geographer gives a list of such rural communities in the Peloponnese which effected a *synoikismos* at various
dates within historic times. In Arcadia, he tells us, Tegea was founded
by a union of nine villages (*demoi*) to resist Spartan aggression, Mantineia of five, under influence from Argos (no doubt after Tegea had
accepted the Spartan alliance).[47] Both places, like other regions of
Arcadia, such as Parrhasia, which never possessed a city, are already
mentioned as units in the Homeric list of contingents[48]; and Mantineia
was at least once broken up again into a group of villages by Spartan
hostility.[49] In western Arcadia, the nine villages of the Heraians, whom
an archaic inscription shows concluding an alliance with Elis for 100
years, about 550, and who struck coins not much later,[50] united in a
city only in the fourth century, under encouragement from Sparta herself,[51] in order to strengthen a friendly protected people; and the Eleians
only built *their* capital city called Elis, to which the inhabitants of the
surrounding villages migrated, about 471, when they also probably
modernised their constitution.[52] In Achaia, 'Aigion was founded by a
union of seven or eight villages, Patrai (Patras) of seven, Dyme of six'[53];
while in eastern Achaia Pellene, threatened by Dorian Sikyon, was
probably a city already about 650.[54]

Sparta herself never built a walled city at all. The reason was that
she, like the highland peoples but almost uniquely among the plain-
dwellers, feared no invader. Already in the dawn of Greek history she
had united the wide plain of Laconia as far as the Parnon range, and
the low, rolling country south of it to the sea. The little sea-port of
Helos, a place with a Homeric past, resisted desperately and was destroyed; its people became serfs, giving their name (like 'Latins' and
'Caerites', more honourably, in the Roman polity, and 'Plataians' for
a time at Athens) to a political class.[55] Assured against death for so long
as they behaved themselves, they worked their lands for a heavy rent

<hr>

[47] *id.* viii, 337.   [48] *Il.* ii, 607f.   [49] Xen. *Hell.* v, 2, 7, Polyb. iv, 27, 6.
[50] Tod, *GHI* no. 5; Head, *HN* 447. (Head's date perhaps too early; cf. W. P. Wallace
in *JHS* LXXIV, pp. 33f. and nn.)
[51] Str. *ib.*   [52] D.S. xi, 54.   [53] Str. *ib.*   [54] *O.P.* 1365.
[55] Paus. iii, 2, 7. The traditional conqueror was King Teleklos, whose eighth descendant
was ruling in 500 B.C. Early access to the sea is indicated by Sparta's relations with Thera
(Hdt. iv, 147) and early reception of Orientalising art, cf. pp. 45, 180, below.

in kind, payable to Spartan landlords. Other villages may have suffered the same fate, for throughout classical times the class of Helots was spread throughout Spartan territory. But many of the larger villages submitted to Spartan overlordship and continued to manage their own village affairs; some were even fortified.[56] Whether their inhabitants were chiefly pre-conquest Achaians (in which case, the feeling that the land had 'always' formed one kingdom, as in Homeric times, may have helped to reconcile them to unity), or whether, as late tradition said,[57] Dorian conquerors had here too driven earlier inhabitants abroad, cannot be said; certainly in classical times the inhabitants of the whole land, including the later-conquered serfs of Messenia, spoke Doric, not Arcadian.[58] If the men of such Laconian townships as Pharis and Geronthrai, *Perioikoi* or 'dwellers around' as the Spartans called them, were indeed descendants of the same horde as the Spartans, this never secured them membership of the Spartan assembly, probably for the simple reason that they lived too far away.[59] The people of the Spartiatai (from Sparte, the 'sown land', the central part of the rich and beautiful Laconian plain) were confined to the men of the neighbouring villages of Mesoa, Pitane, Konooura and Limnai,[60] which as they grew became the quarters of one large, sprawling and, still in Thucydides' time,[61] rural-looking town, and Amyklai, two and a half miles away. Meanwhile beyond Parnon the cultivable patches on the mountainous east coast, with such townships as Prasiai and Epidauros Limera, long continued to own the overlordship of Argos; it may not have been till the sixth century that Sparta asserted her mastery over them and over the continuation of Parnon, the island of Kythera, strategically placed, which in hostile hands could threaten the trade of Gythion, Sparta's port, the successor of destroyed and silted-up Helos.[62]

Though the monarchy survived at Sparta, retaining in particular the command in war,[63] and with the two kings, of different and rival houses, holding priesthoods of Zeus Lakedaimon and Zeus of Heaven, keeping records of Delphic oracles, treated with high honour especially at religious festivals and retaining jurisdiction over property when male

---

[56] e.g., good remains of 'Pelasgic' walling round the strongly-sited Geronthrai (mod. Geraki, under Parnon).

[57] Paus. iii, 2, 6. [58] Thk. iv, 41, 2. [59] So Wade-Gery, in *CAH* ii, 540.

[60] Paus. iii, 16, 6. [61] Thk. i, 10, 2.

[62] 'Kythera, of which our wise man Chilon said, "Better for Sparta if it were sunk under the sea".' – Damaratos, in Hdt. vii, 235.

[63] Hdt. vi, 56, 1 (etc. etc.).

succession failed,[64] – still the tendency in settled communities of land-owners to control the monarchy did not leave Sparta unmarked. The twenty-eight Elders, elected in classical times by the whole Assembly of Spartiates over thirty (though by a 'childish' method of acclamation) *from* men over sixty of certain families only, sat with the Kings for internal deliberative purposes, and for many judicial purposes as a High Court; and they held office for life, even if senile.[65] Another check, more effective than the need to gain the assent of the Assembly (*Apella*) for innovations, was the existence of the Ephors ('Overseers'), elected annually by and from among the whole people.[66] In classical times they were five in number (perhaps one from each village); and the list of them was believed to extend back to 754 or 757.[67] A story was often quoted of King Theopompos, who agreed to the establishment of this new magistracy, being asked by his wife if he was not ashamed to hand on the royal power to his son less than he inherited it; laconically he replied, 'It will last the longer for that'.[68] Theopompos, mentioned by the poet Tyrtaios, who lived only two generations after him, is certainly a historical person; but unless early Spartan generations were much longer than those of fully historic times, his date, eight generations before his descendant Leotychides at the time of Xerxes' invasion, can hardly have been so early; and the list, as known to later Greece, at least *may* have been compiled by fifth-century scholars.[69] Later generations attributed both the foregoing and almost every other detail of the classical Spartan polity to the mysterious legislator Lykourgos; but whether he was god or man, the Delphic Oracle itself did not know (pp. 268f).

The development of the city-state, the work of what in art-history is called the Geometric Period, was determinative of the whole life of Greece. Concentrating the people physically, it concentrated also the life of the communities with that intensity in which the Greek way of

[64] *ib.* 51f, esp. 52, 8.   [65] *ib.* 57, 5; Ar. *Politics*, ii, 1270b–1271a.   [66] Ar. *ib.*
[67] 757, Jerome; 754, Synkellos. This date, like that of Lykourgos, has been endlessly discussed by modern scholars; recently, and with eminent common sense, by W. den Boer, in *Laconian Studies*, Amsterdam, 1954, chaps. i–iv. The point to note, as we shall see hereinafter, is that some classical Greek scholars, whose names we do not know, calculated rightly that the mid-eighth century was an 'epoch-making' period. This led them to assign to it numerous epoch-making events, some of them very wrongly: e.g. the foundations of Cyrene, Naukratis, Sinope, Kyzikos, and the career of Thales! (All in Jerome). Theopompos must really be nearer 700.   [68] Ar. *Politics*, 1313a.
[69] Den Boer, *op. cit.* (against Kroymann, *Pausanias und Rhianos*, p. 140): 'On the contrary, the *anagraphe* of the ephors is the termination of a laborious evolution.'

life and Greek art and thought were forged. Destructively, by accentuating that articulation into separate communities which the distribution of mountains and plains first imposed, it led also to the incessant wars of Greece. Where men lived scattered 'in villages, in the ancient manner',[70] disputes between mountain shepherds or border farmers could remain of only local significance, whether settled by right or by might; but the more the land-holding farmers drew in, to become citizens of the town, the more the borderers of the other city over the hill became 'foreigners' to them, and the more the city community might feel that encroachment or robbery by foreign borderers was a matter that touched them all. To let *that* debatable land go might expose land nearer home; and to fail to support fellow-citizens who lived at the other end of one's own plain was inexpedient if one might wish for their support in turn. Tegea and Mantineia fought fierce battles over the border-lands in the 'waist' of their hour-glass-shaped plain, and especially over the disposal of the spring flood-waters that periodically inundated them[71]; Chalkis and Eretria, if less often, over water-meadows along the Lelantos torrent.[72] Where neighbouring communities were of different sizes, the stronger might settle all disputed questions by imposing its will, as did the five villages of Sparta upon their 'dwellers around', and Argos, when strong, upon the smaller cities of Argolis, despite their bronze-age walls. If the smaller communities were stubborn, they might be destroyed, as Thespiai destroyed Hesiod's Askra.[73] Usually they submitted, sullenly; but then, from the point of view of the larger, there arose the necessity of seeing to it, for the sake of security, that they did not join together to regain their freedom, as the five villages of Megaris did against Corinth, or seek the protection of some greater and remoter overlord. Thus, with the rise of Sparta in the sixth century, the smaller cities of Argolis joined her as a protector and stuck to her even when others fell away; except some, perilously near to Argos herself – Tiryns, Mykenai, Asine, Nauplia – which Argos destroyed, Asine as early as about 700,[74] Tiryns and Mykenai after 470, at a time when Sparta was prevented by other preoccupations from helping.[75] In Boiotia Thebes, large and central,

---

[70] Thk. i, 10, 2.   [71] *id.* v, 65, 4.   [72] Str. x, 448.
[73] Proklos, schol. on *WD* 631, q. Plutarch.
[74] Asine destroyed by Eratos, King of Argos, in the time of Nikandros, father of Theopompos, at Sparta: Paus, ii, 36, 4; iii, 7, 4; cf. p. 76 and n. 34, below.
[75] Hdt. vi, 83, D.S. xi, 65, Paus. v, 23, 3, viii, 27, 1.

struggled with imperfect success to impose her will, as something more than *prima inter pares*, upon a dozen other cities, some of them with a Mycenaean past, and several times destroyed a recalcitrant: in the north the Minyan Orchomenos, in the west Plataia, which escaped for a time by 'giving herself' as an ally to more distant Athens, and Thespiai the destroyer of Askra, all felt the weight of her hand.[76] In Phokis, on the other hand, where there was no predominant city, and where many small, fortress-townships joined to worship at a common sanctuary, any internal bickerings that there may have been leave no mark in history; and a united Phokis was capable of preserving her identity and even regaining a temporarily lost independence against the formidable feudal cavalry of a united Thessaly (pp. 203f).

Any success that a major power gained in buttressing her security thus brought her only within sight of wider horizons and similar problems on a larger scale. Every city did its best to secure its lands against raiding by asserting its supremacy over smaller neighbours, and every city, as its population grew, tried to provide itself with more cultivable land; a problem presently solved, on a large scale, by the great enterprise of oversea colonisation. But at home, inevitably, local 'imperialism' brought contact with other expanding 'spheres of influence' of communities as large or larger. Thebes, attacking Plataia, was foiled by Athens; Argos, trying to preserve her 'heritage of Temenos', the Conqueror, clashed with the more solid power of Sparta. Communities which had a common enemy lying between them naturally tended to become allies; thus Sparta, conquering Messenia and invading eastern Arcadia, which received intermittent support from Argos, found an ally in Elis, which on a smaller scale was doing the same thing, bringing into her orbit the Heraians of western Arcadia and conquering the 'Three Peoples' of Arcadian-speaking Triphylia, which bordered Messenia on the north[76a]; and beyond Argolis, Sparta found friends in sixth-century Athens and Corinth, both enemies of Aigina. But between the intensely city-centred and so self-centred city-states there could in the long run be no relations except those of lord and subject, or of jealousy. Both with Elis and, on a major and tragic scale, with Athens, and even with faithful Corinth, Sparta clashed in the long run.

[76] Plataia, Thk. iii, 55, 3; 61, 2; Orchomenos, D.S. xv, 79; Demosth. *Leptines*, p. 490; Thespiai, Thk. iv, 133, 1; Thespiai and Plataia, Xen. *Hell.* vi, 3, 1.
[76a] Hdt. iv. 148, 4.

Such was the nemesis of the city-state, a nemesis which arose out of its very intensity of life, which in its prime successfully resisted unification by conquest, and shrank from any adequate degree of union by confederation. What prevented genuine union was, in the language of international law, the problem of sovereignty; in the language of personal and economic relations, each group's unwillingness to trust the members of other groups to the extent of surrendering its 'freedom and autonomy'; in the language of morals, pride.

The rare cases in which sovereignty actually was surrendered 'prove' the rule instructively. The most striking, that of the union of fourth-century Corinth with Argos and acceptance of Argive citizenship,[77] was the work of a democratic party in Corinth, in reaction against Sparta and the oligarchic government which she favoured; and in face of the opposition of these forces it was short-lived. The union of inland Stiris and its port of Medeon, in south-east Phokis, attested by an inscription,[78] is that of two tiny states, already members of the Phokian confederacy; and even so, it belongs to the last century of Hellenic independence. Finally, in the development of federal institutions in the Achaian and Aitolian Leagues, the last practical experiment of Greek political wisdom was made only in response to overwhelming pressure, and already too late; and equally characteristically, even then the two leagues always remained hostile to each other.

More frequently, even the friendly relations of cities show a meticulous care for the preservation of independence. A fifth-century treaty between two Cretan cities, Knossos and Tylissos, using the good offices of Argos as mediator, delimits boundaries and provides, *inter alia*, that while a man of Tylissos, the smaller city, may possess real property in the land of Knossos, a Knossian may not do so at Tylissos.[79] The larger city welcomes the closer relations that the holding of land by the same proprietors on both sides of the frontier would entail, but the smaller, with an eye to the preservation of its identity, does not reciprocate.

A clause in the treaty which reads comically to us is one which provides that nothing in it shall prevent Tylissians – a hill-people, presumably tough and backward even by classical Knossian standards – from raiding where they will, 'except in regions subject to the city of Knossos'; a clause which Knossos may perhaps have found convenient, as it might encourage other outlying neighbours to accept Knossian pro-

[77] Xen. *Hell.* iv, 4, 6; v, 1, 34.   [78] *IG* ix, 1, no. 32.   [79] Tod, *GHI* no. 33.

tection. There is no doubt that border-raiding after cattle and so forth
is what is recognised. Thucydides mentions it as still considered an
honourable pursuit in the north-western mainland[80]; Xenophon describes the cattle-raider's mimic war-dance (probably it had once been
held to have magical virtue) of the Ainianes west of Thermopylai[81];
and Thucydides goes on to remark on how, in these regions, where the
city had not developed, men still always carried their arms (like the
'ancient', that is Homeric Greeks, as he says, and like the Sphakiots in
Crete down to our own times), 'because their dwellings were unforti-
fied, and because of the general social insecurity'.

By sea, piracy lasted even longer,[82] though some Greeks after the age of
colonisation might patriotically rob only Phoenicians and Etruscans.[83]
But Greeks still robbed Greeks in the Aegean until piracy was for a
time suppressed by fifth-century Athens; a major centre of the industry
in the sixth century being so large and civilised an island as Samos (see
pp. 219, 314). And from the northern shore of the Corinthian Gulf we
have, inscribed on a bronze tablet, the text of a treaty between two
little Lokrian sea-ports, Oiantheia (the modern Galaxidi) and Chaleion,
regulating and limiting the practice of piracy as between the contracting
parties.[84] Seizure of goods is forbidden under penalties from within
the harbours of the cities, and *proxenoi*, citizens of the home state, are
recognised as representatives at law of visitors from any foreign state
which has appointed them; but the high seas, it is explicitly recognised,
remain open to piracy or acts of private reprisal.

Such was the state of insecurity against which, at least on land, in
southern and eastern Greece the city-states made head. Already early
in our period the lowlanders with their walled towns and their mounted
infantry had over wide areas tamed the local hill-men, chasing their
raiders, harrying their villages and either enslaving or expelling their
remnants, or binding them over to be of good behaviour – 'having the
same friends and enemies', as later treaties used to say, as the city. After

---

[80] i, 5 (referring to Homer, *Od.* iii, 71-4, where 'Are you pirates?' is a civil question).
[81] Xen. *Anab.* vi, 1, 7-8.
[82] Cf. the surprising 'Law of Solon' quoted in the Digest, xlvii, 22, 4, providing for the
enforceability before the state courts of private contracts between 'members of communes
[Demoi] or clans ... or shipmen ... or pirates or merchants ... unless they contravene
public enactments'; i.e., one must not raid people with whom one's city had an agreement,
like Eupeithes of Ithaka, who got into trouble for joining a Taphian party in raiding the
Thesprotians on the adjacent mainland, 'and we had an agreement with them': *Od.* xvi,
424-8. Cf. Ormerod, *Ancient Piracy*, pp. 64ff.
[83] Like Dionysios of Phokaia, Hdt. vi, 17.   [84] Tod, *GHI* no. 34.

this stage, wars were no longer between citizens and casual raiders, as in the mountainous north-west, but between city and city, usually over border-territory or the right to protect and control the policy of some smaller 'third party'. The land that was fought for, and the land *in* which the armies usually clashed, was the limited and precious cultivable land. This led to a change in the character of Greek armies during our period (cf. p. 175). At its beginning we are in a 'cavalry period'; we have few descriptions of battles, between the infantry and chariot battles of Homer and the purely infantry 'push of pike' battles of the early fifth century; but it is clear both from literary allusions and from the popularity of mounted warriors as a subject of early Greek works of art, that a cavalry epoch intervened. Not only on the plains of Thessaly and Boiotia and in Ionia, but in Euboia, where the archaic chariotry also makes a belated appearance in a religious procession; at Sparta, where the royal bodyguard of three hundred continued to be called 'Knights'; and even in rocky Crete, cavalry were for a time of great importance.[85] Accordingly, there was also an epoch when, in the most liberal form of constitution, which in some states replaced the early, closed oligarchies, ability to provide oneself with armour and a horse constituted the qualification for 'first-class' citizenship, as at Asian Kyme and Kolophon and, later, in the Solonian 'timocracy' at Athens.[86] But by the end of our period this epoch has passed. The 'Knight', dismounted (like the English knights at Crecy and Agincourt), fights in the ranks. Neither Athens nor Sparta used any cavalry in the Persian Wars; and in classical Greece the 'hoplite' democracy is one of the standard forms of constitution.[87]

In the warfare of the mature cities, for a city to be actually captured was rare; and nearly all the cases that we do hear of involve either treachery[88] (the result of faction within) or the use of overwhelming force, such as was at the disposal of the Sicilian dynasts of the Persian War period, or of imperial Athens, or of the temporary leagues which

[85] Cf. the archaic frieze from Prinias in the Herakleion Museum, with the horses proudly made of exaggerated size. Euboia (Eretria), Str. x, 448; Sparta, *id.* 481-2 (from Ephoros).

[86] Herakl. Pont. *Kymaion Politeia* (fr. 11); Ar. *Politics*, iv, 1289b, 1290b; *Ath. Pol.* 7, 3, where Knights *may* have been eligible for the archonships; there is no record of any later extension of eligibility from 'five-hundred-bushel men' to all knights.

[87] Ar. *Politics*, iv, 1297b, vi, 1321a; Thk. viii, 97; Hasebroek, *Griech. Wirtschafts- und Gesellschaftsgeschichte*, pp. 184ff.

[88] Cf. the 4th-century tract of Aineias 'Taktikos' *On Siege-Warfare*, in which the possibility of betrayal is the chief preoccupation of a defending commander.

deleted two cities that dominated important sanctuaries: two acts of pious atrocity which no doubt had an economic aspect. The two cities were Melia, which dominated the afterwards Panionian sanctuary at Cape Mykale, destroyed by the Ionian League probably before 700,[89] and Krissa which dominated Delphi about 600, and was destroyed by the united efforts of Athens, the dynast of Sikyon, and the Thessalians (see below, pp. 200ff). Without such a pious motive (with which, indeed, belligerents in classical Greece often tried to provide themselves, accusing their opponents in an ultimatum of some such act of impiety as cultivating sacred land), to destroy a 'kindred' city was felt to be an atrocious act; and most neighbours were kindred. Thus Herodotus implicitly condemns the early destruction of Arisba in Lesbos by its neighbour Methymna[90]; and the religious league of the Amphiktyons or 'Neighbours' who met at Thermopylai (later, also at Delphi) has to its credit an oath, annually exchanged, not to destroy or cut off from supplies of running water any member-state.[91] In later days, the extra ferocity of imperialism or class-war usually underlies any such atrocity, as in the later days of the Athenian Empire,[92] or in the destruction of Sybaris by Kroton (pp. 383ff). In any case, to attack the defenders of a city-wall with scaling-ladders or the battering-ram was not an enterprise which Greek citizen-soldiers generally cared to undertake; sapping and mining, or the construction of a siege-mound, required more man-power than a city-state could usually deploy; and blockade, with or without continuous entrenched lines, required more time than citizen-soldiers would often spare from their farms. The united armies of the Peloponnesian League at the height of its power failed to storm little Plataia in 429. The exceptional man-power and élan of democratic Athens captured Chalkis in 507,[93] and Athens gained a rather un-deserved reputation for proficiency in siege-operations, presumably as a result[94]; but as a rule, it was only the formidable despotisms of Assyria and Persia, with 'expendable' man-power, that could conduct successful siege-operations.

The city wall thus marked off the security and order of city life from the disorder or rule of force in the world outside. It became a symbol. 'The people must fight for its laws *as for its walls*', says Herakleitos of

[89] Vitruvius, iv, 1; Steph. Byz. *s.v.* Melia, q. Hekataios.
[90] i, 151.   [91] Aischines, *On the Embassy*, p. 43.
[92] Skione, Thk. v. 32; Melos, v, 116 (and the Spartans at Hysiai, v, 83, 2 – A.A)
[93] Hdt. v, 77.   [94] Hdt. ix. 70, 2, Thk. i, 102.

Ephesos (p. 400). The Wall and the Law were the external and internal defences of the Greek way of life, and how a city could fight for its walls may be exemplified in a story told by Xenophon[95] as an example of brave deeds which tend to be forgotten when they do not conspicuously affect the course of history. The event takes place in the fourth century, during the wars between Thebes and Sparta; but we may use it as an example of the courage with which, throughout their history, the miniature cities of Greece defended and preserved themselves. It is equally characteristic of the besetting sin of the Greeks that the episode took place because the city concerned had driven into exile some members of a minority party, and because the exiles were prepared to capture their city with the help of outside enemies in order to regain power.

The inland city of Phlious, whose external history is of one long struggle for freedom from Argos, had for this reason continued to stand by Sparta in the hour of defeat. ' . . . And while the Arcadians and the men of Elis were marching to join the Thebans [near Corinth], the exiles proposed to them that if they would do no more than put in an appearance near by, they could capture Phlious. They agreed; and the exiles and others, to the number of about six hundred, took up a position by night, with scaling ladders, not far from the walls. Then, when the look-out post on Mount Trikaranos signalled 'Enemy approaching', and everyone's attention was turned that way, the dissidents [within] signalled to the ambush 'Come'; and they scaled the walls [of the citadel], capturing the arms of the guard,[96] and chasing the men of the day-watch, who numbered ten, one out of each section of five. Of these they killed two, one still asleep and another who fled to the sanctuary of Hera. The others jumped down the wall facing the city; and there were the attackers in undisputed possession of the citadel.

'But now the alarm reached the city, and the citizens came to the rescue. At first the enemy in the citadel sallied out against them, and fought in front of the gates leading into the town; but soon they were driven back inside the citadel, as more citizens came up; and the towns-

---

[95] *Hell.* vii, 2, 5ff.

[96] Xenophon, as usual in his *History*, takes a great deal of background knowledge for granted. Evidently the citadel had a night guard of 50, of whom 40 had 'stood down' at daybreak, leaving their arms piled, while even the ten left on duty were not as alert as they should have been. The defective discipline is also characteristic of Greek citizen-soldiers.

men got inside along with them. The inner baily of the citadel thus became a no-man's-land; the enemy mounted upon the walls and towers and from thence shot and struck at the citizens, while they, from below, guarded themselves and tried to fight their way up the stairways leading on to the wall. Then the townsmen got possession of some of the towers on both flanks, and hurled themselves in desperation upon the attackers hand to hand. By this gallant attack, the invaders were gradually pressed back into a smaller and smaller space. Meanwhile, the Argives and Arcadians came round the city, and tried to breach the wall of the citadel where it joined the high ground; but the defenders, some on the walls and some even from outside, attacked them as they mounted, while still on the ladders, while others continued the fight against those who were already up, upon the towers. They found fire in the tents and attacked the towers with it, throwing on bundles of hay, which grew on top of the citadel and had been mown. Now the men on the towers began to jump down for fear of being burnt; those on the curtain-wall gave way before the assault of the townsmen; and once they began to give way, very shortly the entire citadel was clear of the enemy. Then at once the cavalry of Phlious charged out of the gates; at the sight of them the enemy retired, abandoning their ladders and their dead and even some men who were alive but lamed. At least eighty of them were killed, either in the fighting inside or by jumping from the walls. And there was the spectacle to be seen, after the saving of the city, of the men greeting one another and the women bringing them drink, weeping for joy, and everyone, in literal truth, laughing and crying at the same time.'

The story is probably an eye-witness account from one of Xenophon's sons, who rode with the cavalry of Phlious (just sixty in number!) in some other operations about this time.

The unrecorded history of Greece must have been full of such episodes of heroic action; and there were not less heroic decisions. It is worth while, for instance, to try to imagine the debate that must have taken place in the assembly of Plataia in the year 490.

Plataia had been saved by Athens from the rapacity of Thebes. But that had been when Athens was under a dictatorship. Since then, she had had a revolution; also, she had meddled in an Ionian revolt against Persia, and was in consequence being attacked by a Persian punitive expedition, which had already conquered Euboia. Even Athens herself was not united; her exiled leader was in the Persian camp. Was it prudent to risk the man-power of Plataia in Athens' quarrel?

But prudence was not allowed to turn the scale in face of oaths sworn (probably) 'to have the same friends and enemies' as Athens. So old men and boys made ready to hold the walls, if need be, against the Thebans. The field-army paraded, in a rather scratch collection of armour, one imagines, such as farmer-citizens could afford; the shepherds of Kithairon with their wolf-spears, perhaps even the sheep-dogs, those formidable beasts, which fought on many early Greek battlefields.[97] Men made vows to the gods, and women wept, and the six hundred men of Plataia marched to Marathon to fight the King of the East.

[97] Pollux, v, 46, ὁ Μάγνης κύων; Polyainos, vii, 1; Aelian, *VH* xiv, 46; BM Klazomenai sarcophagus, *c.* 525 B.C. (J. M. Cook, *The Greeks in Ionia and the East* (1962), p. 109).

PART II

The Expansion of Greece

CHAPTER III

Greece and the East

THE influence that was to transform Greek society and to set its maritime cities on the paths of political experiment and its 'wise men' on those of intellectual speculation was, in its economic foundation, that of greatly increased trade, leading to the growth of new classes of workers producing for export, and of new mercantile interests among the existing aristocracies; and the situation that led to greatly increased trade was produced by oversea colonisation, especially the great outpouring of population to Sicily and south Italy that set in towards 700. Colonisation seems to have produced a new mood of confidence. Where the food-problem was solved and wealth increased, readiness for experiment and eagerness to enjoy the good things of a new and larger world replaced the conservative and traditionalist mood of the age of Geometric art and of Hesiod; so, at least, it is natural to explain the fact that, very soon after the foundation of the first Sicilian colonies, geometric art was swept away in favour of the new, opulent and exciting products of Orientalising schools. Greece had been in touch with the east long before this, as is shown by scattered finds of Greek geometric pottery; but it was not until the age of western expansion that Greeks permitted their own art to be revolutionised. It is therefore appropriate, and in accordance with chronological order, to look first at the history of Greek contacts with the east.[1]

[1] T. J. Dunbabin, *The Greeks and their Eastern Neighbours, passim*; early pottery in the east, pp. 27ff, 72ff. D. G. Hogarth, in *Ionia and the East* (1909), argued that the influence of Asia Minor, especially the civilisation of Phrygia, upon Ionia in the 8th-7th centuries was more important than that of Phoenicia and Syria; and it was commonly accepted in his generation that Ionia was in every respect the 'centre of gravity' of the early historic Greek world (as was maintained notably by Beloch, *Griech. Gesch.* I.1 (1912)). Since then, under the influence of more detailed studies of the eastern affinities of Greek Orientalising art, and especially of Woolley's excavation of Al Mina on the Syrian coast, the importance of the contacts by sea with the Levant have been re-established (see Woolley in *JHS* LVIII; C. M. Robertson in *JHS* LX; Sidney Smith in *AJ* XXII; and R. M. Cook's important article 'Ionia and Greece' (*JHS* LXVI, pp. 67-98) represents a 'swing of the pendulum' against excessive emphasis on Ionia. But it must be remembered that the history of the states nearest to Athens receives the most allusions in ancient books written

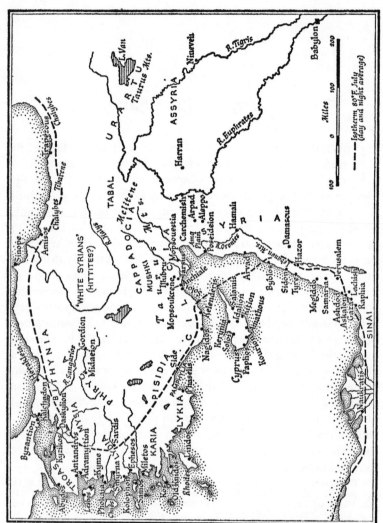

The East

Syria between 1000 and 800 B.C. was the scene of a more advanced civilised life than Greece. It was the home of many and varied peoples. Hittites, driven from Anatolia by early iron-age migrations, in the north, Philistines, probably from the eastern Aegean, on the south-western coast, Aramaeans (the 'Syrians from Kir' of Amos) at Hamah (Hamath) and the desert-port of Damascus, Hebrews out of the desert, including a 'mixed multitude'[2] driven or escaping from Egypt after being enslaved when Egypt expelled the 'Shepherd Kings'; all these were among the elements which mingled and fought with older-established Amorites and Canaanites; and these latter, Chna as they called themselves,[3] known to the Greeks as Phoinikes or Red Men, maintained themselves, after they had lost the interior, in their sea-ports and island strongholds, Tyre, Sidon, Byblos (Jebail, Gebal), Arvad (Ruad), between Mount Lebanon and the sea. The migrations had been very destructive in their time, nowhere more than in Palestine, which suffered the Wahabi fanaticism of the Chosen People; but the older civilisation was stronger in Syria than in the Aegean, agriculture more widespread and towns more numerous; and the iron-age recovery was correspondingly more rapid. While Greece was still illiterate, kings and merchants in the Syrian cities had already their state archives and business records; Syria, like Greece, had its epic theogonies and hymns to the gods and popular lyric poetry; but alongside these, also, in the royal chronicles, the beginnings of a literature in prose.[4] That so much promise was to flow, like the rivers of Damascus, into desert sand, into the stagnation of the well-meaning but despotic Persian Empire, was due to historical causes: to greed, aggressiveness and competitiveness, both within and without. The gulf between rich and poor yawned

from an Athenian point of view; and the results of the American excavations at Gordion, still in progress in 1958, especially that of the 8th-century royal tomb opened in 1957, show that there may have been more truth in Hogarth's view than some have supposed. See R. Young's interim reports in *ILN* 3 Jan. 1953, 17 Sept. 1955, 10 and 17 Nov. 1956 and (especially) 17 May 1958; and *AJA* for these years.

2 '. . . Saith the Lord: Have not I brought up Israel out of the land of Egypt, and the Philistines from Caphtor and the Syrians from Kir?' Amos, ix, 7; 'And there went up also with them a mixed multitude', *Exodus*, xii, 38.

3 Chna, Hekataios fr. 254 Müller, *FGH* I F 272; 'Sanchuniathon', i, 8; also q. by Euseb., *Praep. Ev.* i, 27 (end).

4 The tablets from Ugarit (Ras Shamra) suggest that the alleged *Phoenician History* of Sanchuniathon, preserved in the alleged translation of Philon of Byblos (c. A.D. 60), universally dismissed as a mere forgery by 19th-century criticism, must be seriously reconsidered; for a bibliography of the recent literature, see O. Eissfeldt, *Sanchunjaton von Berut und Ilumilku von Ugarit*, in the series *Beiträge zur Religionsgeschichte des Altertums*, Halle (Saale), 1952.

wider and wider: from Israel we have the reactions to it of the prophets, in their declamations against social injustice. Political division
weakened the resistance of the states to the militarism of Assyria; and
when Assyria had bled herself to death, it was the turn of the Medes.

But first, Syria had its brief springtime. There was no one 'Syriac
civilisation'.[5] What was and is most stimulating about the Levant
region is precisely the variety of its ethnology, geography, scenery and
manners of life. Its history is not a Toynbeian 'intelligible field of study';
Phoenicia alone, or Israel alone, comes nearer to being such. To the
ancient world, it was a 'geographical expression'. The Persians called
it the satrapy of 'Beyond the River' (Euphrates); the Greeks, Syria (a
corruption of the name of Assyria); and they distinguished the northern
Hittites, especially those still north of Taurus, as 'White Syrians', from
the Semites and the Philistines of 'Syria Palaistine'.

Early iron-age Syria, like early Greece, was a greener and more fertile
world than that which deforestation and overgrazing have since made it.
The patches of cleared land round the cities and villages were still varied
by vast forests: the cedar forests of Lebanon, the forest of Mount
Ephraim in central Palestine, where, after David's battle with Absalom,
'the forest devoured more men than the sword devoured'. There was
much wild life. Greek horsemen in Xenophon's time chased ostriches
on the desert edge; and engraved ostrich-eggs were among Phoenicia's
exports of ornaments as far as Etruria. The lion and the bear, as well
as wolf and jackal, were enemies of the shepherd when David kept
sheep; and elephants splashed and trumpeted on the upper Euphrates.
The last were killed perhaps in the royal *battues* of ninth-century Assyrians. After that, and even earlier, as the local product became scarce,
ivory was among precious goods for import; under Solomon's commercial treaty with Hiram, King of Tyre, Phoenician ships operating
from the Gulf of Akaba brought up the Red Sea the famous 'gold and
silver and ivory and apes and peacocks'; a late Phoenician writer, Philon
of Byblos, in whose alleged sources there now seems no reason for
wholesale unbelief, adds to the same list 'pearls and precious stones and
ebony and pepper and parrots, and many other things'. Philon adds
the information that an earlier attempt by Hiram to secure a through
passage for his merchants via the Persian Gulf had been defeated by the

---

[5] As I have argued in *History*, N.S., XLI, review-article on Toynbee's *Study of History*;
see pp. 6f.

opposition of Indian merchants, already installed in Babylon; and that the source of the merchandise was a great island far to the east, apparently Ceylon.[6]

The ivory trade of Syria is of importance to us here, for it gives the first clear evidence of Greek contact with the east since the breakdown of Mycenaean commerce. Long before Greek pottery surrendered to the glamour of the east, eastern ivories, to which no local product stood as a rival, were being imported; and before long – it is characteristic of the Greeks of the Geometric age to prefer their own work – the heavy and costly teeth themselves were being imported and worked on the spot, at places including Samos, Ephesos, Kameiros in Rhodes, Sparta, Corinth and Athens. In the stratified series from the sanctuary of Artemis Orthia at Sparta, the reflections of oriental influence have been described as 'curiously confused and distant . . . perhaps because they are conveyed through some intermediary which we do not at present know' – perhaps Cilician.[7] This is in contrast to the clay masks from the same sanctuary, in which Phoenician inspiration is immediate and obvious. Sparta had close political and commercial relations with Samos, which colonised in Cilicia (pp. 48, 63) and some contact with Ephesos, the home of a famous find of ivories of somewhat later date, *c.* 650 to 550.[8] The art of Anatolia in our period, still known only fragmentarily, included the products of those 'Maionian and Karian' ivory-workers who painted their products, as mentioned in a famous passage of Homer.[9]

Ivory, this unique material, obtained from reticent and 'cagey' foreign middlemen, in the absence of any knowledge of the animal that produced it, developed a mythology of its own. In the barbarous story of how Tantalos (said, at least later, to have been a Lydian) served up his son Pelops to the gods at dinner, and how, when one of his shoulders had been eaten beyond hope of reconstitution, the gods restored him

[6] 1 *Kings*, x, 22; Sanchuniathon, vii, 7. The Hebrew words for 'apes and peacocks' are 'of unmistakable Indian origin' – R. D. Barnett, 'Early Greek and Oriental Ivories', *JHS* LXVIII, p. 1, n. 4.   [7] Barnett, *op. cit.* p. 14; perhaps Cilician, p. 25, n. 153.
[8] Much Laconian pottery (and two bronzes) at Samos: E. A. Lane, in *BSA* XXXIV, p. 179; cf. Hdt. iii, 47; Spartan-style 'spectacles' fibulae, with the springs expanded into two spirals of wire, imitated 'inorganically' in ivory in numerous specimens found at Ephesos (also Paros, Delos), Blinkenberg, *Fibules grecques et orientales*, xv. Date of the Ephesian Foundation-Deposit, Jacobsthal in *JHS* LXXI, 85ff, and, on the coins, E. S. G. Robinson, *ib.* 156ff. The early dates suggested long ago for the earlier Artemis-Orthia deposits at Sparta would seem to be due for detailed re-examination in their turn.
[9] *Il.* iv, 141ff. Further on Ivories, Dunbabin, *op. cit.* (n. 1) 38f.

to life with an artificial limb, ivory is the material used; and so it is also in the story of Pygmalion, whose statue came to life; a story staged, it may be noticed, at Amathous, in the south-eastern 'barbarian corner' of Cyprus, the island whence also the worship of the Paphian Kypris influenced the Greek concept of Aphrodite.[10] Pygmalion's name itself is a Hellenised form of something Phoenician, which appears also in the story of Dido; the story of the statue, as it stands, seems to be one of the cases in which Hellenic or Hellenistic fancy has made an agreeable fairy-tale out of some oriental myth or ritual. Even the word *elephant*, applied to ivory long before Greeks had seen the living animal, appears to have a Syrian origin; it has been plausibly derived from Hittite *ulubadas* (perhaps pronounced *ulubandas*) an ox; Hittites, when they first saw the Syrian elephants, may well have called them 'Syrian oxen', using the name of the largest animal they had hitherto known, just as the Roman soldiers, meeting King Pyrrhos' elephants in Lucania, called them 'Lucanian cattle'.[11]

The course of Phoenician trade is more difficult to trace than that of Greek trade, since Phoenicia did not, like Greece, produce and export a characteristic painted pottery. Phoenician trading settlements were also far smaller than most Greek colonies; the Phoenician homeland and population were much smaller; and Phoenicia never seems to have exported peasants from the home country to form true *coloniae*. In these circumstances the traces left for the archaeologist by the Phoenician trade, of which we have literary tradition, are often slight to vanishing point. It is only of late that the traces of early Phoenician trade with Tripolitania have been detected, at Sabratha, in the form of a few post-holes for huts, and the ashes of the camp-fires of many years, on the sea-beach.[12]

As a result of this, and of the discovery by nineteenth-century archaeology that the beginnings of civilisation in Greece, especially in Boiotia, where they were attributed to 'Kadmos the Phoenician', were indubitably native Aegean, there has been a tendency in the last generation to doubt the traditions of *any* important Phoenician western commerce earlier than the time of the Greek expansion itself. This, it now seems clear, was over-sceptical. Good authorities find the earliest Phoenician

---

[10] Pindar, *Ol.* i, Ovid, *Metam.* vi, 404ff; *id. Metam.* x, 247ff; Barnett, *op. cit.* p. 2, n. 6.
[11] *id. ib.* 6–7, n. 37.
[12] British School at Rome, excavations by Miss K. M. Kenyon; *The Times*, 1 Dec. 1951; *ILN* 29 March 1952.

tombstones in Sardinia as well as in south-east Cyprus to be inscribed in a typical ninth-century script, and compare the oldest masonry at Motya in western Sicily and at Carthage to that of tenth-century Megiddo; while some ivories from Spain (from Carmona in the Guadalquivir valley) present even earlier Syrian analogies.[13] In these circumstances, it seems unreasonable to deny the presence of Phoenician traders in the Aegean, as alleged in many passages of Homer. It may well have been through them that the small island of Kythera gave a title to Aphrodite; and when one remembers the penetration of European liquor to the remotest outposts reached by early modern trade, even among peoples who had their own native alcohol, it seems not impossible that the mysterious 'bibline wine', mentioned by Hesiod as a luxury drink,[14] may actually have been wine of Phoenician Byblos.

But at an early date Greek piracy began to make the Aegean too unsafe for foreign traders. The chronicles reported by Philon of Byblos (an anti-Hellenist, though he writes in Greek) describe 'the barbarians in the islands' as, already in the ninth century, cutting off the Phoenicians from their earlier penetration north of Rhodes[15]; and in the eighth, Greek traders, no doubt also pirates when opportunity offered, were already conducting their own commerce with Levantine ports. One of the most fruitful of modern archaeological discoveries has been that of an early Greek colony at the mouth of the Orontes: probably Poseideion, which receives a bare mention from later Greek writers.[16] The earliest Greek pottery found in bulk is geometric in island styles, especially Euboian; then, about 700, there is a catastrophe, the town is rebuilt on a new plan, and the pottery for a generation is predominantly that of Cyprus. We are reminded of a local tradition reported by a Byzantine writer, that Kasos, a prince of Cyprus, gave his name to the local Mount Kasios, having founded a settlement there, peopled by Cretans and Cypriotes, and married the native princess Amyke, the eponymous heroine of what is still called the Amq Plain. It seems clear that Cypriotes, either led by a historical Prince Kasos or venerating a hero of that name, seized the town by violence for the

---

[13] W. F. Albright, in *AJA* LIV (1950), 174ff. (But, *contra*, Rhys Carpenter in *AJA* LXII (1958), 34ff.)

[14] Kythereia (from Askalon), Hdt. i, 105; Dunbabin, *op. cit.* (n. 1), 51f. Wine, Hes. *WD* 14 589.

[15] Sanchuniathon, viii, 11.

[16] Identification argued by Woolley in *JHS* LVIII, 28ff; name in Hdt. iii, 91, Str. xvi, 751, etc.

sake of its trade. Cypriote wares dominate the pottery market for some twenty-five years, after which, and especially after a period of necessary replacement of the first 'conquest' buildings, the sub-geometric wares of Rhodes and the Aegean, on their superior merits, are gradually more and more imported again.[17]

The Rhodians spoke Doric, and the Cypriotes the archaic Arcadian dialect, inherited from their bronze-age 'founding fathers'; but the name by which Greeks became known in the east was Yawani, the Iawones of Homer, later contracted to Iones, Ionians. Of Ionians proper as colonists in the Levant, we hear only of Samians, who at an unspecified but probably early date colonised Nagidos and the melodiously named Kelenderis in Pamphylia.[18] Aiolic Kyme, an important and progressive city at this time, colonised Side, a famous pirates' nest in later days; Rhodian Lindos, Soloi and, probably later (690 tr.), the important city of Phaselis.[19]

In Pamphylia these Greeks were reinforcing earlier migrants, Arcadian-speaking like the Cypriotes, and so assignable to the age of the great sea-raids. Eastward the 'Yawanis' penetrated into Cilicia (not yet known by that name; the Kilikes, mentioned by Homer in the Troad, were still north of the Taurus), following in the steps of the saga-heroes and seers Kalchas, Amphilochos and Mopsos, whose name survived in the place-names of Mopsos' Spring and Mopsos' House (Mopsoukrene, Mopsouestia). The bilingual inscription in Phoenician and Hittite, found at Karatepe, which has provided the key to Hittite hieroglyphics, shows us an eighth-century king with an Anatolian name, Asitawandas, describing himself as King of the Dananiyim, the Homeric Danaans, and of the House of Mopsos; and the people of the plain of Tarsos itself, in the days of Xerxes (Kilikes proper by this time) are still recorded by Herodotus as having been called 'of old' Hypachaioi, men of 'Lower

---

[17] Summary of conclusions in Woolley, *A Forgotten Kingdom* (Pelican, 1953), 179ff. The Antiochene legend in John Malalas' *Chronographia*, viii, p. 257 Dindorf; Dussaud in *Syria*, X (1929), 301ff. J. Boardman in *BSA* LII (1957) identifies as Euboian much early ware formerly called Cycladic. Woolley perhaps exaggerated the break and the Cypriote interlude. – (A.A.)

[18] Pomponius Mela, i, 13.

[19] Side, Str. xiv, 667; Soloi, Mela, *l.c.*; cf. *Lindos Temple Chronicle* Entry 33 (p. 28 Blinkenberg), alleging a dedication by the Solians for a success against the natives. *Ib.* 24 (p. 20), a similar dedication alleged to have existed, from 'the men of Phaselis under their Founder, Lakios' – who is named also in the foundation-legend given by Athenaios, vii, 297; but while some writers made him a brother of Antiphemos, the founder of Gela (p. 84), others made him an associate of the colonising hero Mopsos, in the heroic age: Philostephanos, in Ath. *ib.*

Achaia'.[20] This is the context of the Hebrew genealogical document which makes 'Javan', the eponymous ancestor of the Yawanis, along with the 'fathers' of the peoples of Anatolia, a son of Japhet; in Greek, Iapetos, the proverbial 'great-grandfather', and husband or father-in-law of the nymph Asia, whose name is originally that of a district of Asia Minor.[21]

Syria by this time was feeling the weight of the terrible hand of Assyria. Pul or Pulu, a great soldier, emerging victorious about 745 from civil wars in Assyria, took an ancient Assyrian royal name, Tiglath-Pileser, and like many a usurper turned his arms abroad. In 743 he attacked Arpad, north of Aleppo, drawing down to the rescue, out of their native mountains, the forces of Sarduris II, King of Urartu (Ararat), the metal-working kingdom round Lake Van, whose export-route to the Mediterranean was threatened. Sarduris was routed, Arpad fell after a three-years' siege, and the Assyrians reached the sea. The kings of Kuweh (Cilicia), Tyre and Damascus did homage, and Mena-hem, who had usurped the throne of Israel, 'gave Pul a thousand talents of silver, that his hand might be with him to confirm the kingdom in his hand'. Syria, however, was not crushed, and adventurer after adventurer arose to lead local rebellions or to try to concert resistance.[22]

Fifty years of invasions and the sack of cities followed; it was the ruin of the once promising Syrian civilisations; and the current confusion encouraged more than one Greek soldier of fortune to try to carve himself out a lordship there, even as the 'Latins' fell upon the Byzantine world when it was weakened by the Turks. What archaeology has shown us of the Cypriote interlude at Poseideion prepares us to read of a similar episode in Philistia, another land of old sea-raider settlements, where, about 720, an adventurer known to the Assyrians as 'that ac-cursed Yawani' temporarily made himself king of Ashdod.

The Assyrians were pushing farther and farther south. Rezon, King of Damascus, was killed, his city sacked, and his ally Pekah chased from

[20] Hdt. vii, 92; Str. xiv, 668, 675-6; Karatepe inscr. tr. by A. Dupont-Sommer in *Jahrb. für Kleinasiatische Forschung*, II (1952). Early Gk. pottery from Cilicia discussed by H. Goldman in *AJA* 1938, 1940; Garstang in *LAAA* 1937, 1939, *AJA* 1943. On Mopsos, cf. now D. Hereward in *JHS* LXXVIII, with full refs.

[21] Asy, a land associated with Keftiu (a name transferred from Crete to Cilicia?) in a triumphal inscr. of Thothmes III, Hall, *CAH* II, 279ff. Asia a nymph, Hes. *Theog.* 359; wife of Prometheus (son of Iapetos), Hdt. iv. 45; wife of I., Apollod. i, 2, 2. Javan, s. of Japhet, *Genesis*, x, 2.

[22] *CAH* III: Sidney Smith, pp. 32ff; Hogarth, 138f; Sayce, 178f; Israel, 2 *Kings*, xv, 19

Samaria in 733-2, Ahaz, King of Judah, for the sake of protection against his immediate neighbours, providing Assyria with a fifth column; Hanun (Hanno), King of Gaza, fled into Egypt. A king of Hamath (Hama) led another concerted rising, and his city was sacked about 720 ('Where are the gods of Hamath and of Arpad?'). Finds of Greek geometric but no later pottery in the ruins of Hamath provide a useful synchronism.[23] It will have been the confusion caused by this rebellion that gave the Ionian his opportunity at Ashdod; but it was not for long. Sargon, the second successor of Tiglath-pileser, had already brought to an end in 722 the three-years' siege of Samaria, begun by Shalmaneser (Shalman-Asshur), and made an end of the northern Israelite kingdom; and in 720 too an Egyptian army of the Ethiopian XXVth Dynasty was routed, and Hanno of Gaza captured at Raphia on the Sinai desert-edge. The Ionian fled, but was captured by some desert or Delta prince-ling, anxious to make his peace, and handed over to the tender mercies of the Assyrian king.[24]

Further north too, Assyria at her furthest west crossed swords with Greeks pushing eastwards, and also, repeatedly, with a king known to Greek legend: Mita of Mushki (Meshech of the Bible), who is none other than that Midas, King of Phrygia, at whose touch all things be-came gold. At home the Phrygians, Midas' more westerly subjects, were to Herodotos 'richest in crops and in sheep of all the peoples that we know'[25]; and Midas was also developing east-to-west trade, along the routes between the parallel mountain ranges, between the metal-workers of Urartu and the Aegean. Greek Kyme, under a King Aga-memnon, was his port for the west (pp. 57, 69). As early as 717, Sargon first mentions 'Mita', who, like the Nubian Pharaohs of Egypt, was a natural ally, but a 'bruised reed'[26] to border states in revolt. Rusas, King of Urartu, was crushingly defeated and the capture of his principal treasury claimed by Assyria in 714; the rebel kingdoms of Tabal and Meliddu, the Tibarene and Melitene of the Greeks, suppressed and placed under direct Assyrian rule in 713-12; and in 709, the Assyrian commander in Kuweh penetrated the Taurus passes, defeated Midas' army in its own territory, and returned with prisoners and spoil. Midas accepted defeat and sent 'presents'. The Assyrians, like the Moham-

---

[23] 2 *Kings*, xv, 27ff, xvi, 9. *Rapport preliminaire sur . . . Hama* par H. Ingholt, Copen-hagen (E. Munksgaard), 1940, pp. 84-118, esp. 97f. Isaiah, xxxvi, 19. Dunbabin, *op. cit.* (n. 1), p. 30.
[24] S. Smith, *CAH* III, 42, 57-8; xvii, 2 *Kings*, 1-6, 23ff.   [25] v, 49, 5.   [26] Isaiah, *l.c.*

medan Arabs, never occupied territory in Anatolia, with its severe winters; but their frontiers had no more trouble from him.[27]

In the same year, Sargon himself was busy on the neighbouring coast. It looks as if he, like the Persians after him, was able to use the sea-power of Tyre and Sidon against their Greek trade-competitors. He claims to have 'drawn the Ionians like fish from the sea, and given peace to Kuweh and Tyre'. That it was no empty boast is shown by the fact that Cyprus submitted; not only does Sargon claim the homage of the 'seven kings of Yatnan', but he was able to have a monument with his portrait set up on its soil, in a newly fortified Phoenician stronghold at Kition, called Karti-hadashti, 'new town'.[28] Since the Cypriote interlude at Poseideion begins about this time, it looks as if the destruction of the earlier Greek settlement may have been Sargon's work, and the refoundation by 'Kasos the Cypriote' carried out under Assyrian overlordship.

That there was no future for large-scale Greek colonisation on these coasts was shown again in 696 under Sennacherib. Kirua, the Assyrian governor of Illubru, a city facing the main pass from Cilicia through the Taurus, rebelled, and was supported by the people of Tarsus and 'Ingira', probably Greek Anchiale, 'Near the Sea'. The episode is probably to be identified with one mentioned by late Greek writers, drawing on the Babylonian and Assyrian chronicles through the work of the Hellenised Babylonian priest Berosos (Bar-Osea). According to them considerable Greek forces were engaged (had Kirua invited Greek colonists?), and a Greek fleet was routed off the Cilician coast (presumably by Assyria's Phoenician allies); after which Sennacherib set up a monument with his sculptured portrait and an account of his victory, and founded (or rather refounded) Tarsus 'after the pattern of Babylon'; perhaps meaning that he secured both banks of the river Kalykadnos.[29] Assyria never again had to fight Greeks, so far as we know, and when Sennacherib's son Esarhaddon (Asshurhaddon) and grandson Asshurbanipal invaded Egypt in 680 and 668, kings of 'Yatnan' brought contingents to their fleets. Several of them, in 668, bear

[27] S. Smith, *op. cit.* 54ff.
[28] *ib.*; Ed. Meyer, *Gesch. des Altertums*[2] (1937), III, p. 43; Hall, *Anc. Hist. of the Near East.*
[29] Meyer, *op. cit.* 64ff; long extract from Alexander Polyhistor, based on Berosos' Greek version of Babylonian chronicles, in Euseb. *Chron.* i, 4f, see Müller, *FHG* III, p. 503; Clinton, *Fast. Hell.* I, 270ff, along with the parallel passage of Abydenos. See further p. 68n.

names which, in their cuneiform dress, appear as recognisable Greek:
Eteandros of Paphos, Damasos of Kourion, Pylagoras of Chytroi,
Onasagoras of Ledroi (names beginning with Onasi- or Onesi-, 'profit',
were common in Cyprus) and Aigisthos of the little sanctuary-town of
Dali, Idalion.[30]

In Lykia and Pamphylia too, Greek colonisation had no great future;
the mountaineers were able to defend themselves. Memories of Rhodian invasions survive in the record of dedications to Athena of Lindos,
engraved on stone in the third century: 'The men of Phaselis under
Lakios their founder . . . helmets and scimitars, taken from the Solymoi.'
The Solymoi appear in Homer as opponents of Bellerophon in this
region, and their 'scimitars' (*drepana*, 'sickles') are the ugly, curved
knives which were the national weapon also of Karia.[31] 'The army
which operated in Lykia under Kleoboulos' (of Lindos, one of the
Seven Sages, cf. pp. 207ff) dedicates 'eight shields, and a golden wreath
for the Statue' of the goddess. Such wreaths of gold leaves, of beautiful
workmanship but economical of the precious metal, are among the
treasures of many museums. Later, the men of Soloi dedicate 'a cup,
with a Gorgon-face in gold in the middle, and the inscription "The
Solians to Athana Lindia, a tithe and firstfruits of the spoil which they
took with Amphilochos from the Metablyreans and S—"' (the name
is broken away). But their victories did not save the Solians from
becoming notorious for the barbarisms of their dialect[32]; even Phaselis,
which prospered, became so identified with the interests of its eastern
trade that, after the repulse of Xerxes, it resisted 'liberation' by an
Athenian and allied fleet until persuaded by the good offices of its
friends, the Chians; and it was still having trouble with the mountaineers in the time of Alexander.[33]

The armament of the Asiatics made so strong an impression on the
Greeks that they adopted several features of it. The characteristic classical Greek fore-and-aft horse-hair crest with its long tail falling behind
seems to have been known to early Greece as the 'Karian' plume,[34]
but its origins were remoter than that. Reminiscent of that borne on

---

[30] J. L. Myres in *EB*[11], *s.v.* Cyprus; Gressmann, *Altor. Texte*, p. 123.

[31] *Temple Chronicle*, Entry 24. *Drepanon*, the Karian weapon, cf. Hdt. v, 112, vii, 93;
for its appearance, cf. painted bas-relief from Koniah, Texier's *Asie mineure*, pl. 103.

[32] *Chronicle*, nos. 23, 33 (see n. 19 above); Kleoboulos, D.L. i, 6, 89ff, Clem. Alex.
Strom. iv, 19, Plut. *Mor.* 392e (*on the E at Delphi*, 3). Dialect, Str. xiv, 663, D.L. i, 2, 51
('solecisms').   [33] Plut. *Kimon*, 12, 3; Arrian, *Anab.* i, 24 (end).

[34] Alkaios, in Str. xiv, 661; cf. Hdt. i, 171.

the heads of Egyptian XIXth-dynasty chariot horses, it came to be worn by foot-soldiers in Urartu and among the Syrian Hittites, and from them was adopted by the Assyrians for some infantry regiments.[35] A file of soldiers wearing the fore-and-aft crest and armed with round shield and six-foot spear, among the dado-slabs found by Hogarth at Carchemish, are evident fore-runners of the Greek hoplite.[36] Another characteristic of the hoplite array, which Greeks also ascribed to borrowing from Karia, was the round shield held by a hand-grip, and the painting of blazons thereon.[37] Many a vase-painting of the seventh and sixth centuries shows men-at-arms bearing the tusked Gorgon-face that was to strike terror into the enemy, or some individual or family blazon. Later, in a more democratic age, armour becomes less decorative and more workaday, and the heraldic blazon gives place to a city-badge or the initial letter of the city's name, like the capital Λ for Lakedaimon, which must have merged into a single zig-zag along Sparta's battle-front.[38]

But the most important of all Greek borrowings from the Levant was that of the alphabet, the letters which Greeks long continued to call *Phoinikeia*[39] (with *grammata*, 'scratches', understood). Their names, which have an obvious etymology in Phoenician but not in Greek, reveal their origin. Alpha, aleph, originally written ∠ (it was characteristic of the Greeks to think that it would look better 'standing up', A) = 'ox'; it is easy to imagine an ancestral form in which the eyes would be shown. Beta is Beth, 'house', as in Bethel, Bethlehem, etc.; on the Moabite Stone, the famous inscription of King Mesha, the contemporary of Ahab, it still has a 'gabled' top. Gamma, gimel or gamel, originally written ∧, = 'camel', apparently represented by that animal's most distinctive feature; Delta, daleth or delt, Δ, = 'tent-door', E perhaps 'lattice window'; and so on through the alphabet.[40] The story that the 'Phoenician' Kadmos invented them, believed by Herodotos, is a product partly of well-meaning mythological systematisation, and partly of clerical forgery, aimed at giving more venerable antiquity to certain relics, which Herodotus saw at Thebes.[41] Homer

---

[35] *CAH* Plates I, 219, 221; H. E. Stier, *Probleme der frühgriechischen Geschichte und Kultur*, in *Historia*, I, figs. 1–10 (pp. 203ff).
[36] Weber, *Hethitische Kunst*, pl. 31, Hogarth, *Carchemish*, I, pl. B. 8.
[37] Hdt., Str., *ll.cc.*; Str. 'Anakreon on 'Karian hand-grips'.
[38] p. 282, below.
[39] *Phoinikeia* alone, meaning 'letters', see the Teos inscr., Tod, *GHI* no. 23, end.
[40] Cf.table in Albright, *Archaeology of Palestine*, pp. 192–3.   [41] Hdt. v, 58f.

has no reference to writing, except in the saga of Bellerophon's journey to Lykia, perhaps a genuine tradition of the Mycenaean age; but Greece had passed through centuries of illiteracy since then. The date at which Greeks adopted the alphabet has been vigorously debated; but since the earliest extant specimens of Greek writing are from *late* geometric pottery, and a high proportion of early specimens either are complete alphabets or emphasise the craft of writing, it may be concluded that the introduction of writing was fairly recent, i.e., it took place probably after 750.[42]

This alphabet was not the unconditioned creation of one genius, nor of the Phoenicians alone. Many men had a hand in the development both of this script and of other forms of simplified writing, which appear in the commercial, international, Levantine world of the Early Iron Age. Evidently a need was felt for a system simpler than the existing hieroglyphics, cuneiform and other syllabaries; and several such systems were invented. The city of Ugarit (Ras Shamra) had its simplified 'alphabetic cuneiform'; early iron-age Cyprus, a syllabary of some fort y signs, some at least of them selected, with apparently arbitrary assignment of values, from the Mycenaean 'Linear B'; and the most serviceable of all, the Phoenician alphabet, seems to have been derived from signs used within the Egyptian empire, by the managers of the turquoise-mines of Serabit-el-Khadem in the Sinai peninsula. Meanwhile in Egypt, professional scribes clung to the use of the ancient writing, whose very complications endeared it to them, as making them indispensable. Scanty but sufficient fragments of this 'Sinaitic' writing found on potsherds at Lachish and, recently, at Hazor provide connecting links between Sinai and Phoenicia.[43]

The Phoenician script still bore one token of its origin from the

---

[42] e.g., among the names and frivolous remarks roughly (though deeply) cut on the rock behind the gymnasium at Thera, the words 'Enpedokles [*sic*] cut this'; I.G. XII, iii, 536, and additions in suppl. Fasc. iii; so-and-so 'himself wrote' (this), on a geometric pot, fig. 1 in Rodney Young's article in *AJA* XXXVIII (1934). See lively controversy on the dates in *AJA* XXXVII, XXXVIII, XLII, between Rhys Carpenter, advocating a date after 700, C. W. Blegen, considering this 'much too late', on the strength of inscribed geometric sherds from Hymettos, A. N. Stillwell (8th-century pots from Corinth), J. P. Harland, R. Young, B. L. Ullman; A. A. Blakeway in *JRS* XXV. Relevant is the fact that western colonies usually follow the alphabet adopted in their mother-cities. Albright (*op. cit.* 196) favours a date before or more probably soon after 800. Cf. also the very competent writing on a sherd (Attic, *c.* 710?) from Aigina, publ. by Boardman in *BSA* XLIX, pp. 183ff.

[43] Good summary by Albright, *loc. cit.*; Hazor, see Yigael Yadin in *ILN* 1 Dec. 1956, 3 May 1958.

earlier syllabaries; it had no vowels. Our vowel-system is the invention of Greeks, probably in Ionia and in the islands round Delos, where, it has been pointed out by Wade-Gery, the reference to the mimicry of 'the speech of every man' by the girl singers of the *Hymn to Apollo* implies a lively interest in the nuances of pronunciation in different dialects. Early inscriptions from Naxos show two ways of writing the long E (perhaps something like French *é* and *ai*), and others from Paros two ways of writing O.[44] For their five basic vowels, which survive in the Latin alphabet, they used Semitic consonants and 'breathings' which Greek did not require: aleph, alpha, was a Semitic unaspirated breathing, O was a Semitic guttural, I the 'jot', iota; while hē became E, and a new sign, Y, was invented for Ü. H, another guttural, became our H; later, in sixth-century Ionia, where the aspirate was dropped, it was used for long E, and about the same time a new sign for long O was invented. The Phoenician script was probably first borrowed by traders; but the invention of the vowels may, it has been attractively suggested, have been intended from the first to provide a notation for the writing down of Greek poetry.[45] Byblos exported a type of cordage for shipping, which is mentioned in the Odyssey; and if this was the papyrus rope, well-known later, it may be that papyrus paper, supplementing skins (*diphtherai*, 'parchment', a word which the Ionians long continued to apply to paper), was available to Homer.[46]

While contact with the Levant thus seems to have been the most important of the fertilising contacts of 'geometric' Greece with the east, it was not the only one. The most important contact with Egypt was later, after about 650; but one earlier Pharaoh was remembered as a personality: Bokkhoris, son of Tnephachthos (Tefnakhte), who, after the rout of the Ethiopians at Raphia in 720, had asserted himself against the southerners as king of Lower Egypt. 'Physically feeble, but sagacious beyond all his predecessors'; wise, crafty, a great law-giver and 'in character most avaricious', are the accounts of him given by Diodoros, from an unknown source (perhaps Kastor of Rhodes, who used oriental sources); adding that he reformed the law of contract, providing that contracts not set down in writing were not enforceable at law; the alleged debtor against whom there was only verbal evidence might 'take an oath, and be free of the debt'. Anyone who made

[44] *The Poet of the Iliad*, pp. 17f.   [45] *op. cit.* 11ff.   [46] *ib.*, before the foregoing.

frequent use of this provision fraudulently, comments the historian, would naturally lose his credit.[47] But Phoenicia was at this time probably in closer touch with Egypt than Greece was; its ports had no sufficient territory from which to feed themselves and, especially during the Assyrian wars, probably found Egyptian corn important. Phoenicia earlier than Greece felt the influence of Egyptian art, and in the decoration of their 'trade-goods' for export Phoenicians combined Egyptian and Assyrian motives without either understanding or caring about their original significance.[48] At home, it should be added in justice to a much maligned people, their art shows more integrity, running, it is true, not to ideal forms, but to an often attractive realism in figures of animals and in the portraiture of anthropomorphic sarcophagi, as may best be seen in the National Museum at Beirut. But even the 'trade-goods' were eagerly accepted in the west, especially in Etruria, where migrants from Asia Minor had imposed themselves, perhaps in the ninth century, as conquerors over a native 'Villanovan' peasantry. This aristocratic society was already being deluged with near-eastern trade goods, and orientalising its own art, before 750; but the earliest object found in Italy and datable through written evidence is a blue faience vase decorated with Egyptian scenes, and bearing the name of Bokkhoris. If, as is conceivable, it is a good Phoenician imitation, it may have been produced slightly after his time; if genuine Egyptian, it cannot; for the end of the XXIVth Dynasty was that the Ethiopians (Dynasty XXV) once more invaded the Delta, captured Bokkhoris and, presumably regarding him as a rebel, burnt him alive.[49] Their occupation of Lower Egypt lasted only a generation; for under Esarhaddon and Asshurbanipal the Assyrians, supported by ships from Cyprus and Phoenicia, invaded Egypt, sacking Thebes itself in revenge for a final Ethiopian counterblow in 663, and governing through Egyptian vassals, one of whom, Psammetichos (Psamatik), son of Necoh of Memphis, was destined to a distinguished future (pp. 128f).[50]

In the west the Greeks, having some mines of their own which made

---

[47] D.S. i, 79.

[48] Conspicuously so in the series of late 8th-century silver and bronze bowls ((Myres, *Enc. Brit.*[11], *s.v.* Cyprus); *JHS* LII; Della Seta, *Italia Antica*, figs. 74, 75), found chiefly in Cyprus, but also at Nineveh, Delphi, Olympia, and in Etruria; Frankfort, *Art and Architecture of the Ancient Orient*, pp. 195ff, figs. 96-98, pll. 171-3. Shields from Crete (and Delphi and Miletos) in similar style, Dunbabin, *op. cit.* (n. 1) 40f, pl. IX.

[49] Euseb. (Armenian and Synkellos), Dyn. XXIV.

[50] Hdt. ii, 152ff; Hall, *CAH* III, 280ff.

them less dependent on the western metal trade than the Phoenicians, had been less quick to explore; but by 750 their seamen had crossed the Ionian Sea. In the Odyssey, there is mention of a Sicilian slave-trade, and Taphian sea-captains from north-west Greece, who range as far as Sidon, both trade in slaves and exchange iron, probably from Greece itself, for the copper probably of Cyprus.[51] The western seas, of which Odysseus tells his more extravagant tales of gods, monsters and pastoral savages inclined to cannibalism, are still a fairy-land in the poem; but this may be due both to the poet's awareness that he is writing about a remote past, and to the willingness of the first explorers to discourage competitors. The Greek world was on the eve of its great westward expansion; but what concerns us here is that its earliest westward trade seems closely linked with another eastern contact, that with Anatolia under the Kings of Phrygia, who bore, probably alternately, the names Gordieus and Midas.

This is the context of the elder Pliny's story that one Midakritos was 'the first to import lead from the island of Cassiteris' – 'Tin Island'; though where this much-travelled name may have been located first is unknown.[52] This fits in with the stories that Midas dedicated a throne at Delphi, the first oriental potentate to have connections with that sanctuary, and that a Midas married Damodike, daughter of Agamemnon, King of Kyme.[53] Midakritos is probably a sea-captain of Kyme, named by his father after their royal patron, just as several Greeks in the next two centuries were named after Pharaohs. Damodike, or Hermodike (from the river Hermos, an important trade-route), as another version calls her, is also said to have introduced coinage into Kyme[54] – anachronistically, if we understand this of true coinage, which did not come into use until after Midas' kingdom had fallen; but coinage, like the alphabet, was only the most successful of a series of experiments made in this age. Cast (not struck) half-shekels of gold, silver and copper were current in the Assyrian world,[55] and may well have reached the Aegean. D. G. Hogarth, a generation ago, in his *Ionia and the East*, may have over-stressed the importance of Anatolian influence on Greece at this time at the expense of Levantine; but the evidence of the current excavations at Gordion shows us a Phrygian monarchy

[51] *Od.* i, 184, xv, 427, xx, 383, xxiv, 211.
[52] *Nat. Hist.* vii, 56 (57)/197.   [53] Hdt. i, 14; Pollux, ix, 83.
[54] Herakl. Pont. *Kym. Pol.* (*FHG* II, p. 216); cf. Pollux, *l.c.*
[55] Inscr. of Sennacherib, cited by Smith, *CAH* III, pp. 76, 97.

rich, artistic and literate already in the eighth century; and that it influenced Greece, e.g. in the introduction of the conical stamp-seal (not the Babylonian cylinder-seal) remains probable.[56]

Such were the circumstances in which Greece received those first seeds of new ideas in art and also in the science and mathematics of the ancient east, which were to germinate later. They were a small matter in comparison with what was to grow from them; but they were not negligible. The Greece of the 'Greek Renaissance' did not emerge in isolation; and Hellenistic scholars, with the help of translated Oriental sources, seem to have known more about some aspects of this history than Herodotos. One document preserved to us out of their researches is the curious List of Sea-Powers, quoted by Eusebios from a lost book of Diodoros, who probably derived it from the *History of Sea-Powers* of his contemporary, Kastor of Rhodes.[57] As it stands, it is a rather fatuous document, in which one sea-power vanishes from the scene when another succeeds it; and its chronology, 'stretched' to cover the period from Xerxes back to the Trojan War, cannot be pressed; but its point of interest here is the fact that it records sea-powers successively of Rhodes, Phrygia, Cyprus, Phoenicia and Egypt, *before the rise of Miletos* (pp. 128ff). These may be at least plausibly associated with the arrival of island geometric pottery in Syria; the activities of Midas and Midakritos; the Cypriote period at Poseideion; the Assyrian use of Phoenician shipping in Cilicia, Cyprus and Egypt; and the restoration of Egypt after the fall of Assyria.

This age saw also the development of the types of ship which were to compose and protect the great colonising convoys. Greek nautical vocabulary shows little of such borrowing from Semitic as we find in some other departments of civilised life (*byssos*, linen, *biblos*, papyrus; but also *gaulos*, merchant ship); no doubt Greek and Phoenician shipbuilding developed in conscious competition. One development,

---

[56] Cf. n. 1, p. 41 above; esp. the evidence for 8th-century Phrygian literacy from the royal tomb described by Young in *ILN* 17 May 58.

[57] Kastor was an orientalist, who also wrote a chronographic work on the Babylonian and Assyrian as well as the Greek (e.g. the long Sikyonian) lists of kings, which was among the chief sources of Eusebius; and the recently discovered Khorsabad king-list (published in *JNES* I, II), compared with the Greek lists, shows that Hellenistic oriental studies have to be taken seriously, though not uncritically. We do not know what evidence K. had for his *History of Sea-Powers*; but at least it is most unlikely that he compiled it out of his head, merely bringing in every people who furnished a squadron to the fleet of Xerxes, as was argued by W. Aly (*Rhein. Mus.* LXVI, 1911). The list=D.S. vii, fr. 13 Dindorf; cf. Myres, in *JHS* XXVI; Fotheringham, *JHS* XXVII.

unknown to the bronze age, is that of the specialised fighting ship, the 'long' ship, with a sharp ram on the waterline; and such ships appear almost simultaneously, as far as our evidence goes, on the late geometric 'Dipylon' vases of Athens and on Assyrian sculpture, showing Phoenician ships.[58] The Dipylon ships are of the simple *pentekonter* type, with a single row of twenty-five oars a side. Only nineteen or twenty men are usually shown, with, in one case, twenty-two oar-blades, but this is probably only for lack of space; while the upper row of oarsmen sometimes shown does not imply a second 'bank' of oars; they are the rowers on the other side of the ship, shown in accordance with the same geometric convention which, in rendering a funeral procession, will show the corpse as well as the hangings which 'cover' it, both wheels of each chariot and all eight legs of two horses. But in the Assyrian sculpture we see that a decisive step has been taken in answer to the question how to pack in more oars a side without making the ship so long as to break her back. This step is the invention of the *bireme*, in which an upper tier of rowers, rowing over the gunwale as in the old open boats, is placed in échelon, each man above and between two rowers of a lower tier, whose oars pass through port-holes. Some Greeks claimed this invention for Erythrai in Ionia, one of the most important Greek cities of early times.[59]

On the basis of the bireme, a further step was taken, in which *three* tiers of oarsmen were somehow ingeniously échelonned in three dimensions, probably by means of an outrigger (the meaning of the Greek word *parexeiresia* ?) to support the rowlocks, or rather thole-pins, of the uppermost and outermost tier; and thus was produced the *trireme*, the standard battleship of classical Greece.[60] The precise arrangement of the oars still remains unclear; the trireme, a difficult subject, is unrepresented in vase-painting, and a classical Athenian relief shows merely that only the top tier of rowers was visible to an external view. The names of the three tiers are suggestive: *thranitai* or 'stool-men', who sat high, received the most pay, and were sometimes armed to serve as marines; *zeugitai* or 'cross-bench men', who sat in the primitive posi-

---

[58] 'Dipylon' ships (and sea-battle), *CAH* Plates I, p. 283; Buschor, *Gr. Vasenmalerei*, fig. 21; Lane, *Gk. Pottery*, pl. 10b: relief from Nineveh in BM (*Guide*, 1922, p. 53); illust. in L. Casson, *Ancient Mariners*, Pl. 6 (c).

[59] Pliny, *NH* vii, 56(57)/207, q. Damastes of Sigeion (late 5th century).

[60] Best discussions, J. S. Morrison, in *The Mariner's Mirror*, XXVII (Jan. 1941); *CQ* XLI (1947); J. A. Davison in *CQ*, 1947.

tion; and *thalamitai* or men in the hold, corresponding to the lower tier
in the bireme; while a passage in Thucydides[61] makes it quite clear that
one man (not three, as in the mediaeval Venetian 'triremes') pulled each
oar. The date of invention of the trireme is equally mysterious. Late
tradition ascribes it to the men of Sidon, probably enough; Thucydides
says that *in Greece* such ships were built first at Corinth; and he appears,
though he is not quite explicit, to connect the invention with one
Ameinokles of Corinth, who 'built four ships for the Samians . . . about
300 years before the end of "this" war' (so, 704 or 721 ?). Herodotos
perhaps means to describe Pharaoh Necoh (*c.* 600) as using triremes;
but the word appears first in Hipponax (*c.* 540), and Thucydides *is* quite
explicit in saying that it was not until shortly before the Persian Wars
that whole fleets of triremes existed. Polykrates of Samos, about 520,
dominates the Aegean with 100 *pentekonters* (p. 314). Possibly earlier
Greek states may have kept only a few of the expensive triremes, along
with larger numbers of fifty-oars, for chasing pirates and coast-raiders.[62]

The existence of the specialised warship must have had an important
effect on the development of the city states; it demanded corporate
activity of a new kind: the levying of taxes to pay for expensive units
which were unproductive except by way of piracy. We hear, it is true,
of the Ionians of Phokaia doing their trading 'not in round ships but in
pentekonters'[63]; but that was later, in the western Mediterranean, in
the face of active Phoenician hostility, and in pursuit of such valuable
cargoes (the silver of Spain, which could be used as ballast) as could
pay for the maintenance of such a large crew. For the exchange of
surpluses nearer home and in less dangerous waters, the 'round' ship,
dependent on her sails, with a much smaller crew and more space for
cargo, was the only economic craft. Occasionally, too, we hear of
some very rich man paying for a whole ship and its crew in time of
war,[64] just as every fairly rich man served with his own horse and
armour; but ships, for the most part, had to be provided by the State,
and this must have involved a quite new development of state action,

[61] ii, 93.
[62] Clem. Alex. *Strom.* i, 16, 65; Thk. i, 13, 2-3, 14, 2; Hdt. ii, 158, 1, iii, 39, 3; Hipponax fr. 49 Bergk, 45 Diehl; Davison (see n. 60) denies any triremes before *c.* 540; and R. T. Williams, in *JHS* LXXVIII, suggests that Thk. wrote ναῦς δικρότους (*biremes*) and that this underlies the reading τεσσαρας καὶ ταῦτα (for δ' καὶ ταῦτα?) in *O.P.* XII, no. 1620, much our oldest text of Thk. i, 13, 2.
[63] Hdt. i, 163, 2.
[64] Like Kleinias of Athens, Hdt. viii, 17; Philip of Kroton, *id.* v, 47.

and in men's ideas of what the State was and could be expected to do. Contracts would have to be given and the satisfactoriness of work supervised by some appropriate body, as by the Council in later Athens; money would have to be voted, the size of navy estimates discussed, and taxes raised; and in states possessing both a coast and a hinterland, the principle would have to be decided, whether 'ship-money' was to be levied from inland districts. This question was pressing in Athens, with her large inland territory, and, doubtless not without discussion, it was answered in the affirmative. The whole land was divided into forty-eight *naukrariai* or 'ship-building districts'; and before long, in the normal course of events in a developing administration, we find that the 'Presidents of the Naukraries' have acquired wider importance (cf. p. 286).[65]

In the early seventh century, *after* a generation of *western* expansion, came the revolutionising of Greek art by the orientalising movement. In city after city, almost overnight, the geometric convention, which had expressed the spirit of the community defending itself behind its walls, began to seem dull and lifeless compared with the exciting and opulent art to be seen on rich men's imported eastern textiles or silver or bronze cups and bowls: the rich, curvilinear, conventionalised veget-able ornament, the lions, deer, griffins and sphinxes, the human figures in battle or hunting. For a century, Greek pottery-painting runs riot under the new influences, before the emergence of a severer style, the Black-Figure of Athens. Many details are taken over complete. The rosettes, popular as filling-ornament between the figures (for one legacy from the geometric past was a *horror vacui*), copy those which we see on the sculptured robes of Assyrian kings. The palmette (and much else in the orientalising repertoire) derives from the eastern Tree of Life; the earliest Greek examples naturally are the most luxuriant and the nearest to their model, often imitated *in toto* (not only the leaf), before the palmette settles down to a classic restraint, and finally into a late-classical convention. On a seventh-century vase from Rhodes two wild goats are actually eating one![66]

[65] *Ath. Pol.* 8, 3-4; cf. Hdt. v, 71, 2. For the elaboration of city finances by the 6th century, see C. Sterghiopoulos, *Les Finances grecques au VIe siècle* (Athens, *Institut français*, 1949).
[66] Lane, *Gk. Pottery*, pl. 16A; for other early Gk. examples, cf. pl. 34; Buschor, *Gr. Vasenmalerei*, fig. 50 (another view of the same); *id.* fig. 90, the François Vase (handles); architectural terracottas from the early Temple C at Selinous, D. S. Robertson, *Greek and Roman Architecture*, fig. 28 (=*CAH* Plates I, 387 (a)); etc. Palmettes also appear in eastern

The classic egg-and-tongue moulding derives from Egyptian friezes of lotus (i.e. water-lily) buds (the 'egg') alternating with open flowers, whose central pistil is the tongue or 'dart' of the moulding, while the wide-open petals lie back, curving concavely, parallel to the convex curve of the buds.[67] The 'Ionic' pillar-capital with its volute ornament is an adaptation of a motive first seen in late bronze-age ivory and metal-work, e.g. in the form of symmetrically opposed coils of wire on either side of the leg of a caldron-stand; but it was already in regular use *as* a pillar-capital, before its adoption by the Greeks, in Syria, where it is reproduced in miniature among the ivory-carvings, and in Cilicia; it appears on window-pilasters of the city of Illubru, depicted in the sculptured record of Sennacherib's campaign in 696.[68]

The southern Greek islands, Cyprus, Rhodes and Crete, which today, in spite of differences of environment and of recent history, show common elements of dialect and folk-culture,[69] were among the first Greek lands to show the effects of the new movement. Cyprus, which had escaped the last or Dorian wave of the great migrations, had had a 'mediaeval' period less disturbed than that of the Greek mainland, and preserving some Mycenaean features: the old Aegean 'bathing-drawers' as a dress for men; the monarchy, with a king in each chief city, dwelling in a Minoan-style palace with wide flights of steps rising from a courtyard; the chariot, still used in war down to the Persian period;

art without the whole 'tree'; *e.g.* Schäfer and Andrae, *Kunst des Alten Orient*, 495 (ivory from Nimrud in BM) and pl. 29 (tiles from throne-room of Nebuchadrezzar, Berlin). The classic representation of the Tree (with attendant demons), see Frankfort, *Art and Architecture of the Ancient Orient*, pl. 90.

[67] e.g. Ahiram's sarcophagus (Frankfort, *Art and Architecture*, fig. 76). The original pattern, on a 6th-century Gk. vase, Buschor, fig. 72; but the origin is forgotten and the pattern developing independently, already in mouldings from 6th-century temples at Ephesos and Naukratis, Robertson, *op. cit.* (n. 66) figs. 41, 45 (=*CAH* Plates I, 389). Good illustrations of the whole development in W. H. Goodyear, *The Grammar of the Lotus and Ancient Sun-Worship* (London, 1891), esp. pl. xxi, though the text is prejudiced by a theory.

[68] Demargne, *Crète dédalique*, pp. 238ff, fig. 39 (bronzes); fig. 23 and pl. I (ivories from Crete and Mycenae, the latter found 1892 and previously unpublished); supporting window-sill, Frankfort, *op. cit.* (n. 67) pl. 170 (B), cf. text, p. 194; window-frames at Illubru, Layard, *Monuments of Nineveh*. The first monumental examples probably from Cyprus, Demargne, p. 154; there were many, apparently from bases or small monuments, in the Persian siege-mound at Old Paphos (Kouklia). Elaborate exx. from Aiolic Asia (Neandria, Larisa), *CAH* Plates I, 391 (b), 393 (b); others exist in the museum at Mytilene and on the site at Klopedhi, N.-E. of Kalloni. Was Kyme the connecting link?

[69] e.g. the verbal 3rd pl. in -si (mainland -n); the peasant 'rücksack' (*vouria, vourka*), replacing the mainland one-handled *tagdri*.

a long, decadent survival of the grand style of Mycenaean vase-painting, with bulls, birds, chariot scenes and royal personages sitting at their ease or taking refreshments; the Trojan War saga, and the Mycenaean-looking Cypriote syllabary. Cyprus at this time resembles a minia-ture Byzantine world, over against the dark-age barbarism of the west. Cypriote terracottas reached the Aegean, notably Samos; and in the seventh century the island seems to have been the first Greek land where full-scale sculpture in stone was practised after Mycenaean times, imi-tating, if with little trace of inspiration, Syrian or Assyrian models before the later influence of Egypt became prevalent.[70]

But Cyprus was not destined to be to Greece all that Byzance was to western Christendom. It contributed indeed something to post-Homeric epic poetry: the *Kypria[epe]* or Cypriote Verses, an epic or collection of epic poetry whose title was variously explained; it was ascribed to Stasinos or Hegesias of Cyprus or said, in late legend, to have been written by Homer and given to Stasinos his son-in-law as a wedding present.[71] It began at the beginning of the Trojan saga, with the Bridal of Thetis and the Apple of Discord, and continued through the first nine years of the Siege to the beginning of Homer's *Iliad*, where it stopped; it thus clearly belongs to the post-Homeric develop-ment of the epic cycle.

Otherwise, Cyprus contributed curiously little, though its own local brand of archaic Greek civilisation developed, until stunted by Persia, with considerable opulence. Little seems to have been borrowed *from* Cyprus by other Greeks; they derived their oriental art-motives from Asia and later from Egypt direct. Proud of its ancient traditions, and in contact with the alien civilisation of the Phoenicians, who never lost their foot-hold at Kition (Larnaka), Cyprus, though rich, stagnated. In spite of the evidence of early trade with the east, and the tradition of an early 'thalassocracy', the island's lack of good harbours was a handi-cap; and a fact significant of the islanders' attitude to the outside world was their clinging to their unhandy script, out of unwillingness, per-haps, to be beholden to the Phoenician neighbour. It is an interesting example of the stiffening effect which a frontier position, *plus* ancient traditions, can have on a society.

Rhodes and Crete present points both of likeness and difference.

[70] Terracottas, Dunbabin, *op. cit.* 50; stone sculpture, Myres, *Handbook to the Cesnola Collection*, pp. 133ff, 193ff.   [71] Ath. viii, 334, xv, 682; Tzetzes, *Chil.*, xiii, 638ff.

Here, there *had* been a Dorian conquest. In eastern Crete, 'True-Cretans', Eteokretes, seem to have preserved their independence and a non-Greek language; a few inscriptions from Praisos and one from Dreros, nearer the centre, of the sixth century and later, use the Greek alphabet for writing this unknown tongue.[72] Elsewhere, notably at centrally-placed Knossos, Dorian lords ruled over a country population reduced, by classical times, to serfdom.[73] There was no such continuity as in Cyprus. Both islands, however, lying on the sea-route from Syria to the west, were exposed to the influence of eastern art, carried no doubt both in Phoenician ships and in their own. Rhodes is credited (by the local patriotism of Kastor?) with a brief thalassocracy, *before* Phrygia, Cyprus and Phoenicia, and if Crete, at this time, is not, this is no doubt because she had had her hour under Minos, and because Kastor only lets each thalassocrat 'bat' once. To the same source we probably owe Strabo's reference to Rhodian activity in the west 'long before the Olympic Games were founded'.[74] Crete lacks a *sacer vates* for this phase of her history; but Cretan geometric pottery is strongly represented (along with Rhodian and Cypriote) among the traces of early Greek contact with Sicily[75]; contact *before* that colonisation of the west, in which we find Rhodians and Cretans acting together.[76]

At home, accordingly, the Geometric period in both islands seems to be enriched by more foreign contacts than on the mainland. Their proto-geometric pottery, with its favourite designs of concentric circles and quadrilaterals, is closely inter-related, and shares, with some differences of treatment, the characteristic motives of contemporary Cyprus; and in the age of the mature geometric, imported ivories and bronze-work show the oriental subjects which dominate Greek pottery of the next century: lions, gryphons, warriors with the hoplite helmet, the nature goddess.

Cretan geometric, especially around Knossos, is of particular interest.[77] It breaks with the preceding period, both in vase-forms and in decor-

---

[72] M. Guarducci, *Inscrs. Creticae*, III, 6, nos. 1-6 (Praisos); H. van Effenterre in *Rev. de Philologie*, XX (1946), new find from Dreros.

[73] Sources in Ath. vi, 263, 267; also xv, 695-6, q. the War-Song of Hybrias; Willetts, *Aristocratic Society in Ancient Crete*, esp. ch. v.

[74] xiv, 654; John of Antioch, fr. 30 (*FHG* IV, p. 552), also refers to Rhodian 'thalasso-cracy' in the next line to the foundation of Carthage.

[75] Dunbabin, *The Western Greeks*, pp. 4-5, 472ff; but note reserve expressed by R. M. Cook, review in *CR* LXVI (1949), esp. p. 116.

[76] Thk. vi, 3, 3.

[77] Payne, in *BSA* XXIX, XXXI; Demargne, *Crète dédalique*, 100f.

ation. Cypriote forms largely replace the foregoing (mostly derived from Mycenaean), and the vase-painting, still angular and so far 'geometric' in style, achieves large figures, executed with a competence which makes Attic Dipylon work, for all its competence and precision, look jejune. A *chef-d'oeuvre* of the style comes from Arkades, in central Crete: the Mistress of Beasts (Artemis, they probably already called her) stands the full height of the vase, between two cranes, and holding aloft a geometrically stylised Tree of Life in either hand.[78] Little if at all later, sculpture too began to be practised: wooden images, known to us only from the references of Greek writers, and presently also statues put together out of bronze plates fixed to a wooden core, before the invention of the classical *cire perdu* process. This was the age of 'Daedalic' Crete: that of the first Greek statues to attempt to break away from pure geometric formalism, to 'open their eyes and take a step with their legs and stretch out their arms', as Diodoros puts it, centuries later[79] – explaining that this was what was meant by the legend that Daidalos, the servant of Minos, made statues that walked. These statues, the point of departure of the whole movement of Greek sculpture, were the work of Cretan artists of the generations about 700.

Daedalic Crete exercised a wide influence. Corinth itself, destined to produce the most brilliant of all orientalising vase-painting, was indebted to Crete for 'the first exotic influences'[80]; and later Greek art-history ascribed many primitive sculptures, when not to 'Daidalos' himself, then to Endoios, his pupil, or to Dipoinos and Skyllis, sixth-century Cretans, said to have worked at Argos, Sikyon, Kleonai, Tiryns and in Aitolia, and to have taught mainland sculptors working also at Sparta, Delos and Olympia.[81] Crete itself produced a rich series of orientalising vases, as did Rhodes; but by about 650 both islands were feeling the counter-influence of Corinth.

Rhodes, never insignificant, through its position and the enterprise of its people, was divided politically between three cities: Lindos, Ialysos and the smaller Kameiros. The three states usually acted together; Herodotos speaks of 'Rhodioi' as though of one state[82]; but it was not till after the *synoikismos* of the three and the foundation of one city of Rhodos after 411, that the stage was set for the island's great political

---

[78] Demargne, *op. cit.* pl. X, after Doro Levi, *Arkades*, fig. 431.
[79] iv, 76.   [80] Payne, *Necrocorinthia*, pp. 4, 5.
[81] Paus. i, 26, 4, ii, 32, 5, v, 17, 1, iii, 17, 6, vii, 5, 9; Pliny, *NH* xxxvi, 4/9; Stuart Jones, *Ancient Writers on Greek Sculpture*, pp. 7-14.   [82] ii, 178.

importance. To the Greek renaissance, apart from its attractive pottery, with friezes of wild goats and orientalising ornament, Rhodes contributed one epic poet, Peisandros of Kameiros, author of a *Herakleia*; he first is said to have equipped Herakles with the famous lion-skin, club and bow, instead of ordinary armour, as in the Hesiodic *Shield of Herakles*; and the popularity of Peisandros is shown by the fact that the vase-painters follow him. He probably also standardised the classic series of the Twelve Labours. The nobles of Rhodes claimed to be Herakleids, and there is said to have been an earlier Rhodian *Herakleia* by Peisinos of Lindos, on which Peisandros drew.[83] Later (after 600 ?) Kleoboulos, the despot of Lindos, who campaigned in Lykia (p. 52), gained a reputation for wisdom and a place among the Seven Sages (pp. 207ff).[84] For the rest, the three cities occupy an honourable but not distinguished place in the history of the eastern Aegean.

Crete, apart from her sculptors, produced in our period only one name of note: that of Epimenidas (*fl. c.* 600), prophet and religious poet, also of the Seven Sages, who was said by legend to have slept a Rip van Winkle sleep for many years in a cave. He *may* have tried to bring the religion of his people into line with the Olympianism of Homer, and been scandalised by the fact that (since in Crete the Greek invaders had given the name of Zeus to the Adonis-like Cretan Young God) Zeus at Knossos was a Dying God, and his tomb was shown. The sour comment of 'a Cretan prophet', *perhaps* Epimenidas, that his fellow-islanders were 'always liars' has, through an allusion by St Paul, become one of the most famous tags of Greek poetry.[85] For the rest, Crete by his time was already falling somewhat behind and holding somewhat aloof from the main stream of Greek history, its cities much occupied in internal wars (with Knossos, the largest, attempting a policy of local imperialism) but capable sometimes of getting together (the *synkretismos* of later Greek writing[86]) to resist outside intervention.

The fading of this early promise of Crete has puzzled many modern writers; yet it seems to be adequately explained by Cretan social conditions. The 'Cretan constitution', described by Aristotle (who says

[83] Str. xv, 688.
[84] Clem. Alex. *Strom.* vi, p. 266; Str. xiv, 655; D.L. i, 89ff (almost completely worthless).
[85] *Ath. Pol.* 1; Str. x, 479; D.L. i, 109ff; Plut. *Solon,* 12. On the Dying Zeus and 'Cretan liars', Kallimachos, *To Zeus,* 8f; *A.P.* vii, 275. Paul, *To Titus,* i, 12.
[86] Plut. *Mor.* 490b; probably a ref. to the *Koinon* of Crete, which is Hellenistic, see Willetts, *op. cit.* (n. 73) 225ff.

nothing of local variations) and revealed also in a fifth-century inscription giving the laws of Gortyn, was still in classical times archaic.[87] The typical Cretan polity was a military aristocracy, with a Dorian citizen body dominating the rural 'dwellers around', presumably pre-Dorian, and including the classes of *mnoitai*, paying tribute for their land, which was deemed to belong to the city, and *aphamiotai* or *klarotai*, villeins working on the private estates (*klaroi*) of citizens, with a status servile but protected by law, including some rights in the property if the possessor, *pastas*, died childless.[88] The word *klaroi*, 'lots', implies that the titles to these lands went back to an original 'allotment', no doubt after the Dorian conquest. *Perioikoi* were forbidden to bear arms or to engage in military exercises; and however much the cities might war among themselves, no government would stir up trouble among the serfs of another; to do so would have been suicide for Dorian Cretan society.

Among the military citizen class there were both economic and political inequalities. City kingships had disappeared, and the highest executive military and judicial authority rested as a rule with a board of ten Governors, *Kosmoi*, elected by the citizen assembly, but from the members of certain families only, which thus formed an inner aristocracy. The Kosmoi differed in this from the Spartan Ephors. After their year, the Kosmoi were eligible for, but did not pass automatically into, the city Council, membership of which, once acquired, was held for life. The citizen assembly, apart from electing the Kosmoi, voted only on such questions as the Kosmoi and Council laid before it. All citizens, however, and their families, were assured of maintenance by the state; the city revenues, in kind and later also in cash, received as tribute from the Perioikoi, were applied largely to the provision of food for the Men's Messes, *andria*, in which all citizens, divided into Clubs, *hetaireiai*, met for meals, and to some similar provision for their wives and children.

The Cretan citizen, rich or poor, was thus a soldier, a privileged person, and did no menial or productive work. His education was calculated to fit him for this station in life. He was literate, at least in classical times, and knew well the traditional poetry and songs that

[87] Ar. *Politics*, ii, 1271b–72b. The Laws of Gortyn, Guarducci, *Inscr. Creticae*, IV, no. 72; detailed discussion in Willetts, *op. cit.* (n. 73); select bibliography, *ib.* p. 4, n. 2.
[88] Laws of Gortyn, col. v, lines 25ff; Willetts, pp. 10, 46–51; sources, see n. 73.

enshrined and idealised his way of life; but first and foremost his training was athletic, fitting the boy for the day when, at seventeen, he was
enrolled in one of the Herds, *agelai*, each led by a son of a noble family,
which trained together as soldiers, and fought mimic battles with each
other on festal days. Cretan society, like that of Sparta at a somewhat
later date, had become stereotyped. The men's club-life, like the para-
sitism of the military Dorians upon an alien peasantry, is reminiscent of
some uncivilised peoples in other parts of the world; and, as at Sparta
and in some other military societies, homosexuality was considered
respectable.[89] With the tradition carefully preserved between the cities,
that in no circumstances did one countenance revolt even by an enemy
city's serfs, and with the sea as a barrier to outside interference, the
Cretans held down their subjects without great difficulty; but it was
at a price: the price of never developing beyond the level of culture
reached at the beginning of the historic period. Of incident there was
no lack. Kosmoi were accused of corruption or illegal action and in-
duced, by riot or by pressure from their colleagues, to resign; riots
were engineered when some powerful nobleman did not choose to
submit to a legal decision; and since the laws left room for many arbitrary decisions by the Kosmoi, this could often happen. Sometimes
these riots led to the suspension of the office of Kosmos (*akosmia*), and
the establishment of a dictatorship, the very negation, comments Aristotle, of civic order.[90] For the rest, the Dorian Cretans fought, hunted,
loved, sacrificed and sang and ran races and feasted on festal days; the
peasants tilled the land, and looked on, no doubt cynically, at these
proceedings, and conducted their own agrarian religious rites. Plato,
the grand reactionary, found much to admire in Crete. Meanwhile, the
rise of classical Greece went on elsewhere.[91]

[89] Str. x, 483; Ar. 1272a.   [90] Ar. 1272b.
[91] Cf. Demargne, *Crète dédalique*, pp. 348ff ('l'Arrêt brusque de la Renaissance Crétoise');
Dunbabin, reviewing Demargne in *Gnomon*, 1952, 195ff.

Further to n. 29 (p. 51): For the archaeology, see now H. Goldman, *Excavations at
Gözlü Kale, Tarsus*: III, *The Iron Age*; especially, therein, Hanfmann on the Greek pottery,
arguing that Orientalising pottery associated with the sack necessitates an *earlier* date
than that established by Payne for the beginning of proto-Corinthian. But Boardman
in *JHS* LXXXV (1965), (review, p. 232, and article, pp. 5-16), doubts whether this pottery
can be so closely associated with the sack of 696. On this and following chapters, see
now also Boardman's excellent *The Greeks Overseas* (Pelican, 1964).

CHAPTER IV

Greece and the West, and the Rise of Corinth

CARTHAGE, a new development in Phoenician colonisation, being not only a trading-post but a New City (another Karti-Hadasti), was founded, according to later computations, about 813 or earlier, by Dido or Elissa (both good Semitic names), sister of Pygmalion, King of Tyre, who had killed her husband.[1] At this time Greek sailors were just beginning to penetrate the western Mediterranean. Proto-geometric pottery had already reached the 'heel' of Italy, and mature geometric in some quantities reached Etruria, Latium and the Bay of Naples; pottery believed to originate from Crete, the Cyclades, Corinth, Argolis and perhaps Cyprus; though reserve is necessary over the acceptance of at least some of these identifications.[2] The eighth-century trade implied seems to have by-passed south-east Italy; it was Etruria, already penetrated by oriental art-styles, that offered attractions, especially the metals which Greece wanted in increasing quantities.

About 750 took place an epoch-making event; one wonders whether the example of Carthage contributed to it. Kyme in Aiolis, the ally of Midas of Phrygia (p. 57), joined with Chalkis and Eretria to found a large, permanent outpost, outside the Etruscan area, but not far from it – some two days' sail for a merchant ship under favourable conditions. The place selected was of a kind often to be favoured by Greek colonists: on the neck of a peninsula, which, though hilly, could shelter thousands of men and beasts in case of war. Inland, beyond low hills, lay the plains of Campania, which the Greeks were to dominate for a time.[3] The peninsula, the western promontory of the Bay of Naples,

---

[1] 815, Timaios in D.H. i, 74; 818, Velleius, i, 6; 825, Justin, xviii, 7. Topography and archaeology, see Lapeyre and Pellegrin, *Carthage puhique*, Paris (Payot) 1942. Archaeology, as usual, suggests a considerably later date – hardly before 725! Cf. Rhys Carpenter in *AJA*, 1958; Demargne in *Rev. Arch.*, 1951, reviewing Cintas, *Céramique Punique*.

[2] Dunbabin, *The Western Greeks*, pp. 3ff; cf. review by R. M. Cook in CR LXIII, pp. 113ff, esp. 116; and n. 4 below.

[3] Date from archaeology, some 20 years before Syracuse, Dunbabin, *WG* 5; topography, A. Maiuri's guide, *I Campi Flegrei*, illustr.

had already been visited and perhaps even settled on a small scale by Greeks, including Rhodians according probably to the Rhodian Kastor; and finds of Euboian geometric pottery in burials antedating **the**

South Italy and Sicily

large-scale colonisation warn us at least not to dismiss the tradition out of hand.[4]

To this site Hippokles of Kyme and Megasthenes of Chalkis[5] (their names are preserved, no doubt through the 'hero' cult paid to them as founders) conducted their great convoys; it must have been one of the most ambitious and best organised enterprises ever undertaken by

[4] Str. xiv, 654 (from Kastor?). The pottery Euboian, see Boardman in *BSA* LII (1957).
[5] Str. v, 243.

Greeks at such long range; and there, no doubt, like the Founding Father of the Phaiakes in the Odyssey, they 'drove a wall round the city, and built houses' (protection first, shelter second) 'and established temples of the gods, and divided the ploughland'.[6] The legends of Odysseus were much in the minds of the pioneers on this coast, and a cult of the hero grew up at several points.[7] The pastoral savages, no doubt still to be found among the hills, may even have given Homer the details of his picture of the cave-dwelling, dairy-farming and non-agricultural Cyclops.[8] The perilous strait between Skylla and Charybdis was identified with the Straits of Messina, and the rocks where the Sirens sang were found, appropriately, near Sorrento. Thus was born the first Greek western colony; Chalkis was revered as its official mother-city, while Kyme gave it its name, which for distinction we may render in its Latin form, Cumae: a division of privileges between joint founders which more than once recurs.[9] Centuries later, her coins still preserved the memory of the city's double origin.

Chalkis, whose name means Copper-city and is one of the few city-names significant in the Greek language, was famous for swords,[10] and no doubt for other metalwork; hence her special interest in the western trade. With Eretria, her southern neighbour and sister, she had doubt-less fought over the rich plainland between them, divided by the Lelantos torrent; wars perhaps not very lethal, and marked by chival-rous conventions, such as one 'not to use long-range weapons'.[11] The battles were fought out by their knightly cavalry, the low-class archer or slinger being excluded. But now they went into close partnership, and Eretrians also figure in the earliest western enterprises. Eretrians occupied the island of Corfu (Kerkyra),[12] an invaluable staging-post on the way to Italy; and the two cities together occupied the volcanic 'Monkey-Islands' (Pithekoussai) off Cumae, now Ischia and Procida, where they found gold. The volcanic soil too was rich; but presently the colonists were driven away by violent volcanic outbreaks, 'fire bursting from the ground', accompanied by earthquakes.[13] They then crossed the water to the neighbouring headland. Livy says that this

[6] *Od.* vi, 9f.
[7] E. D. Phillips, 'Odysseus in Italy', in *JHS* LXXIII.
[8] *Od.* ix, 112ff, 218ff, on the Cyclopean economy.
[9] Str. v, 243, cf. below, pp. 73, 84.
[10] Alkaios, fr. 54 Diehl (in Ath. xiv, 626), l. 5; Aesch. (fr. 356 Nauck) *ap*. Plut. *Mor.* 434a.
[11] Str. ix, 448. There is no *record* of wars before *c.* 700.
[12] Plut. GQ xi.   [13] Str. v, 247.

island settlement preceded the official foundation of Cumae; finds of geometric pottery give colour to this story, while a solitary Mycenaean sherd hints at the possibility, here as in the Lipari Islands, of still earlier Aegean predecessors.[14]

Trade, especially the metal-trade, therefore did introduce Greeks to the western Mediterranean; but soon after the foundation of Cumae, there develops a new phenomenon: the settlement of thousands of peasant families in the west, upon sites often chosen not, or not only, for their commercial advantages but for the sake of land. This, the first and greatest outburst of Greek colonisation, was organised by the new landed oligarchies. It may seem surprising that such governments should interest themselves in such an enterprise; but the connection is not far to seek. Wealth in land was becoming more and more unequally distributed, largely no doubt through the division of holdings between sons in the more fertile families, and their engrossing by inheritance in the less fertile; hence the importance, especially to the chief property-owning families, of those 'laws about heiresses' which are brought to our notice so frequently in accounts of Greek constitutions.[15] While the rich grew richer, the poor clamoured for a 'redistribution' (cf. pp. 274, 300). While there was a king reigning, it was to him that the appeal would be addressed; and in reducing the monarchy to a cipher the rich were incidentally insuring themselves against the possibility that such a thing might be done. But having done this, they found themselves directly responsible for dealing with peasant land-hunger. If conquest of more land near home was impossible, colonisation abroad was a sovereign remedy. Colonisation long remained in aristocratic eyes, including those of Plato, the great, painless method of averting social revolution by draining off the despised, uncultured and potentially dangerous poor.[16]

In this movement the Chalkidians, with their experience gained in the foundation of Cumae, played a leading part. We shall hear of them colonising in company with men of Andros and Naxos and with Messenians, as well as with Eretria and Kyme; and probably man-

[14] Livy, viii, 22; Dunbabin, *WG* 6.
[15] e.g. in Athens, *Ath. P.* ix, 2, lvi, 6; Sparta, Hdt. vi, 57, 4; Crete, Laws of Gortyn, col. vii, 15ff. Willetts, *Aristocratic Soc. in Anc. Crete*, ix, 69ff; Plato, *Laws*, 740, and Ar. *Politics*, 1274b (Thebes) on 'preserving the number of Lots' (preventing engrossment).
[16] *Laws*, 735-6.

power from many other sources helped to populate the numerous colonies of Chalkis.

Comparison of pottery from native settlements in eastern Sicily with the earliest from Greek burials at the colonies shows that some trade had developed here too, in the years between the first contact with central Italy and the colonisation of the island coast. At Leontinoi, in the plain of the Symaithos, south of Etna, archaeology suggests some twenty years' duration of a joint Greek and Sikel settlement, before the foundation of the exclusively Greek city.[17] This must have been before the beginning of the main Chalkidian colonisation, at least if we are to believe Thucydides, who gives the impression of a series of expeditions, mounted as a deliberate military operation, all within a few years:

'The first Greeks in Sicily were Chalkidians of Euboia led by Theokles, who founded Naxos and set up the altar of Apollo the Guide which still stands outside the city; sacred embassies from Sicily offer sacrifice at it before setting sail.' 'Other Ionians', mentioned by Ephoros, presumably included Naxians, who gave the city its name. Five years later 'Theokles and the Chalkidians set out from Naxos and colonised Leontinoi, driving out the Sikels by force of arms, and thereafter Katane, where the Katanaians chose one Euarchos as Founder for themselves'.[18] That is to say, the Chalkidians first secured their base, at a point sheltered from the interior by Etna and the northern mountains, and close to the first landfall for coasting vessels. Sikel settlements long continued to exist in those hills, importing Greek pottery and metal-work, and apparently friendly.[19] Theokles was not concerned with that rough country; he was after a greater prize. After only five years for consolidation, he leads his men to a swift conquest of the plain of the Symaithos, first securing Leontinoi, on its far side, and lastly Katane, nearer Naxos, where the official Founder was the propitiously named Euarchos.

This piece of ruthlessness at the expense of inoffensive barbarians with whom the Greeks had had peaceful dealings for years, may have been assisted by treachery. A late writer tells how, the Chalkidians having settled peaceably in Leontinoi along with the Sikels, and being bound by oaths not to molest them, Theokles introduced some Megarans, who had settled on the coast, set *them* to attack the Sikels, and

[17] Dunbabin, *WG* 45.   [18] Thk. vi, 3, 1 and 3; Str. vi, 267.
[19] Dunbabin, *ib.*

later ejected them in turn and had the place to himself.[20] This does not fit very well into Thucydides' brief narrative; though he does mention a short-lived participation in the colony at Leontinoi by these Megarians, who, after this and various other false starts, during which their leader Lamis died, finally founded Megara Hyblaia, 'Hyblon, a Sikel king, having betrayed the land to them'.[21] Once more we have the suggestion of treachery and, what treachery presupposes, peaceful relations intervening between episodes of open warfare. The treachery itself, and not least the sharp practice over oaths, is, alas, no less typical of Greek history than the ruthless assertion of the right of the stronger.[22] It is historically quite incorrect to describe early Greek expansion and dealings with more backward races as typically 'gentle'.[23]

Other Chalkidian colonies grew up in the same region: a Kallipolis, a new Euboia, both destroyed by later despots of Syracuse[24]; but meanwhile, it is significant that Theokles took no measures to secure the Straits. Pirates from Cumae were the first settlers at Messina; they called it Zankle, after the native name of its sickle-shaped harbour, for 'the Sikeloi call a sickle *zanklon*'.[25] Later 'a large body from Chalkis and the rest of Euboia came and divided up the land', under Perieres of Cumae and Krataimenes of Chalkis.[26] Rhegion, whose name means 'the Breach', across the straits among the mainland Sikels, was founded probably not much later; and it also was a famine-relief settlement. Chalkis, in a year of bad harvest, 'devoted' one-tenth of its population to Apollo; the men of Zankle invited them to the adjacent site; and Antimnestos of Zankle with Artimedes of Chalkis organised the colony.[27] The newcomers brought with them a group of Messenian nobles and their dependents, and these nobles, it is interesting to hear, came to form a dominant group (through their prestige and being accustomed to command?) among the Ionian-speaking peasant majority.[28] Long afterwards (about 490), one of their descendants, Anaxilaos,

[20] Polyainos, *Stratagems*, v, 5.   [21] Thk. vi, 4, 1.
[22] Cf. Polybios, xii, 6, on Lokroi (below, p. 80).
[23] As maintained by Toynbee, *Study of History*, V, 210ff (esp. 214).
[24] Hdt. vii, 154, 2 (Kallipolis), 156, 3 ('the Euboians in Sicily'), cf. Str. vi, 272, ix, 449; unless 'Euboia in Sicily' is indeed a ghost-name, Hdt.'s ref. being to the Euboians in Sicily generally and Str. having assumed a city so named. Such a city is usually accepted by modern scholars, though no such site has been identified; cf., e.g., Dunbabin, *WG* 128.
[25] Thk. vi, 4, 5.
[26] Thk. *ib.*; Str. vi, 268 (inferior).
[27] Str. vi, 257, from Antiochos of Syracuse, D.H. xix, 2 (Artimedes).
[28] Str. *ib.*

despot of Rhegion, gained possession of Zankle also; and it was then that the city obtained its still current name.[29]

Zankle at some early date founded a daughter-colony twenty-five miles to the west, at Mylai,[30] a strong position on the neck of a roomy peninsula, and this completed the tale of the early Chalkidian colonies in Sicily.

The event which brought the Messenians to the west must be mentioned here, for it was a vitally important event in the age of Greek expansion, and one destined, indeed, to distort tragically the whole course of classical Greek history. While Chalkis and other cities were learning to expand overseas, Sparta, at the expense of Messenia, was uniquely successful in expanding by land. A small-scale map gives little hint of why Sparta should have been able to conquer Messenia, rather than Messenia Sparta; but to visit the Taygetos range is to see the fateful superiority of Sparta's position. From their group of villages, standing high (about 600 feet) and hard by the foot of the main mountain chain, the Spartans dominated that range and held its passes, especially the famous Langadha. The ascent from Messenia is much longer and starts from a lower, often hot and enervating plain almost at sea-level. It followed that in war, raiding of the rich farm-lands of Steny-klaros, the economic centre of Messenia, would be regular and very hard to stop, while any Messenian raids into Lakonia would be difficult. The Messenians had indeed a refuge, in the great mountain amphitheatre of Ithome; but their tragedy was that it, and all the hill-country of western Messenia, lay for defensive purposes on the wrong side of the plain.

At the present day, and without reference to ancient history, the Messenian plain-dwellers seem rather afraid of the mountain people, whom they still call Lakones, and are careful not to offend them; but it was, we are told, a Messenian outrage, by some youths against some Spartan girls at a festival at a border sanctuary, which gave Sparta the *casus belli*, the cause necessary to rouse normal human nature from simple covetousness – they could see the rich plains from their nearest pass – to fighting point, with sexual honour to avenge, and a sense that the gods would be with them. The Messenians refused satisfaction; perhaps they felt that the Spartans intended aggression anyhow; and

[29] Thk. vi, 4; cf. Dunbabin, *WG* 396.
[30] Str. vi, 272; *perhaps* the 'Chersonessus in Sicily' of Jerome, 716-5 B.C.; Dunbabin, *WG* 12, is too positive.

a peace-party (were they those whose lands were certain to be ravaged first?), finding themselves assailed as defeatists, abandoned their country and emigrated to the west; they chose, as it proved, the better part. Twenty years of warfare followed; land-hunger added to Spartan desire for revenge the persistence characteristic of economic motives. King Theopompos, eighth ancestor of Damaratos and Latychidas in the generation of 500-480 (so, about 700),[31] the realist who had acquiesced in the election of the Ephors to limit his power at home, the 'first historical Spartan',[32] became the hero of the war. By its end, Ithome had become untenable; with the plain exposed to continual devastation, it was impossible to keep large numbers of people living there, and without that, there was nothing to check the invaders. 'Forsaking their fertile farms, they fled from the high mountains of Ithome', says the Spartan poet; and those who did not choose to abandon all were permitted to cultivate the plain under Spartan lordship, paying a crushing tribute: 'like asses heavy-laden beneath great burdens; rendering to their masters under grim compulsion the half of all the produce of their fields.' As a token of subjection, they were also required to take part in mourning for the deaths of their lords; especially, probably, in the great public mourning for Spartan kings.[33] It was the status of helots.

Sparta had won 'Messene good to plough and good to plant', and mastery of the hill-country to the west and south-west soon followed. At the port of Asine in the south, perhaps previously called Rhion, the Spartans gave a home to the people of Asine in Argolis, recently expelled by Argos; the story, told by Pausanias, is confirmed by the fact that the site in Argolis, which yields copious pottery from the bronze age to late geometric, was left desolate exactly at this epoch.[34] Sparta was to repeat the step two generations later, after the great revolt in Messenia (pp. 182ff), in favour of another dissident sea-port population of Argolis, the people of Nauplia[35]; these she settled at Methone or

---

[31] *Accessit* 786, Eusebios; but the reigns of Spartan kings in both lines in the 5th-4th centuries average about 25 years (like those of France, England and Scotland in historic times), and it is most unlikely that those of archaic Sparta were much longer.

[32] Wade-Gery (from lecture-notes, 1923).

[33] Tyrtaios, the 8-line fr. built up from quotations by Pausanias, iv, 6, 5 (ll. 1, 2), 15, 2 (4-6), 13, 6 (7, 8), and schol. on Plato, *Laws*, 629a (3); cf. Str. 279 (ll. 5-8); the only fully authentic and near-contemporary evidence on the war. Tribute, and 'Mourning for their masters', Tyrt. *ap.* Paus. iv, 15, 5; cf. Hdt. vi, 58 (for Sp. kings).

[34] Str. viii, 373; Paus. iii, 7, 4, iv, 14, 3; date confirmed by the Swedish excavations at Asine. Rhion, 'opposite to Tainaron' (Str. viii, 360), named by Ephoros among cities of early Messenia (*ib.* 361).   [35] Paus. iv, 24, 4; 35, 2.

Mothone in the extreme south-west, where the Messenians, in the generation before the conquest, are reported to have built a port 'though their land had others too'[36]; a step evidently intended to provide them with a profitable port of call for shipping bound for the west.

Sparta, with her increased territory and population of serfs to till it, became one of the richest states of the seventh century. The perils of her position were not yet apparent. But the strain of the long war left her with an aftermath of trouble among her own citizens. That a revolutionary conspiracy which now occurred was entirely the work of the disenfranchised sons of Spartan mothers, who had formed liaisons with other men during the absence of their husbands (as the story has it[37]) may be thought unlikely; that such people had a part in it is not. In any case, as a sequel to the war, Sparta made her one contribution to the colonisation of the west. Those who might have been troublesome at home were sent off to a site with a good, land-locked harbour and fishing-ground under the 'heel' of Italy, and founded the important city of Taras (Taranto).[38]

Other mainlanders too followed the Chalkidian example; especially coast-dwellers of the westward-facing Corinthian Gulf. The people of Achaia, with no room to expand between the Arcadian mountains and the sea, sent out to Italy in a generation or two a prodigious number of colonists, and occupied most of the best land on a coast that must have seemed a paradise after their cramped quarters at home. Probably the earliest colony (720 tr.[39]) was built in a spacious and lovely plain, girdled by forested mountains, on the narrowest part of the 'instep' of Italy, where the rivers Sybaris and Krathis (both named after waters of Achaia[40]) unite to flow to the sea. Hither one 'Iselikeus' (Is of Helike, the federal meeting-place of Achaia?) led a band of his countrymen and a contingent from Troizen, a minority which was presently driven out after a quarrel.[41] Despite these growing-pains, the city of Sybaris prospered enormously (pp. 383ff). Its population, on the most modest

[36] *id.* iv, 3, 10.
[37] Ar. *Politics*, 1306b; Antiochos of Syracuse, *ap.* Str. vi, 278f, Ephoros, *ib.* 279f; etc.
[38] Str. *ib.* 'Skymnos', 330ff, Justin, iii, 4; Polyb. viii, 28 (the Spartan festival Hyakinthia observed at T.); the fishing interest, Ar. *Politics*, 1291b.
[39] 'Skymnos', 256ff; 709-8 B.C., Eusebios. Archaeological evidence is said to show that Poseidonia (a daughter-colony, see n. 44) was itself occupied as early as 700, see *Not. d. Scavi*, 1937; but the precise dating of early Greek pottery itself depends upon the literary evidence for the western colonies. Cf. Dunbabin, *WG* 24f and nn.; 439ff; Vallet and Villard in *BCH*, 1952.
[40] Str. viii, 386.
[41] Str. vi, 263; Ar. *Politics*, 1303a.

ancient estimate, which seems entirely probable, reached 100,000.[42] Its walls were six miles in circumference. Its territory, beyond its fabulously fertile plain, extended over the hills to the western sea, with ports at Laos and Skidros, and included twenty-five dependent townships and the lands of four subject native tribes.[43] Very shortly, Sybaris founded a daughter-colony at Poseidonia (Paestum), half-way to Cumae, and across her isthmus she too traded with Etruria.[44] Further south, in a more breezy and bracing situation north of the Lakinian headland, where now one column of a temple of Hera stands, a monument to so much life, Myskellos of Rhypai founded Kroton,[45] sister-city and ally of Sybaris until a class-war supervened, a city only less rich and populous; she expanded on the side away from Sybaris, with an ally in Achaian Kaulonia, founded by Typhon of Aigion, and subject boroughs at Skylakion on another isthmus and Terina north of it, both on the western sea.[46]

Thus at a very early date an Achaian 'sphere of influence' was growing up in south Italy, outstripping in potential wealth the Chalkidian in north-east Sicily and the Straits region. The appetite grew with what it fed on; the Achaians aspired, it is said, to exclude other Greeks from the region,[47] and perhaps viewed with some concern the arrival of the Spartan 'Parthenioi' at Taras. Taras was too far away for interference, but Sybaris and Kroton, joining forces, seized the site of Metapontion, only twenty-four miles from it, presumably in order to deny ground to a rival.[48] A certain Daulios, despot of Krisa, the port of Delphi, is also said to have taken part in this venture, even as the official Founder[49]; but the famous ear of corn on Metapontine coins (after 550) testifies to the character of the community as land-minded and agricultural.

But, with their resources of manpower thus fully extended, the Achaians were unable to hold all the stretch of coast between Metapontion and Sybaris; and an Ionian swarm settled in between: a colony from Kolophon, a cavalry-state (like Chalkis and Eretria at this time),

[42] 'Skymnos', 341.

[43] Str. *l.c.*; Laos and Skidros, Hdt. vi, 21; position of Laos, Str. v, 253. Fertility of the plain, Varro, *On Agriculture*, i, 44.

[44] Str. vi, 251f; 'Skymnos', 248f; Sybarite luxury, trade with Etruria and with Miletos (in wool), Timaios, *ap.* Ath. xii, 519. Date of P., cf. n. 39.

[45] Str. vi, 262, 'Skymnos', 325.

[46] Kaulonia, 'Skymn.' 318ff, Paus. vi, 3, 10; Skylakion, Str. vi, 261; Tereina, 'Sk.' 306f.

[47] Justin, xx, 2.   [48] Antiochos, *ap.* Str. vi, 264f.   [49] Ephoros, *ap.* Str. *ib.*

whose city, like Athens, lay a few miles from the sea.[50] Kolophon's
cavalry had just been overwhelmed, after years of invincibility,[51] by
that of Lydia, newly aggressive under Gyges (pp. 102f). (The date may
thus be about 675.[52]) Her lower city had been overrun,[53] her lands
(we may presume) much curtailed. It must have been a swarm of the
dispossessed, perhaps guided by sailors of Rhodes, who are said to have
visited the place earlier,[54] which sailed to the navigable river-mouths
of the Siris and Akiris, destroyed the local settlement of the Chones
(a tribe whose name recalls that of the Epirote Chaones), and founded
a city called Polieion,[55] in honour of their Ionian Athena Polias. Greeks
commonly continued, however, to call it Siris, after the name of the
river, already familiar.[56]

At the other end of their domain, too, the Achaians were unable to
exclude interlopers. Euanthes of Lokris, in 673 tr., led a colony of his
people to the Zephyrian Cape, so-called because it gave shelter from
the west wind, between Kaulonia and Rhegion; soon afterwards they
moved to a hill-position fifteen miles further north.[57] The ports of
departure for this expedition may well have been in the western Lokris,
over against Achaia on the Corinthian Gulf; but it was to the Hundred
Houses of Opus, near Thermopylai, which seems to have been reckoned
the senior Lokrian city, that the aristocracy of Epizephyrian Lokroi
traced its descent – through the mother, according to the ancient Lokriau
custom.[58] The two Lokrian areas, though physically separated, kept in
touch, and may well have acted together. Among the rank and file
of the settlers there are said to have been many outcasts, like the Parthenioi of Taras, flotsam from the upheaval of Sparta's Messenian War;
it is possible enough, though the character of the tradition does not inspire confidence.[59] It is conceivable that, in both cases, what had really
happened was some stricter definition of the conditions for citizenship
in an aristocracy, and that the later story that Lokroi was colonised by
'runaway slaves, adulterers and kidnappers', or Taras by illegitimate

---

[50] Hence Beloch (*GG*² I, ii, 241f) dogmatically denied that Kolophon ever colonised!
[51] Str. xiv, 643.   [52] Cf. p. 103, below.   [53] Hdt. i, 14.
[54] Str. vi, 270; cf. xiv, 654. [Now (1967) confirmed by finds of early Rhodian and
Ionian pottery; see *Herakleia Studien*, = *Röm. Mitt.*, Suppl. 11, forthcoming.]
[55] Str. vi, 263.
[56] Archilochos, *ap.* Ath. xii, 531; cf. Gela (Lindioi), p. 84; Borysthenes (Olbia), p. 115;
Tyras (Ophioussa), *ib.*   [57] Str. vi, 259.
[58] So, Ephoros, *ap.* Str. *l.c.*; contrary to *a priori* probability as well as to most Greek
writers (see 'Skymnos', 314ff), and therefore probably from definite evidence.
[59] Ar. *ap.* Polyb. xii, 8, *q.v.*

children, arises from the founding of colonies for those excluded. In Homeric society, fathers could treat their base-born sons as members of the family, and so of the aristocracy, but under classical Greek laws, the laws of a crowded country, this was often forbidden.[60] Entirely credible, though in its details perhaps embellished, is the companion story of how the Lokrians by treachery drove out the Sikel natives: they made peace with them (promising to take no more land) 'for as long as these heads remain upon our shoulders and we stand upon this earth'; and having thus lulled the Sikels to security, the Lokrians, who had taken the precaution of putting earth in their shoes and heads of garlic on their shoulders under their shirts, attacked them unaware.[61] It is completely in the Greek manner to consider that the gods would not be offended if one avoided literal, verbal lying[62]; and the phrase 'How the Lokrians kept the Treaty' became a proverb.[63]

The gods, it seems, were not offended. Lokroi prospered, if less resplendently than its Achaian neighbours, extending its bounds, like them, to the western sea at Hipponion and Medma.[64] But the most interesting thing about its history is the statement that Lokroi was the first of all Greek cities to have its laws published on stone.[65] The codifier's name is given as Zaleukos, which scholars have believed to be an epithet of a god; but it is not otherwise known as such. The date assigned to him by the chronographers is 660 – soon after the foundation of the colony, 673 tr.; and archaeology seems to confirm that it was the last Italian 'primary' foundation.[66] The laws are said to have been crude and simple, and later writers studied them in search of archaic curiosities.[67] Not very much later is said to have been the code of Charondas at Katane.[68] The two codes together, though little is known about them, are a portent of the new age of literacy. They are also characteristic of the effect of colonisation upon Greek society. Beyond the sea, and often with mixed populations, men were unable to rely in

---

[60] e.g. in classical Athens, *Ath. P.* 42, and orators.

[61] Polyb. xii, 5ff, Polyain. vi, 22.   [62] Cf. e.g. Thk. iii, 34.

[63] Zenobios, *s.v. Lokron synthêma* (but cf., *aliter*, Oldfather in *Philologus*, LXVII; *PW*, Lokroi, col. 1315).

[64] 'Skymnos', 308.   [65] *id.* 314ff.

[66] Or 661, 677 (Jerome); foundation-date confirmed as considerably later than Syracuse, etc., by the earliest pottery from the site, Johansen, *Vases Sicyoniens*, p. 182; but cf. discussion by Dunbabin, *WG* 35, n. 6.

[67] Ar. *Politics*, 1274a; Ephoros *ap.* Str. vi, 260; D.S. xii, 20f (who makes him a Pythagoreian!); numerous later fables about him, cf., e.g., Ath. xi, 429a, Aelian, *VH*, ii, 37, xiii, 24.   [68] Ar. *ib.* a-b; 1252b; 1296a; 1297a; Her. Pont. 25.

all things upon implicitly accepted custom, which was what *nomos*, literally 'distribution', had hitherto meant. For particular disputes, particular *themistes*, 'layings down' of the law by a magistrate, might suffice; but men wished to know the principles on which the magistrates operated; especially in the colonies, where populations, drawn from the economically frustrated or politically defeated at home, would from the first be out of temper with arbitrary *themistes* based ostensibly on divine inspiration.[69] It is characteristic that it was first in the west that codes were published, associated with the name of a human legislator or codifier, who would himself have to think out what in the ancestral customs was essential and of universal import, and what only local and accidental. In the old country itself, the introduction of written laws could not then be long delayed, and by 600 was probably widespread; but aristocracies tended to resist an innovation which limited the powers of judges; and here, consequently, the Codes are typically a product of an age of revolution.

But the city which was to play the greatest part of all in the increased western trade, and through which its effects were to react most strongly upon old Greece, was Corinth, through the foundation of Syracuse.

Syracuse, in classical times the strongest city of the western Greeks and their champion against Carthage, had her own historians, the earliest of whom, Antiochos (*fl. c.* 424), was used by Strabo for his account of the colonisation, and is often supposed to have been used by Thucydides; who, however, names no source and differs in several particulars. We have many references to the foundation of this great city, some of which synchronise it or bring it into close chronological relations with no less than four other colonies: Megara, Naxos, Kroton and Kerkyra.[70] Since the date implied (not directly given) by Thucydides for Syracuse (not later than 733[71]) had a rival, based on a generation-count, viz.

[69] Thus Str. 260 says that Z. defined penalties by law, instead of leaving them to the judges.

[70] S. founded 'in the next year after Naxos' (whose priority was too well known to be disputed), Thk. vi, 3, 2, or 'about the same time', Str. vi, 269; founders of S. and Kroton consult Delphi simultaneously, *ib.*; S. and Kerkyra founded by the same expedition, *ib.*; Megara already founded at that time, *id.* 270, cf. 'Skymnos', 272. This last is supported, with archaeological evidence, by G. Vallet and F. Villard in *BCH*, 1952, who find the earliest pottery from M. perhaps 20 years earlier than any from S.

[71] Megara founded 245 years before its destruction by Gelon (which was a few years before 480; Dunbabin, *WG* 416, reckons it to have been in 483), and after some false starts (5 years?), beginning 'about the same time' as the colonisation of Syracuse.

757/6,[72] and since the stories implying the priority of one or the other city are incompatible at many points, it is clear that no precise chronological record was available to the classical Greek writers. Their computations, however, compiled first by fifth-century scholars, and based presumably on genealogies and on synchronisms, derivable sometimes from early poetry, produced results not unworthy of respect. Archaeology confirms the Greek tradition that nearly all the primary colonies, from Taras to Syracuse, were established in one generation, and that the distant Cumae was older than any other of them, and Lokroi the youngest.[73]

A detail which Syracusan tradition, claiming that the city was all but as old as Naxos, will have been at no pains to preserve, was that at both the great Corinthian western colonies there are traces of Euboian forerunners; Eretrian colonists at Kerkyra,[74] and probable Euboian placenames, those of the Chalkidian spring Arethousa and the 'Quail Island', Ortygia, at Syracuse.[75] That both places became Corinthian strongholds may be connected with the tradition that at the height of their success, and in early times, while a king, Amphidamas (perhaps the contemporary of Hesiod) still ruled at Chalkis,[76] the two Euboian cities quarrelled, and fought one of their fiercest wars over the Lelantine Plain. In the new age, the quarrel was no longer a matter of only parochial interest: 'the rest of the Greek world took sides in the ancient war between Chalkis and Eretria', according to Thucydides, more than in any other in an age, for the most part, of mere border wars between neighbours.[77] East of the Aegean two neighbours and inveterate enemies, Samos and Miletos, helped Chalkis and Eretria respectively[78]; and though it may be a mistake to speak, as some scholars used to, of the Greek world as divided between two 'trade Leagues' at this date, a great deal of scattered evidence shows prominent states as falling into two camps, relations within each of which are predominantly friendly, while relations between the two are almost always hostile (pp. 90ff). The cavalry of Thessaly, now beginning to emerge, like Sparta, as a great land-power, helped the knights of Chalkis to victory in the main

---

[72] Parian Marble, *sub anno* (though Jacoby, *FGH* IID, 685, argues otherwise); Archias the founder 'tenth descendant of Temenos'.
[73] Dunbabin, *WG* App. I, v; pp. 452ff.
[74] Plut. *GQ* 11; cf. Str. x, 449.   [75] Str. *ib.*
[76] Hes. *WD* 656, and schol.; discussed by Plut. *Sympos.* (*Mor.* 156).
[77] Thk. i, 15, 3.   [78] Hdt. v, 99.

theatre of war[79]; and while we have no mention of direct participation by Corinth, we have the much-quoted detail from Thucydides, that, about 704 tr., Ameinokles, a Corinthian naval architect, 'built four ships for the Samians'.[80]

It may very well, then, have been as an ally of Chalkis that Chersikrates of Corinth occupied Kerkyra, ejecting Eretrian settlers,[81] and that during the same period, when Chalkis' hands were full, Archias, said to have been Chersikrates' brother, quietly took over the Chalkidian claims ('securing the place from hostile occupation'?) at Syracuse; 'driving the Sikels first from the Island (now a peninsula) on which today the inner city stands', says Thucydides. Later, he says (archaeology adds, very little later), 'as the population grew great, they fortified the outer city too'.[82]

Syracuse in its beginnings (whatever the case at Kerkyra) was a typical western agrarian colony. Many of the settlers came from one inland Corinthian village, Tenea[83]; and the lure that drew them was the prospect of land. A tale recorded by a poet within living memory of the event, as that of a byword for improvidence, was that of one Aithiops, who traded, Esau-like, his rights for a honey-cake on the voyage out.[84] The leaders of both expeditions were, naturally, of the Bakchiad nobility; and it is a characteristic story, even if contaminated with legend, which describes them as young men, whom a drunken riot had involved in a scandalous homicide.[85] That leaders to go abroad should be men involved in a blood-feud between important families is typical of 'Homeric' early Greek society.

Late and poor evidence also mentions a King in early Syracuse: one Pollis, an Argive. The story cannot be rejected out of hand; there is a parallel to it at Megarian Byzantion (p. 114). Both were perhaps priestly officials; and Argos long retained a recognised religious primacy among her Dorian neighbours.[86]

---

[79] Plut. *On Love*, 17 (*Mor.* 760). [80] Thk. i, 13, 2; cf. pp. 59f and nn.

[81] Plut. GQ 11; though Strabo (269, end) only mentions hostilities against 'Liburnians' (Illyrians). An odd fact is that (much later) Dorian Kerkyra used Euboian designs on some of her coins; possibly, in view of her usual bad relations with Corinth, taking up ancient tales of her pre-Corinthian past.

[82] Thk. vi, 3. [83] Str. viii, 380. [84] Archilochos, *ap.* Ath. iv, 167.

[85] Plut. *Mor.* 772; schol. on Ap. Rhod. iv, 1212. The evidence re-collated: G. Huxley in *BCH*, 1958.

[86] Ath. i, 31b, q. 'Hippys of Rhegion'; Pollux, vi, 16, q. Aristotle; Aelian, *VH* xii, 31. But cf. Dunbabin, *WG* 93-4: 'Hippys' is a forgery, a 'Pythagoreischer Schwindelautor' (Jacoby, in *PW* viii, 1927ff), and some of Pollux' Aristotle-citations are from pseudepi-

Slowly, Syracuse expanded over south-east Sicily. Thucydides quotes some time-intervals, such as we have not for the Italian cities, which remind us that the colonies were not full-grown from birth. Akrai, 'the Cliffs', twenty-five miles inland in the hill-country, was founded some seventy years after Syracuse, and became an important subject borough; Kasmenai, in a position unknown, twenty years after Akrai; and finally, 135 years after Syracuse (598 tr.), Kamarina on the south coast, which aspired to be an independent state, and more than once suffered for it.[87] In the meantime, with the growth of economic in-equalities among the settlers (starting with such improvident indivi-duals as Aithiops), and perhaps still more with the growth of a floating population of merchants, sailors, craftsmen and political exiles, the citizen Land-Holders, *Gamoroi*, had become an oligarchy[88]; and Syra-cuse, like Leontinoi and other colonies, was troubled in the sixth century by much the same political stresses as old Greece in the seventh.

Meanwhile, forty-five years after Syracuse, according to Thucydides (688 tr.), Antiphemos of Rhodes and Entimos of Crete 'leading addi-tional colonists' (*epoikous*; i.e. perhaps reinforcing a trading settlement, of which archaeology gives evidence), founded Lindioi, almost due west of Syracuse on the south coast, laying down 'Dorian customs'.[89] This sounds as if the bulk of the colonists were from Crete. Lindos in Rhodes provided the official name of 'the present citadel and the first place to be fortified' (cf. Cumae, Naxos); but the state continued to be called, like Siris in Italy, by the name of its river, Gela or 'Coldstream'; the Sikel language was akin to Latin. Antiphemos sacked Omphake, a hill-fort of the Sikans west of the Gelas, and dedications at Gela and at Lindos commemorated this and other early campaigns.[90] The pres-ence of much Cretan and Rhodian ware, both in the colony and in earlier native settlements, and the absence of geometric, confirm what the literary sources tell us, both of the origin of the settlers and of the date of their arrival, nearly half a century after the founding of Syracuse.[91]

grapha; and Pollux (contrary to 'Hippys') distinguishes Polis the Argive from Pollis the king. The only fact alleged about P. is the introduction of 'Bibline wine' (cf. Hes. *WD* 589) into Sicily, where it was called 'Pollios'. A King at Taras, in the late 6th century, Hdt. iii, 136; prestige of Argos, even later, *id.* vi, 92, where A., when militarily impotent, imposes fines upon Aigina and Sikyon, and S. even pays a proportion. Vallet and Villard (*BCH*, 1952), reject Jacoby's scepticism.

[87] Thk. vi, 5, 3-4.   [88] Cf. Hdt. vii, 155.   [89] Thk. vi, 4, 3.
[90] *Lindos Temple Chronicle*, 25; Paus. viii, 46, 2; ix, 40, 4.
[91] Orsi, *Mon. Ant.* XVII; Blakeway, in *BSA* XXXIII, p. 183.

With Gela and Lokroi, two enterprises by states new come to the colonial field, the primary colonisation of the west ended; it recommences after half a century in an entirely new form, with thrusts into the far western Mediterranean by eastern Greeks, and into western Sicily by men of the colonies already established (Ch. VII). Meanwhile the established colonies grew in population and expanded their territories. But colonisation had also an effect perhaps unanticipated by its promoters, in the enormous expansion of trade. The colonies had been planted mostly in sites selected for their fertility; and they wanted the luxury goods which were manufactured at home or imported from the east. The painted pottery, the archaeologist's stand-by, survives to bear witness, where finds of eastern metalwork are rare, and textiles, perfumes and wine perish. The growth of trade gives the answer to a question, no less important than the question why colonisation started when it did: the question why it stopped. The answer is that to import food reduced the need to export men. But imports had to be paid for; and the consequent growth of trading and industrial classes set in motion a process, often violent and painful, of social change.

In this process Corinth, with the fine harbour of Syracuse in friendly hands and the halfway house at Kerkyra kept as long as possible under direct control, played a leading part; and it was at Corinth that there took place the most brilliant development of the new orientalising art.

This was an art inspired, as we have seen (pp. 45, 61), by oriental models already familiar. Oriental motives had long since influenced and been imitated in Cretan geometric art, and at the end of the geometric period in other regions (notably Attica) we seem to see an attempt to copy the warriors, beasts and goddesses of Phoenician metal-work, instead of the neat, black, little silhouette-figures of the past.[92] The result looks, not infrequently, merely undisciplined; if the matter had ended there, one might have said that this was merely a typical case of a respectable, traditional folk-art being undermined and corrupted by oversea trade-goods. But in the generation after the opening up of the west, artists at Corinth, in Crete and Rhodes and later in the Cyclades, and in Euboia and Attica and Ionia, where the direct influence of the east crosses with that of the Corinthian school, launch out on a course essentially their own (no oriental *pottery* anticipates the new Greek

[92] e.g., *CAH* Plates, I, 196 (The Mistress of Beasts, on a sherd from Boiotia); *ib.* 358 (=*JHS* XXXII, plates X, XI); recent discoveries in Eleusis Museum.

styles), but with a repertoire including the copying of many eastern motives. For instance, Payne noted on Protocorinthian vases a type of lion still recognisably Syro-Hittite, even though borrowed through Cypriote and Cretan intermediaries. This is at a time (before 650) when the Assyrian Empire already dominated Syria; and the appearance of a more Assyrian-looking type of lion, Assyrian rosettes, Assyrian influence in rendering horses, and other 'indications of a more direct contact'[93] comes only with the development of mature Corinthian art, after 640, just when Assyria was dying on her feet and her grip on the Levant coast was failing. The curious time-lag in transmission is probably to be explained by the continued importance of east-Greek intermediaries.[94] Corinth stands on the west side of her isthmus, and though trade came to her from all sides, her own sailors always sailed chiefly to the west.

But the importance of these oriental influences must not blind us to the elements of originality. The Corinthians, in particular, used what they borrowed with a native vigour that makes of a foreign model a servant, not a master. Even motives which might be expected to lose their vitality along with their religious significance, such as the Sacred Tree with its boughs bound with ribbons – to the Greeks, if not 'foolishness', at best only an attractive and intricate pattern – even this 'floral complex' is handled, in Crete and Corinth, with such confidence and competence as to establish itself in its own right, merely *as* a pattern.[95] Even what is frankly misunderstood is exploited to good purpose. The seventh-century Greek griffin, the ferocious though fabulous monster, particularly popular as an adornment of bronze caldrons, is also of Asiatic origin. In a Syrian example, he has a lock of mane, between his horse's ears, ending in a curling 'quiff' on the forehead. In early Greek examples this becomes a meaningless knob (what the artist saw, he copied; but were none of the examples that reached Greece in new condition?).[96] But the knob then develops, in many Greek bronzes, into a formidable, spear-headed spike; one wonders if this is an early stage in the evolution of the unicorn.[97] Varying the naturalistic lions or wild goats, often of great charm and vigour, which process round the vases also of east-Greek schools, Protocorinthian artists are particu-

[93] Payne, *Necrocorinthia*, pp. 53-4.   [94] Dunbabin, in *JHS* LXVIII, p. 66.
[95] Cf. p. 61, n. 66.
[96] W. Lamb, *Greek Bronzes*, pp. 70-2, fig. 8; *JHS* LXVIII, pl. xi, d, e; *CAH* Plates I, p. 353(b).   [97] In lit., first in Ar. *Hist. An.* 499b.

larly fertile in the invention of such Beasts for Bad Children as the plastic lion's head, on an aryballos found in Rhodes, with a second lion on the back of it and female human heads in Egyptian wigs facing sideways[98]; or two-headed beasts, or even a creature with two bird-bodies extending opposite ways on the flanks of a jug (is it meant to be the same body seen from two sides?) and meeting in front in a gorgon face and a lion's fore-paws.[99] As a contrast, realistic scenes, such as a line of hoplites advancing in battle array, are executed with amazing precision, sometimes on a fantastically tiny scale. The exquisite little Macmillan Aryballos in the British Museum, topped by an open-mouthed plastic lion's head, has two armies advancing against each other for its main band of decoration; a band of racing horsemen; a band of animals and a band of triangular 'rays' or *Strahlenkranz*, dark on light, radiating from the foot; all this on a vase only 2¾ inches high! Floral or vegetable ornament, the chief motive on some other vases, is rendered with 'an astonishing sense of the expressive power of simple, sweeping curves'.[100] It is the spring-time of Greek art, and one is not seldom reminded of Hopkins' line: 'Whence come all this juice and all this joy?'

Armed with so much of sheer merit, in addition to Corinthian prowess in sea-faring and foreign policy, Corinthian art and trade invaded the west. It may be saying too much to speak of a 'Corinthian monopoly' in the century after the founding of Syracuse,[101] but it is beyond question that Corinthian pottery far exceeds in quantity all other wares of that century found in the west. The only other ware to appear in significant quantities is Rhodian. At Gela, Cretan pottery is much used in the first fifty years, but wages an unequal struggle, and finally is driven from the market. No other rival could compete with Corinth's advantage of position; cargoes from the Aegean must either break bulk at the Isthmus or go round the dangerous Cape Malea. The Corinthian Gulf states which had colonised South Italy had no manufactures; the southern Peloponnese was disturbed and set back in its development by Sparta's wars of aggression.[102] Corinth was not

[98] Payne, *Protokorinthische Vasenmälerei*, pl. 23.   [99] *id. Necrocorinthia*, fig. 12.
[100] Johansen, *Vases sic.* pl. 6, 1; Payne, *Protok. Vasenm.* 7, 3; 8, 1; *Necrocor.* fig. 4. (Examples from the Argive Heraion, central Crete, and Cumae.)
[101] As did Blakeway; see R. M. Cook's important review of Dunbabin, *WG*, in *CR* LXIII (1949), pp. 113ff.
[102] Thus, Sparta imported *less* later Corinthian than Protocor.; Payne, *Necrocor.* p. 185.

only the nearest by sea to the west, but the largest producer; and so she could also presumably undersell other goods even of comparable quality. 14,000 votive cups from one sanctuary, that of Persephone at Lokroi, give some idea of the scale of this trade. Distant Cumae, Etruria and Carthage, not yet hostile, were insatiable buyers.[103]

Corinth was not without her own problems in external affairs, in this generation in which the state-system of classical Greece was crystallising. The Megarid, since its colonisation by the Dorians, had been not a city-state, but divided between five villages. Its people had looked to Corinth for protection when necessary, and had taken part in the public mourning for deceased Bakchiad rulers.[104] It was probably still as vassals of Corinth that Megarians took part, with Corinth and Chalkis, in the colonisation of eastern Sicily, attempting, though unsuccessfully, a joint settlement with Chalkidians, and finally settling only ten miles from Syracuse. But with increasing prosperity they grew unwilling to admit the hegemony of Corinth, just as, at the same time, Corinth herself and other Dorian neighbours ceased to admit that of Argos. Corinth is said for some time to have maintained her hegemony over the five villages by fostering quarrels between them; but even when they fought, the northern villagers did so with a chivalry, particularly in such matters as the treatment of prisoners, which was eloquent of the growth of a common feeling.[105] Finally they drew together under the leadership of Megara, and Corinth attempted a direct reconquest. It failed. The Megarian leader and hero of this war of independence was Orsippos, an Olympic victor, winner of the footrace in 720, or about nine years after the foundation of the western Megara, according to later Greek belief; this was presumably before he won military fame.[106] The Megarians however were unable to hold the southern part of the five districts; at an unknown date, probably early, the Corinthians captured Krommyon, on the east coast,[107] Peraia, 'the land beyond', i.e. the land across the sea as one looks from Corinth, and the Temple of Hera, close to the point dividing the east end of the Corinthian Gulf, where sailors seem to have made and paid their vows

[103] Payne, *ib.*; on Carthage (and her colonies), cf. A. Vives y Escudero, *Estudio de Arq. Cartaginesa: la Necropoli de Ibiza* (Madrid, 1917), esp. p. 113.
[104] Said to be the explanation of a proverbial phrase 'Megarian tears'; Zenob. v, 8 (with unconvincing details); schol. on Pindar, *Nem.* vii, 155; Wade-Gery in *CAH* III, 535n.
[105] Plut. GQ 17 (*Mor.* p. 295).
[106] Paus. i, 44, 1, supported by the (reported, not extant) inscr., *CIG* 1050.
[107] Str. viii, 380, ix, 390.

for safe return, at the place still known as Perakhora. These were probably the lands of the 'Piraians' and Heraians, named in Plutarch's list of
the Five Villages.[108] The temple, conspicuous on the promontory
above its tiny harbour, continued to flourish. Ivories, bronzes, seventh-
century Egyptian scarabs, painted vases, including many of the most
exquisite Protocorinthian works, filled its precincts until many had to
be taken out and buried to make room for more. Under excavation
Perakhora has yielded the greatest of all hauls of treasure for the study
of Corinthian art.[109] By 540, the frontier of Megara was pushed back
to the Geraneia mountains. Her fertile lands were limited to the good
but modest-sized plain between Geraneia and Patéras, with the western
port of 'The Springs', Pagai, ten miles from the city; and the scenes of
her considerable later exploits lay east oversea (pp. 113f, 120f).

Of Orsippos the story is also told that he was the first Olympic
victor to run naked; his loin-cloth, such as all athletes wore in early
times, became detached – Pausanias opines that he dropped it on purpose. That Greeks were just at this time becoming emancipated from
the ideas of decency which were still held, with all the strength of a
tabu, throughout western Asia,[110] is no less characteristic of the age
than the increasing self-consciousness and consequent separateness of
the city states.

Unable to compete with Corinth, and with the best sites in the nearer
west already occupied, Megarians, Euboians, other islanders and the
eastern Greeks generally turned to the north and north-east for new
lands to conquer.

[108] I disagree here with Dunbabin, 'Early History of Corinth', in *JHS* LXVIII, and
agree with Hammond in *BSA* XLIX.

[109] H. G. G. Payne, *Perachora*. The pottery must be dated by the scarabs, cf. Vallet and
Villard in *BCH*, 1958.

[110] Paus. i, 44, 1; cf. Hdt. i, 10, Thk. i, 6.

CHAPTER V

The Aegean and Asia Minor, c. 700-640

THE eastern like the western Greek world did its expansion to the accompaniment of colonial wars and a continuation of old border bickerings, often unmentioned by historians in this context. Yet, if one omits the essential violence of early Greek history, one is giving a false picture.

'It was particularly,' as Thucydides says and as we have already noticed, 'in the early war between Chalkis and Eretria that the rest of the Greek world took sides as allies.'[1] We have no formal list of these allies; but Herodotos' allusion to help given by Samos and Miletos to Chalkis and Eretria respectively[2] shows the important fact that the alliances spanned the Aegean. Immediate neighbours were nearly always 'natural' enemies, and a state is, in consequence, often recorded to have had friendly relations with a neighbour's neighbour on the other side. A linking-up of such feuds and friendships, in the new age of increased traffic by sea, was equally natural; though, as to how many of the recorded hostilities were directly connected with the struggle in Euboia, we have no further information.

Thus, in Ionia, the islanders of Chios tried to found a colony at Leukonia, on the adjacent mainland, for a body of nobles involved in a blood-feud; they had killed Hippoklos, the King of Chios, in a riot arising out of a misunderstanding among drunken men at a wedding. But the men of Erythrai, the neighbouring mainland city, then very powerful, claimed the area as theirs and starved the colonists out.[3] Chios, a natural enemy also of the Samians, who were perhaps even more piratical in their habits than most early Greeks (cf. p. 219), then, probably at this juncture, got help against Erythrai from Miletos.[4]

---

[1] i, 15; cf. p. 82 above. [2] v, 99.
[3] Plut. *Brave Deeds of Women: The Chians*; Polyainos, viii, 66. For sources on Chian-Erythraian relations, cf. Ath. vi, 258-59; ix, 384e; from Hippias of Erythrai and Antikleides. [4] Hdt. i, 18.

Erythrai joined forces with Paros to found Parion in the Dardanelles,[5] a colony probably later seized by Miletos.[6] The Chian colony of Maroneia, in Thrace, unsuccessfully fought the Parian colonists of Thasos for possession of Stryme[7]; and Mytilene and Kyme, friendly to Miletos (cf. pp. 98f, 119), successfully drove Thasians away from Ainos (p. 97).[8] Chalkis colonised in the north Aegean together with Andros, and after a dispute they called in Samos, Paros and Erythrai to arbitrate between them.[9] Corinth, we have seen, was friendly to Samos, lending her the services of a naval architect (p. 60); and the use which Samos could make of a reinforced navy, at a time when a king, Amphikrates, still ruled in Samos, is illustrated by a story of how Amphikrates led an expedition against Aigina, which resulted in a bloody and destructive though indecisive war.[10]

Aigina, an active trading community with connections both by sea with the Levant[11] and, by mule caravans, with the interior of the Peloponnese,[12] was a trade-rival of Corinth. Having specialised in commerce since the geometric period, she seems not to have felt the pressure of population, and took no part in early colonisation. She also continued, it seems, to acknowledge the primacy of Argos without embarrassment. Pheidon, the last powerful king of Argos (pp. 177ff), is said to have had his mint in Aigina,[13] producing the first coinage west of the Aegean.[14] Samos was also interested in the 'long sea' route to the further west, and so developed friendly relations with the rising enemy of Argos, Sparta, which now controlled the south-west Peloponnesian ports; she assisted Sparta against the revolt of the Messenian helots[15] and was on terms of close friendship with Cyrene. A

---

[5] Erythrai the official *metropolis* (Paus. ix, 27, 1), while Paros gives the name; cf. above, Cumae, Naxos, Lindioi. *Exetastai*, an Erythraian magistracy, also at Parion: inscrs. *ap.* Bilabel, *Ionische Kolonisation*, p. 49. (But *exetastai* are surely too common to be evidence? —W.G.F.)

[6] Str. xiii, 588; that the Milesians came in by conquest is conjecture from their early hostility to Erythrai.

[7] Archilochos (who probably fought in the war) *ap.* Harpokration, 171, 4; cf. Hdt. vii, 108.

[8] Thasians at A., Dionysios of Byzantion fr. 30 (*GGM* II, p. 47); but A. in later times is Aiolic, cf. n. 41.

[9] Plut. GQ 30.   [10] Hdt. iii, 59.

[11] Distribution of her coins in Cyprus, Cilicia, Pamphylia: Hill, *Historical Gk. Coins*, p. 5.

[12] Paus. viii, 5, 8.

[13] Ephoros, *ap.* Str. viii, 376; but Hdt. vi, 127, mentioning Ph.'s weights and measures, says nothing about coinage. E. may be romancing.

[14] But hardly before 625; cf. E. S. G. Robinson, in *JHS* LXXI, p. 166.

[15] Hdt. iii, 47.

Samian captain was said to have given help at a critical moment to the founders of Cyrene, which was a colony of the Lakonian islanders of Thera, and maintained close economic relations with Sparta herself.[16]

In the Peloponnese, Elis appears as a natural ally of Sparta against Arcadians, Messenians and Argives; Pheidon of Argos once marched into her territory, and 'committed impiety' by taking charge of the celebration of the Olympic games.[17] Megara, at odds with Corinth, appears later as an enemy of Samos (p. 218), and is able to colonise in the north-eastern region dominated by Miletos, as do Teos and Klazomenai, the landward neighbours of Miletos' and Chios' enemy, Erythrai (pp. 108, 119). Erythrai, thus surrounded and outweighted, ceases to play a prominent part in history; and Miletos, until she also 'helped to wound herself', emerges as the greatest city of all eastern Greece in the seventh century.

Athens, which down to about 600 could still export corn, played no part in colonisation, and scarcely any in recorded seventh-century history; but her earliest recorded wars are with Aigina and, inevitably, with her neighbour, Megara; her earliest distant venture brings conflict with Mytilene (p. 221) and she duly appears later as an ally of Corinth.[18]

Thus a considerable amount of evidence, scattered but consistent, shows the chief colonising cities of the Aegean and states of mainland Greece divided into two groups, between which we have constant accounts of hostility, *not* only between neighbours, but *within* each of which we hear only of friendly relations, at least until new developments in the sixth century brought some changes of circumstance.

The two lists of allies (if the term is not too strong) may be conveniently given in parallel colums[19]:

In Eastern Greece:		Miletos	Samos
		Chios	Erythrai
(probably)		Lesbos	
,,		Teos	
,,		Klazomenai	

[16] Hdt. iv, 152; cf. pp. 141f, below.
[17] Hdt. vi, 127, to which later writers add little except an improbably early, mid-8th-century date: Olympiad 8 (748 B.C.), Paus. vi, 22, 2; 'tenth from Temenos', Ephoros, *ap.* Str. viii, 358.
[18] Hdt. vi, 89.
[19] Cf. further Burn in *JHS* XLIX.

In the Central Aegean:	Naxos?	Paros
		Andros
	Eretria	Chalkis
West of the Aegean:	Megara	Athens
	Aigina	Corinth
In Northern Greece:		Thessalians
In the Peloponnese:	Argos	Sparta
	Arcadians	
	Messenians	Elis

It will be seen that while the Milesian alliance predominates east of the Aegean, the allies of Samos, Chalkis and Corinth predominate west of it, and gain the support of the rising land-powers, the Thessalians, Sparta and Athens. The remarkable Samian interventions west of the Aegean certainly won her some good friends. At home on their mountainous island the Samians, in ancient as in modern times a tough and soldierly people, never seem to have been seriously threatened by Miletos; abroad, the westward direction of Samian efforts is as noticeable as the eastward direction of Megara's, after the break with Corinth.

The Islands and the North Aegean

Such was the situation in which the Greek expansion to the north and north-east took place. In the south Aegean there were still a few islands not inhabited by Greeks, or thinly enough peopled to attract colonists.[20] Miletos occupied Leros,[21] to the south-west, and Ikaria,[22] west of Samos, doubtles to the Samians' displeasure; but this island, steep-sided and harbourless, had no significance for commercial or naval purposes. Semonides of Samos, a satirical poet of note about 630 tr., led a colony to Amorgos,[23] a south-eastern Cyclad with useful harbours; Megara, at an unknown date, occupied Astypalaia,[24] with fine harbours but little cultivable land, between Amorgos and Rhodes. But such island-grabbing could do little to allay land-hunger in the long run.

It was therefore to the north that the main movement turned. The

---

[20] Thk. i, 15.   [21] Str. xiv, 635.   [22] *ib.*
[23] *Suda, s.v.* Simonides. Hellenistic decrees of A. begin 'The Samians dwelling at Minoa of Amorgos . . .'; see Bilabel, *Ionische Kolonisation.*
[24] 'Skymnos', 551.

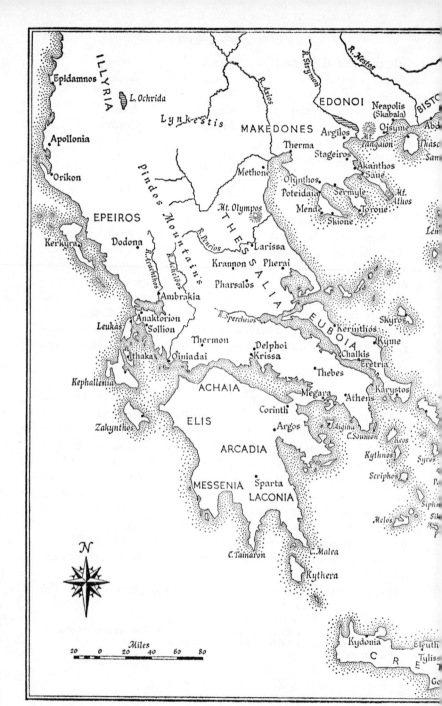

The Aegean

R. Hebros

BISTONES
Dikaia
Maroneia
Stryme
Zone?
Sale?
Abdera
Thasos
Samothrace

ODRYSAI
Heraion
Teichos
Selymbria Byzantion
Perinthos

Kalchadon
BITHYNIA
Astakos

Ainos
Kardia
Kallipolis
Alopekonnesos
Limnai
Imbros
Madytos Abydos
Sigeion
Tenedos
Achaion
Kolonai
Assos
Methymna
Antissa
Eresos
Lesbos
Arisba
Pyrrha
Mutilene

Naxos
Sestos
Lampsakos
Parion
Priapos
Kyzikos

Prokonnesos
Artake

Kios
Myrleia
Daskylion
Apollonia

Miletoupolis
R. Rhyndakos

TROAS
Troy

Antandros
Adramyttion
Gargara

MYSIA

PHRYGIA

Lemnos

Kyme
Phokaia
Larisa
Chios
Erythrai Klazomenai
Teos
Kolophon

R. Hermos

LYDIA
Sardis

Smyrna

R. Kaystros

Andros
Tenos
Syros
Kos
Mykonos
Rhenaia Delos
Paros
Siphnos
Sikinos
Pholegandros
Thera

Ikaria

Ephesos
Magnesia
Melia?

Samos
Miletos
Priene

R. Meander

KARIA

Labranda

Leros
Kalymnos
Kos

Halikarnassos

LYKIA

Naxos
Amorgos

Astypalaia

Old
Knidos
Kameiros
Rhodes
Ialysos
Lindos

Karpathos

Eleutherna
Tylissos Knossos
Dreros
CRETE
Arkades
Gortyn
Praisos

Minor

Euboian cities found an outlet in the three-pronged peninsula called (much later, after Olynthos had been given to the Chalkidians by Artabazos the Persian) Chalkidike. This movement began probably *after* the great first generation of colonisation in Sicily; no Greek pottery earlier than the seventh century has yet been found there, and not much of that.[25] Eretria, by no means obliterated by the Lelantine War, and perhaps under pressure after the loss of the disputed territory, founded the prosperous city of Mende[26] and probably others in the fertile promontory of Pallene; Dikaia, further east[27] and Methone, on the mainland coast to the west, which was said to have provided a home for the Eretrians driven from Kerkyra.[28] Chalkis founded Torone (Terone on its coins) in the central Chalkidic peninsula, with its high all-but-island citadel, known as Lekythos, 'the Bottle'[29]; she was also connected with a scatter of small settlements here and on the adjacent coast and on the rocky bays of Mount Athos, where the Greeks mingled with 'Pelasgian' natives.[30] On the east coast of the main peninsula, a joint expedition from Chalkis and Andros captured Sane from the natives, and then Akanthos. This place, after a dispute about priority of occupation, was assigned by the arbitration-board from Erythrai, Samos and Paros to Andros, whose scout had hurled his spear into its abandoned defences while his Chalkidian colleague was trying to secure priority by running ahead; after which Andros broke off friendly relations with Paros, which had given a minority vote.[31] Andros was also the founder of Argilos[32] further north, and of Stageiros,[33] later to be world-famous as the birthplace of Aristotle.

Further east, Paros secured a major prize, the large, inshore mining island of Thasos. The mainland opposite included the rich gold-mining area of Mount Pangaion, and the Parians were quick to try to secure it as a 'Peraia', or possession on the 'land opposite', like those held by Rhodes or Mytilene. But they did not find this easy. The Thracians were no Sikels to be cheated and bullied with impunity. Big, fairish men, 'red-haired and grey-eyed',[34] thorough northerners, with a language from which a few words survive (they include *brüzo*, 'I brew',

---

[25] R. M. Cook, in *JHS* LXVI, p. 77.   [26] Thk. iv, 120.
[27] D. 'of the Eretrians' in Ath. tribute-lists, distinguished from 'D. by Abdera'.
[28] Plut. GQ 11.   [29] Thk. iv, 110.
[30] *id.* iv, 109; names in Hdt. vii, 22.
[31] Plut. GQ 30; cf. Thk. iv, 84; date 654, Euseb.
[32] Thk. iv, 103.   [33] *id.* iv, 88.
[34] Xenophanes, *ap.* Clem. Alex. *Stromateis*, vii, 22.

and *bria*, 'burgh', a walled stronghold[35]), they fought with the 'great Thracian swords' mentioned by Homer[36]; their charge was terrible, and as in the early Gallic wars of Rome or the claymore-versus-bayonet battles of early modern Scotland, the Greek line of pikes gave way before it not once nor twice. The Thasians were defeated by the Saioi,[37] and it was only gradually, as the advantages of Greek trade penetrated the Thracian consciousness (more especially the seductions of Greek wine, for which it was said that the mountain people would trade their own children), that 'trading-posts of the Thasians' were able to flourish: Oisyme, another Galepsos and Skabala, near that later Neapolis where St Paul landed in Europe, and which at the present day bears the name Kavalla.[38]

Further east again, Chios and her allies colonised. The Thracians were no more amenable. Timesios of Klazomenai, at the later Abdera, was driven out by the Bistones (about 650 tr.), and that great city was not established till about 540 (p. 316)[39]; but the Chians made good their settlement at Maroneia, under the southern slopes of Mount Ismaros, said by Homer to have been the source of the priest Maron's wine that made the Cyclops drunk.[40] Ainos, once called by the Thracian name of Poltyobria, 'Poltys' burgh', on the 'swift Hebrus', in a position well favoured for trade with the horse-riding Odrysians, had a stormy beginning: first founded, perhaps, as a small trading-post by the Lesbian colonists of Alopekonnesos, across the 'Black Gulf' in the Gallipoli Peninsula (p. 91), then seized by Parians of Thasos, driven from the Bosporos by Megarian rivalry, and finally secured again by Aiolians in force, from Mytilene and Kyme. A joke about its Thracian climate, 'eight months' winter and four months' dirty weather', also repeated about the north coast of the Black Sea, was current; but with fertile land and good trade-routes inland, it flourished.[41] It may well have been through it in part that the legend of Orpheus, destined to be fruitful in Greek thought, came first, like the head of Orpheus in the legend, 'down the swift Hebrus to the Lesbian shore'. There were also

[35] *Brüzo*, Archil. *ap.* Ath. x, 447; *-bria*, in place-names, =polis, Str. vii, 319.
[36] *Il.* xiii, 577; cf. xxiii, 808.   [37] Archil. *ap.* Plut. *Spartan Customs.*
[38] 'Skymnos', 656-7; Thk. iv, 107; cf. Hdt. vii, 118; *ATL* I, Gazetteer.
[39] Hdt. i, 168; 650, Euseb.; Ol. 32, Solin. x, 10.
[40] 'Skymnos', 678; Archil. *ap.* Harpokr. 171, 4; *Od.* ix, 196ff.
[41] Dion. Byz. (see n. 8 above); Harpokr. *s.v.* Ainos; Poltyobria, Str. viii, 319; *id.* fr. 52; climate, Ath. viii, 351 (cf. Hdt. iv, 28, on Scythia); advantages, J. M. F. May, *Ainos, its History and Coinage* (London, 1950), esp. pp. 39ff.

certain 'forts of the men of Samothrace' (also probably Aeolic Greeks) on the neighbouring coast; perhaps the little places, Zone, Sale and Drys, of later Athenian tribute-lists.[42] The displaced Parians retired to Stryme; here again, members of the rival league tried to eject them, this time the Chians of Maroneia[43]; but both Maroneia and Stryme survived the war.

Meanwhile in north-west Asia Minor, a slow expansion of Aiolic peasant settlements in Mysia and the Troad seems suddenly to have been overtaken and passed by a wave of systematically planned and reconnoitred expeditions from Ionia. At first there is a general movement, chiefly to the Dardanelles and to sites just beyond, by all the eastern colonising cities; then Miletos takes the lead, and launches out into the Black Sea, even to sites where the Greek way of life could only be lived with difficulty; as in the later West, colonies seem to be planted now not only to win land, but explicitly for trade; simultaneously, Miletos appears to have taken over, probably forcibly, several colonies originally planted by her rivals. Her associates, Megara, Mytilene, Teos, Klazomenai, appear much later beyond the Straits; but hostile Samos forces her way in only in 599 tr., after a struggle with Megara, at a time when Miletos herself was under a new government with a different foreign policy (pp. 218ff).

The Aiolic expansion in the Troad was probably not much earlier than 700, though poets and their audiences liked to connect it with the heroes of the Trojan War; they even developed a legend that Penthilos the son of Orestes the son of Agamemnon led a migration by land through Thrace, and that Gras, Penthilos' grandson, occupied Lesbos after passing through the Troad.[44] The legend served both to link up the Penthilidai, the nobles of Lesbos, among whom there may have been a Thracian strain,[45] with what was rapidly becoming the national epic, and also to justify territorial claims in the favourite Greek manner.[46] The men of Kyme seem from archaeological evidence to have captured the native fortress bearing the old Aegean name of Larisa, eight miles from their walls, only about 700[47]; previously, it had been watched for many years by Kymaian Neon Teichos, 'New Castle', only five miles from the city.[48] Further north Mytilene had a *peraia* with some villages,

---

[42] *ATL* I, 517ff. An Aeolic inscr. from Samothrace, *BCH*, 1954, p. 145.
[43] See n. 7, above.   [44] Str. xiii, 582.
[45] Cf. the name Pittakos, borne by a Thracian chief in Thk. iv, 107.
[46] Cf. below, pp. 219f.   [47] Schefold, in *Arch. Anz.* 1933.   [48] Str. xiii, 621.

which she is said to have kept under control partly by maintaining a monopoly of the benefits of education[49]; a curious story, but, in the early days of literacy, perfectly credible. Adramyttion, in the corner of its gulf, and the neighbouring Antandros, long remained in native hands; but to the west of them Methymna in northern Lesbos secured Assos, high on a crag above its harbour, where excavation has revealed a temple with sixth-century archaic sculpture.[50] Assos in turn colonised Gargara, on the promontory demarcating the inner Gulf of Adramyttion.[51] Outside it, the Aiolic islanders of Tenedos had their own *peraia*, with the strongholds of Achaion, another Larisa (Strabo enumerates thirteen occurrences of this name in all)[52] and Kolonai, 'the Mounds'.[53] Then Mytilene went further, occupying Sigeion hard by ancient Ilios[54]; Ilios itself; Madytos and Sestos, across the water on the narrows of the Dardanelles, to which the Greeks perhaps now began to restrict the application of the name Helles-Pontos, Helle's Sea, an early name for the whole north Aegean.[55] Sestos, with its small but powerful citadel, from which two straight lines of wall descended like 'legs', as the Greeks said, for two hundred yards to opposite sides of the harbour,[56] could never be a large city, for sheer lack of space; but it was strategically very important. It lay on the Narrows, where in modern times the guns of Kilid Bahr, the Key of the Sea, cross their fire with Chanak; also, the set of the current, sweeping from the Black Sea with the outflow of Dniepr and Don and Danube to replenish the sun-evaporated Mediterranean, tended to carry shipping into Sestos, besides making it difficult for east-bound traffic, except under the most favourable conditions, to get up the Straits at all. 'Because of the current,' says Theopompos, 'Sestos controls the passage.'[57] Across the peninsula Aiolians, unspecified, occupied Alopekonnesos, 'Fox Island', probably in a position protected on the land side by a lagoon[58]; and from thence the first settlers ventured across to Ainos, above-mentioned, north of the Black Gulf.[59]

For none of these settlements have we any indications of date; but the fact that nearly all the Ionian colonies lie farther afield makes it

[49] Aelian, *VH* vii, 15; 'Myt. coast', Str. xiii, 605.
[50] Steph. Byz. *s.vv.* Adramytion, Antandros, citing Ar.'s *Politeiai*; F. Sartiana in *Rev. Arch.*, 1913, 1914.
[51] Str. xiii, 610f, from Hellanikos and Myrsilos; both of Lesbos.
[52] *id.* 604; cf. ix, 440.   [53] *id.* 604.   [54] *id.* 599.
[55] 'Skymnos', 709-10; Str. (vii) fr. 58.
[56] Theopompos, *ap.* Str. xiii, 591.   [57] *ib.*   [58] 'Skymnos', 706.   [59] n. 41, above.

likely that the Aiolic group is earlier than the Ionian movement, which begins about 675.

The East in the Seventh Century

Western Asia in these years was in a turmoil, which ended by checking any expansion of Ionia by land; which left, indeed, some Ionian cities in ruins and others hard pressed. Loss of land probably contributed to the subsequent outbreak of colonisation by sea.

Before 700 there lived north of the Black Sea a people, not without skill in weaving, metallurgy, wagon-building and other arts derived from the ancient east, who were called the Kimmerians. Their name survived in classical times in the name of the Kimmerian Straits, between the Crimea and the Caucasus, Kimmerian forts and barrows, a Kimmerian Mountain and a Kimmerian City on the straits.[60] Their language was akin to that of the eastern Thracians, if we may judge by the names of native kings of the Crimea in classical times: Kotys, Rhoimetalkes, Rheskouporis, Spartokos (Spartacus).[61] They were now overtaken by disaster. Central Asia was in eruption, as in the days of the Hunnish and the Tartar invasions, and the nomad Scyths (Skutha), driven on by other hordes from the east, burst into south Russia. Their mobility and powerful archery made them as irresistible to the Kimmerians as the Huns, horsemen and archers, were to the Goths, horse and foot swordsmen, in the same part of the world. Some Kimmerians held out in the Crimea, where the splendid gold-work, produced by Greek artists for fourth-century Crimean kings, shows their handsome warriors in battle against brutish Scyths[62]; but a great horde of them, with vast wagon-trains, retired through the Caucasus, to the dismay of the civilised world.

Urartu was the first civilised state to feel their strength. In 708 an Assyrian officer near the frontier reports that King Argistis, son of Rusas (p. 50), is preparing a powerful army; but it proved not to be against Assyria. Argistis marched northward; 'but', reports the crown prince Sennacherib to his father, 'when the men of Ararat went to Gamir, they were defeated'.

---

[60] Hdt. iv, 11-12; Str. vii, 309, xi, 494; culture, Rostovzeff, *Iranians and Greeks in South Russia*, pp. 39ff. (But the names Krim Tartary, Crimea, are believed by Russian scholars to derive from Turkish *Quirim*, a ditch (cf. Russian *Perekop*): Vernadsky and Karpovich, *Hist. of Russia*, 1943, vol. I, p. 53, n. 27.)

[61] And still in inscrs. of the city of Tanais in Roman times, Rostovtz. *ib.*

[62] Rostovtz. *op. cit.* p. 40; illust. *ib.*; also *CAH* Plates I, 254; etc. etc.

Gamir, the biblical Gomer, is the land of the Kimmerians. But Argistis had saved his kingdom, at a heavy cost, and the hordes moved westward. King Sargon himself took the field in Tabal, west of Urartu, in 706-5, and was killed in battle against one Eshpai of Kullum; it has been suggested that the Iranian-sounding name of this formidable enemy may also be Kimmerian.[63] The Assyrians saved his body, and brought it home for burial. The hordes had been sharply checked, and for some thirty years they seem to have remained quiescent in Cappadocia. They occupied Sinope, from which the Crimea was only two days' sail away. They are said here to have destroyed an early Milesian colony, killing Habrondas, its founder; but it is not certain that there was a colony here so early. The story may be only a later Greek historian's theory.[64]

Then, a new generation having grown up, the 'Gimirrai' became active again. They overran (before 675?) the Phrygian kingdom, where the last King Midas is said to have drunk poison in despair.[65] Esarhaddon of Assyria (680-668) fought them again north of the Taurus, near Komana: 'Teushpa (Teispes?) of Gimirrai, the Umman-manda, whose name is remote . . . with all his army I destroyed.' Ummanmanda was an already ancient name for northern barbarians; not only later Greeks, but even the Assyrians, who knew a good deal about them, were vague about the relationships of these migrant tribes. The dreaded Skutha themselves had by this time penetrated through the Caucasus in turn, 'in pursuit of the Kimmerians' says Herodotos, unhistorically. Just as late Roman emperors used Hunnish mercenaries against the Germans, so did Esarhaddon propose to use 'Bartatua, King of the Ashguzai', the Protothües of Herodotos,[66] against Kimmerians and Medes, his nearer enemies, while another Scythian, Ishpaka, is counted as their ally.[67] About 670 a barbarian named Mugallu captured Meliddu, Melitene, south of the Taurus, Assyrian regular troops failing to save it. Asshurbanipal (*accessit* 668) made peace with him, exacting tribute but leaving him in possession. 'Mugallu of Tabal, who against the kings my fathers had planned enmity, the fear of my lords Ashur and Ninlil overwhelmed him.' He sent his daughter to join the Assyrian king's harem, with 'great horses' from Cappadocia; in 651 he sent nearly 600 of these. '—ussi his son yearly his rich tribute sent, and

[63] Sidney Smith in *CAH* III, 53, 59.
[64] Hdt. iv, 12; 'Skymnos', 948 (note the word 'it seems'); discussion, Busolt, *GG* I, 465f
[65] Str. i, 61.   [66] Hdt. i, 103.   [67] Minns, in *CAH* III, 188.

prayed my lordship; by the great gods my lords I made him swear.'
But later he broke his oath: 'with Dugdammi, the king of the seed of
Khalgate he conferred . . . Dugdammi, king of the Sakai-Ugutumke,
the arrogant . . .'.[68] The ethnology is again vague; Sakai and probably
Khalgate (cf. the Skolotoi of Herodotos[69]) are names of the Scythians
or similar nomads, whereas Dugdammi was a Kimmerian; but with
his name we have a link with the Greek side of the story; for Dugdammi seems to be that Dügdamis, by later Greeks miscopied as the
Aegean name Lygdamis (Λ for Δ) under whom the horrors of barbarian invasion impinged upon Ionia.

The destruction of the Phrygian kingdom had probably been foreshadowed, not only by the process of growing hollow within, by loss
of contact and solidarity between rich and poor, government and
governed, the usual prelude to the fall of a civilisation, but by a more
specific economic calamity: the closing by the Kimmerian migration
of the east-west trade routes, which had brought the gold of Kolchis
and the steel of the Chalybes to Miletos or Kyme. The same situation, it
may be guessed, set the stage for a revolution in Lydia. Arselis, King of
Karia, swooped upon Sardis, killing the king Myrsilos, whose 'divine'
or official name was Kandaules, 'Taker of the Spoil',[70] and carrying off
among other loot the Double-Axe of Sandon, the divine ancestor of
the 'Herakleid' kings, to grace his own 'Place of the Axe', Labraunda[71];
and a soldier named Gyges, of a northern family which had long been
on bad terms with the dynasty, made common cause with Arselis and
seized the throne.[72]

Gyges, like Midas, became a figure of legend. It is likely that he
figures in the Book of Ezekiel, as 'Gog, Prince of Meshech and Tubal'
(Moschoi and Tibarenoi).[73] One famous tale made him a shepherd,
who gained the throne through finding a magic ring that gave him
power to become invisible.[74] Herodotos tells the equally famous

---

[68] Campbell Thompson and Mallowan, *A New Inscr. of Asshur-bani-pal*, in *LAAA* XX,
pp. 96-7; lines 138-62.   [69] iv, 6.

[70] Plut. GQ 45; Radet, *La Lydie et le Monde grec*, p. 133; *ib.* 66. Tzetzes renders the
name K. as '*Skylokleptes*'. Hipponax, *ap.* schol. on Lykophron, 219 (=fr. 4 Diehl),
renders the same as 'Dog-strangler' – perhaps rightly, if the word is Indo-European; so
Prehn in *PW* X, col. 1860.

[71] Labraunda, cf. Hdt. v, 119. That Arselis, as Plut. says, 'came as an ally to Gyges'
looks like a biased Lydian version of the story.

[72] Nik. Dam. fr. 49 Müller; more rationalistic than Hdt. i, 8ff, and perhaps based on
some real tradition, e.g. from the Lydian historian Xanthos.

[73] Ezek. xxxviii, 1, 6 and *passim*; xxxix, 1ff.   [74] Plato, *Republic*, 359.

story (also not unconcerned with seeing unseen) of the Guardsman's Dilemma: of how the virtuous Gyges was given no choice but regicide or death, by the Queen when the foredoomed Kandaules had caused him to see her naked. This is perhaps simply a naughty Greek rationalisation of an official propaganda-line, i.e. that the new king was the beloved of the Naked Queen, meaning the Ishtar-like mother-goddess; for Lover of the Goddess was an Asian royal title.[75] Herodotos' story became the theme of a Greek drama or, it is possible, was itself derived from an early Athenian play[76]; while his contemporary Xanthos the Lydian seems to have given a different, more rationalistic, though not on that account necessarily more historical, version of an intrigue between Gyges and the queen.[77]

So the House of the Hawk, the Mermnadai, became kings of Lydia. There is at least no doubt about the existence of Gyges, for all his aura of legend. He is mentioned both in Assyrian records and by his Greek contemporary, the poet Archilochos; and his name and that of Lygdamis-Dugdammi give the first synchronism in terms of proper names between Assyrian and Greek chronology. The latter, as calculated by later Greek scholars, proves worthy of respect, though some dates, including those of Herodotos for Gyges himself, are shown to be too early.

Gyges at the beginning of his reign (about 675?) does not appear to have feared trouble from the Kimmerians; indeed, if we may trust a story, probably from Xantho, that she was born and brought up 'in the land of the Syrians above Sinope', whither his father Daskylos had fled into exile,[78] he may even have had connections with them. Like many military usurpers, he plunged into foreign wars; he was the first Asian ruler to cut short the boundaries of Ionia. He failed to take Miletos and Smyrna, at the mouths of the Meander and Hermos; probably he cut short their territory, but there is no reason to disbelieve the obvious hypothesis, that he had also an eye to the dues that might be levied in their ports. His interest in the west is shown by the story that he, like Midas, made dedications at Delphi. In central Ionia he won his chief success, when he routed the hitherto invincible cavalry of Kolophon, and rode victorious into their probably unwalled lower

[75] Barnett, in *JHS* LXVIII, p. 22.
[76] So, Lobel in *Proc. Brit. Ac.* XXXV; Page, *A New Chapter in the Hist. of Gk. Tragedy* (C.U.P., 1951).
[77] Nik. Dam. fr. 49, cf. n. 72 above.   [78] *ib.*

city.[79] He then made peace with Miletos and let her colonise Abydos, opposite Sestos.[80] The name of two of Gyges' ancestors appears in the same northern region, in the native city of Daskylion (cf. n. 78). He had cause to pay attention to the Straits, for Thracians, some of them already long settled in Asia Minor, were a possible source of danger, especially if reinforced from across the sea; one of their tribes, the Treres, appears soon after, taking part in another round of destructive barbarian raids.

Against the Kimmerians Gyges concerted action with Assyria, thus appearing in Asshurbanipal's records: 'Guggi, King of Ludi, a far land at the crossing of the sea' (or perhaps 'across the sea'; Gyges' envoys would have had to go by sea) 'of which the kings my fathers had not heard the name, was told of my great empire in a dream, by Asshur, the God my creator, saying "Take the yoke of Asshurbanipal, King of Asshur, the beloved of Asshur King of the gods, Lord of all." . . . From the day when he took the yoke of my kingdom, he smote the Gimirrai, the plunderers, who did not fear my fathers nor me. Two chiefs, whom he took prisoner from among them, he sent to me in fetters of iron, with many presents.' (But later) 'He discontinued the sending of envoys; he disregarded the will of Asshur; he trusted to his own power and hardened his heart. He sent his forces to the aid of Psamatik of Egypt, who had rebelled against me; and when I heard of it, I prayed to Asshur and Ishtar, "Before his enemies may his corpse be thrown and may they carry off his (attendants?)".'[81]

Psamatik, son of that Necoh whom Asshurbanipal had left as governor of Egypt (p. 56), had succeeded his father about 660 and, taking advantage of Assyria's other preoccupations, turned out the Assyrian garrisons. Asshurbanipal had, indeed, many troubles. His own brother was in revolt in Babylon, and this struggle was followed by a desperate and sanguinary war with an old enemy, the tough and well-organised kingdom of Elam. The son of Mugallu of Meliddu, who was still paying his tribute in 651, threw off the yoke and made an alliance with Dugdammi (n. 68); but false friends to Assyria were not necessarily friends to each other; and while Asshurbanipal's troops sacked Babylon and fought their way, losing heavily, towards Susa, 'Dugdami the Arrogant', with his rear secure, fell once more upon Lydia. The Thraci-

[79] Hdt. i, 14; cf. Str. xiv, 643; Theognis, 1103.　　　[80] Str. xiii, 590.
[81] G. Smith, *Hist. of Assurbanipal*, p. 64; Bury-Meiggs, *Hist. of Gce.* pp. 860f.

ans in the north-west seem to have joined him, especially one Kob, leader of the Treres, now first heard of[82]; and perhaps also Lykian mountaineers from the south.[83] Gyges fell in battle (the Assyrian king joyfully records the literal fulfilment of his prayer) and his son Ardys was unable to save even Sardis, except its citadel rock.[84]

So the invasion reached Ionia. The towns on the central promontory escaped it, but its full fury fell upon those inland. Magnesia on the Meander, a great city, recently victorious over Ephesos, fell 'through its pride' in a sack which became proverbial[85]; but Ephesos held out, encouraged by the spirited verses of Kallinos, some of which, the earliest extant elegiac poetry, still survive.[86] Then pestilence, ascribed to the wrath of Ephesian Artemis, smote the invaders, and the great wagon-trains rolled away eastward, in search of lands where the 'arrows of God' were not so deadly.[87] Ardys regained his kingdom, though some Kimmerians remained at Antandros in the north-west for a century.[88]

Dugdammi's ally, the son of Mugallu, died of sickness, welcomed by Asshurbanipal as the judgment of God, about the same time. Assyria too, though fearfully weakened, was emerging victorious from the Elamite war. Dugdammi himself thought it prudent to make peace, and sent tribute of 'great horses' and, we are assured, his own chariot; but he soon broke his oaths; then he fell sick and died in his turn.[89] Strabo merely says that he 'was destroyed in Kilikia'.[90] His horde, probably defeated by Assyrian troops, drew off northwards under his son Sandakshatra (the name, if it is indeed mixed Asian-Iranian, meaning 'Warrior of Sandon', is an interesting one). Kob and his Treres were 'driven out' (whence is not stated) by Assyria's dangerous ally,

[82] Str. i, 61, xiii, 586; cf. Kallinos, *ap.* Steph. Byz. *s.v.* Treres.

[83] Str. xiii, 627, on the rather dubious authority of Alexander's romantic court-historian Kallisthenes, who alleged *two* captures of Sardis, (*a*) by the Kimmerians, (*b*) by the Treres and Lykians (perhaps merely from different passages of Kallinos, whom Kallisthenes was using?).

[84] Hdt. i, 15.

[85] Str. xiv, 647, citing Kallinos and quoting Archilochos; cf. Theognis, 603f, 1103. Ath. xii, 525, mentioning the same two poets, says M. was taken by the Ephesians (but not that Kallinos said so); this seems less probable. Clem. Alex. (*Strom.* i, 144), citing the same poets, adds nothing.

[86] Discounting Sir M. Bowra's view that Tyrtaios is so early. – 20 lines, the only considerable fr., in Stobaios' *Anthology*, 51, 19; one fine line in Str. 647.

[87] Kallimachos, *Hymn* iii, 251ff; the reference to wagons is interesting, but *may* be only part of a traditional picture of northern steppe-people.

[88] A. hence called 'Edonian' or 'Kimmerian'; Aristotle (who knew the region), *ap.* Steph. Byz. *s.v.*

[89] *LAAA* XX (cf. n. 68).   [90] Str. i, 61.

Madys, son of the Scythian Bartatua.[91] Sinope was occupied by the Milesians about 630.[92] There were still Kimmerians in Anatolia till they were driven east by Alyattes,[93] grandson of Ardys, *c.* 600; but after the days of Dugdammi's raid and the great sickness, they were never formidable again.

[91] Str. *ib.* (who makes M. a Kimmerian; a mere slip, for S. knew his Herodotos); cf. Hdt. i, 103.

[92] Eusebios (Jerome), 629; cf. 'Skymn.' 949ff. This date is consistent with the archaeological evidence, including that from E. Akurgal's and L. Budde's excavations; cf. *Anatolian Studies*, V (1955), p. 23.

[93] Hdt. i, 16.

Additional note: On the Kimmerians in the Crimea, see now V. D. Blavatsky and T. V. Blavatskaya, cited (p. 97) in E. Belin de Ballu, *Histoire des Colonies grecques du littoral nord de la Mer Noire*, on which see further, p. 127.

CHAPTER VI

The Greeks and the Black Sea

SUCH were the circumstances in which the Ionians, who had previously had enough land at home, began to expand overseas. Their large-scale expansion, in which the great organiser of colonies was Miletos, begins just when Lydians and Kimmerians cut them short on the land side; though the sequence of events has been obscured by the existence of certain dates calculated in classical times according to the inflated chronology.

Here as in the north Aegean, we have little archaeological evidence for dating the earliest colonies; and what we have does not suggest that any of them antedate the seventh century.[1] The date, 756, assigned by Eusebios to the Milesian settlements at Kyzikos and at Trapezous (itself a daughter-colony of Sinope), belongs to a system in which Naukratis and Cyrene (both elsewhere dated about 630) as well as Syracuse, and various other 'epoch-making' dates including the *floruit* of Thales of Miletos (pp. 404ff), are all dated *c.* 760-745. A Milesian Thalassocracy was naturally assigned to the same period. Synchronisms with events in oriental history, given by later Greek scholars, on the other hand fit well with the slight archaeological indications. That Eumelos, the Bakchiad poet of Corinth, who wrote a Processional Hymn for the Messenians before their conquest by Sparta, called his three Muses Kephiso, Achelois (after the great river of north-west Greece) and Borys-

---

[1] So, R. M. Cook in *JHS* LXVI, pp. 76-7, 82; Rostovtzeff, *Iranians and Greeks in S. Russia*, pp. 63ff. It is still sometimes repeated that the Gk. pottery from Berezan island, off the Dniepr estuary, goes back to geometric; see the Russian *Matériales pour l'Archéologie de Russie*, XXXIV (plates 1-8); summary by Minns in *JHS* LXV, p. 111. On a recent visit to the Odessa Museum, I did not succeed in meeting any senior museum official; but the excellent public exhibition, well labelled in Russian and Ukrainian, has nothing pre-7th-century: some fine fragments of white-ground 'wild-goat' plates and vessels; other 7th-6th-century E. Gk. ('Rhodian', 'Samian', 'Naukratite') and Corinthian. An Attic sherd showing part of a warship is 6th-century BF, though placed among older material. The 'geometric' sherds reported by the early excavators must, it seems, have been simply those which did not have animal or curvilinear decoration. The earliest pottery from Olbia was, as always reported, slightly later than the earliest from Berezan. Cf. also P. N. Ure in *CAH* IV, p. 105. [But see, *contra*, Andrewes, p. 127, below.]

thenis (after the river Dniepr) and named a nymph Sinope, is interesting if true; but Corinth took little interest in this region thereafter. Excavation at Sinope has found no remains earlier than c. 625.[2] Meanwhile, the best evidence we have for the dating of exploration here is the personal name Istrokles, from Istros, the River Danube, the name of an artist who signed a mid-seventh-century vase found at Smyrna.[3] He must have been born and named about 670 at latest; and before that, his father, presumably an Ionian sailor, who named his son, as Greeks often did, after an achievement of which he was proud,[4] had been on a voyage or voyages as far as the Danube. Since he was proud enough of the achievement to name his son after it, he may also have been among the pioneers.

As we have seen, Ionian colonisation in the Marmara region begins geographically, and so probably chronologically, where Lesbian leaves off. Limnai, 'the Pools', beside the Suvla Lagoon in the Gallipoli Peninsula, was a Milesian colony[5]; Kardia, on the Bulair Isthmus, 'the largest city on the peninsula', was Milesio-Klazomenian.[6] Across the water Abydos, which like Sestos and Arisbe is the home of Trojan allies in the *Iliad*, and had since had Trerian and other Thracian occupants,[7] was, as we saw, occupied by Milesians with the encouragement of Gyges. Fifty miles up the coast, Parion (p. 91) was a foundation of Erythrai, the official founder, and the Parians of Thasos, who gave the name.[8] The alleged presence of Milesians too at Parion[9] may be due to Milesian conquest; but the connection with Erythrai was not lost.[10] Many small Milesian settlements are recorded in this region later: Kolonai, Paisos (another city of Trojan allies in Homer), Priapos, from which an obscene local god made his way into the later Greek pantheon.[11] Milesian also, according to the very explicit statement of Strabo, was Lampsakos,[12] which became wealthy and important, swal-

[2] Cf. p. 106n. Nymph Sinope, cf. Aristotle ap. schol. on Ap. Rhod. ii, 943; Borysthenis (?). Tzetzes, Schol. on Hes.*WD* 1. *Borysthenida* is actually a modern emendation; *vv. ll. Barysthenida, Erysthenida, Orysthenida, Thoprysthenida.* (But cf. p. 127n.)

[3] John M. Cook, in *ILN* 28 Feb. 1953, p. 329; *BSA*, 1959, p. 16.

[4] e.g. Telemachos, Tisamenos (s. of Orestes), in saga; Eurymedon, Naxiades, Karystonikos (the last two from the Erechtheid casualty list, *IG* I², 943 +) in 5th century Athens.　　　　[5] Str. xiv, 635.　　　　[6] *id.* vii, fr. 52.　　　　[7] *id.* xiii, 585f.

[8] Dion. Byz. fr. 30 (in *GGM* II); Paus. ix, 27, 1; date 708, Jerome (too early, if the Thasians were there from the first).

[9] Str. xiii, 588 (with Er. and Parians); Paus. *l.c.* mentions E. and P. only.

[10] Inscrs. in Bilabel, *Ion. Kol.* p. 49.

[11] Str. xiii, 589, xiv, 635 (from Anaximenes of Lampsakos); the god Priapos, a local vine-spirit, 'not in Hesiod', *id.* 587.　　　　[12] *id.* 589.

lowing up Priapos (with its god) and Paisos; but the local historian Charon, with confirmation from inscriptions,[13] makes it clear that the origin believed in locally was different.

It is here that Phokaia, destined to fame later, makes its debut in colonisation, modestly and not very early (654 or 652, Euseb. Jerome). A romantic story, told by Plutarch on the good authority of Charon,[14] gives one of our few glimpses of a colony's early days. Phobos, a young Phokaian of 'power and kingly position' (some kind of limited monarchy still surviving at Phokaia?) had sailed to Parion on business, and was entertained by Mandron, chief of a small tribe of the Thracian Bebrykes in a district known to Greeks as Pityoëssa, 'the Pine-Woods'. Mandron invited him to send a colony to settle among the Bebrykes and help them in their tribal wars (as later the Dolonkoi of the peninsula invited Miltiades). Phobos, 'having persuaded his fellow-citizens', sent them, under Blepsos his twin-brother. They duly won victories and spoil; but, though Mandron remained friendly, the Bebrykes became jealous and then afraid, and plotted, in the absence of Mandron, to massacre them. Lampsake, the chief's young daughter, vainly tried to dissuade her kinsfolk and finally, as a last resort, warned the Greeks. They acted promptly. They announced a great sacrifice and feast outside the walls, and invited their Thracian fellow-citizens; then, having previously divided themselves into two bodies, 'with the one they occupied the walls, while the other slew the men'. They invited Mandron to return as chief, along with their own leaders; he was too distressed to do so, but asked them to send out to him the families of the men killed; and this they did. Lampsake fell ill and died; and the Greeks re-named the city after her, honouring her at her tomb as a heroine, and later as a goddess.

The story is entirely convincing, though no doubt it tells less than the whole truth about the growth of ill-will between colonists and natives. It dates from before the age of Ephoros, the great romancer, and the tomb and cult of Lampsake were there to keep her story alive. The tragic end to a story of initially friendly relations is, alas, only too easy to parallel.

---

[13] Bilabel, *Ion. Kol.* p. 50: names of months at L. (Lenaion, Heraion) are not Milesian, and are consistent with Phokaian origin; and L. sends a deputation with an honorary decree to Marseilles 'because the Massalians are our brethren'. (But on the months, cf. Tréheux in *BCH*, 1953.)

[14] Plut. *Brave Deeds of Women*, 18 (Charon of L. fr. 6 Müller).

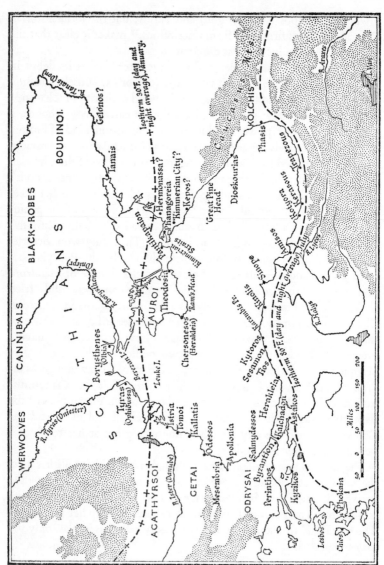

The Black Sea

Lampsakos had a fine harbour, and aspired to power on both sides of the Straits. The little town of Kallipolis, on a headland directly across the water, is the Gallipoli that gives its modern name to the Thracian Chersonese; lying 'in the *peraia*', as Strabo says, only five miles from Lampsakos,[15] it was probably the bone of contention over which the Lampsakenes fought the later Athenian colonists (p. 311).

Miletos' great success in colonisation hereabout was further east, in the ideal colony-position of Kyzikos, on a spacious island (now a peninsula) twenty miles across and so close to the shore of Asia that Alexander the Great had the strait bridged by two causeways.[16] Here the city was built, guarding, with the help of a flourishing navy, all access to the island; a daughter-colony bearing the Thracian name of Artake, faced the Sea of Marmara. The adjacent Prokonnesos was also colonised from Kyzikos, 'at about the same time as Priapos and Abydos'.[17] This fits well enough with the later and more moderate of the chronographers' dates for Kyzikos, 675. The colony is there ascribed to Megara, and its later Ionic inscriptions do not *disprove* this; inscriptions of Dorian Halikarnassos are also Ionic.[17a] But Eusebios, who *also* gives the 'traditional' date 756 (!) *may* be confusing with Kalchadon.

Kyzikos later became a great entrepôt for the north-eastern trade; but it was on her own local resources that her wealth primarily depended. The natives on this coast and further east were no longer Thracians, but the less formidable Phrygians,[18] peasants and shepherds accustomed to obey and be protected by their own high-king, and now, by the fall of Midas, left without one; there were also Pelasgians, one of the scattered remnants of that old sea-people, speaking a non-Greek language, whose name the Greeks came to use for all Aegean aborigines.[19] These were probably ready enough for friendly relations; and

[15] xiii, 589.

[16] *id.* xii, 575; Pliny, V, 32/142. Topography in F. W. Hasluck, *Cyzicus.*

[17] Str. xiii, 587. The pottery going back to *c.* 700, reported by Dr E. Akurgal from a site 20 miles inland from K. (*Anatolia*, I, 1956, pp. 15ff), if earlier than the foundation of K., must show trade with Ionia by land, before the Gks. had learned to navigate the straits, with their strong adverse currents, by the dexterous use of back-eddies and, when necessary, by towing. (Cf. Dion. Byz. *Anaplous Bosporou*, on the still more formidable problems of the Bosporos; A. J. Graham, in *Papers of the London Institute of Classical Studies*, V, 1958, pp. 25ff). Akurgal's site is, he believes, probably Daskyleion, the home of Gyges' ancestors. The question whether Gk. *warships* could *row* against the current (Rhys Carpenter, in *AJA* LVII, 1948, cf. Labaree in *id.* LXI, 1957) is, as Graham argues, not relevant; our concern is with merchant ships.   [17a] Mr D. M. Lewis reminds me.

[18] For the boundaries, cf. Str. xii, 576ff, xiii, 581.

[19] For development of the theory in ancient Greece, cf. Myres in *JHS* XXVII.

pockets of them survived, speaking their characteristic language (also found in parts of Chalkidike) down to the time of Herodotos.[20] The Kyzikenes were able to occupy territory on the mainland, including gold-mines; when coinage came into use, the gold Kyzikene stater became one of the most widely used currencies, surviving even when imperial Athens suppressed Aegean silver coinages[21]; and the tunny-fish, a badge on those coins, presumably indicates that fisheries also played an important part in the Kyzikene economy.

East from Kyzikos the Milesians at unrecorded dates expanded even inland, to the wide lakes between the sea and the Mysian mountains, one of whose peaks the Greeks named Olympos. Here rose the cities of Miletoupolis and Apollonia-on-the-Rhyndakos.[22] A Hellenistic decree of the latter, found at Miletos, thanks the people of Miletos for having made search in 'the relevant histories and other records' and certified that Apollonia 'was in truth a colony of theirs by the action of their forefathers, when they sent an army to the lands along the Hellespont and the Propontis and overcame in war the barbarians who dwelt there, and founded the Greek cities, including our own, under the leadership of Apollo of Didyma'.[23] In the same region was Myrleia, a colony of Kolophon,[24] and beyond it Kios, the easternmost Milesian Propontic colony, and the latest (627 tr.).[25] Beyond this point came the colonies of Megara.

The Lydian kings, who encouraged Greeks on the Propontis, while they attacked them in Ionia, were pursuing a coherent policy. They wanted, and took with a firm hand, the 'Asian meadows' by Hermos and Kaystros; they wanted too, if they could get them, the Ionian ports to pay taxes to Lydia instead of taking a middleman's profits from her. But Greek colonies on the Propontis took their land at the expense of Thracians or Phrygians, not of Lydia, though sometimes of Lydia's outlying subjects. Also, Greek cities in that region with their war-galleys provided the best defence against any more Thracian hordes.

---

[20] Hdt. i, 57; on the Athos peninsula, cf. Thk. iv, 109.

[21] Cf., e.g., Xen. *Anab.* vi, 2, 4, etc.; Lysias, *Against Eratosthenes*, 11 (p. 121). For the developed economy of early K., cf. the 6th century decree of exemption from taxes, with five (!) exceptions: Dittenberger, *SIG*[3] i, 5.

[22] Both in K. territory under Rome, Str. xii, 575, cf. 576.

[23] *Milet.* iii, no. 155; not (as per *CAH* II, 561) evidence of aggression against *Greeks.*

[24] Pliny, *NH* v, 32/143; later Apameia, Str. xii, 563.

[25] Pliny, *NH* v, 32/144; Ar. *Ki. Pol. ap.* schol. on Ap. Rhod. i, 1177 (fr. 514 Rose); later Prousias (Broussa), Str. *l.c.*; date Jerome, Synkellos.

Miletos, which organised so many colonies on the Propontis, and more in the Black Sea, was frequently at war with the successors of Gyges, once the Kimmerian threat was removed; but they aimed at putting economic pressure upon her, not at her ruin. Gyges' son Ardys captured the small neighbouring port, Priene; his grandson and great-grandson, Sadyattes and Alyattes, kept up the pressure for eleven years (*c.* 620–610 tr.), invading the land in oriental state, with music playing, and devastating the crops, but carefully *not* destroying the farm buildings, that the Milesians might still have something to lose. Finally, failing to reduce the city to extremities, Alyattes made terms, restoring twofold the temple of Athene at Assessos, which had been accidentally burned (p. 210). We do not hear what concessions the Milesians made. They may well have lost territory; earlier in the war they and their Chian allies had given battle far afield in the plain of the Meander, beyond their (later?) boundaries and sustained a great defeat there.[26] A commercial convention must surely have formed part of the treaty. But even this pressure, by the denial of supplies from inland to Miletos' growing population, must have stimulated a new development in Ionian trade: the importation of food from north of the Black Sea.

To the development of colonisation so far away and amid a climate and scenery so unfamiliar, the Megarian colonisation on the Bosporos formed a stepping stone. Cut short at home by her quarrel with Corinth, Megara turned east in search, initially, of land. One Archias led her first eastern colonists to a peninsular position, on the Asiatic side of the Bosporos, at Kalchadon, the Chalcedon of the Romans, among the Thracian Bithynians (675 tr.).[27] Later Kalchadon founded Astakos, in the easternmost corner of the Marmara; the chronographers' date for this city (708) must therefore belong to the inflated systems.[28] In Thrace their first settlement was on the open shore at Selymbria, 'Selys' burgh'[29]; and it was not till seventeen years after Kalchadon that they occupied the splendid site on the Golden Horn, towards which the set of the current tends to carry shipping from the Black Sea. Here rose Byzantion, named, it was said, after one Büzas, perhaps again a Thracian

---

[26] Hdt. i, 15-22; in 18, 1, H. describes the *other* M. defeat as 'in their own territory'.
[27] Str. xii, 563; 675 Eus. Arm., 683 Jerome.
[28] Charon Lamps. *ap.* Phot. *Lex. s.v.* Ostakos (*addenda*, 34a, in *FHG* IV; ref. misprinted in *CAH* III, 659n.; Jacoby, *FGH* 262, F 6); later Nikomedeia (Ismid), the name used by Jerome, *s.a.* 709.
[29] 'A few years before Byzantion', 'Skymn.' 715; the name, Str. vii, 319.

name; for the official Founder, according to a learned Byzantine writer, was a 'king' Zeuxippos (perhaps an Argive, as at Syracuse) whose name was preserved in that of the early market-place.[30] The same local and learned author, whose tradition is to be preferred to that of the chronographers, gives a foundation-date thirty years later than theirs: 628; and if this is right, the date of Kalchadon in turn must come down to 645. A Persian general, long afterwards, remarked that the founders of Kalchadon must have been blind, to miss the finer site opposite them. His remark was scarcely justified, for the trade that made the fortune of Byzantion was hardly yet in existence. Even the Golden Horn itself was first valued as a fish trap. But it became a popular saying, and was even unblushingly claimed by the Delphic Oracle, which built up a corpus of mostly apocryphal stories about inspired advice given to early colonists.[31]

The two Bosporos cities supported one another politically, and prospered, extending their power over a wide area by Greek standards, at the expense of the Bithynians, whom they harried ruthlessly.[32] Megara's appetite for expansion was thus glutted for two generations, and she left it to Miletos to be the pioneer of the Pontos. The appearance of Samians in these waters, with the colonies of Perinthos and Heraion Teichos, 'Fort Hera', belongs to a later phase in the history of Greek sea power (pp. 218f).[32a]

Beyond the Straits the Black Sea spread islandless and unfriendly, *Axeinos*, as the Greeks called it, possibly corrupting an Asian name, Askanian (cf. Biblical Ashkenaz); very unlike their bright Aegean. The contrast has struck later Balkan Slavs also; it is they who have christened the two seas respectively the Black and the White; and curiously black, between dark sands and overcast skies, the Black Sea waters can be. Exploration, as we have seen, was early enough for an Ionian baby to be named Istrokles by 670; but no colony here is certainly earlier than 650. When they did pass the straits in force, however, the Milesians acted on a large scale; one may suspect that, like the Chalkidians, they organised the man-power of other states besides their own.

[30] John the Lydian, *On the Roman Magistrates*, iii, 70.
[31] 17-year interval, Hdt. iv, 144; Megabazos, *ib.*; oracle, Str. vii, 320, Tac. *Ann.* xii, 63; the Horn as a fish-trap, Str. *ib.*; strategic advantages, Polyb. iv, 38.
[32] Cf. D.S. xii, 82 (416 B.C.); Bith. made serfs, Phylarchos, *ap.* Ath. vi, 271b.
[32a] Hēraiōn Polis, Hdt. iv, 90; H. Teichos, Demosth. *Olynth.* iii, 5.

The city of Istria, south of the Danube delta, with a short land route to the main course of the great river, may have been the oldest; it was founded 'at the time of the Scythian raids into Asia'[33]; if so, after 640 (656, Eusebios). A neighbouring native settlement, at a place now called Tariverde, was importing Greek pottery quite early in the sixth century. Borysthenes, named for another great river, the Dniepr, and to some extent succeeding an older station on Berezan island (the Karkinitis, 'Crab-land', of Herodotos, not mentioned later as a city?), is dated 646 (Jerome), or 'in the time of the Median Empire', which should mean after the fall of Assyria (612).[34] Tyras, similarly named from its river, the Dniester, with the alternative name Ophioussa, 'Snakeland', is undated, but probably of the same epoch[35]; and so is Sinope (630/629 Eusebios). At Pantikapaion, with its native name, on the Crimean shore of the Straits of Kertch, seventh-century pottery is also said to have been found.[36] Three cities, Sinope, Pantikapaion and Borysthenes, officially Olbia, 'Prosperity', played the leading parts in the development of trade with the vast north-east.

Wild and dangerous, the Pontos seemed a worthy place to be entered with prayers to the gods and to the heroes who, in mythology, had opened up the ends of the earth. Apollo, patron of Miletos, gave his name to a city on an offshore island, at the north end of the eighty miles of harbourless shoal coast beyond Byzantion; a horrible place in the frequent north-east winds, where the Thracians of Salmydessos got a bad name as wreckers.[37] Among heroes, men revered especially Achilles, whose death after his victory over Memnon, son of the Dawn, was recounted by Arktinos of Miletos in a sequel to the *Iliad*. He was worshipped as Pontarches, Lord of the Pontos.[38] His shrine and 'grove' (though there was not a tree in the place, remarks Strabo) lay at the west end of 'Achilles' race-course', the immense sand-spit east of Borys-

[33] 'Skymnos', 768ff (probably from his chief authority on the Pontos, the local writer Demetrios of Kallatis, 'Sk.' 719). I. named, Hdt. ii, 33. Pottery of late 7th century, R. M. Cook in *JHS* LXVI, pp. 76-7; G. A. Short in *LAAA* XXIV, p. 142. 'Nothing so far pre-610'—(W.G.F.) Tariverde, *id.*, from a visit.

[34] 'Skymn.' 804ff; Karkinitis city, Hdt. iv, 55 and 99; Gulf, Str. vii, 307ff. Berezan, cf. n. 1, above. Chian pottery, 7th-6th C., acc. to V. M. Skudnova in *Sovietskaya Arkheologija*, 1957.

[35] 7th-century pottery according to V. Parvan, see G. A. Short, *ib.*; called Ophioussa in the 4th-century *Periplous* attrib. to 'Skylax', but Tyras by later writers.

[36] Rostovtzeff, *IGSR* p. 43.

[37] Xen. *Anab.* vii, 5, 12ff; cf. the epode in a Strassburg papyrus (*Sitzb. Berl. Ak.*, 1899), usually attributed to Archilochos (fr. 79 Diehl). But a marginal note names Boupalos, the enemy of *Hipponax*.   [38] *CIG* 2076-7.

thenes; another, with a settlement called Achilleion, lay opposite to
Pantikapaion on the Kimmerian Bosporos; and the lonely and un-
inhabited White Island, thirty miles off the Danube mouths, with its
temple 'tended' by swarming sea-birds, unafraid of man, was held
sacred to him.[39]

Along the southern shore, men remembered Jason and Homer's
'world-famous Argo'. The land of Aia at the end of the world was
identified with Kolchis, at the end of the Black Sea. The Golden Fleece,
which Iason the Healer went to fetch, when the Cloud-Nymphs had
fled the land and the seed-corn was parched and the sacrifice of the
king's children had been prevented – the fleece of the Flying Ram,
surely the golden clouds of a 'red sky at morning' – this Fleece of
legend seemed to have found its perfect rationalisation, when it was
found that south of the Caucasus some peoples pegged out sheepskins
in the torrents, as a method of collecting alluvial gold.[40] Even the
terrible journey 'round the back', which Jason and his new-won bride
Medeia ('the Wise Woman') had to make to escape from Aietes, the
Man of Aia, was interpreted later as a journey round the back of the
known world, up the Danube and so to the Adriatic (the northern
trading people called the Sigynnoi had in fact a trade-route that went
that way[41]); a journey leading to the mysterious Eridanos, a river of
Greek legend, whose name was at one time attached to the Po.[42] The
Unfriendly Sea might seem less terrible when one was following in the
wake of the Heroes; and before long it was rechristened euphemistic-
ally, Euxeinos, Hospitable.[43]

Sinope, half-way along the south coast, claiming Autolykos, an Argo-
naut, for her first Founder, occupied, like Kyzikos, the neck of a peninsula; not so spacious, but still a useful refuge, with fertile ground at the
top of jagged and uninviting rocks on the sea sides. The headland
shelters, moreover, the only first-class natural harbour in 700 miles;
and it lies just at the narrowest part of the great sea, where, as Strabo

[39] Ach. Dromos, Str. vii 309; Ach. village and sanctuary, *id.* xi, 494; White I. and its
birds, 'Skymn.' 793ff, Arrian, *PPE* 32ff.

[40] Str. xi, 499; 'a primitive anticipation of the grease-process', as Myres says, reported
as still practised locally 'within living memory' (*CAH* III, 662).   [41] Hdt. v, 9.

[42] The name was Greek, Hdt. iii, 115; that of a rivulet at Athens, Paus. i. 19, 5, etc.
The rumoured river flowing into the northern sea (Hdt. *ib.*), where poplars grew and
amber was found, must surely have been the Vistula, at the end of the immemorial
amber-route; but it is the Po in Ap. Rhod.; an identification on which Strabo (v, 215)
pours critical scorn. For the scenery, cf. Eur. *Hippolytos*, 753ff.

[43] Str. vii, 298-9.

correctly states, the high promontory which Greeks called the Ram's Head, in the Crimea, and that of Karambis, west of Sinope, can be seen simultaneously on a clear day in mid-passage.[44] Sinope was thus a staging-post not only for merchants seeking the gold of Kolchis and the steel of the Chalybes with their magnetite ores, but for the traffic across the Euxine.[45] On the land side it was shut off by forested mountains; but these yielded good and accessible ships' timber, and Sinope had also a profitable export trade in the 'Sinopic vermilion' (perhaps cinnabar, the ore of mercury) with which Greeks loved to colour their ships' bows and other gear of their colour-loving civilisation. Like 'Stilton' cheese, it was called Sinopic 'not as being produced but as being marketed there'; it came from inland.[46] Sinope also took toll of the west-bound shoals of tunny-fish on their way to the Bosporos, which swarmed along the coasts and were caught in fish-traps under her headland; though it was noted that the fish were not yet full-grown when they reached this point.[47] This was, in fact, a wasteful and destructive fishery, which has ended by all but destroying the once teeming shoals.

But it was as a commercial centre especially that Sinope grew great. Smaller colonies, from whose poor anchorages coastal traffic probably plied, to tranship at Sinope or Byzantion, multiplied along the coast: to the west, Karambis, Kinolis, Koloussa, Kytoros famous for its box-forests, Kromna, Sesamon, Tios or Tieion (the last three later forcibly united into Hellenistic Amastris)[48]; to the east, Sinope's daughter-colonies Kotyora, Kerasous, whence Lucullus, conqueror and epicure brought back the cherry (and its name); and the most important Trapezous, Trebizond, named for the near-by 'Table Mountain' which now carries an aerodrome; a city with a strong citadel, standing back from the sea between two ravines, and destined to a long and eventful history.[49] Amisos (Samsoun) also, east of Sinope, near the mouth of the 'Wolf River', which gives good routes inland, is explicitly said by Strabo to

[44] Str. vii, 309; 'Skymn.' 956-7; D. M. Robinson, *Sinope* (Baltimore, 1906); W. Leaf in *JHS* XXXVI.

[45] Cf. Str. *l.c.*, 'Many of those who have crossed report . . .' etc.

[46] Str. xii, 546; Eustath. *ad Dionys.* 1180; W. Leaf, *l.c.* (n. 44).

[47] Str. xii, 545, cf. vii, 320.

[48] 'Skylax', 90 (a list); Kytoros 'a trading-post of the Sinopians', Str. xii, 544; box forests, Catull. vi, Verg. *Georg.* ii, 437, etc.; Amastris formed from a group of Milesian settlements, 'Skymn.' 958ff; Tios, Arrian *PPE* 19.

[49] Kotyora, Xen. *Anab.* v, 5, 3ff; Kerasous, *id.* v, 3, 2, Plut. *Lucullus* 19; Trapezous, Xen. *Anab.* iv, 8, 22, etc.; dated 756 (!) Euseb. *Arm.*

have been colonised by 'Milesians first'; indeed, it seems scarcely possible that they could have missed it. But here later comers were to take a hand.[50]

Beyond Trapezous on the fabled shores of Kolchis, some of the 'colonies' that figure on some modern maps are 'not proven' ever to have existed. Patous or Bata seems to have been a native name, perhaps Hellenised by Roman times in the form Bathys Limen, 'Deep Harbour', now famous as Batoum. No Greek city is reported there, nor yet at Megas Pityous, 'Great Pine Head' (mod. Russian Pitsounda, Georgian Pitfinda), under the Caucasus further north, named by Strabo only as a natural feature.[51] It is still pine-wooded. Ancient finds have been reported there, but access is forbidden on security grounds. Between them however, Milesian Phasis on its river held the seaward end of a caravan-route, with a 'made' road in Roman times, from the navigable Phasis in four days' journey to the Kur, flowing to the Caspian. The Greeks of Phasis were renowned for their humanity to shipwrecked sailors, whom they would send home at the city's expense. Arrian was shown in their city a great seated statue of the unnamed Phasian Goddess, in orientalising style – and also the alleged anchor of the *Argo*, on which he remarks that the iron did not look old enough.[52] Further north Dioskourias, Milesian too, with its temple of the Great Twin Brethren (also named among the Argonauts) traded with the wild tribes of the Caucasus, shameless in love and reputed cannibals. Their chief art was the indelible printing of the figures of beasts on their garments – the northern 'animal style' of art, well-known in metal-work, here at least extending to textiles. Like many mountain populations they exhibited extreme linguistic diversity; the most moderate travellers' tales said that seventy languages (others said 300) could be heard in Dioskourias market-place. They bartered gold and slaves, flax, hemp, and pitch, against wine and salt, and had invented spiked crampons for snow-walking. Otherwise they were chiefly remarkable for their extreme dirtiness; one tribe was called the Lice-Eaters, says Strabo, 'by reason of their squalor and filth'. Next to them dwelt the Soanes,

[50] 'Milesians first', Str. xii, 547, q. Theopompos; after which an account of a second settlement has dropped out, and we read of a third, from 5th-century Athens. See p. 120 below.

[51] Patous, 'Skylax', 72; Bata, Str. xi, 496; Portus Altus, the Peutinger Map; Megas Pityous, Str. *ib.*; anchorage there, Arrian, *PPE* 27.

[52] Str. xi, 498; Her. Pont. fr. 18; Arr. *PPE* 11.

more powerful, but not appreciably cleaner. They smeared their
arrow-heads with a poison of horrible septic power. Well might the
Hellenes hold together and treat each other as brothers in such an
environment.[53]

On the west and north coasts, the route to the early river-mouth
stations was gradually filled by intermediate colonies. Milesian Apollonia, on an islet off the southern cape of the Gulf of Burgas, among the
Thracian Astoi, is dated 'so years before the accession of Cyrus' (c. 610);
archaeology agrees.[54] It is said to have been first named Antheia, and
is called a colony of 'Milesians and Phokians' (i.e. Phokaians?). This is
the only mention of Ionians other than Milesians hereabout, and the
change of name perhaps indicates forcible annexation (cf. p. 120).
Odessos, the modern Varna, with poor anchorage but a plain sheltered
from the north wind, is dated 'in the time of Astyages' (before 560)[55];
Tomoi, undated, where Ovid shivered among the half-Scythian Getai,
lay thirty miles south of Istros.[56] The Kimmerian Bosporos (Strait of
Kertch) was secured, according to recent archaeological findings,
before 600.[57] Milesian Pantikapaion, 'mother city' of the settlements here, dominated the Taman Peninsula, as the predominance of
her coins there shows, and probably founded Theodosia (Feodosia),
south-west, in the Crimea.[58] By that time, however, Miletos was rent
by faction, and other cities, of the group friendly to her, make an
appearance as colonisers. Phanagoreia, across the strait, is ascribed to
Phainagoras of Teos, at the time when the Teians evacuated their city
in face of Cyrus' invasion,[59] when others of them founded Abdera
(c. 540; pp. 315ff). Another human name, that of Hermonassa, east of
the Sea of Azov, was said to be that of the wife of Semandros of Mytilene, who carried on his work when he died before the colony was
fairly established[60]; Kepoi, 'the Gardens', near by, was Milesian,[61] but

[53] Str. xi, 497–8; Arr. *PPE* 14. On the mountain tribes, Hdt. i, 203; languages, Str.
498, exports, *ib.*; salt-trade, crampons, *id.* 506; 'lice-eaters' and Soanes, 499.
[54] 'Skymnos', 730ff; position, Str. vii, 319; cf. Short in *LAAA* XXIV, pp. 144ff; Cook
in *JHS* LXVI, 76–7, 82.   [55] 'Skymnos', 748f; Str. *l.c.*; Mela, ii, 2; Short, *op. cit.* p. 146.
[56] 'Skymnos', 765; Str. *l.c.*; Mela, *l.c.*; Ovid, *Tristia, Letters from Pontus.*
[57] V. D. Blavatsky, *Excavations of Pantikapaion*, 1952, 1953 (in Russian); summary in
Belin de Ballu (see p. 127n.), p. 140.
[58] Str. vii, 309; Arrian, *PPE* 30; Ionic and Attic vases from *c.* 540 on show Th. existing
before its colonisation from Megarian Herakleia, which is probably 5th-century, Rostovtzeff, *IGSR*, pp. 63, 65.
[59] 'Skymnos', 886f; 'Skylax', 72; Steph. Byz. *s.v.*; Rostovtzeff, *l.c.*, believes in a
7th-century date here too.
[60] Arrian, *ap.* Eustath. *Comm. ad Dionys.* 549.   [61] 'Skymnos', 899.

'look-out posts of the Klazomenians' on the coast further north attest the presence of yet other Ionians.[62] Finally, the cities of the Kimmerian Bosporos themselves established far-off Tanaïs, bearing the name and standing at the mouth of the River Don; unnamed by Herodotos, who repeatedly mentions the river, it became a full-blown city only in 328; it became, however, second only to Pantikapaion locally, importing wine and textiles in exchange for hides and slaves and the other products of the steppe.[63]

In the south, one other Ionian city colonised in the Pontos. About 563 Phokaia, at the zenith of her power, a generation after the foundation of Marseilles, occupied Amisos with good routes inland, in the heart of the Sinopian preserve and perhaps even a Milesian colony (cf. above, p. 117).[64] Miletos was in no state to interfere, and Phokaia is credited with being in the middle of a forty-four-year 'thalassocracy' at that time; it looks as if the foundation of Amisos marks the breaking of a long Sinopian monopoly (p. 221).

But it was Megara which at that late epoch began a contribution to the Hellenisation of the Black Sea, second only to that of Miletos. Megara supplied the sailors; Boiotia some, very likely the greater number, of the colonists. Herakleia-in-Pontos, founded *c.* 559, 120 miles east of Byzantion, was not primarily a commercial port, but an agricultural colony in the old Dorian style. It became all the stronger for that. The number of settlers must have been large, from the first. The native Mariandünoi, a tribe of the Thünoi (Sea – or coastal Thünoi?) were conquered, like those round Kalchadon. Those at a distance became tributaries, those nearer the city serfs, bound to the soil and used as oarsmen in the fleet.[65] They were not however liable to be sold abroad; and their naval service, it must be remembered, was such as free men at Athens rendered to their city. Voyages and naval campaigns were usually short; the Mariandünoi were not galley-slaves, chained for months to the oar. Herakleia became probably the most populous of the Pontic cities, and herself colonised in turn; Herakleia-in-the-Chersonese, usually known as Chersonesos for short, was her

[62] Str. xi, 494.   [63] Parian Marble, B7; Str. *ib.*
[64] 'Skymnos', 917ff; topography, J. A. R. Munro in *JHS* XXI. An odd sherd from this site (Louvre, CA 2244), perhaps Aiolic, is said to resemble some from Marseilles: Vasseur, *Origines de Marseille*, pl. VII; R. M. Cook, *op. cit.*
[65] 'Skymnos', 972ff; Paus. v, 26, 5 (a dedication for the successful conquest); Justin. xvi, 3, who mentions a recent Boiotian defeat by Phokis. Naval service, Ar. *Politics*, 1327b,

daughter-colony (perhaps Ionian earlier)[66]; and so was Kallatis on the western shore, founded *c.* 520.[67] Last of this group of Dorian colonies was Mesembria, under the seaward spurs of the Balkan range, with a native name, Menebria or Melsambria, Menas' or Melsas' burgh; assimilated to the Greek word for mid-day or 'south', which it partly faced. It was founded by refugees from Byzantion and Kalchadon when Otanes the Persian took those towns, in revolt after Dareios' retreat from Scythia about 512.[68]

The Black Sea area always remained somewhat detached from the main stream of Greek development: a 'colonial' area, of immense importance as a source of food and raw materials, but contributing little to Greek poetry, thought or art. In the early days the struggle for self-preservation and commercial wealth was too hard; and even in the fourth century and later, when Herakleia, Sinope and Pantikapaion, often under the overlordship of more or less Hellenised native dynasties, were at their most populous and wealthy, policing their own seas with well-appointed navies, young men in search of higher education tended to go to Greece for it, and if of intellectual distinction often remained there, like Diphilos the writer of comedy and Diogenes the Cynic, both from Sinope.[69] A reason for this, at least contributory, was the severity of the climate; the more sheltered portions of the north coast may provide health-resorts for Russians, but to the Greeks, whose way of life at home was not adapted to keeping warm, it was intimidating. 'Four months cold weather and eight months winter' was a popular account of it. 'And such a winter': in those months, 'if you pour water on the ground you will not make mud, but if you light a fire you will'. Metal wine-jars had been known to burst, leaving their contents standing. The very sea froze, so that battles had been fought on the ice, and the Scythians had crossed the Sea of Azov with horses and wagons. Even in summer (but not in winter) it was 'always' raining, with frequent thunder. Earthquakes, on the other hand, the Greeks noted with surprise, were considered a prodigy.[70]

---

[66] Str. vii, 309; 'Skymnos', 824ff; Rostovtzeff, *IGSR* p. 65.

[67] Str. vii, 319, xi, 542; 'Skymnos', 761ff (with date). Mela, ii, 2, makes it Milesian.

[68] 'At the time of Dareios' Scythian expedition', 'Skymnos', 740. Hdt. vi, 33, puts the refugee colonisation in 493; but cf. v, 26, where B. and K. are in revolt, and reduced, directly after D.'s retreat.

[69] Str. xii, 546.   [70] Hdt. iv, 28; wine-jars, Str. vii, 307.

The economic magnets that drew men to such a region were correspondingly powerful; the gold and steel, flax and hemp, hides, fish and slaves; but above all, the corn of the Ukrainian Black Earth Belt, of which the ports were Tyras and Olbia. When Herodotos visited Olbia, the symbiosis between natives and traders from lands economically so complementary had gone a long way. The descendants of Ionians who had settled in the countryside to grow corn had 'gone native', intermarried with the local people (probably pre-Scythian, for the steppe gave place to forest east of the lower Dniepr) and produced a mixed race, the Kallippidai, the Mixellenes of later inscriptions. North of them a native population, which still did not eat bread, had taken to growing corn for sale; and on the left bank of the Dniepr above the forests there were 'Scythians' (or perhaps pre-Scythian subjects of the nomad kings) who farmed on their own account. Only beyond them did one come to the nomads, dwelling in their covered wagons, among whom the Royal Scyths held sway after the manner of the later Golden Horde.[71] Greek traders had even sailed far up the great rivers and settled there; Herodotos tells of Gelonos, a great stockaded city of wooden buildings by a river, in the forest country north of the steppe, inhabited by a half-Greek population. From such adventurers the Greeks heard tales of the wild tribes inland: the gold-wearing Agathyrsoi north of the Danube, who practised group-marriage (or perhaps rather used 'classificatory' kinship-terms, which the traders misunderstood), and decorated their palisades with the heads of enemies; otherwise their culture was 'like that of the Thracians'; the Werwolves (Neuroi), extending to the Pripet marshes – the Cannibals, further north-east; the blond Boudinoi, 'lice-eaters', dwelling among forests and marshes full of otters and beavers, beyond Gelonos, and often called Gelonoi themselves, to the indignation of the Greek Gelonians.[72] Finds of Greek coins and other metal-work have been made as far afield as Poznan province and Brandenburg; and the influence of Greek upon native art has been traced across Great Russia as far as the Kama.[73]

[71] Hdt. iv, 17-20, 46, 59-80.

[72] Hdt. iv, 20-26, 102-9.

[73] Rostovtzeff, *op. cit.*; Minns, *Scythians and Greeks*, p. 440; on the finds of 36 early Attic ('heraldic') coins and one of Minyan Orchomenos in 1824 at Schubin (Poznan) and of Ionic gold-work (pectoral and shield-device, dagger-sheath, earrings) not 50 miles away at Vettersfelde, Brandenburg, in 1882, C. T. Seltman, *Ath. History and Coinage*, pp. 133f.

Greek art was not influenced by Scythian, except for a few pieces made for native chiefs, although the Scythian 'animal style' was by no means contemptible. By the time the two peoples were in close contact Greek art was well advanced on the path towards classical humanism, a very different ideal. But if the artists (men whose success in their profession depended upon their being thoroughly 'central' in their society) were now no longer disposed to learn from barbarians, it was otherwise with Greek religious thinkers. To them, as to the cheerful and worldly genius Herodotos himself, the fact that there were other ways of life and systems of cosmology was itself significant.[74] There is little trace of actual borrowing of cult or ritual from the north, with the important exception of a group of cults from Thrace, such as those of Bendis and Kotytto in classical Athens[75]; but influences from Thrace profoundly affected the sixth-century recrudescence of the agrarian, probably pre-Olympian cults of Greece itself (pp. 346ff).

Of the speculations connected with the name of the Thracian prophet Orpheus, more must be said below (pp. 366ff). Here it may be observed that the appearance of a religious teacher and ascetic in early iron-age Thrace (if this is what Orpheus was) is not unique, nor even very surprising; though it did surprise Strabo, who shows a good deal of resemblance to a scholar of the nineteenth century. Strabo himself quotes, though he disbelieves, Greek authors who spoke of the existence of a class of ascetics in Thrace, the so-called 'Smoke-Walkers' (did they walk barefoot on hot ashes, like the Anastenarides of modern Macedonia?); and Aeschylus, in a lost trilogy on Orpheus, had witnessed to the impressiveness of the drum and tambourine rhythms that accompanied Thracian worship.[76] The Balkan Peninsula in later times has repeatedly been the home of religious movements, though they have usually achieved only the status of heresies: the Bogomiles in the late Byzantine world, the modern Bektashis in Muslim Albania, the modern Bulgarian Danovists. In east Thrace, among the horse-riding Getai, whom Herodotos calls 'the most righteous of the Thracians', and who 'disbelieved in the existence of any god but theirs', a prophet, Zamolxis or Salmoxis, had preached a doctrine of immortality to the chieftains and had been deified (identified with the sky-god Gebeleizis), having

---

[74] Hdt. iii, 38; cf. p. 329.   [75] Cf. Plato, *Republic*, i, 354.
[76] Aesch. *ap.* Str. x, 470f; contrast Str. vii, 296. On Anastenarides, cf. *The Times*, 4 June 1960.

risen again, it was said, after three years in the tomb. His doctrines were in some respects so like those of the Greek Pythagoreans that a hostile Pontic Greek tradition, representing Salmoxis as a charlatan, said that he had learned his doctrines in Samos, having lived there in Pythagoras' house as a slave. Herodotos quotes the story with his usual critical reserve, ending 'But I think Salmoxis lived many years before Pythagoras' and suspending judgment as to whether he was a man or a local god. Whatever adumbrations of a higher religion Salmoxis may have preached, there was still plenty of barbarism and superstition among his people. When Gebeleizis thundered and lightened, they defied him, shooting arrows at the sky; and every four years they would 'send a messenger to Salmoxis' (like some chiefs in nineteenth-century West Africa), choosing a man by lot, and tossing him into the air, to be caught on their points by three men with spears. 'And if he does not die, they blame the messenger, calling him a bad man.'[77] Still in Strabo's time the kings of eastern Thrace would resort for advice to hermits, living in caves and abstaining from animal food; and there was said to have been a continuous succession of these since 'Zalmoxis' himself.[78] Elsewhere in Thrace, Herodotus tells of a tribe which practised suttee; a favourite wife was killed by her nearest kinsman at her husband's grave, and buried with him, and the members of a man's harem would compete for the honour; and of another tribe whose pessimism led them to mourn over a newborn child and rejoice at a funeral. In general in Thrace, 'to be idle' (and especially 'to live by war and robbery') was considered 'most honourable, and the peasant the most ignoble'; and to be tattooed was also a token of nobility.[79] In short, the Thracians were warlike barbarians; yet among these people, with their pessimism and their grim but genuine religious feeling, there was something capable of striking an answering chord of feeling in Greek hearts in a time of social change.

Even Scythia, it appears, exercised some influence on Greek thought. Among the early Greek philosophers some were not merely rationalists, but rather prophets, claiming inspiration; religious teachers, whose personalities attracted a cycle of miracle-stories, sometimes even within living memory. Pythagoras is their prototype; Empedokles, through his own poetry, the best known to us (below, Ch. XIX). In their

[77] Hdt. iv, 94–6; cf. F. Pfister, in *Studies Presented to D. M. Robinson*, pp. 1112ff.
[78] vii, 297f.   [79] v, 4–6.

combination of the characters of prophet, healer of the sick and teacher about the nature of the soul, it has been pointed out that these 'healer-seers', *iatromanteis*, have something in common with the Shamans (holy men and inspired bards) of Siberia; and such shamans may have been the *manteis* mentioned by Herodotos in Scythia. Such a one is Abaris, who, according to a legend that Herodotos found unconvincing, 'wandered over the world carrying an arrow', which (Aristotle adds) guided him on his way until he met Pythagoras, who took it from him and 'made him confess' – what, we are not told (p. 378). Shamans today claim to ride on arrows on their voyages to the home of the gods. Another supernatural voyage was that of Aristeas of Prokonnesos, said to have travelled, 'rapt by Apollo', far into the great steppe, and to have written an epic about the griffin-fighting Arimaspians; apparently genuine figures of central Asian folk-lore. Back at his home, Aristeas was said to have entered a barber's shop and there fallen, apparently dead; but after the barber had locked up his shop and gone to report the matter, he met two men who said they had seen Aristeas alive, walking towards Kyzikos; and when he returned to the shop, the body had disappeared. Over 200 years later, Aristeas was said to have appeared at Metapontion in Italy; and this gives a clue to the origin of these tales as Herodotos heard them. They belong to the Pythagorean cycle of legends, which he heard in south Italy, and their historical importance is that they show that among these 'Greek shamans' Pythagoras' circle at least owed a debt to Scythia.[80]

The religious *rites* of Scythia did not influence Greece; but there were points to interest Herodotos here too. There was a conspicuous absence not only of cult-images, but even of temples or altars to the Sky-God Papaios or to any other member of the pantheon except the War-God; to him there was a vast mound built of (or revetted with?) brushwood, surmounted by 'a rectangular sanctuary, with three steep sides and one accessible'; it sounds rather like a Mesopotamian ziggurat, from which indeed it may have been derived. Here stood the symbol in which the god was held to be embodied, an iron short sword of antique pattern; and here not only beasts, but prisoners of war, 'one in every hundred', were sacrificed.[81]

---

[80] Hdt. iv, 13ff, 36; cf. Pindar (fr. 271 Bgk.) *ap.* Origen *Agst. Celsus*, iii, 26-7; Dodds, *The Greeks and the Irrational*, 140ff and nn.; K. Meuli in *Hermes*, 1935.

[81] Hdt. iv, 59 and 62.

Some northerners in turn were attracted by Greece, and not only by Greek trade-goods. The Scythian prince Anacharsis travelled to Greece (*c.* 510?) and was received with an interest less patronising than that taken by England in a Pocahontas from Virginia or a Honi Heke from New Zealand. Greeks felt that he might have something of interest to contribute on the nature of the universe, on which their own ideas were in flux. What Anacharsis may have said to them is lost; but later, in a more sophisticated Greece, men delighted to think of what he might have said, or to father their own thoughts on this 'noble savage'. Thus Anacharsis came to be numbered among the Sages (pp. 207ff); a large collection of his alleged sayings grew up (*inter alia*, he was said to have praised the authoritarian Spartan constitution, which seems possible; but Herodotos is sure that even this was a Greek fabrication); and his name has achieved a curiously lasting fame, rising once more in the generation of Rousseau.[82]

But the ideas of nomad society were not in flux. The Scythians were savages, using the skulls of their enemies as cups and their scalps as towels or for decorative purposes; but they took their own ways. seriously. Like the Hebrews, they refused to keep the pig (a forest animal) in their country and especially to use it for sacrifice; and they regarded Greek cults as Elijah the rites of Baal. Anacharsis, homeward bound, made a vow at Kyzikos to the Mother of the Gods, for his safe return; but when he paid it, going into the woods of 'The Bush' for the purpose, his own brother the king, being led to the place, drew his bow and shot him. In Herodotos' time, a similar fate befel Skyles, a king himself. He was son of a woman of Istros, who 'taught him the Greek language, and letters'. He used to make long visits to Olbia, where he had a Greek wife and a house 'surrounded by sphinxes and griffins in white stone'; an archaic Greek palace. So far no objection was raised; but when a Greek boasted to the Scyths that their king had become a devotee of Bakchos, they rebelled against him and, when he fled to Thrace, secured his extradition by threats, and put him to death; 'for the Scythians say that it is outrageous to invent a god who makes men mad'.[83]

Herodotos' work is the final distillation of what Greeks learned in their period of expansion, of lands unlike their own and the strange

[82] *id.* iv, 76f; D.L. i, 101ff ('*Life*' of A., among the Seven Sages).
[83] Hdt. iv, 63-6 (customs); 76 (fate of A.); 78-80 (Skyles).

ways of their inhabitants. He is the father not only of history, but of anthropology; an observer of customs untrammelled by the desire to fit all that he has seen into a theory; a reporter of what he has seen even if he does not understand it, and of what he has heard, if it seems for any reason worth reporting, without his necessarily believing it.[84] He is nowhere greater than in his account of the northern peoples, in which he ranges from the institution of 'blood-brotherhood' (the term is modern) among the Scyths – the practice of sealing an alliance by the chief contracting parties mingling their blood and drinking it – to an account of lake-villages in the western Balkans.[85] He shows us what a variety of experience the physical expansion of the Greeks had brought within their ken; a stimulating factor, which took its full effect when the old patterns of Greek society were disrupted by the growth of new ways of life in the new trading world.

[84] e.g. iv, 42 (p. 131, below); cf. vii, 152: 'I am bound to report what is said, but I am not bound to believe it; and this shall be my principle for all narratives.'
[85] iv, 70; v, 16.

Addition to n. 1 on p. 107 above:
'I would still contest all this.... I doubt if you have established that there was a [chronological] *system*.... The primary question is Sinope and that area: a source of metal, not more remote from Miletos than Etrurian metal from Euboia. As with Cumae, this would be starting far away, suggesting that in the middle of the [8th] century trade was more the object than land (Al Mina also.)' – A.A.
Cf., however, pp. 404ff.

On recent Soviet work, see now E. Belin de Ballu, *Histoire des Colonies grecques du Littoral nord de la Mer Noire; Bibliographie annotée des Ouvrages et Articles publiés en U.R.S.S. de 1940 à 1962* (Leiden, E. J. Brill, 1965). The summaries are useful; the overall picture is supplemented, but not greatly altered.
See also J. Boardman in the Hellenic Society's *Archaeological Reports for 1962-3*.

CHAPTER VII

Egypt, Cyrenaica and the Further West, c. 640-500

THE century c. 750-650 in the Levant had ended with a Greek recession in face of Assyria. But now, Assyria was weakening. Asshurbanipal (d. 626) in his old age complains that his god has forgotten him, for all his unwearied piety. The terrible war with Elam, ending in Kadmeian victory about 640, had drained Assyria's manpower. The peoples of the future, the Medes and Persians, appear on the horizon:

'After the victorious weapons of Asshur had overcome and destroyed all Elam, Cyrus the King of Parsumash, Pishlume the King of Khudimeri, kings whose home is distant, who dwell beyond Elam, the fear of Asshur, Nin-lil and Ishtar of Irbil overwhelmed them. . . .' They sent presents and 'kissed my feet'.[1] The Persians, migrating south-east from an earlier Parsumash on the borders of Armenia, were moving in, still with tactful politeness to Asshur, into areas which Assyria had devastated but could not occupy. This Cyrus could be, though the generations are rather long, the royal grandfather named by Cyrus the Great.

In Egypt, as we have seen (p. 104), Psamatik, the Psammetichos (variously spelt) of the Greeks, between 660 and 650, got rid of the Assyrian garrisons; the more easily, since Assyria needed the troops elsewhere. He did not gain supreme power, however, without opposition at home. In the story told to Herodotos, the period after Psamatik's 'flight into Syria from Sabakos the Ethiopian (Shabaka) who had killed his father Necoh' and restoration by the Egyptians of Sais, appears as the time of the Twelve Kings. Egyptian tradition for tourists drew a veil over the Assyrian invasions, except for a story of how, as in the Bible, a supernatural disaster (a plague of mice (or plague-carrying rats?) sent by Apollo Smintheus, the plague-sending god of the Iliad) compelled the hasty withdrawal of Sennacherib.

[1] Campbell Thompson and Mallowan, in *LAAA* XX (1933), p. 95 (lines 115ff).

Psamatik, driven into the Delta fens by his rivals, was promised by an oracle that he would win supreme power 'when bronze men appeared from the sea'. The bronze men duly appeared, in the form of Ionian and Karian pirates. Psamatik made an alliance with them, used their arms against his rivals, and recruited more mercenaries from Asia Minor. Some, it will be remembered, were sent by Gyges of Lydia; a step of which Asshurbanipal, who by now regarded Psamatik as a rebel, took an unfavourable view (p. 104).

Thus far the Egyptian and Assyrian views of the matter. A Greek tradition, reported by Strabo, describes another phase of what was going on: a considerable colonising expedition, sent by Miletos: 'Sailing with thirty ships, in the time of Psammetichos, they put in to the Bolbitine (western) mouth of the Nile' and founded the Fort of the Milesians; 'and some time later, sailing up into the province of Sais, they defeated the fleet of Inaros and founded the city of Naukratis, ('Sea-Power'), destined to fame. Inaros, not otherwise known, but bearing a common Lower Egyptian name, must have been a rival of Psammetichos; we have here Greek and Egyptian accounts of the same events.[2]

Thus Psamatik was established as Pharaoh, with the backing of his armoured Greeks; and the XXVIth (Saite) Dynasty, the last flourishing ancient Egyptian monarchy, saw also the golden age of the Greeks in Egypt. They came in swarms, 'both to trade, and also to see the country', as the Greek phrase repeatedly says: wise men like Solon of Athens (p. 301; also Thales of Miletos and Pythagoras of Samos, according to dubious but plausible tradition); cheerful young aristocrats like Charaxos, brother of Sappho of Mytilene (p. 226), who, like Solon, traded while seeing the world; traders with their ships' crews by the hundred, and soldiers by the thousand; Psammetichos gave his Ionians and Karians quarters on both sides of the Nile near Memphis, at the place called The Camps. For him they secured Ashdod, a trading port and gate into Asia, after a long siege. His son, the Pharaoh Necoh of the Bible (609-593) led them again in action.

South-west Asia presented a tempting spectacle. Assyria was crumbling under the assault of the Medes, newly formidable with a centralised monarchy and military discipline, learned from Assyria; Babylon,

---

[2] Sabakos, Hdt. ii, 137, 139, 152; 'Sanacharibos', *ib.* 141 (cf. Isaiah, xxxvii, 36-7, 2 *Kings*, xix); Ps. and the 'bronze men', Hdt. ii, 151-4; Naukratis, Str. xvii, 801.

so often conquered, rose once more under the desert-edge dynasty of the Chaldaeans. An attempt to use the invading Scythians against the allies proved as perilous as late Roman attempts to make use of Huns; the nomads swept over Media and Syria even to Askalon, but retired from the hot plains riddled with disease. The Medes are said to have got rid of those settled in their country by a kind of 'Sicilian Vespers'. Nineveh fell in 612 before Kyaxares the Mede and Nabopolasser of Babylon, in a sack vividly celebrated in the fierce verse of the prophet Nahum; but Asshuruballit, the last Assyrian king, held out at Harran, in the great western bend of the Euphrates. As his ally, no doubt with ulterior motives, Necoh marched out (608?), overcoming on the way Josiah, King of Judah, who was killed in the Pass of Megiddo. Necoh is said to have dedicated to Apollo of Branchidai, near Miletos, 'the garments that he wore in the battle', a tribute to the god of his Greek soldiers. But while Necoh tarried, imposing Jehoiakim as a puppet king in Jerusalem, Harran fell, Scythian troops, now serving Nabopolasser, sacking its great temple of the Moon-god; and at Carchemish in 605 Nebuchadrezzar, Nabopolasser's son, routed Egyptians and Greeks and made an end of the Assyrian remnant. Hogarth and T. E. Lawrence, in 1913, discovered among the burnt ruins of the city a vivid relic of the fighting: a doorway, shot full of bronze arrowheads and finally burnt in, and among the ashes a shield adorned with a grinning Gorgoneion; that of some dandified Greek mercenary who had fought to the last.[3]

Nebuchadrezzar overran Syria, 'mopping up' enemy remnants near Hamath; but he was recalled by the death of his father, and sped home in a dramatic desert ride to secure the kingdom. Necoh was given a respite, and in 601, on his own frontier, checked Nebuchadrezzar severely; the latter needed a full year to refit his army. But the 'bruised reed', as an Assyrian had once called Egypt, did nothing to support Judah. 'The king of Egypt came not again any more out of his land; for the king of Babylon had taken, from the brook of Egypt unto the river Euphrates, all that pertained to the king of Egypt.'

In Egypt itself Necoh prospered, attempting to restore, with ruthless expenditure of the lives of his fellahin, the ancient 'Suez Canal' from

---

[3] Ashod, Hdt. ii, 157; Kyaxares and the Scythian raids, i, 103–6; Megiddo (Magdolos), ii, 159, cf. 2 *Chron.* xxxv, 20ff; Carchemish, Jeremiah's poem, chap. xlvi (Lydians, *ib.* 20); Woolley, *Carchemish*, II, p. 125; D. J. Wiseman, *Chronicles of Chaldaean Kings*, pp. 23ff, 68f.

the Nile to the Bitter Lakes, and sending a famous Phoenician expedition down the Red Sea to see if there was a way round Africa. In three
years, camping twice to grow corn on the way, the Phoenicians
succeeded, though they showed also that this 'south-west passage' was
too long to be useful. The search for it is probably to be connected
with the prowess of Greek piracy, which was making the Mediterranean
route to the west risky for Phoenician trade. Herodotos' account of
this great voyage is famous for an example of his sound reporting, even
of details which he does not believe: 'They said, what I cannot believe
but another may, that as they were sailing round Africa, they had the
sun on their right.'[4]

The impact of Egyptian civilisation on that of Greece struck fire.
The mere fact that, as in Scythia, so many things were different
prompted realisation of the relativity of human customs. The impressiveness of the Pyramids, the huge temples and statues, made the travellers very ready to believe in 'the wisdom of the Egyptians' and to
exaggerate its philosophic profundity. The Egyptian rules of land-
measurement, generalised by Greek thinkers and treated as subjects for
philosophic contemplation, *theoremata*, formed a basis for *geometria* (cf.
pp. 332ff). The myths of Osiris the Dying God and Isis his *Mater
Dolorosa*, embodying ideas not unfamiliar in the stories of Dionysos and
Persephone, were known to Herodotos, and may have influenced the
religious movements of the sixth century (Ch. XVIII). Above all
ranks the stimulus to the already dynamic art of Greece. Monumental
stone temples, replacing those of brick upon stone foundations, with
wooden pillars and terracotta decoration, began to arise. There was no
slavish imitation; the Greek temple plan remains that of a bronze-age
king's 'hall', with its tree-trunk pillared porch at one end, and whether
the concave fluting of the Doric column was influenced by the convex
fluting of the Egyptian is disputed; but both in architecture and in
sculpture the monumental use of stone received a great stimulus; and
in sculpture, already adumbrated in Cyprus under Assyrian influence,
the wig-like treatment of the hair, especially in Crete, is eloquent of
Egyptian influence. Here too, however, Greeks were quick to leave
their models behind. It was left for Plato, in the heyday of naturalism

---

[4] Wiseman, pp. 29, 71; Isaiah, xxxvi, 6; 2 *Kings*, xxiv, 7. Nebuchadrezzar's ride,
Berosos, *ap*. Jos. *Against Apion*, i, 19. Canal, Hdt. ii, 158; navy, 159; voyage round Africa,
iv, 42. Meyer, *GdA*[2] III, 148, does not share the scepticism with which some have treated
this story.

and in revolt against all that his world took for granted – democracy, Homeric mythology, 'Orphic' salvationism, and the view that sculpture aspires to the condition of a waxwork – to argue that the Egyptians alone had managed these things properly, having worked out, ten thousand years before (*sic*), the forms of religious art, and then straitly forbidden artists to innovate.[5] The archaism of late Egypt, looking back to the Old Kingdom and spurning all that had happened since (just as Herodotos was told of hardly anything that had happened between the times of the Pyramid-builders and Psammetichos) afforded some excuse for his misconception of Egyptian art-history.

Even the sheer antiquity of Egypt was impressive, opening up new vistas to a society whose longest pedigrees went back in sixteen or twenty generations to the Homeric gods. It is true that Hekataios' priestly informants overstated the case if, as Herodotos tells us, they showed him 345 statues, alleged to be those of a hereditary line of priests, with no divine ancestor even then.[6] But it is in Egypt that Herodotos is inspired to make his most striking geological observations. Basing his conclusions on the evidence of 'shells on the mountains' far inland, on the deposit of silt by the Nile flood and on the evident silting-up of arms of the sea by the rivers of Ionia and the Troad and by the West-Greek Acheloos, he arrives at his bold conclusion that all Lower Egypt is of recent geological origin and 'the gift of the Nile' – and that if the river chose to change its course and flow into the Gulf of Suez, 'I think the Arabian Gulf would be silted up within 20,000 years, or even 10,000.'[7]

Excess of reverence was never a Greek failing, and it was not long before jokes about Egyptians became as popular as a respect for Egypt's art and supposed philosophy; especially since, from the first, Greeks had learned to despise the Egyptians as soldiers. The most popular expression of such contempt was the Story of Busiris, popular already in the sixth century, and dramatised by Epicharmos of Syracuse early in the fifth. King Busiris (the name is really that of a city, Bu-Osiris) was told by a foreign prophet that if he sacrificed a stranger to the gods every year the land would prosper. Busiris accepted the advice, and sacrificed the prophet. He then continued the practice, with excellent results, until Herakles passed through Egypt on the way to one of his labours, and they tried to sacrifice him. The hero, never very quick in

[5] *Laws*, 656 D – E.   [6] Hdt. ii, 143.   [7] *id.* ii, 10, 12; 'gift of the river', ii, 5.

the uptake in the comic tradition, went quietly at first; but when he found the altar in front of him, he became restive, and ran amok. Busiris had grown very corpulent from long prosperity; Herakles lifted him up and dropped him, and he burst (like Judas, as used for comic relief in some of the old mystery-plays); and after routing everyone else within reach the hero (true in this also to his comic character) retired to gorge himself in the royal larders. A sixth-century Ionian, the great comic draftsman of the so-called Caeretan hydrias (Caere in Etruria imported several), has immortalised the central scene. A huge red Herakles is routing a crowd of small, negroid or yellow-faced, white-robed priests. One is grasped by the neck, another by the ankle and seems about to be used as a flail; another is caught in the crook of each of Herakles' elbows, and he is standing on two more; the king, marked out by his serpent-headed *uraeus* diadem, has just arrived on the top step of the altar, nose first. Round the back of the vase come five hefty negroes, armed with sticks: the police, arriving too late.[8]

Some Greek studies of the negro, it is fair to add, are marked by deep sympathy; the same is true of the African animal, the monkey, which makes its appearance in Greek art about the same time.[9] But the general attitude of the Greek in Egypt was one of cheery irreverence. He was more often than not a soldier, and some of his names for Egyptian things are in the true tradition of military humour. The vast tombs of Cheops and Chephren they called 'buns', *pyramides*; certain other characteristic monuments, 'skewers', *obeliskoi* (cf. 'Cleopatra's Needle'). Ostriches they called *strouthoi*, which means 'sparrows', and crocodiles *krokodeiloi*, as Herodotos tells us, 'comparing them to the (little lizards called) *krokodeiloi* on the dry walls at home'.[10]

Some of the men who made this sort of joke are known to us by name. Psammetichos II (594-589 B.C.) had occasion to march beyond the First Cataract, seeking to bring back a body of frontier troops who had deserted; and a column, including some Greeks, went up to the Second. During a halt, on their return, some of these Greeks cut their

[8] Epicharmos, *ap.* Ath. x, 411b; the vase, Buschor, *Gr. Vasenmälerei*, fig. 79, etc.; fragments of another, from Naukratis itself, *JHS* XXV, pl. VI.

[9] e.g. the pensive face of the faience monkey (a scent-bottle) from Kameiros in the Ashmolean Museum, Oxford; the negro head, illust. in *ILN* 1931, p. 959, from a 6th-century sanctuary at Agrigento; the late but exquisite BM bronze, *ib.* 1955, p. 681.

[10] ii, 69.

names, as any foreign soldier might if not restrained, on the leg of one of the colossi of Rameses II at Abu Simbel (now doomed to disappear sooner or later beneath the waters stored by a high dam).

'When King Psamatichos came to Elephantine, this they wrote who sailed with Psammatichos the son of Theokles. They came above Kerkis, as far as the river let them; and Potasimto led the foreigners, and Amasis the Egyptians.'

The tomb and sarcophagus of Potasimto (Pedisamtawi) have been discovered. Amasis (Aahmes) however can hardly be the general who later became king, as *he* lived until 525; the name is a common one. Psammatichos the son of Theokles must, it would seem, have been a second-generation *poulain* (as the crusaders said), born in Egypt to a Greek father, and named after the king.

Then come the signatures:

> . . . And Archon the son of Amoibichos and Axe, son of Nobody [or perhaps a name, Pelekos, son of Eudamos] wrote me [the inscription].
> Helesibios of Teos.
> Telephos of Ialysos wrote me.
> Python, son of Amoibichos.
> Pabis of Qolophon [Kolophon]
>   with Psammatas.
> Hagesermos.
>   Pasiphon, son of Hippos.
> Krithis wrote [this].

And, on the leg of another colossus (a text recently deciphered for the first time):

> Anaxanor the son of Er—— of Ialysos, when the king marched his army the first time, (that is) Psamatichos.[11]

Naturally, these brash and favoured foreigners were not popular, and about 570 they were threatened with serious trouble. Apries, son of Psammetichos II (the Pharaoh Hophra of Jeremiah xliv, 30, who campaigned ineffectually against Nebuchadrezzar) sent an expedition, probably not including Greeks, against the Greek colony of Cyrene (pp. 137ff), but was defeated with heavy loss. Jealousy against the

---

[11] Improved readings given by André Bernard in *Rev. des Et. Gr.* LXX (1957); Ditt *Syll.*[3] I, 1, Tod, *GHI*, 4, etc. Elephantine garrisoned, Hdt. ii, 28; Ps. II's expedition, 161, 1.

Greeks burst into a flame; the Egyptian soldiers mutinied, chose as their leader a coarse, efficient officer named Amasis, whom the king had sent to reason with them, and overthrew the king and his Greeks and Karians in battle at Momemphis. Amasis thus became ruler of Egypt; Apries survived, powerless, for the moment, but trying to regain his position failed and was killed, and Amasis remained as Pharaoh.[12]

He was constrained to curtail the position or at least the conspicuousness of the Greeks; but having no wish to lose either their services or the Greek trade, he craftily gave back with one hand most of what he took with the other. He forbade the free movement of Greeks, but concentrated their trade in one 'treaty-port' at Naukratis. 'If anyone sailed into any other of the Nile mouths, he had to swear an oath that he had not come there intentionally, and then sail his ship to the Canobic mouth; or if contrary winds made that impossible, he had to take his cargo round through the Delta to Naukratis in barges.' Naukratis thus became a unique 'international settlement', like nineteenth-century Shanghai. 'To the Greeks who came to Egypt, Amasis gave Naukratis to dwell in, and to those who did not wish to settle, but made voyages thither, he gave sites for altars and precincts for their gods. The greatest, most famous and most used of these precincts was called the Hellenion, and was founded by the following cities: of Ionia, Chios, Teos, Phokaia and Klazomenai; of the Dorians (of Asia) Rhodes (sc. the three cities), Knidos, Halikarnassos and Phaselis; and of Aiolis, Mytilene only. These are the cities to which this sanctuary belongs, and which appoint Directors of the Market; any claims thereto made by other cities are unfounded. And separately, the men of Aigina founded a sanctuary of Zeus, and the Samians of Hera, and the Milesians of Apollo.'[13] Aigina, it is noteworthy, is the only city west of the Aegean here represented; Corinth is a conspicuous absentee, though her pottery reached Egypt, and a prince of Corinth, born probably about 620-610, was named Psammetichos (p. 194). Naukratis flourished exceedingly, until its prosperity was reduced by the Greco-Persian wars, and became famous, among other things, for the particular charm, attested by Herodotos, of its Greek geisha-girls or *hetairai*, some of whom (the Thracian Rhodôpis, Doricha, probably

[12] Hdt. ii, 161-9, iv, 159; inscr. of Amasis, *CAH* III, 303.
[13] Hdt. ii, 178-80, cf. 154.

not the same, though Herodotos thought so) even achieved a niche in Greek literature (p. 226).[14]

Cyrenaica

The Greek colonisation of Cyrenaica was coaeval with the penetration of Egypt. Herodotos has a long account of it, valuable, in spite of some romantic details, as our only narrative of the early development of a colony. After a mythological prologue, in which in a familiar manner he tries to make history out of the heraldic pedigrees of the Kings of Cyrene, reaching via Sparta back to Jason and Kadmos, he tells how the first expedition was stimulated by a long drought on the Dorian island of Thera, in which 'all the trees died but one'[15] (presumably a local way of accounting for the treelessness of this fantastic, volcanic island). The Delphic Oracle is said to have promoted the colony, forcing the idea upon a population of home-biders; the Oracle figures, indeed, perhaps suspiciously often; but its fame as an adviser on colonisation probably was high by this time, having been first built up, no doubt, among the numerous westward colonisers dwelling round the Corinthian Gulf.

An inscription of *c.* 380 from Cyrene, renewing arrangements for common citizenship between colony and mother-city, purports to quote the foundation-decrees; and since inscriptions at Thera show that writing was in general use there in the seventh century, these documents may well be genuine. One son from each estate is sent as a conscript, on pain of death for deserters, while other Theraians are free to join as volunteers; other settlers are to be admitted later; and if the colony cannot be held and has to be evacuated within five years, the colonists are to be received back, with full rights to share in the family property (in contrast, for instance, to Eretria's treatment of her colonists driven out from Corfu, p. 96). A fascinating and primitive-looking detail is then added: 'They invoked curses upon those who transgressed and did not abide by these provisions, either of those about to settle in Libya or of those remaining. They made 'giants' of wax and burnt them in a general assembly both of men and women and boys and girls: (praying) that any who should not abide by these oaths . . .

---

[14] ii, 134–5. R. became a figure of saga, 'a fellow-slave of Aesop' of the Fables, Hdt. *l.c.*; hence probably (despite the anachronism) her identification with Doricha, named by Sappho; Ath. xiii, 596, distinguishes them.
[15] Hdt. iv, 145–9 (cf. Pindar, *Pyth.* iv).

should melt and waste away like the images, himself and his posterity and his property; but that to all who should abide by them . . . there might be great prosperity both to them and their posterity.'[16]

Herodotos describes the first timid reconnaissance, from which the exploring party, 100 in number, returned to Thera and were forcibly denied a landing (no doubt it was to prevent a repetition of this that the oaths were sworn); the first settlement on an off-shore island, where the reconnaissance-party had left their Cretan guide, Korobios, a purple-fisher, to 'hold the fort'; the detail of how Korobios had meanwhile run short of food, and been reprovisioned by Kolaios the Samian, bound for Egypt, who was then blown out of his course by an unremitting east wind, and discovered the silver-trade of Spain by accident (cf. p. 147); and at last, after two years, under further pressure from Apollo, the settlement on the mainland coast, whence, after six more years, the settlers are guided by the natives, peaceable but not wholly unsuspicious, to the inland site of Cyrene. Here they settled, ruled by a king, their founder, Aristoteles, surnamed Battos, which signified in Greek 'the Stammerer' (a detail taken up in the Delphic legend), but in the Libyan language, as Herodotos soundly points out, meant 'king'.

For two generations, under Battos and his son Arkesilaos, the colony remained small; but under the third king, Battos II, surnamed the Prosperous, 'the Delphic prophetess in an oracle urged any Greeks to sail to join the Cyrenians . . . for the Cyrenians were inviting them, promising a redivision of the land. . . . So a great multitude collected; and the neighbouring Libyans, under their king Adikran, being deprived of their land and oppressed by the Cyrenians, sent and placed themselves under Apries, the king of Egypt.'[17] This was the origin of Pharaoh Hophra's disastrous expedition, c. 570 (p. 135).

The day of small things and of comparative innocence at Cyrene was now at an end. The next king, Arkesilaos II, quarrelled with his brothers, who moved west with their followers and founded Barka; while 'at the same time they encouraged the Libyans to revolt from Cyrene'. Greco-Libyan relations were being strained by the arrival of the thousands of new Greek settlers, and complicated by the existence of a large population of mixed blood. It has been shrewdly remarked that evidence of such mixture of blood is usually strongest in colonies

[16] *SEG* IX (1938-44), No. 3   [17] Hdt. iv, 150-9.

Greece and the West

of colonies,[18] and this is certainly true of Barka; it is also natural, since colonists were recruited chiefly among the less privileged classes, to which the offspring of mixed marriages would usually belong. Arkesilaos marched against the rebels, driving them east, away from their friends at Barka; but at a place called Leukon, far from his base, they turned desperately upon him, and destroyed most of his army. 7000 Cyrenians are said to have perished, in the first on record of many disasters suffered by armoured Europeans pursuing lighter-armed enemies in arid country.[19]

Arkesilaos did not long survive his defeat; he is said to have been smothered while lying sick by his brother Laarchos, who then seized power as regent for the king's son, Battos (III), a child, and also lame from infancy. Laarchos ruled despotically until he was murdered in turn by the brothers of the queen-mother Eryxo, whom he had aspired to marry. The conspirators, noblemen not of the royal house, then 'proclaimed Battos king, and restored the ancestral constitution'.[20] Strong rulers in this century (like Kleomenes later at Sparta, with which Cyrene had close links) aspired to win a despotic position by acting as reformers and leaders of the people, while 'the traditional constitution', *patrios politeia*, became the slogan of aristocratic and conservative elements. Cyrene in later times had, like Sparta, traditionally the mother-city of Thera, a Senate or Council of Elders, *Gerousia*, and annually elected Ephors, 'Superintendents'.[21] We may infer that the 'ancestral constitution' was one in which, as at Sparta, the monarchy was checked and controlled by the aristocracy.

But in a commercial city with a large and mixed population, such as Cyrene now was, plebeian elements were soon clamouring for recognition. The conservative classes had been weakened by the recent losses of the armoured infantry, and were unable to maintain their old dominance.[22] In this crisis recourse was had once more to Delphi; and by its direction (very characteristically) an arbitrator was invited from the innocent and conservative republic of inland, Arcadian Mantineia. Mantineia nominated one Demonax (his name, 'Lord of the Demos', suggests an aristocratic family with democratic sympathies); and he

[18] Dunbabin.   [19] Hdt. iv, 160.
[20] Plut. *Mor.* 260, N.D. fr. 58 Müller, Polyainos, viii, 41, amplify and probably correct the one sentence in Hdt. *l.c.*
[21] Herakl. Pont. *Kyr. Pol.* (see *FHG* II, p. 212); cf. *SEG* IX, 1, ll. 82ff; Chamoux, *Cyrène sous les Battiades*, 214ff.   [22] Cf. Ar. *Politics*, v, 1303a.

'having come to Cyrene and studied the situation' produced a typical sixth-century moderate reform. He divided the people into three new tribes, presumably replacing the three ancient tribes of the Dorians; this was a frequent action of Greek reformers[22a] (cf. pp. 194, 198), and would have the effect of placing the later settlers, now enrolled in the tribes, on a level with the older citizens in voting rights: 'one tribe of the Theraians and *perioikoi* (the partly Libyan country-dwellers?), one of the Peloponnesians and Cretans, and one of all (other) islanders; he assigned to the king Battos certain sacred estates and priesthoods; and all the other former prerogatives of the king he distributed to the people'.[23]

While Cyrene was weakened by the Libyan disaster and her internal crisis, Barka seems to have taken the lead for a time in attempting to expand westward, pushing into the Syrtes and defeating the Phoenicians in a naval battle.[24] Four new cities, including Euhesperides (Benghazi), making up with Barka the later Pentapolis of western Cyrenaica, may date from this time.[24a] Greek aggressiveness in this quarter was being actively encouraged by Delphi. Unfulfilled oracles that Spartans were destined to colonise the island of Phla in Lake Tritonis in southern Tunisia and that a hundred Greek cities should grow up round the lake are of some interest, as showing that not all recorded prophecies are *post eventum*.[25] But an attempt by a Spartan prince, Dorieus, disappointed of the succession, to colonise the region of the River Kinyps, near modern Tripoli, was defeated by the Libyans with help from Carthage (after 520); Dorieus, we are told incidentally, had *omitted* to consult Delphi[26]; and the frontier between Greek and western Phoenicians came to rest finally at the Altars of the Philainoi, at the southern point of the Syrtes, near El Agheila.[27]

Neither the power of Barka nor the peace at Cyrene lasted long. The next king, Arkesilaos III, was ambitious to regain power. Defeated in civil war, he fled to Samos, where he 'collected men indiscriminately by the promise of a redistribution of land'.

Meanwhile his fierce and strong-minded mother, Pheretime, went to Cyprus and tried unsuccessfully to get military aid from Euelthon, King of Salamis; 'this Euelthon', remarks Herodotos in passing, 'dedi-

[22a] *op. cit.*, vi, 1319b.   [23] Hdt. iv, 161.   [24] Servius, *ad Aen.* iv, 42.
[24a] One at least, Taucheira, from before 600; see the publication of important stratified archaeological deposits by J. Boardman, *Tocra*, 1963-65.
[25] Hdt. iv, 178-9; Macan, *ad loc.*   [26] *id.* v, 42.
[27] Mela, i, 7; Sall. *Jugurtha*, 79; S. used Punic records in translation, *op. cit.* 17.

cated at Delphi the censer which is preserved in the Treasury of the Corinthians and is well worth seeing'.[28] The evidence of continued Cypriote interest in the west is of interest. With his army of land-hungry men from Samos, however, Arkesilaos successfully assailed Cyrene and took revenge on his enemies. Many fled into exile; those whom he captured he despatched to Cyprus to be put to death, but when the ships carrying them put in at Knidos (another city with western connections, notably with Taranto) the people liberated the prisoners and sent them to Thera. Others held out in a castle in the countryside, until Arkesilaos burned the castle with them in it.

To secure his position, Arkesilaos then acknowledged the overlord-ship of Cambyses, King of Persia, who had conquered Egypt *c.* 525; but becoming nervous that he had disobeyed a cryptic oracle from Delphi, deprecating revenge, and must avoid 'the place between the waters', which he took to mean Cyrene, he handed over the govern-ment to his mother and retired to the protection of his father-in-law, Alazeir, King of Barka. (This native name of a king is striking.) But his fate followed him. Cyrenian exiles and men of Barka slew him 'when out shopping' and Alazeir also. Pheretime fled to Egypt, and the Persian Satrap Aryandes, after a refusal from Barka to surrender the assassins, sent an army under an Egyptian general, yet another Amasis, and a fleet under a Persian to subdue Cyrenaica (*c.* 512). Cyrene seems to have submitted. Barka stood a siege for nine months, during which a local smith devised an ingenious method of detecting Persian mining operations by laying a bronze shield on the ground at suspected points, where its concave metal acted as a sound-amplifier. But Amasis captured it finally, under cover of treacherous peace-negotiations. Pheretime took a savage revenge on her enemies – when she died, 'eaten by worms', it was considered to show the anger of heaven – and the invaders, after sending a column as far as Benghazi, returned to Egypt, carrying off many of the inhabitants of Barka; King Darius deported them to Bactria, where their descendants were still recognisable in the time of Herodotos.[29]

It is, as usual, the bloodier episodes of history that figure in our sources; but the prosperity and the artistic development of Cyrene continued with scarcely a check. To the former, and also to continuing interest in Cyrene in mid-sixth-century Sparta, witness is borne by the

[28] iv, 162.   [29] *ib.* 162–7; 200–5.

famous Arkesilaos Cup, one of the masterpieces of vase-painting of a Sparta not yet sterilised by Spartan-ness. The King of Cyrene, duly named in writing, sits on a folding stool under an awning, wearing a wide-brimmed sun-hat; its conical crown rises to an ornamental spike, no doubt a royal prerogative. Before him, his servants are weighing and stowing into nets certain bottle-shaped objects, perhaps tubers of the medicinal silphium plant, second only to grain among his exports, and famous because unique; below, men are storing the filled nets in a vault, of which the curved roof appears on the left. Some have taken the awning for the sail of a ship, but the method of attachment by rings is against that; moreover the sail would hardly be set during the operation of loading. Birds and a monkey perch on the great beam, from which the balance is hung; a crane flies overhead, and a lizard, a gekko on the wall, is visible behind the king. The whole scene is full of brightness and movement, the wealth and glamour of sixth-century Cyrene.[30]

The House of Battos reigned for two more generations. Under Battos IV, the Handsome, Cyrene struck coins of great fineness and variety,[31] of silver, Attic or western, gained by her agricultural wealth and her position on the southern route to the West. The late-archaic statues of youths and maidens that adorned her temples are scarcely outshone by those of Athens. A Cyrenian poet, Eugammon (named for the god Ammon?), about 560 is said to have written the last poem of the post-Homeric Trojan Cycle, bringing the story down to the death of Odysseus.[32] Under a fourth Arkesilaos, whose diademed head in bronze has been found in Cyrene, the royal racing-chariot won glory with a victory in the Pythian Games (462), celebrated in the most splendid of all the odes of Pindar; perhaps also commemorated by the chariot-group of Battos the Founder, which Pausanias saw at Delphi, centuries on. Telesikrates of Cyrene won Olympic and Pythian victories in the race in armour and in the 400 yards; at Cyrene 'in the yearly feast of Pallas, many a victory he won; and every maiden prayed in silence that she might have such a husband or such a son'.[33]

[30] Illust. *CAH* Plates I, 378, Buschor, *Gr. Vm.* fig. 79, etc., etc.; discussion, see Chamoux, *Cyrène sous les Battiades*, pp. 258ff.
[31] E. S. G. Robinson, *B.M. Coin-Catalogue: Cyrenaica*; further bibliography in Chamoux, *op. cit.* pp. 29-30.
[32] Proklos, *Chrestomathia*, ii; date, Eusebios; though his absence from earlier records, e.g. the list of distinguished Cyrenians in Str. xvii, 837-8, suggests some doubts as to whether the list known to the Neoplatonists was genuine.
[33] Pind. *Pyth.* iv and v; Paus. x, 15, 6-7; Telesikrates, *Pyth.* ix (171ff).

The bronze head, of about 450, is one of the earliest works of Greek portraiture.[34] Monarchy lent itself to such glorification of the royal individual, whereas in most of the Greek world as yet republican modesty delayed this development. When it was cast Arkesilaos was already faced with trouble. He secured himself for a time by means of colonists personally obliged to him for their lands, whom he settled at Euhesperides; but his position was anachronistic, and a revolution made an end of him and a democracy of the city about 440.[35]

The Further West

In the west, as we have seen, there had been a pause in colonising activity, after the prodigious outpouring of the generation 730–690 tr.; a pause to be accounted for by the solution of food problems provided by emigration and the import of corn. The earliest literary allusion to imports of Sicilian corn to the Peloponnese is in Thucydides[36]; but Greek literature so seldom mentions economic matters that absence of earlier evidence is not evidence of absence. Of the manufactures which must have paid for the corn, apart from luxury goods and the ubiquitous painted pottery, we hear only a very few details, such as that Megara, much later, specialised in the production of cheap clothing,[37] and that Miletos imported wool from Sybaris, no doubt for industrial use.[38]

But after the primary colonies had been in existence for two or three generations, some of them in turn, it appears, felt the need to expand; and we hear of a drive into western Sicily, with the foundation of two cities, almost sixty years after that of Gela. These were Megarian Selinous, where the Founder Pamillos came from the mother city but most of the colonists from colonial Megara,[39] and Chalkidian Himera, with three joint Founders, perhaps representing respectively Zankle, the organising city, Chalkis the original *metropolis*, and the Myletidai, a body of exiles from Syracuse, who joined the colony in sufficient force to affect its dialect.[40] The two were almost twin-born according to Diodoros, whose dates (Selinous 650, Himera 648) are probably too early; Thucydides dates Selinous about 630 and gives no date for

---

[34] Pernier in *Africa Italiana*, II (1928); Chamoux, *Cyrène*, 368ff.

[35] Cf. Hdt. iv, 163, the prophecy (*post eventum*?) of a monarchy limited to eight reigns; Herakleides (*FGH* II, p. 212; Theotimos of Cyrene, *ap.* schol. Pindar, *Pyth.* V. 33).

[36] iii, 86. Cf. Sophocles, *Triptolemos, ap.* D.H. 1, 12, on western corn.

[37] Xen. *Mem.* ii, 7, 5; Aristoph. *Ach.* 519.

[38] Timaios, *ap.* Ath. xii, 519.   [39] Thk. vi, 4, 3.   [40] *ib.* 5, 3.

Himera.[41] Both cities are pushed forward, on the south and north coasts respectively, as though under a concerted plan, to secure as much ground as possible in face of the Phoenicians at Motya and the Elymoi of Eryx and Egesta; prehistoric immigrants by sea, these latter, and said to be descended from 'Trojan refugees', i.e., as archaeology makes increasingly likely, from non-Hellenic eastern sea-farers.[42] That there was such a plan is likely, for it was just in these years that Greek sailors began to penetrate the western Mediterranean. The epoch-making voyage of Kolaios the Samian to Spain (p. 137) must have taken place, at earliest, only just before the foundation of Selinous. Himera and Selinous strike the earliest coinage in the west, soon after 600, soon followed by Himera's mother-city, Zankle.[43] It has been plausibly suggested that the silver of which Himera's early and beautiful coins were made came from southern Spain, now being regularly visited by the ships of newcomers to the west, the Ionians of Phokaia.

'These Phokaians,' says Herodotos in a famous passage,[44] 'were the first Greeks to make long voyages, and it was they who first revealed the Adriatic and Etruria and Iberia and Tartessos; and they made their voyages not in merchant vessels, but in fifty-oared galleys'; in ships of war. Pompeius Trogus, the learned historian from Provence epitomised by Justin, adds some details: 'Compelled by the narrow boundaries ... of their territory, they paid more attention to the sea than to the land; by fishing, by trade, and frequently also by piracy, which was then considered honourable, they secured a livelihood.'[45] About

[41] D.S. xiii, 59 and 62. Archaeologists used to prefer the later date for S., but partly because the accepted dates for Gk. pottery are based on Thk.'s dates for the colonies; cf. Payne, *Necrocorinthia*, pp. 23f; Dunbabin, *WG* 437f. Now, however, that by the re-excavation of pottery from Selinous long unseen in the vaults of the Palermo Museum, a considerable quantity of Late Protocorinthian and Transitional pieces have been discovered, the acceptance of Diodoros' date becomes a line of least resistance; see the publication and careful argument of G. Vallet and F. Villard in *BCH* 1958. To keep Thucydides' date, it is argued, would leave too little time for the development of the successive Ripe Corinthian styles. This argument, however, it is admitted (*ib.* p. 24), is subjective; and to scale down the whole system of dates for archaic pottery, however troublesome, would have the advantage of 'keeping in step' with the dates for early coinage, necessitated by the re-examination of the material from Ephesos as well as with the hitherto troublesome evidence of the Perakhora scarabs. Cf. pp. 178 and n. 10, 89, above.

[42] Thk. vi, 2, 3; cf. Bernabo Brea, *Sicily Before the Greeks*, pp. 108, 125ff, for Mycenaean pottery in the Lipari Islands; though similar evidence from the Elymian area itself is still lacking, and Brea (p. 176) doubts the tradition. Hellanikos (*ap.* D.H. i, 22) brings the Elymoi from Italy, like the Sikels.

[43] J. G. Milne in *Numismatic Chronicle*, 1938. Cf. Stesichoros' interest in Tartessian silver, Str. iii, 148 (below, p. 152).   [44] i, 163.   [45] Justin, xliii, 2.

600 tr., they crowned their efforts by the foundation of Massalia, Marseilles.[46] They are *not* named as founders of Spina, a 'notable Greek city' just south of the Po, which at one time policed the northern Adriatic with its fleet, had a shrine at Delphi and imported great quantities of classical Attic pottery[47]; but this foundation must surely have had some connection with their exploration of the Adriatic, a sea which, through the fierceness of the natives on its eastern and the harbourlessness of its Italian shore – perhaps also through its considerable summer rainfall, uncongenial to the Greek way of life – remained comparatively little visited by early Greek sailors.[48]

In making the Phokaians also the 'discoverers' of Etruria, Herodotos does less than justice to Aiolic Kyme; but his statement serves to draw attention to a curious fact. Phokaia replaces Kyme. She becomes prominent, especially in the west, as Kyme declines; and as the two cities were near neighbours, it seems as if there must have been some connection between their changes of fortune, whether through some attack on Kyme from inland, to which Phokaia, on its promontory-site, would be less exposed, or through the silting-up of a harbour or through some other unrecorded cause. Phokaia seems to have been as closely connected with Lydia as Kyme of old with Phrygia; and, though Ionian in speech and customs, she also inherited Kyme's old connections with Lesbos. A fourth-century inscription records a monetary convention under which Phokaia and Mytilene co-ordinate their coining operations; and that this connection was ancient is shown by the fact that many early Mytilenean coins are found, along with Phokaia's, near Marseilles itself, at Emporiai and Rhode (Ampurias and Rosas), Massalia's daughter-colonies in Spain, at other sites in Spain, at Hyele (Velia), Phokaia's refugee-settlement of the Persian invasion period on the west coast of south Italy, and at Volterra in Tuscany.[49]

[46] Timaios, *ap.* 'Skymnos', 209ff; 598 Jerome, 593 Eus. Arm.

[47] Str. v, 214; R. L. Beaumont in *JHS* LVI; Dunbabin, *WG* 346 (refs.); *ILN* 4 Dec., 1954, 8 Dec., 1956. The pottery is nearly all 5th century.

[48] Comparatively; but cf. Beaumont, *The Gks. in the Adriatic* (*loc. cit.*). Michel, *Recueil d'I.G.*, no. 8.

[49] Convention, *IC* XII, ii, 1; Tod, *GHI* II, no. 112; J. F. Healy in *JHS* LXXVII. Coins (esp. the Auriol hoard, 6th century): see G. Vasseur, *L'Origine de Marseille* (= *Annales du Musée de M.*, XIII, 1915); P. Gardner, *History of Ancient Coinage*, p. 62, who also mentions numerous early Myt. coins at Ampurias, Rosas, other Spanish sites, Velia and Volterra. Vasseur classifies the hoard, of c. 2160 coins, all early (anepigraphic), as about half Lesbian 'by their types'; but it would perhaps be hard to prove that many of these are not Phokaian; cf. C. T. Seltman, *Greek Coins*, p. 29, for Myt. coinage 'modelled on' Ph. Most of the rest are likewise NE Aegean; well-represented are Lamp-

Even the rather dull, grey 'bucchero' pottery of Phokaia and the Phokaian west is characteristic also of Mytilene.

At Marseilles and also at the native hill fortress of Ensérune, near Béziers, on the trade-route to the Atlantic now followed by the Canal du Midi, it has been claimed that the earliest datable Greek pottery, Protocorinthian and eastern Greek, is of the mid-seventh century.[50] It is perhaps questionable whether these earliest sherds have not been antedated; but clearly there will have been a period of commercial contact before definitive settlement. It is, indeed, reported that Massalia was founded by merchants who had 'gained favour with the Kelts (really an anachronism at this time, for "Ligurians") on the Rhone'.[51] Trogus calls the tribe the Segobrigii, a name later recorded in central Spain, perhaps displaced thither by the advance of the Gauls.[52] Euxenos of Phokaia was said to have been present at a feast given by their king Nannos, who was that day to betroth his daughter Petta to the suitor of her choice; and the girl, on a sudden inspiration, handed the symbolic cup of water to the Greek, who renamed his bride Aristoxene, 'Good to the Stranger'. Their son Protos or Protis became the Founder of Marseilles, and ancestor of a family, the Protiadai.[53] Trogus' version makes Protis himself and his Segobrigian wife Gyptis the hero and heroine of the story. There is nothing impossible in this tale of a Ligurian Pocahontas, but the variations in the names and the significance of some of them leave room for speculation. Were the names Aristoxene, Euxenos (the Well-Received) and Protis (First) perhaps symbolic names attached to cult-statues, and did the romance grow up round these? When we notice that another woman, Aristarche (Best of Leaders), a priestess of Ephesian Artemis, whose oracle the

sakos, Kyzikos, Abydos; Smyrna, Kolophon, Teos, Klazomenai, and Lesbian Antissa and Methymna.

[50] Vasseur, *op. cit.* (also in *Comptes rend. de l'Ac. des Inscrs.* 1910) speaks of Protoattic, Protocorinthian, Naukratite, Rhodian, 'Cyrenaic' (Laconian) from 650 on. Cf. also Jacobsthal and Neuffer in *Préhistoire*, II. R. M. Cook, *op. cit.* in *JHS* LXVI, agrees that there is much more E. Gk. than usual on a western site, but doubts J.'s and N.'s claim that much is specifically Phokaian, and suggests that Vasseur's pl. I, nos. 1, 4, 6, are Aiolic. On dates he agrees only that a few published pieces are definitely pre-600 and one very much earlier. Payne dates the Corinthian 'at least as early' as 600–575 (*Necrocor.* p. 184). At Ensérune the earliest Corinthian piece in the museum is claimed to be late 7th century; but cf. now n. 41 above. The next oldest four or five are definitely 6th century. See now J. Jannoray, *Ensérune*; Vallet and Villard, *op. cit.* (n. 41) p. 24; Villard, *Céramique Grecque de Marseille* (Paris, de Boccard, 1960).

[51] Plut. *Solon*, 2.

[52] Town of Segobriga, Pliny, *NH* iii, 3/4; for 'Ligures pulsi', cf. Avienus, 133.

[53] Ar. *Const. of Massalia, ap.* Ath. xiii, 576.

Phokaians consulted, also plays a part in the Massalian saga, bringing with her a cult-image of the goddess[54]; that yet another native heroine saves the city later by betraying to her Greek lover a plan of the now jealous natives, to take it by treachery[55]; and when we remember the similar story current at Phokaian Lampsakos (p. 109), we are constrained to believe that these Ionians had an unclassical liking for stories containing female characters and love-interest. Such an interest appears, it may be noted, also in several stories invented or developed by the first great poet of the Greek west, Stesichoros of Himera.[56]

The real story of the western metal-trade was romantic enough. Already the Phoenicians had explored 'Tarshish', as Ezekiel addressing Tyre says,[57] 'with silver, iron, tin and lead they traded for thy wares'; and even earlier, bronze-age sailors from the Levant and the Aegean, as archaeology is now confirming, had penetrated the west, bringing some rumour of eastern civilisation to the Megalith-builders, themselves no mean travellers. Now came the Greeks, and Arganthonios, King of Tartessos, whose name perhaps means the Silver Man (cf. El Dorado), became legendary among them. He was said by Herodotos to have reigned for eighty years and by Anakreon for 150.[58] Perhaps the name was dynastic. Glad, no doubt, to meet competitive buyers, the king received the Greeks with open arms. Kolaios, the Samian pioneer, was said to have made the largest profit ever heard of, 'except that of Sostratos of Aigina, which is beyond all competition' (unfortunately we hear no more about this). The natives are said, even in the third century, to have used silver for mangers and storage bins, and early Phoenicians to have come home with their ships ballasted with silver and using pigs of it for their anchors.[59] Tin and lead played their more prosaic part. A line of colonies spread from Marseilles along the coast of Spain as far as Mainake, somewhere near later Phoenician Malaga, with which it was sometimes confused.[60] Rhode on the Costa Brava was claimed as originally a Rhodian foundation, and some

[54] Str. iv, 179.
[55] Justin, xliii, 4.
[56] Cf. the plots of his *Daphnis, ap.* Aelian, *VH* x, 18, *Kalyke* (Aristoxenos, *ap.* Ath. xiv, 619) and *Rhadine*, Str. viii, 347.
[57] xxvii, 12; cf. Jer. x, 9 (silver); this evidence, from the generation about 600, is conclusive against the theory of Schulten (*Tartessos*, 4, 16ff) that the Tyrians had ceased, since the Assyrian conquest, to visit the west.
[58] Hdt. i, 163, Anakr. *ap.* Str. iii, 151.
[59] Kolaios, Hdt. iv, 152; mangers etc., Str. iii, 151; anchors etc., D.S. v, 35.
[60] As Str. iii, 156, points out.

Rhodian vases (aryballoi) and faience have in fact been found at the neighbouring Ampurias. Rhode, under the modern Rosas, remains unexplored.[61] Greek pottery at Ampurias goes back well into the sixth century[62]; in Corsica, a stepping-stone to Marseilles, a Phokaian colony at Alalia is dated by Herodotos about 560.[63] Half-way between Ampurias and Mainake, Strabo refers to three other small colonies of Massalia. One, the post of Hemeroskopion, 'the Watchtower', where the Massaliotes built a temple of their Ephesian Artemis, is probably to be identified south of the Cabo de la Nao, where a superb, sea-washed 'pillar-rock' commands a wide view southward; no doubt it played a distinguished part in the inevitable Graeco-Phoenician waru as it did later in the days of Sertorius.[64]

For all this was not achieved without fighting. The rallying of the western Phoenicians under Carthage was a natural reaction to the Greek invasion of the west, and Carthage gained her first foothold in Spain when she took Gaddir, Cadiz, under her protection against the natives (the date is not indicated).[65] Already 'at the time of the foundation of Massalia', according to Thiscydides, Phokaians had defeated a Carthaginian fleet. Further successes were gained later, presumably off Spain, 'in a war arising out of the sezure of some fishing boats', but Mainake was lost, perhaps about the end of the century.[66] Before that, Phokaia itself had been evacuated by many of its inhabitants in face of Cyrus the Persian, and the refugees, reinforcing Alalia in Corsica and engaging thence in piracy, had been forced to evacuate it after a desperate 'Pyrrhic victory' in a battle against the allied navies of Carthage and Etruria. The survivors retired to Rhegion, and then settled at Velia (Elea or Hyele), about 535, guided thither by a friendly citizen of the Sybarite colony of Poseidonia (Paestum).[67] Most of the Massaliote colonies on the south coast of France, such as Agathe (Agde), Antipolis (Antibes), Nikaia (Nice) and at the temple of Herakles of the Lonely House, Monoikos (Monaco) have not so far yielded early

[61] Str. iii, 160, xiv, 654; Dunbabin, *WG* 233.
[62] M. Almagro, *Breve Guia . . . de Ampurias* (Barcelona, 1943), fig. 5; pll. XXIII-XXV; A. Frickenhaus in *Anuari* II, 1908. Schulten, *Tartessos*, 46, rejects this on the flimsy ground hat Rhodians are not mentioned here by Avienus.
[63] Hdt. i, 165.
[64] Str. iii, 159; Rhys Carpenter, *The Greeks in Spain*, 19ff, 117ff.
[65] Justin, xliv, 5 (6th century, Schulten; but J.'s next sentence refers to Hamilcar Barca).
[66] Thk. i, 13; Justin, xliii, 5; ruins of Gk. Mainake, Str. iii, 156.
[67] Hdt. i, 166-7.

pottery, and may represent a later, fifth-century, more intensive consolidation; though Olbia may be nearly as old as Marseilles. By then, Tartessos had been conquered by Carthage; but Marseilles still profited by holding the hither end of the route to the Atlantic via Ensérune.[68]

In Sicily, meanwhile, Greek expansion continued. Gela, neighboured on the east by Syracusan Kamarina, the foundation of which was resented, and which became more than once a bone of contention between the two greater cities, sent a colony (c. 582) to Akragas, forty miles west along the coast. Greek traders had long left their traces here by the sea, while the Sikans continued to occupy the rocky hills two miles inland. The Greeks under Aristonöos and Pystilos (they included new-comers from Gela's mother-city, Lindos), now occupied these: a superb site, which may be compared to a saucer, tilted to the south, the ground dropping steeply in broken limestone cliffs almost everywhere, outside its raised edge. The southern cliffs, rising 350 feet above sea-level, though only 30 or 40 above the sloping plain at their foot, were soon crowned by walls and by a line of small temples in brick, timber and terracotta, replaced in the fifth century by the magnificent stone buildings which still stand, the glory of ancient Sicily. North of them, the ground slopes a little to a stream and rises again, gently for half a mile and then steeply to the northern ridge, over 1000 feet above sea-level and falling in cliffs again on its outer side. From its west end, the Acropolis, now crowded with the houses of the mediaeval town, the Temple of Athena, patroness of Lindos, looked out from a height of 1150 feet, far over land and sea. North of this citadel ridge, the *Rupe Atenea*, the hillside descends in a tremendous sweep to a low col, whence two streams diverge to join the Akragas and Hypsas torrents, flowing below the eastern and western walls of the town, to meet south of it. The city was thus all but surrounded by the streams, whose erosion has left the cliffs that carry its walls beetling on all sides over the surrounding country. These walls enclosed an area of about $1\frac{1}{2}$ square miles, by no means solidly built up; in the lower, southern part of the 'saucer' especially, the houses of the well-to-do stood among

[68] Pottery in the museum at Agde is 5th century and later; at Narbonne, a little 6th century and much good 5th century may have been imported by natives, as at Ensérune (n. 50). On the Garonne route, Narbonne to Bordeaux, cf. Pytheas of Marseilles (4th century), quoted sceptically by Str. iv, 190; tin from Cornwall, shipped from the tidal islet of Iktis (St. Michael's Mount?) and carried by pack-trains in 30 days across Gaul to the Rhone mouths, D.S. (c. 50 B.C.), v, 22. Olbia, Dunbabin, *WG* 339.

gardens, no doubt largely of vines, olives and fig-trees, well watered by two rivulets. Here grew up the largest and wealthiest Sicilian city except Syracuse, hailed as 'the most beautiful of mortal cities' by Pindar, who knew it in its early classical prime.[69]

Less happy was the fate of another East Dorian venture, about the same time. About 580, a Knidian and Rhodian expedition under Pentathlos of Knidos descended upon Lilybaion, the westernmost point of Sicily, completely commanding the island-sheltered bay of Motya. The men of Selinous, with whom the venture must surely have been concerted, were already at war with Segesta, across the island to north of them. But the Elymian and Phoenician opposition proved un-expectedly tough. Pentathlos was killed in battle; Lilybaion proved untenable; and the remnant of his followers sailed away to occupy the Lipari islands, just north of Sicily, long since a port of call for Mycen-aean sailors. Here they founded a semi-communist republic, in which the ownership of land on the main island (at first, on all the islands) remained vested in the community; and supplemented a living gained from agriculture and fishing by piracy in the Phokaian manner, at the expense of all and sundry, at least among non-Greeks.[70]

Selinous, for a time, gave up aggression; the plentiful Corinthian pottery which reached Carthage may, it has been thought, have been largely re-exported from here and from Akragas; and when probably before 550 Malchus, the first Carthaginian general whose name is known, campaigned in Sicily, it is not known that he fought Greeks; he may only have been attaching the non-Hellenic west to the new Carthaginian empire. He was next transferred to Sardinia, where he was defeated by the natives; being refused permission to return home, he then turned his arms against Carthage, overthrew the government and put to death ten of his opponents in the Senate; but soon afterwards he was accused of intending to establish himself as monarch, and paid the penalty with his life.[71] The pattern of the grim, 'classical' Carthage was taking shape.

Selinous, Himera and the far-flung Massalia, over against the newly

[69] Thk. vi, 4, 4; Pindar, *Pyth.* xii, 1ff; cf. also his *Ol.* ii, iii, *Pyth.* vi. Rhodians, cf. *Ol.* ii and scholia, quoting a lost ode of Pindar (fr. 119 Schroeder). Archaeology, Dunbabin, *WG* 305ff, criticising P. Marconi, *Agrigento*. Plan, Dunbabin, 306.

[70] Paus. x, 11, 3 from Antiochos of Syracuse; D.S. v, 9, with date 580; Euseb. dates Lipara 627; Str. vi, 275 (warfare against Etruscans); Livy, v, 28 (Roman embassy to Delphi held up, but afterwards escorted; cf. Herakl. Pont. *ap.* Plut. *Camill.* 22: 'R. a Gk. city'). [71] Justin, xviii, 8.

formidable Carthaginian power, seem to have been stimulated to cling the more to their Hellenic civilisation. Massalia, where, after the overthrow of an early, narrow oligarchy, a merchant aristocracy retained power for centuries by prudent attention to the people's welfare, had its own editions of the *Iliad* and *Odyssey*.[72] Selinous, perhaps the first Greek city to be systematically planned, with its central 'Broadway', and grid of streets, had presently its range of temples, as at Akragas and Poseidonia, of a splendour unparalleled in old Greece. The earliest pediment known bears a terrific, apotropaic, terracotta Gorgon. Then comes the earliest and greatest school of stone sculpture in the west. Akragas, for all her architectural splendours, had nothing like this. The development of styles at Selinous may well have lagged behind that of Athens; but it culminated, probably well into the fifth century, in mature archaic works of unsurpassed charm and dignity: the metopes now at Palermo, with the bridal of Zeus and Hera and the Amazon falling before Herakles, with an expression of despair which one might suppose oneself to have imagined if it were not confirmed by detailed examination. The lips, which keep a trace of their original colour, are parted, as in some of the contemporary struggling figures in the west pediment at Olympia, and the teeth are shown, though they could never have been visible when the slab was *in situ*, high above the temple colonnade. Syracuse, Leontinoi, Gela, Akragas and Selinous itself have yielded more or less complete remains of early free-standing statues; from Selinous survives a fine archaic bronze youth, no doubt a victorious athlete; but the architectural sculptures of Selinous remain the loveliest of Sicilian sculpture.

Selinous was also second only to Himera in striking coins. The earliest bear for obverse the *type parlant* of the city, the wild celery or wild parsley (*selinos*) plant. Himera used the device of a cock, which, if this is a punning device (the 'cock that crowed in the morn', for *hemera*, 'day'), sheds some light on early Greek pronunciation. But Himera's chief contribution to the arts was that of a great poet, the first in the Greek west, Tisias, surnamed and commonly known as Stesichoros, the Choir-Master.

Stesichoros' date is variously given; he may have been one of the earliest colonists, migrating or brought by his parents from Matauros

[72] Ar. *Politics*, v, 1305b, 1321a; Str. iv, 179f; text of Homer, cf. scholia on *Iliad*, i, 298 and *passim*.

in the territory of the western Lokroi, and living on until 556–553, the 56th Olympiad. Some later poets seem to have used his name, to the confusion of chronographers.[73] With Alkman the Laconian (pp. 180ff), whose work was probably unknown to him, he shares the honour of being the first composer of choral songs for festivals whose work was preserved, and many of his odes were of great elaboration and beauty. Like his follower Pindar, he would often recount a whole story 'sustaining', as Quintilian says, 'the weight of epic with his lyre.' Simonides brackets with him Homer as an authority on the ancient myths; but he also used local stories, some of them vegetation-myths, which he transmuted and humanised into tragic love-tales. Among them was that of Daphnis, originally the Spirit of the Bay-Tree, famous in the later pastoral poetry of the west. Others may have been or purported to be based on stories of real people, like that of Rhadine, from the western Peloponnese, married to a despot of Corinth, who slew her in jealousy. Stesichoros also dealt fully with the story of Herakles and his capture of the cattle of Geryon, the daemon of the far west; he was the first to localise it in Spain, 'by the unfailing, silver-rooted springs of Tartessos' river, in the caverns of a crag'.

Of his free treatment of stories already famous, the classic example was that of his Palinode on Helen. He had spoken ill of the Tyndarid princesses, 'twice and three times wedded and deserting their husbands', and the tradition said that he went blind (had he himself alluded to a purely spiritual blindness?); but his sight was restored when he wrote his *Recantation*, in which he audaciously explained that she never went to Troy at all; a phantom of her went with Paris, that the doom of Troy might be fulfilled; but Helen herself, spirited away by Aphrodite to Egypt, remained there blameless for seventeen years, to be found by her wedded lord after the war was over. The corollary, that the war was fought for a shadow, was to appeal to Euripides.[74]

---

[3] Teisias, b. at Matauria (Matauros, Steph. Byz.) Ol. 37, d. Ol. 56 at Katane, *Suda, s.v.* (a better notice than many in that compilation). His tomb at Katane, Photios, *s.v. panta okto*. Fl. 610, d. 559, Euseb. But as the oldest and almost the only anecdote about him (Ar. *Rhet.* ii, p. 1393b) associates him with Phalaris of Akragas, and as he was impressed by an eclipse, which *might* have been that of 557, solar, total at Himera, it is not unlikely that the 'vulgate' calculations were here again rather too early. A 'Stesichoros' at Athens, 485 and again *c.* 370, Parian Marble, lines 50, 73; cf. Wilamowitz, *Sappho und Simonides*, 233ff. Eclipse, Pliny, *NH* ii, 2/9; see Fotheringham in *JHS* XLVII, p. xxxii.

[74] Simon. *ap.* Ath. iv, 172. Quintil. x, 1, 62. Love-stories, n. 57, above. Geryon at Tartessos, Str. iii, 148. S. *Helen*, q. schol. on Eurip. *Orestes*, 249; story of his blindness, and q. from his *Palinode*, Plato, *Phaidros*, 243a; cf. Eurip. *Helen*, Isokr. *Helen*, 64.

Stesichoros was one of the formative influences on the splendid classical Greek choral lyric. He was credited by some with the addition to the Strophe and Antistrophe, which the choir chanted as they danced to right and to left, of the Epode or tailpiece, sung standing; these were the proverbial 'Three (elements) of Stesichoros', which not to know was the mark of the illiterate.[75]

Treasuring their Hellenic culture, these far-western colonies maintained close links with the centres of Greek religion. Among the cities which set up 'Treasuries' (small shrines, destined to protect offerings of gold or ivory against thieves and the weather), at Delphi and Olympia, the rich Greeks of the west were strongly represented. Syracuse, like Sikyon (cf. p. 202) had treasuries at both holy places. At Olympia, in a row of ten such buildings that looked across the sacred Grove from the foot of the Kronian Hill, eight were from colonial cities, six of them western: Sybaris and Metapontion, Syracuse, Gela and Selinous, and Epidamnos (p. 195) on the way to the Adriatic, along with Cyrene, Byzantion, Sikyon and Old Megara[76]; and twenty-one early Greek brooches (half of all those found at Olympia down to 1925) were of characteristic western styles.[77] A runner of Kroton is said to have won the sprint in 588, the first of a series of his countrymen, breaking a Spartan predominance in this event which had endured for a hundred years; but a wrestler of Syracuse had won the first recorded western victory in any Olympic event, as early as 648.[78]

At Delphi, among the 'treasuries' and other major dedications recorded by Pausanias and often also attested by surviving inscriptions or remains, the states of the Greek mainland play a larger part, along with eastern cities and islands (the Treasuries of Siphnos and Knidos, the Naxian Sphinx); but here too appear early offerings made by the cities of the west, or on the way thither (Kerkyra); several of them commemorate victories over non-Greek enemies. Marseilles dedicates for a victory at sea over the Carthaginians, the colonists of Lipara for one over Etruscans, Taras for a defeat of her Messapian neighbours.[79]

---

[75] *Suda, s.v. tria Stesichorou.*

[76] Paus. vi, 19, 1 and 7 to 12. J. Boardman considers there are archaeological pointers to the Megarian Treasury being western too; though P. speaks of Old Meg. offerings in it.

[77] Blinkenberg, *Fibules grecques et orientales* (refs. scattered through the book.)

[78] See Euseb. ed. Schoene (or Clinton, *Fasti Hellenici*): 5 Krotonians out of 8 in Ol. 48 to 55, and again 7 out of 8 in Ol. 68 to 75; no doubt from Hippias of Elis.

[79] Paus. x; Knidos, 11, 1; 3; 5; 25, 1; 32, 1; Siphnos, 11, 2; Kerkyra, 9, 3ff; Massalia, 18, 7; Lipara, 11, 3; 16, 7; Taras, 10, 6ff; 13, 10. Inscrs. of the last two survive; see n. 82.

The mysterious Spina, hard by the mouths of the Po, is also credited with a 'treasury' by Strabo, as is, still more surprisingly, the Etruscan city of Agylla or Caere[80]; but one may suspect that this, like what was called 'the Treasury of the Carthaginians' at Olympia, may really have got its name because it contained spoils won from these Etruscans. Two of the earliest (sixth-century) inscriptions from Delphi are on the tombstones of a man of Selinous and a man of Marseilles.[81] One of the most Simonidean of the epitaphs unreliably attributed to that great poet commemorates the dangers that men faced to keep up these communications[82]; one may venture to translate:

> These, bringing Tuscan spoils to Phoibos, found
> Their end, one sea, one night, one plot of ground.

[80] Spina, Str. v, 214; Beaumont, *Gks. in the Adriatic*, in JHS LVI; Agylla, Str. 220. Treasury of the Syracusans at O. called 'of the Carthaginians', Paus. vi, 19, 7, from the spoils which it contained.

[81] Dittenberger *SIG*³ nos. 11, 12. Slightly later inscrs. attest worshippers from Lipara (*id.* no. 14); Taras (21 and 40); Kerkyra (18); Etruria (24); Metapontion (25); Kroton (30).

[82] *A.P.* vii, inserted after no. 650; also, with *v.l.* 'from Sparta' for 'Tyrrhenian', *ib.* no. 270. Our text reading is more likely to have been corrupted into the other than *vice versa*.

PART III

The Revolution in Greek Society

CHAPTER VIII

The New Age and the New Poetry: Archilochos

OVERSEAS expansion opened the eyes of many Greeks to the possibilities of other ways of life. It produced also many uprooted individuals, more ready to attempt these ways than those still settled on the land. And the pressure of population upon food-supplies, though relieved locally by imports, reappeared elsewhere. In Attica (pp. 285ff), a crisis develops precisely at the point where the produce of the land can no longer feed the population; and even in the colonising cities, new strains and stresses developed. The invention of *coinage*, of which adumbrations had appeared in the Assyrian world and in commercial Lydia, increased facilities for the accumulation of wealth – and for losing it. Debts, in money, and usury introduce new complexities. Town workers, producing partly for exptor, are threatened, when times are bad, not only with having to tighten their belts, like the hill-foot crofters, but with actual starvation; and being grouped together in one place they are in a position sometimes to put pressure upon governments. They may also make common cause with hard-pressed crofters, in debt to richer landowners, with the typical revolutionary demand for a redistribution of the land. Repeatedly, they find a leader, often a man of noble birth, divided from the majority of his class by some stain on his ancestry or merely by the usual rivalries of great families. In city after city, such a leader makes himself *tyrannos*, a name for a despotic ruler applied to Gyges and then used to mean a political boss holding power by means of armed supporters and not according to law.

'Tyrants', since the basis of their power was force, which they sometimes misused, and since they overthrew aristocracies, got a bad name from Greek writers, who were mostly upper-class. The normal modern use of the word is far from the original sense. A large measure of popular support was essential to a *tyrannos*; without it, even the occupation of the citadel by armed force might prove a barren victory, as Kylon of Athens found (p. 286f); and when they lost popular favour, armed force in the hands of mercenaries alone never proved strong enough to preserve tyrant dynasties.

Such support inevitably came from unprivileged classes, including even newly rich bourgeois, excluded from the aristocratic Councils. To call the 'tyrants' 'democratic' would be obviously erroneous. Most of them were aristocrats themselves. It is not necessary on that account to assert that when they removed felt grievances or assisted the poor they were invariably moved only by vindictiveness against old rivals, or by a purely cynical awareness that they needed support. They were men of their age, brought up on the codes of Homer and Hesiod, in which justice, which did not include social equality, was due to all men with whom one was at peace, and flagrant injustice was displeasing to the gods.[1] Hospitality was due to strangers; even the outcast tramp might be given a crust and a bone and allowed to sleep on the veranda, like Iros and the disguised Odysseus. The herdsman in his hut received the homeless wanderer, and the nobleman in his hall the travelling nobleman, as a man and a brother, and gave him of his best. One might be receiving 'angels unawares', like Laphanes the Azanian who 'as the story goes in Arcadia, received the Great Twin Brethren in his house, and after that entertained all' who passed by.[2] Friendship was due to friends, and to the children of old friends and hosts; gratitude and support to humbler supporters; but the code did not exclude the exercise of the full rigour of the law against the insolvent debtor, who was often enslaved; and for vengeance a good man would risk his life.[3] Men's secret motives are beyond the reach of our knowledge, and to judge them is idle. We may take note of their words, when we know them, but our main concern is with what they did. What the *tyrannoi* effected, in the long run, was to 'break the cake of custom'; to break old political systems, with the result that, even where democracy did not follow, customs that had wholly outlived their usefulness did not grow up again.

In this age of movement, set in motion by colonisation and trade,

---

[1] *Iliad*, xvi, 385ff; Hes. *WD* 213-85.
[2] Hdt. vi, 127.
[3] e.g. Achilles, *Il.* xviii, 97ff.; Ar. *Politics*, 1315a (on tyrants).

we meet with the first Europeans known to us through their own word, in the persons of Greek poets. In the days of the Geometric vase-painters, poetry had been as anonymous as art was traditional. The great poet of the Iliad does not abide our question; a 'me' in an appeal to the Muse is the nearest we get to him. In the Odyssey, one such 'me' appears in the first line: 'Tell me, O Muse, of the resourceful man....' That is all. In the *Little Iliad*, the short sequel to the *Iliad* ascribed to Lesches of Mytilene, the poet uses the first person: 'Of Ilios I sing and Dardania rich in horses.'[4] Hesiod, son of a sailor of Kyme who had migrated back from Asia to Boiotia, uses the epic form for new purposes, expostulatory and didactic, and incidentally tells us about his origin, and much about his world and circumstances. He lived in the new sea-faring age, but mistrusts it, and recommends adherence to well-tried ways. A generation or two later, individual self-expression in poetry bursts into full view with Archilochos of Paros.

Archilochos, in lines noted by later writers as historical evidence, mentions Gyges, who was killed in battle between 652 and 644, as a type of wealth and power. He mentions the sack of Magnesia by the Kimmerians (probably just after the fall of Gyges), in a poem written during or after his days as a colonist in Thasos; and he mentions, in connection with his ill-starred love affair at Thasos, a total eclipse of the sun, which, accordingly, could be that of 6 April 648 (the ' – 647' of astronomers) or that of 27 June 660, total at Thasos but not at Paros. He did not reach old age, being killed in battle. His life therefore must fall entirely within the first two-thirds of the seventh century, and the Parian colonisation of Thasos, in which he took part (*not* in 'an early reinforcement' as some moderns have alleged) and which his father led, must be dated not *c.* 720 or 708, as the ancient scholars calculated, but a generation later.[5]

No doubt the forms of personal poetry and choral song, of which we now hear, were traditional. Love-songs, hymns to the gods, war-chants, laments, even satire in many places,[6] have existed in illiterate societies all over the world and performed an important social function. What happened in the Greek Renaissance was that they began to be

[4] *Il.* xii, 176; xvi, 112; *Od.* i, 1; *Little Il. ap.* Proklos, *Chrestomathy.*
[5] For the history, cf. pp. 96-106, above; eclipse (also the Gyges fr.) Ar. *Rhet.* iii, 1418b; cf. Jacoby, *The Date of Archilochos*, in *CQ* XXXV, in reply to Blakeway in *Greek Poetry and Life*, pp. 34ff.
[6] e.g. in the Irish heroic age, and still at the present day among the Bantu.

written down, as the great epics already had been; and the first personal poems to be so honoured were those of Archilochos.

Two other features of Greek literary history arise from this transition from the 'oral society' to literacy. One is the attitude of poets to the work of their predecessors.

In the absence of literacy, there can be no literary property. A poet or rhapsodist from abroad may be welcome because he may have new things in his repertoire; but once he has delivered his recitation, no one can be prevented from repeating it or reconstructing it if he can. Naturally, in an 'oral society' with a strong poetic tradition, metrical turns of phrase and poetic expressions, as well as whole passages which become traditional or proverbial, heroic, pathetic, erotic, etcetera, will be preserved in men's memories; and traditional material will be freely re-used in the composition of new poems. The process can be observed in the ballad poetry of English and Scots, modern Greek and many other languages, and its relevance to the question of Homer's use of earlier material is recognised.[7] In Greece itself, where, in the mountains of Crete and of the mainland, the 'oral society' is only now giving way under the influence of the press, the radio and the school, old *tragoudia* of resistance to the Turks were laid under contribution for the composition of new or only slightly adapted songs and ballads of the guerilla resistance to Germans and Italians.[8] Naturally also, in archaic Greece, old social habits did not immediately disappear with the introduction of writing. The remains of early Greek personal poetry, scanty though they are, show us many instances of poets quoting, paraphrasing or adapting a predecessor's work. It was a compliment to the predecessor. The practice is not extinct in the Attic tragedians[9]; and when, for once, we have a collection of over 1200 lines of personal poetry attached to one name, that of Theognis (pp. 247ff), it is hardly surprising (though it *has* surprised scholars of a sophisticated, literary society) that this nobleman's 'proverbial philosophy' contains quotations and adaptations scattered among his original poems. What we do find is the

---

[7] e.g. Milman Parry, *L'Epithète traditionelle dans Homère*, Paris, 1928; Bowra, *Heroic Poetry*, 1952.

[8] I collected a number of these in 1945 in Crete and the Pindos. Cf. the publication by Notopoulos, forthcoming.

[9] Cf. pp. 260f; also Aeschylus' use of Phrynichos' *Persians*, according to the editorial note. Vergil's frequent echoes and paraphrases of Ennius or Naevius, attested by Servius, are as much part of the epic tradition as his choice of a metre.

notion of 'literary property' *beginning* to come in; some of the proverbial philosophers or 'gnomic poets' are anxious enough to preserve
the attachment of their names to their works to 'sign' them, even at
the cost of having to introduce 'Thus said Phokylides' or 'Proverb of
Hipparchos' into sayings of one couplet or of one line (pp. 216, 319).
Theognis seeks the same end by constantly addressing his friend Kyrnos
by name. The first literary quotation of modern type in extant Greek
literature, with reference to its source, is in Simonides of Keos, quoting
Homer; though Solon of Athens before him names and addresses his
older contemporary Mimnermos, in order to correct him.[10]

The introduction of writing had also a second effect, characteristic
of the history of Greek and, to a lesser extent, of all later literatures.
Once a particular kind of poetry had been composed superlatively well
and preserved in writing, it gave less satisfaction to a younger poet to
do the same kind of thing again. The existence of 'classics' in a genre
inhibited, to some extent, further work on the same lines. No one, in
our age, can write another *Hamlet*, nor could any later Greek epic poet
match the *Iliad*. Only second-rate (not always unmeritorious) men
could even get satisfaction out of trying. The original spirits continually 'move on' to the development of new branches of literature, until
at last a time came when it seemed that everything had been done and
that there was no new thing under the sun. This process combines
with the rapid development of Greek social, economic and political
life, introducing continually new problems, to produce the effects, so
conspicuous in the history of Greek literature, of the *successive* development of the different types of major poetry and then of prose to a
classical perfection, followed by comparative sterility as in an over-
cropped field. Plato as a youth is said to have written tragedies[11]; and
there can be little doubt that a man with the brain of Aeschylus, born
into the fourth century, would have been known among the philosophers.

Archilochos was the son of Telesikles the son of Tellis, a leading man
in Paros.[12] His own name, 'Leader of a company', is aristocratic
enough; boys were often named according to what their fathers were

[10] Sim. fr. 85 Bergk (Stob. *Fl.* 98, 29), line 2, *Il.* vi, 144; Solon and Mimnermos, *ap.*
D.L. *Solon* (i, 60).
[11] D.L. iii, *Plato*, §5.
[12] S.B. *s.v.* Thasos; Paus. x, 28, 3.

doing at the time of their birth. But Archilochos was a bastard, son of a slave woman named Enipo.[13] The circumstance left its mark on him for life. As his father's son (once his father had decided to rear him) he knew something of well-to-do society; but as a bastard, he could not inherit; the true-born kinsmen, sons of wedded and dowried mothers, would not have stood it. So he grew up with 'a chip on his shoulder', not one of the most unfortunate of men, but a man with an intelligible grievance. And he had genius.

'His poetry is all but lost', says the author of three inspired pages on him[14]; 'his life little more than a startling rumour. The ancients, who had him all to read, spoke of him in the same breath with Homer. He was not only so great a poet, he was a new kind of poet. . . . This Archilochos sings about himself. We hear in him a voice as personal, as poignant, as in Villon or Heine or Burns; it is a revolutionary voice. Modern literature has nothing to teach Archilochos. One can see that in the miserable scanty fragments of his astonishing poetry that have come down to us.'

In his youth, if one may judge from his poems, which contain much about the sea and little about activities on land other than warfare, he worked in boats and ships for his bread and olives. He did not love the sea. Too many of his friends and neighbours had died in it, 'with their lives in the embrace of the waves'; and he knew well how men

> To fair-tressed Pallas in the deep sea gray
> For sweet home-coming urgently did pray.

Probably an early elegy, from his days in Paros, lamented his sister's husband, lost at sea and receiving no rites of cremation:

> Oh, could we but have laid upon the fire
> His head and comely limbs, in clean attire.

Without this, as men believed, his homeless spirit would wander, an unquiet ghost. Characteristically, Archilochus ended the poem by turning to creature comforts,

> For not by tears shall I charm grief away,
> Nor make it worse by drink and being gay.

[13] Kritias, *ap.* Ael. *V.H.* x, 13.
[14] J. A. K. Thomson, *Greeks and Barbarians*, 26ff.

Another shipwreck is commemorated in the quotation, 'Of fifty men, gentle Poseidon left us Koiranos.' (Gentle Poseidon!) The poem apparently told how one Koiranos of Paros, who had saved a dolphin caught by some fishermen off Byzantion, bought it and let it go, was later wrecked in a ship from Miletos in the strait between Paros and Naxos (still a place where dolphins may often be seen). A grateful dolphin then came up under Koiranos and carried him to shore. It is one of the many classical stories of the tameness of these engaging, warm-blooded sea-mammals, which, though regularly exaggerated and made into fables, are not always so absurd as modern writers have thought.[15]

Sometimes the sea is merely a nuisance, as when the boatmen say, '... For we will not take you over free of charge!' 'But the thrilling line *Let us hide the bitter gifts of the Lord Poseidon* breathes rather an imaginative horror.'[16] The 'gifts' are perhaps corpses washed up on the shore. In another poem he is on shipboard himself, and the consolation during a dreary watch is, as usual, wine:

> Along the rowers' benches bring your cup,
> And lift the lids of the big wine-jars up
> And drain the good, red wine; we can't, 'tis clear,
> Be sober all the time we're watching here.

He went fishing, in Parian waters; he praises a friend

> Good with his trident, and a clever cox;

and when he speaks of the coming of a sudden Aegean storm (a metaphorical storm; a war-cloud from Euboia) he writes in terms of a landmark visible from his own island's north-east coast:

> Glaukos, look the sea is troubled; rising waves the surface tear;
> Dark the clouds above the Capes of Gyra stand up high in air;
> 'Tis the sign of storm; and terror comes upon us unaware.

Gyra is apparently in Tenos; Glaukos (also called 'dandy Glaukos') a friend named several times (cf. p. 165). The metaphor calls up occasions when two boys in a boat would have to hoist a half sail and run for Paros in good time.

[15] *IG* XII, v, 445, col. 1; Ath. xiii, 606 (from Phylarchos); Aelian, *Nat. Hist.* viii, 3; etc. A dolphin which had become tame was not only reported but photographed recently, playing with bathers off a beach in New Zealand (Opononi, north of Auckland, 1955).
[16] J. A. K. Thomson, *l.c.*

He probably visited the western colonies. Island pottery was reaching that market, and he speaks of the 'lovely land around the streams of Siris', perhaps with personal knowledge. And in due course something that looked like a career opened before him, as before thousands of young and landless Greeks in his time, with the offer of a place in a colony which Telesikles his father was to lead to Thasos. There would be a bit of land for everyone and the chance of a fortune from the goldmines, which existed both in the island (already heavily exploited in the Bronze Age, by 'Phoenicians' as the Greeks said)[17] and on the mainland opposite. Archilochos closed with the offer readily.

He left home without unnecessary tears: 'Never mind Paros, and those figs, and a seaman's life.' But unfortunately he did not like Thasos any better. 'This place sticks up like a donkey's back, crowned with wild woods. There is no good land here, nor lovely nor desirable, as around the streams of Siris.' Like some modern emigrants, he had not realised that his bit of land would be a bit of forest. 'All the trouble of all Greece has run together here in Thasos.' It sounds as if the Parians, like other colonisers of the time, had recruited widely, and as if Archilochos did not much like his land-hungry fellows.[18]

There was trouble with the natives too. The Thracians, as we have seen, were big, blond, formidable men; and yet the Greeks could not resist the temptation to try to overreach them. A long but sorely damaged Hellenistic inscription from Paros gives us fragments of an account of the life and times of Archilochos, built up from the allusions in his poems by Demeas, a local historian.[19] From this it appears that the Parians made a treaty with the Thracians, promising not to interfere with their mining operations, but that some of them afterwards broke it; Archilochos, in his disillusioned way, did not hesitate to say what he thought about this; *he* was probably in favour of honest brute force. He also jeered at the misfortunes of some other Greeks, not Parians, who having killed some Thracians were afterwards 'some of them

---

[17] Hdt. vi, 47; cf. ii. 44.

[18] Frags. 18, 53, 54, Diehl. Refs. to the fragments of early Gk. poets will *not* be regularly given here, except where the context is informative, which often (in quotations by grammarians and writers on metric) it is not; while the most informative frags., few as they are, can generally be easily found in the various collections (Bergk, *Poetae Lyrici Graeci*, 1882, before the Oxyrhynchus papyrus finds; Diehl–Beutler, *Anthologia Lyrica*; J. M. Edmonds, *Lyra Graeca*, 2nd ed. 1928, and *Elegy and Iambus*, 1931 (Loeb), with full quotation of contexts.

[19] *IG* XII, v, 445.

drowned by the Parians, and the rest carried off by the Thracians as slaves'. It might be an allusion to the fighting over the post at Stryme, east, along the coast, against the Chians of Maroneia (p. 98). Archilochos took an active part in all this. In some lines quoted in the inscription, he seems to be praising his friend Glaukos for a victory in a single combat; and of himself, he boasts superbly, 'I am the servant of the God of Battles; and I know well the lovely gift of the Muses.'

Of Glaukos, the world has now a precious, almost contemporary relic: a monument discovered by the French excavators in the market-place of ancient Thasos, with an inscription in archaic lettering.[20] It must have been set up not long, perhaps immediately, after his death. In the archaic manner, the stone speaks:

> MONUMENT OF GLAUKOS SON OF LEPTINES AM I: SET UP BY THE
> SONS OF BRENTIS.

Of the Sons of Brentis we know no more. Glaukos, it would appear, lived in Thasos to an honoured old age. The life of his poet friend was to be less happy.

At Thasos, Archilochos fell in love. The girl's name was Neoboule, daughter of Lykambes. He had seen her

> As with a leafy myrtle-spray she played
> And a sweet rose, and her long tresses made
> Over her shoulders and her back a shade.

And he remembers

> ... her scented breast and hair above;
> Even an old man would have fallen in love!

Archilochos vowed himself hers: 'Lykambes' daughter only.' He believed that he had been accepted; but something went wrong, and they did not marry. Possibly Lykambes felt some doubts about this fierce, unconventional and sometimes blasphemous young man ('Gentle Poseidon', in a poem about a shipwreck!), who was in any case poor. Or perhaps it was the poet's behaviour, his words and attitude more than actual military misconduct, when the colonists sustained a defeat on the mainland and the Servant of the God of Battles fled with all speed, abandoning his shield. As much had happened to plenty of other men, but it was not a thing one talked about, unless the shield-

[20] J. Pouilloux in *BCH* 1955, pp. 74ff, pl. III.

loser was a personal enemy.[21] For one thing, shields were not only needful but expensive; in some communities possession of full armour was a necessary qualification for membership of the Assembly. The *timê* (price) of a shield was part of the *timê* (price, status, *honour*) of a man. What made this occasion unique was that Archilochos made a poem about it:

> My trusty shield adorns some Thracian foe;
> I left it in a bush – not as I would!
> But I have saved my life; so let it go.
> Soon I will get another just as good.

And again,

> That man, my friend, who cares what people say
> Will not find many pleasures come his way.

Whatever the reason, the wedding was off. Archilochos was stunned; he obviously had the egoism of his kind, and he had never imagined that anyone could do that to *him*. When an eclipse of the sun startled the north Aegean, he remarked that, after the way he had been treated, that was the sort of thing that would happen nowadays:

> Nothing now is unexpected; none can say, 'This cannot be';
> Nothing's wonderful, since Father Zeus Olympian, even he
> Turned the noonday into night and hid the light whereby we see!
> Then on mortal men did terror sore and grievous lay its hold;
> Now henceforth will men believe and now will hope for things untold;
> Now let no one of you marvel any more, though he behold
> Beasts of earth unto the dolphins give their pasture in exchange,
> Though to them the salt sea-deep and echoing waves of ocean strange
> Sweeter than the land became, and dolphins loved the mountain range.[22]

The context was a suggestion that Lykambes should remonstrate with his daughter to this effect[23] (so girls, we notice, had some say in the choice of their partners). But he was disappointed; Lykambes took the same view. Archilochos appealed in vain to alleged oaths sworn and to the bond of 'salt and table'. He pleads: 'Could it but be mine to touch Neoboule's hand.' He storms, dropping into an obscene account of exactly what he would like to do. Finally –

[21] E.g. Aristoph. *Clouds*, 354, *Wasps* 20. K. J. Dover suggests that Arch. was not speaking *propria persona* (Hardt Foundation *Entretiens* X, v; 1964); but the ancient world unanimously assumed that he was.
[22] Based on a version made by David Graham (Fr. Nicolas Graham, C.R.) at Uppingham, 1935.   [23] Ar. *Rhet.* iii, 1418b.

One great thing I know: how to repay with bitter wrong wrongs done to me.

He let go at Neoboule and all her family a torrent of abuse so savage and so horribly brilliant that she, her sisters and her father were said to have hanged themselves. (Modern scholars have suggested that what the words mean was that they would for ever hang their heads; but the former was the universal ancient tradition.)[24] In any case, public opinion did not turn in favour of Archilochos. Archilochos cursed the whole 'thrice-miserable' colony. Then, having between this quarrel and the loss of his shield made himself, as Kritias the Athenian said, 'unpopular in Thasos',[25] he threw up everything and went out into the world, a 'clanless, lawless, homeless man' in Homer's phrase.

Following his bent, he became a mercenary soldier: 'Well, then, I will be called a mercenary, like a Karian.' Karians were considered the lowest form of human life; a proverb 'Try it on a Karian' was a recommendation of a *corpus vile*.[26] 'With my spear I earn my bread, and with my spear the Thracian wine, and on my spear I lean to drink.' He writes of the wars in Euboia: 'Not many bows are bent, nor many slings are there, when the War-God joins his battle in the plain; but there is the grim work of swords; in such fighting they are skilled, the spear-famed lords of Euboia.' Hardship and lust and a soldier's defiance of fate breathe in his fragments. Kritias blamed him for revealing himself as an adulterer. Demeas had something about his taking a concubine away with him when he left Thasos, whom he claims to have married and later abuses roundly; the love-quarrel with Neoboule was not his last. 'Go to bed with a Seriphian island frog' seems to be one injunction to his consort. Another lady he characterises as 'Fig-tree of the rock, feeding many crows, – simple Pasiphile (Love-of-all) who makes strangers welcome.'

He knows the glamour of the soldier 'tossing his Karian plume'; the Asian, ex-Assyrian and Urartian, fore-and-aft horsehair crest was becoming 'the only wear', and it developed sometimes in fantastic shapes and sizes. In one example, from south Italy, where lived the richest men in the Greek world, from the crown of the helmet rises a neck, on which is a splendid ram's head, in the round, and the fore-and-aft plume is replaced by a great (and unpractically fragile) sheet of thin

[24] e.g. schol. on Horace, *Ep*. vi, 15, Photios, *s.v. κύψαι*; Edmonds, *E & I* II, pp. 84, 116.
[25] *Ap*. Ael. *VH* x, 13.   [26] Eurip. *Cyclops*, 654; etc. etc.

metal, reproducing the plume's shape.[27] One wonders if the owner's name was Krios, 'Ram'. The gaudy or would-be-terrifying blazons on shields at the same time were developing a heraldic character: a horse's or a lion's head probably as the *types parlants* of men with names like Hipparchos or Leon, or the three legs joined at the hips (*triskeles*) borne by the Athenian Alkmeonidai. The front rank of a hoplite army, where stood (as in early Rome) the men with the best arms, must have been as magnificent as it was in intention a daunting spectacle. But Archilochos, as one would expect, like a good professional soldier, reminds us that dandyism was not the same thing as efficiency. In memorable lines, surely a portrait from life, he gives his picture of a Greek *petit caporal*:

> Not for me a tall and dandy captain with a shaven chin,
> Flaunting all affectedly his dainty lovelocks as he struts;
> I'd prefer one short and bandy-leggéd, with a heart within
> Stout and good, and firmly planted on his feet, and full of guts.

He also delights in exposing war's unglamorous aspects. 'Of seven who fell, whom we overtook by running, a thousand were we the slayers!' 'Thick was the foam about his lips' runs one fragment; and another (quoted by a grammarian to illustrate the Instrumental Dative) 'Tickled by lice'.

Perhaps he mellowed with age. Some poems (but we cannot date them) breathe a more stoic air:

> Let him do his will; for, sure, the War-God is the same for all

– with an echo of Homer. Or:

> Heart of mine, now so upset by irremediable woe,
> Up, defend yourself and firmly set your face against the foe.
> Meet the ambush hand to hand and neither show, if foemen fly,
> Exultation, nor defeated lay you down at home and cry;
> But rejoice in times of joy, and in reverses, sorrow then,
> Not Too Much; but understand the tide that rules the lives of men.

Or, in lines put into the mouth of one Charon the Carpenter, a kindred spirit of the Miller of Dee:

[27] In the City Art Museum, St Louis, Missouri; illust. by T. T. Hoopes in *ILN* 5 Aug., 1950, 6 Feb., 1951.

> For Gyges' gold I do not care;
> I do not envy him, nor dare
> High heaven, nor lust for power of kings;
> Far from my eyes are all such things.

The word translated 'power of kings' is *tyrannis*; the first extant appearance of the word.

Several of his poems, *epodes* as they were called, written in alternate iambic trimeters and dimeters, were animal fables. The Fox met the Ape walking alone . . .; a pair of crafty scoundrels, but we do not hear what passed between them; or the Fox went into partnership with the Black-Rumped Eagle; then the Eagle treacherously carried off the Fox's young; but the Fox prayed to Zeus, and the Eagle (as in Aesop) was probably punished when he carried off meat from a burning sacrifice, and set his nest on fire.[28] We should know more of Archilochos' fables if Aesop of Samos, a century later, had not become the fable-teller *par excellence*; he certainly worked over some of Archilochos' stories. One famous saying became proverbial:

> The fox knows a hundred tricks; the hedgehog, one good one.[29]

Another epode metre was an even more startling mixture; dactylic hexameters alternating with iambics, which check the heroic metre in full career and bring one down to earth with a bump; as it were Don Quixote riding a-tilt, with Sancho interjecting his earthy comments. Archilochos used several variations of this mixed metre, chiefly for personal attacks. It may not have been his invention, for a famous mock-heroic poem, *Margites*, 'The Booby', ascribed popularly to Homer, is said also to have used this alternation of rhythms. Archilochos' work as a sheer inventor of metres can be exaggerated; his greatness is in the fact that he used them superbly well.

His fame spread over the Aegean world; and it is pleasant to find that while he was still in vigorous middle-age he was able to go home; not to Thasos of the bitter memories, but to settled, civilised Paros, where the islanders defeated their neighbours of the larger island, Naxos, perhaps more than once in his life-time, and were at the height of their prosperity. In an age in which poets were highly valued, so

[28] Cf. the Byzantine *Aesop*, i, 1 (so, R. Pfister to London Classical Conference, Sept. 1959).
[29] Karpathos, Zenob. iv, 48; hedgehog, *id.* v, 68, where he says 'A. refers to' (perhaps 'quotes') 'this'; Edmonds, frags. 152, 118.

that princes – *tyrannoi* – competed to have them at their courts, the
nobles of Paros who had known his father may have been glad to
invite him, and to overlook his faults for the sake of his genius. To his
last years in Paros we may attribute, at a guess and with no certainty,
a couple of occasional pieces attributed to him in the Palatine Anthology; a mock epitaph, exulting over the deaths of 'the pillars of Naxos',
two great champions, and a couplet to accompany the dedication of
her veil to Hera by a bride; perhaps also a line from a poem by the old
soldier before a battle:

> Bid the young men keep their courage; victory is heaven's to give.

He was fighting as an honest citizen-soldier when a man of Naxos
killed him.

The story goes that his slayer, Kallondes, surnamed 'Crow', was later
repulsed by the Delphic priestess when he wished to consult the oracle,
and when he protested that killing in battle brought no stain was told
first to placate the poet's ghost, since he had slain 'the servant of the
Muses'.[30]

It is fifty years before another poet appears before us as a character
with the vividness of Archilochos; but there are other personalities
among his contemporaries. Semonides, a noble of Samos, said to have
been born about 664 (in another version 794!) is usually named
Semonides of Amorgos, after the south-eastern Cyclad to which he
led a colony (*c.* 630?); so he also was both writer and man of action.
He gained a reputation as a writer of iambic satires, which it is not easy
to understand on the evidence of his fragments. His sense of humour
is rudimentary, and he is not a poet, as Aristotle would say, 'except for
the metre'. Of two pieces preserved, perhaps complete, in Stobaios'
Anthology, in 118 and in 24 lines (would that we had as much of
Archilochos!), the shorter is a reflection on life for the benefit of the
young, in which his riper wisdom points out that the future is uncertain,
that human hopes are often disappointed and that ambition is a waste
of time. Some men grow old before they grow rich, some die of
disease, some are killed in war or drowned at sea, and some live to
hang themselves. His moral is, more strikingly, an approximation to
the Christian 'Do not worry for tomorrow': 'If men would obey me,

[30] Her. Pont. fr. 8; Plut. *Delays of Divine Vengeance,* 17.

we should not love our troubles, nor torment ourselves by dwelling upon them.' It is not un-noteworthy that a successful and honoured man in what may seem to us the bright days of Greek expansion could, in middle life, be disillusioned: 'For we shall be a long time dead; and the days of our life are few and evil.'

The longer piece is a Satire on Women, characteristic of the men's world of Ionian society, taking the same generally low view of the sex as Hesiod (whom in another place he paraphrases)[31] or as many speakers in Aristophanes and Euripides. God had made women of various natures: of mud, of the treacherous sea, or like the fox, the sow, the cat, the dainty mare ('a fit wife only for a king or tyrant'), the ape, the ass or the bee; the last is the only good one, and in speaking of her Semonides shows some tenderness. She loves her husband and brings up good children, and does not sit about with other women exchanging lewd talk.

In sharp contrast to each other are two great elegiac poets of Ionia, Archilochos' older and younger contemporaries. Kallinos of Ephesos (cf. p. 105) stirred his countrymen to battle when hard pressed by their neighbours of Magnesia, and then by the still more formidable Kimmerians:

> Now the Kimmerian host comes onward, the workers of terror.

> How long lie ye so idle, and when will your valour be rousing,
>   Young men? Feel ye no shame? Think of your neighbours at hand;
> What will they say of your sloth? What, think ye in peace to be drowsing?
>   Not so! War is abroad over the face of the land.

The sense goes on, after a break,

' ... and let him that falls shoot, dying, his last shot. Honoured and noble it is for a man to fight for country, children and wedded wife; and death shall come, when the Fates have so ordained it. ... No one can escape that, though he were of immortal descent. Though often he comes back safe from carnage and the thud of the javelins, yet in his own house the fate of death will find him. But then he is not loved nor regretted by the people; but the other is mourned by small and great if he fall. All the people lament for a stout-hearted man when he

---

[31] S. *ap.* Clem. Alex. *Strom.* vi, 744, cf. Hes. *WD* 702-3; a very close paraphrase despite the change of metre.

dies, and while he lives he is prized as a demigod. Men look on him as a tower; for he does the work of many all alone.'

It is the earliest that we have of many statements of the city patriotism, in which each man's love for 'land and children and wife' is summed up and bound together. In the preservation of the community, in an honoured memory, and in the posterity that would give him burial and honour his tomb, the citizen-soldier found his immortality. Of such was Tellos of Athens, who lived when his city was prosperous, who had plenty of this world's goods 'as we Greeks count wealth' (not the wealth of a King of Lydia); whose sons all grew to manhood, who saw his grandchildren, and who fell splendidly in the moment of victory in a battle at Eleusis and was given a public funeral; whom the wise Solon, in Herodotos' story, counted the happiest of all men of whom he knew.[32]

Kallinos does not omit to pray; and like many later Greek intellectuals he prays to Zeus, to the High God and to no other Olympian, not even to 'great Artemis of the Ephesians'. 'Have pity on the Smyrnaians' (Smyrna was the name of a part of Ephesos 'behind the citadel',[33] and he uses the name instead of the unmetrical Ephesioi); 'remember, if ever they burned fat thighs of oxen to Thee.' But prayer is no substitute for action. For Kallinos, Heaven helps those who help themselves.

Very different is the outlook of Mimnermos of Kolophon (*fl. c.* 630 tr.). Kolophon had been the most powerful of all the Ionian land-powers before the rise of Lydia. 'On to the top he put Kolophon', had said someone (some elegist?), in a phrase that became a proverb,[34] in the days when Kolophon's cavalry were the force that could turn any scale. Xenophanes, of the same city, who sailed to the west about 540 when all this was a fading memory, speaks of the magnificence of those knights:

> But they learned useless luxuries from the Lydians, while still they were free of hateful tyranny. They would come to the place of meeting in robes all purple, a full thousand of them, flaunting their proud locks and bedewed with scent.

Mimnermos himself commemorates a champion of old, 'driving the

[32] Hdt. i, 30.
[33] Hipponax, *ap.* Str. xiv, 633 (along with this line of K.).
[34] Str. xiv, 643.

dense ranks of the Lydian horsemen upon the plain of the Hermos with his ashen spear'. But there were none like him now. The weight of Gyges' cavalry had been too great (pp. 103f).

So Mimnermos, with a great poetic gift, grew up in a shrunken society; and in him we see, as always when the city-state lost its pride and ceased to be something to live and die for, the limitations of the Greek view of life. The melancholy that pervades his sweet and melodious verse foreshadows poetry of the Hellenistic age. Youth is fleeting, and after it there is nothing to look forward to except death or, worse still, a prolonged old age, helpless, neglected, ugly, and repulsive to the still lovely young.

> Though one were lovely, when his prime is past
> Not even his sons will honour him at last.

Many a historical instance, even those of such honoured names as Pericles and Sophocles, bears out this tragic truth. In the pre-Christian world, there was indeed much 'natural virtue'; but disinterested kindness was rare. Even gratitude, it became a commonplace of the rhetorical schools, was a chilly emotion, which easily passed over into a kind of resentment.

Mimnermos' most famous fragment (hardly a whole poem, in view of the emphatic 'But we' at the beginning) is on the same theme:

> Yes; but we, as the leaves of the spring in the season of flowers
>   Grow so swift on the bough, bright in the rays of the sun,
> Even as they, for a cubit of time, in the spring that is ours,
>   Joy in our youth, and nought know of the ill that is done
> Neither the good. But at hand are the dark Fates, standing beside us,
>   One with a destined pain: Age, when our prime shall be done;
> One with death; how short, how short are the days that betide us,
>   Harvest days of our youth, yet with us under the sun.
> Then, when the destined end is arrived, when youth is behind him,
>   Then for a man to be dead, rather than life, is a gain;
> Troubles are his, manifold; so often in age he may find him
>   Poorer than once, when want comes with her toil and her pain.
> Many an old man mourns for the loss of his children dying;
>   Grieving he goes from the earth, down to the Lord of the dead;
> Many again in sickness, the heart out-wearied, are lying;
>   There's not a man, but Zeus trouble upon him has shed.

Rather characteristically, he thought the sun must get tired:

> The Sun, his lot is labour all his days;
> No rest from riding on the self-same ways
> For him or horses, once the roseate morn
> Leaves the sea-deeps and up the heaven is borne;
> For back his soft bed bears him, fast asleep,
> The bed the Smith-God fashioned, through the deep,
> Golden and wingéd, swift across the seas
> From orchards of the far Hesperides
> To uttermost east; there, in the black men's land,
> Till earliest dawn, horses and car will stand.

He was known especially as a love-poet, the first in Greece to make love his main theme; here too, when free political life ended, Hellenistic poets followed him. Of his chief work, an elegiac sequence to Nanno, a flute-girl, very little remains; but it includes the saying

> Let there be truth twixt me and thee;
> Of all possessions that is best.

His final prayer, equally characteristically, is

> Without disease and sore anxiety,
> At sixty years of age – so may I die.[35]

[35] The lines criticised by the robuster Solon: 'No, Mimnermos – say eighty!' (D.L. i, 60). But for a more favourable impression of M. the man, cf. J. M. Cook in *BSA* LIII-LIV, pp. 27f.

CHAPTER IX

The Peloponnese in the Seventh Century

IN old Greece, neither Sparta's conquest of Messenia nor the colonising movement had yet produced all their destined effects. There
was a generation of increasing prosperity. The art of the east reached
even Arcadia, its products brought up from the coast on caravans of
donkeys, by bagmen from eastward-trading Aigina.[1] The delicate and
accomplished Protocorinthian pottery reached Argos and the interior
by land, as well as the west by sea. Attica's Protoattic was big and at
first clumsy by comparison, its very crudity eloquent of the overwhelming impact of the new ideas, but at the same time, its bigness is
eloquent too, eloquent of the ambition and large conceptions that were
to make Athens an artistic metropolis, once a disciplined tradition had
emerged again. But this, like Athens' political development, lay still
in the future. In 600, she could still export corn.[2]

But social change was afoot, manifested not least in the conditions
of war. The men who could afford armour were still, and remained
for centuries, the lords of the battlefields, and battles took place on and
for the economically vital plains; but, with increasing wealth, more
men could afford armour, and the weight of the mass of spearmen, the
phalanx, became increasingly the decisive factor. Not all in its ranks
possessed the almost impenetrable but very heavy corselet of bronze;
some even preferred the lighter, more flexible and probably cheaper
quilted jerkin of linen cord, as did Alexander the Great long after, and
the little, quick-moving Lokrian Ajax according to the Iliad.[3] In the
new circumstances, in which city armies fought each other rather than
chased outland raiders, those who possessed enough pasture to keep
horses still rode to the field; but often there was little point and much
danger in arriving there ahead of the foot. The result was, in Greece

[1] Cf. Paus. viii, 5, 8, dated in the time of Pompos and Aiginetes, kings in Arcadia just
before the 1st Messenian War; which is only a little too early.
[2] As is shown by Solon's prohibition, 594/2.
[3] Cf. below, the 'Megarian Oracle' (p. 176), l. 6; gl. ii, 529; Plut. *Alex.* 32, 5.

south of Thessaly, a diminution in the use of horses for war, and even in the tendency to keep them, unless for breeding mules or for racing chariots. In the sixth century we still hear of cavalry at Megara (cf. p. 253), but by the early fifth they had temporarily disappeared from the south.[4] This meant an increase in the military importance and therefore in the potential political weight of a new middle class.[5]

Some time in the seventh century the Megarians, independent of Corinth and beginning to colonise eastwards, consulted Delphi as to where they stood among the states of Greece; the search of a new power for recognition. But the oracle was partial to the great western colonisers, and the enemies of Corinth, who had expected justice from Apollo, were, like a lord of Sikyon after them (p. 197), severely snubbed. The response gives us a glimpse of an unfamiliar Greece:

> Pelasgian Argos' fields are past compare;
> Horses of Thrace and Sparta's maids are rare;
> Best warriors drink of Arethusa fair;
> (But better still are they who dwell between
> Tiryns and Arcady's sheep-pastures green,
> The linen-armoured Argives battle-keen;)
> But you, Megarians, neither third we call
> Nor fourth, nor twelfth, nor anywhere at all.[6]

The people of the Pelasgian Argos, the fertile plain on the Spercheios, were no doubt pleased; Spartan men, perhaps less so; but the choral poetry of Alkman, written for Spartan girls (p. 180), sheds light on the oracle. The compliment to the soldiers of Chalkis, 'who drink of Arethusa', suggests as date the morrow of the Lelantine War. But the oracle became proverbial, and lines 4 to 6, inorganic and indeed positively inconsistent with line 3, look like a later addition, dating from the generation in which the Peloponnesian Argives defeated Sparta on the field of Hysiai (669 tr.). Hysiai is some fifteen miles south-west of Argos and six miles from the sea, which suggests that Argos regained some part of the east coast strip (p. 27).

It **is** tempting to connect the Argive victory (but no ancient source

---

[4] Hdt. vi, 112; Sparta, Thk. v, 72; Hdt. viii, 124.
[5] Cf. Andrewes, *The Greek Tyrants*, 31ff.
[6] Theokritos xiv, 49; the oracle quoted, schol. *ib.*; cf. Kallimachos, *ep.* 26; in *A.P.* xiv, 73 the v.l. Aigians (of Achaia) for Meg. is due to later scholars who did not appreciate the 7th-century situation.

does so) with the reign of King Pheidon, under whom Argos was for the last time the leading power in the Peloponnese.

Pheidon is called 'tenth from Temenos' (inclusively), which on the traditional chronology would date him about 750. He was said to have marched west to Olympia and presided over the Games of the eighth Olympiad (748), to the displeasure of the Eleians; but the other traditions about him suggest that he belongs rather to the seventh century. Starting as a hereditary monarch with greatly reduced powers, he made himself absolute; he was 'a king who became a *tyrannos*'.[7] He then 're-united the heritage of Temenos, which had been divided'; he reasserted Argive suzerainty over her neighbours, and even over Aigina, where he is said (by Ephoros, in the fourth century) to have struck coins.[8] Aigina certainly did strike the first coins in Europe: the silver *staters* or 'standard pieces', with their badge of a turtle (later changed to a tortoise), which, spreading through the mainland and overseas to the Levant, show us the ramifications of the island's trade (p. 91).

But the earliest coins known from Ionia are now dated, following the re-examination of Hogarth's discoveries at Ephesos, after 650, and those of Aigina can be little before 625. This is, in fact the approximate date at which Herodotos, who gives our earliest mention of Pheidon, does place him, though in a context of saga which has led some to doubt its historical value. Moreover, Herodotos does not mention Pheidon's alleged coinage, but only his march to Olympia and the standardisation of weights and measures, which is certainly historical; the standards became widely current in the Peloponnese and even in Attica, and were long known as 'Pheidonian' (p. 295).

Certainly also, a 'vulgate' tradition about Pheidon, probably from Ephoros, placed him in the eighth century, and it was wrong. The horror-story known from later writers, about how Archias the founder of Syracuse *or* Chersikrates of Kerkyra had to go into exile for causing the death of the boy Aktaion, whose father *or* grandfather had saved Corinth from Pheidon uses this dating[9]; but if it were right we should expect to find the Pheidonian standards in the colonies, which we do

---

[7] Ar. *Politics*, 1310b. Ephoros, *ap.* Str. viii, 358; Parian Marble, 30, has '11th from Herakles'. At Olympia (and Ph.'s son *fl. c.* 570!), Hdt. vi, 127.

[8] Str. *ib.* cf. 376.

[9] Plut. *Love-Stories* (*Mor.*, p. 772); *aliter*, schol. on Ap. Rhod., iv, 1212. Date defended still by G. Huxley in *BCH*, 1958. A. Andrewes in *CQ*, 1949.

not. The Sicilian Greeks used, rather curiously, a native weight-standard, that of the *litra* divided into twelve *ounkiai*, with intermediate 'thirds' and 'sixths' called *triantes* and *hexantes*. The resemblance of the terms to the Latin *libra*, *uncia* (ounce), *triens*, etc. is obvious; the Sikel language was close to Latin (cf. Gela, p. 84), and the original measure of value, in Sicily as in Latium, must have been a pound of copper. Thus at Akragas later, the silver *dekalitron* was equated with ten *obols* (1⅔ drachmas) of Aigina.

The word *obolos* was a by-form of *obele*, a spit or skewer, and *drachme* means 'a handful'. This shows the origin of the terms; they were derived from an earlier, primitive currency of iron bars, six of which made a 'drachma'. Pheidon dedicated in the great Temple of Hera near Argos such 'handfuls of spits', some of which are in the National Museum at Athens; perhaps as specimens of his standard weights but perhaps, alternatively, as a dedication, in accordance with a common Greek practice, of something with which one had finished.[10]

Thus the figure of Pheidon bulks large but shadowy. A chronology based on generations antedated him about 750, *as also the foundations of Sinope, Naukratis and Cyrene*, all really founded about 630. It may be that this dating resulted in detaching him, in the chronographic 'vulgate' tradition, from connection with a probably better tradition of an anti-Spartan and anti-Eleian reaction in the Peloponnese in the seventh century: the Battle of Hysiai, and the rebellion of the pre-Eleian inhabitants of the hill-country south of Olympia against the domination of 'Hollow Elis'.[11] The 'three peoples' of Triphylia are said by Pausanias to have called in Pheidon against the Eleians in 748, but *also* to have seized the sanctuary in 644 (Ol. 34), and retained their inde-

[10] Aig. coinage hardly before 625, 'and if Pheidon had anything to do with it, . . . then his date must be brought down also': E. S. G. Robinson, in *JHS* LXXI, p. 166, citing further Llewellyn Brown in *Num. Chron.* 1950. Ph.'s *metra*, Hdt. vi, 127. The Sicilian *litra*, divided into twelve *ounkiai*: Ar. *Const. of Akragas* and *Const. of Himera* (frags. 476, 510, Rose), *ap.* Poll. iv, 174, repeated ix, 80. Ph.'s dedication of 'spits' in the Heraion, Herakleides of Pontos, *ap.* Orion, *Etymolog. s.v. obolos* (Ar. fr. 481 Rose); derivation of the word *drachma*, Ar. *ib.* and in Plut. *Lysand.* 17. Iron currency, Aristoph. *Clouds*, 249; Pollux, vii, 102; ix, 78.

[11] Hysiai, Paus. ii, 24, 7 (dated by an Olympiad). But Paus. puts Ph.'s intervention at Olympia in Ol. 8 (748), in accordance with the traditional chronology of Ph. 'Ol. 28' in Paus. (vi, 22, 2, his only mention of Ph.) is an emendation. Such emendations are un-doubtedly right, in some *other* passages of Paus. (cf. Wade-Gery, *CAH* III, 761); but note that Str. also (viii, 358, cf. 355) does not name Ph. in connection with the Pisatan domination of O. after Ol. 26. To introduce Ph. at this date is modern theory.

pendence for some sixty years, in the reigns of Pantaleon and his two sons, Damophon and Pyrrhos, who styled themselves Kings of Pisa.[12]

If Pheidon was a *seventh*-century restorer of the strength of Argos, it may well be that he drew upon a new source of man-power, the expanding class of *hoplites*; a middle class, such as has in many ages supported a strong monarchy against an aristocracy. His weights and measures betoken an interest in trade; the name of his son Lakedes, 'who cares for the People', may be significant; and the phrase 'linen-armoured Argives', if connected with his army, suggests that his 'battle-keen' spearmen were not limited to those who could afford the heavy and expensive bronze.

But his work was without a future; and the reason for this we may see in the fact that he was, as a Marxist would say, involved in a contradiction. Himself a Herakleid king, his natural ideal was the restoration of the power of the House of Temenos. But this involved him in strife with his fellow-Herakleids, the junior branch in Sparta, which had expelled that in Messenia, and with his own kindred, the nobles of Argos. Against them, as against the conquest-aristocracy of Elis, he could enlist the help of subject classes and peoples; but these, of mixed blood or not Dorian at all, could feel no enthusiasm for his Herakleid monarchy as such. At Sikyon, which was part of the 'lot of Temenos', the next century was to see an explicitly anti-Argive and anti-Dorian movement; and at Corinth, which he may have dominated for a time, his name was expunged from the tradition, and certain Pheidonian laws which existed there, aimed at preserving the numbers of landed full citizens by limiting the concentration of property (favouring hoplites against aristocracy!), these were attributed to an otherwise unknown local namesake.[13] Pheidon is actually said to have met his death 'when intervening as a friend in civil strife at Corinth'.[14] With the disappearance of his personality, the strong monarchy and the resurgent military power of Argos disappeared also. His grandson Meltas was dethroned and a king named Aigon *elected*[15] (a recovery of power by the aristocracy); and in the trading cities the leadership of the *bourgeois* movement passed into uninhibited, anti-Dorian hands.

In the south, the defeat of Sparta at Hysiai seems to have unleashed a storm that was to do permanent damage to Greek civilisation.

---

[12] Paus. vi, 22, 2-4.   [13] Ar. *Politics*, 1265b.
[14] Nik. Dam. fr. 41.   [15] Paus. ii, 19, 2; Plut. *Mor.* 340.

Sparta, with her lands augmented by the conquest of Messenia (especially the rich plain of Stenyklaros) and her postwar unrest settled by the foundation of Taranto (pp. 75-7), had become one of the most opulent states of Greece. She imported ivory for her craftsmen to work; brooches in bronze, or with ivory plaques, dedicated at her great sanctuary of Artemis Orthia, show oriental motives, such as the bronze couchant lion with its tail ending in a serpent's head; the shape of the Doric bronze 'spectacle' fibula, with its originally functional ornament of two coils of bronze wire, was also imitated in ivory, and in its ivory form had a vogue abroad, at Corinth and even at Ionic Ephesos and Paros[16] (p. 45). Sparta had also close relations with Samos, which must have used Sparta's ports on her route to the west (pp. 90ff, cf. 184). Lakonian vase-painters, like those of Corinth and Athens, were developing a characteristic, orientalising, local style (p. 141). Spartan noblemen took pride and pleasure in male and female beauty, in athletic prowess, in the fame of their Herakleid descent; their poet Tyrtaios was to rebuke them for it in later and grimmer years (p. 183). The oracle's compliment to Spartan ladies finds an echo in Alkman's Song for Maidens, preserved by chance in papyrus, sometimes difficult to interpret – we should need to know the relationships of all the girl choristers whom the poet names – but among the most beautiful surviving fragments of early Greek lyric.[17] Later Greeks, knowing only 'Spartan' Sparta, were at a loss to know how such a poet could have come out of such a place, and fastened on a passage in his poems where someone is addressed as 'no rustic nor (mere northern Greek) nor shepherd, but from high Sardis born'. Some later Greeks (not all) accordingly alleged that he was a Lydian slave; but what we now know of early Spartan art makes this theory unnecessary.[18] A fragment, which Goethe imitated, ranks with the best Homeric similes or the lyrics of Attic tragedy, in Greek nature-poetry. The scene is the vale of Lakedaimon, where the great peaks and buttresses of Taÿgetos tower above the sea of olive and fruit trees and the corn of the plain:

[16] Lion brooch, Blinkenberg, *Fibules grecques*, xvi, 2g; ivory 'spectacle' type at Paro and Ephesos, *ib.* xv; at Corinth, Payne in *ILN* 2 May, 1931.

[17] Mariette Pap. in Bibl. Nat., Paris; latest ed. by D. L. Page, *The Partheneion*.

[18] Alkm. *Parth.* ii, *ap.* S.B. *s.v.* Erysiche (a place in Akarnania). A. a Lydian, *A.P.* vii, 18 and 709; Krates, in *Suda, s.v.*; but there was also a tradition that he was a Lakonian of Mesoa, *ib.*

Now lie sleeping the peaks of the mountains and the gullies,
Buttresses and water-courses;
The creatures, even all that the dark earth nurses;
Wild beasts in the mountain caves, and honey-bees,
And monsters in the deep of the purple sea,
And now sleep all the birds,
The race of the slender wings.

Über allen Gipfeln ist Ruh,
In allem Wipfeln hörest Du
  Kaum einen Hauch.
Die Vögelein schweigen im Walde;
  Warte nur, balde
  Ruhest Du auch.

Alkman was not only a great poet, but a learned man after the fashion of his day, who took himself seriously. He knew the Homeric Cycle intimately, and was prepared to supply the names of peripheral characters such as Priam's mother (and, presumably, Hecuba's), which Homer did not.[19] He knew of Polymnastos, the famous musician of Kolophon.[20] In geography, he was indeed so proud of his knowledge in that Age of Discovery, that he paraded it, giving much trouble and harmless pleasure to later scholars.[21] He knows of the Enetoi or Veneti (those of the Adriatic or south of the Black Sea), with their swift horses, and even of the upper-Asian Issedones, east of the Scythians.[22] He knew, too, of the tendency then developing in the west for 'intelligible' Greek-speakers to adopt a common name for themselves. The name that prevailed was Hellenes, already used by Homer in a more limited sense; Megale Hellas, Great Greece, was the land of the growing cities in south Italy; but some of the Italian natives used a north-western Hellenic tribal name, Graioi, Grai-ikoi, *Graeci*.[23] Alkman is the first to record for us this name 'Greeks', which the Hellenes did not finally come to use for themselves, and was at pains to account for it, making a lady named Graika the mother (since the father's name was otherwise given) of the hero Hellen.[24] He got into deeper water, and

[19] Schol. on *Il.* iii, 250.   [20] Plut. *On Music*, 5.
[21] Cf. numerous citations by S.B., collected by Edmonds, *Lyra Graeca*, I, pp. 112ff.
[22] Enetic horse, papyrus, line 51: 'Essedones', S.B. *s.v.* Issedones.
[23] Graioi a people of Epeiros, and an old name for Hellenes, Ar. *Meteor.* i, 352a, Apollod. *Myths*, i, 7, 3; J. Bérard, *Le nom des Grecs en Latin*, in *Rev. des Etudes Anc.* LIV (1952).
[24] Alkm. *ap.* S.B. *s.v.* Graikes.

laid himself open to some later mockery, by giving among names of tropical peoples that of the Skiapods or Steganopods, the people with one enormous foot, large enough to be used, when the owner was in a recumbent posture, as an umbrella[25]; a legend destined to a vigorous old age (it was resuscitated in the sixteenth century), after starting, apparently, as an early Greek traveller's experiment in what the people at home would swallow.

But it was as a love-poet and a worshipper of beauty in young people that he was especially remembered. When he grows old, it is still to the girl dancers before Artemis that he addresses himself. He alludes to the mythology of the Halcyon, probably the kingfisher, which does haunt Mediterranean coasts, and was said to float its nest on the open sea at mid-winter; wherefore the gods afford an interval of calm weather, the 'halcyon days'. The myth also said that when the *kerylos*, the male halcyon, grew old, the females carried him on their backs. Alkman is perhaps regretting that he is too old to join in the dances:

> No more now, dear maids sweet-throated, delightfully singing,
> My limbs bear me; would, how I would, that a bird I could be
> Over the flower of the foam in the kingfishers' company winging,
> Careless for ever at heart, spring's harbinger, blue as the sea.

But probably before Alkman's death, the events had taken place which were to lead to the transformation of Spartan society. Six reigns before the invasion of Xerxes (so, about 630?) Messenia rose in revolt, with support, it is said, from Argos (but Argos does not seem to have done anything effective), from Arcadia (Sparta must have encroached upon south-east Arcadia to reach Hysiai) and from the resurgent Triphylians. Kings make a late appearance in all these regions as strong war-leaders: Aristokrates of the Arcadian Trapezous or Orchomenos, Pantaleon of Pisa.[26] A Messenian hero, Aristomenes (but some versions of the saga placed him in the original conquest-war and one *c.* 490!) gained fame in song, apparently as a guerilla leader:

> To highest hills, to Stenyklaros hollow
> Did Aristomenes the Spartans follow.[27]

The Messenian stronghold this time was not at Ithome but at Eira in

---

[25] Str. i, 43.
[26] Paus. iv, 17, 2ff, 22, 1-7, viii, 5, 13; vi, 21, 1, 22, 2ff; Str. viii, 362.
[27] *Ap.* Paus. iv, 16, 6.

the northern hills, in touch with their allies. The war dragged on and on. Sparta was near exhaustion; and there was acrimonious division between those whose estates in Stenyklaros had been ravaged by raiders and those more fortunately placed in old Laconia, from whom the harassed settlers west of Taÿgetos claimed compensation.[28] But the Spartan squires, 'ladies' men' though they had been counted, rallied and endured the crisis. In the darkest hour they were stirred to renewed effort by the poetry of Tyrtaios, whom later Athenian tradition, probably first in comic parody, made into a lame schoolmaster of Athens (a very low form of life in Greek social estimation), despatched contemptuously to Sparta in answer to a cry for help. The story only shows that nothing was known of Tyrtaios' personality (perhaps he used the word 'teach'?; but his elegiacs were not autobiographical). There is no reason to believe that he was anything but a patriotic Spartan, in close touch, as some argumentative lines in defence of the constitution appear to show, with the Kings and the Elders of the Council. According to Strabo, he spoke of himself as a general.[29]

It was no provincial or backward city that produced Tyrtaios. His metre is that of Kallinos; the dialect the literary Ionic of Homer; and he uses a wide range of mythology and eastern history for examples:

> I count no one a man worth anything
> For speed of foot or skill in wrestling-ring;
> Though tall and strong as the Cyclopean race,
> Though he outran the northern wind of Thrace,
> Though he were comelier than Tithonos was,
> And rich as Midas or as Kinyras;
> Though kinglier-born than Pelops' lineage
> And honey-tongued, more than Adrastos sage;
> Though, but for courage, every gift were his,
> For all is nothing worth in war but this,
> That amid carnage one endure to stand
> And thrust against the foemen hand to hand.
> This, this is excellence, this to attain
> The noblest prize there is for youth to gain.[30]

The eastern names are no more than one should expect, in a com-

---

[28] Ar. *Politics*, 1306b (from Tyrtaios).
[29] viii, 362, a good and critical passage; T. *ib.*; cf. T. *ap.* Plut. *Lykourgos*, 6 and D.S. vii, fr. 14 (T. fr. 3 Bgk.).
[30] *Ap.* Stob. *Anth.* 51, 1.

munity with Sparta's oversea connections. Sparta is, indeed, recorded to have received help from Samos in these wars.[31]

Spartan persistence, and no doubt better armament than was available to Arcadian hill-men and revolted serfs, had their way in the end. King Aristokrates betrayed his allies at the Battle of the Great Trench (a trench dug apparently *behind* the combatants to deter attempts to withdraw).[32] For all the commando daring of Aristomenes, the cultivable plains were increasingly made safe for Spartans and their serfs and denied to the insurgents. Eira became untenable and a pitiful remnant of Messenians with their women and children withdrew to the highland hospitality of Arcadia – the fate that Tyrtaios had foretold for his countrymen if they failed under the strain, to become refugees.[33] Thence many of them made their way overseas. Aristomenes is said to have died at Ialysos in Rhodes, where his alleged tomb was shown, and where the great athletic and military family of Diagoras claimed descent from him; Damagetos their ancestor, King of Ialysos, having been advised to take in marriage the daughter of 'the best man in Greece'. Through other daughters, descent from him was claimed by families of Phigaleia and Lepreon in Triphylia and of Heraia, in Arcadia.[34]

Sparta's territorial expansion was at an end, though she attempted to continue it. A Spartan band is said to have entered Phigaleia, only to be driven out again by 100 men of Oresteion in Arcadia.[35] The villagers of south-east Arcadia united to found the walled city of Tegea (p. 26), and before it, at some date before 550, the Spartans suffered defeat; when Spartan prisoners are said to have been bound in their own fetters.[36] The Triphylians held Olympia till 572 tr., when the Eleians, now in alliance with Sparta, defeated them and regained control (p. 179). Methone, the Messenian port, is said to have been made over by Sparta to the men of Nauplia, lately expelled by Argos,[37] like the men of Asine earlier (p. 76). But the revolution in Spartan policy and polity that followed this crisis belongs to a later section of our story.

Aristokrates is said to have come to a bad end, being stoned by his

---

[31] Hdt. iii, 47.
[32] Paus. iv, 17, 2ff; for this use of trenches, cf. Ar. *Eth. N.* 1116a and schol. (q. Edmonds, *El. & Iamb.* I, p. 68), citing Tyrtaios.
[33] T. *ap.* Lykourgos of Athens, *Against Leokrates,* 107 (fr. 10 Bgk.).
[34] Paus. iv, 24, 1-3.   [35] *id.* viii, 39, 3f.   [36] Hdt. i, 66.   [37] Paus. iv, 24, 4.

people on the discovery of his treachery.[38] He had been a considerable
figure in his time; his fame outside Arcadia is shown by the statement
that his daughter married Prokles of Epidauros, who, as leader presumably of the traders and the 'Dusty-Footed' countrymen against the
Dorian aristocracy, had made himself tyrant.[39] And this leads us to a
consideration of the developments which were simultaneously taking
place in the Isthmus cities and in the sea-faring world of the Aegean.

[38] *id.* viii, 22, 6f.
[39] D.L., *Periandros* (i, 94); 'dusty-feet' at E, Plut. *GQ* 1.

Additional note: Objection has been taken to my placing of Alkman before Tyrtaios.
The view in the text is that taken long ago by Wade-Gery in *CAH* III (1925), ch. xxii,
and in Oxford lectures, which still seems to me reasonable; Alkman depicting a pre-
'Lycurgan' Sparta, Tyrtaios the poet of the *Eunomia*. The *floruit* often given for Tyrtaios,
685, is from Pausanias' date for the Messenian revolt, Ol.23.4 (Paus. iv.15). But as the
war is six *reigns* before Xerxes' invasion (and 5th-4th century Spartan reigns average
about 25 years), this is much too high. Alkman is dated by the *Suda* to Ol.27 (672).
How vague was the evidence on which ancient Greek scholars did their best to date the
early poets may be seen in the copious quotations collected by Clinton, *FH* I, pp. 183,
189, 361ff, etc. More to the point however is the fact that the recently published (though
fragmentary) papyrus *Commentary on Alkman* (O.P.2390, ed. Lobel, in Vol. XXIV,
1957) names, and makes it likely that Alkman named, a King Leotychidas, presumably
the king named by Hdt. viii, 131 as great-great-grandfather of his namesake who fought
in 479; Lobel, *op. cit.*, pp. 53f. This might bring Alkman *and* the Messenian revolt down
even after 600; for according to Rhianos, Pausanias' admittedly unreliable sources,
Leotychidas was king at that time. (Paus. *loc. cit.*). In that case Alkman *is* a contemporary
of Tyrtaios, perhaps even a younger one; and what he illustrates is the *continuation* of
Spartan gracious living for some time even after the *Eunomia*; a continuation to which,
as I have already observed (below, pp. 280f), Spartan sixth-century art also bears witness.
    On this now see further F. D. Harvey in *JHS* LXXXVII, pp. 62ff.

CHAPTER X

The Isthmus and the North: The New Lords

CORINTH is the city from which we have the fullest account, the type-specimen as it were, of the early *tyrannis*. The great sea-faring and artistic city was full of merchants and sailors, rising in prosperity and prepared to resent the exclusive government of two hundred Bakchiadai (pp. 21, 83); all the more so since the invention of the specialised warship; for the government had to distribute the financial burden of providing these vessels. Dissatisfaction came to a head when Bakchiad policy was not even successful. Kerkyra, the major staging-post on the way to the west, rebelled. The first naval battle of which Thucydides had heard was fought, about 664 he believed, between Kerkyra and Corinth. We have no details; but Kerkyra remained independent, and hostile; and within ten years, if the traditional dates are consistent, the Bakchiad government was swept away.[1]

The popular leader in this revolution was Kypselos, son of Eëtion, son of Echekrates of the Rock, the village of Petra, said to have traced his descent from the pre-Dorian Lapithai. Eëtion married Labda, daughter of Amphion, a Bakchiad; the Bakchiadai usually married within the clan, but Labda, who was lame, had been unable to find a spouse. Kypselos, like Archilochos, was thus connected with the local charmed circle, but shut out of it. Legend added that he was a child of fate, his destiny foretold by the Delphic oracle, and his life threatened, while still in swaddling clothes, by the jealous government.[2] A later story, more probable though perhaps only through rationalising, implies that he was not suspect; he rose through his personal qualities

---

[1] Thk. i, 13. Tyranny at C., 660–586, Jerome; minor variations in other edns. of Euseb. The modern 'vulgate' (655/4 to 582/1) seems to be arrived at by adding Aristotle's figure for its duration ($30 + 44 + 3 = 73\frac{1}{2}$ years (mss.), *Politics*, 1315b) to the date for its end deducible from Sosikrates, *ap.* D.L. *Periandros.* I believe the correct dates to have been fully thirty years later.

[2] Hdt. v. 92.

to command in the army.³ That it was a distinguished soldier who overthrew the narrow and now discredited government is entirely probable. Kypselos then ruled Corinth for some thirty years, *c.* 655-625 tr., popular to the end. Aristotle notes that he never had a bodyguard.⁴

Corinth flourished; market and harbour dues were a fruitful source of revenue. Trans-shipment of east-west cargoes at the Isthmus was easy enough, says the ancient geographer, to make many merchants prefer it to the risks of the long sea-route, including that of being held up by contrary winds (the prevailing summer north wind) while trying to round Cape Malea; 'and also the tolls of those trading in or out of the Peloponnese by land fell to those who held the keys'. Later, too, the Isthmian Games, in honour of Poseidon, 'attracted multitudes, and the Bakchiadai when in power ... reaped a harvest without stint from the market'.⁵ The new monarchy could afford to be moderate in its exactions, and won the willing support of the trading and producing classes, delivered from the burden of supporting the aristocracy. The first coinage of Corinth was struck under the *tyrannis*,⁶ and probably the first stone temples were erected, though the famous temple of Apollo, some of whose pillars still stand, is later, hardly before 540.⁷ Kypselos made alliance with Thrasyboulos, the great tyrant of Miletos⁸; thus Miletos later could trade with western Sybaris,⁹ while Samos, no longer friendly, used the southern route.

Parallel movements were taking place in the neighbouring cities. At Sikyon Orthagoras, son of one Andreas, described as a cook, is said to have risen, like Kypselos, in the army, in war against Achaian Pellene; and like Kypselos, he overthrew a Herakleid aristocracy and made himself *tyrannos*.¹⁰ So did Theagenes of Megara (pp. 248, 286),

---

³ Nikolaos of Damascus (fr. 57J, 58 M), the court-historian and 'cultural attaché' of Herod the Great, whose frags. 56-60 (from the 'Vatican Excerpts'), give our most detailed account of the dynasty. That he researched deeply is unlikely; but he may well reproduce Ephoros. The *judicial* functions ascribed to K. as polemarch (the only functions mentioned in our excerpts) do, however, look anachronistic, and arouse suspicions that somebody is romancing.

⁴ *Pol.* 1315b. ⁵ Str. viii, 378; cf. Thk. i, 13, 3, on the Isthmus as a *land* route.
⁶ But not much before 600, Robinson in *JHS* LXXI, p. 166; Llewellyn Brown in *Schweiz. Münzenblätter*, 4 (1955), pp. 49-51.

⁷ As shown by the developed Cor. pottery found in the 'fill' of its foundations: S. Weinberg in *Hesperia*, VIII, 191ff.

⁸ The alliance seems to be already in being when K.'s son sends to Thr. for advice, Hdt. v, 92, 6. ⁹ Implied by Hdt. vi, 21.

¹⁰ Ox. Pap. XI, 1365; (*FGH* 105 F2). Andreas a 'cook', Libanius, *Against Severus* (p. 251 Reiske). D.S. vii, fr. 24.

recorded to have 'slaughtered the cattle of the rich, when they had been turned out to graze by the riverside'[11] (had there been strife over land between cattlemen and crofters?). That the poor, who formerly 'dressed in goatskins and kept out of town', were now giving themselves airs is one of the complaints of Theognis, later (p. 249). But that the tyrants were not felt immediately and everywhere to be Bolsheviks and enemies of all gentlemen is shown by the fact that Theagenes' daughter was taken in marriage by a young noble of Athens, Kylon, distinguished by an Olympic victory. Kylon then proceeded, with troops sent by his father-in-law, to try to make himself tyrant of Athens. He was overthrown by the people under Megakles of the Alkmeonidai,[12] who claimed descent from Nestor; but this did not prevent later Athenian nobles, Alkmeonid and Philaid (claiming descent from Ajax) from marrying into the houses founded by Kypselos and Orthagoras (pp. 205f, 310).[13] Their objection was to being under another man's lordship, not to power in itself.

Theagenes founded no dynasty; he was expelled, and replaced by a government based on a comparatively broad Assembly (p. 248). The House of Kypselos, on the other hand, it is said, reigned for seventy-four years (655-581 tr.; the real dates are probably later) and that of Orthagoras for a hundred (*c.* 650-550).[14] Kypselos fought no wars with his neighbours; Corinth needed only peace. His eldest son Periandros married the daughter of Prokles, tyrant of Epidauros; a story tells that it was a love-match, beginning when Periandros saw Melissa ('Honey-Bee') in a summer frock, handing out wine, in Homeric fashion, to the harvesters in her father's fields.[15] He made peace too with Kerkyra; for when Kerkyra seized the harbour-site of modern Durazzo and founded the city of Epidamnos (626 Jerome), she invited colonists from Corinth as well as 'other Dorians', and, in accordance with traditional good manners, a Founder from her mother-city, Phalios, son of Erato-kleidas, a Herakleid.[16] Old Kypselos died about this time, and Peri-andros, who succeeded him, was probably not sorry to see Phalios go; to get rid of a prominent nobleman and a number of his henchmen, with their own goodwill, by encouraging them to go where their leader could both be second to none and serve the interests of the

---

[11] Ar. *Politics*, 1305a.   [12] Hdt. v, 71, Thk. i, 126.
[13] Hdt. vi, 128, where the unsuccessful candidate for the Orthagorid match is himself related to the Kypselidai.
[14] Ar. *Politics*, 1315b.   [15] Ath. xiii, 589.   [16] Thk. i, 24.

mother-state, was a measure that commended itself later to Athenian tyrants (pp. 310ff). Another colony, founded directly by Kypselos, was the important city of Ambrakia,[17] on the north side of its gulf, with a fertile alluvial plain by the river Arachthos; that Arachthos where Arniadas of Kerkyra fell 'fighting by the ships', as his epitaph tells us, whether against the natives or against Corinthians.[18] The Founder was Gorgos, Kypselos' second son; the date, hardly before 635 tr., if a younger brother of Periandros (d. 585 tr.), was old enough to lead it.

Periandros, we are told, 'was a fighting man and continually at war; he built warships and was active on both seas'.[19] The slipway, by which ships could be hauled across the Isthmus from sea to sea, dates from his time.[20] Anaktorion, across the Gulf from Ambrakia, was colonised under his base-born half-brother Echiades; the peninsula of Leukas, just to the south, under another, Pylades[21]; Apollonia, near modern Valona, under a certain Gylax, after whom it was at first named Gylakia. The pseudo-Skymnos says that Kerkyra had a share in founding this place[22]; possibly the Kypselids merely captured Gylakia and changed its name.

A golden bowl, said to have been found at Olympia, bears the inscription, 'The sons of Kypselos dedicated this from the spoils of Herakleia.'[23] There was a place of this name near Anaktorion (perhaps a colony of Kerkyra; for the Akarnanian natives, though Greek-speaking, had not yet developed city life). The bowl may well be a thank-offering for the success of Echiades. The princes probably remained as governors of the new cities; Gorgos certainly did so at Ambrakia, where he passed on his principality to his descendants, Periandros and Archinos.[24] Of the origins of the smaller and nearer

---

[17] Str. x, 452; 'Skymnos', 453ff.
[18] *IG* IX, 1, 868, from Kerkyra; Tod, *GHI* 2.   [19] N.D. fr. 59.
[20] Dated not far from 600, by the forms of letters carved on the walls that prevented the ships, carried on trollies, from going off the 'tramway' (a paved road with two deep grooves; the gauge is five Greek feet, 4 ft. 11 in.). Report by Ephor N. M. Verdelis in *ILN* 19 Oct., 1957; Hood, *Archaeology in Greece, 1956* (BSA and Hell. Soc., 1957), p. 7.
[21] Str. x, 452, puts both these earlier, under Kypselos; N.D. 58 (with names of the Founders), under Periandros.
[22] Gylakia, S.B.; 'Sk.' 439f; dedication at Olympia for Apollonia's (later) capture of Thronion from the Abantes, Paus. v, 22, 3.
[23] *SEG* I, 94; in Boston Museum of Fine Arts. 'If a forgery, it is most masterly, and its genuineness is here accepted', Wade-Gery in *CAH* III, 551n. For this Herakleia, 'a city of Akarnania', cf. S.B. (no. 21), Pliny, *NH*, iv, 5. But 'I wish I knew why the dedicators named themselves Kypselidai – most unusual.'–A.A.   [24] Ar. *Pol.* 1304a; *Ath. P.* ch. 28.

colonies, Sollion, Molykreion and Chalkis, on the coast of Aitolia,[25] there is no record.

From the coast of the mainland (Epeiros, not yet a proper name) Corinthian trade penetrated inland. An oracular shrine among oak-forests was identified (637 tr.) as Homer's and Hesiod's Dodona. Silver mines at a place called Damastion, mentioned by Strabo, may have been exploited for Periandros' coinage[26]; and a magnificent find of archaic Greek bronze vessels and golden death-masks, from a grave at Trebenishte, near Ochrida, shows the native chiefs here too prizing Greek art.[27] The up-country Macedonian kings of Lynkestis, who claimed Herakleid descent, learned to connect their ancestor Arrhabaios with the Bakchiadai; their rivals, the House of Karanos in the plain of Macedonia, went one better and traced theirs to Temenos.[28] Kerkyra can hardly have welcomed this penetration; but Periandros was not the man to brook rivalry. He subdued Kerkyra and installed his son Lykophron as viceroy.[29] Becoming aware of the existence of the natural route from Albania to the Aegean, later followed by the Egnatian Way, Periandros next secured a footing near its eastern end with Corinth's only Aegean colony: Poteidaia, in a strong position bestriding the isthmus of Pallene, the peninsula that already held the cities of Mende and Skione (p. 96); the Founder was his son Euagoras.[30] The area was Euboian, and the Euboians too can hardly have unani-mously welcomed this intrusion; but Euboia was not unanimous. We hear of a seventh-century tyrant or dictator, one Tynnondas; Chalkis had tyrants, probably early[31]; and Kypselid intervention in Euboia is the subject of a quatrain preserved among the works of Theognis[32]:

> Fie for our weakness! for Kerinthos ta'en,
> For ravaged vineyards in Lelantos' plain,
> For nobles banished, while low villains boss
> The state; God damn the house of Kypselos!

Kerinthos, with a citadel dominating a useful harbour, now silted up,

---

[25] Mentioned, Thk. iii, 102; ii, 30; i, 108, respectively.
[26] Str. vii, 326; J. M. F. May, *The Coinage of Damastion*, 1ff.
[27] Filov, *Die archaische Nekropole von Trebenischte*; cf. Payne, *Necrocorinthia*, p. 186; illust. in *ILN*, 1930, p. 1163. On Dodona, see Jerome, *sub anno*.
[28] Str. vii, 326; Hdt. viii, 137.   [29] Hdt. iii, 52, N.D. 60.   [30] N.D. 60.
[31] Tynnondas, mentioned as comparable to Pittakos of Mytilene, and earlier than Solon, Plut. *Solon*, 14. For two tyrants of Chalkis, mentioned by Ar., Antileon, followed by a restored oligarchy (*Pol.* 1316a), and Phoxos, dethroned by an alliance of nobles and people (1304a), we have no dates.   [32] 891ff.

on the north-east Euboian coast, would have been good as a half-way post on the way to Poteidaia.

Periandros' fame spread abroad, not only as a man of power, but as one of the Seven Sages (pp. 207ff), historical figures who appear as a group in a popular legend. Later tradition, which became very hostile to his memory[33], disputed his right to this honour, and substituted other figures, such as his cousin, Periandros of Ambrakia, or Anacharsis the Scythian (p. 208); but a more favourable picture of him also survived. The characteristic of the Sages was a practical wisdom, expressed in pithy, proverbial utterances[34]; most of them, like him, were masters of statecraft. Periandros also appreciated the culture of his age, and entertained the Lesbian musician Arion of Methymna, the first poet to make a set literary form of the Dithyramb or hymn to Dionysos, which was to influence the birth of Tragedy. Hitherto it had been, if we may judge by a mention of it by Archilochos, only a form of traditional improvisation over the wine.[35] The Sage was also expected to have a reputation for justice and incorruptibility, which was part of Periandros' character in his legend ('Do nothing for money; for the gainer must gain' – i.e. there is always a catch in it). And that such really was Periandros' reputation in his own day is shown by the fact that he was invited, outside his own sphere of operations, to arbitrate after a war between Athens and Mytilene over points of vantage on the Dardanelles (p. 221).

His difficulty, which was to be the ruin of his reputation, was that his personal government was no longer, like his father's, automatically welcomed in contrast to that of the Bakchiadai. He grew suspicious and jealous of opposition. Tradition told how he did not permit all who wished to live in town, how he forbade men to keep slave households and to sit idle in the market-place.[36] These prohibitions make sense only as applied to the leisured class, the landed gentry. Traders

---

[33] E.g. characteristically, Plato, *Protagoras*, 343a.   [34] D.L. Book I, *passim*.

[35] 'Well I know', says Arch. characteristically, 'how to lead the song of Lord Dionysos, his dithyramb, having thunderstruck my wits with wine' (*ap*. Ath. xiv, 628). Hdt. (i, 23) says, in contrast, that Arion 'first among men of whom we know *composed dithyramb and gave it a name and taught it*' (sc. to a choir) at Corinth in the time of Periandros. Solon is said by John the Deacon, a Byzantine commentator, to have attributed to him the first tragedy; (the fragment rescued from oblivion by Rabe in *Rhein. Mus.* LXIII, 150; Edmonds, *El. & Iamb.* I, p. 518); but how accurate this is it is impossible to say. That tragedy in some sense 'grew out of' dithyramb is Aristotle's well-known view (*Poetics*, 1449a). Cf. p. 198 below on 'tragedy' at Sikyon.

[36] N.D. 59; cf. Ar. *Politics*, 1313a–b.

and manufacturers could only live in town, and to the employment of slaves in work for export he cannot have objected. But leisure, likely to be employed, as always in Greece, in political talk, he felt was dangerous. 'He was always devising some work for the citizens, to keep them busy.' For the poor, this might be described as a full-employment policy; those rich enough to be 'fined for being idle' were presumably forced to contribute to their lord's public works. Periandros was making himself a king. Above all things, there must be no one to rival him in wealth and influence. A famous story told how, early in his reign, he sent a messenger to Thrasyboulos of Miletos, an expert in prince-craft, asking him for advice on how to maintain power; and how Thrasyboulos, too cautious to put such advice into words, took the messenger for a walk along a field of standing wheat, during which he kept decapitating with his walking-stick any stalk that stood out above the rest; then he bade the man go back to Periandros and tell him what he had seen. Aristotle, repeating this story, presumably from memory, makes the Corinthian *give*, not receive, this object lesson; his mistake is evidence for the later feeling that no one could ever have had anything on tyranny to teach Periandros.[37]

The more favourable picture of him, Periandros the Wise, makes him a puritan: he limited expenditure on funerals, and 'drowned all the procuresses'. It attributed to him such apophthegms as 'Quiet is good'; 'Goodwill is a better bodyguard than arms'; even 'popular rule is better than tyranny', which is in such flat contradiction to the prevailing picture that it almost looks genuine. An intelligent man in the loneliness of power might have expressed himself to some Arion or other visitor in a disillusioned manner. More in accord with the tyrant picture is 'Punish not only those who are doing wrong, but those who are likely to'. He knew well that there could be no quiet for him; he held a wolf by the ears. One of the 'public' facts recorded about him is that he kept a bodyguard, 300 strong. The number was ample against conspirators (many nobles, indeed, are said to have been killed or exiled); but that it was no stronger shows that he still kept the goodwill of the mass of the population.[38]

Corinth was never richer. Its exports reached every corner of the Mediterranean world. Corinthian potters could not keep up with the

[37] Hdt. v, 92, 6; Ar. *Politics, twice*: 1284a, 1311a.
[38] Herakl. Pont., in Rose, *Ar. Fragm.* 611, 20. Sayings, D.L. i, 94; bodyguard, N.D. 59.

demand for their goods, the richly decorated vases with their fighting men and chariots, their friezes of processing animals; their details picked out in red or purple, the figures black on the buff ground, and every vacant space conscientiously crammed with rosettes, derived from oriental embroidery. Indeed we notice, ominously for the future, that the pressure to produce more and more was undermining the vase-painters' integrity. No doubt, to meet the pressure of demand, the master potters had to take on all the hands, slave or free, that they could get and train; training was scamped, and the quality of some of the new workers was marginal. In Ripe Corinthian, the rosettes grow smudgy, or commercial art even resorts to such devices as elongating the bodies of its lions (or front-facing lions, like the heraldic 'leopards' of England, conventionally called panthers) in order to save time by getting round the vase in four lions instead of six.[39] But the market could take it, so far; for a long time yet, Greeks and barbarians would go on asking for Corinthian and accepting what they got. Roof-tiles are said to have been a Corinthian invention; and from this industry developed another ceramic art, the production of terracotta slabs for the decoration of brick and timber temples; *metopes*, to block the spaces between the ends' of roof-beams and prevent birds from nesting, *akroteria* to decorate roof-ridges and corners. Boutades of Sikyon, working at Corinth, was said to have invented the practice of decorating these with a human head; and we have revetments from Aitolian Thermon and Kalydon of this period, on which 'instructions to builder', incised on the inner surface before firing, show that the slabs were exported, 'pre-fabricated', from Corinth.[40]

Periandros seems to have made war on Sikyon; a Roman writer tells how his friend Thrasyboulos captured its harbour-town[41]; it is a warning of the vast gaps in our knowledge that we know no more of this. The House of Orthagoras certainly survived the onset. Family tragedies preoccupied the great tyrant during his last years, and ended his life in gloom. He is said to have murdered his wife Melissa in a fit of rage inspired by the slanders of some concubines, whom he after-

[39] 'The dachshund type' of lion, Payne, *Necrocor.* p. 48; 'a particularly well-bred specimen', illust. at fig. 11.

[40] Payne, *op. cit.* chap. xvii; van Buren, *Greek Fictile Revetments in the Archaic Period.* Boutades, Pliny, *NH* XXXV, 43/151; on Corinthian roof-tiles, *IG* II, 1054(4), 58ff; Dittenberger, *SIG³* p. 402; Pollux, x, 157, 182.

[41] Frontinus, *Stratagems*, iii, 9, 7.

wards burnt. He tried to keep the details of her death from her sons, Gorgos-Kypselos and Lykophron; but something leaked out to her father, Prokles of Epidauros, and he hinted his suspicions to his grandsons. Gorgos-Kypselos, of subnormal intelligence, did not take it in; but Lykophron turned savagely against his father, refused to speak to him, and finally perished trying to raise a rebellion against him in the countryside. Gorgos was killed in a chariot accident; their halfbrother Euagoras died in his governorship of Poteidaia. Periandros took his revenge on Prokles, capturing Epidauros. But in his old age came a final blow, when his only remaining son, Nikolaos, the 'most moderate' of the family, who was governing Kerkyra, was killed there by a conspiracy. Periandros descended upon Kerkyra in fury. He reduced it, put to death fifty of those responsible for the trouble, and carried off 300 boys of their families, whom he despatched to Alyattes of Lydia to be made eunuchs; but they were rescued on the way by the Samians. As the new governor of Kerkyra he left the son of his brother Gorgos the founder of Ambrakia, another Kypselos, surnamed Psammetichos after the Pharaoh of Egypt.[42] Psammetichos succeeded him when he died, old and embittered, and is said to have reigned for three and a half years, before losing his throne and presumably his life in a revolution (581 tr.).[43] Corinth retained as bitter memories of the *tyrannis* as any Greek state.

The restored republican polity was comparatively liberal; the population was divided into eight 'tribes', which implies that pure Dorian blood was not essential for citizenship. Each tribe elected a member of a 'Cabinet', the eight Probouloi, and its quota of members of a deliberative Council, probably of eighty. There was probably a property-qualification for voting rights, and a higher one for eligibility to office; but on this we have no evidence. It was all very unlike the oligarchy of the Bakchiadai.[44]

The tyranny at Ambrakia may have lasted a little longer; the second and last tyrant was Periandros, brother's son to Periandros of Corinth. Archinos, a Kypselid of Ambrakia, married Timonassa, daughter of

---

[42] Hdt. iii, 48ff, N.D. 60. That it was another son and not Lykophron (as Hdt. has it) who was killed at Kerkyra seems a detail which N.'s authority (Ephoros?) is not likely to have invented. The mistaken identification of the two (cf. the Harmodios story, pp. 321f) is more probable.

[43] Ar. *Politics*, 1315b.

[44] N.D. *ib.*; Photios, *Suda, s.v. panta okto*, 'Eight of everything'.

Gorgilos, a nobleman of Argos, probably in the 560's; Corinth and the Kypselidai were evidently by then on opposite sides. Periandros had contracted a liaison with a youth of good family, and then insulted his sensitive Greek 'honour', not by the immoral relationship but by making a joke in company at his 'girlishness'; a conspiracy was formed which overthrew the tyrant, and then 'the people, having joined with the conspirators in expelling Periandros, transferred the government to themselves.[45] The whole episode is typical; one of the great charges against tyrants in general was that youth and beauty were never safe from them. Both the occasion of the conspiracy and the subsequent self-assertion of the people are paralleled later at Athens.

After this Leukas, Ambrakia, Anaktorion, Poteidaia, and the smaller Corinthian Gulf colonies are usually found following Corinth's lead, a unique and stable little Greek colonial 'empire'. Poteidaia even had Corinthian 'high commissioners' alongside her own magistrates as late as 432. Epidamnos flourished in isolation, fortifying herself in face of the Illyrians by electing an unusually strong chief executive, responsible to a committee of 'tribe chiefs', *phylarchoi* (later, to a larger Council) and practising some elements of state socialism. Slaves producing for export were state-owned (a feature which reminded Aristotle of Plato's Republic), and all trade with the natives passed through the hands of an official controller. She built a 'treasury' at Olympia, and one Kleosthenes of Epidamnos was even rich enough to win a chariot-victory there in 516; he commemorated it by dedicating a chariot-group with a statue of himself; a new precedent. Kerkyra, with a constitution relatively democratic, celebrated her deliverance by the construction of a temple with pediment-sculptures of tremendous archaic power. As isolationist as Epidamnos, she was in the fifth century the second naval power in Greece, and as hostile to Corinth's imperial claims as ever.[46]

At Sikyon, the Orthagorid monarchy culminates in the thirty-year reign of the 'crafty and formidable' Kleisthenes, 'son of Aristonymos, the son of Myron, the son of Andreas' the cook. Orthagoras, if this

---

[45] Ar. *Pol.* 1311a; 1304a. Timonassa, *Ath. Pol.* 17, 4.
[46] Hdt. viii, 45, ix, 28, the 'Serpent-column' (C. allies in 480-79); Thk. i, 24-61, etc. (*epidemiourgoi* at Poteidaia, i, 56); Epidamnos, Ar. *Pol.* 1267b, 1287a, 1301b; controller of mainland trade, Plut. GQ 1; Olympia, Paus. vi, 19, 8 and 10, 6-8. Republic of Kerkyra, *IG* IX, 1, 867, 869, cf. 682 (later); Richter, *Sculpture and Sculptors of the Greeks*, pp. 4, 36.

genealogy in Herodotos may be trusted, thus seems to have been succeeded by his brother's family. Myron is credited with a chariot-victory at Olympia (648 tr.), after which he built a 'treasury' to house his dedication of two bronze 'chambers' (miniature shrines), which Pausanias the traveller saw, 'one in the Doric and one in the Ionic style'; one of them bore the inscription that it was the offering of 'Myron and the People of Sikyon'; evidence of the Sikyonian monarchy's 'constitutional' character.[47] This is the earliest known appearance west of the Aegean of the 'Ionic style', with its oriental volute capitals.

About 600 a second Myron, grandson of the first and also descended from Orthagoras (through his mother?), reigned for seven years, and compassed his own ruin in the too familiar manner; he seduced the wife of his brother Isodemos (the name, with its reference to 'popular equality' is significant), during the latter's absence on a voyage to Libya. Isodemos is represented as an easy-going and simple character; but the intrigue was revealed to him by his younger brother, the ambitious Kleisthenes, who so wrought on him that he contrived to catch his wife and brother together, and slew the adulterer. Then, overcome by remorse, for the murder of a near relative was a formidable pollution whatever the cause, he listened to a friend suborned by Kleisthenes, who advised him to go abroad for a year and undergo purification. He retired to Corinth, and Kleisthenes then accused him in Sikyon of conspiring with the Kypselidai. Kleisthenes thus secured sole power at Sikyon with popular support as a champion of independence, and the sea-borne attack on the city by the powerful Thrasyboulos quite failed to check his progress. Kleisthenes was no obstacle to Periandros' colonial ambitions; and once Corinthian support for Isodemos was dropped (we hear no more of him), the paths of the two cities did not cross – except, as will be seen, in a purely geographical sense.

Sikyon, with a much more fertile plain than Corinth, was much less a naval power. She had never colonised; Kleisthenes may have been the first to develop a navy there, and he used it for an operation inside the Corinthian Gulf (pp. 201ff). When coinage begins, probably after Kleisthenes' time, its chief foreign distribution is in eastern Arcadia, at Tegea and Mantineia, reached by way of the Sikyonian river Asopos,

[47] N.D. 61; Hdt. vi, 126; Paus. vi, 19, 2 (the date, 648, too early?).

Phlious, Stymphalos and Orchomenos.[48] A legend accounting for the rise of the tyranny as a 'scourge of God' for the excesses of the oligarchy represents Sikyon, even before Orthagoras, as holding inland Kleonai, which is nearer to Corinth, as a vassal-state, and Kleisthenes also as holding it for a time.[49] Kleisthenes' chief efforts in foreign policy were, in fact, directed to south and north, not east and west. The state with which he did become embroiled was Argos. We have no details of fighting; but a circumstantial story, undated, tells of Sikyonian troops besieging Orneai, more than half-way to Argos, and the period of the tyranny is the likeliest time for such a bold enterprise. The Orneatai, we are told, made a vow in desperation, if they were delivered, to worship Apollo at Delphi with a procession and sacrifices every day; which vow they paid by dedicating a relief of a procession and sacrifice, in bronze.[50] It is an interesting glimpse of the reasoning that probably prompted many Greek votive images.

What we do hear about Kleisthenes is about his *Kulturkampf* with Argos. Argos still enjoyed a religious prestige among the surrounding cities; Sikyon at a later date actually paid, in part, on religious grounds or for the sake of her southern trade, a fine imposed by Argos, at a time when Argive military power had been shattered.[51] Kleisthenes was led to attack this prestige in a way which none of his predecessors had thought necessary: 'Having gone to war with Argos, he stopped the competitions of rhapsodists reciting the Homeric poems, because they were full of the praises of Argos and the Argives; and, as there was (and still is) a hero-shrine right in the market-place of Sikyon, of Adrastos the son of Talaos, Kleisthenes wanted to banish him, as an Argive, from the country.' He consulted Delphi, but was severely snubbed: 'Sikyon's king was Adrastos; but you are a mere stone-thrower' (perhaps meaning a low-class light skirmisher, not a good hoplite; compare 'club-bearer', one of the old abusive names for the Sikyonian poor). Nothing daunted, however, though he did not now venture to demolish the shrine, he imported from Thebes the alleged bones of the hero Melanippos, who, in the repulse of the Seven Against Thebes had killed Adrastos' brother and his son-in-law Tydeus. He allotted to Melanippos a precinct in the most honourable possible

[48] A. Jardé, *La Formation du peuple grec*, p. 139 and n.; from V. Bérard, *Cultes Arcadiens.*
[49] Plut. *Delays of Divine Vengeance*, 7.
[50] Plut. *On the Pythian Oracles*, 15; Paus. x, 18, 5; both referring to the monument.
[51] Hdt. vi, 92.

place, in the grounds of the town hall. 'Now the Sikyonians had been accustomed to honour Adrastos, and to commemorate his disaster with tragic choruses (not in honour of Dionysos, but of Adrastos). Kleisthenes now transferred the choruses to Dionysos, and the rest of the rite, the sacrifice, to Melanippos; and he changed the names of the Doric tribes, so that they might not be the same at Sikyon as at Argos.'[52] He called his own (non-Doric) tribe, the Aigialeis or Coast-Dwellers, 'Rulers', *Archelaoi*, and the others 'Hyatai, Oneatai, and Choireatai', meaning Pigmen, Assmen and Swinemen. 'These names remained in use at Sikyon during Kleisthenes' reign and for sixty years after his death.'[53] The childishness of the story makes it almost incredible, but 'sixty years after Kleisthenes' death' brings us down almost to living memory when Herodotos wrote; presumably there is some element of truth behind it.

The story of the cult-changes, on the other hand, gives another glimpse of the *naïvetés* of Greek religion. The solemn transfer of a hero's alleged bones for political reasons is paralleled both from Athens and Sparta.[54] The phrase 'tragic choruses' in Herodotos must mean something like *what he knew* as tragedy in Athens; it was there performed in honour of Dionysos, the vegetation-god, and had developed out of some form of earlier mimic dancing, commemorating the sufferings of the dying and resurrected god.[55] This peasant worship was then rising in prominence and penetrating the cities, with the rise of the peasants in prosperity and civilisation. Kleisthenes' patronage of a cult, which from its nature was unconnected with conservative aristocratic priesthoods, finds a parallel in Athens under her tyrants (p. 310). Adrastos is the only other personage recorded to have been worshipped in this manner; it is possible that he was originally more than a hero or ancient king, and that his name, '(he from whom there is) No Running' denoted a power, central in later tragedy, that of inevitable Fate.

[52] *id.* v, 67.   [53] *ib.* 68.
[54] 'Bones of Orestes' from Tegea to Sparta, Hdt. i, 67f; of Theseus, from Skyros, Plut. *Kimon*, 8.
[55] Cf. Ar. *Poetics*, 1447b, on the claim of 'some Peloponnesians' to have 'invented' tragedy; and 1449a on its humble and rustic origins in the dithyrambic improvisations (cf. n. 35, above). Dithyramb may have been *distinct* from pre-literary 'tragedy', as Pickard-Cambridge used to argue (see his *Dithyramb, Tragedy and Comedy*), but clearly they had much in common; not only were both Dionysiac, but Ar. singles out the dithyramb, along with tragedy and comedy (though he also adds 'and other kinds of music') as *mimetic*, *ib.* 1447a.

Art also was active in Sikyon. The earliest names recorded of Greek sculptors working on the mainland are those of the Cretans Dipoinos and Skyllis, called pupils of the mythical Daidalos (which implies extreme chronological vagueness) who migrated to Sikyon, and executed works also at Argos, Tiryns and Kleonai and in Aitolia.[56] Their time must have been *about* the time of Kleisthenes. It is possible that some of the works attributed to them which Pausanias saw may have borne their signatures; but none such have yet been found.

Cretan works of art were also, until about 600, still reaching Delphi; the legend, that the first priests of Apollo at the great shrine had been 'Cretans from Minoan Knossos', brought there by the special providence of the Dolphin-God when they had only meant to go to Pylos, may be founded on facts archaic as well as 'Minoan' in our sense.[57] Argos too, had made public dedications at Delphi, which help to account for the oracle's snub to Kleisthenes. The shortest route from Crete to Delphi lay through Argos and Sikyon; and converging lines of evidence suggest that this route was still in use down to Kleisthenes' time.

Among these Argive works were the two great statues in island marble, of about 600, by (Poly)medes of Argos, the first extant Greek signed statues. Delphians added, later, the note on the plinths: 'Kleobis and Biton drew the (their?) mother for forty-five furlongs, setting themselves to the yoke.' They are the original works, in connection with which Herodotos probably heard the story that he tells in a famous passage: the story of the two young Argives, both athletic victors, who thus dragged their mother, the priestess, from Argos to the Heraion, when 'their oxen had not arrived from the farm in time'; for whom their mother prayed the Goddess to reward them with 'what is best for men'; and who then, in their hour of glory, lay down to sleep in the holy place and never rose up again, but died there. These were the men whom the wise Solon counted the happiest mortals of whom he knew, next to Tellos of Athens (p. 172); happy because, after fame and prosperity in life, 'as we Greeks count prosperity', they had, as Solon explained to Croesus, all died well.[58]

[56] 'Pupils of Daidalos', Paus. vi, 19, 14; works, *id.* ii, 15, 1, 22, 5; Pliny, *NH* xxxvi, 4/9, with the story of their movements (Crete, Sikyon, Aitolia), and date 'before Cyrus, i.e. *c.* 580'.

[57] Homeric *Hymn to the Pythian Apollo*, 391ff; Guarducci, *Studi e Mat. di Storia delle Religioni*, 19-20, pp. 85ff.

[58] Hdt. i, 31. The statues are extant at Delphi, with their inscription. Paus. (ii, 20, 3) saw another pair, at Argos, unsigned.

Across the Gulf of Corinth, or of Krissa as many called it, one of the best south-to-north routes lay through the port of Krissa near modern Itea; thence through Lokrian Amphissa, over the Gravia Pass to Phokis, through the Asopos gorge by Thermopylai and so to Thessaly. In Krissa's territory, on a shelf of the huge crags of Parnassos, lay the Delphic sanctuary, already rich and famous, the 'navel of earth' as legend said. An ancient conical *baitylos* or fetish-stone was held to mark the exact spot. Krissa also, profiting by trade (she had taken part in the colonisation of south Italy, p. 78) and by the transit of pilgrims to the sanctuary, was prospering greatly, greatly enough for her wealth and her position to excite cupidity.

From this, and from the oracle's rebuff to Kleisthenes, arose what Greek history knows as the First Sacred War.

Thessaly, potentially the greatest military power in Greece, but in the classical age paralysed by the rivalries of her baronial families – Aleuadai of Larissa, Skopadai of Krannon, Echekratidai of Pharsalos – was at this time united under an organisation ascribed to Aleuas the Red; and her aristocracy, with their thousands of vassal cavalry and with footmen from the subject hill tribes, were setting out on the paths of empire.[59] They had long since intervened triumphantly in the Lelantine War (pp. 82f). Phokis had fortified Thermopylai against them, but Malian hunters who knew the hill routes had guided them round and up to the 'Fair Race-Course', the upper greensward between the two crests, that accounts for the name of the ridge Kallidromos.[60] Thus the pass fell, by no means for the last time; Phokis was overrun, and the Thessalians dominated the Amphiktiony or League of Neighbours whose delegates (Hieromnemones or Sacred Remembrancers, a title surely older than the alphabet, and Pylagorai or Speakers at the Gates) met at the sanctuary of Demeter near the hot springs, in the

---

[59] Theokr. xvi, 34ff (with ref. to Simonides) and schol.; Aleuadai, also Pindar, *Pyth.* x and schol. *ad. init.*; Skopadai, Kallimachos, epigram *ap. Suda, s.v. Simonides*; an Echekratidas, *A.P.* vii, 142, ascr. to Anakreon; organisation and military potential of Thessaly, Xen. *Hell.* vi, 1; work of Aleuas the Red (the four Tetrarchies; quota of 40 horse and 80 foot from each estate), Ar. *Thess. Pol. ap.* schol. on Eurip. *Rhesos*, 307, and Harpokr. *s.v. tetrarchia.* Ar. frs. 498, 497 Rose; Hellanikos fr. 28M=52J). Menon of Pharsalos (5th century) joined the Athenian forces before Amphipolis with '300 mounted tenants' (*penestai*) of his own, Demosth. *Against Aristokrates*, 199. – J. S. Morrison (ed. Wade-Gery) in *CQ*, 1942, however casts doubt upon Echekratidai as a separate clan (a view based upon Thk. i, 111) and argues that this name is Aleuad, and of Larissa; see refs. *ib.* pp. 60-1.

[60] Hdt. vii, 215; topography, Burn in *Essays presented to D. M. Robinson*.

pass of Thermopylai.[61] The Gates which named this famous pass between the cliffs and the sea were perhaps man-made: the gates through the Phokian Wall.

A connection between the League and Delphi dates from before 625. Legend connected its foundation with Pylades, whose name is derived from Pylai, the friend of Orestes and son of a King of Krissa[62]; and Kypselos of Corinth had thought fit to give the name Pylades to a son of his (p. 189). But now Corinth drops out of the story, perhaps simply because the aged Periandros had his hands full with the wars with Epidauros and Kerkyra.

The Thessalians, in control of inland Phokis, inevitably dominated Delphi. Their votes and those of their satellites, the Perrhaiboi, Magnetes, Ainianes, Malians and now Phokis, controlled the Amphiktiony. But Krissa (herself probably Phokian) held out; she had still her transit trade between the mainland, including Delphi, the Peloponnese and the west. The port was an obvious objective for Thessalian aggression, and a cause for quarrelling could be found in maintaining that the tolls were excessive, or even that, from pilgrims or ambassadors bound on a sacred mission, it was impiety to levy them at all. Krissa was also accused of acts of violence against pilgrims; and since it would have been clearly against her interests to commit or permit such acts in normal times, we may guess that such 'incidents' occurred when the city was already under hostile pressure.[63]

Behind her walls, Krissa could, at a price (the price paid by Athens in 431), have defied the Thessalian horsemen; but she had other enemies too. The oracle had insulted Kleisthenes, and he was ready, both for personal and for economic reasons, to eliminate these middlemen. A Sacred War or crusade was proclaimed. The oracle, under Amphiktionic influence, exhorted the faithful to make war on Krissa and on the Kragallidai (probably their leading family) 'by day and by night, and to devastate their country and sell them into slavery, and to dedicate their land to Apollo and Artemis and Leto and Athena Pronoia

[61] On the League, cf. my *World of Hesiod*, p. 224 and n. 3.

[62] Agathon, *ap.* schol. on Soph. *Trachiniai*, 639; Parke and Wormell, *The Delphic Oracle*, I, 101-2, 112 n. 5; W. G. Forrest, *The First Sacred War*, in *BCH* LXXX (1956), i, p. 43, n. 3.

[63] Str. ix, 418; Ar. *Record of the Pythian Victors*, in Plut. *Solon*, 11. Kallisthenes, Ar.'s nephew, who was associated with him in his Pythian researches and was honoured therefor with him by the Delphians, adds the detail about violation of women pilgrims: Kall. fr. 1, Jacoby, *FGH* 124. Jacoby, *ad loc.*, is sure that this is a piece of Kallisthenic romance. Romance, perhaps, but is it K.'s invention, or war-propaganda?

to be uncultivated for ever'.[64] Eurylochos of Thessaly, probably Tagos or elected captain-general of the Thessalian League, came south with his army in 592 tr.[65]; and Kleisthenes brought up his fleet, the first recorded Sikyonian navy, and blockaded Krissa on the sea side.[66]

Others hastened to join the winning side and to 'liberate' the holy place from its impious enemies; the Myanes or Myoneis of Lokris, for instance, had a victory-offering at Olympia housed in the Treasury of the Sikyonians[67]; and Alkmaion of Athens with a body of his country-men. Delphi had given advice to Kylon in his attempt to make himself tyrant of Athens (p. 286). The attempt had failed, and while Kylon escaped, his supporters were massacred by troops under the archon Megakles, Alkmaion's father, some of them, it was said, at the very sanctuary of the Furies, the avengers of blood. This involved the Alkmeonid house in formidable blood-feuds. Delphi, when consulted, had declared them accursed; it recommended the purification of the city by the sage and holy man, Epimenidas of Crete (one of the last traces, it has been remarked, of the Cretan connections of Delphi under the old management) and the Alkmeonidai were exiled.[68] Later Athens was proud of her participation in this 'crusade', and claimed that her own wise man Solon had taken a leading part in it; but of this there is no trace in Plutarch's extensive quotations from his poems. It seems, indeed, quite possible that Alkmaion the Athenian leader took part in it *as an exile* with his kinsmen and partisans, glad to find employ-ment, and incidentally to join in 'liberating' the holy place from the sacrilegious enemies who had perverted it against his family. The sequel certainly was that the Alkmeonidai reappear in Athens, and developed a close connection with Delphi, and with Kleisthenes.

The doomed Krissaians held out to the last, as they well might; according to tradition for ten years, for which there was epic precedent; but neither Corinth nor anyone else made a move to help them. The besiegers had only to wait till starvation did their work for them. The sentence of the oracle was carried out with all the savagery of ideo-logical warfare. Eurylochos returned home, leaving a subordinate named Hippias to deal with guerilla resistance in the hills, which

---

[64] Inscription (no doubt set up much later), Aischines, *Against Ktesiphon*, 107.
[65] Schol. on Pindar, *Pythians* (introduction).
[66] Schol. on Pindar, *Nem.* ix, 23 (from Menaichmos of Sikyon).
[67] Paus. vi, 19, 4f.
[68] Plut. Sol. 12 (cf. *Ath. P.* 1); Forrest, *op. cit.* (n. 62) p. 41.

continued for six years longer (588-2?); and in 582 Eurylochos, hailed as 'the new Achilles', and Kleisthenes took part in the foundation or refoundation of the Pythian Games, from which the Pythiads, held in the second year of each Olympiad, were thenceforth counted.[69]

The Thessalians at one time overran even Boiotia; but their empire was not to last. There are too many places in Greece where a horse cannot go; and more where it cannot go fast. Thessaly's footmen were serfs or mountain allies, half-hearted when fighting abroad and likely to be outfought by men fighting for home and freedom on their native rocks. Far into Boiotia, but off the main route and *off the plain*, not far from Hesiod's Askra, is the probable site of Keressos, a hill-fort where, 'more than 200 years before the battle of Leuktra' (i.e. before 571), some Boiotians stood a long siege by the Thessalian Lattamyas and finally (the countryside gathering to their aid?) drove him away in such plight that Boiotians claimed this for a decisive victory that 'liberated the Greeks'.[70]

This claim must mean that the Boiotian victory started the crumbling of the southern Thessalian empire; and the central episode of this, otherwise undated, was the rebellion of Phokis, which rose with a fierce desperation reminiscent of modern Greek struggles with the Turks. 'They massacred the governors and tyrants (Phokians appointed by the Thessalians?) in the Phokian cities, all of them in one day; and the Thessalians clubbed to death 250 Phokian hostages.' The Phokians can hardly have been unaware that this would happen. 'Then, in full force, they invaded Phokis.' The Phokians were powerless to meet them in battle array; they planned to fall by night on their camp, but failed; a reconnoitring force of 300 men was discovered and ridden down by the Thessalian horsemen. The Phokians fell back and back, rallying for a last stand in the south-east corner of their country, where a narrow tongue of plainland along a brook led to Hyampolis and the oracular shrine of Apollo at Abai. At Kleonai, probably behind Hyampolis, with their backs to the hills, they gathered their women and children with such treasures as they had been able to carry, beside a vast funeral pyre, and left guards with them, to kill them if the battle went ill. Someone suggested that the women might be consulted about this. The women applauded, and garlanded Daiphantos of

[69] Schol. Pind. *l.c.* (n. 65).
[70] Plut. *Camillus*, 19; *Malignity of Hdt.* 33; Paus. ix, 14, 2f.

Hyampolis, the author of the proposal. 'Phokian desperation' became proverbial. Then, Daiphantos leading their outnumbered cavalry and Rhoios of Ambrysos the foot, they gave battle. The Thessalians advanced shouting 'Athena Itonia' – the name of a sanctuary in Phthió-tis, and of another in Boiotia; they were fighting for their empire; the Phokians met them, shouting 'Phokos' – their eponymous ancestor – and won an astonishing victory, commemorated for ever after at the feast of Artemis the Stag-Shooter, in whose month the battle took place, and at whose festival this Phokian national saga was preserved.[71]

Phokis was not quit for ever of the Thessalians. They came down the Kephissos again 'not long', says Herodotos, before Xerxes' invasion, to be routed again on the narrow-fronted Hyampolis position (the two battles are *not*, I think, to be confused, though Pausanias does identify them). The Phokians caught them in a cavalry-trap of 'pottes', as Robert Bruce's chronicler would call them; literal pots, buried in the ground, thinly covered and with dust spread over them; and their infantry, trying to rout out the Phokians from the massif of Parnassos, were routed by a night attack led by six hundred Phokians, charging in silence, with whitened armour and faces, whom the invaders took for ghosts; so, at least, the Phokian saga said. The Phokians claimed to have captured four thousand shields, 'of which they dedicated half at Abai and half at Delphi; and from the tithe of the spoils were made the big statues which stand round the tripod before the temple at Delphi, and the others like them at Abai'.[72] Long after this, the Thessalians still kept up relations with Athens; but their unity was breaking down, amid quarrels between their leading families; it was not till the fourth century that Jason of Pherai showed once more, for a moment, what the power of a united Thessaly might have been.

Alkmaion of Athens prospered. His family, whatever the date of their first exile, was again powerful in Athens. After his prominence in the Sacred War he was in a position to assist Lydian ambassadors at Delphi as Herodotos says, and was richly rewarded. Herodotos tells the charming and disrespectful story of how 'Croesus' (the name is an anachronism) invited him to go into his treasury and help himself to as much gold as he could carry, and how Alkmaion went in wearing

[71] Paus. x, 1, 3-10; Plut. (who according to Photios wrote a *Life of Daiphantos*, un-fortunately lost) *Brave Deeds of Women*, 2.
[72] Hdt. viii, 27ff; Paus. x, 1, 3 and 11.

wellington boots ('buskins') and a large belted tunic, filled boots and
bosom with gold dust (which would pack more closely than coins),
sprinkled his hair with gold dust, took a big mouthful of it, and came
out looking scarcely human; whereat the king laughed heartily and
presented him with as much again. Alkmaion kept race-horses and
won the proudest honour open to Greek wealth, a chariot-victory at
Olympia.[73] His son Megakles married the daughter of his old com-
rade in arms, Kleisthenes of Sikyon.

Kleisthenes, says the story,[74] having himself won a chariot victory
at Olympia (about 572?), made proclamation inviting suitors for the
hand of his daughter Agariste, and entertained them at a great house-
party, 'first asking each about his family and descent, and then for a
year making trial of their manliness and spirit and culture and character,
both in personal conversation with each and with them all together.
He arranged athletic sports for the younger men, and especially
watched their behaviour at dinner.' The details, a *locus classicus* for
aristocratic Greek life, are often dismissed as mere saga; but the list of
suitors is *not* drawn, as is sometimes said, from 'the whole Greek world',
but from those parts which may reasonably be supposed to have been
in touch with Sikyon. Ionia and the east, Sicily and the further west
are not represented. From Italy come Damasos of Siris, 'the son of
Amyris, called the Wise', and Smindyrides the Sybarite, 'who of all
mankind went furthest in luxury'. Later Greek stories of him were
numerous (p. 383). From the north-west and north come a suitor
from Epidamnos (which, like Sybaris, built a treasury at Olympia)
and one from the Molossian kingdom in Epeiros; a Thessalian, Diak-
torides of Krannon; and a brother of Titormos, the strongest man in
Greece, the Paul Bunyan of the Aitolian backwoods. From Elis comes
Onomastos, son of Agaios ('Renowned, son of Glorious'), a name full
of pride; from Arcadia two, one of them Laphanes the Azanian, son
of that Euphorion 'who, as the story goes in Arcadia, entertained the
Great Twin Brethren in his house, and after that showed hospitality
to all men'; from Argos Lakedes, son, according to Herodotos, of the
great Pheidon. An Eretrian from Euboia and two Athenians make up
the party, and of the latter, Hippokleides the son of Teisandros, of the
great Philaid family, won particular favour, 'both for personal prowess
(*andragathia*) and because he was related by descent to the Corinthian

---

[73] Hdt. vi, 125; cf. Pindar, *Pyth.* vii, 14.   [74] Hdt. vi, 126ff.

Kypselidai'. Corinth, we note, is no longer implacably hostile. The climax of the whole story, how Hippokleides, flown with wine and success, danced Ionian measures, while Kleisthenes looked on 'and felt the deepest misgivings', and finally brought open rebuke upon himself by doing hand-stands on a table (in a kilt), is probably derived from a folk-tale; it appears in India as that of the Dancing Peacock.[75] But Hippokleides is a historical person; he may be the Archon of Athens of 566, in whose year the great Panathenaic Festival was founded, and he is undoubtedly a relative (nephew or younger brother?) of Kypselos of Athens (daughter's son to the Corinthian tyrant?), father of that Miltiades who became prince of the Chersonese (pp. 310f).[76]

So Megakles and Agariste were married; 'and to them was born', says Herodotos, 'the Kleisthenes who organised the (new) tribal system and democracy of Athens, and was named after his mother's father the Sikyonian, and Hippokrates; and to Hippokrates, another Megakles and another Agariste, ... who, being married to Xanthippos the son of Ariphron and being with child, dreamed that she brought forth a lion; and after a few days she brought forth Perikles to Xanthippos.' It is Herodotos' one mention of the great statesman whom he knew.

The betrothal gives us our last glimpse of Kleisthenes of Sikyon. He died still in power, and his monarchy continued under one Aischines, perhaps his nephew. Finally Sparta, now asserting a claim to the leadership of the Peloponnese, overthrew Aischines, shortly after the Ephorate of Chilon at Sparta (555/4 tr.)[77]; an epoch-making figure (cf. p. 278). Kleisthenes' tribal arrangements lasted still longer, for the Sparta of Chilon was *not* posing as the champion of pan-Dorianism; she aimed at conciliating Arcadians and other non-Dorians, no doubt in opposition to Argos, which had meanwhile founded or refounded the Nemean Games of Kleonai (evidently regained from Sikyon), in honour of the dispossessed Adrastos (572 or 568).[78]

---

[75] Rhys Davis, *Buddhist Birth Stories*; cited in Macan, *Comm. on Herodotos*, App. xiv.
[76] Philaid pedigree (from Pherekydes) in Marcellinus' *Life of Thucydides*; unfortunately corrupt at this interesting point. See discussion by Wade-Gery in *CAH* III, pp. 764-5, and stemma, p. 570; also his *Miltiades* in *JHS* LXXI (and now, *Essays*, 155ff.); *aliter*, stemma in my *Pericles and Athens*, pp. 242-3.
[77] Rylands Papyrus 18 (Bilabel, *Klein. Hist.-fr.* 1); date from D.L. *Chilon* (i, 68), as interpreted by T. G. Cadoux in *JHS* LXVIII, p. 109.
[78] Ol. 52 or 53, Euseb., Jerome.

NOTE ON THE SEVEN SAGES

A list of the (evidently already famous) Seven *Sophoi* of early Greece appears first in extant literature in Plato's *Protagoras* (343A): Thales of Miletos, Pittakos of Mytilene, Bias of Priene, Kleoboulos (son of Euagoras, a Herakleid, D.L. i, 89), tyrant of Lindos, Solon of Athens, Chilon of Sparta, and Myson (son to a tyrant (or chief?), some said, D.L. i, 106) of the village of Chên in Mount Oita, west of Thermopylai. Diogenes Laertios, however, whose *Lives of the Philosophers* (Book I) is our chief source on the famous Seven, and who quotes, though uncritically, a large number of earlier writers (some 200 in his whole work), including early poets, indicates (ch. 30) that in most lists, instead of the obscure Myson, appeared Periandros of Corinth.

All were historical figures and men of note in their communities; and all were alive during the early sixth century. Dikaiarchos of Messene (*ap.* D.L. i, 40) commented soundly that they were not philosophers in the later sense of the term, but men of statesmanlike intelligence, *synetous kai nomothetikous*. Kleoboulos (p. 52) and Periandros ruled their cities, Pittakos and Solon were chosen to legislate for theirs (pp. 243ff, 292ff). Chilon was Ephor at Sparta, in 556 tr. (Pamphile *ap.* D.L. i, 68) – but Herodotos, the earliest author to mention him (i, 59) makes him already prominent before the birth of Peisistratos, i.e. about 600 tr. Bias won fame as a judge and ambassador (p. 215), and Thales as a political adviser as well as the first scientist. The earliest extant mentions of them are, respectively:

Thales: Xenophanes, *ap.* D.L. i, 23.
Pittakos: Alkaios, *ap.* D.L. i, 72ff, and in papyrus fragments (pp. 240ff); Simonides, Plato's *Protagoras*, *loc. cit.*
Bias: Demodokos of Leros (see p. 215), Hipponax and Herakleitos (p. 398); all *ap.* D.L. i, 84.
Kleoboulos: Simonides, *ap.* D.L. i, 90.
Solon: his own poems, q. by many later writers, pp. 290ff.
Chilon: Hdt. i, 59; vii, 235.
Periandros: *Id.* i, 20ff; iii, 48ff; v, 92, 95.

The legend, which probably first brought them together as a group, told in its commonest version how a golden tripod, fished up out of the sea off Ionia, after quarrels over its possession was adjudged by an oracle to 'The Wisest'. It was therefore offered to Thales; but he said that another of the Sages was wiser, and he, another, until, having gone the round of all the Seven, it was by their common consent dedicated to the Delphic Apollo. There were many variations of the story (D.L. i, 28ff); it is also told by other writers, e.g. Diodorus in an excerpt of Book ix. The first author recorded to have written it down was Andron of Ephesos (D.L. i, 30), a contemporary of Theopompos (Euseb. *Praep. Evang.* x, 3, 7); but it must have been a popular story, orally transmitted, long before that. There are the numerous variations; and there is the presence of Periandros, which must date from before his *damnatio memoriae*. The predominance of eastern Greeks (four) suggests an eastern Greek origin, probably before the ruin of Ionia in the Persian Wars. Herodotos, however, does not mention the story.

The Sages were also credited with the authorship of the three injunctions inscribed round the entrance to the Delphic temple, often mentioned by Plato (e.g. *Philebos*, 48c; *Alkib.* i, 124ff; *Charmides*, 164f): NOTHING TOO MUCH. GO BAIL AND RUIN IS NEAR. KNOW THYSELF. With a little forcing (making *engya* in the second into a spondee) they could be read, in this order, as one oracular hexameter. In the same, the original intention presumably was not to discourage 'going bail' for a neighbour, but to warn against being sure about the future; which is typical Greek moralising. Kritias the 'tyrant' and cousin of Plato ascribed KNOW THYSELF to Chilon; this is our earliest mention of these inscriptions (from schol. on Eur. *Hippolytos*; Krit. fr. 6A, Edmonds). He is followed by Aristotle (Rhet. ii, 12.14). Plato in the *Protagoras* makes his Socrates attribute both this and NOTHING TOO MUCH to the Sages jointly, meeting at Delphi and wishing to leave an offering of their wisdom; while in the *Charmides* (*l.c.*) he attributes KNOW THYSELF to 'the god' and calls the other two inscriptions 'later'. (The inconsistency is a good example of the fact that Plato did not consider himself personally bound by anything said in the *Dialogues*, as he makes clear in the *Seventh Letter*, and generally took them much less seriously than most of his readers.) So Delphi claimed to have witnessed a meeting of the Seven. Romancers enjoyed imagining what their conversation might have been; and Plutarch used a *Dinner of the Seven Sages* as framework for a dialogue.

The damnation of Periandros created, for later generations, a vacancy in this *collegium* of the Great and Good. A name early substituted was that of the Noble Savage Anacharsis (said by Sosikrates to have visited Athens in 592-588, D.L. i, 101); but very soon somebody invented and told, against him, a story that replaced him by a personification of Greek peasant wisdom in the person of Myson, Plato's candidate, already known to Hipponax (*id.* i, 107) as 'he whom Apollo named the wisest of men'. Anacharsis, this version said, rashly asked the Oracle if any man was wiser than he was, and was told 'Myson of Chên'. Having enquired where that was, Anacharsis went to look for him, and found him, on a summer day, mending his plough. 'But, Myson,' said Anacharsis, 'it's not the right season for the plough.' 'It's the right season for fixing it' said Myson. Another version made Chên a Laconian village, and Chilon the great man whom Apollo placed second to a rustic (*id.* i, 106, cf. 30).

In this way began the practice of composing variant lists of the Seven, which provided endless amusement for scholars. Some later writers rejected the little-known Kleoboulos; some (anti-Spartans?) rejected Chilon. In their places were introduced Epimenidas of Crete (p. 287), Pythagoras, the early prose-writers Akousilaos of Argos and Pherekydes of Syros, the early dramatist Lasos of Hermione (p. 319) or any of half-a-dozen other names. One Hellenistic scholar enumerated seventeen in all (Hermippos of Smyrna, *ap.* D.L. i, 41-2). The names of Thales, Bias, Pittakos and Solon kept their places in all lists (Kleoboulos for Solon in Parke and Wormell, *The Delphic Oracle*, p. 389, is a slip). Romance or forgery provided them with highly unconvincing letters, duly recorded by Laertios, and also, in the person of one Lobon of Argos, with contributions to lyric poetry; the fact that these show a common style and are all in metres of the same type has led to general agreement that these are forgeries too, though Beloch, usually the most sceptical of historians, breaks with his usual custom by accepting them (GG I, 2, xvi; 2nd edn., pp. 327ff).

CHAPTER XI

Power and Poetry in Ionia

MILETOS during the sixth century was to give birth to the most momentous of all Greek achievements, that of 'natural philosophy'; but at the century's beginning there was in Ionia only the same 'revolutionary situation' as in the Isthmus region, exacerbated by the continuing pressure of Lydia. King Alyattes, at the beginning of his long reign (c. 617-560 tr.), 'inherited', as we have seen, from his father a war with Miletos (p. 113); but though his horsemen won two bloody victories over the Milesians and Chians, the sea-faring economy of Miletos was not to be broken so. The city held out under Thrasyboulos, the 'expert in tyranny'. After six years, having fallen ill and ascribing the blow to the anger of Athena of Assesos, whose temple (being thatched?) had been set on fire by sparks from the burning corn and burnt down, Alyattes gave it up. On the advice of Delphi, he negotiated for an armistice to restore the temple; and Thrasyboulos, given timely warning of this by his friend Periandros, was able to strengthen his bargaining position by letting the Lydian herald find the city keeping high festival, with no sign of exhaustion. Miletos obtained an alliance, which stood her in good stead for a century; and Alyattes, restored to health, built the offended goddess two temples instead of one.[1]

Upon Kolophon, subdued already by Gyges, Alyattes secured his hold by treachery; he summoned its still powerful cavalry to Sardis, and massacred them,[2] ending Kolophon's career as a major city. But later (after 590) he had his own borders to defend. Kyaxares the Mede (p. 130) pushing through Armenia, further west than any Assyrian king had gone, came up against the Lydian kingdom, probably on the line of the River Halys. He must have heard of Lydia, and the first contacts may not have been hostile. But aggressive war was an honourable pursuit for kings in that world; Lydian suspicion of the

[1] Hdt. i, 17-22.   [2] Polyainos, *Stratagems*, vii, 2.

formidable Mede was inevitable, and in due course war broke out, over Alyattes' refusal to extradite some Scythians in Kyaxares' service, who had considered themselves insulted by a reprimand, avenged themselves by a murder and fled. Alyattes marched, with Ionian contingents in his army, and held his own in several severe campaigns.[3] The end of the war came after an incident which marks the birth of western science: Thales, a young Milesian (he was still active nearly forty years later), foretold an eclipse of the sun during the current year; probably that of 21st September, 582.[4] Thales' cosmology was flat-earth and geocentric, and he cannot therefore have known the cause of eclipses; but he may have been aware of their cyclic recurrence, known empirically to Babylonian priests through their observations and systematic records kept through many hundreds of years. The important thing about Thales is his scientific attitude to such phenomena, of which more hereafter (p. 331). The eclipse, as it happened, was visible in Asia Minor that forenoon; it made Thales' reputation and, though only about three-quarters total, it made sufficient impression on the kings, already disappointed of easy victory, to cause them to make peace. Two interested neutrals, Nebuchadrezzar of Babylon and Syennesis (a dynastic name or title) king of Cilicia, mediated. The Halys frontier was confirmed, and alliance was cemented by a ceremony of blood-brotherhood and by the marriage of Aryenis, a daughter of Alyattes, to Astyages the son of Kyaxares.[5]

Alyattes turned west again, attacking this time northern Ionia; and his tactics showed an ominous development, learned probably from the east. Miletos he had tried to exhaust by harrying her territory. Smyrna he now assaulted in the Assyrian manner, throwing up a vast ramp, submerging whole olive gardens in its course, against the walls.[6] Up it his attacking infantry surged; the town fell, and was dismantled, ending its career as a city-state until Hellenistic times. Theognis of Megara reflects on history in the melancholy couplet:

> By pride fell Kolophon, Magnesia fell,
> And Smyrna; surely so shall you as well!

Alyattes pressed on along the coast into the central Ionian peninsula;

---

[3] Hdt. i, 16, 73f; order of events, Busolt, *GG* II, p. 469.
[4] Beloch, *GG*² I, ii, p. 355; 585, Pliny *NH* ii, 12/53; 584, Jerome.   [5] Hdt. i, 74.
[6] *id.* i, 16; the mound was cut through by the excavations of 1948ff; E. Akurgal, *Bayrakli* (Ankara, 1950); J. M. Cook in *BSA*, 1958-9.

but from before Klazomenai 'he came off not as he hoped, but severely defeated'.[7] The men of Klazomenai (perhaps reinforced by their neighbours) may have used war-dogs, long known in Ionia, against the Lydian horses; for the great sixth-century sarcophagus from Klazomenai in the British Museum, with scenes of Greek hoplites, war-dogs and hostile cavalry in battle, probably commemorates just this victory. That the enemy are, as used to be thought, Kimmerians (not recorded to have entered the peninsula) is unlikely; the style of the drawing is much later than the time of their raids.

Ephesos, slightly inland, which had survived its perils in the days of Kallinos and doubled its territory by annexing that of its old enemy Magnesia, probably profited further from the misfortunes of Kolophon, and was treated with respect by Alyattes. It must have been at this time one of the greatest cities in the Greek world. Its school of ivory-carving is famous (p. 45). Though not a sea-power or a colonising city, it had its oversea contacts, probably through Samos, and so with Sparta, and the return-influence is shown in Ephesian brooches. Over thirty of those found there (along with eighty of Asian and island types) are adorned with ivory plates in the form of two or four connected discs; the form derived from the imitation in ivory of the 'spectacle-fibula' with its coils of bronze wire, characteristic of Sparta and the north-west. In its original bronze form the type did not cross the Aegean; but Paros, friendly to Samos and its allies, shows the same western influence, with ten ivory disc-brooches out of twenty-one recorded.[8]

Politically, Ephesos had passed through the same revolution as Corinth, Miletos and Erythrai. Its royal house, the Basilidai, were relegated to priestly functions, retaining the royal robe, chief seats at festivals and priesthood of Demeter Eleusinia[9]; and a *tyrannos* had arisen, one Pythagoras.[10] The tyrant Melas, perhaps his son, actually married a daughter of Alyattes[11]; no small honour from the father-in-law of the prince of Media. About this time too (and not 100 years earlier, as used to be thought) the first great stone temple to Artemis was begun on the classical site[12]; but there were clouds on the horizon.

[7] Hdt. *ib.*   [8] Blinkenberg, *Fibules grecques*, iv, x, xii, xv.
[9] As still under Augustus: Str. xiv, 632f.
[10] *Suda, s.v.* Pyth. q. Baton of Sinope (who wrote *On the Tyrants of Ephesos*, see Ath. vii, 289).
[11] Aelian, *VH* iii, 26; Polyain. vi, 50.   [12] Jacobsthal in *JHS* LXXI.

Alyattes was growing old, and among his many sons by several wives there were rivals for the throne. One was Pantaleon, with his Greek name and a Greek mother. But the successful candidate (probably not the eldest, if he was really born in the twenty-third year of his father's reign) was Kroisos, Croesus, the son of a Karian woman.[13]

The supporters of the two princes were not divided on racial lines; striking evidence of the interpenetration of Greek and Lydian civilisation. 'The Lydians have the same customs as the Greeks', says Herodotos, 'except that their daughters engage in prostitution', thus 'earning themselves dowries; and they select their own husbands.'[14] Presumably the prostitution was religious, as in Babylonia. A story is told of Croesus, as governor of Adramyttion, opposite Lesbos, being summoned to join his father for a campaign, and finding himself short of money to pay his contingent. He tried to borrow from Sadyattes, a rich Lydian merchant, but was kept waiting and finally refused, on the ground that Sadyattes 'could not afford to finance all Alyattes' sons'. The man was really a supporter of Pantaleon. Croesus then resorted to Ephesos, and there secured a modest loan from one Pamphaes of Priene; when he gained the throne he is said to have repaid Pamphaes with a wagon-load of gold (a typical Croesus-story) and tortured Sadyattes to death.[15] Whether Pantaleon escaped is not recorded.

Croesus was thus quite kindly disposed towards Ephesos, but he desired the city as a subject, not as an ally; and when the young tyrant Pindaros, his sister's son, refused submission, he assaulted it, using the new Lydian siege-tactics. A tower collapsed, probably undermined; it was remembered thereafter as 'the traitor tower'. Pindaros then ordered his people to 'place the city in sanctuary' by running out a cable from the walls to the Temple of Artemis, 1400 yards away (evidently the town was not surrounded) and opened negotiations for peace. Croesus smiled at the stratagem, but refused to make peace with Pindaros personally; he must leave Ephesos. Pindaros laid down his power, making over the treasury to representatives of the people and appointing one Pasikles as guardian of his young son and private property, and retired with those chiefly compromised against Croesus

---

[13] Hdt. i, 92; C. was 35 at accession, and A. reigned 57 years, *ib.* 26, 25.
[14] *ib.* 94, 93.
[15] Hdt. 1, 92; N.D. fr. 65, Aelian. *VH* iv, 27; for an attempt by 'C.'s stepmother' (i.e. Pantaleon's mother?) to poison him, cf. Plut. *Pythian Oracles*, 16, a story told to account for the statue at Delphi called 'Croesus' Cook'; she was said to have saved his life.

to the Peloponnese, affording one of the most attractive memories on record of a patriotic Greek ruler.[16]

Thus Ephesos escaped the fate of Smyrna. Croesus treated the city, or at least its goddess, with favour. 'The golden oxen and most of the pillars' at the great temple were noted by Herodotos as his dedications, in fulfilment of a vow, promising the Goddess the property of the unfortunate Sadyattes if he won the throne; and pillar-drums with fragments of inscriptions recording that 'King Croesus set this up' are in the British Museum. Against the other Ionian cities his siege-craft continued to prevail; in a few years he was undisputed master of the mainland, and began to cast covetous eyes upon the islands; but he was wise enough to adjourn his proposed naval operations. Bias the wise man of Priene is said to have deterred him by posing the question what his reactions would be if he were told that the islanders were collecting cavalry for a march on Sardis.[17] Ephesos survived to produce, in the next generation in its old royal house, one of the most profound of all Ionian thinkers (pp. 395ff).

Miletos alone retained her relative independence; but she made poor use of it. 'After the fall of the tyrants Thöas and Damasenor', says Plutarch, 'two parties divided the city called the Plutis and the Cheiro-macha'[18]; the names are almost translations of 'Capital and Labour'. Between these parties there developed a class-war of an extreme bitterness and atrocity. There was a racial side to the struggle, to embitter the economic, for the 'workers' are also called Gergithes, the name of a native people also found in the Troad[19]; presumably natives reduced to servitude by the Milesians, themselves not unmixed with Asian blood.[20] The people gained control and, 'collecting the children of those who had fled on threshing-floors', brought up oxen and trampled them to death. 'And then the rich, gaining the upper hand in turn, burnt all their prisoners, coating them with pitch, and their children with them. And as they were burning, many evil omens occurred; among other things, a sacred olive-tree caught fire spontaneously. For this the God [probably Apollo of Didyma] for a long time repelled them from his oracle and when they asked why, he replied:

I am concerned for the Gergithes slain, who were warriors never;
Death in the coats of pitch, and the tree now blasted for ever.[21]

[16] As n. 11.   [17] Hdt. i, 27.   [18] GQ 32.
[19] Str. xiii, 589.   [20] Hdt. i, 146.   [21] Herakl. Pont. *ap.* Ath. xii, 524.

In these horrors, it is worthy of notice, not all sections of the population of Miletos were implicated. The revolution and counter-revolution affected chiefly the trading and industrial population, the seafarers and the water-front. The plutocracy became known as the *Aeinautai*, the 'ever at sea'; they are said to have had the habit of going out in a ship to confer together,[22] a sound security precaution. Some landowners went on 'cultivating their gardens', leaving the progressive world to its bloodshed (p. 216); the priests of Apollo, who condemned the atrocities, probably belonged, as in most cities, to the old landed families. To the mid-sixth century belongs an exchange of incivilities between landsmen and seamen in the persons of their elegiac poets, Phokylides of Miletos and Demodokos of Leros, the island colony, perhaps part of the Milesian state (p. 93), with good harbours, the possibilities of which were recognised by the Milesian sage and geographer Hekataios[23] and again by fascist Italy.

> The Lerians – thus saith Phokylides –
> Are bad; not some, but every single man.
> I make one sole exception: Proklees;
> And Proklees himself's a Lerian.

The lines have often been imitated; one version ascribes the authorship to Demodokos and makes the butt the men of Chios.[24] More certainly by Demodokos is the couplet

> Thus saith Demodokos: Milesians are
> Not fools; but they behave as if they were.[25]

Demodokos had a considerable reputation as a satirist, but only a few lines survive. One couplet ascribed to him in the Anthology is on the snake that bit a Cappadocian, and died of it. A trochaic line praises a legal decision, said to have been successfully proposed *ex parte* by Bias, the sage, under whom little Priene maintained her independence against both Miletos and Samos[26]:

> If you sit in judgment, let the judgment be Prienian!

But the details of this Greek 'judgment of Solomon' are not preserved for us.

[22] Plut. GQ 32. [23] Hdt. v, 125.
[24] Phok. *ap.* Str. x, 487; (Dem.) *A.P.* xi, 325.
[25] Ar. *Eth. N.* 1151a. [26] Plut. GQ 20; D.L. *Bias* (1, 84).

Phokylides is a more considerable figure, and a representative of the party under which Miletos at last attained peace. Exhausted, the warring factions agreed to arbitration by Paros. The Parian delegates, says Herodotos, 'went through all the Milesian territory, and wherever they saw an estate well cultivated in the devastated land, they wrote down the name of its owner; . . . and they did not find many such. Then they returned to the city and summoned an assembly, and nominated these men to form the government.'[27] The decision, though reactionary in the strictest sense of the word, gave peace; and by the end of the century, Herodotos tells us, Miletos was once more the leading city of the eastern Greek world.

This was the political experience which lies behind the thought of Phokylides; if he wrote, as is rather likely, before the Parian Arbitration, his was one of the voices which helped to prepare public opinion. He, like not a few in his generation, had seen enough of wealth and power and the lust for them:

> This too Phokylides did say:
>   A little city on a hill
>   With ordered life is better still
> Than fury in great Nineveh.

> This also said Phokylides:
>   What profits one his noble birth
>   If his advice be nothing worth
> Nor in his words be grace to please?

> Many things are best in mid degree;
> Of middle station I would wish to be.

> Would you be wealthy? Tend your fertile field
> And like a Horn of Plenty it will yield.

Elsewhere, somewhat cynically: 'First get a living; virtue after that!' (As in the Yorkshire saying, 'First get on, then get honour, then get honest!') But also, strikingly if not consistently, 'In justice all of virtue is summed up.'[28]

In all of this, Phokylides is typical of a new movement in Greek thought. The doctrine of moderation which he preaches was not

[27] v, 29.
[28] Q. as a proverb by Ar. *Eth. N.* 1129b; ascr. to Phok. *or* Theognis, schol. *ib.*

something inborn in 'the Greek character' as some writers would superficially have it; it was an achievement by some of the sages of that age, in reaction against the fierce struggle for wealth and power. More than one of the surviving quotations from him is owed by us to his spiritual descendant, Aristotle. In Phokylides' own time the Delphic Oracle was also making the doctrine of the Golden Mean its own, with the laconic inscriptions NOTHING TOO MUCH and KNOW THYSELF (p. 208). In the latter we have an *internalising* of ethical feeling, just as, in the last of our quotations from Phokylides, we have a *moralising* of the idea of 'virtue' or ARETE, a word which in earlier Greek could include intellectual and even physical qualities; a horse or a sword could have *arete*. It was one of the new ideas of the sixth century that the characteristic goodness of a man is moral goodness. In Greek society at large, the word *arete* must have been suffering a shift or development of meaning, or Phokylides' dictum would have been incomprehensible. As it is, it is original, within its author's limits; Phokylides' significance lies not in originality but in being typical. Solon of Athens had anticipated him in much of his teaching, not least in the doctrine of moderation; even Theognis of Megara (Ch. XIII), a fierce partisan, could quote NOTHING TOO MUCH; and the vase-painters of Athens, after the excitement and licence of the orientalising movement, were turning again to discipline in the conventions of a new style, the Attic Black-Figure.

Phokylides looks both forward and back. He can repeat other men's sentiments in the traditional manner of pre-literate days (cf. pp. 160f), as when he paraphrases the *Satire on Women* of Semonides, comparing feminine temperaments to those of different animals, with no more change than is necessitated by the change from iambic to elegiac metre; while at the same time he is keen to claim 'property' in his own more original utterances, like Demodokos and like Hipparchos of Athens (p. 319), by prefacing them with his name. He is significant both as being a central figure, 'middling' in every way (he would have liked the idea), and as shedding a light on how his city, after its ferocious class-war, could settle down again and play the leading part in the inauguration of Greek science (Ch. XVII).

In the meantime, however, Miletos had ceased to dominate the Black Sea trade routes or, for a time, to play any part in oversea politics. In the Thalassocracy-List her name is followed perhaps by that of Megara (if an emendation proposed long ago by the present writer is correct),[29] as founder of Kalchadon and Byzantion, and then by that of Lesbos (presumably united for a time under the leadership of Mytilene). But already soon after 600, when Miletos was under pressure from Lydia and in alliance with Periandros, there came a series of events which brought new-comers to the Dardanelles and in part reversed the hundred-year-old verdict of the Lelantine War. These events affected the fortunes of four cities, with whose revolutions and culture we have still to deal: Mytilene, Megara, Samos and Athens.

The seventh century had seen a division of spheres of colonisation: Chalkis with Paros and Andros monopolised the north-west Aegean, Miletos with Megara and Lesbos the north-east. Early in the sixth century, as we have seen (p. 190), Periandros occupied Poteidaia in Chalkidike, and apparently interfered in Euboia in order to secure Kerinthos, on the way thither. Further Corinthian activity here may have been prevented only by the troubles of Periandros' last years. But further east, Samos and Athens now made a bid to secure footholds in the Propontis.

Samos, in 599 tr., sent a colony to Perinthos on the north coast of the Marmara, which succeeded in establishing itself[30]; but not without a struggle. Byzantion and Kalchadon, the colonies of Megara, reacted violently (the Samians may already have had a reputation as pirates) and called in help from their mother-city to place the new settlement under siege. Samos in turn sent a relief squadron of thirty ships (rather a small number for Samos; perhaps a first-line squadron was already there). Two of these are said to have been 'destroyed by lightning as they sailed out of harbour' (no doubt an intrusion of myth); but the result of the expedition was a complete victory for the Samians, who took 600 prisoners.

The sequel to this however was disastrous to the Samian government. Samos had already had a *tyrannos*, one Demoteles, and got rid of him by murder, the government reverting to the landed *Geomoroi*. The victorious sailors now determined on revolution, and gained the support of some, at least, of their generals. The fleet returned, bringing the prisoners, whose capture had been reported, to be exhibited in a

[29] *Megareis* for *Kares*, in a passage shown to be corrupt by the absence or corruption of the figures (probably already in Eusebios' copy of Diodoros); Burn in *JHS* LVII.
[30] Str. vii, fr. 56; date, Synkellos, p. 238.

victory parade, 'bound in their own fetters'; but the fetters had been sawn through and loosely secured; the prisoners had been provided with concealed daggers; and by arrangement with their captors, they proceeded to massacre the Council assembled to receive them. The revolutionaries thus achieved the purpose of avoiding the blood-guilt, which would have been incurred by themselves shedding the blood of their fellow-citizens.[31]

It may have been not long after this that there rose to prominence in Samos one Aiakes, son of Bryson; an inscription records him as having 'levied for Hera (her tithe of) the booty, according to his stewardship'. He is perhaps identical with Aiakes, father of the famous Polykrates, under whom Samos prospered as a commercial and piratical state, in the next generation (pp. 314ff).[32]

Of the Megarians who carried out the massacre, any who wished for it were offered citizenship in the new Samian popular republic; evidently their home government was not one to which they would automatically wish to return. As to those who did return home, we should like to know, but do not, what part they played in the revolutions of their own city (Ch. XIII).

Megara intervened no further in the Propontis; she had her own troubles at home. It was the misfortune of this once promising state to be sandwiched between larger and more powerful neighbours, Corinth which encroached upon her southern territories, and now Athens which, lately a corn-exporter, had reached the 'saturation point' at which she urgently needed more territory or food from abroad. Athens set out to secure both. She claimed the island of Salamis, which was in Megarian hands; whether by recent capture, as the Athenians alleged, or as an ancient possession cannot be known. The Athenian claim, when the question was ultimately submitted to Spartan arbitration, used the evidence of Homer (had not Ajax in the Iliad beached his ships next to those of the Athenians?) and, interestingly, of archaeology, that is of the ancient burial customs revealed by tombs on the island. Both points would be consistent with a Megarian occupation dating from the Dorian invasions. The Megarians replied by producing their own text of Homer, which made Ajax lord also of

---

[31] Plut. GQ 57.
[32] Tod, *GHI* no. 7, *SIG* no. 10; Mary White, 'The Duration of the Samian Tyranny', in *JHS* LXXIV, suggests that he may have been *tyrannos* himself. But 'the script must surely be later than Polykrates' father' – R.M.

the ancient villages of the Megarid, and by pointing out that the
regulations for the diet of the Athenian priestess of Athena Polias,
including a taboo on foreign cheese, banned also that of Salamis; to
which the Athenians replied that they banned also cheese from other
inshore islands such as Helene (modern Makronisi) off Cape Sounion.
The question was almost as academic then as now; the expansion of
Athens was, in words that were used of the American occupation of
Texas, 'a biological phenomenon'; and Sparta found in favour of
Athens, the state now in possession, the friend of her ally, Corinth, and
the enemy of Aigina, which had long looked towards Argos.[33]

Theagenes had tried to anticipate the danger by helping his son-in-
law Kylon to seize power in Athens (p. 188); he had failed, and
Theagenes himself had since been driven into exile; but in the fighting
for the island Megara with her well-developed sea-power at first did
well. The Athenians were losing heart and in a mood to call off the
operations when a man destined to fame, the young Solon, burst upon
the scene with his fiery elegiac poem, including the lines:

> Rather would I be a poor Pholegandrian or Sikinetan,
>   Changing country and home, than an Athenian then!
> 'Look!' they'd say, 'Here comes an Athenian, one of the beaten,
>   One of the famed "No-more-fighting-for-Salamis" men!'[34]

Pholegandros and Sikinos are two of the smallest inhabited Cyclades.
Later legend had it that a decree had actually been passed forbidding
any more proposals for an offensive on pain of death, and that Solon
had to feign madness in order to recite his poem; but this does not
seem to be borne out by his words, which speak of the acceptance of
defeat only as a shocking possibility. In any case, Athens listened, and
tried again. She was potentially far stronger than Megara; and the
island remained finally in Athenian hands.

Warfare, like the wars of the fifth and fourth centuries, probably
went on intermittently but interminably; once (about 570?) the
Athenians actually captured Nisaia, the port of Megara, but, being
themselves also divided by faction, failed to hold it (p. 250). Our
information, based on oral traditions written down long after, or on
later writers' deductions from early poetry, enables us neither to give
a precise chronology, nor to relate these events to the Delphian Sacred

---

[33] Plut. *Solon*, 10; Str. viii, 394f.   [34] D .L. *Solon* (i, 47).

War, or to other events of Athens' early history; to an Athenian defeat in an 'ancient quarrel' with Aigina, for example, which Herodotos describes with a wealth of mythical-looking detail, but without indications of date.[35] But it was also in this generation (605 Jerome) that Athens for the first recorded time sent a fleet far afield, seizing a vantage-point at the mouth of the Hellespont, Sigeion, in the Plain of Troy and in an area hitherto monopolised by Mytilene. Since Athens and Samos were both thus at war with Megara and both forcing their way, as interlopers, into the Hellespontine area, it is highly probable that they were acting in concert. No ancient writer says so, but in view of the nature of our tradition, fragmentary and largely biographical, this is not surprising.

Some details of these operations will concern us later (pp. 240, 250); but the net result of them was that Athens, with her large territory and great manpower, proved too powerful to be kept out. She held Sigeion against Lesbian attacks, and was confirmed in possession by the arbitration of Periandros; though Mytilene retained an outpost inconveniently near, at the traditional Barrow of Achilles.[36] Later, Athens secured a stronger foothold across the straits, dominating and colonsing the Gallipoli Peninsula (pp. 310ff). The author of the Thalassocracy-List dates the end of Lesbian predominance at sea *c.* 585, but the 'successor' was not Athens, now preoccupied with internal strife, but Phokaia, friendly to Mytilene (pp. 145, 226). Phokaia's reassertion of her power in the north-east is marked by her colonisation of Amisos (566 tr.) in the heart of the Pontos (p. 120). With good river-valley routes to Cappadocia, its commercial potentialities for the trade in Chalybian iron and oriental goods were enormous. Fifth-century Athens reinforced it, and there was Milesian influence too; inscriptions of the Hellenistic age, when Phokaia had lost importance, show Amisos cherishing Milesian connections.[37]

One major Ionian sea-power took no part in all this: the island city of Chios. With the strongest navy in Greece (100 ships) in 494,[38] she does not figure among the 'Thalassocracies'. The reason is of some interest.

Up to a point Chios had developed like other cities. She had had a

---

[35] Hdt. v, 82-8; cf. Dunbabin in *BSA* XXXVII (early 7th century?).
[36] Str. xiii, 599-600.
[37] Myres in *CAH* III, p. 663.   [38] Hdt. vi, 8.

dynasty of kings, one of whom, Hektor, may have given his name to
the great Trojan hero of Chian Homer[39]; she had seen this followed by
an oligarchy which fell when members of the aristocracy themselves
became dissatisfied with the 'despotism' of the executive.[40] Chians had
colonised, at Maroneia (p. 91), and had probably gained territory on
the Ionian mainland, with the help of Miletos, at the expense of
Erythrai (pp. 90ff). Possession of mainland territory would help to
account for their readiness to support Miletos against Lydia (p. 113).
Their merchant seamen and sea-captains were numerous enough to be
a recognisable political force.[41] They exported textiles, their famous
wine, figs, other fruit and the gum mastich, to this day a famous Chian
product.[42] But after Maroneia Chios, like Aigina, where Aristotle
makes the same observation on the numbers of the merchant seamen,
seldom if ever colonised; and the reason was the same: Chios developed
production for export and (followed in this too by Aigina), was the
first Greek city to acquire a vast population of imported, barbarian
slaves.[43] Long afterwards, Thucydides remarks that Chios had 'more
slaves than any other city except Sparta'[44] (though Sparta's helots are
more properly called serfs). Controlling them was a problem; indeed
a story is told of how at one time (much later) the runaway slaves in
the island's wooded and mountainous 'interior' were organised by
one Drimakos into a band, which harried the farms, evaded capture,
and at last (the gang-leader turning 'protector') made terms with the
republic, promising to limit their depredations, give receipts, and, in
order not to swell their own numbers inconveniently, send back any
further runaways, unless they could satisfy Drimakos that they had
really been ill-treated. 'And the slaves after that ran away much less,
fearing his judgment.'[45]

[39] Wade-Gery, *The Poet of the Iliad*, pp. 6ff (source, Ion of Chios *ap.* Paus. vii, 4, 8ff).
[40] Ar. *Politics*, 1306b.   [41] *ib.* 1291b.
[42] Textiles, Kritias (*ap.* Ath. i, 28), 6f (reading μαλλόν; Edmonds, *El. & Iambus* I, p.
484); Wine 'invented' in Chios, Theopomp. *ap.* Ath. i, 26; cf. the amphora on Ch. coins
(from 6th century on); Horace, *Od.* iii, 19, 6, etc. etc.; Mastich, Pliny, *NH* xii, 36/72.
[43] Theopompos (himself a Chian) *ap.* Ath. vi, 265b, c. The whole passage, Ath. pp.
262–73, it may be observed, contains most of the information commonly quoted on the
development of slavery and serfdom in the Greek world, together with all the figures of
alleged huge slave populations (470,000 at Aigina according to Ar. *Aig. Pol.*, 460,000 at
Corinth acc. to Timaios, 400,000 in Attica in 312, with only 31,000 free males, acc. to
Ktesikles' *Chronika*, citing a census taken by Demetrios of Phaleron). Ath. quotes nearly
thirty historians, philosophers and poets, and anyone familiar with these few pages will be
saved a great deal of page-turning in the *corpora* of collected fragments.
[44] Thk. viii, 40.   [45] Ath. 265–6, from Nymphodoros of Syracuse, of unknown date.

Such a slave-economy was, contrary to non-specialist modern belief, not normal in *early* Greece, nor, in the less 'progressive' regions, even in classical times; a friend of Aristotle in Phokis, who had 1000 slaves, was accused of 'depriving citizens of employment'.[46] Chios was the first specialised Greek 'slave-state', producing in the process such unlovely characters (as their own contemporaries thought) as the dealer Panionios, whose speciality was the collecting of handsome boys to be made eunuchs for sale in Ephesos or Sardis.[47] With slave labour she built up her production for export, and found, like Aigina, no need to export her men. Thus she became, in the language of the 1930's, a 'sated power', and though she could fight toughly if attacked (as against Persia in 494), she played no part in colonial wars.

Chians had a reputation among their neighbours as pawky and dishonest[48]; but they were not solely given up to money-making. A famous family of sculptors in stone spans, in three generations, the whole sixth century: Mikkiades, his son Archermos and *his* sons Athenis and Boupalos. The names of Mikkiades and Archermos appear on an early statue-base at Delos which may be actually that of the famous flying Victory, the earliest signed major Ionian work; that of Archermos also at Athens, where island sculptors may have helped to inspire or even have contributed to the beautiful series of archaic Maidens on the Acropolis. Lesbos also commissioned at least one of his works. Athenis and Boupalos, working in their turn at Delos, added an epigram reminiscent of modern advertising, saying that Chios was famous not only for vines but for the works of the sons of Archermos.[49] They gained a more oblique fame as the result of their rashness in caricaturing, as the story goes, the satirical poet Hipponax of Ephesos, who, having offended the Ephesian tyrants Athenagoras and Romas, was living in exile (*c.* 540 tr.). Hipponax, however, if ugly and undersized, was a spirited little man, the inventor, it is said, of the queer 'limping iambic' or *skazon* line with a spondee or trochee for its last foot. He hit back with his own weapons if not also with nature's: 'Hold my cloak, I will hit Boupalos in the eye – for I am ambidextrous,

[46] Timaios, *ap.* Ath. 264c, d, on Lokris and Phokis; and of course there were no slaves in the Golden Age (nor any work), cf. the comic utopias quoted at 267-9.
[47] Hdt. viii, 105-6 (duly q. by Ath. 266e). Beloch, *GG*[2] (1924) I, i, p. 270.
[48] Aristoph. *Frogs*, 970; cf. *A.P.* xi, 235.
[49] Inscrs. in Stuart Jones, *Anc. Writers on Gk. Sculpture*, p. 19; Pliny, *NH* xxxvi, 4/11ff; schol. on Aristoph. *Birds*, 573; on the connection with the Victory, cf. Richter, *Archaic Greek Sculpture*, 118f.

and never miss!' For the rest, he is a minor figure to us, though popular
with lexicographers for his vocabulary from the common speech of an
Ionian street, especially names of fish and other foodstuffs. He was
credited also, perhaps wrongly, with the saying, popular with Greek
men, that the two best days of married life are those of the wedding
and of one's wife's funeral.[50]

Chian society itself produced no more world-famous poets after the
Blind Poet of the Delian Hymn (p. 12); but the clan or guild of the
Homeridai preserved and recited the great epics until Athens was ready
to edit them in a form probably substantially that which we still read
today. Whether anonymous Homeridai have contributed much or
anything to that form is one of the questions on which much argument
has shed little light. In later days, too, Chios had considerable literary
figures in Ion the tragedian, writer of memoirs and friend of Sophocles,
and Theopompos the historian.

In politics, the prosperity based on slave-labour and the necessity
for all free classes to hold together to control it were perhaps responsible for a willingness to compromise, which produced the apparently
peaceful emergence – at least, we hear of no convulsions – of an
advanced constitution known from a single inscription, found in the
island in 1908, and recently rediscovered after decades of inaccessibility
among the neglected treasures of the last Turkish Sultan.[51] Dated now
about 550 (rather than 600 as was formerly thought), it may perhaps
show borrowing from Solonian Athens (pp. 299ff) rather than the
other way; but it is undoubtedly our best evidence for the machinery
of a forward-looking sixth-century Ionian state. It is the text of a law,
dealing with courts, fines and the duties of officials. To publish such
texts at all was a democratic proceeding; oligarchies preferred to keep
the secrets of the law locked in the breast of aristocratic judges. (The
site of Corinth, which never achieved democracy, has produced
extraordinarily few pre-Roman inscriptions; and those of Athens
become numerous all of a sudden after the democratic reform of 461.)

The Chian text, written in the archaic manner with lines running in
alternate directions, left to right and right to left, or, on three sides of

[50] Pliny, *l.c.*; the lines on marriage, assigned to H. by Stobaios (iv, 22, 35), seem to be
given to another author in Berlin Papyrus 9773; see Diehl-Beutler, *Anth. Lyrica* (1952)
III, p. 139.
[51] Tod, *GHI* no. 1; new edition and discussion by L. H. Jeffery in *BSA* LI, 157ff and
pl. 43.

the stone pillar, up and down, is fragmentary; but phrases in it are full of significance. There is reference to persons 'serving as Demarch or King'; and the fact that the Demarch (itself a democratic title) comes first suggests that he, like the Athenian Archon, ranked above the Kings, who are plural and, no doubt, like the King-Archon at Athens, religious officials. There is also reference, twice in succession, to the 'People's Council', *demosie boule*; and there could surely be no point in referring to it otherwise than simply as 'The Council', *tout court*, unless there had existed also another Council which was not 'the People's'. The evidence is clear that Chios about 550 was some sort of a democracy; and the implied coexistence of two councils, a People's Council and, probably, some august aristocratic survival like the Areopagus, is a striking parallel to the state of affairs at Athens. The laws, of which we have here a fragment, were not the least achievement of the city of Homer.

CHAPTER XII

The Lyric Age of Lesbos

LESBOS, with an area of 630 square miles and a population of 140,000 (1940), is the largest and richest eastern Aegean island; green, except in the high summer, even today; hilly, with outcrops of rock, like all Greek islands, but without high mountains like those of Chios and Samos; the highest, called Olympos, in the south, is a little over 3000 feet. In ancient times, with a smaller population and considerable remains of forest, it was shared by Mytilene and four smaller cities – Methymna and Antissa in the north, Eresos in the west and Pyrrha on the land-locked central gulf; there were also openings for younger sons on the neighbouring mainland. Here the Aiolians thought of themselves as heirs of the Achaians of the Trojan War[1]; and the Trojan cycle was a favourite source for Lesbian poetry. Mytilene itself faces east, and had close relations with Phokaia, as earlier with Kyme; and her oversea interests were not confined to the coasts visible from her own hills. Alone of Aiolic cities she shared in the foundation of the Hellenion at Naukratis, where a brother of Sappho went to trade and dallied, to her indignation, to spend his money on one of the famous Naukratite courtesans[2]; and, still more striking, the archaeology of the Phokaian west gives evidence of economic ties with the whole of the north-eastern Aegean area. The utility pottery of early Marseilles was the grey *bucchero* of Lesbos and north-west Asia Minor; and the great Auriol hoard of 2160 archaic coins, all anepigraphic, contained about 50 per cent coins of Lesbos (or of Phokaia itself, which later had a convention with Mytilene for a joint currency), one-third coins from north of Lesbos, and one-sixth from Asia Minor south of it.[3]

The ruling class, still in power about 600, consisted of clans descended from the kings; we hear of Penthilidai, Atreidai in their own

---

[1] Implied by the terms of the Athenian counter-claim, Hdt. v, 94.
[2] Hdt. ii, 178, cf. 135. [3] Cf. above, p. 145, n. 49.

conceit, through Penthilos, son of Orestes.[4] Another great house were styled Archeanaktidai, 'sons of the ruling Lord'; an Archeanax, no doubt a member of it, was credited with having fortified Sigeion (pp. 240f) with stones taken from the ancient walls of Troy.[5] These nobles had not let the rising tide of commerce flow past them; they had, at least some of them, gone into trade themselves, like Sappho's brother. They took a hard-headed view of the importance of money. 'Money's the man', declaims Alkaios, quoting by name Aristodamos the Spartan, a friend of Chilon the wise, 'and no poor man is held in account or honour.'[6]

Into this rich, tough, enterprising aristocracy Sappho, the daughter of Skamandronymos and Kleuis,[7] was born, late in the seventh century. Through her writings and through later authors who knew them, we know the names of her family circle: her brothers, Erigyios (a rare name, but one still known in Lesbos in the fourth century), the errant Charaxos and the youngest, Larichos, sometime page of honour or Cup-Bearer at Council dinners in the Town Hall.[8] She was married, probably at a fairly tender age, and had a daughter, whom she named after her mother: 'Kleuis my beloved, fair as the golden flowers, for whom I would not take as price all Lydia nor lovely . . .' (Lesbos?).[9] We hear nothing of any other children, nor, except in a confused article in a Byzantine encyclopaedia, of her husband; probably he died early. Sappho lived on, respected in her own society, as ever since, for her poetry. She was no beauty by Greek canons, being (the tradition may well come from her own words) little and dark[10]; typically Greek, in fact; but the Greek ideal of beauty was to be tall and blonde, like the painted marble or gold-and-ivory goddesses. It is with respect, almost with awe, that the warrior-poet Alkaios addresses her – if, we are compelled again to say, the first line is really his, which is not explicitly stated.[11] He remembered her smile; her face in animation:

---

[4] Ar. *Politics*, 1311b; mentioned, Sappho, fr. 71 Lobel and Page; Atreids, cf. Alkaios (*O.P.* 1234) with D.L. i, 81, on Pittakos' marriage; legendary pedigree, Str. xiii, 582.

[5] Alk. E. 1, 24 Page; Str. xiii, 599. [6] *Ap.* schol. on Pindar, *Isthm.* ii, 17.

[7] *O.P.* 1800 (in Edmonds, *Lyra Graeca*, I, p. 430); Skamandronymos, Hdt. ii, 135 (named for the Trojan river).

[8] Erigyios, *O.P. ib.*; cf. E. son of Larichos of Mytilene, one of Alexander's cavalry officers, Arrian, *Anab.* iii, 11, etc. (descended from the same family?). Larichos, S.'s brother, cup-bearer, Ath. x, 424e.

[9] Hephaistion, *On Metre*, 98; fr. 132 LP. [10] *O.P. ib.*; etc.

[11] Ar. *Rhetoric*, i, 9 (2nd line and S.'s reply – in Alcaics!); 1st line only in Hephaistion. *op. cit.* 44.

'Violet-tressed, holy, honey-sweet-smiling Sappho, I wish to speak, but reverence restrains me.' A detail, which makes it rather more likely that the lines *are* by Alkaios, is the fact that they are twelve-syllable lines in an unusual metre. Docked of a syllable at the beginning, they would equal one of the first three lines of a Sapphic stanza, and docked of a syllable at the end, one of the two first lines of an Alcaic. The metres, later to be called after the two great poets, were in fact favourite metres with them respectively.

Sappho's poetry gives us a few glimpses of a Greek society at peace and, what is even more rare, of women's life; our only view of this between the *Odyssey* and the red-figure vase-painters. Naturally, it is a selective view; we are among the gentry, not among the poor, and the subjects of poetry are those which stir emotion: places of beauty, high occasions; a religious festival, and the sacred grove where it takes place; a parting, a wedding; love remembered in absence; passion, especially when its sweetness is laced with bitterness; jealousy and hate.

What the world has remembered about Sappho is her passionate love of some of her girl friends. They may have been pupils, sent to Sappho, sometimes from abroad, to be taught music and poetry; for in an 'oral society', such as that of Greece still was in its social habits, poetry is not the concern only of a few peculiar individuals. It has its social functions, satirical, religious and other, and to be able to compose and improvise or adapt, as well as quoting and drawing aptly upon the existing stock of poetry, is a social accomplishment. That the poet, like the athlete, the soldier, the scientist and the public speaker, later becomes a specialist and sometimes a professional is a product of increasing sophistication, which sets in in classical Greece and, inevitably as the unfolding of a rose, leads on (in combination with other social causes) from culmination to disintegration. In classical Athens we still find occasional poetry produced by such all-round figures as Kritias, Thucydides, Plato; and the practice survives today, both in parts of Africa and the West Indies, in parts of Soviet Asia, and in Greece itself, especially among villagers in Crete and Cyprus. Some individuals excel as poets, just as some excel in athletics; but composition is widespread.

Some of Sappho's girl friends are said to have come from abroad: Gongyla from Kolophon, Anaktoria perhaps from Miletos[12]; and if so,

---

[12] Both named repeatedly in the papyri; their home-towns, *Suda, s.v.* Sappho, I (*if* Anag ora' may be emended to Anaktoria).

they came for a purpose other than mere conversation. Later writers repeatedly speak of her as *teaching* them; though it must be added that the conclusive evidence of her own words is lacking. A line 'Hero I taught, from Gyara, the strong runner', could be hers, without implying that she also gave training in athletics; but it is not certainly hers, being quoted only to illustrate a form of the accusative used by 'the Aiolians'.[13] What is quite certain is that poetry was composed by Lesbian women, plural, with all that that implies of participation in the life of their society. We hear of only one other noted poetess (Erinna); but Sappho herself takes her position for granted and is in no way self-conscious about it like one doing something exceptional.

It is clear, too, that Lesbian song already had a long history. The poetic vocabulary, the metres, the conventions, were not created in a day out of nothing, not even the metres by the great poets who made them famous. Among Lesbian men Arion of Methymna, who had won fame at the court of Corinth and in the further west (p. 191), was a probably older contemporary of Sappho; and still earlier (*c.* 645 tr.) was Terpandros of Antissa, whose name means 'the delight of men'; who was invited, perhaps as an exile, into the society of cultured Sparta, and whose music was said to have restored morale in a time of pestilence and depression. Many legends were told about him, among others that he invented the seven-stringed lyre with its octave of notes; this is not true, since such an instrument appears in late Minoan painting on a famous sarcophagus from Aghia Triadha; but there is no reason to doubt his real existence or authorship of a few lines, of much charm, preserved in quotation.[14] High mountain peaks rise from high plateaux, and great creative individual achievements out of great traditions.

About the erotic element in Sappho's love for these girls there is no doubt. Her expression of it is as candid as it is ardent. Also, she makes no secret of an equally passionate jealousy. Atthis was a girl of Mytilene, one of her earliest friends; Sappho reflects on the unaccountability of love; 'Long ago I loved you, Atthis, when still my maiden life was full of flowers; (yet) I saw you as just a little girl and without grace'. Later she nearly broke Sappho's resilient heart: 'Love, who sets one

[13] Cf. context, from Aldus' *Thesaurus*, in Edmonds, p. 234.
[14] Date, *Parian Marble*, 34; fragments, in hexameters and spondaic dimeters, from such respectable authors as Plutarch (Lykourgos, 21), Strabo, Clem. Alex., see Diehl, Edmonds (I, pp. 30ff).

quivering, shakes me: the bitter-sweet, irresistible monster. O Atthis, you have come to hate the sight of me, and fly to Andromeda!' It is perhaps of Atthis too that she writes, in a papyrus fragment: ' . . . and honestly I wish I were dead. With many tears she left me, and this she said: "Oh, what a cruel fate! Truly, Sappho, unwillingly I leave you." And this I answered: "Go, be happy, and remember me; you know how we cared for you." But if you do not, I will call to your mind . . . our happiness. . . .' The following lines are mutilated; but they show that what Sappho 'called to her mind' was a memory of girls in the fields garlanding each other with flowers.

Maximus of Tyre, under the Roman Empire, a scholar and rhetorician who knew his Sappho, compared her circle to that of Socrates, and he is our authority for the view that Andromeda was a rival teacher[15]; it is not *proved* by actual quotation. Sappho reviles her as 'a country wench who does not know how to drape her rags over her ankles'. She is the Andromeda elsewhere recorded smugly to have 'made a fine bargain' (or 'been nicely paid out') and she *may* be the 'woman of no education' savaged by Sappho in another famous invective: 'Once dead, dead you will be, nor shall there be any remembering of *you* ever again; never a rose bloomed in the hills of song for *your* plucking; but inglorious still, even in Hades' halls, you will flit to and fro, one of the dead nameless eternally.'

It might be just the poetess crowing over a woman who made no such pretensions, and incidentally boasting that immortality is hers to convey; but it has very much more point if the woman attacked *did* claim to be a poetess.

There were other sorrows. 'Little Timas' – the Timas who once sent from Phokaia a purple kerchief for Aphrodite – died young:

> Here Timas lies: before her wedding-day
> 　Persephone's dark house received her, dead,
> And all her year for mourning sheared away
> 　Their hair, the glory of each comely head.

Normally, of course, it was precisely to get married that girls left the circle; and that, like death, was at least part of the order of nature. Sappho took part in the rejoicings, and wrote poems for weddings, including some heavy humour (jokes about the size of the bridegroom's feet, for example), which was presumably traditional. There was not

---

[15] *Op.* 24 (Edmonds, p. 154).

the bitterness of being abandoned in favour of another woman. All the same, she did feel jealous, as she shows in the famous poem which Catullus translated, and through which his Clodia gained the name of 'Lesbia' to immortalise her:

Matched with the gods he seems to me, the man who sits facing you and hears close by him the gentle voice, the sweet laugh, that for me makes the heart shiver within my breast; for when *I* see you, my voice fails, my tongue is tied, a thin flame creeps beneath my skin, I cannot see, there is a throbbing in my ears, the sweat runs down, I tremble all over, I am paler than grass, I seem not far from death. . . .

How can the man be so calm?

Largely through Sappho's fame, the sentiments of Lesbian women for each other and their alleged practices got an ill repute, already in ancient Greece, which has lasted ever since. It gained for Sappho's poetry (still much read in later antiquity, as is shown by the frequency of quotation and allusion and by the number of papyrus fragments) the hostility of the Church under the Christian Empire, which is said to have been responsible for the destruction of her works; and the church, with the example of later pagan morals before it, can hardly be blamed. But it is difficult today, with so much of history past – the corruption of later pagan slave-civilisation, the Christian revolt against it, and finally the all-pervading, commercialised sex-stimulation of our own society through advertising, press and cinema, to recapture the *naïveté* of pre-classical Greece. To say 'innocence' would be over-statement. Whatever of innocence Greece may ever have had was rapidly being lost in Sappho's time. In the renascent culture there is rather something adolescent; and the loss of innocence is part of it. Nevertheless, to read into the personal sentiments, then being given literary expression for the first time, the feelings of guilt that would have been inevitable later is anachronistic. The absence *of shame* is a characteristic of Sappho, for which classical Greek moralists were the first to blame her. It was a social situation that could only occur once. The disintegration of the tightly-enclosed Geometric 'bud' swiftly produced, as one of its aspects, the 'schism in the soul' in its attitude to sex (as well as in other matters) which might lead to repression, as in sixth-century puritanism,[16] or cynicism, as in all too much of the

[16] See below, pp. 363ff.

Anthology, or sublimation, as in Plato. But in Sappho, in Theognis and even in her contemporary the wise and virtuous Solon, all this is not yet. It is widely recognised today that the nature of human beings is normally to some extent bi-sexual. The social arrangements of Greece for its young people, which were not coeducational, led naturally to the formation of homosexual attachments among them. In some, this did lead, disastrously, to adult homosexual 'fixation'; and some of the young and beautiful, especially boys, were very badly spoilt; Alkibiades is the classic example. But in Sappho the openness with which she expresses herself, her very 'shamelessness', is still a proof of innocence, of a kind. She loved many of her girls, as she wrote her poetry, with a fire of which few are capable; and she said what she felt.

It must be remembered too that our tradition *about* Sappho, as transmitted by late antiquity, is distorted and literary. When, at the end of the Peloponnesian War, Athens fell on evil days and her morale could no longer tolerate political comedy, dramatists looked for less dangerous subjects. They found some in the presentation of 'comic history'; and among the characters, safely dead, who could be caricatured, none were more popular than the figures of literature best known through their own works. The *Frogs* of Aristophanes inaugurates this Middle Comedy. Archilochos was a useful butt, the first drunken, truculent, Braggart Soldier of the Greek stage; peaceful bourgeois could get much satisfaction out of being reminded that *he* threw away his shield. Sappho naturally lent herself to presentation in a dramatic tradition which had not quite lost its connection with a religious carnival in which obscenity was not only tolerated but expected: Sappho the lesbian in the basest sense of the word, or Sappho lovesick for the 'he-man' Phaon and throwing herself over the Leukadian Cliff (in western Greece!) to assuage her hopeless passion.

Phaon was the pagan St Christopher, the good ferryman, who would take the poor across free of charge. The gods heard of him; Aphrodite herself came down to test the reports, and after he had duly ferried her across the local strait in the likeness of a poor old woman, she rewarded him with the gift of a box of ointment which made him irresistible. More than one despairing admirer leapt off the local White Cliff for love of him. Unfortunately, misusing the gift of the deity, he ended by being taken in adultery and murdered.[17] This naughty story was perhaps a comic version of a myth explaining the apotropaic ritual of the White Cliff of Leukas. From it a human scape-goat, a condemned criminal, attached, it is said, by strings to a large number of seagulls as a form of parachute, was annually precipitated on a feast-day of Apollo, while boats waited to rescue him if possible and expel him to the mainland.[18] The introduction of Sappho into the story (as figures from different fairy-tales may be mixed in a panto-mime) was probably a further development. Yet another ingenious dramatist introduced into one play Sappho along with the satirists Archilochos (*fl.* 700 tr.) and Hipponax (540 tr.) as contestants for her favours.[19] Naturally, well-informed members of the audiences knew that this *was* pantomime; but the character Sappho in the common imagination of late antiquity came, in the absence of serious biography, to be the Sappho of lewd farce; just as for us, with slightly better excuse, the character of Richard III is the Richard III of Shakespeare.

It is refreshing to return to 'the real Sappho', in the only form in which she is known to us, the author of the fragments; but it is difficult to make her known in any real sense, to anyone who cannot read those fragments in the original. The thought expressed has nothing remark-able about it; nor has the feeling, except for its intensity. In translation, little survives beyond an attractive *naïveté*, as of ballad poetry. The wine will not travel. The Aiolic dialect was one of particular beauty, and for what Sappho could do with it, her age-long reputation – 'the tenth Muse', as Plato called her – must be the evidence. The metaphors that come to mind in speaking of her are significant: gold, fire, sunlight. It was the poet Meleagros of Gadara who, when collecting the little elegiac pieces by many poets for his *Garland*, the first Greek Anthology, compared each author's work to a different flower, and called those of Sappho 'few, but roses'.

What survives in translation is just, therefore, the picture of Sappho's Lesbos and its still rural life: her word-pictures, like that, surely from a wedding-song, of evening outside the village, when men and women and children and their beasts, by ones and twos and half-dozens, are coming in: *Hespere panta pheron hosa phainolis eskedas' Auos* – how

---

[17] Aelian, *VH* xii, 18; Servius, *ad Aen.* iii, 279; Edmonds, pp. 150ff.

[18] Str. x, 452 (on the western isle of Leukas), quoting Menander as introducing Sappho.

[19] Diphilos, *ap.* Ath. xiii, 599 (cf. viii, 339, x, 450, xiii, 572, naming three other drama-tists who wrote on Sappho); Edmonds, 152ff.

much is lost in translation! 'Hesperos, thou bringest all that the bright Dawn parted asunder; thou bringest the sheep, thou bringest the goat, thou bringest the child to its mother.'[20]　Rural again are the two hexameter similes, probably from a wedding poem for choirs of boys and girls answering one another, such as Catullus composed in imitation of the Greek: *Oion to glükümalon . . .*

> As the apple ripens and reddens, up on the tree so high,
> High on the topmost twig – and the pickers have passed it by –
> No, not that; but they could not reach it if they should try!

And the reply: *Oian tan hüakinthon . . .*

> As the bluebells grow on the hills, till the shepherds' trampling feet
> Beat them down, and bright on the ground is the bloom so sweet . . .

Rural and out-of-doors, groves, not city temples, are the places where she and her maidens worship:

> Come hither, come, out of the Cretan land
> To this thy shrine, within whose orchard glade
> Of apple-trees thy altars fragrant stand
> 　　　With frankincense.
>
> Cold water falls between the apple-trees
> And climbing roses over-arch their shade,
> And rustling in the leafy boughs the breeze
> 　　　Lulls every sense.
>
> Here is thy meadow, pasture fair for steeds
> With spring-time flowers, and the breezes blow
> Sweet-scented . . .

and with that the text, scribbled in this case on a fragment of pottery, becomes fragmentary.[21]　Again: 'The full moon shone, and the maidens took their places round the altar. . . .' The moon, the brilliant Aegean moon which gives objects even some slight colour, is much in her writing; more than once used for comparison with the surpassing beauty of some girl who seems to extinguish 'lesser lights', as in the lines, full of the clear, hard, *a*-sounds in which her dialect was rich:

---

[20] Fr. 104(a) LP. Cf. imitation by A. E. Housman, *Epithalamium* (*Last Poems*, xxiv).
[21] Fr. 2 LP; Page, *Sappho and Alcaeus*, pp. 34ff.

Asteres men amphi kalan selannan
aps apükrüptoisi phaennon eidos
oppota plethoisa malista lampei
gan epi paisan.

Around the fair moon every star
Is hidden again, though bright they are,
When full and strong she shines afar
On all the earth.

Seventeen of the thirty-eight vowels and diphthongs have the broad *a*, including nine of the twenty long vowels; and of these, six have *a* followed by a nasal sonant and the other three by a sibilant (*ast-*, *aps*, *ais-*).

She (or the supposed speaker) is out of doors, it seems, even in the sad little fragment on an assignation not kept: 'The moon has set, and the Pleiades; it is midnight; the time is passing; and I lie alone.'

The moon shines again in another poem, written to comfort the afterwards faithless Atthis, when one of her friends has married and gone to live in Sardis. (It may be Anaktoria the Milesian, who figures as an absent friend in another poem with mention of Lydia.) 'And in Sardis often her thoughts turn hither' (the beginning is fragmentary, but this seems to be the sense). ' ... For she honoured you like a goddess, and in your songs took most delight. And now she shines among the women of Lydia as, when the sun is down, the rosy-fingered moon excels all the stars; and her light spreads over the salt sea and over the flowering fields, and the sweet dew falls, and roses grow, and soft chervil and flowering clover; and as she goes her ways, she remembers gentle Atthis with longing.... But in that place to come ... us ...' The papyrus falls into fragments again.

Love, worship and play, no less than work and public life, take place under the sky, never more than a few minutes from the country even when in the narrow, twisting streets of the little towns, hugging the lower slopes of their citadel rocks, between the home plain, the sea and the wooded hills. But it is no rustic or provincial society. It was travelled and international. Mytilene imported much Corinthian painted pottery; the home-produced ware was plain. Her coins are of the finest workmanship – much finer than those of Phokaia, which used similar badges. Evidently the nobles of Mytilene were willing to

pay more to secure the best artists. A few pillar-capitals that survive
show a rich and luxuriant variety of the volute type; some have called
it 'Aeolic', which is misleading; the variety belongs not to a region
but to a period, *this* period, after which Ionic architecture, like other
branches of Greek art, settles down towards greater classicism and
chastity. Sappho's own Aphrodite, as the poetess in her most famous
ode pictures her appearing, is 'Aphrodite of the many-coloured throne',
Aphrodite 'smiling with thine immortal face'; smiling, we may venture
to think, an archaic smile. The words suit all that we know of the
archaic seated statues, where everything, statues, bases, architectural
features, was brilliant with colour, even to the sphinxes' wings, as a
find with its colour preserved by a unique chance has shown us; a find
from Aphrodite's own island and city, Paphos in Cyprus, where in a
conflagration during a Persian siege some works of art or fragments of
them had been calcined; some left, for their colour to fade normally;
just one fragment had been just enough 'fired' to preserve its red, black,
dark blue and brilliant green, as evidence for the almost overwhelming
colourfulness of an early Greek sanctuary.

Sappho's was, moreover, a military society, as appears in a poem, a
letter-poem perhaps, sent to Anaktoria in Lydia.[22] The comparisons of
human beauty to that of 'an army with banners', though familiar to us
from the *Song of Songs* and imitated from Sappho by the pseudo-
Anakreon, is not an obvious comparison. Might one guess that Anaktoria had written to Sappho after seeing the Lydian army in review,
and being thrilled by it? I, Sappho answers, would rather see *you*:

> Some call a host of cavalry
> And some of foot the finest sight
> Of all; and some a fleet at sea;
> But I would say, the heart's delight.
>
> Nor is the fancy hard to prove:
> She, who the beauty of mankind
> Excelled, fair Helen, all for love
> The noblest husband left behind;
>
> Afar, to Troy she sailed away,
> Her child, her parents, clean forgot;
> The Cyprian led her far astray
> Out of the way, resisting not.

[22] Fr. 16 LP; *S. and Alc.* pp. 52ff.

[Ever, we see, was woman weak,
Turned to the fancy of a day;]
And now, remembrance I will seek
Of Anaktoria far away,

The marvel of whose living grace
And laughing eyes I'd rather see
Than chariots all of Lydian race
And armoured lines of infantry.

There was more, but it is lost, and the first half of the fourth quatrain is lost in part; the sense *may* have been as here given.

War and public affairs were indeed about to change profoundly that gay society. Of the years of revolution at Mytilene we know chiefly, though not exclusively, through the poems of Alkaios.

Alkaios, indeed, also has his poems of peace; to what Sappho shows us of girls' life, with its dancing and chains of flowers and miseries of jealousy, he adds some robust cavalier drinking songs, with a few 'background' touches. Now it is the summer heat that gives the occasion for drinking: 'Wet your lungs with wine; for the (dog-)star is coming round, and the season is fierce, and everything is thirsty with heat. The sweet cicada chirps from among the leaves . . . , the artichoke flowers, and women are at their worst and men are weak, for Sirius parches head and knees.' The whole passage is a close paraphrase of Hesiod's *Works and Days*, 582ff. Now again it is the winter cold: 'Zeus rains, there is a great storm out of the sky, the streams are frozen fast' (i.e. their headwaters in the mountains are iced up. It can still rain lower down.) . . . Shut out the storm, pile high the fire, mix the sweet wine generously; and put a soft cushion behind your head.' The scene is supplemented in another fragment, describing a hall, decorated with splendid arms: 'The great hall flashes with bronze and all the house is adorned with shining helmets, from which white plumes of horse-hair nod, a glory to the heads of men; and bright greaves hide the pegs they hang upon, a defence against strong archery; and there are corselets of new linen thread, and hollow shields laid by; and there are broad swords from Chalkis, and many girdles and jerkins; these we must not forget, in the work we have undertaken.'[23] The 'work' may be either

[23] Ath. X, 430a (cf. also n. 34, below); Hor. *Odes*, I, xxxii, 5ff, cf. Cic. *Tusculans*, iv, 71.

foreign or civil war; the context fails us. At another time it is 'Drink, for life is short', with a reference to Sisyphos, who tried to cheat death and paid dearly for it; at yet another, 'Drink, why wait for the lamps? The day is almost done,' and wine is the gift of a god, Dionysos, to men. In short, Alkaios is a true toper and, as Athenaios observes, any reason will do. Horace, supported in general terms by Cicero, also describes him as writing amatory poems to boys, such as the black-eyed Lykos, which is quite probable; but none of these remain.

But there is much more in Alkaios than this. He was a serious poet, and a great master of metre; of the fragments rendered above, the winter poem is in the four-line stanza that bears his name; the Sisyphos poem is in dactylic lines,

$$\_\cup \ \_\overset{\smile}{}\cup\cup \ \_\cup\cup \ \_\cup\cup \ \_\cup\_$$

arranged in couplets; the 'armoury' poem in a kind of glyconic couplet,

$$\overset{\smile}{}\overset{\smile}{} \ \_\cup\cup \ \_\cup\_$$
$$\_\_\cup\cup \ \_\cup\_ \ \cup\_\cup\_$$

and the other two in the beautiful choriambic Major Asclepiad line,

$$\cup \ \overset{\smile}{} \ \_\cup\cup\_ \ \_\cup\cup\_ \ \_\cup\cup\_ \ \cup\_$$

this also arranged in couplets in the papyri. His reputation extended across the Aegean, and he was invited to compose a Hymn to the Delphic Apollo. In this he retold, with the licence that was the prerogative of the inspired poet, the myth of the arrival of the god at Delphi, of his sojourn among the Hyperboreans of the uttermost north (in disobedience to the will of Zeus, says Alkaios somewhat surprisingly), and his return to Delphi at midsummer in his chariot drawn by swans, in answer to the prayers of his servants, while all nature rejoices. The nightingales, the swallows and the cicadas sing his praise, the Kastalian Spring flows silver, the Kephissos rises up in waves. The hymn, known to us only in a paraphrase by a late rhetorician, was evidently a highly original composition.[24] Of other hymns to the gods we have some stanzas: to Hermes, in which he seems to have added to the Homeric Hymn's story of the divine infant's theft of Apollo's cattle the tale that while Apollo was rebuking him Hermes abstracted his bow

[24] Himerios, *Oration*, xiv, 1of; text and trn. in Edmonds, pp. 316ff (with one of that scholar's over-venturesome 'restorations'); Page, *S. and Alc.* 244ff.

and arrows[25]; and to the Great Twin Brethren, saviours of men at sea, believed to be manifest in the electric discharge from mastheads and yard-arms later called St Elmo's Fire: 'Leaping upon the mastheads of fine ships, shining afar as you run upon the yards (?), bringing light to the dark ship in the bitter night.' Another poem, striking in quite a different manner, is a dramatic lyric, put into the mouth of a woman in trouble. There is a parallel in Theognis (ll. 275ff, cf. 861ff); if we had more of the early Greek personal poetry we might find such sophistication less strange. As it is, these pieces are unparalleled before the Alexandrian age; a hint of what we lack, through the loss of nearly everything between Hesiod and Aeschylus. The poem was in the 'Ionic' metre, once used by Horace – also, and probably not by accident, about a girl in love; though *his* lyric is not dramatic, i.e. he does not put the lines into her mouth:

> Tibi qualum Cythereae puer ales, tibi telas
> operosaeque Minervae studium aufert, Neobule . . .

Sappho too has some lines put into the mouth of a girl who, like Neobule in Horace, cannot mind her work for thinking of her love:

> I cannot mind my loom, mother,
> subdued by Love's desire.

Was it from a poem that began with her speaking? We cannot say; but there is no doubt about that of Alkaios. Its *first* line ran, 'Wretched I, who not an evil, not a mischance have escapéd.'[26] It is of some interest that the Lesbian like the Megarian gentleman could show this amount of sympathy.

The events that were to upset Alkaios' life had begun when he was a boy, if not before he was born.

Mytilene, as we have seen, was still governed by the Penthilidai, claiming descent from Agamemnon. When opposition developed, their reaction was to deal with it as Odysseus dealt with Thersites, with a stick. But the days when this could be done with impunity were over. A day came when their opponents came out with arms, probably concealed; their leader was one Megakles, otherwise unknown;

---

[25] Hor. *Odes*, I, x, and Porphyrion, *ad loc.*; Page, *op. cit.* 252ff.

[26] Hephaistion, 72; scanty fragments of some more lines, O.P. 1789, schol. on Soph. O.T. 153, Herodian, ii, 941; Edmonds (edn. 2), p. 448, Page, *S. and Alc.* 291ff.

but his name, 'Very Famous', indicates that his parents were people who thought well of themselves. 'Megakles with his friends slew the Penthalidai (*sic*) as they were going about striking people with their clubs; and later, Smerdes slew Penthilos' (presumably a member of the same family) 'after he had been beaten and dragged away from his wife.'[27]

The unrest culminated in the rise of a *tyrannos*, Melanchros; but he was soon overthrown and killed by the nobles. Prominent among these was Pittakos, with his Thracian name, son of one Hyrras, and with him were two elder brothers of Alkaios, Antimenidas and Kikis ('the Strong', cf. Homeric *akikys*, 'weak'). Alkaios mentions Penthiles (perhaps the same) in a morsel of papyrus which adds the words 'for I was still a little child sitting by . . .'.[28]

A somewhat more widely based government, still aristocratic (Archeanaktidai, Kleanaktidai figure in the fragments), now probably held power for some years. Alkaios was grown up when the ranks were closed by the Athenian intrusion on the Hellespont. Pittakos commanded the Lesbian forces, and distinguished himself by killing in single combat the Athenian general, the great athlete Phrynon (named in another papyrus scrap of the poet). But the Athenians held fast to Sigeion, and there was at least one Lesbian defeat, when Alkaios threw away his shield, a mishap which, like Archilochos, he reported in unabashed terms to his friend Melanippos:

> Tell them, Alkaios from the stricken field
> Has come back safe, but not, alas, his shield;
> By now, the tough war-hide that he let fall
> Adorns grey-eyed Athena's temple wall![29]

Finally came the reference of the dispute to Periandros, before whom the Lesbians, probably quite seriously, adduced the evidence of Homer to show that the plain of Troy was ancestrally theirs by right of conquest; to which the Athenians (or Atticans, as they may have been calling themselves for a time just then)[30] replied that they had just as

[27] Ar. *Politics*, 1311b.

[28] D.L. *Pittakos* (i, 74); Kikis (etymology) *Etym. Mag.* 513, 33 (Edmonds, p. 404); Alkaios a child (ref. to this time?), *O.P.* 1234, 6, 7ff (fr. D.17 LP).

[29] Restoration of the fr. from a paraphrase, Diehl, p. 411; fr. Z 105(b) LP; the history see Hdt. v, 95 D.L. *l.c.* and pp. 218ff above; Page, *S. and Alc.* 152ff.

[30] For Attikos as a noun, cf. Alk. *l.c.* with Solon, *Salamis* (*ap.* D.L. *Solon*, i, 2).

good a claim, since there were Athenians in the Trojan War too. The peace, leaving Sigeion itself in foreign hands, amounted to a defeat for the home side, and broke the Aiolic monopoly of landing-places and watering points on the straits. It did nothing, therefore, to allay unrest and before long there was violence at Mytilene once more. A new popular leader arose, one Myrsilos, a Kleanaktid. His name resembles that of more than one Hittite king, over 600 years before; but whether it was really Asian, or a chance resemblance, there is no evidence. What is significant is that Pittakos, who had sworn oaths of alliance at some stage with Alkaios' party, broke off the alliance and gave Myrsilos his support.[31]

Alkaios was naturally furious; he calls down curses upon the 'son of Hyrras' in the name of the gods by whom he had sworn: Zeus; the 'Aiolian mother of all'; and Dionysos (spelt Zonnysos); an interesting triplet; it is rather surprising to find the vegetation-god bracketed with Zeus in the prayers of an aristocratic party so early. What Pittakos might have said about it we naturally do not know; but all that we hear about Pittakos except from Alkaios is to his credit. We may infer that there was more to be said for Myrsilos than for Melanchros, and that Pittakos felt that oaths sworn against Melanchros did not apply against him.

Myrsilos had been in exile at one time, but returned in a small ship provided for him by one Mnamon; Alkaios, rather surprisingly, said in a lost poem that he did not want to quarrel with Mnamon for that; presumably it was before Myrsilos had shown himself dangerous. Now, Alkaios' party plotted to kill him, but the plot was discovered. Threatened with arrest, they fled to Pyrrha, some twenty miles away, on the central 'sea-loch'; so says a note on another almost entirely lost poem.[32] What sort of poems Alkaios wrote there, we do not have to guess; portions remain of his *stasiotika*, 'partisan songs', heaping insults upon his enemies and calling upon his friends to stand fast, play the man, and not be unworthy of their noble ancestors. One or more of them speak of the state or of his party under the likeness of a storm-tossed ship: 'I cannot understand this tumult of winds; the waves come this way and that, and we in the midst are driven onward in our black ship, battling with a monstrous storm. The mast-foot is awash, the sail

---

[31] Alk. papyrus fr. G 1 LP; *S. and Alc.* 161ff; P. allied with Myrsilos, fr. D 12.
[32] Marginal notes in papyrus frags. E 2, V 1 i LP; *S. and Alc.* 179ff.

lets daylight through, there are great rents in it, the anchors drag. . . .'
The metaphor of the Ship of State was a new one then. In another
poem he writes to one Agesiläidas of the miseries of banishment:

> . . . sad indeed
> a boorish peasant's life I lead,
> longing to hear in Square and streets
> ·he Herald's cry, 'Assembly meets'
> or 'Council'; where my father's race
> grew old and had their rightful place
> among these graceless burgesses;
> but I am driven away from these
> and live like Onomakles afar
> in forests where the wild beasts are.

Onomakles must have been some locally famous outlaw or misan-
thrope. After two mutilated lines, containing the words 'war' and
'revolution' (*stasis*), he goes on to describe a country shrine where, he
says, 'I dwell, keeping out of trouble', and adds the interesting detail
that beauty-contests were held there:

> Where Lesbian maids for prize compete
> in beauty, trailing to their feet
> their robes, and women's voices clear
> hallow the feast-day year by year.

The contests, like those in singing and in athletics, are, we see, an act
of worship, offering one's best to God. One would like to know
whether the winners were commemorated by statues.

In Mytilene, Myrsilos provided himself with a bodyguard, the
typical mark of a tyrant, and prepared to deal with the exiles. Presently
he marched against them. 'Between Pyrrha and Mytilene', according
to another fragment of commentary, 'they . . . some of the bodyguard,
as Alkaios says to Bykchis. For Myrsilos . . .'[33]

What did they do to some of the bodyguard? Suborn? Ambush?
And what was Myrsilos doing? We know only the end of this chapter;
Alkaios and his party triumphed once more. 'Now to get drunk,' says
our poet characteristically – Horace translated the opening, *Nunc est
bibendum* – 'for Myrsilos is dead!' There was a triumphant return;
Sappho too may have shared in it and in the previous exile, for the

[33] Lower margin of D 2 (a) LP.

word 'exile' appears in a fragment of hers, next door to 'Kleanaktida(s?)' (Myrsilos?), and in a context in which she seems to be celebrating something.[34]

But there was something lacking to complete the triumph. Pittakos survived. Worse still, the people rallied to him, and a mass meeting elected him Dictator, *aisymnetes*. Alkaios, naturally, used a different word: 'They have set up the low-born Pittakos as tyrant over our gutless and godforsaken city, amid cheers from the crowd!'[35] The low-born Pittakos: and yet his family may have been that of the Archeanaktidai, a sufficiently noble-sounding name, and his father, Hyrras, a 'king', probably holder of a priestly office, in Mytilene.[36] His Thracian (maternal?) ancestry was evidently no bar to this.

Pittakos took effective steps to avoid sharing the fate of Myrsilos. He chased the rival nobles not only out of Mytilene but out of the whole island. Alkaios raved, descending to the verbal resources of a fishwife: among his epithets for Pittakos are splayfoot, potbelly, cracks-between-the-toes, supper-in-the-dark (meaning that Pittakos was too stingy to have the lamp lit) or clean-and-polished, meaning that he wjas neither.[37] But it was no use; the people wanted him.

The ex les scattered; perhaps in defeat they quarrelled. Sappho is said to have gone to Sicily (as we have seen, Lesbos had western connections); Alkaios, now or at some stage in his life, went to Egypt; regrettably, the fragments so far tell us nothing more about his travels.[38] If he joined Pharaoh's 'Ionian' guard, he ran some slight risk of meeting in battle his brother Antimenidas, who joined the Babylonians. However, it did not happen. It was Antimenidas, enlisted under the hard-riding Nebuchadrezzar, who had the adventures, including, probably, the Palestinian campaigns. At some point, the Babylonian sacked

[34] Alk. *ap.* Ath. x, 430a; Sappho (papyrus) fr. 98 (b) LP.

[35] Ar. *Politics*, 1285a, quoting these lines (fr. Z 24 LP), defines an *aisymnetes* as an elected *tyrannos*, and adds later (1295a) that the difference was that he ruled over a willing people. The question whether a given *aisymnetes* was a *tyrannos* therefore resembled the question 'When is a conquest a liberation?'

[36] Marginal note 'Pittakos' opposite 'or Archeanaktid' in the text of a mutilated papyrus (Alk. fr. E 1 LP, lines 23f); but for lack of other evidence, some have supposed that the note refers to something in the next column; discussion in *Sappho and Alcaeus*, pp. 174f. For Hyrras as *basileus*, see schol. on Dionysios Thrax, quoted *op. cit.* p. 170 n. 8; the scholiast notes 'tyrannos'; but in the constitution of Pittakos, the chief magistrate is a *prytanis* and the *basilees* are plural (as in 6th-century Chios, cf. p. 225 above); see Theophrastos *ap.* Stob. *Florileg.* xliv, 22.   [37] D.L. i, 81.

[38] Sappho, Parian Marble, 36 (598 B.C.); A. in Egypt, Str. i, 37. A reference to quarrels that had profited only the enemy, Pittakos, appears in *O.P.* 1234, 2, i; fr. D 12 LP.

Askalon, the spoils and prisoners of which (not necessarily newly taken) are mentioned in a document of 592. It may have fallen in 604, but the name is unfortunately mutilated in the Chronicle for that year.[39] It adds point, in any case, to the appearance of the same name in a papyrus fragment, which preserves the following apparently Asclepiad line-ends:

> sea
> (leave?) to be borne;
> of what was borne
> overtakes
> of holy Babylon
> Askalon
> rouse the grim (battle?)
> utterly.
> and brave man
> (to?) the house of Death
> to devise
> garlands for us
> all these things[40]

In its suggestions of intriguing possibilities, while never once telling us all that we want to know, it is all too typical of the evidence for early Greek history.

At Mytilene, Pittakos ruled firmly and overhauled the laws; he did not alter the form of the constitution.[41] One of the forces which he considered needed curbing was drink; judging by Alkaios, one may conclude that he was quite right. Alkaios, incidentally, had once devoted some verses to the drinking habits of (it seems) Pittakos' father, alleged to have kept it up noisily day and night, drinking neat wine till the ladle was hitting the bottom of the barrel. The better to check violence, Pittakos laid down that offences committed under the influence of drink should be punished doubly – once for the crime, and once for being drunk enough to commit it.[42] He strengthened his position by marrying a daughter of Drakon the brother of Penthilos; gossip said that she looked down upon him and henpecked him.[43] Popular talk could even refer to him as 'king', as in a traditional labour-song:

[39] D. J. Wiseman, *Chronicles of Chaldaean Kings*, pp. 28, 69, 85.
[40] *O.P.* 1233; Alk. B 16 LP.   [41] Ar. *Politics*, 1274b.
[42] Ar. *ib.*; on P.'s father, *O.P.* 1234, 2, ii; D 14 LP.   [43] D.L. i, 81.

> Grind, mill, grind,
> For Pittakos also grinds
> Who is king in great Mytilene.[44]

Whether his 'grinding' was supposed to be metaphorical is, as usual, uncertain. Croesus of Lydia is said to have tried to place him under an obligation with a gift of money, and to have been rebuffed; if there is anything in this story, it is another indication that the traditional chronology, which made Pittakos' 'reign' end fifteen years before Croesus' accession, dates Pittakos too early.[45]

But he had not heard the last of the die-hard exiles. After several years they gathered in Lydia, to make one more attempt, as Alkaios had put it earlier, 'to rescue the people from its troubles'.[46] The idea of 'liberation' willy-nilly is, we observe, not new. Antimenidas was there, displaying a splendid sword of oriental workmanship; a reward for valour presented to him after he had slain a giant, some Goliath or Phrynon, whose challenges to single combat were having a bad moral effect. Alkaios greets him:

> You are back from the uttermost bounds of land,
> With an ivory hilt to the sword in your hand
> Bound round with gold, that in fight you won
> For signal service to Babylon,
> When you killed in combat a monstrous man,
> Who of five king's cubits lacked but a span.[47]

The royal cubit was longer than the standard one, and the giant's stature as alleged would be over eight feet. The 'bounds of the earth', since Alkaios and other Lesbians were well acquainted with Egypt, must be somewhere more remote than Syria; Antimenidas and his comrades must also have campaigned far inland, in Arabia or on the eastern frontiers of Nebuchadrezzar's empire.

Croesus, whether as King of Lydia or still as prince and Governor in the north-west (cf. p. 213) was willing to help; it was his obvious policy to secure a friendly government in the island. To this point in the story may belong the lines:

[44] D.L. *ib.*; Plut. *Banquet of the Seven Sages*, 14.   [45] D.S. ix, 12, 2.
[46] G I LP, line 20.   [47] Z 27 LP; from paraphrase in Str. xiii, 637.

Father Zeus, the Lydians, indignant at these misfortunes, gave us two thousand staters, if we could enter the holy city, though they had never had any service from us, nor even knew us; but *he*, like a crafty fox, chose the easy course and thought not to be found out![48]

The 'fox' is presumably Pittakos, and the allusion will be to the Lydian subsidies proffered to him, an episode on which Alkaios naturally takes a different view from the later Pittakos-saga.

When all was ready, the exiles made their bid; but Pittakos was far too wary to be taken by surprise. Alkaios himself is said to have been captured – and released, for all his insults, with the Pittakeian adage, 'Forgiveness is better than revenge.'[49] Thus Alkaios was able to reach old age, no doubt in reduced circumstances, but in peace. The last glimpse of him that we have is in the fragment

> On my buffeted head pour down the myrrh,
> And on my grizzled breast . . .
> While men drink; trouble . . .
> They gave me, but among others . . .
> Mankind; and he that does not . . . [50]

After this fashion the hand of time quietly fades him out.

Pittakos remained in power for ten years, a long term popular with early Greek states that wanted a strong executive[51]; then, once more surprising his critics, he resigned power and lived, it is said, ten years longer. Voted an estate, he dedicated it as a sanctuary; it was long known by his name. Many adages and proverbs were ascribed to him, including the famous 'Power reveals the man.' 'Asked "What is best?" ' – which seems to have been a question that early Greeks were fond of addressing to a sage – 'he replied, "To do the present thing well." '[52] One saying, which may seem naive to us, puzzled Simonides of Keos: simply, 'It is hard to be good.'[53] For a man who, with honest intentions, had risen to supreme power in times of revolution, it was full of meaning. Again, 'Never announce what you intend to do, or you will be laughed at if you fail.' His is one of the few Greek historical biographies which has a happy ending.

[48] *O.P.* 1234; D 11 LP.   [49] D.S. ix, 12, 3; D.L. i, 76.   [50] *O.P.* 1233, 32; B 18 LP·
[51] D.L. i, 75; cf. Strabo xiii, 617. For long terms, cf. Ar. *Politics*, 1310b (also the ten-year archonship, doubted by most scholars, in early Athens acc. to the chronographers).
[52] Sayings collected at end of D.L.'s 'Life'.
[53] In Plato's *Protagoras*, 339aff.

CHAPTER XIII

Theognis and the Decline of Megara

THERE is no happy ending to the story of another poet whose city was involved in the Hellespontine War: Theognis of Megara. Theognis is not one of the great thinkers, but he did think; sometimes originally though naively, sometimes according to the *mores* of his knightly class. Like Phokylides, a very different character, he is typical of his age. Nor is he one of the greatest Greek poets; but in many of his pieces there is a bitter sweetness that is haunting and attractive. In others, written in defeat, poverty and exile, counter-revolution and revenge, there is only bitterness.

His work, a collection of short elegiac pieces amounting to some 1400 lines, the only 'collected works' of his age to have come down to us, presents a celebrated problem. He is repeatedly quoted by Plato, Xenophon, Aristotle; but all their quotations come from the first third of our text, whereas later Greek writers quote from all parts of it. This looks as if the complete collection had been made later, perhaps at Alexandria; and the appearance in the later part of the book of numerous couplets which repeat or imitate, often in inferior form, lines which occur earlier, would be consistent with the view that an editor or editors attempted to collect Theognis' complete works by adding pieces believed to be his from miscellaneous sources. We cannot be certain, in these circumstances, that everything in the book is really his; but there are no sufficient grounds for denying to him almost everything except the collection of maxims addressed to his friend Kyrnos. In particular, the appearance of fourteen short passages (forty-nine lines) which are also quoted by Greek writers as from other poets (including three passages adapted from Solon, in the early part of our text) is no argument against Theognis' authorship of most of the corpus, or even of these lines. It was, as we have seen already, customary and good manners to quote, adapt and paraphrase other men's lines (pp. 160f, 259f); it was even a compliment, unless severe criticism was implied, to the poet quoted.

Leaving detailed discussion to a note (pp. 258ff), it will therefore be assumed that we have in the book a body of verse mostly, and much of it practically certainly, by Theognis of Megara, dated by the chronographers *c.* 548–540.[1] The political circumstances implied suit Megara in old Greece at this time; and if Plato alone, and censured by his commentator, makes him a citizen of Sicilian Megara, it may be that he was made a citizen there after going to Sicily (as indeed some lines in the collection say), probably as a political exile. Herodotos of Halikarnassos was, we are reminded, often called Herodotos of Thourioi, where he settled.[2]

Theognis' whole life probably fell within the sixth century. It was an age when his city, which had played a distinguished part in colonisation, continued to have achievements to her credit; but, sandwiched between two powerful and aggressive neighbours, Athens and Corinth, she fell on evil days. We cannot confidently associate particular poems of his with events in Megarian history; but that history provides a background against which his poems stand out in gloomy silhouette.

Theagenes the tyrant, about 640 tr., who 'slaughtered the cattle of the rich' (p. 187), had been a popular revolutionary leader. Like Peisistratos at Athens, he obtained a bodyguard from the people, and overthrew the government. His aqueduct, of which some remains survive, bringing water to the centre of the town, provided a necessity rather than merely an amenity to the growing city, and must have been particularly appreciated by the families of the urban poor.[3] But perhaps, like many tyrants, he lost favour through arrogance and self-aggrandisement. Some time after the failure of his bold attempt to secure a friendly g,overnment in Athens by supporting Kylon (p. 286), he was driven out and, according to Plutarch, a 'moderate' (i.e. conservative) government held power for 'a short time'.[4] But (as after Napoleon in France or Cromwell in England) things would never really be the same again. Theognis, a 'knight' and a tory, views the

---

[1] 548 Euseb.; 542 Jerome; Ol. 59 *Suda.*

[2] *Laws,* 630a; censured by Didymos, *ap.* schol. *ad loc.,* who suggests that Th. may have become a citizen of the western Megara.

[3] Bodyguard, Ar. *Rhetoric,* i, 1357b; aqueduct, Paus. 1, 40, 1, cf. 41, 2; illust., e.g., in Highbarger, *History and Civn. of Ancent Megara,* Pl. v.　　　　　　[4] GQ 18.

society of his time with a jaundiced eye. 'Wealth has mixed the breed', he complains; any low-born rich man or rich man's daughter can marry into one of the best families, and it is not in accordance with the principles of eugenics as applied by any stock-farmer.[5] The use of the same word *eugenes*, 'well-bred', of the 'best families' and of the best rams or donkeys, naturally made this conclusion self-evident. That the rich merchants, grandsons of men who took part in opening up the Black Sea, considered themselves as good men as the landed squires, is no less natural. Theognis turns an equally disdainful eye upon the new working classes, 'who in former times knew nothing of justice and law, but were dressed in goatskins and kept outside the city, like deer; and now they are "good men", Kyrnos, and the former nobles are poor creatures now; who can bear to see this?'[6] It is first-hand evidence, all the better for being the evidence of a man who heartily disapproves, that to many poor men, descendants of shepherds and crofters, the new age had brought material betterment: woven clothes instead of skins, and a situation in which, massed in the city and working largely for export, they could venture to stand up to the nobles and talk about their 'rights'; necessarily when trade was slack and landless men faced starvation.

In an extremity, there was one other alternative: to borrow food, or the wherewithal to buy it. Borrowing was all the easier from the arrival of money. Aigina, which struck the first coins in Europe about 625 (p. 178), was Megara's neighbour, and had common enemies in Corinth and Athens, and even her heraldic badge on those coins, a turtle (later a tortoise) was also sacred to the Megarian god or hero Skiron.[7] But with money came the idea of usury. In a trading community no doubt it assisted many an enterprising merchant; but it was a terrible thing for the poor man; for if times continued bad and interest accumulated beyond hope of repayment, the debtor's ultimate pledge in a system of unlimited liability was the labour-power, the actual persons delivered into chattel slavery, of himself and his family. Some, as we read in the poems of Solon of Athens, evaded this fate by running away abroad[8]; but the prospect of going out into the world as a penniless alien, without status or protection, like the beaten men

[5] 183ff.   [6] 53ff.
[7] For the Megarian or 'good' version of Skiron, cf. esp. Paus. i, 44, 6.
[8] Solon, *ap. Ath. P.* 12, 4; lines 10ff.

in Tyrtaios or like Homer's 'displaced person', must have been daunting except to the young, strong – and single.[9] Among the commons of Megara there was fierce resentment against the money-lenders. There was therefore no solidarity between rich and poor in the town of Megara, any more than between 'Knights' and rich bourgeois; rather, indeed, less.

Add to this that Megara's trade-routes were being threatened and her territory cut short by powerful enemies, and it is not surprising if a 'revolutionary situation' developed. With Miletos neutralised, Samos, Athens and Corinth were far too strong for Megara to check. The relief of Perinthos and defeat of Megara's fleet in the Propontis were followed by the loss of Salamis at home; the harbour town of Megara itself, Nisaia, fell, perhaps in the 560's, to the Athenians under their young and dashing general, Peisistratos[10]; though this at least was recaptured when Athens herself was internally divided, by a last effort of the Megarians, to many of whom the loss of the port would have meant starvation. On the other front, the Corinthians at some unknown date pressed their advance right up to the Geraneia range, whence they looked down into the home plain and the very town of Megara; an event to which we have perhaps an allusion in some lines of Theognis[11]:

> How can you play and sing, when eyes can trace
> Our country's frontier from this market-place?
> – The frontier of the land whose acres bear
> The very food you eat, the wreaths you wear?
> Cut your hair short for sorrow! End this play
> And mourn the fertile lands now reft away!

Evidently some people did not take such a serious view of the loss of territory out of sight from the town (beyond Geraneia) as the poet; or else they preferred to drown their regrets and anxieties in wine and song. The poem is not addressed to Kyrnos, but to one Skythes, 'Scythian' (a well-known Greek personal name,[12] and one which might well become established at Megara with her interests in the Black Sea); but both the serious attitude to life and the censorious attitude to people whose standards were less high are typical of Theognis.

The period was not all gloomy; amid the city's reverses there were

---

[9] The *atimetos metanastes* – a displaced person with no one to exact price or *wergild* for him: *Il.* ix, 648; refugees, Tyrtaios, *ap.* Lykourgos, *Against Leokrates,* 107 (frag. 6 Diehl), 3ff.   [10] Hdt. i, 59.   [11] 825ff.   [12] e.g. Hdt. vi, 23f.

also positive achievements. Athens and Samos, amid their own revolutions, did not prevent the last and highly successful Megarian colonising venture in the Black Sea at Herakleia (pp. 120f; 559 tr.). The new colony started its career as a democracy,[13] which is evidence for the political condition of its mother-city at the time; and colonists were contributed to it also by Tanagra,[14] whose coinage starts around 550. Other Boiotians probably also took part. The Boiotian League was a natural ally for Megara against Athens, though not in this century a very successful one.

At home, the democracy of Megara witnessed a significant development in popular poetry: before the Athenians, as their descendants claimed (and Aristotle at Athens does not deny it), Megara developed something recognisable by classical Greece as Drama, comedy.[15] Comedy, 'the song of the village', emerged from the choral dance and song, with which peasants worshipped the vegetation gods, and especially Dionysos, the god perhaps originally of all vegetation, though particularly of the vine.[16] With the dance and song were probably associated, as they certainly were in Attica, satirical or *iambic* recitations, made up for the occasion, in which, with traditional licence and obscenity, people mocked their neighbours, especially (naturally) the prominent; for the spring festival had also the character of a Feast of Folly, when normal respect was laid aside; and obscenity was part of the sexual element in village rites 'for the fertility of the crops and of the people'. It is no accident that both in Megara and in Attica (and later, with Epicharmos, at Syracuse) the rise of the drama from peasant magic to a major art-form in the city comes with the rise of the peasants to full citizenship.[17]

---

[13] Ar. *Politics*, 1304b.   [14] Paus. v, 26, 6.

[15] 'At Megara under the democracy', Ar. *Poetics*, 1447b, 1449a; cf. schol. on *Ethics*, 1123a; introduction from M. into Attica, *Parian Marble*, 39 (between 580–512 B.C.).

[16] Cf. D. Dendrites, Plut. *Table-Talk* (*Mor.* 675f); D. Phloios, 'of the bark', *ib.* 684d; Kissos, 'Ivy', Anthios, 'of the flowers', Myrrhinousios, 'of the myrtle', Paus. i, 31, 4 and 6, in villages of Attica; apples and pomegranates as well as the vine, among his decorations on the Chest of Kypselos, *id.* v, 19, 6; Karpios, 'of the fruit', on an inscr. seen by Leake in Thessaly (*Travels in Northern Greece*, IV, pl. 43); Farnell, *Cults of the Greek States*, vol. V.

[17] While in the villages the peasant ritual, rooted in sympathetic magic, continued; cf. Plut. *Mor.* 527d for the rustic Dionysia in Boiotia still under the Roman Empire; Dawkins in *JHS* XXVI for a detailed account of 'Dionysia' among modern Christian villagers in Thrace (at Viza, anc. Bizye): a masquerade of men dressed in goat-skins (cf. the word *trag-odia*), the parade of a wooden *phallos*, a 'marriage', the 'slaying' of a goatman, keening by his 'wife' (acted by a youth), and his resurrection; after which the mummers yoke themselves to the plough and pray for a good harvest.

With all this Theognis the Tory reveals no sympathy. Zeus, Apollo, Artemis, the Muses and the Graces, the spirits of traditional poetry, are the gods whom he worships; the name of Dionysos occurs once (976), in a poem on wine. Poems of love and wine represent the highlights of his youth, in so far as they are really his; some of the sage advice on moderation at a drinking party has been suspected, on linguistic grounds, of being later (p. 258); and if 'Book II', eighty-four couplets chiefly on the love of boys, is really his in any great part, it is surprising that Athenaios, with his flair for scandal, evidently had not heard of it (p. 262). Any of these that are his own may, it has often been suggested, have been rejected from the collection used as a school-book in Athens; for Athenian bourgeois morality, contrary to much uninstructed opinion, was strict on this subject. (The young men who gathered round Socrates and whom he taught, often in vain, belonged to an aristocratic, 'emancipated', Spartanising set.) Among these poems are the lines of warning to young Kyrnos (1353ff):

> Bitter and sweet and charming and unkind
> Is young love, Kyrnos, in its blossoming:
> Crowned, it is sweet; but if no end we find
> Pursuing, that is life's most bitter thing.

Theognis certainly knew what he was talking about. There is an almost adolescent bitterness of jealousy about some lines in the main collection (599-602):

> Out on the public wagon-way,
> Just as before, I saw you go,
> When first you did my love betray
> – And do you think I did not know?

> Go, and be damned, then, where you must,
> Whom no gods love, nor man can trust,
> And cherish by yourself apart
> The adder's poison of your heart.

But it was the poems of his maturity, also addressed to Kyrnos, that gave his name immortality, and the name of Kyrnos too, as he had promised. The tone of these poems of advice is manly and sincere, though full of aristocratic prejudice; this indeed was one of the things that endeared him to undemocratic circles in Athens. Be slow to speak; moderate in drink; above all things, loyal to friends; but be mistrustful, especially mistrustful of the bad (usually identified with the common people).

> Many are friends in meat and drink; but few
> When there is any noble work to do. (115-6)

Immediately after his introductory prayers and the 'dedication' to Kyrnos he sets out his theme, in lines (27ff) well known to Plato and Xenophon (p. 260):

> I'll give you, as your friend, advice I had,
> Kyrnos, myself from good men as a lad:
> Be wise; and never do a dirty deed
> For honour's or ambition's sake, or greed;
> Attend to that! And never with the low
> Consort, but always with the nobles go;
>
> .   .   .   .
>
> Good lessons come from good men; with the bad
> You'll shortly lose even the sense you had.

With Kyrnos he rode to war (549ff):

> A wordless message wakes the war,
> Kyrnos; the beacon shines afar.
> Bridle the swift-foot horses, ho!
> For now, I think, we'll meet the foe.
> Near and advancing they will be
> If gods are not deceiving me.

So, like Dante, he did his military duty to his faction-ridden city. But he was full of misgivings. Bad leaders, he felt, were arising; the people, whom he so despised, appear on occasion as their innocent victims; he fears a renewed tyranny (39ff):

> The city is pregnant, Kyrnos; I fear that there may be born
> A man to be an avenger of violence, pride and scorn,
> For still the people are sound at heart, but the leaders all
> Have turned aside, and to every evil are like to fall.

He feels that the best potential leaders are not appreciated (233f):

> Kyrnos, a noble man is a rock and a castle wall
> To the witless people; but from them he gets no honour at all.

Like high-minded members of a dethroned upper class in many ages, he is sincerely sorry to see the people putting their trust in plausible, shallow or self-seeking demagogues. Unfortunately, the behaviour of the aristocracy when in power had been such that the people preferred their own leaders at any price. As the 'Old Oligarch' of Athens was to say a century later, 'blowing the gaff' with much urbanity about political realities, 'The people make up their minds that (some low fellow's) ignorance and crudity and loyalty is better for them than a gentleman's nobility and wisdom and disloyalty.'[18]

He was happily married, as two lines (1225-6) testify, not in the manuscripts, but quoted by Stobaios:

> There is no sweeter thing in life,
> Oh Kyrnos, than a loving wife,
> As I myself have proved; and you,
> My friend, I hope shall prove it too.

If we hear no more of his wife, that, in Greece, is not very surprising. But the couplet is a needful reminder (unless someone is to be supposed to have forged it, complete with the name of Kyrnos) that we must not imagine this early Greek society, with its passionate friendships between men and boys, to have been merely rotten with homosexuality; though some circles did become so. There is no doubt, either, about a passionate element in Theognis' own feeling for Kyrnos in their young days; he is quite capable of jealousy and possessiveness; the 'Kyrnos book' itself ends, after claiming to have given the youth immortality ('after all I've done for you!') with the lines (253-4), 'and yet I get not even a little respect from you, but you put me off with words like a child'.

But apart from this, he feels that the world is going bad; 'Hope alone is left' (ll. 1135-6); though in this, indeed, he is only echoing Hesiod's *Works and Days*. He looks back nostalgically to days of relative innocence; the great world has fouled the springs of his youth with its trampling feet:

> A spring rock-shadowed, clear and cold, I knew, and I would think
>   How sweet and good the water, years ago;
> Now it is foul and muddied all; and I will go to drink
>   Another – or the river, far below!

Part of the point is, as A. E. Zimmern pointed out, that Greek rivers, being mountain torrents, usually turgid or dry, do not often give pure drinking-water.

But there was worse to come.

Some time after about 550, the 'bourgeois democracy' of Megara broke down. Debt was widespread. Extremist leaders gained complete control of the Assembly. A measure was passed commanding the refund by money-lenders of all the interest they had ever received; and bands of the poor would invade the houses of the rich and demand to be feasted.[19] An outrage is also reported, in the time of this 'unbridled democracy', against a *theoria*, a band of pilgrims from the Peloponnese on their way to Delphi; presumably the Megarians regarded them for some reason as 'class enemies'. 'They encamped at Aigeiroi beside the lake' (there is no lake in the Megarid now, and the place is unidentified) 'with their wives and children, in their wagons; and the most violent of the Megarians, flown with wine, in their brutality and cruelty rolled over the wagons and pushed them into the lake, so that many of the pilgrims were drowned. The Megarians, such was the disorder in their state, took no steps to deal with the outrage, but the Amphiktyons, since the party was a sacred one, sentenced some of the guilty to exile and some to death; and those descended from them were called "the wagon-rollers".'[20]

It was probably at this time that Theognis with many others lost his lands and was driven into exile.[21]

> I heard the crane a-calling
>   O Kyrnos, calling clear,
> That comes with word for mortals
>   That ploughing time is near;
>   It grieved my heart to hear.
>
> Others my fields have taken;
>   It's bitter thinking, how
> No mules of mine this season
>   Will drag the curvéd plough;
>   For I'm a sailor now.[22]

---

[19] Plut. GQ 18.

[20] *id. ib.* 59. The lake can hardly be, as Dunbabin thought, that near Perachora, for that is not on the way to anywhere except the Heraion; the wagons must have been *en route* for Delphi by land. Possibly it was a sea-lagoon, since silted up.

[21] Cf. Ar. *Politics*, 1304b; no date given, but probably 6th century.

[22] 1197ff; last line corrupt; the reference *might* be to a disastrous trading voyage; but Th. elsewhere manifests great contempt for trade.

Other lines (783ff), if they are his, describe his wanderings:

> I've been to Sicily; the vines I've seen
> Of rich Euboia, and where Sparta stands
> Gracious beside Eurotas' rushes green,
> And everywhere I met with friendly hands,
> Yet got no joy wherever I have been;
> So sweet is home, beyond all other lands.

He may have lived for a time at Thebes (1209ff). Often he groans over poverty, 'worse than death or ague', which to avoid, a man would do better to throw himself upon the sea (173-82, etc.). Friends abroad grew tired of the embittered exile, or at least were not going to involve themselves in a war to restore him; Theognis himself could say (333f),

> In help to exiles, Kyrnos, do not set
> High hopes; once they are home, they soon forget.

From the other side of the picture (209f),

> No loyal comrade can an exile find;
> A thing, even than exile more unkind.

His thoughts grow tougher and more cynical (363f):

> Speak your enemy fair; but when he is at your feet,
> Then offer no excuses, but gather your vengeance sweet.

He prays for vengeance (341ff):

> O Zeus, grant me a favour, Olympian, hear my prayer:
> Grant in return for my trouble a little of fortune fair.
> Grant me death, if I cannot at last from my cares obtain
> Respite, and to be giving instead of receiving pain;
> That would be just. Not a chance of revenge so far do I see
> On the men who have got my possessions and hold them, taken from me,
> Seized by force – while I like a dog got through the ravine,
> Shaking my coat of the wild flood-water in which I have been.
> O God, grant me to drink their blood, and may fortune kind
> Give me this satisfaction of all the desire of my mind!

His prayer seems to have been granted. The democracy at Megara, once launched on the course of satisfying its supporters and financing the state by confiscations, found it all too easy to go on – indeed, difficult to stop; Greek revolutions, not only democratic ones, usually did.[23]

[23] Cf. the very similar rakes' progress of the 'Thirty Tyrants' of Athens, Xen. *Hell*. ii, 3, 12ff, Lysias, *Against Eratosthenes*, 5ff.

More and more angry and embittered men gathered abroad, and the despoiled bourgeoisie, once natural allies of the poor against the squires, became equally natural allies of the nobles against the 'bolshevik' poor. Finally the democracy sustained a defeat, perhaps in a foreign war first, 'through its indiscipline and disorganisation'. The exiles came home in arms and bore down opposition; and a new oligarchy was formed, in which the initial qualification for office was 'to have been with the exiles in the campaign'.[24]

As we should guess from Theognis, they were in no forgiving mood (847ff):

> Stamp on the witless people, and smite with the ox-goad keen!
> Fasten them under a yoke, bitter to bear; for not one
> People, for sure, so fond of a master shall ever be seen,
> No, not in all mankind under the rays of the sun.

('They like it really'!) But reprisals against democrats are not among the traditions that came down to Aristotle and Plutarch.

Theognis and Kyrnos reached old age, if we may so interpret the rather cryptic lines (819f):

> Kyrnos, we've reached the trouble all men pray for;
> So now, to die together's all we stay for!

But there is no peace in his poems; only a gloomy cynicism:

> I do not care, when life is gone,
> What kingly couch they lay me on,
> But that my fate to me may give
> Some good fortune while I live.
> Thorns are as good as softer bed
> To lie upon when one is dead,
> And we'll not know in coffin barred
> Whether the wood is soft or hard.   (1191-4)

Four lines sum up not only his melancholy, but all 'the melancholy of the Greeks'; much quoted, and echoed by Sophocles in his old age in a famous chorus (425-8)[25]:

> Not to be born is best of all for mortal men;
> Never to look upon the blazing sun on high;
> And being born, to pass the gates of Hades then
> Soonest is best, beneath the mounded earth to lie.

[24] Ar. *Politics*, 1300a; again, dateless but probably 6th century.
[25] O.C. 1225 (where a schol. quotes Th.) and often by later moralists; cf. n. 3 above.

THE THEOGNIDEIA

Among the 1388 lines (exclusive of mere repetitions) preserved under the name of Theognis, fifteen passages, fifty-one lines in all, are also quoted by later writers with different attributions.

Since it is impossible to use Th. as historical evidence without taking up a position on this matter, it will be worth while to summarise the facts.

The following are the fourteen alternative attributions:

LINES	ATTRIBUTED TO	BY (AUTHORITY AND COMMENTS)
147	Phokylides	Theophrastos in his *Ethics*, acc. to a schol. on Ar., *N. Eth.* 1129B, where it is q. as 'a proverb'. The schol. himself believes it to be by Th., or a proverb q. by both poets. (The sentiment, 'All goodness is summed up in justice', suits Ph. very well; but this very fact might have led to a slip of memory by Theophrastos.)
153-4	Solon	*Ath. Pol.* 12, with slightly different text.
227-32	Solon	Stobaios, *Fl.* ix. 25; with a slightly different text; as last lines of a seventy-six-line reflective poem.
255-6	?	Ar., *N. Eth.* 1099A, q. as from 'the' (evidently well-known) 'inscription at Delos'. (But the inscr. itself may have used lines by Th.)
315-8	Solon	Plut., *Sol.* 3 (with a γὰρ at the beginning, implying an extract from a longer poem, for Th.'s τοι). Stobaios, *Fl.* i, 4, q. the lines as Th.
472	Euenos	Ar., *Metaph.* 1015A. The line ('All forced action is painful') is from the poem, Th. 467-96, addressed to one Simonides (a common name), on behaviour at a wine-party. Hence Bowra, Edmonds and others assign both this and two other poems addressed to S. (Th. 667ff, 1345ff) to Euenos, finding them linked also by similarities of language, e.g. the conjunction οὕνεκα or τοὕνεκα, found in all three and only once elsewhere in the collection (852, repd. 1038A). But both Ath. (x, 428) and Stobaios (*Fl.* xviii, 14), who q. Euenos four times, assign this poem to Th.
527-8	Besantinos	*A.P.* ix, 118. The name of Bes., attached also to one other epigram in the Anthology, is otherwise unknown.

LINES	ATTRIBUTED TO	BY (AUTHORITY AND COMMENTS)
585–90	Solon	Stob., *Fl.* ix, 25, 65–70 (immediately before Th. 227–32, q.v. above). But two small verbal changes in the Th. version make it stand better as an independent poem, and entirely change the point.
719–28	Solon	Plut., *Sol.* 2; but Th., acc. to Stob., *Fl.* xcvii, 7.
795–6	Mimnermos	*A.P.* ix, 50.
935–8	Tyrtaios	Stobaios; the lines are an extract from a forty-four-line elegy of T., q. in *Fl.* li, 1 and 5. But in the Th. mss. they are prefaced by a couplet, not in T., which entirely alters the sense.
1003–6	Tyrtaios	Stobaios; earlier in the same poem, but again with a change in the sense, this time by the substitution of one word, σόφῳ for νέῳ.
1020–2	Mimnermos	Stobaios, *Fl.* cxvi (*In Dispraise of Old Age*), 34; a fragment, beginning with a pentameter; the preceding lines, Th. 1017–9, should probably go with them.
1155–6	Mimnermos?	Anon., *A.P.* x, 113; Planudes assigns to Th. A prayer not for wealth but for contentment, q. by many late writers, ranging from a schol. on Lucian to St Basil; Stob., *Fl.* ciii, 14, q. as from Th. both this and Th. 1153–4, wishing for wealth *and* contentment.
1253–4	Solon	Hermias on Plato, *Phaidros* 231E. Pl. also q. the couplet in *Lysis*, 212D, without attribution ('The poet who says'). The couplet, 'Happy is he to whom boys are dear' (*or*, 'who has dear children') 'and hoofed horses and hunting dogs and friends in foreign lands', is the only one in 'Book II' (on which see below) attributed to an author other than Th. If it was originally meant to be paederastic (which is not certain), it would not be the only such poem attributed to S.

It is evident that not *all* the rival attributions are themselves given on high authority. The strongest cases for other authorship are those where lines in the Theognideia are adapted from longer poems by Tyrtaios and Solon; and even these may have been deliberately taken over by Theognis. Simonides of Keos quoted Homer, or Solon criticised Mimnermos (pp. 160, 174); and paraphrase, often in a different metre, did not even require acknowledgment. It was a compliment to the poet paraphrased, and the cultivated hearer (rather than reader) who recognised the source had the Aristotelian pleasure of recognising 'that this is that'. It was a usage that must have come down from the still recent pre-literate past, in which the same singer, *aoidos*, the living repository of a community's traditional poetry, was often (perhaps usually) also a composer himself. Among our scanty remains of seventh- and sixth-century poetry we find Alkaios (in Proklos, on Hesiod, *WD* 582ff) turning that passage into Asclepiads; Semonides of Amorgos paraphrasing *WD* 702ff (Clem. Alex., *Strom.* vi, 13 – an important chapter, on what Cl. regards as plagiarism among the pagan poets); Phokylides in turn summarising in elegiacs Semonides' iambics on women (Stobaios, lxxiii, 60 and 61). The list could be prolonged (cf. T. W. Allen's paper, 'Theognis', in *Proc. Brit. Ac.* XX, 1934). The Attic tragedians paraphrase passages from Th. himself (see below); Aeschylus is said in the 'Argument' to his *Persians* to have drawn heavily on the *Phoenician Women* of Phrynichos; Euripides in his satyr-play *Autolykos* paraphrased Xenophanes' diatribe against athletes, and the passages are quoted side by side by Athenaios (x, 413). Even Vergil, faithfully following the traditional custom, is said by his commentator to have introduced into the *Aeneid* many echoes of the earlier Roman historical epics. *Unus qui nobis cunctando restituis rem* is a famous example. If we had more of the early Greek personal poetry, we should no doubt find more examples; though not more in direct proportion, since these examples are preserved, not by chance, but by later scholars who noticed them as examples of borrowing.

It would therefore be in accordance with the practice of his age, if Theognis used and adapted lines of Solon or Phokylides in his own exposition of traditional wisdom for Kyrnos; 'such things' (he says, Th. 28-9) 'as I myself learned from good men as a boy'. Similarly, the line attributed to Euenos *may* have been borrowed by him from Theognis.

But it does not follow that there is nothing in our mss. of Theognis that is not from his hand. Our collection does appear to have grown, to have had additions made to an earlier and shorter book; it is a striking fact that, whereas late Greek writers quote from all parts of our Book I (1-1220), extant quotations by Attic philosophers and moralists are all from the first 500 lines. There are enough of these to make the fact significant.

The following lines are q. by authors before 300 B.C. from Th. by name:

Line   14 q. by Aristotle, *Eud. Eth.* 1243A.

      22-3 q. by Xenophon, acc. to Stobaios, lxxxviii, 14.

      27ff q. by Plato, *Menon*, 95D; Xen., *Mem.* i, 2, 20; *Symp.* 2, 4; and   Ar., *N. Eth.* 1170A, alludes to it.

      77-8 q. by Plato, *Laws* 630A.

      177 q. by Ar., *Eud. Eth.* 1230A (and by many later writers).

183ff q. by Xen. and Ar., acc. to Stobaios (as on 22, above); the
    passage (on eugenics) became a commonplace, and is
    much q. by later writers, often erratically.

425ff q. by Epicurus, censuring the sentiment ('Not to be born is best'),
    acc. to D.L. x, 126; and by many later writers (as on
    183ff).

429ff q. by Plato, *Menon* 95D, contrasting the doctrine (that virtue is
    neither hereditary nor teachable) with that of 27ff (q.v.
    above); also by Ar., *N. Eth.* 1179B.

Two passages from the same part of our text are also q. by Ar. with attribution
other than to Th. (above, pp. 258f); Th. 255f as from 'the Delian inscription',
and 472 as from Euenos.

Probable paraphrases or echoes of Th. also occur in several plays of Sophocles
and Euripides; and these also seem always to refer to the same part of our
text, viz.,

221ff, cf. Soph., *Ant.* 705ff.
255ff, cf. Soph., *Kreousa, ap.* Stob. ciii, 15 (Ar.'s 'Delian inscr.', above).
305ff, cf. Eur., *Elektra* 367ff.
309ff, cf. Eur., *Elektra* 940ff.
425ff, cf. Soph., *O.C.* 1225ff.

On the other hand, from the later part of our text, the phrase 'the razor's edge
of danger' (Th. 557, cf. Soph., *Ant.* 996) is already known from Homer, *Il.* x,
173, and from a famous epitaph of the Persian Wars attributed to Simonides by
Plutarch (*Mal. Hdt.* 39); and the expression 'an ox has set its foot upon my
tongue', i.e. 'my lips are sealed' (Th. 815, cf. Aesch., *Agamemnon* 36), *may* be a
case of use by both poets of a homely proverb, or, it has been suggested, of a
liturgical tag from some mystery-cult. So also in line 17, the phrase *hoti kalon
philon esti* (cf. the refrain in Eur., *Bakchai* 881, 901, *hoti kalon philon aiei*) may be
from a common source; both passages, it will be noticed, come in a Theban
context.

Later Greek writers, in contrast, notably Athenaios and Stobaios, quote from
all parts of Book I; though the favourite quotations continue to be those already
popularised by the Athenian writers. These clearly became commonplaces, and
variant or inaccurate quotations of them are only what we might expect. In
English, 'fresh fields and pastures new', a misquotation of 'fresh woods' etc. in
the last line of Milton's *Lycidas*, is a familiar example.

Even Stobaios and Athenaios did not have exactly our text before them.
Stobaios, out of forty-five quotations, has three couplets (all addressed to
Kyrnos, so probably genuine) which are not in our Th. mss. (printed as lines
1221-6 in modern editions); and Ath. (x, 457B) has a cryptic couplet (printed

as 1229-30 Edmonds) beginning with '. . . for . . .', so that at least one lost couplet must have stood before it. Athenaios also almost certainly did not know our Book II or *Mousa Paidike*, transmitted only in the one good ms., *A*. For he delighted in attributing weaknesses of the flesh, and in particular homosexuality, to famous men of the past, and he did not omit Theognis from this imputation; yet he expresses himself with unwonted reserve, and quotes in support only some lines (993ff) which are at most ambiguous. If he had known Book II, he could surely not have failed to quote it here (Ath. vii, 310).

The *Mousa Paidike*, otherwise unquoted by the ancients and barely preserved, has the strange distinction of being represented by what may be the earliest independent quotation of Theognis. On an Attic vase of about 480, there proceed from the mouth of a bearded man on a dining-couch, as he reaches down to feed a pet rabbit on the floor, the words 'O most beautiful of boys . . .', the beginning of l. 1365; from a couplet which may itself be a parody of 1117f, a couplet in bitter mock-adoration of the God of Wealth (see *Ath. Mitteilungen* IX, pl. 1). On the other hand, it would be naive to suppose that this line-opening could only have been excogitated once in the history of Greek poetry.

We have now to try to account for the absence of early quotations from the last two-thirds of our collection (except for the vase-fragment); and also for the appearance, especially in the last quarter of Book I, of a considerable number of repetitions or adaptations and re-workings of earlier couplets.

Most of our collection shows little trace of arrangement, though sometimes a group of poems on the same subject is placed together (e.g. in 467-510, five poems on the right and wrong uses of wine). A section which does show arrangement is the opening, ll. 1-254, beginning with prayers to Apollo, Artemis, the Muses and Graces, continuing with the 'dedication' to Kyrnos, introducing the poet's name and city, followed by 200 lines of political and social comment and admonition, and closing with the poet's claim that he has immortalised Kyrnos and might have hoped for gratitude. This, with the next 200 lines (about 45-50 separate poems, according to how we divide them; highly miscellaneous, and with only six addressed to Kyrnos, as against twenty-nine in the first section), makes up the part from which the Athenian writers quote. This part, then, may represent the 'Theognis' well-known as a school-book in Athens, being commended to the Athenian leisured and literary classes by its conservative and indeed sardonically aristocratic tone. If, however, the *Mousa Paidike* was known in Athens about 480 (we note that it also contains a couplet attributed to Solon), the poems contained in it would, in the normal course of events, have been likely to be omitted from the selection. This was probably the origin of the semi-detached existence of our Book II.

At a later date, then, some scholars tried to collect the 'complete works' of Th., and one such corpus is that which has come down to us in mss.; Stobaios, we saw, quotes three couplets, addressed to Kyrnos, which are not in our mss.

It was probably easy to collect a considerable body of verse that passed for Th.; he enjoyed fame as a moralist and anti-Jacobin. But it must often have been impossible to distinguish certainly what was really his. Lines addressed to Kyrnos are his, unless we are to suppose what is possible but rather unlikely, that some people deliberately composed pseudo-Theognideia, complete with the dedicatee's name. One *collection*, other than the original Kyrnos-book, seems to have been incorporated; we have what may be a new beginning at 757ff, with prayers to Zeus and Apollo, and lines on the duty of a 'servant of the Muses', *preceded* by lines which could have stood at the end of a collection. Moreover, the two prayers both make reference to the 'Median menace', which a poet who knew something of Ionian history (cf. 1103f, to Kyrnos) might well have felt immediately after Cyrus' conquest of Ionia, *c.* 540.

But there was also an enormous quantity of elegiac poetry in circulation in the Hellenistic world, much of it attached, more or less unreliably, to famous names. Some of it was collected by Meleagros of Gadara in his *Garland* of love-poems. The natural tendency to try to attach anonymous poems to known authors is exemplified in the Palatine Anthology's attribution of many war-memorial epitaphs to Simonides, including some that must date from after his death. We know very little about the conditions under which books circulated in the Greek world; but it is clear that many texts circulated privately, borrowed and copied by those who wanted them; as when Plato depicts some scholars travelling from Klazomenai to Athens to borrow the notebook reported to contain the contemporary notes of a debate between Socrates and Parmenides. Lovers of poetry might possess books, but they kept far less in books and more in their capacious memories than we do. Occasional poetry, including probably most elegiac pieces, in particular must very often have circulated *sporadên*, as the Greeks put it; and if Theognis himself arranged and made available to his friends in writing some collection or collections of his work, it does not follow that *all* he ever composed was so treated. Oral transmission gave every opportunity for misquotation, imperfect memory, or re-use of lines with adaptation to present circumstances; and it seems certain that most of the poems *repeated* with variations, misquoted or adapted, in the later part of our Book I must have been preserved in this way. We should probably imagine our editor adding them to the collection, in his personal copy, for completeness' sake. Sometimes he might well have saved himself the trouble, having written down a better version already; but one has to remember how very much less easy and convenient it was to look up a reference in an ancient roll than in a modern book, even without an index.

There seems, then, to be a strong *prima facie* case for the genuineness of all Kyrnos-poems, and of everything else in the 'school-book', from which we have early quotations; including the lines taken over from Solon. Secondly, it should be noticed that much of the poetry that is genuine beyond all reasonable doubt is also highly personal, referring to particular times and situations; so much so, sometimes, as to make its precise original significance inaccessible to us. Such poems, even if not in the Kyrnos-book or 'sealed' with the name of Kyrnos (*if* that is the meaning of the word *sphregis* in l. 19) are still quite likely to be by Theognis, especially if they fit the circumstances of sixth-century Megara as known to us from Aristotle and Plutarch; though mistaken attribution is always possible. The poems about which we can be least certain are the numerous *gnomai* and admonitions, of applicability not limited to any particular situation, if not addressed to Kyrnos nor found in the first 450 or so lines; for these are the poems which may have been made up anywhere and assigned to Th. because they were thought suitable to his style, like the Persian War epitaphs to Simonides.

The position here adopted on the *Theognisfrage* is thus a moderate conservative one, closer to those of T. W. Allen (in *Proc. Brit. Acad.* XX, 1934) or E. Harrison (*Studies in Theognis*, 1902) than to that of T. Hudson-Williams or J. M. Edmonds among editors or of Sir Maurice Bowra (*Greek Elegy and Iambus*); while I cannot dogmatically reject the possibility of what Sir Maurice believes, that some Athenian poems have been included, and that the Simonides and Onomakritos addressed in some poems are the famous ones, both members of the Peisistratid literary circle. Among 'radical' writers on the subject, I have learned much from Jacoby's interesting and characteristically learned study, printed as a *Sonderausgabe* from the *Sitzungsb. d. Preuss. Akad.*, 1934. I must also express especial gratitude to Mr Douglas Young, poet as well as scholar, and on this subject a conservative, for the loan of an unpublished paper (See now *Miscellanea Critica*, Teubner, 1964, I, pp. 307-390); and for stimulating oral discussion; while not laying upon him responsibility for my own views.

In any discussion of the Theognideia, it is necessary above all to try to put oneself in the position of an editor of poems transmitted orally or in private manuscripts, to which additions might be made by an owner, without necessarily adding details of the authorship of each piece. Such transmission still occurs sometimes in the case of frivolous verses, such as limericks or epigrams. For the things that may happen to a text in such conditions, reference may be made to a scholarly *opusculum* which the learned may find not unstimulating: the edition of the *Balliol Rhymes* by W. G. Hiscock (Blackwell, Oxford, 1939); a collection of rhymes on Balliol College celebrities of the Jowett period, in the manner of an old English masque (the characters introduce themselves), of which twenty-five copies were privately printed (two were known by Hiscock to survive); along with variant versions due to errors in oral transmission or attempted improvement, such as has also befallen some of Edward Lear's limericks, and with additional and later rhymes in the same manner (as it were pseudo-Theognideia), on other Oxford celebrities.

CHAPTER XIV

Sparta and Reaction

THE period of instability at Megara ended with Megara's acceptance of an alliance with Sparta; no date is given, but a probable one is 519, when a Spartan army, the first recorded as operating so far north, was in the Megarid under the young and active king Kleomenes.[1] Sparta had constituted herself, as far as the Isthmus region, the protector of respectable, conservative governments, that is of oligarchies or middle-class 'timocracies' with political rights graded according to property, such as probably existed in classical Corinth. Corinth supported Kleomenes' proceedings on the borders of Boiotia[2]; and the question arises, how Sparta had arrived at this dominant position.

Sparta by this time had become the unique, 'national socialist', military aristocracy at which other Greeks marvelled, and which they sometimes envied amid the frequent instability of their own freer institutions. Weakly babies, who failed to pass the scrutiny of the tribal elders, were exposed to die on the slopes of Taygetos. Boys from the age of seven were brought up in 'packs' supervised by youthful prefects under the general control of a director of education, the *paidonomos*. They slept in dormitories on beds of rushes, which they gathered themselves by the Eurotas; they wore one 'plaid' summer and winter; their food – its staple, a grey porridge, a more ancient confection than leavened bread – was rationed. They used to supplement it by stealing from the farms; if caught, they were beaten – not for dishonourable conduct but for bad scouting. Book-learning was minimal, though they learned to read; but poetry and music – warsongs, marching-songs, and the elaborate choral dancing and song before the gods – learned in the 'pack' and performed competitively on feast-days, made the Spartan gentleman something more than a

---

[1] Thk. iii, 68, 3, cf. Hdt. vi, 108.   [2] Hdt. *ib.*

mere boor. Team fights with nature's weapons and violent team ball games between the 'packs' were part of the training of the future soldier; music and passionate friendships were the sweetening of life, and the desire to shine in the eyes both of people in general and of one's beloved in particular added fervour to the young Spartan's efforts never to fall short of a standard of stoic bravery that flinched from nothing.[3]

The famous contests in endurance of flogging by adolescents have been supposed by some to date only from the Roman Empire, which preserved Sparta as a 'museum piece'; but they pretty certainly existed in classical times, being mentioned by Plato and Xenophon. The form of them then, it seems, was that, at a festival of Artemis Orthia, youths from the older year-classes of the 'packs' snatched cheeses from the steps of the altar, running the gauntlet, at each approach, of guards armed with whips, which they were expected to lay on with their full strength; and the 'Victor of the Altar' – he who succeeded in collecting the most cheeses – gained life-long glory.[4] The origin of the curious custom is lost in the mists of antiquity; but the whipping may well have been in origin both a pre-manhood initiation test of endurance, as in the *Sharo* whipping ceremony, voluntarily endured by youths of the nomad Fulani in northern Nigeria, and also considered to avert the envy of the gods from the community.[5]

In adult life no less, the classical Spartan belonged to the State. He ate in the mess of about fifteen members, to which he was elected at the age of twenty, and which formed his section in the army. Election, carried out by secret ballot in the mess with bread pellets, had to be unanimous; one blackball – a pellet squeezed flat when dropping it into the urn – excluded, and the fear of failing to gain election to such a fraternity, on which his whole civic and social status depended, was

[3] Xen. *Lak. Pol.* ii; Plut. *Lykourgos*, 16-18, *perhaps* from Ar. *Lak. Pol.*, cited in cc. 1, 5, 6, 14, 28, 31 but not here; music, *id.* 21, q. Terpandros and Pindar; porridge, *id.* 12, cf. Ath. iv, 142e, 143a, q. Phylarchos and a comedy of Antiphanes; team-fights, Paus. iii, 14, 8ff, Cicero, *Tusc. Disp.* v, 27/77.

[4] Plut. *Lyk.* 18, Paus. iii, 16, 10, N.D. fr. 114 Mül. = 90, 103 z 11 Jac., Hyg. *Fab.* 261, Philostr. *Apol. Ty.* iv, 31, Tertul. *To the Martyrs*, 4. All these late authors definitely suggest a popular and sadistic spectacle. Bosanquet in *BSA* XII, Rose in *Artemis Orthia* pp. 399ff, point out that the theatre facing the altar is of Roman date. But the cheese-snatching ritual is mentioned by Xen. *Lak. Pol.* ii, 9, and Plato, *Laws*, 633b. Cf. discussions by Michell, *Sparta*, 175ff, den Boer, *Laconian Studies*, 261ff.

[5] K. M. T. Chrimes, *Ancient Sparta*, p. 261; Frazer on Paus. *l.c.*; Grote (II, ch. vi) also compared Red Indian initiations. Fulani, *Sharo*, see *ILN* 1964, p. 485.

among the spurs which would have made the young Spartan rather
die than fail in any way in his youthful training. Each member contributed fixed measures per month of grain, cheese, wine and figs, from
the lands farmed by his helots. The standard food was still the same
grey porridge, but when a member offered sacrifice or had game in
plenty, from the hunting which was the Spartan's chief recreation, he
might entertain the whole mess at home. Conversation was 'laconic',
pithy and hard-hitting; the Spartan had to be able to 'take' chaff, and
nothing said in the mess might be repeated outside. Boys not of
Spartiate descent might, it seems, be admitted to the training, and
thereafter to a mess, through the patronage of noble families; they were
called *kasens* (=Ionic *kaseis*, 'brothers') of the young Spartiates with
whom they had been brought up, or in a slang term *mothakes*, 'upstarts'.
The Spartan military class thus never quite became a caste; but what
were the limits of this outside recruitment, and how numerous were
the *mothakes*, some of whom seem to have come from loyal helot
families, the evidence is lacking.[6] To remind every Spartan of the
obedience that he owed even in the minutest detail, the Ephors annually
proclaimed to all, on coming into office, 'to cut their moustaches short
and observe the laws'.[7] When he died, he was buried simply in his red
military tunic, among twigs of olive. The burial of grave-goods was
forbidden, and no epitaph recording even the individual's name is said
to have been set up, 'except over the grave of a priest killed in warfare,
or a priestess'.[8]

Girls also, we are told, received an athletic training, such as to fit
them to be mothers of soldiers. They ran and wrestled in the open,
gymnai; probably not naked but 'scantily clad' in short 'gym tunics',
like the girl runners portrayed in Laconian bronzes and in a famous
stone statue in the Vatican.[9] Marriage took place when a girl was full-
grown, in contrast to many other Greek states, where it followed soon
after puberty.[10] There was no wedding party. As a *rite de passage*, the
bride wore a boy's tunic and her hair was cut short; the bridegroom
came to her secretly and after dark, and for years afterwards, perhaps

[6] Plut. *Lyk.* 212, to which the numerous 'fragments' in Ath. iv, 139ff add little of
interest. *Mothakes*, Phylarch. *ap.* Ath. vi, 271e, f (who says Lysandros was one); identified
with *kasens*, Chrimes, *op. cit.* ch. iii, 3, pp. 95ff, *The Social Structure of the Agelai*.

[7] Ar. *ap.* Plut. *Kleomenes*, 9.   [8] Plut. *Lyk.* 27; cf. den Boer, *Lac. Stud.* p. 294.

[9] Xen. *L.P.* i, 4, Plut. *Lyk.* 14; dress, Plut. *Comparison of Lyk. and Numa*, 3, q. Ibykos,
Sophokles, Euripides (*Androm.* 598); Thk. i, 6, 4.

[10] Plut. *Comp. L. & N.* 4, *Lyk.* 15; contrast Ar. *Politics*, 1335a.

until the husband was turned thirty and qualified to vote in the
assembly, he visited her only by stealth[11]; chaff in the mess was
probably the 'sanction'.

The date and nature of the revolution which so transformed Sparta
has been and continues to be the subject of endless discussion.[12] The
primitive appearance of the 'men's house' club life, the severe initiation
of the boys, the absence of normal family life and the fact that many
features of Spartan society appear also in Dorian Crete (whence
Spartans said that their institutions were derived) might make it appear
that these institutions were survivals from a state of society which other
Greeks had outgrown; but against this appears to stand the fact that
seventh-century Sparta, with its art, poetry and luxury-imports (e.g.
ivory) appears as a powerful, wealthy, otherwise normal aristocratic
community, which only becomes 'spartan' by a subsequent reaction.
Probably these institutions really are survivals, nevertheless; and we
might find parallels to them if we knew more about other *early* Greek,
especially Dorian, societies. We do find parallels in Crete, where
another aristocratic society dominating a serf population became
'frozen' even earlier (pp. 66ff). Just when much of Greece was
evolving towards the 'modern', classical culture, and probably abandoning many archaic customs, Sparta deliberately re-enforced and
developed them. The reason for the change is to be found in the aftermath of the great Messenian rebellion, after which Spartans realised
that if they were to hold their position as lords, delivered from the
necessity of work for men on the farms and for women at the loom,[13]
the necessary condition was one of constant vigilance and preparedness
for war.

Classical Sparta claimed to be living under the laws of Lykourgos,
of whom the Delphic Oracle had said

> I know not if to hail thee man or god,
> But rather, O Lykourgos, god I bode.

Lykourgos, then, according to this earliest evidence about him, probably was a god; but since he was not among the gods of Homer and

---

[11] Plut. *Lyk.* 15, Xen. *L.P.* i, 5.

[12] Amid the immense literature in periodicals, mention may be made of Blakeway's
review of Ollier, *Le mirage spartiate*, in *CR* XLIX (1932); Andrewes, in *CQ* XXXII
(1938); Wade-Gery in *CQ* XXXVII and XXXVIII (now in *Essays in Gk. Hist.* pp. 37ff);
Hammond, in *JHS* LXX (1950).

[13] Xen. *L.P.* i, 4.

Hesiod, and since many codes of laws were associated with the names of human law-givers, classical Sparta chose to regard him as a man. But his name did not appear in the lists of kings either; a point in favour of the genuineness of these lists, for it surely would have, if they had been concocted in classical times. To which royal family he belonged was disputed, and as to when he lived, men agreed only that it was a long time ago; some said in the ninth century, making him an 'earlier founder' of the Olympic Games, some earlier still, 'at the time of the Conquest'.[14] Antique venerability, that is to say an ancient cult (more ancient than the time at which the rites due to gods and to heroes were differentiated) was evidently the most important thing about him. Presumably he had always been connected with the customs and government of the community; and new enactments may have been successfully fathered on him by the expedient of a leading question to the Delphic Oracle, of the form 'Was this what Lykourgos willed:....?' But for the rest, since the mainspring of Spartan policy was a desire for conservation of what she had, later elaborations could as easily be attributed to him as those of Leviticus and Deuteronomy to Moses.

'Some say', continues Herodotos after quoting the above oracular lines, 'that the prophetess also declared to him the present Spartan constitution' (a Delphic account?); 'but according to the Spartans themselves, Lykourgos as regent for his nephew Leobotes, King of the Spartans, introduced this from Crete. For, as soon as he became regent, he changed all their customs, and provided sanctions against contravention; and then, their military arrangements, establishing the *enomotiai* ('sworn brotherhoods') and Thirties and messes; and also the Ephors and the Elders.'

The *enomotiai*, platoons of thirty-two according to Thucydides,[15] were thus probably the same as the 'Thirties', the smallest Spartan unit. No other Greek army seems as yet to have been subdivided below the battalion level; and the manoeuvrability given by organisation and drill, together with unrivalled morale, rendered the Spartan army long invincible.

Herodotos' 'Spartan account' had thus made of Lykourgos a human law-giver and fitted him into the Agid royal pedigree; though a rival

---

[14] Oracle in Hdt. i, 65; variant accounts of L.'s date and parentage, Plut. *Lyk.* 1-2, q. Simonides, Apollodoros, Xen. (*L.P.* x, 8), etc.; a valuable passage. Thk. (i, 18) dates the *eunomia* '400 years before the end of this war', and does not name L.

[15] v, 68, 3.

version, as early as the poet Simonides,[16] put him in the Eurypontid line. Later writers gave additional details about him as the tradition developed, no doubt in the course of oral instruction for the young, until Plutarch was actually able to write a 'Life' of him; though he was too good a scholar not to know and record the existence of many discrepant details.

Herodotos describes the reform as a transition to *Eunomia*, 'good law' or discipline; for, as Aristotle was to say, *eunomia* does not consist in having good laws on paper and not obeying them.[17] There was a poem of Tyrtaios called *Eunomia*; and from its title, and from the occurrence in it of lines which read like a versified form of the *Rhetra* or basic 'commandment' ascribed to Lykourgos, it is possible to ascribe the decisive adoption of 'good discipline' to the late 7th century.

The *rhetra* itself, preserved by Plutarch, is older. Archaic to the point of unintelligibility in places (a state of affairs accentuated for us by the fact that the manuscripts are corrupt in at least one passage), it looks like a genuine, early 'ordinance' preserved in writing. It was the only one of its kind; for in after years Sparta also attributed to Lykourgos the command NOT TO USE WRITTEN LAWS.[18] In this respect also Sparta appears as turning her back upon a modern development after making early use of it. The text so far as intelligible, runs:

> Having founded a sanctuary of Zeus Syllanios and Athena Syllania [usually emended to Hellanios, Hellania]; having preserved [*or* 'constituted'] tribes and obised [probably 'constituted'] *obai*; having established a Council of Elders thirty with the Chief Rulers; from season to season to hold Apella between Babyka and Knakion: so, to introduce (business) and to dismiss (the people); and [probably, but here the text is corrupt] the people shall have right to reject, and power.[19]

---

[16] See n. 14.   [17] *Politics*, 1294a.

[18] Plut. *Lyk*. 13. 'An act of the Spartan Ekklesia', Wade-Gery, *Essays*, p. 37.

[19] Plut. *Lyk*. 6. Syllanios, -a, is unexplained, but as it occurs twice it is unsound to emend to Hellanios; *potius difficilior*. Hesychios has a form *Skyllanios*, proposed by von Blumenthal in *Hermes*, LXXVII; cf. the sacrifice of a puppy (*skylax*) to the War-God before the boys' team-fight, Paus. iii, 14, 9; but the suggestion is still hazardous. 'Right to reject' translates *antagorian*, as approved by Treu in *Hermes*, LXXVI (1941), Wade-Gery, *op. cit.*, den Boer, *L.S.* p. 154 n. 2; but I do not feel very happy about it; *antagoria* is a rather abstract word for archaic Sparta. The mss. have the unintelligible γαμωδανγοριαν. —'Miss Jeffery suggests the rhetra purports to be an oracle of the founders' time (which would account for Xenophon and maybe more), *archagetai* being the original kings who led them to Sparta. I rather like the look of this.' - A.A.

Plutarch explains *obai* like tribes, *phülai*, as divisions of the people; Chief Rulers, *archagetai*, the two kings; *Apella*, the Assembly, held, Aristotle said, between the brook Knakion and the bridge of Babyka, in an unadorned open space later known as Oinous.[20]

Rhetra, etymologically simply a 'pronouncement', from the root *rh*, 'say', signifies in its next oldest appearance the treaty of peace between the Eleians and their neighbours, the Arkadians of Heraia (p. 277). It may have the same significance here. It regularises the position of Kings (not called kings), *Senatus* of twenty-eight members beside the two 'Chiefs', and Assembly; it provides for the holding of statutory meetings of the latter in a specified place (not somewhere inconvenient of access) and recognises the people's right to reject proposals; and its date, before the reign of Theopompos, who lived eight generations before the invasion of Xerxes, takes us back to the epoch when monarchies were disappearing from the progressive parts of the Greek world, or being temporarily preserved, as by Pheidon of Argos, by a strong hand.

As often, notably in the Roman Republic's 'Struggle of the Order', the enactment of a reform was followed by a reactionary move to reduce its effectiveness. The Spartan Apella had not secured, and never did secure, the right of initiative. Plutarch continues: 'And when the people were assembled, no one else was allowed to make a proposal, but the people had sovereign power to judge the proposal put forward by the Elders and the Kings. Later, however, when the multitude were distorting the proposals by excisions and additions, the kings Polydoros and Theopompos wrote this amendment into the *Rhetra*:

But if the people pronounce[21] crookedly, the Elders and Chief Rulers shall be dismissers

– that is, not ratify the business, but withdraw and dismiss the assembly, as perverting and changing the proposal contrary to what was best. And they secured support for this, claiming that this was the God's command, as Tyrtaios seems to commemorate in the lines

> Thus from Apollo's oracle they heard
> And brought from Pytho his prophetic word:
> The god-appointed Kings, who love the land,

[20] *Ap.* Plut. *l.c.*
[21] Keeping ἔροιτο, the ms. reading, and translating '*say*' (not 'ask'); some texts emend, ἔλοιτο, 'choose'.

> Shall lead in council; next, the Elders stand,
> And after them the Commons of the state,
> Returning answer back with *rhetras* straight.'

Diodoros, who gives lines 3ff with a different initial couplet, and represents them as the original oracle given to Lykourgos, adds four more[22]:

> Good shall they speak, and all things rightly do
> Nor for the city counsel ought untrue;   [*This line mutilated.*]
> The people shall prevail, and power shall be
> To them; for thus Apollo did decree.

Diodoros is a poor source, but it will be seen that he does here make the poem end, like the prose *rhetra*, with emphasis on the decisive power, *kratos*, of the *demos*.

Theopompos, like the Roman aristocracy, saw that all was not lost so long as *demos*, having the last word, did not have the initiative too; business could almost always be arranged and presented by the kings, with the assistance of twenty-eight old men of ancient families, to such purpose that a well-timed mass-meeting, addressed by members of the government only, would give the desired plebiscite.[22a] He did, however, have to agree to another guarantee of popular rights, which was ultimately to change the balance of the constitution; the election of the annual *ephors* or 'overseers' (of what the government was doing) by the people and from among the people, to see that the government of the people was not flagrantly arbitrary. Monthly they received an oath from the kings, that they would govern according to the laws; and in return, they gave only a conditional oath: that *so long as* the kings obeyed the laws, they would vouch for it that the people obeyed the kings.[23] This was the reform, on which Theopompos' wife was said to have chid him, for consenting to hand on the royal power to his son less than he had received it; and the King to have replied laconically, 'It'll last the longer' (p. 28). The story is *ben trovato*. Actually, no early poem or document is quoted as mentioning the ephors. Their importance in Theopompos' time was still secondary. Writers of the Roman period compare them to the tribunes.[24] The kings at this time were still the government; and the ephors, like a

---

22 D.S. VII (Exc. Vat.), 12. 6.   22a For this power of the elders, cf. Plut. *Agis.*, 11.
23 Xen. *Lak. Pol.* xv, 7.   24 Cicero, *Rep.* ii, 33, *Laws*, iii, 7; Val. Max. iv, 1.

mediaeval House of Commons, were far from being what they afterwards became.

This, then was the 'mixed constitution' whose bonds the Spartans drew tighter after the great Messenian rebellion. They probably accentuated the rigours of their education, or rather military training. They adopted no more written laws, thus leaving the more discretion to judicial authorities, of whom the highest were the kings and senate.[25] By making full citizen rights depend on membership of the regular army and therefore of the Messes, so that no Spartiate could practise in business or trade, they stopped for ever the rise of a Spartiate *bourgeoisie*. A hexameter line, attributed to Apollo, had declared, 'The love of wealth alone shall ruin Sparta.'[26] The new Sparta set her face against even the possession of the new, coined silver and gold, and kept for her sole currency the old, iron currency bars, such as Pheidon of Argos had dedicated in the Heraion (p. 178); a 'money' so bulky that 'a thousand drachmas worth would be a wagon-load'.[27]

But the reforms did not, as we have seen, prevent boys of other than old Dorian families from being introduced, through Spartiate patronage, into the boys' 'packs' and the men's messes, and so into the body of soldier-citizens; and this raises the question of what the constitutional status of such citizens was. It may be that to provide citizen units, parallel to the Tribes, for such 'plebeian' soldiers was the function of the otherwise mysterious *Obai*. Etymologically, the word may mean 'groups of kinsmen'[28]; but the *obai* known to us from inscriptions of the Roman Empire seem to be local. Of seven names known, four are those of the villages which had grown together into the town of Sparta, Konooura, Mesoa, Limnai, Pitane; one is that of Amyklai, early incorporated[29]; one, that of the Neopolitai, may have been a later creation, and the last, the *Oba Arkalon*, perhaps not Spartan but a community of the Lakonian *perioikoi*.[30] It may be that, under the *Rhetra*, all Spartan soldiers, whether members of old Spartiate families

[25] The kings, only as presidents of the Gerousia, except in specified cases affecting the family (and so, titles to property) and public highways: Hdt. vi, 57; the Gerousia was the homicide court, Ar. *Politics*, 1275b.

[26] Ar. *Lak. Pol. ap.* schol. on Eur. *Androm.* 446, Zenob. ii, 24, etc. (fr. 544 Rose).

[27] Xen. *Lak. Pol.* vii, 5, Plut. *Lyk.* 9.

[28] As argued by Beattie in *CQ* XLV (N.S. I), p. 48. (But ὠϜά, 'village', is better supported, by numerous Hesychios glosses – A.A.)

[29] The 'Ball-game Players'' inscrs., *IG* V, i, 674-687, and 26 (Amyklai); cf. Paus. iii, 16, 9; Ehrenberg in *PW s.v. Oba.*

[30] *SEG* XI, 475a; discussed by Beattie, see n. 28 above.

and of the Dorian *phülai* or not, were made members of the obes, and that membership of an obe gave, at the age of thirty and after passing through the training, membership of the Apella. All members of the Apella elected and were eligible as ephors; and this, comments Aristotle, together with the right of electing the senators, left the obscurer citizens content[31]; content, we may conjecture, to accept the Amendment of Theopompos and Polydoros, leaving initiative to the Government, as against the more prominent citizens who might have ideas of their own.

Polydoros was also credited with a redistribution of the land, adding another 3000 estates, *kleroi*, to an original 6000 ascribed to Lykourgos.[32] This would represent the distribution of the lands of Messenia and, together with the colony at Taranto (p. 77) satisfied Spartan land-hunger for a long time.

Meanwhile the old families retained the right of eligibility to the Senate. Twenty-eight men over sixty, elected for life – so that some would always be decrepit – must have made up a less formidable body than a larger council would have been; but they naturally acted as a sheet-anchor of ancient custom. The method of election was by acclamation; a group of judges, shut up in a building near by, was required to judge which cheer was the loudest, when the names of candidates were proclaimed to the Assembly in an order unknown to them.[33] 'A childish method', says Aristotle[34]; and, we may add, primitive, like so much else at Sparta. It resembles the proceedings of tribal meetings observed by anthropologists in Africa and the Pacific, in which voting does not occur, but discussion proceeds until a 'sense of the meeting' is reached, or, as it has been less kindly put, until a majority shouts the opposition down.

Such, then, seems to have been the development of Sparta's constitution. It does not follow that the three Dorian tribes were abolished, though evidence is lacking[35]; but it is noteworthy that King Kleomenes at the end of the sixth century disowns any narrow Dorianism. A revolutionary monarch, it is perhaps not surprising if he felt more at home in Arcadia than in conservative Sparta; but he also stressed (as a Herakleid) his Achaian, not Dorian, ancestry, when the priestess told

---

[31] *Politics*, 1294b.   [32] Plut. *Lyk.* 8.   [33] *id.* 26.   [34] *Politics*, 1271a.
[35] Chrimes, *Anc. Sparta*, pp. 306-19, criticising the views of Wade-Gery in *CAH* III, 558ff.

him that Dorians were not admitted to the Temple of Athena at Athens.[36] The invincible, early-classical Spartan army was not based on the three tribes; but neither was that of classical Argos, where the Dorian tribes certainly still functioned.[37] Sparta, like Argos, had five regiments, until a further reorganisation in the fifth century; and they were probably at one time local. Herodotos, who had been at Sparta and was a good observer though not a military man, calls one of them 'of Pitane'; and Pitane is the name of a Spartan village, and of an *oba* (p. 27). For this he is censured by Thucydides, who *was* a military man, and had also visited Sparta; but it seems rather likely that Thucydides, who adopts a somewhat feline attitude towards his predecessor, is being pedantic.[38] Local recruitment cannot have remained a binding practice, in view of the system of election to messes and the adoption of *kasens*; and also certainly the *names* of the five early-classical regiments were different. They are given by late scholars, perhaps drawing on Aristotle, as Edolos or Aidolios, Sinis ('Ravagers'), Arimas or Sarinas, Messoages ('Centre-breakers', perhaps, rather than the *v.l.* Mesoates, from the name of the village), and Ploas, perhaps 'Sea-farers'; such a name may seem surprising, but early Sparta had some sea-power, and had at least once captured an island, that of Kythera, from Argos.[39] Later the district of Skiritis, round the headwaters of the Eurotas, was incorporated, and its men given the honourable status of a separate 'highland' battalion, with the dangerous privilege of going 'before the Kings' and doing advanced-guard work.[40]

There is thus nothing in the early 'mixed constitution' that need have prevented Sparta from developing otherwise than she did. For the origins of spartan Sparta, it is reasonable to look to the aftermath of the rebellion and to a tightening of discipline, the *Eunomia* for which Tyrtaios pleaded. If so, it was two generations (which indeed is natural) before the full effects of the change had worked themselves out in culture and in society. Sparta did not intentionally turn her back upon

[36] Hdt. v, 72.
[37] *IG* IV, 517 (Solmsen, *Dialektinschr.* no. 26); casualty-list, ed. Meritt, *Hesp.* XIV; Thk. v, 72 (the 'Five Lochoi', plus an élite 1000).
[38] Hdt. ix, 53; Thk. i, 20, 4 (cf. Gomme, *ad loc.*). Hdt. knew people at Pitane, cf. iii, 55.
[39] Schol. on Thk. iv, 8, and on Aristoph. *Lysistr.* 453; Ar. q. on this subject by Hesych. *s.v. lochoi,* Harpokr. *s.v. moron*; Chrimes, *Anc. Sparta,* p. 315nn. Kythera, Hdt. i, 82.
[40] Thk. v, 67, Xen. *Lak. Pol.* xiii, 6, *Kyroup.* iv, 2, 1; Geyer in PW *s.v.* Skiritis; Michell, *Sparta,* p. 250.

art and poetry, but only upon those things, new or old, that made for weakness or 'decadence'. Her fine pottery continued to be produced and exported until about 550. The generation of 600 was the age of Gitiadas, poet and sculptor, and architect of the splendid new Temple of Athena, the House of Bronze, named from the bronze plates that sheathed its walls. (Remains of them, and of the nails that fixed them, have been found.) The new (second) Temple of Orthia was built about 585.[41] Nor was the Spartan army immediately as invincible as it afterwards became. In the time of Kings Leon and Agesikles, according to Herodotos, i.e. *c.* 580-560, it suffered defeat, its last defeat for a long time, before the new walls of Tegea (p. 184).[42]

Sparta, indeed, with two-fifths of the Peloponnese subject to her, was at full stretch to hold it; victory at Tegea, with yet more serfs, might have been more disastrous than defeat. Defeat sobered her, and under the next pair of kings, Anaxandridas and Ariston, there was a change of policy. The famous Chilon, numbered among the Seven Sages, was Ephor in the year 556-5 tr. (p. 207); with him the ephors appear for the first time not merely as a check on the kings, but as directing policy with them. Chilon was reputed author of the famous proverb, Nothing Too Much (p. 208). He disliked the sea, and regretted the existence of Kythera[43]; and from his time Sparta called a halt to her attempts at conquest. To Tegea (after another and more successful war, or so the Spartans said) she granted free alliance, no doubt on the terms that she should 'have the same friends and enemies'; and Tegea became, with few interludes, her loyal ally for 200 years.[44]

But to acquire no more serfs was only the negative side of a policy. Rich in land, and so vastly outnumbered by their subjects, the Spartans dared not tolerate potentially dangerous neighbours. Like other 'sated powers', Sparta embarked on her classical foreign policy, in quest of security. Forswearing further attempts to conquer the Peloponnese, she set herself to lead it. Argos, deprived long since of the coast east of Parnon, must have looked with alarm on the alliance with Tegea. About 546 tr., war broke out over the border district of Thyrea. There was an attempt at limitation of armaments; 300 champions from each side were to engage in the ordeal by battle; but after the mutual

[41] Paus. iii, 17, 2 and 18, 8; Lane in *BSA* XXXIV.
[42] Hdt. i, 62; Paus. viii, 47, 2.
[43] Hdt. vii, 235; Chilon had reason, cf. Thk. iv, 53ff.
[44] Hdt. i, 67.

slaughter of nearly all the combatants had led only to a disputed decision, a general battle took place after all.[45] Thoroughly beaten, Argos was tamed for a generation. Sparta gained Thyrea, her last annexation, and made lasting alliance with Phlious, Epidauros, Hermione and Troizen, the neighbours over whom Argos aspired to rule.[46] In Arcadia too, her new policy towards Tegea enabled her to gain further allies. The eternal neighbourly enmity between Tegea and Mantineia made it difficult to be friendly with both at once, but at least both were never hostile at once.[47] Beyond Arcadia, Elis, having shared common enmities, was a natural ally; she aspired to dominate the Arcadian-speaking 'Three Peoples' of Triphylia on her southern borders; and, perhaps about the time of Sparta's peace with Tegea, she similarly came to terms with the north-west Arcadian Heraians. A bronze tablet came to light long since at Olympia, naive and archaic, a precious document[48]:

> The *Rhatra* of the Waleians and the Heraians. There shall be alliance for a hundred years, and it shall begin this year. If there be need, either in word or deed, they shall stand by each other in all things, including war; and if they do not stand by each other, those who do the wrong shall pay a talent of silver to Zeus of Olympia for his service. And if anyone deface this writing, whether tribesman(?) or official or community, they shall be liable to the sacred fine written herein.

The Peloponnesian League, that fought the Great Persian War, was taking shape. From it, sea-board Achaia behind its mountains was deliberately omitted. But the Isthmus cities, where 'tyrannies' had overthrown the aristocracies, presented a problem. Spartans could not but feel that these revolutionary monarchies set a bad example. Pheidon of Argos, Aristokrates of Orchomenos, Pantaleon of Pisa had been enemies to Sparta and to her friends in Elis. Also, all tyrants had enemies; if not the nobles as a class, then particular nobles who might appear as rivals. Accordingly, from every city under personal rule there were exiles who had escaped from fear of execution; aristocratic gentlemen, whom, if they visited Sparta (as Theognis may have done) Spartiates could recognise as kindred spirits, and who could promise

---

[45] Hdt. i, 82.
[46] Hdt. ix, 28, Thk. v, 55ff and Xen. *Hell.* iii–v *passim.*
[47] Cf. Hdt. ix, 35, Thk. iv, 134, v, 55ff, Xen. *Hell.* vi, vii.
[48] In the B.M.; Tod, *GHI* no. 5.

the friendship of their cities if only they and their like were restored to power and to their property. All motives concurred; Sparta adopted as a policy hostility to tyrants within her sphere of influence. Among the first to feel her hand was Aischines, last of the 100-year-old dynasty at Sikyon.

'Chilon the Lakonian, who had been Ephor and general, and Anaxandridas' (thus says a papyrus fragment) 'suppressed the tyrannies in Greece: at Sikyon Aischines, at Athens Hippias the son of Peisistratos....'[49] Here the fragment ends. Its last clause is anachronistic; Hippias (pp. 312ff) belongs to the generation after Chilon, and his father Peisistratos, sagacious and diplomatic, from without the Peloponnese maintained friendly relations with both Sparta and Argos.[50]

Plutarch, perhaps drawing upon the same source as the above, mentions the Spartan suppression of Aischines (otherwise unknown to us), the sons of Peisistratos, a number of more distant dynasts whose fate probably belongs to the history of the Persian Wars, and also (first in his list) the Kypselidai of Corinth and Ambrakia.[51] Psammetichos, the nephew and successor of Periandros, fell, after three and a half years in power, in 581 tr.; the date is almost certainly much too early (p. 405).[52] No one else however mentions this as a case of Spartan intervention; and Nikolaos says that Psammetichos was killed by an internal conspiracy. Thucydides, followed by Aristotle, merely says, 'Most of the last tyrants were put down by Sparta'; and a Corinthian speaker in Herodotos, (upbraiding the Spartans for proposing an action contrary to this policy), 'Truly heaven and earth shall change places, and men shall live in the sea and fishes where men lived, if *you*, Spartans, propose to suppress republics and restore tyrannies in the cities.'[53]

Corinth in any case became, as we have seen, a respectable, perhaps rather dull, middle-class republic (p. 194). The advisory Council of Eighty (*ib.* n. 44) probably, as at Sparta, prepared business and invited the Assembly to pass it.[54] No inscription, in spite of much excavation, has shed light on classical Corinth's administrative arrangements.[55] It

[49] Rylands Papyrus 18: Bilabel, *Klein. Historikerfragm. aus Pap.* no. 1; Leahy in *Rylands Library Bulletin*, 1956.
[50] Hdt. i, 61, v, 63, *Ath. P.* 17, 4, but cf. 19, 4.   [51] *Malignity of Hdt.* 21.
[52] Ar. *Politics*, 1315b, cf. Sosikr. *ap.* D.L. i, 95.
[53] N.D. fr. 60; Thk. i, 18, 1; Ar. *Politics*, 1312b; Hdt. v, 92a.
[54] Cf. A. Andrewes' inaugural lecture, *Probouleusis*.
[55] Cf. the meagre fragments in *Corinth*, VIII, ed. Meritt; and contrast the great increase of Athenian inscrs. after 461.

was not the habit of non-democratic states to put up the laws in public (p. 224).

Socially, Corinth was a business men's society. Herodotos notes that no other city in Greece was so free from snobbery at the expense of the artisan or craftsman; Sparta, on the other hand, he found to be the place where these were most despised.[56] Nevertheless, or rather the more because of this very contrast, Corinth and Sparta long remained firm allies. It was partly because of the common enmity with Argos, which Sparta even at the height of her power never tried to destroy; perhaps on a long-sighted calculation that she thus secured the loyalty of all Argos' neighbours; but it was also *because of the contrast*. 'Two of a trade never agree' was the gist of a Greek proverb[57]; and if Corinthians, in face of Argos and (later) Athens, had to lean upon someone, they preferred the strange, dedicated men of Sparta, whom they did not aspire to emulate. 'If you will not protect our interests,' said a Corinthian speaker at Sparta on another occasion of conjugal exasperation, 'we shall have to look elsewhere; but we could never find other leaders as congenial as you.'[58]

Corinth about 550 was beginning to feel the trade rivalry, though not yet to fear the power, of Athens, still under her pacific and popular *tyrannis*. Athenian art was advancing to new conquests, and the fine Athenian black-figure pottery was pouring into Corinth's ancient markets in the west, even to Etruria. In vain Corinthian craftsmen, departing from the old 'orientalising' style, which they had so much debased (p. 193), imitated Athenian work. Corinth's inspiration was gone, and before the end of the century she gave up the struggle. Her vase-painting died (a curious fact) in the same generation as that of Sparta, where the collapse is, perhaps over-glibly, usually attributed to the Eunomia. Yet Corinth was not wholly given up to philistinism. The dignified Doric Temple of Apollo, whose ruins are among the best-known in Greece, dates, it has been proved by the Late-Corinthian pottery fragments found in its foundations, not to the time of the spectacular tyranny, but to that of the republic, about 540.[59]

How far Sparta's claim to be 'liberating' Sikyon or Corinth from oppression could have been justified is an unanswerable question;

[56] ii, 167.
[57] Hes. *WD* 25; q. by Ar. *Politics*, 1312b.
[58] Thk. i, 71, 4; on Sp. as acceptable leaders, cf. Xen. *Lak. Pol.* xiv, 6; Plut. *Lyk.* 30.
[59] S. S. Weinberg in *Hesp.* VIII, 191ff.

Greeks at the time would have disagreed about it no less than later
ideologists. The later literary tradition, predominantly upper-class, is
all for Sparta and against the tyrants; and its prejudice was not baseless.
It may well be that the *tyrannis*, having broken the power of the
aristocracies and held sway for two generations or, as at Sikyon, three,
had completed its mission. Also, as classical writers are never tired of
pointing out, unbridled power in the hands of individuals seldom failed
to corrupt. Many tyrants or their relatives, like Thessalos at Athens
(p. 320), indulged their sexual passions; or their passions and their
tongues, like Periandros of Ambrakia (p. 195); and 'a man will buy
revenge with his life'.[60] The trouble about Sparta's influence was that
having liberated, she did not leave her allies truly free, but, from fear
of her own disinherited subjects, discountenanced democracies. The
sequel was a lack of enterprise in the Peloponnese; its only major
contribution to classical civilisation was sculpture – at Argos.

Sparta as we have said (p. 276) did not deliberately turn her back
upon art. She had several sixth-century sculptors, said to have learned
their art initially from the Cretans, Dipoinos and Skyllis (p. 199):
Hegylos and his son Theokles; the brothers Dorykleidas and Medon;
Syadras and Chartas.[61] There were many works ascribed to them at
Olympia, where Spartan athletes in the century 684-580 (tr.) had carried
off an unrivalled series of victories in the games.[62] Now at the height
of her power, she adorned her sanctuaries with unsurpassed splendour.
At Thornax, north of the town, the Spartans dedicated a colossal
bronze Apollo, which they planned to sheathe throughout in gold.
They sent to Sardis to buy it; and King Croesus, over-estimating the
potential value of a Spartan alliance, gave them all that they wanted.
With this, perhaps more than they had expected to afford, they perhaps
changed their plan and used the gold to cover an even larger statue at
Amyklai, to the south; Pausanias the traveller estimated it as 45 feet
high; standing, helmeted, and holding in its hands spear and bow. But
the quality of their work was already beginning to fall behind. Pausanias, who was not unsusceptible to the 'aura of divinity' of archaic
works, did not think much of this one.[63] He does not name its artist,
and comments that 'apart from its head, hands and feet, it is like a pillar

---

[60] Ar. *Politics*, 1312b (end); cf. 1311a (end), 1314b; Hdt. iii, 80.
[61] Paus. v, 17, 1-2; vi, 4, 4; 19, 8 and 14 (where 'Dontas', mss.; Medon em. Robert).
[62] See Clinton, *FH sub annis*, mostly from Euseb.
[63] Hdt. i, 69; Paus. iii, 10, 8; 19, 2.

of bronze'; and the Apollo at Thornax resembled it. He admired more the 'Amyklai Throne', really a row of thrones which stood behind the statue; it was adorned with a wealth of rather indiscriminately chosen scenes from mythology on panels of bronze, and it was the work of an Ionian artist, Bathykles of Magnesia.[64]

There were works of Gitiadas also at Amyklai; but after Bathykles we hear only of foreign artists at Sparta; she was still proud to commission great sculptors. Klearchos of Rhegion (*c.* 520?) was credited with the bronze 'Zeus the Highest', near the Bronze House of Athena; Kallon of Aigina (*c.* 480?) and the great Polykleitos, though an Argive (*c.* 430?), were to work at Amyklai.[65] But under the developed Spartan system no citizen artist could be produced, and the *perioikoi*, cut off from the outside world by the frequent 'expulsions of aliens', *xenelasiai*, were limited to a provincial, rustic culture. Laconian bronze work continues into the fifth century, but with ebbing inspiration.[66] Sparta produced no prose literature, no poet of any note after Tyrtaios. She imported no more ivory; the votives from the second temple of Orthia are of lead or bone, and, whether from lack of ready money or from deliberate choice, alone among the greater Greek cities she never followed Athens, the 'school of Hellas', in providing herself with a classical 'town centre'. Thucydides comments in a famous passage:

> If Sparta were to be depopulated and only the temples and foundations of the buildings left, posterity would never, I think, believe in later ages in the reports of her fame, . . . because she has no fully built-up area nor elaborate temples and buildings, but only a group of villages in the old Greek manner; . . . but if Athens suffered the same fate, men would infer that her power had been twice as great as it really has, because of what their eyes could see.[67]

But Plato, out of temper with the Athens of his own day and with its realistic 'wax-work' art, admired Sparta and even Dorian Crete because their peoples had achieved stability. It is a Spartan and a Cretan who take part, along with the 'Athenian stranger' who represents Plato himself, in devising the idealised oligarchy of his *Laws*; and

---

[64] Paus. iii, 18, 9 to 19, 1.
[65] *id.* iii, 18, 8; cf. Wade-Gery, *CAH* III, 564.
[66] W. Lamb, *Gk. and Roman Bronzes*, pp. 90, 150f. W. L. Brown on *Archaic Pelopn. Bronzes* (read to the Hellenic Society, London, 20 June, 1958) identifies the great crater found at Vix, France (*The Times*, 15 June, 1953, etc.) as well as those at Trebenishte (cf. Payne, *Necrocorinthia*, 216ff) as products of the Spartan school; Brown dates the Vix *burial* shortly after 500, that at Trebenishte a little earlier. [67] i, 10, 2-3.

Pindar too (admittedly, he composed for any patron who would pay him) praises the city as renowned for 'the counsel of elder men and the spear of the young, and choral dance and music and *aglaia*'; a word which one might translate 'the glory of life'.[68]

Not 'puritanism' is the word to describe the spirit of classical Sparta, but perhaps, in the Churchillian sense of the word, 'austerity'; a proud austerity. The city or group of villages, with many trees growing between the wooden houses, like the great planes that surrounded the boys' riverside 'battle-ground',[69] the 'gracious city' (*aglaon astu*) of a Theognideian poem (p. 256), might look rustic to an Athenian, but it was a home that Spartans could love, even if, under a Lycurgan rule, no tools but the axe and saw might be used in house-building.[70] It was not only, as enemies said in mockery, that the unpleasantness of their life made Spartans willing to die in battle, nor only that war, to which Spartans went as to a festival, was a relief from the horrors of peace.[71] Spartans loved their way of life. The long hair that they combed like dandies, the red, uniform tunics that 'would not show blood to an enemy', the military music, the great Λ (for Lakedaimon) on each shield, that replaced older, individual blazons and made a continuous zigzag along the ordered line, were the badges of men no less determined than Periclean Athenians that this way of life 'should not be taken away from them'.[72] A story was told of a Spartan wrestler in the Olympic Games, who won after a severe struggle, and after refusing a large bribe to let another man win; for in many states an Olympic victor received considerable material rewards. 'What do you gain by that, Laconian?' asked one of those who had offered the bribe. 'A place in the line of battle in front of the King,' said the young man, smiling.[73]

The nineteenth-century developers of the English Public School admired Sparta, finding in its boarding-school education, with prefects, fagging and rough ball games, evidence of a kindred spirit. A stranger

---

[68] *Ap*. Plut. *Lyk*. 21.

[69] Paus. iii, 11, 2; 14, 8, etc.

[70] Plut. *Lyk*. 13 (Leotychides I, dining under a coffered ceiling at Corinth, asked his host whether the trees grew square in that country).

[71] Ath. iv, 138d (anecdote of a Sybarite at Sparta); cf. Plut. *Lyk*. 22.

[72] Plut. *ib*.; Hdt. vii, 208-9 (combing their hair at Thermopylai); red tunics, Xen. *Lak. Pol*. xi, 3, Ar. fr. 542 Rose, *ap*. schol. on *Acharnians*, 340; *lambda* on shields, Photios, *Bibl*. p. 200, q. Eupolis and Theop. Com. (frags. 37 and 18, Meineke, respectively); cf. Xen. *Hell*. iv, 4. 10, Pericles on Ath. patriotism, Thk. ii, 41 (end).

[73] Plut. *ib*.

might suppose that there was conscious imitation by Thomas Arnold, which there was not; Arnold made opportunist use of features of a boys' society which he found existing. A later and more liberal generation, finding in Sparta elements of a 'national socialist' society (militarism, cruelty, eugenics, the negation of individualism), has regarded it with horror. It is desirable that we should see Sparta whole, not deliberately closing our eyes either to the good aspects of it or to the bad.

In Sparta's dealings with the helots, indeed, there is a heavy balance of evil. Every year, Aristotle said, the new ephors on coming into office formally declared war on them, so that it might not be impious to kill them; and the most able of the young men were drafted into a Secret Service, the *Krypteia*, whose function was to murder any helots found travelling at night, and, on occasion, any whose spirit and strength made them appear dangerous. Plutarch is unwilling to ascribe this institution to his idealised Lykourgos; but Aristotle, he himself tells us, regarded this as part of the original Lykourgan polity.[74] Thucydides tells how, during the war of 431-421, two thousand helots were enfranchised for loyal service, and shortly afterwards made away with to a man.[75] It is small wonder if after the defeat of Athens, when Sparta reached simultaneously the summit of her power and her lowest depth of indulgence in greed and power-politics, both helots and the 'lesser' citizens, outside the diminished ranks of the Spartiate *homoioi* or 'peers', were ready, as the conspirator Kinadon put it, if opportunity offered, to 'eat the masters raw'.[76] But at the same time, a surprising fact is not that there were helot revolts, as after the earthquake of 464, but that there were not more; that most of the helots most of the time continued peacefully if not contentedly to feed their masters in peace and war and to cultivate their fields, and that Sparta was not immediately overwhelmed by a mass movement or starved by a general strike when Laconia was invaded by Theban armies after 371. As for the *perioikoi*, though some of them from time to time took part in anti-Spartan movements, yet in general – content, we may suppose, with

[74] Ar. (frags. 538-9 Rose) *ap.* Plut. *Lyk.* 28. – Plato, *Laws*, 633b-c mentions Krypteia only as an example of hardship, and the scholiast explains it as a temporary banishment of the young man, who had to fend for himself in the wilds and *keep out of sight* – a practice which could be paralleled from Africa and N. America. But he does not *deny* that these young men might be used to terrorise the Helots.
[75] iv, 80.   [76] Xen. *Hell.* iii, 3, 6.

the freedom from fear of invasion which Sparta long provided – they fought faithfully and well alongside Spartiates in many campaigns. Clearly the hostility was not universally felt either in all places or at all times. There were even, as we have seen, loyal helots, and when Greece was invaded by Xerxes, 35,000 (were any of them Messenians?) are said to have served in the campaign of Plataia, though chiefly, it may be, as a transport and supply service.[77]

In foreign relations too, it is possible to paint the picture of Sparta's behaviour in too gloomy colours, at least until the defeat of Athens. That defeat itself is something which we can hardly cease to regret; but we can also hardly blame the Spartans, being what they were, for not wishing to be submerged by a rising tide of democracy. Down to 431 Sparta's league, on the whole, made for peace and stability. Spartan armies, it was observed, did not pursue beaten enemies far from the field.[78] Their object was not destruction of other Greeks, but only the preservation of their own position: a doctrine of limited war. Spartan kings in particular, brought up from youth to an awareness of foreign affairs, often showed a concern for all Greece and a breadth of vision beyond most of their countrymen. It was unfortunate that the ephors, the elected representatives of Spartan public opinion, were often able to thwart or overrule them. Kleomenes in 494 refused to destroy Argos when he could have done so; Archidamos in 431 laboured to avoid war with Athens; the young Pausanias in 403 'kept the ring' and permitted the restoration of the Athenian democracy.[79] Above all, it was the Peloponnesian League and Athens, with scarcely any other allies, which drove back Xerxes and saved Greece, sorely weakened by the ruin of Ionia, from further and irremediable harm. Sparta did much to preserve the Greece that has meant so much to Europe; though, at the same time, she did much to check its growth.

[77] Hdt. ix, 28; cf. Xen. *Lak. Pol.* xi, 2, for mobilisation of craftsmen.
[78] Plut. *Lyk.* 22.
[79] Hdt. vi, 81-2; Thk. i, 79ff, ii, 12; Xen. *Hell.* ii, 4, 29ff. See now, further, A. H. M. Jones, *Sparta* (Blackwell, Oxford, 1967).

CHAPTER XV

Athens and the Middle Way

THUS Crete and the Peloponnese had found a temporary end to the class struggle in a reaction which sterilised both. The Greeks of Asia, weakened by the same convulsions, fell rather easily before Cyrus. It was Athens and, to some extent, the western colonies that took up the torch. They gained something from the influx of vigorous Ionian refugees, as a prize rose grows larger through the nipping off of rival heads. Athens also owed much, in her resistance to the Persians, to the fact that she was further off than Ionia, beyond the Aegean. But it was not merely geography that made Athens great. Though human and fallible, the Athenians managed their transition from a peasant to a commercial economy with more success and less bloodshed than most of their neighbours, and nothing is of more importance in Greek history than to see how they did it.

Athens, moreover, because of the interest taken in her past by Athenian antiquaries and also by other Greeks, including Herodotos and Aristotle, becomes in the sixth century less imperfectly known to us than any other Greek city.[1] It is here alone that we can see something of the details of political life: the rivalries of great families cutting across and using for their own ends the issues of the class-conflict. It is a fact of importance for the understanding of the *tyrannis*, and one too little emphasised, that noble families of Athens had not the least hesitation in intermarrying with those of tyrants elsewhere.

Athens in 600, as we have seen, was still exporting corn; and her

---

[1] Especially through the Aristotelian *Athenaion Politeia* (hereinafter cited as *Ath. P.*). Plutarch and the lexicographers regularly quote this as 'Aristotle'; cf. Rose, *Ar. Fragmenta*, esp. fr. 387ff. The reason for doubting Ar.'s personal authorship is not merely its general second-rateness, but the fact that it often differs from the *Politics*, and *almost always for the worse*; and that this is not due to Ar.'s having later 'learned better', since our text is dated not earlier than 329–8 (*Ath. P.* 54, 7). It seems reasonable to ascribe it to a 'research student' in Ar.'s Institute.

'Open war here. There are – after all – second-rate anecdotes enough in the *Politics*, some of which you have quoted. . . . It was a very venturesome research student.' – A.A.

government was probably still the early, close oligarchy (pp. 22ff). The chief Archon annually swore his oath to preserve property in the hands that held it; the annual 'King' presided over festivals and judged religious causes; the Polemarchos, third man in the state (and not first; which is interesting evidence of the civil character of Athenian government at an early date) commanded in war and handled judicial business involving foreigners. In the country the Naukraroi, presidents of the ship-money units, being probably the only local officials of the state government, seem to have gained importance outside their original sphere. The Assembly of the people, probably open to all men of substance (the Zeugitai, owners of a yoke of oxen,[2] roughly the hoplite class) was probably only convened in a crisis, when, for instance, peace or war had to be voted.

There is no particular reason to suppose that the Zeugitai resented the long-familiar government of the Eupatridai, so long as their economic conditions were tolerable. Indeed, the result of their contentment was seen as late as about 632, when the young Kylon, who had won glory by a victory in the foot-race at Olympia and married the daughter of Theagenes, tyrant of Megara (pp. 188, 248), seized the Acropolis with his partisans and Megarian troops, and tried to make himself tyrant. The Archon Megakles, of the formidable Alkmeonid family, called out the levies, and the contingents poured into town under the Presidents of the Naukraries. The citadel was besieged, and though many of the peasant soldiers slipped away to their fields when the initial crisis was past, enough remained to enforce the blockade. Kylon lost heart, and with his brother escaped by night, abandoning his men; and they, reduced by hunger and thirst, surrendered on the promise of a fair trial. Attaching themselves, in order to remain technically 'in sanctuary', to the throne of Athena by a long series of ropes, they began to descend; but when they were opposite the Cave of the Furies, under the cliff of the Rock of Ares, the rope broke. 'The Goddess rejects them', cried Megakles; and there was a rush to seize them. Many were killed 'while trying to escape', a convenient excuse in all ages; some, in the heat of the chase, actually at the altars of the Dreadful Goddesses, the Furies themselves. More effective protection was given, it is said, and a few lives saved, by some Athenian

---

[2] The ancient and obvious explanation; though some, e.g. Andrewes, *Gk. Tyrants* p. 87, suggest 'men of the ranks', *zeuge*, i.e. hoplites.

ladies, wives of men on the government side, at whose feet some of the fugitives threw themselves.[3] First blood had been shed in the Athenian Revolution.

It was an unpromising beginning. Athens was shocked by the massacre, and when reverses were suffered in warfare with Megara the conviction grew that pollution had been incurred. The Cretan holy man, Epimenidas of Phaistos (pp. 66, 209), was called in to purify the city. He gave advice on religious observances, and in particular offered solemn sacrifice at the scene of the massacre. But public opinion, especially among kinsmen of those killed, demanded a scapegoat. Two young men, Kratinos and Ktesibios (we are not told that they were Alkmeonids) are said to have been put to death; and on the principle of 'solidarity of the family', that whole house was also arraigned, before a special court of their fellow-nobles. Against such a religious charge 'reasons of state' did not avail, and the Alkmeonidai were banished; banished 'for ever', we are told, and the bones of their ancestors dug up from their graves and cast out beyond the frontiers.[4] Since, however, it is evident that they did not lose their lands, and since they were back and playing a leading part in Athens before 560, if not even at the time of the Delphic Sacred War (pp. 202ff), these details are probably wrong; they may have been falsified in tradition through court pleadings on later occasions, when enemies found it convenient to rake up the family curse. They cannot have returned under a general amnesty ascribed to the year 594 if, as we are told, that measure expressly excluded persons exiled for 'massacre', unless, as is conceivable, that amnesty did override a verdict of a special court, other than the Areopagus.[5]

Popular discontent was, however, on the increase. A reform conceded about 620 met one new demand: the demand for publication of the laws in writing, so that men might know at least what penalties a magistrate or court had the right to impose. This was done by one Drakon. It was not a reform *of* the laws; and Drakon secured the

---

[3] Hdt. v, 71, Thk. i, 126, Plut. *Solon*, 12 (from the lost beginning of the *Ath. P.*?).

[4] Plut. *ib.*; *Ath. P.* 1; D.L. i, 110ff.—'*Ancestors* is your interpretation' – A.A. (The Gk. says 'they themselves'.) – But surely dead Alk. are called 'they themselves' as Demosthenes calls Athenian of past generations 'you'.

[5] Pleas of justification were admitted in classical Ath. homicide law, *though it remained very archaic*; cf. Demosth. *Aristokr.* 74 (p. 644), *Ath. P.* 57, 3, on the Delphinion Court (and contexts); for survival of the 7th-century homicide laws, *IG* I², 115 (Tod, *GHI* I, 87); *Ath. P.* 7, 1.

powers of judges so far as possible by recording as the penalty for almost every delinquency, in the words of the former British military code, 'Death, or such other penalty as the Court may decide'. A later Athenian said that the old code seemed to be written in blood instead of ink.[6] But there was more serious trouble ahead.

Population was approaching saturation-point. Peasants were still clearing and 'colonising' upland holdings, especially in northern Attica, on both sides of Mount Parnes; but much of this 'marginal land' was poor; and in the plains, small holdings became smaller still through subdivision. The large landowners still had produce to spare; but while Attica exported corn, wine and oil, its own poor went hungry.

Class feelings grew bitter. After the time of Drakon, says the Aristotelian *Constitution*, 'there was a long period of strife between nobles and people; for the constitution was oligarchic in every respect, and in particular the poor were in servitude to the rich, both themselves and their wives and children; and they were called Dependants (*pelatai*, cf. Latin *clientes*) and Sixth-Parters (*hektemoroi*), because they worked the lands of the rich for this hire – and the whole land was in the hands of a few. And if they failed to pay their hire, they were liable to be sold as slaves, both themselves and their children. All debts were on the security of the person, down to the time of Solon; he was the first champion of the people.'[7]

Debt and debt-slavery were the aspect of the problem which finally forced themselves on the attention of prudent men, even among the rich. The appearance of money (though Athens struck no coins of her own until after 600) exacerbated this evil. In earlier times, a poor man might borrow a bushel of corn to tide him over until the harvest, and if the next harvest was better, he could repay and survive. But when debts were reckoned in money, a habit of thought which, since the rich were exporting grain, may well have come in quickly, then the poor man would have to borrow the *price* of enough food to last till the harvest, just at the time of year when food was scarce. If, after the harvest, he sold enough produce to repay, he would be selling when food was cheap; he would therefore have to sell more produce than he had bought with his loan[8]; while if he chose to wait for a better price,

---

[6] Demades, *ap*. Plut. *Sol*. 17; Ar. *Rhet*. ii, 25, 1. Dr.'s existence is denied, characteristically, by Beloch, *GG*² I, ii, pp. 258ff, who identifies him with the sacred snake of the Acropolis; but by no other scholar of note.

[7] *Ath. P*. 2.   [8] W. J. Woodhouse, *Solon the Liberator*, p. 120.

he would have to pay interest by the month; for the practice of usury, long known in the east, had quickly appeared.

The rich were ruthless; we have the unimpeachable evidence of Solon, a Eupatrid himself, for that. The desire to keep abreast of fellow-noblemen acted as a spur, and many desirable luxury goods could only be had from abroad. If a man desired to increase his capital, land was almost the only investment; and the land available was that of peasants who failed to make ends meet. Naturally, the more improvident peasants failed first; they may have seemed to deserve little sympathy, even had Christian charity been a pagan virtue. The same consideration was applied to seizing insolvent debtors as slaves. In the new commercial age, slaves were an export, and it might be more economically profitable to sell a debtor and his family, for instance to Corinth or Aigina, where slaves are said to have been exceptionally numerous,[9] than to keep them on their land as *pelatai* (if that is what *pelatai* were), who would still have to be fed. Many Athenians had been sold, and not always 'justly', Solon tells us, before the process was stopped.[10] An intermediate stage was that in which land had been, as it were, mortgaged, by the Athenian legal arrangement, which in later times was called 'sale with a provision for redemption', if the purchase price could be repaid within a fixed time limit[11]; but the conditions which had forced a peasant family to submit to such a sale were not likely to permit them to free themselves; likely, rather, to lead to their falling still further into debt, until their very bodies belonged to the creditor. In the meantime, hated 'boundary marks' – certainly not, as yet, inscriptions, or some would have been discovered, but posts of wood or stone – were set up round their holding, to denote that it was now legally part of the neighbouring large estate.[12] The 'injustice' to which Solon refers was probably the determination of some creditors to anticipate the inevitable, and to seize debtors for export before they ran away, as Solon tells us some did[13] – facing the rigours of life as labourers abroad, without rights or security, but at least keeping the family together in precarious freedom.

What the previous legal status of the peasantry, now thus threatened,

---

[9] Ar. *ap.* Ath. vi, 272d, cf. *ib.* b.   [10] *Ap. Ath. P.* 12 (Sol. fr. 36 Bgk.), ll. 9ff.
[11] *IG* II², 2749; cf. D. M. Robinson in *Hesp.* XIII.
[12] Solon, *loc. cit.* 6; cf. J. V. A. Fine, *Horoi, Hesp.* Suppl. IX (1951). 'Why not *horoi* with inscriptions on wood – markers rather than boundary stones?' – R.M.
[13] *ib.* 10ff.

had been, is a question which has been much discussed; but the variety of answers given is evidence that our information is not sufficient to pronounce with certainty in any detail. Plutarch, using the Aristotelian *Athenian Constitution* as a source for his *Life of Solon*, understood the *hektemoroi* to be tenants (since 'the whole land belonged to a few') who paid one-sixth of the produce as rent, and substitutes *thetes*, a word meaning hired labourers, for *pelatai*. But other words compounded with *moros* 'part' or 'lot': *isomoros*, 'sharing equally', *okymoros*, 'swift-fated', i.e. early to die, *amoros*, 'luckless', always mean 'having' such-and-such a part. Thus *hektemoroi* should be men who *received* a sixth part of something.[14] If so, they cannot have been rack-rented tenants; they could not have lived. Even Sparta only levied half the produce from her serfs, in fertile Stenyklaros (p. 76). If they were hired labourers, such as might be required at harvest time, with more than one member of a family working, and plying a craft at other seasons, or working 'pocket-handkerchief' properties of their own, their situation seems more possible. If so, too, they were different from the 'dependent' *pelatai*, who may have been in a position resembling serfdom. It seems likely that there was, as we might expect *a priori*, a considerable variety of status among the poor of Attica: dependent *pelatai*; free labourers with or without small plots of their own; and peasants in the stony hill country, or who, in the plains, through the repeated division of farms, had sunk from the class of hoplite *zeugitai* to that of *thetes*. In any case, around 600 there was widespread desperation and fear of slavery; and fear, too, among the rich themselves, lest some other Kylon might arise, with the support of the peasantry this time, and overthrow the aristocratic order, as in the Isthmus cities.

The internal plight of Attica is clearly connected with the attempts about this time to secure additional land by the capture or recapture of Salamis, and to secure Sigeion, on the route to the Ukrainian cornlands: a port for which Athenian merchantmen could make if delayed by weather or if in need of repairs, without being fleeced by foreign chandlers or simply captured by hostile Megarians. These operations cannot be synchronised in detail with developments in Attica; but they all belong to the generation in which the trouble at home came to a head.

[14] Plut. *Sol.* 13; Woodhouse, *op. cit.* 48ff; G. Thomson, 'Greek Land-tenure', in Studies pres. to D. M. Robinson, II; for a *pelates theteuon* (working as a labourer) cf. Plato, *Euthyphron*, p. 4c.

Prudent men, even among the Athenian governing class, saw the danger of insurrection; also, perhaps the impossibility of a bold foreign policy if a process were to continue, which reduced the numbers of potential soldiers and sailors. Their spokesman was the statesman and poet-pamphleteer (he would certainly have written in prose at a later date), Solon the son of Exekestides.

Solon, a Eupatrid claiming descent from King Kodros, was not one of the great landowners. He was a nobleman turned merchant: a man who had 'seen the world'. Still in the prime of life – he is said to have died old in 560 – he was already distinguished as a patriot, since the time when, braving possible resentment, he had demanded a renewal of the attack on Salamis (p. 220). 'A leading man in reputation, but of moderate property and fortune,' says the *Constitution*. He now wrote, fiercely as a Hebrew prophet, denouncing the greed of the rich and the enslavement of men for debt. One poem began

> With bitter pain at heart I understand
> Seeing this old, this first Ionian land
> Thus murdered . . . [15]

Another of which we have probably almost the whole, runs

> Our city by the will of Zeus and all
> The blest immortal gods shall never fall;
> The All-Father's Daughter watches o'er our land:
> Pallas Athene, with protecting hand;
> But citizens themselves now madly lust,
> For money's sake, to lay her in the dust!
> Our rulers bear injustice in their mind,
> On violence bent, its grim reward to find.
> Glutted, they still do not know how to cease,
> To sit back and enjoy good cheer in peace!
>
> .   .   .   .
>
> Their wealth is all from their ill-gotten gain
>
> .   .   .   .
>
> Nor state nor temple treasuries restrain
> Their thieving hands from robbery; the law
> Of Justice stern they do not hold in awe:
> Who, silent, knows their present deeds and past
> And surely comes for reckoning at the last.

[15] *Ap. Ath. P. 5, 2.*

A few lines later, he continues:

> Such evils walk amongst us; of the poor
> Many a man now treads a foreign shore,
> Sold overseas with hands tied, shamefully,
> To labour there perforce in slavery.
> One common evil each man's home invades;
> The doors no more suffice for barricades;
> It leaps the high fence standing in its way;
> In innermost chamber it finds out its prey.
> 'Tell Athens this', my spirit bids; 'tell all
> The evils that from wicked laws befall!'
> But good laws give us right and order strong
> And bind in chains unrighteousness and wrong;
> Smooth out the rough, check violence and greed,
> Wither the blooms that spring of sin for seed,
> Straighten the crooked judgment, soften pride,
> Bring to an end the quarrels that divide,
> Check the fierce hate and bitterness of strife
> And right and reason give to human life.[16]

Solon was a god-fearing man, and repeatedly expresses his conviction that ill-gotten gain can never prosper in the end – though the guilty may die in possession of it, and their innocent children suffer. He had no hankering after great wealth – *he*, at least, was not trying to keep up with the Alkmeonidai. Moreover, as a merchant, he stood rather apart from the main class-struggle of agrarian Attica, just as the farming class did at the time of the Parian arbitration from that of commercial Miletos. He was a man whom both sides could trust. In 594, 592 or 586 according to different authorities (even at Athens, clearly, we are *not* yet in a period for which precise dates could be given), he was elected Archon with supreme powers, after both Council and Assembly had sworn solemn oaths to accept and carry out whatever measures he might ordain. He was, in effect, made *aisymnetes*, like his contemporary Pittakos of Mytilene; probably, like Pittakos and like earlier Athenian Archons till 683 tr., he was given his powers for ten years. Plutarch boldly and justifiably calls both of them, as well as Tynnondas of Euboia, not otherwise known, 'elected *tyrannoi*'.[17]

[16] *Ap.* Demosth. *On the Embassy*, p. 254.
[17] Plut. *Sol.* 14; date 594, Sosikr. *ap.* D.L. i, 61; 592, *Ath. P.* 14; Jerome; 586, D.S. ix, 17 (see Dindorf's note, Teubner, 1866, II, p. xlviii). The Ath. swore to obey his laws for ten years, Hdt. i, 29.

Solon had, we are told, determined already what he would do; later tradition said that in discussions with his friends he had revealed enough to amount to a 'budget leakage', and that the fortunes of some of the great families of classical Athens were founded on speculation thus made possible. A Konon, a Kleinias and a Hipponikos are mentioned. The story is almost certainly untrue; the family whose heads were called alternately Hipponikos and Kallias, for example, were hereditary Heralds of the sanctuary of Eleusis, and drew a fee from every initiate at the Mysteries; they had presumably also been large landowners in the Eleusinian plain since time immemorial; they were the richest family in Attica, and this was not the only envious rumour as to how they came by their wealth[18]; but the mention of these historic names at this date is of interest.

Solon announced his programme, probably immediately, in the context of his oath of office as Archon, instead of taking the customary oath to defend property (p. 23). He did not announce a redistribution of the land; a great disappointment to the poor, who had set their hopes on this. But as an immediate step he cancelled all debts, whether owed to private individuals or to the State (presumptive evidence, it may be noted, that a system of taxation existed); and he forbade for ever that any Athenian should be seized as a slave for debt. There was a great clearance of the hated 'boundary-marks'. Solon boasts of it in an iambic poem, while elsewhere he speaks of himself as 'standing like a boundary-marker between the hostile armies' of the opposing sides.[19] Clearly a *horos* could be the evidence and the guarantee of a right as well as of a felt wrong.

Solon also liberated by his decree all those already enslaved for debt, and, he tells us, 'brought back to Athens many who had been sold, some legally, some illegally, . . . speaking no longer with an Attic accent after their wanderings'.[20] How these were traced and bought out, an operation which must have required large sums of money (and just after a cancellation of arrears of taxes) is a mystery; but the fact shows that the State had considerable resources. Perhaps temple treasures may have been borrowed for this good cause. That many could be traced suggests that many were not far away, e.g. in Aigina,

[18] Plut. *Sol.* 15; cf. his *Aristides*, 5, on Kallias. K. and Eleusis, Andok. i, ii; though the family's 'registered address' in classical times was at Alopeke, near Athens.
[19] In *Ath. P.* 12, 5 and Plut. *Sol.* 16.
[20] In *Ath. P.* 12, 4 (*Sol.* fr. 36 Bgk. 8ff).

Megara and Corinth; slaves, like corn, were a typical export from an undeveloped to a developed area. Others he liberated from slavery 'trembling before their masters'at home in Attica. It has been suggested, though on inconclusive evidence, that *some* land in Attica, the original 'lots' of old-established families, was by law inalienable, so that all the creditor could do with it was to take it over together with its original owners as a sort of serfs.[21] These were presumably liberated without compensation.

For the future, Solon overhauled the laws concerning the holding of property. He explicitly made legal the adoption of an heir by a childless man; an assertion of individual property-rights against the clan, to which the land would otherwise have reverted[22]; and he is said, on the high authority of Aristotle's *Politics*, to have limited the amount of land which any one man might *acquire* (not *hold*, as some have mis-translated; thus the large, ancient estates remained intact).[23] To prevent the competitive 'conspicuous waste' of wealth, he introduced some sumptuary laws; the best attested limited lavish expenditure on funerals,[24] to which, long before, the Dipylon pottery bears witness. And, most far-reaching and important, he forbade altogether the export of agricultural produce except that of the olive.[25] Landowners who wished to pay for imports must hereafter rely wholly – many no doubt already relied largely – on the long-term investment of planting or grafting olive trees, which took the best part of a generation to reach maturity, and on the resulting cash-crop of oil, the chief edible fat, soap and source of artificial light of the Greek world. The olive remained throughout classical times one of the staple supports of the Attic economy. Corn for sale must therefore be sold in Attica at a price which Attic consumers could pay, no matter what higher price might have been obtained oversea. The light calcareous soils of most of Attica were well suited to olive-growing; and the consequent reduction in corn-production need not have been great, since in the plains corn

[21] N. G. L. Hammond, to Hellenic Society, 1957; J. V. A. Fine, *op. cit.* (n. 12 above). Ar. (*Politics*, 1266b) mentions laws forbidding the sale of land, 'e.g. in Lokris'; but he does not name Athens, nor appear to mean that this was the law there, either under Solon (whom he has just named, see n. 23, below) or just before him; nor do our other sources on early Athens indicate such a thing.
[22] Plut. *Sol.* 21.
[23] *Politics*, 1266b. (Perhaps meaning only that S.'s laws helped towards even distribution? – R.M.)
[24] Plut. *ib.*
[25] *id.* 24, q. Solon's 'first column'.

could be, as it still is, grown between the trees. Enough of the bright sunlight penetrates between the trees, which must be well spaced, and access to the trees for the autumn olive-picking in no way interferes with the corn, sown later and reaped in April or May.

Solon's allotted task was to overhaul the whole body of Attic law, the ancestral customs and the judge-made case-law, as reduced to writing under Drakon. Since he is not said to have taken many years over this, it may be assumed that he reproduced, for publication on the wooden boards, joined together in pyramidal structures on pivots,[26] which stood before the town-hall, the existing corpus, with such considerable alterations as he thought fit to introduce. All early Athenian laws thus tended in later times to be ascribed to Solon, except those dealing with prosecutions for murder or homicide, with which he did not meddle, and which therefore continued to be described as Drakon's.[27] The above-mentioned modernisations are those which may with most probability be ascribed to Solon himself. He had firmly directed Athens on to the course of development from a corn-exporting to a corn-importing community; and accordingly he is also said to have insisted on the duty of every father to see that his sons were taught a trade (a measure which doubtless was of little concern to the land-owning classes), and to have facilitated the admission to citizenship of immigrants who were skilled workers and who settled in Athens with their families.[28] Athens must become, as she did, a city of skilled workers if she was to pay for her imported food.

Athens had already had for some fifteen years, some have thought, a coinage represented by some rare silver pieces with the badge of a wine-amphora[28a]; those known are invariably both worn and clipped, but *could* have weighed about 12·3 grammes: two-drachma pieces (the early Athenian standard coin, as the *Constitution* says), on the Pheidonian standard of the Peloponnese, Boiotia and Aigina. Solon is credited

[26] *Ath. P.* 7, 1; *axones*, 'revolving columns', cf. Plut. *Sol.* 25. – 'The most hopeful physical descriptions are in Eratosthenes, *FHG* 241 F37b, and *ET. Mag. s.v. axones.*', – A.A.
[27] The laws were overhauled and re-published on stone late in the 5th century (cf. n. 13 above); the old wooden structures seem to have fallen to pieces ('now used for roasting corn' – Kratinos, *ap.* Plut. *ib.*; though Plut. adds that a few small fragments were still preserved in his time); and on this occasion as well as from time to time by statute there was certainly some modernisation of details; cf. the attack of Lysias on Nikomachos, who, having been commissioned to edit the text 'set himself up in place of Solon as a legislator'; *Lys.* xxx, 2.   [28] Plut. *Sol.* 22, 24.
[28a] But doubt is cast upon these on the ground that the shape is late 6 C. and metallic; not then, a pottery amphora.

with having gone over to the Euboic standard, used also by Corinth, Chalkis and their corn-exporting colonial areas; the new two-drachma *stater* or standard piece was of about 8·4 grammes. A series of such pieces, bearing various types on the obverse is shown to be from one mint by the single series of punches which leave their mark, the 'incuse square', on the reverse. The obverse types include the owl of Athene, the amphora, the forepart of a prancing horse, and the *triskeles*, three human legs joined at the hip, which may have been the heraldic badge of the Alkmeonidai. Others, accordingly, may have been also the 'blazons' of noble houses, members of which may have been in charge of the mint in different years; e.g. an ox-head that of the priestly Eteoboutadai.[29]

Solon's economic policy was successful. Within a generation Athenian manufactured goods were pouring into the west; the evidence is supplied, as usual, by pottery. Black-figure ware, the first classical Athenian style, began to use the fine clay from Cape Kolias, south-east of Phaleron, about this time; skilful firing and an admixture of *miltos*, ruddle, imported from Keos, gave it the bright terracotta background-colour, like the red soil of Attica, henceforth characteristic of Attic wares[30]; and the neat, taut, often masterly drawing of its ornament, including in the high-class pieces scenes from legend or from daily life, outclassed the familiar but now slovenly products of Corinth (p. 279). Corinthian potters, in the effort to hold their market, imitated the colour and style of Attic; but they could not recapture the artistic morale of their ancestors.

It remained to meet, for the future, the claims of the poor for security and of the new rich for a share in the government.

---

[29] *Ath. P.* 10, 2; Seltman, *Athens, its History and Coinage*, pp. 14ff, arguing that these 'heraldic' coins are all from one mint, as shown by the use of a single series of anvils (producing the reverse incuse-square) with the various obverse crests; therefore *not* probably from the cities of Euboia. J. G. Milne, however (*Early Coinages of Athens and Euboea*, in *Num. Chron.* 1941), defends the old attribution to Euboia, with a single mint, e.g. at Chalkis; to the writer, this seems improbable, as do some of Milne's conclusions in *The Economic Policy of Solon*, in *Hesp.* XIV. E. S. G. Robinson also, in *JHS* LXXI, p. 166, makes the first coinage of Athens Solonian, and remarks that 'it would fit better if most of it could be put' later than 590 (since later than the first of Aigina, which is later than the first Lydian and Ionian, now dated post-650). (C. M. Kraay, in *Num. Chron.* 1956, suggests a date 'about 575 or after'). But this sequence, *and* the belief of classical Athenians that there was a pre-Solonian Ath. coinage, can be preserved if the traditional date of Solon's archonship, given as 594 or 592, is like other dates in early Gk. history somewhat too early. Androtion believed the 'devaluation' was intended to lighten debts, Plut. *Sol.* 15.   [30] Seltman, *op. cit.* pp. 11ff.

Solon introduced two revolutionary constitutional enactments: that the Archons should be elected by the Assembly, and that *all Athenians* (*probably* all recognised members of clans or *gene*, whether 'drinkers of the same milk', *homogalaktes*, or attached as 'sharers in worship', *orgeones*) might attend and vote, even the poor *Thetes* or Labourers. The qualification for eligibility was to be the status of a Knight; and this laid eligibility open, at least legally, to rich tradesmen, to 'any carl who throve so' that he could buy enough land to qualify. To do so, he would have to find someone prepared to sell land, which cannot always have been easy; but that it could happen was shown by a thank-offering on the Acropolis: a plaque showing a man with a horse, and the inscription

> Anthemion son of Diphilos gives thanks
> To heaven, from Workers' risen to Knightly ranks.[31]

The classes of Knights, Small-holders (*Zeugitai*) and Workers must have been long familiar. Solon was probably the first to define them in terms of property: Knights as those whose property yielded 300 *medimnoi* (about 200 bushels) of produce, whether oil, wine or grain, per year, and Zeugitai, not less than 200. Knightly status could thus be claimed on as little as about seven acres of first-class land, though naturally it would require much more poor land.[32] The medimnos was sixty-four times the *choinix*, the normal Attic day's ration for a man. If all under corn (which would be unlikely) a minimum knightly holding would thus produce corn (but nothing else) for over fifty

---

[31] *Ath. P.* 7, 4. (This, like Hes. *WD* 341, is against the persistent modern belief that in pre-classical Greece land was normally parcelled into family holdings and was inalienable; there may have been *some* such land, as Hammond believes, but there is no satisfactory evidence of it.) That magistrates were *directly elected* is stated in *Ath. P.* 22, 5 (after 510; but we are told that the tyrants had not changed the law, Thk. vi, 54, cf. Hdt. i, 59 (end), *Ath. P.* 13, 2; 16, 8). We hear of no *extension* of eligibility until the admission of Zeugitai to the archonships in 457. That the nine archons (including the military commander-in-chief) were selected by lot from among 40 elected candidates (*Ath. P.* 8, 1ff) is in contradiction to the statement in 22, 5, as well as inherently improbable. Cf. Hignett, *Ath. Const.* 79ff, 321ff; though Ar. (*Politics*, 1273b-4a) surely does *not* mean that S. left the method of election unaltered, but only the existing archonships.

Whether all Athenian citizens, including immigrants, had to be at least attached to a *genos* as *orgeones* is also uncertain. Here too, the evidence is insufficient to bear the weight of a comprehensive theory. What can be said about *genos* organisation, with the help of epigraphic evidence (*IG* II², 1237), is set forth by Wade-Gery on *The Demotionidai*, in *CQ* XXV (now in *Essays in Greek History*, 115f). Cf. Andrewes in *JHS* LXXX, forthcoming.

[32] In England, the average yield of wheat per acre is quoted as about 31 bushels; but only good land is used.

individuals for a year, or *income* enough to support a household of a dozen or more largely bread-eating Greeks in rustic plenty; while, if most of his 300 medimnoi represented cash-crops of olive-oil or good wine, such a knight's income would be considerably more valuable.

Above this modest minimum definition of wealth (which took no account of cattle or sheep on unenclosed hill pastures), Solon himself probably introduced a new 'top income-bracket', the class of those producing over 500 bushels; their title, *pentekosiomedimnoi*, defined from the first in figures, looks, in contrast to the other class-titles, like an *invented* word. They paid at the highest rate in direct taxes (twice as much as Knights, six times as much as Zeugitai), and from among them the Treasurers were chosen (by lot) – both because rich men might be presumed to be under less temptation to indulge in peculation and because, if any such incident did come to light, they had ample property on which to distrain. Zeugitai were eligible to minor magistracies; Thetes to none.[33]

The Assembly was given also another important controlling power. Meeting as a Court, in which capacity it was called *heliaia* (a word which meant the political assembly in some other states), it received the right to vote on the accounts submitted by magistrates demitting office (in classical times, after audit by a board of scrutineers, the *logistai*). At the same time, other actions of the ex-magistrate might be called in question; if his acts and his accounts were passed without objection or successfully defended, then and only then he passed into the Areopagus.[34] At an unknown date, probably early, the *heliaia* was divided into juries, e.g. of 501, for this and other judicial work; for an important trial, we hear of larger numbers, up to 2501. To the *heliaia* citizens could also appeal in serious cases against decisions of magistrates; and Solon introduced the important principle that 'anyone who wished' might take up the cause of 'the oppressed'.[35] To do just this came later to be one of the regular functions and sources of influence

[33] *Ath. P.* 7, 3; 8, 1; graded tax-rates (at an unknown date), Pollux, viii, 130: 'P. paid a talent, knights a half-talent, z. 10 minas'; though he does not tell us in what circumstances.
[34] Ar. *Politics*, 1274a, ascribes this provision to Solon (though Hignett, *op. cit.* 97, 203ff, doubts this too). *Logistai, Ath. P.* 48, 3; 54, 2. *Heliaia* in an archaic law, Lysias, x, 16, Demosth. xxiv, 105; *haliaia* the political Assembly at Argos, Tod, *GHI* no. 33, l. 45. Recruitment of Areopagus from ex-archons, Plut. *Sol.* 19. *Euthünein* in Ar. *l.c.* unqualified, surely *must* mean what it meant in Ar.'s own time. – But 'surely no financial audit as early as Solon?' – R.M.
[35] *Ath. P.* 9, 1; Plut. *Sol.* 18; Aristoph. *Ploutos*, 907-19.

of a popular leader or *demagogue*; as, in another age, of Tammany Hall.

Thus the Assembly of all the people had received the powers of choosing which Knights should be Archons, of calling them to account, and of voting on any change in the laws. The Knights who in practice were elected long continued to be largely members of the old Eupatrid families, who had experience and influence, and *time* for public affairs. But men of substance of other families *could* be elected; while the ordinary man had safeguards *against* the government, against arbitrary treatment. Rome, 300 years later, under the Lex Hortensia, reached almost the same position. But Athens developed thereafter into a full-blown democracy, which regarded Solon as its father, whereas Rome became once more an oligarchy, controlled by a new official or 'noble' class of patrician and great plebeian families. Just why this happened is a more complex question than is sometimes thought; but a very important factor in the development of Athens was another far-sighted enactment of Solon's: the establishment (as at Chios within the century, cf. pp. 224f) of a second or Popular Council, to prepare business for the Assembly.[36]

The new Council, attributed to Solon by all ancient authorities, had four hundred members, a hundred from each of the four Ionic tribes, of Zeugite or Knightly class, appointed annually, and probably from the first *by lot*, cast among those who volunteered and against whom no objection was raised and sustained at a tribe-meeting. It was therefore, and was intended to be, a body of respectable, average citizens, genuinely representative of the Assembly, whose 'committee' it was; probably much more representative than would have been an elected council, which would naturally have tended to consist of the well-known. This Council (later increased to five hundred in number) continued throughout Athenian history to draft measures and to prepare all the Assembly's business. Changing annually, it developed no such *esprit de corps* as did the permanent 'upper Council' (as Plutarch calls it) of ex-Archons. Its presence ensured that the powers entrusted to the Assembly should not be neutralised, through the adroit preparation of business and choice of 'psychological moments' for bringing it forward by a governing group; whereas at Rome, for lack of a

---

[36] *Ath. P.* 8, 4; its functions, in classical times, 43ff. The title 'of Areopagus' did not occur in Drakon's laws (Plut. *Sol.* 19); it was not necessary.

People's Council, the all-important preparation of business did fall
into the hands of the body of ex-magistrates, the Roman Senate.

The ancient Council *now*, for the sake of distinction from the new
one, came to be known by the name of its meeting-place as the Council
of the Areopagus. Solon left to it the functions of a supreme court, the
'Guardianship of the Laws'. Before it cases of homicide long continued
to be tried, especially the cases, very difficult under the primitive law
of blood-guilt, where the accused admitted blood-shedding but pleaded
accident or justification. It also still had the right to arraign before it
any man on a charge of conspiring against the republic or of breaking
any other fundamental law.[37] Laws, we note, were recognised as
standing on a different footing from administrative or 'police' orders,
against which an appeal lay to the Heliaia. The Areopagus thus had
formidable powers of intervention against any radical reformer, unless
he was very careful of his ground; e.g., if he proposed any controversial measure before the lower council and assembly without first
directly proposing the amendment or suspension of any existing law
to the contrary; and to do this would often be likely to rouse the
sensitive though latent conservative feelings of the Athenian people.

The immediate reaction to Solon's legislation was one of general
disappointment. Many rich men had lost heavily by the cancellation
of debts, and malicious gossip alleged that some of Solon's friends had
profited (p. 293) by hastening to buy land with borrowed money.
The Eupatrids cannot have been pleased at the giving of effective
power to the Assembly with its new Council; and the people were
disappointed that there was no redivision of the land. Some of the new
laws, too, notably that dealing with inheritance in default of heirs male,
gave rise to judicial problems of interpretation.[38] Solon defended his
proceedings in vigorous verse pamphlets, 'turning this way and that',
he says, 'like a wolf among many dogs'. He had 'freed the dark earth',
'uprooting the (creditors') boundary-marks'; he had 'reconciled might
and right' and 'given equal laws to base and noble'. He had freed the
debt-slaves, he had 'given the people more than they formerly ever
dreamed of'. On the other hand, he had resisted the temptation to

[37] *Ath. P. ib.*
[38] *Ath. P.* 9, 2 (mentioning ridiculous suggestions that S. was obscure on purpose, to
increase the power of the courts); Plut. *Sol.* 20.

make himself *tyrannos*, which he could easily have done; but such a course, as he says, could only have led to much bloodshed. He had given the people 'privilege enough', (the essential minimum of power', says Aristotle), while protecting the noble. He had 'protected both sides with his strong shield' and 'stood like a boundary-mark between two armies'. He had 'fulfilled his promises', and he would not 'approve that base and noble should have equal shares in their native land'.[39] Here he speaks the familiar language of an old aristocrat. On the other hand, it is clear that a Theognis would have regarded his proceedings, not least the admission of the new rich to the archonships, as excessive radicalism.

But he grew weary of being 'beset by dogs' – 'badgered', in fact – with requests for interpretation of his own laws, or for amendments, which, under the solemn oaths sworn before he took office, no one else might introduce for ten years. A prolonged dictatorship was not part of his programme. It was for the people to operate his constitution and to learn to live under it. Finally, perhaps at the end of only one year, he left Athens, to travel once more in the Levant, 'both to trade and also to see the world'. He visited and wrote about Egypt: 'At Nile's outflowing by the Canopic shore', says the only fragment that remains; though Plato, brilliant but dubious as a historical source, says that he also recorded tales told him by Egyptian priests about the vanished Kingdom of Atlantis, which, if it is anything but a fable, can scarcely be other than Bronze-Age Crete.[40] He visited and advised Philokypros, king of Cypriote Soloi, on Morphou Bay, who was planning to descend from his hill-fortress and build a more spacious city in the plain; Philokypros, whose son Aristokypros was to fall in battle against the Persians about 498[41]; a detail which suggests (though it does not prove) that the traditional dates for Solon's activities may be too early. A famous legend told how he visited Croesus (who came to the throne about 560) and warned him of the jealousy of heaven towards exceeding riches. The happiest man Solon had heard of, as Herodotos says, was Tellos of Athens (p. 172), who had plenty of this world's goods 'as we Greeks count wealth', and saw all his family grow up, and sons born to them, and died gloriously in battle near the

[39] Solon, poems in *Ath. P.* 12; cf. Ar. *Politics*, 1274a.
[40] Hdt. i, 29; Solon, *ap.* Plut. 26; *Ath. P.* 11; Plato, *Timaios*, pp. 21ff, *Kritias* (esp. 113).
[41] Plut. *ib.*; Hdt. v, 113.

Megarian frontier; and next, he ranked Kleobis and Biton (p. 199), who performed a mighty deed of piety and died immediately after it. What all three had in common, as the sage pointed out, was that they had not outlived their happiness.

Solon returned to Athens in his old age, to find violent party strife in progress; and before he died, it had been quelled with a strong hand by his young kinsman, Peisistratos. But it would be a misconception to regard his work as a failure. In the following century Athens shot ahead of all her neighbours in power and wealth. Her 1000 square miles of territory provided a basis for this achievement; but a basis is not all. Much larger territories did not save Thessaly from being paralysed by internal feuds, nor Sparta by the fear of her own serfs. The naval power of Corinth and Aigina never grew beyond its sixth-century level; and both these cities were renowned for their immense slave-populations. No doubt many of the slaves were non-Greeks, imported; but we have seen that an evil, from which Solon saved Athens, was precisely the depression into slavery of thousands of her poorer freemen. Where there was no Solon to check the process, nor governing class wise enough to give him his way, what developed was a widening division between the rich and a proletariat, in part descended from those who had once been full citizens.

[See now, particularly good on the subjects of this and the following chapter, the book of W. G. Forrest, learned, independent and sometimes controversial, *The Emergence of Greek Democracy* (Weidenfeld and Nicolson, 1966).]

CHAPTER XVI

Athens and the Aegean, 590-510

CLASSICAL Athens and the People's State (*Demo-kratia*), whose zeal provided its amazing springs of power,[1] were not built in a day, but in roughly a hundred years from the time of Solon; and the early growing-pains of the Solonian republic were sharp, though mild compared with the revolution at Megara.

Solon had provided machinery by which class-conflicts, and not only the rivalries of leading men, *could* be settled with constitutional weapons. To be elected Archon, a coveted honour,[2] it was now necessary to secure the votes of farmers and townsmen. But rivalries were fierce, and parliamentary traditions take time to grow. Four years after Solon set out on his travels, and again four years after that, according to the *Constitution of Athens*, the divisions in the Assembly were such that no Archon could be elected. The word *anarchia* figured in the list set up in classical Athens; the state had no head, and presumably the lesser magistrates carried on the administration.

Four years later again (the symmetry suggests a later scholar 'restoring' the list with rather unsatisfactory materials), one Damasias was elected archon and remained in office, or secured re-election, contrary to custom, for a second year, and the beginning of a third. He was virtually a *tyrannos*; but his supporters, once the opposition was thoroughly roused, proved not to be strong enough: after another two months 'he was driven out of the archonship by force'. Then those who had combined to eject him formed a provisional government, a board of five noblemen, three peasants and two craftsmen; 'and these held the archonship' (presumably the eponymous archonship, the headship of state, in commission as it were) 'for the year after Damasias'.[3]

---

[1] Hdt. v, 78 (on the Athenian victories of 507); the word he uses is *isegorie*, equality of speech. *Demokratia*, Hdt. vi, 43, 3; 131, 1.
[2] *Ath. P.* 13, 2.   [3] *ib.* 1 and 2.

The explicit class basis of this emergency coalition government is interesting; the farmers and craftsmen, to whom Solon had given limited rights, already play a real part in politics. The fact emerges again in the appearance of regular parties in the Assembly: a party of 'the Plain', the rich landowners, who would gladly have gone back to the pre-Solonian régime, and a party of 'the Coast', who supported the new order. Leader of the former was Lykourgos the son of Aristolaïdes, head, perhaps, of the Eteoboutadai, the noble and priestly family to which the fourth-century orator Lykourgos belonged; of the latter, Megakles the Alkmeonid, son-in-law of Kleisthenes of Sikyon, son of the Alkmeon of the Sacred War (pp. 204ff), and grandson of the Megakles of the 'Kyloneian sacrilege'. Both the facts, that they had oversea connections, like Solon, and enemies among the other aristocrats, through the Kyloneian blood-feuds and through mere jealousy, made the Alkmeonidai, intelligent, ruthless and incalculable, always liable to be found in opposition to their peers. Both parties, we are informed, 'took their names from the districts in which their farms lay'.[4]

This remark has given rise to needless argument as to whether these parties were class parties, or local, or really dominated by the struggles for power of great families. The answer is 'All three'. No doubt some of those who supported the Solonian order were coastal farmers; the coastal landowner was often (like Hesiod's acquaintances) an oversea trader, and if a trader bought land, as some did, he would prefer it near the coast. But the town workers, who owed their political rights to Solon, must have supported the party too. As to the contests of noblemen for the Archonship, they were evidently a conspicuous feature of Athenian life; but to get elected now meant courting the voters, and these were presumably divided, not very reliably, into those who could be influenced by the families to which they were attached and those who would vote independently.

The need to build up a party of loyal voters and supporters, if one would attain power under the new conditions, was seen by the most clear-sighted politician in Athens: Peisistratos the son of Hippokrates, who claimed descent from Peisistratos the son of Nestor. Like Julius Caesar, he combined military prowess with great personal charm. He was the general who, at some unknown date (and certainly not before

[4] *ib.* 4; Hdt. i, 59; on the 4th-century Lykourgos, ps.-Plut. *Lives of the Attic Orators.*

600, as Plutarch has it, for he lived till 528) had temporarily captured Nisaia, the port of Megara. He now took up the cause of those whom Solon had left delivered from the fear of slavery, but otherwise out in the cold: the hill-foot crofters, farmers of stony soil and too poor, many of them, even to afford the best tools. They were numerous in the Diakria or Uplands of northern Attica, well-known to Peisistratos, whose own family estates lay in the north-east.[5]

With the help of their votes, Peisistratos might well have hoped for a year as Archon; but matters took a more dramatic turn. One day he drove his mule-chariot at headlong speed into Athens, both himself and his beasts bleeding from flesh-wounds. His enemies, he said, had waylaid and tried to murder him as he was coming in from the country. He appealed for protection. The Assembly (to a meeting of which he may well have been driving) voted the People's hero a bodyguard; not a bodyguard of regularly armed soldiers, but fifty citizens with cudgels. The proposer was Aristion of Marathon, a neighbour of Peisistratos at home; very probably the grandfather of that Aristion whose fine grave-monument, of about 500 B.C., was found between Marathon and Brauron. But this nucleus of a 'private army', with Peisistratos' personal popularity, was enough. With murder in the air, the popular leader could not draw back. Not long afterwards, he seized the Acropolis and took over the government.[6]

The republican tradition, which dominates all our sources, says uniformly that Peisistratos' wounds were self-inflicted, with the deliberate aim of obtaining a bodyguard, and that the aged Solon saw this at once, and said so in the Assembly. No ancient source even mentions any other possibility; but it must be evident that, if Peisistratos' enemies did try unsuccessfully to murder him, no other story was open to them when they wished to deny it. The story of self-inflicted wounds to gain credence for a piece of deception was a popular one in Greek story-telling.[7]

But Peisistratos' *tyrannis* was not established immediately. Before long, 'while his power was not yet firmly rooted', the Coast and Plain parties rallied against him. Peisistratos, ever a realist, withdrew, perhaps only to safety among his partisans in northern Attica, and waited

[5] Plut. *Sol.* 10.
[6] Hdt. i, 59, *Ath. P.* 13, 4; 14, 1; Ar. *Politics*, 1305a.
[7] e.g. *Od.* iv, 240ff.; Hdt. iii, 154ff (Zopyros the Persian).

for them to quarrel again. He did not have to wait long. Megakles, out-weighted by the conservatives, made overtures to him; and, says Herodotos, 'they devised a most childish stratagem . . . , considering that the Athenians were considered to be the most intelligent of the Greeks. There was a woman of Paiania' (east of Hymettos) 'named Phya, five feet and nine inches tall, and beautiful; they dressed her in armour, and arrayed her in the most glorious possible manner, and drove into the city, sending runners before her' to proclaim that the Goddess Athene was bringing home Peisistratos 'to her own Acropolis. And the report spread to the villages that Athene was bringing home Peisistratos, and in the city men believed that the woman was the goddess herself, and worshipped the mortal woman, and received Peisistratos back.'[8] It has been surmised that this story, which shocks Herodotos, may have arisen from a votive monument, showing Peisistratos coming home in triumph under the protection of the goddess.[9] In any case, it appears that he returned without fighting, and married Megakles' daughter.

But the marriage was childless. Rumour shortly said that this was by Peisistratos' intention, since he already had sons, and the Alkmeonidai were said to be accursed. The girl went back to her parents, and with the Alkmeonid faction once more hostile and Megakles now personally incensed, Peisistratos once more withdrew. This time he 'left the country altogether', says Herodotos. The *Constitution* adds that he and his partisans went off to found a colony in the north Aegean.

His first settlement was at Rhaikelos on the Gulf of Therma (the later Thessalonika). Thence he moved east into the Pangaion region, the gold-mining country. 'Thence he acquired wealth, and hired soldiers, and after ten years came to Eretria, and made his first attempt to regain power by force.' He found many allies among the states near Athens; from which it may be surmised that the growing city was proving a troublesome neighbour. Men calculated that Peisistratos, who never used force unnecessarily, would be preferable to the republic. The ruling Knights of Eretria let him use their city as a base; Thebes made him a generous grant of money, and 1000 volunteers from Argos joined his army. They were brought in by his young son Thessalos,

    [8] Hdt. i, 60; *Ath. P.* 14, 4 (with impossible chronology).
    [9] e.g. by Beloch in *Rhein. Mus.* XLV; *aliter GG*[2] I, ii, p. 288; relief from the Themisto-clean Wall, in Seltman, *Ath. Hist. and Coinage*, fig. 33.

surnamed Hegesistratos, 'Army-leader', borne to him by another wife, Timonassa, daughter of Gorgilos of Argos and widow of Archinos of Ambrakia, of the now fallen Kypselidai. Another eager volunteer, who brought in both men and money, was a popular leader in exile, like himself: Lygdamis of Naxos, a nobleman who had taken the people's side when they rose in arms to avenge a drunken outrage by some young nobles against a popular rich farmer named Telestagoras and his family.[10]

His plans completed, Peisistratos crossed the straits and landed unopposed at Marathon. His supporters from the northern uplands rallied to him, and many slipped out to join him from Athens itself. The city government in Athens must have been at sixes and sevens. They had taken no effective counter-measures; and even when he set out to march on the city by the road east and south of Mount Pente-likos, they were only in time to hold the wide gap between Pentelikos and Hymettos, some seven miles from the city, near Pallene. Here he was joined by a prophet, Amphilytos of Akarnania (a western high-lander, like most of the prophets mentioned by Herodotos), who enunciated the hexameter lines

> The net is cast, the drag-net opened wide,
> The tunnies come, swift on the moonlit tide.

One wonders whether the prophecy, with its suggestion of an envelop-ing movement by night, became known to both sides. Peisistratos, exclaiming reverently that he 'accepted the oracle', chose to interpret its reference to the moon as an oracular description of broad daylight, and gained a complete surprise by attacking in the heat of the day. 'The Athenians from the city at that time had turned their attention to taking their mid-day meal, and after that some of them sat down to play knuckle-bones, and some took a siesta.' There was an immediate rout; and Peisistratos bade his sons mount their horses (we see that they had dismounted for battle) and lead the pursuit; not slaying, but bidding the Athenians 'not to be afraid, and disperse and go home'. Thus for the third time, and finally, he became master of Athens.

Not long after this, he paraded the citizen army for a review and inspection of arms at the sanctuary of Theseus (not the 'Theseum' of

[10] Hdt. i, 61, *Ath. P.* 15; on Lygdamis, also Ar. *Nax. Pol. ap.* Ath. viii, 348b-c; *Politics*, 1305b.

modern tradition, which is the Temple of Hephaistos, but not far from it) and began to make a speech, but was deliberately inaudible. There were shouts of protest; whereat Peisistratos bade them come up to the entrance-steps of the Acropolis, so that they could hear better. Leaving their arms piled, the citizens trooped after him, up the hill into the saddle between the Citadel and the Hill of Ares, where they settled to listen. Meanwhile some of Peisistratos' personal adherents 'collected the arms, and locked them up in the buildings near the Theseion, and went and signalled to Peisistratos. He then, having finished the other things that he had to say, told the people what had been done with their arms, and that they should not be surprised or afraid, but go away and mind their own private affairs; and "I", he said, "will look after *all* public business." '[11]

There was no doubt about it; this was monarchy. 'Having thus seized Athens for the third time, Peisistratos rooted his tyranny firmly, with many foreign mercenaries' (probably including Scythian archers, who now begin to appear frequently on Attic vases) 'and with revenues both inland and from the River Strymon' (i.e. from his Pangaian gold-mines); 'and he took hostages from among the Athenians who stayed and had not promptly gone into exile, and deposited them in Naxos; for Peisistratos captured that too, and handed it over to Lygdamis.' When he felt himself secure, however, as also in his short earlier periods of power, he governed remarkably gently, 'constitutionally rather than tyrannically', 'not abolishing the existing magistracies nor changing the laws; but he administered the city on the basis of the existing constitution'. Archons were still elected, the despot simply taking care that they were always members of his family or otherwise 'reliable'. The Areopagus still met, and on one famous occasion Peisistratos actually appeared before it to defend himself on a charge of homicide; but the man who had ventured to cite him lost his nerve and did not appear. To settle disputes in the countryside, he appointed travelling 'rural justices', so that farmers might not have to neglect their work and come into town to go to law; also, in the usual manner of enlightened Greek tyranny, so that partisanship over suits in the city might not stir up excited crowds.

With his revenues from the mines, he was also in a position to do something concrete for the poorer peasants, his earliest supporters.

[11] Pallene, Hdt. i, 62f; disarmament, *Ath. P.* 15, 4.

He made loans at moderate rates of interest for the purchase of farm tools and equipment. Production soared, and Peisistratos' investment was doubly profitable; for in addition to the interest on his loans he took, as his sole direct tax, a levy of ten per cent on produce. Thereby hangs another good story. Peisistratos kept no ostentatious state; one of the great sources of his popularity was that he was accessible and friendly; when he felt himself secure, he could even walk in the country, almost unattended, settling disputes when occasion arose, like one of his own justices. Once on such a walk, at the foot of Hymettos, he caught sight of a peasant working away with his mattock at what appeared to be 'absolute stones'. He was probably clearing for himself a field out of what had hitherto been waste – a process which has gone on in Greek mountain country to this day. Admiring his industry, Peisistratos sent his servant to enquire what he was getting out of that field. 'Only aches and pains', said the peasant, who had not recognised the Chief; 'and of these aches and pains Peisistratos must have ten per cent.' Peisistratos was delighted with his free speech, and sent back the message that that field should be tax-free; and 'Tax-free Farm' became the name of the place for many generations.

Like many tyrants, he was also a great builder. Very welcome to working-class wives was his improvement of the water conduits, bringing a clean supply within easy reach; that, for example, south of the Acropolis, called 'the Fair-Flowing', an ancient source, from which in classical Athens people still drew the water for wedding ceremonies and other sacred occasions. 'After the tyrants' (perhaps Peisistratos' sons) 'had adorned it' with a built-up fountain-house, says Thucydides, 'it came to be called the Nine Fountains.' Peisistratos also designed a vast temple east of the Acropolis to Olympian Zeus, which was never finished until the emperor Hadrian took it in hand. He was ever attentive to the gods – probably sincerely, though in this too he was politic; and one of his measures, incidentally asserting the new power of Athens in the central Aegean, was a purification of Delos, where 'from all the area within sight of the Sanctuary, he dug up the graves, and transferred the bodies to another part' of the island.[12]

The foundations of classical Athens were being laid. Among the

[12] Hdt. i, 64 cf. 59 (end); *Ath. P.* 16; Ar. *Politics*, 1315b; Kallirrhoe, Thk. ii, 15, 4; archons under the tyrants, Thk. vi, 54; Olympieion, Ar. *Politics*, 1313b; completed by Hadrian, Paus. i, 18, 6.

other developments of the century (as also at Megara, p. 251f) was that of the agrarian ritual drama into an art-form. One Thespis is said to have gone about Attica with his troupe of mummers, presenting his masques on a wagon for stage; Plutarch tells a legend of how the aged Solon saw him acting. Tragedy, 'the goat-song', perhaps so-called because a goat was sacrificed to Dionysos, was still hardly distinct from *komoidia*, comedy, the 'village song', as yet rustic and 'rejected with scorn by the city'; but within a life-time it was to become the art-form of Phrynichos and Aeschylus.[13]

Abroad, in addition to keeping up his mining colony, Peisistratos consolidated Athens' position in the north-east. He retook Sigeion from the Mytileneans, whom we must suppose to have regained it while Athens was in confusion – unless, indeed, it was he who secured this outpost for the first time, in which case our traditional dates for Alkaios, Sappho and Pittakos need to be brought down by many years – and installed his son Hegesistratos as governor. Mytilene remained hostile, and Hegesistratos held his position 'not without fighting'[14]; but presently a golden opportunity opened of securing the other side of the straits as well.

Even the will to power of other noblemen could be used to good effect. Miltiades the son of Kypselos (so, a relative to Hippokleides the suitor of Agariste, p. 206), of the 'four-horse-chariot-keeping' house of the Philaidai, had not gone into exile. His family estates were near Brauron, so he may well have been a confederate or even kinsman of Peisistratos; but he felt restive under the monarchy of one of his peers. 'He was sitting on the porch of his house', says Herodotos, when he saw a group of men passing, whose outland dress and spears (for men no longer went armed in Attica) marked them as foreigners. With Hellenic hospitality and curiosity, he invited them in, and over his entertainment they explained who they were. They were Dolonkians, of a small Thracian tribe still independent of the Greek colonies, in the interior of the Gallipoli Peninsula; but they were now threatened by the Apsinthioi, a more powerful mainland tribe. They had consulted Delphi, and the god had bidden them invite to their country as a Founding Father the first man who invited them into his house after they left the shrine. Miltiades was that man.[15]

---

[13] Ar. *Poetics*, 1448a (end); Plut. *Sol.* 29; *Parian Marble*, 39 (date between 580 and 562).
[14] Hdt. v, 94.   [15] Hdt. vi, 34ff; Plut. *Sol.* 10.

Perhaps the offer was not quite so unpremeditated as this charming story says; but in any case nothing could suit Peisistratos better than to see the formidable Miltiades go abroad with a band of like-minded volunteers, and by the same stroke to get the Thracian Chersonese into Athenian hands.

Having consulted Delphi on his own account, Miltiades set sail. His career in the Chersonese was adventurous. He shut out the Apsinthioi by means of a wall, four miles long, across the isthmus, but was subsequently captured in a war with Lampsakos, across the straits (a colony of Mytilene's ally, Phokaia, p. 109), and only released as the result of a peremptory demand by Croesus of Lydia. Dying childless, he left his principality to Stesagoras, the son of his maternal half-brother Kimon; the family history makes it presumable that their mother was a kinswoman of both her husbands; probably an heiress, who by Attic custom would be expected to marry her nearest male kinsman. This Kimon had gone into exile to escape from Peisistratos; but he remained wealthy enough to continue a race-horse owner, and won a chariot victory at Olympia, which he caused to be announced in the name of Miltiades. 'At the next Olympic festival, he won again, with the same team of mares, and caused the victory to be announced in the name of Peisistratos, and for resigning the victory to him was allowed to come home in peace. Then he won another Olympic victory with the same mares, and was murdered by the sons of Peisistratos, who was now dead' (at least, their guilt was alleged later); 'they set men to lie in wait for him near the Prytaneion', where, as an Olympic victor, he was probably dining as a state guest. 'He is buried before the city-walls, beyond the Hollow Way' (as one approached from Peiraieus), 'and opposite him are buried those mares, which won three Olympiads. This is a feat which has been achieved by one other team of mares, those of Euagoras the Laconian, but by no other horses ever.[16]

Stesagoras, Kimon's son, was murdered in turn; war broke out again with Lampsakos, and he was 'struck over the head with an axe in his prytaneion, by an enemy who pretended to be a deserter'; and then the Peisistratidai sent out his brother, the young Miltiades, whom they had already elevated to the Archonship in 524,[17] 'in a ship of war, to take

[16] Hdt. vi, 103. ('To accuse the Peisistratidai would have sounded well in 490!' -M.M.)
[17] Mentioned to fix a date, D.H. vii, 3, 1; cf. T. J. Cadoux, *The Athenian Archons*, in *JHS* LXVIII.

over'. The Peisistratids clearly regarded the Philaïd principality as an Athenian outpost, and their complicity in the murder of Kimon the race-horse owner (or The Booby, as some people uncharitably called him) was still unheard of. The young Miltiades had to cope with some active or suspected disaffection. He started as he meant to go on, by holding an official mourning for his late brother and placing under preventive arrest all the leading men, who assembled from the peninsular cities for the occasion; and a certain Aratos remained in arms against him until his castle was taken by force – a success which Miltiades thought fit to commemorate by a dedication at Olympia: an ivory cornucopia, seen long afterwards by Pausanias the traveller.[18] Miltiades remained long in power, keeping five hundred mercenaries, and marrying Hegesipyle, daughter of Oloros, a Thracian king. One of their sons was another Kimon, the great general of classical Athens; and one of their descendants another Oloros, the father of Thucydides the historian.[19] Miltiades himself lived to acknowledge the overlordship of Darius the Persian, to take part in his expedition north of the Black Sea, to rise against him in the Ionian Revolt, and when it was crushed to flee to Athens, where he gained a world-famous name as the victor of Marathon. Of this 'crowning mercy' we have perhaps a material relic in the shape of a helmet, lately found at Olympia, with the laconic but metrical inscription 'Miltiades dedicated'.[20]

Peisistratos had died in 528-7, old and respected, and his sons succeeded him jointly, the eldest, the able and sagacious Hippias, conducting the administration. A fragment of an inscription set up under the democracy in the Agorá appears to be from a list of Archons, covering the beginning of the new reign:

> ? On)ETO(rides?
> H)IPPIAS
> K)LEISTHENE(s
> M)ILTIADES
> ? Ka)LLIADE(s
> ? Peisi)STRAT(os

Of these the first, perhaps Onetorides, one of the handsome young

[18] Hdt. vi, 39; Paus. vi, 19, 6.
[19] Hdt. *ib.*; Plut. *Kimon*, 4; Marcellinus, *Life of Thucydides.*
[20] Now in the Olympia Museum; *SEG*, XIV, 351.

men named on Athenian vases with the epithet 'Beautiful', was probably appointed for 527-6 before Peisistratos' death. Then comes
Hippias, holding the titular headship of the state as a Roman emperor
might hold a consulship at the beginning of his reign; and then,
startlingly, the heads of the two other most prominent families:
Kleisthenes, the son of Megakles by Agariste, daughter of Kleisthenes
of Sikyon; and Miltiades (elsewhere mentioned as archon for 524-3,
which enables us to date the list). The name following these might be
that of a chief of the rich, priestly family of the Heralds of Eleusis, who
used the names Kallias, Kalliades and Hipponikos; and the last name
on the fragment, only half preserved, that of Peisistratos the younger,
Hippias' son, who dedicated the Altar of the Twelve Gods in his
archonship, as an inscription recorded (before 519).[21] There was, it
seems, a general 'honeymoon', in which an archonship could be
allotted even to the chief of the Alkmeonidai, who later preferred to
suppress the fact (unrecorded by Herodotos) that they had ever
collaborated with Hippias.

Beyond the Aegean, Croesus of Lydia fell with a daunting crash
before Cyrus the Persian; but Greeks might still hope that Persia, like
Lydia, would come no nearer. Cyrus fell in battle far away on his
eastern frontier (*c.* 529), and his son Cambyses was busied with the
conquest of Egypt. Lygdamis of Naxos consolidated his power at the
expense of his old enemies, his fellow nobles. Naxos had a flourishing
school of sculpture (its most famous product, the famous Sphinx at
Delphi), and at the moment of the revolution several rich patrons were
having imposing male statues prepared at different points on the island.
They remained unfinished, among the rocks out of which they were
being carved; and they remain to this day. A curious story alleges that
Lygdamis offered to sell them, unfinished as they were, to the original
patrons or other highest bidders, to count as their own dedications;
also that he confiscated the property of those who fled into exile, but
later, unable to find purchasers at a reasonable price for so much land,

---

[21] See Meritt in *Hesp.* VIII, 59ff; date from D.H. vii, 3, 1. The altar should be that at
which the Plataians sat as suppliants (Hdt. vi, 108) in 519 (Thk. iii, 68, 3). The lettering
of the companion inscr. on the same P.'s altar of Apollo (Thk. vi, 54, 7), which is extant
(*IG²* I, 761), is however thought by epigraphists to be later than 500; cf. Bizard in *BCH*
XLIV (1920); possibly added later by supporters of the family?
Mr Lewis points out that the name Kalliades has not been found in the Heralds' family.

permitted those who could offer ready money to buy their own land back again.[22] It appears that, like Peisistratos, he was not vindictive, and also that some Naxian like some Athenian exiles escaped with enough gold and silver to be still well-to-do. But perhaps his most important action was to give support to the most spectacular figure in the Aegean world of his time: Polykrates of Samos.

Polykrates the son of Aiakes (*perhaps* that Aiakes who, we saw, 'levied the tithes of piratical gains for Hera', p. 219) had already been using his great wealth to court popularity. When he was ready, with some help from Lygdamis but with a minimum of force (fifteen men, said one story) he seized the seat of government. At first he ruled jointly with his brothers, Pantagnotos and Syloson ('Preserver of Booty', a name typical of the family); but before long he had murdered the former, while the latter fled, to take service with the Persians in Egypt. Polykrates led Samos to piratical triumphs, 'ruling the waves' in a manner that reminded men of the legends of Minos. He had 100 galleys, and 'held up all men without distinction, saying that his friends were more grateful when he gave them their property back than they would have been if he had not taken it'. He was a pious corsair, seeking, like Peisistratos before him, the favour of Apollo of Delos; he made Delos a present of the adjacent and larger islet of Rheneia, attaching it symbolically by a chain across the strait. He terrorised Miletos; with Athens he was probably friendly, through Lygdamis, and he certainly proved an ally to her in practice; for he inflicted a crushing defeat on the fleet of Mytilene, which came south to help Miletos, taking a great haul of prisoners, with whose forced labour he 'dug the whole ditch around the walls of Samos'.[23]

Polykrates was also a great builder, completing (for it had probably been started earlier) the Temple of Hera, 346 feet long; the largest Greek temple known to Herodotos (though those of Selinous and Akragas were as large). He provided his capital (now Tigani, officially Pythagorion, on the south side of the island) with a good harbour by the construction of its mole, curving out into deep water and nearly a quarter of a mile long; often repaired, it still shelters many caiques.

[22] (Ar.) *Oikonomika* ii, 3.
[23] P.'s use of his wealth, Alexis of Samos, *ap.* Ath. xii, 540; Lygdamis and P., Polyainos i, 23; P. 'rose with 15 men', Hdt. iii, 120; Delos (and Minos), Thk. i, 13, cf. iii, 104, cf. H. W. Parke in *CQ* XL; other details, Hdt. iii, 39. View that P.'s father had been tyrant before him (which is against the literary evidence), M. White in *JHS* LXXIV.

Most striking of all, he supplied the city with water (like other *tyrannoi*), by means of a tunnel pierced through the watershed of the island, 1100 yards long. Its architect was Eupalinos of Megara, who knew the earlier and far less ambitious water-conduit of Theagenes (p. 248); for Polykrates was prepared to attract foreign craftsmen by handsome salaries; just as he also enticed Demokedes of Kroton, the famous doctor, by offering a higher retaining-fee than the Athenians, who had previously enticed him from Aigina. His gangs started operations from both sides of the ridge, and met, with an error of only about six feet, in the middle; a remarkable testimony to the accuracy of the *geometria* which Greeks had learned in Egypt. These operations provided work and pay as well as amenities for the poorer Samians, at the expense of the rich who were taxed to pay for them. It is, naturally, the latter aspect which impresses later writers.[24]

Like Peisistratos, Polykrates took thought for the economic foundations of his society. He imported, according to a local historian, the best breeds of sheep from Attica and Miletos, of goats from Naxos and Skyros, of dogs (for hunting and protection of the flocks) from north-west Greece and from Laconia.[25] He kept royal state in a splendid palace, collecting a library and enjoying the works of Samian artists and craftsmen, who were already famous: Rhoikos the son of Telekles, architect of the Heraion, Theodoros the son of Phileas, who had worked for Croesus, making the silver bowl which Herodotos saw at Delphi. He was the artist of the famous ring which was Polykrates' most treasured possession; late writers also credited him with the creation of the famous golden plane-tree and golden vine, which a wealthy Lydian prudently presented to Darius, and which long remained among the chief treasures of the court of Persia.[26]

Polykrates entertained, too, the last great lyric poet of Asian Greece: Anakreon, in whose story the shadow of Persia falls across the Aegean

[24] 'P.'s works', Ar. *Politics*, 1313b. (Hdt., who describes them (slightly over-estimating the length of the tunnel) in iii, 60, does not name P.). Attraction of *technitai*, Alexis of Samos in Ath. xii, 540d; Demokedes, Hdt. iii, 125, 129ff (esp. 131).

[25] Alexis, *ib.*; 'Klytos the Aristotelian, in his book on Miletos' (*ib.*), adds pigs from Sicily.

[26] Palace, Suet. *Caligula*, 21; library, Ath. i (epit.), 3c; Rhoikos, Hdt. iii, 60; Theodoros, *id.* i, 51, iii, 41, Plin. *NH* xxxiv, 83; Rh. and Th. 'first to cast bronze', Paus. viii, 14, 8 (an anachronism; Overbeck, *Schriftq. d. ant. Kunst* supposes there were two Theodoroi; Hdt. does not explicitly say Th. himself worked for P.). The vine and plane, given to Darius, Hdt. vii, 27; cf. Xen. *Hell.* vii, 1, 38, Ath. xii, 514f; ascr. to Th., Himerios, *Ekl.* 31, 8, Phot. *Bibl.* 612; melted down by Antigonos in 316, D.S. xix, 48.

scene. His city of Teos was one – the only one except proud Phokaia –
whose people refused submission to Cyrus' generals. Instead, they
manned their ships, took their families and such possessions as they
could, and sailed, not indeed to the west, like such Phokaians as did
not repent of the decision, but across the sea to Thrace, to Abdera,
'where before this Timesios of Klazomenai founded a city but got no
profit of it; he was driven out by the Thracians, but the Teians of
Abdera now sacrifice to him as a hero'.[27]

The Thracians had grown no softer, and the new colony made good
its ground only by long fighting. Pindar of Thebes, a generation later,
recalls these wars in a paean commissioned by the colonists:

> ... Of a new city am I; I have seen my mother's mother utterly
> smitten by the enemy's fire.... (My fathers) gained this land by
> war, this fertile land, planting prosperity when they drove out the
> Paionian spearmen. Misfortune was theirs; but when they endured,
> at last the gods wrought with them. He that does bravely shines
> with the flame of glory; and upon them came a light supreme, facing
> the foe before the Dark-Wooded Hill. Hail, Paian, Hail! May
> Paian never leave us.

Anakreon probably bore his part in all this without discredit; at
least, he was said to have stayed long enough in Abdera to write an
epitaph for one of its heroes:

> Great fighter, fallen on Abdera's front,
> Agathon's pyre was mourned by all the town;
> There was no youth his match, whom in the brunt
> Of war blood-thirsty Ares has cut down.

Another, ascribed to Anakreon but unlocated, runs

> Good soldier was Timokritos, whose grave
> This is. War spares the coward, not the brave.

Abdera might well wish to claim a famous authorship for the inscriptions on her war-memorials; but on the other hand, the tradition is the
more likely to be true, for the fact that this was *not* the sort of verse for
which Anakreon was famous. It was becoming a tradition, too, since
Archilochos and Alkaios, for poets to laugh at their own military
efforts; and Anakreon duly did so. But he was, in truth, not a fighting

[27] Hdt. i, 168.

man by choice; and when an invitation arrived for him to join the court of Polykrates, he took it.[28]

> Fill high the bowl with Samian wine;
> We will not think of themes like these;
> It made Anakreon's song divine;
> He served – but served Polycrates –
> A tyrant; but our masters then
> Were still, at least, our countrymen.

But the alien lordship was drawing closer. Polykrates made alliance with the old Pharaoh Amasis, who, like the Ptolemies, had made Cyprus an Egyptian outpost; but when Cambyses mobilised the sea-power of Phoenicia against Egypt, and the kings of Cyprus went over to him, Polykrates' nerve failed, and he too sent a squadron to join the Persians. The aristocratic captains mutinied, and turned back from Karpathos in the Dodecanese to attack him; but they were defeated after landing, and sailed to get help from Sparta, their old ally (p. 184). A Spartan expedition in turn, the first recorded to have crossed the Aegean, effected a landing, but failed after fierce fighting in an attempt to storm the town, and retired after a six-weeks' siege for lack of provisions. Evidently they received no help from the country people, who could have supplied them if they would. The exiles, left to their own devices, held the gold-mining island of Siphnos up to ransom for 100 talents and then seized Kydonia in Crete; but, after five years, they were destroyed by their old enemies the men of Aigina in alliance with the Cretans.[29]

But Polykrates did not long survive. The famous story that he threw his cherished ring into the sea in a vain attempt to avert the jealousy of heaven, and had it brought back to him in the belly of a fish, *could* be perfectly true; a gruesome parallel to it was recorded in 1787, when Mr Ephraim Thompson of Whitechapel had returned to him a watch, numbered 1369 by the maker, Henry Warson, which he had given to his son, who was lost overboard from his ship off Falmouth; it had been found in the belly of a sick shark, caught in the Thames.[30] That it was Amasis of Egypt who advised Polykrates to take this step, and

[28] Pind. *Paian*, ii, esp. 5, 28ff, 60ff; Mt. Melamphyllon, Pliny, *NH* iv, 11/50. Epitaphs, *A.P.* vii, 226, 160.

[29] Hdt. iii, 44-7, 54-9.

[30] *id.* iii, 40ff. Story from the *Annual Register*, 1787, in *The Observer*, 4 Oct. 1926.

who was the first to break off his alliance, calculating that Polykrates' luck was too good to last, is the most improbable part of the story; it sounds like a pro-Polykratean excuse. That there was gloomy for-boding in his entourage, as the threats to his position multiplied, is likely enough; but Polykrates himself went off in high good-humour to the mainland to pick up the satrap Oroites, who said that he was under suspicion and threatened with death; snubbing his daughter, who reported an ill-omened dream, with the words 'You'll live to be an old maid if I come back safe, my girl.' With that he went, was arrested by Oroites, who was not in disgrace, and was put to death and his body impaled (about 523).[31]

The tyranny and the sea-power of Samos did not fall at once, being held together by Polykrates' Secretary, Maiandrios. Maiandrios dedi-cated his late master's gorgeous furniture in the Temple of Hera, and meditated laying down the tyranny; but he found that 'he who rides on a tiger cannot dismount'. Thus, says Herodotos, 'wishing to be the most righteous of men, he was frustrated'. The Thalassocracy-List makes the power of Samos last till 517. Then Darius, now firmly on the throne after the chaos following the death of Cambyses, sent an expedition to restore, as his vassal, the exiled Syloson. Maiandrios retired without resistance (his brother Lykaretos even entered the Persian service, and was later governor of Lemnos); but fighting broke out after the surrender, and led to a massacre, giving rise to the proverb, 'thanks to Syloson, there's room!'[32]

Maiandrios went to Sparta, where he is said, improbably, to have tried to bribe King Kleomenes to restore him; but Sparta did, it appears, send a fleet to the Cyclades to try to consolidate resistance to a further Persian advance. Now or earlier, she suppressed Lygdamis of Naxos; and a two-year Spartan 'Rule of the sea' is recorded (517-515), after which Naxos, under the upper-class government set up through Sparta's intervention, emerges as head of a short-lived Cycladic con-federacy. She was said to be able to mobilise 8000 hoplites; and though after 505 her sea-power is said to have been dethroned by that of Eretria, she was still strong enough to beat off a Persian-Ionian attack as late as 500.[33]

[31] *id.* 120ff.
[32] *id.* 139-47; Lykaretos, cf. v, 27; proverb in Str. xiv, 638.
[33] *id.* 148; D.S. 'Thalassocracy-List', *ap.* Euseb. (I, p. 225 Schoene), 13-16; Plut. *Mal. Hdt.* 22; on Naxos, Hdt. v, 30ff.

Hippias of Athens, less spectacular than Polykrates but more prudent, took no hand in these stirring doings. Friendly at once to Argos and Sparta and also to the lords of Thessaly, he must since the beginning of his reign have been acknowledging Persian overlordship at Sigeion. Living in peace, he seems even to have reduced his father's direct tax on produce, from ten to five per cent.[34] But he was quite capable of pursuing a robust foreign policy on his own borders. He was married to a daughter of Charmos, his father's general, as well as to Myrsine, daughter of Kallias and mother of his five sons[35]; and when Kleomenes of Sparta, in the Megarid in 519, advised the Plataians to commend themselves to Athens, for protection against Thebes, he accepted the offer, defeated the Thebans and pushed his north-western frontier forward to the Asopos.[36]

Meanwhile his brother Hipparchos interested himself in poetry and religious matters; among those who gathered at his court were Simonides of Keos, famous alike for choral lyrics and elegiac occasional verse; Lasos of Hermione, a dithyrambic poet and wit, said to have taught Pindar; Pratinas of Phlious, who introduced into Athens the Satyr-play, a form of burlesque, with its chorus of the horse-tailed and horse-eared wild men, the companions of Dionysos; and Onomakritos the expert on oracles, who, however, presently got into trouble and was expelled, having been caught by Lasos in the act of interpolating his own compositions into his collection of the prophecies of Mousaios.[37] When Polykrates fell, their ranks were swelled by the addition of Anakreon, whom Hipparchos rescued from Samos, sending a warship to fetch him.[38] Hipparchos was a minor poet himself, and adorned the pillars bearing the head of Hermes, god of trade and traffic, which he set up to mark half-way points between Athens and the chief villages, with brief, metrical exhortations to morality.

> Hipparchos said: Walk thou with honest thoughts

ran one of these; and another

> Hipparchos said: Do not deceive a friend.

---

[34] Thk. vi, 54, 5.
[35] 'Kleidemos in his *Returns*, Book viii', *ap.* Ath. xiii, 609c-d (perhaps a garbled ref., as a book of this *title* is ascribed elsewhere to Antikleides; but the *detail* suits Kl. the Atthidographer); Myrsine, Thk. vi, 55, 2.   [36] Hdt. vi, 108; date from Thk. iii, 68, 3.
[37] *Ath. P.* 18; cf. ps.-Plato, *Hipparchos*, 228c (Simonides); Lasos, Hdt. vii, 6; Thomas, *Life of Pindar*; his witticisms, e.g. Ath. viii, 338b, Stob. *Anthology*, lxx, 29; Pratinas, *Suda*, *s.v.*; Onomakr. Hdt. *ib.*   [38] Ps.-Plato, *ib.* (also on H.'s own lines, below).

But the nemesis of tyranny, the lust of power and the fear of rivals, poisoned the atmosphere here too. Peasants and craftsmen might prefer Peisistratid lordship to the aristocracy, inasmuch as it was easier to support one family of lords than many in continual rivalry; but Philaïds and Alkmeonids might be suspected of envy. The head of the former family, Kimon the race-horse owner, had been eliminated, it is alleged, by a preventive murder, though the Peisistratids disclaimed all knowledge of this, and continued to support his family in the Chersonese. Kleisthenes the Alkmeonid, archon in 525, at some later date went into open opposition and headed an armed rising. A body of aristocrats and their partisans fortified Leipsydrion in the northern hill-country; but the Peisistratids were still too strong for them. A drinking-song, one of the 'cavalier songs' of Athens, took the form of a lament:

> Oh false Leipsydrion, weak to save
> Our friends, the noble and the brave:
> The nobly born, in valiant deed
> Who there in battle proved their breed.[39]

Kleisthenes with his family now took refuge at Delphi, where long ago his grandfathers had met over the ruins of Krissa, and found a use for his business talents and for his family's varied connections. The great temple had been accidentally burnt down (548 tr.), and since then, while the Delphians themselves set out to raise a quarter of the cost of rebuilding, subscriptions had been solicited in all parts of Greece and the Levant. Even Amasis of Egypt had subscribed 1000 talents of alum (perhaps for fire-proofing roof-timbers); the Greeks in Egypt raised 2000 drachmas, a miserable sum; they were evidently not much interested in the westward-facing sanctuary. Enough money was now in hand for building to be undertaken, and the great Athenian exile obtained the contract.[40]

At home, as so often, it was the failure of a dynast to control his sexual desires that precipitated disaster. Thessalos-Hegesistratos conceived a passion for a youth named Harmodios, of a family which traced its descent to the companions of Kadmos; but the boy was loyal

---

[39] *Ath. P.* 19, 3; cf. Hdt. v, 62.
[40] 548, Paus. x, 5, 13. The fire, Hdt. i, 50; subscriptions, ii, 180; 'the Alkmeonidai' take the contract, *Ath. P.* 19, 4.

to another admirer, his cousin Aristogeiton. Affronted, Thessalos paid him out by a shabby, public insult. Harmodios' sister was one of the maidens chosen to carry the baskets of offerings in the procession at the Great Panathenaia, the four-yearly, most splendid religious festival of Athens; but a few days before the feast Thessalos (presumably helping Hipparchos, who loved pageantry, with the preparations) told her abruptly to get out; the procession, he added, was for girls of good families, whereas *she* was the sister of that 'pansy', Harmodios. Thereat Harmodios and Aristogeiton, in fury, determined with a band of confederates (whether few or many, the stories differed) to kill the Peisistratids on the feast-day itself, when they could get near them in the crowds, with daggers which they could conceal in ceremonial bunches of myrtle.

We are left wondering whether the two angry young men conspired entirely on their own, or whether their indignation made them suitable tools for some larger enterprise. In any case, they selected for their first destined victim not Thessalos, but the ruler, Hippias.

On the summer morning of the feast, Hippias went up to the Acropolis, where, in front of the gaily painted archaic temple, he would receive the procession escorting the beasts and other offerings for sacrifice. Hipparchos was marshalling the procession, down beyond the Agora by the Sacred Gate, where various 'properties' were kept. Harmodios and Aristogeiton were already waiting their chance among the crowds of spectators, when they were alarmed to see one of their confederates talking intimately with Hippias himself. Jumping, in a panic, to the conclusion that they were betrayed, 'they held off from attacking Hippias as being forewarned', but 'wishing to effect something before they were arrested, they went down from the citadel, rushed off prematurely without their confederates, and murdered Hipparchos as he was marshalling the procession; and thus they ruined the whole plot'. Harmodios was killed on the spot by Hipparchos' bodyguards. Aristogeiton escaped in the crowd, but was arrested soon after, and perished after prolonged torture to make him reveal the names of his accomplices. Hippias, thoroughly shaken, redoubled his security precautions, and the remaining four years of his reign were a reign of terror.[41]

[41] *Ath. P.* 18, 'correcting' (?), on some details, Thk. vi, 54-8, who expands his own account in i, 20, and that of Hdt. v, 55f.

The Athenian democracy of classical times looked upon Harmodios and Aristogeiton as its heroes and martyrs. A point of interest about their story is that, though the main facts of it were accessible to those who enquired carefully, and though history was being written at Athens within living memory of the event, the version which lived in 'folk-memory' was quite different and much simplified. The murdered Hipparchos was supposed to have been head of the government, and also the villain of the story; and immediate liberation was supposed to have been the result. A drinking song ran

> I will carry my sword in a myrtle bouquet
> Like Harmodios and Aristogeiton, when they
> The tyrant did slay
> And gave back to Athens fair laws to obey.

Other versions are also quoted, and catches to cap these lines (they are not all a single song for one voice); one, beginning as above, ended

> On Athena's high day
> The tyrant, the mighty Hipparchos, did slay.

One 'capping' verse ran

> Belovéd Harmodios, not dead and cold,
> In the Isles of the Blesséd you live, it is told,
> With Achilles of old,
> Fleet-footed, and great Diomedes the bold.[42]

The democracy set up statues of the Tyrant-Slayers, early enough to be carried off as booty by Xerxes in 480; and their deed was among the very few episodes of recent history to be illustrated by vase-painters[43]; the modern equivalent would be to qualify for inclusion in a stained-glass window. Once the legend had captured the popular imagination, research toiled after it in vain; even one prose-writer, the author of the dialogue *Hipparchos*, calls him 'the Tyrant'.[44] The tradition stands as a warning that in most of the picturesque stories, of which Greek history is full, what is handed down to us is not first-hand reporting, but what popular repetition made of it. Thucydides was aware of the difference; Herodotos, though an excellent reporter himself, was not.

[42] Ath. xv, 695, q. all four quatrains; they were attrib. to Kallistratos, *q.v.* in Hesychios.
[43] RF *stamnos* in Wurzburg; cf. M. Hirsch in *Klio*, XX, 1926; Beazley in *JHS* LXVIII.
[44] And the Parian Marble, in 263, reproduces the whole popular tradition!

At Delphi, Kleisthenes was following a more promising line. He had gained great influence through his restoration of the temple; a story said that, though his contract specified that it should be built of *poros* stone (limestone), he gave it, of his own generosity, a façade of Parian marble. Another story, less friendly, said that, having large sums of money in his hands, he used some of it to bribe the prophetess to give oracles in his interest. In any case it appears that under his influence the Oracle, whenever Spartans consulted it, 'whether the Spartan state or individuals', would return the answer, 'You must liberate Athens.'[45] The prestige of the oracle, soon to be tarnished by its defeatist attitude in the Great Persian War, still stood high; and it was already Spartan policy not to tolerate tyrants within their sphere of influence. But Peisistratos and his sons had always been good friends to Sparta; and to embark on adventures beyond the Isthmus was a policy which King Kleomenes, when offered the willing alliance of Plataia, had eschewed (p. 319).

At last, however, Sparta determined to obey the command of Apollo, and about 511 a fleet with troops under one Anchimolios (like some other sea-borne expeditions it was not under a king) sailed to the Bay of Phaleron. But Hippias was forewarned, and had obtained help from his allies, the barons of Thessaly: 1000 cavalry under their 'king' (or *Tagos*?) Kineas of Koniaia. On the plain of Phaleron, which Hippias had had cleared of trees in readiness, a cavalry charge broke the ranks of the Spartans, killed Anchimolios, and drove them to their ships with heavy loss.

But Sparta's prestige was now involved. A much larger army marched by the Isthmus under Kleomenes himself. Debouching from the west into the plain of Eleusis, it beat off the Thessalians with the loss of some forty troopers; whereat the Thessalians accepted defeat and rode away home. Kleomenes marched into Athens and 'together with those of the Athenians who wished to be free', besieged the Peisistratidai in the 'Pelargian Fort' on the Acropolis. The fortress was well supplied and, says Herodotos, could have outlasted the Spartans' willingness to conduct a blockade; but a misfortune befell the defenders. The children of the Peisistratidai were captured in an attempt to smuggle them out of the country, and with them as hostages Kleomenes and his Athenian friends drove the bargain that the Peisistratids

---

[45] Both versions in Hdt. v, 62f, followed by *Ath. P.* 19, 4f.

should leave Attica, with their personal belongings, within five days.[46]

So ended the fifty years of what many Athenians, in the troublous times that followed, looked back upon as a golden age, an 'age of Kronos' before the iron age of the younger gods. At the moment, all was rejoicing; prominent citizens breathed freely again; yet even so, there was remarkably little animosity against the fallen lords. An inscription was presently set up, recording the names of all members of their family, who were to be exiled for ever; but even known and prominent partisans of theirs 'who had not done evil during the troubles' were allowed to stay. Among them, biding his time, was Hippias' brother-in-law, another Hipparchos, son of Charmos the general. Despotism itself, or the attempt to establish it, was decreed punishable, not by death but by loss of citizen rights; though it must be remembered that the implications of such *atimia* – 'outlawry' – were much more formidable when the early law was passed than when the Aristotelian scholar recorded it: 'This is the statute and ancestral custom of Athens: If any persons raise rebellion in order to rule as tyrants, or if any man join in establishing tyranny, he shall be outlawed, both he and his posterity.'[47] Even the Tyrants' Scythian archers, most strikingly, were neither massacred nor sold abroad, but kept on and kept up to strength by the republic as a permanent police corps, to figure repeatedly in the plays of Aristophanes.

To Hippias the Thessalians, perhaps a little ashamed, offered the lordship of Iolkos, whence the *Argo* set sail; Amyntas, King of Macedonia, on whose borders Peisistratos had dug for gold, offered him Anthemous on his own coast. Hippias, however, declined both offers and retired to Sigeion. Hippoklos, tyrant of Lampsakos, whose son married Hippias' daughter, had recently gained favour with Darius for guarding his communications on the Danube, when the Great King had invaded Scythia and found himself in grave difficulties.[48] The Persian, overlord of Ionia and all the East, might prove a more potent protector and avenger than either Thessaly or Macedon.

[46] Hdt. v, 63–65, *Ath. P.* 19, 5f.
[47] *Ath. P.* 16, 10; 22, 4.
[48] Hdt. v, 94, cf. iv, 138; Thk. vi, 59.

PART IV

The Revolution in Greek Thought

CHAPTER XVII

The Natural Philosophers

THE same troublous sixth century saw the beginning of the achievement which makes the Greek contribution unique in human history: the development of the first scientific thought.

The Axis Age (p. 3), the age of the first philosophies and the first higher religions, was not exactly simultaneous wherever it occurred. The age of the prophets of Israel, in centrally placed Syria, begins earliest, about 750, with the social protest of Amos. Zoroaster in Persia cannot be securely dated; Thales lived until about 540, Confucius and Gautama Buddha till about 480. But that all these original and unprecedented movements of thought should begin, in regions between which it is most unlikely that there was communication (scarcely even possible, unless between Israel and Persia), even so nearly simultaneously as this, remains remarkable.

As to why the new movements were *possible* in this age, and not before, a tentative suggestion has been made (pp. 3ff). This does not detract from the originality of the great thinkers; nor from their courage. The prophets of Israel risked, and some lost, their lives; and even in Greece, where persecution was rare, the classical thinkers had to make the bitter discovery that men would not change their manner of life and the conduct of their society merely because of an exposition according to reason.

It is noteworthy that Mesopotamia and Egypt, where the old civilisations had not completely disintegrated, did not produce new movements of thought at this time. Rather, priests and people clung the more desperately to their outworn faiths when times were bad. It must have been axiomatic to them that the highest duty was to *preserve* a familiar way of life. But in this way, their societies became 'fossilised'. The metaphor is suggestive.

The record of literal fossils in palaeontology shows us how in remote ages, in competition between powerful organisms, some of the strongest took to flesh-eating, and some of their victims developed armour or weapons: the plate-armoured fish of the Devonian epoch; the armoured and horned or club-tailed dinosaurs of the late Mesozoic. But the future was not either to weapons or armour. The armoured creatures perished when times changed, when seas dried or diminished or grew too salt, or when winters grew colder with the advance of the polar ice. Each time, the following age was one in which a less limited life was lived, by creatures descended from inconspicuous ancestors; from creatures soft-bodied, defenceless, but more adaptable; from fish something like the modern lung-fish and mud-skippers, surviving precariously in shallow creeks and corners, or, when a pool dried, dragging themselves over land to find another – the ancestors of amphibians, reptiles, and ultimately mammals and birds; and again after the great age of the reptiles, from unknown species, probably small of body, surviving and evolving in colder regions with hair or feathers, constant body temperature and a relatively larger brain. Something strangely analogous has happened more than once among human societies. In the *Achsenzeit* it was, in the west at least, in small states and either in outlying regions or among oppressed peoples that thought took new forms: in outlying and divided Greece, and in Israel, central indeed to the ancient world (it is only our maps, limited to the Roman Empire, which place Judaea in a corner) but caught and ground painfully between Asia and Egypt, the upper and the nether millstone.

In India and China, where archaeology is even younger than in the west, we know correspondingly less of the background; but it is already clear that there too, on the Indus and in Honan, there had been advanced bronze-age cultures, which in their ripeness fell a prey to barbarians. Confucius belonged to a class of civilian officials called the *Ju*, which appears to have the curious meaning of 'Weaklings'[1]; they may have been descendants of officials of the bronze-age (Shang) culture, thus called by the warrior retainers of iron-age chiefs, to whom, like Boethius under Theodoric, they had made themselves indispensable. The fact that the Warring States of Confucius' time (*c.* 551-480), like the Greek states, signally failed to restore an earlier unity, may have helped the *Ju* to maintain their position, by leaving the rival 'Dukes', in a competitive situation, unable to neglect their help. On the

[1] Liu Wu-chi, *History of Confucian Philosophy*, pp. 14ff.

Ganges in the same century we find likewise a society divided among local kingdoms, but of their earlier history we know nothing at all. But the tradition tells us that it was the human suffering which he encountered outside the gates of his father's palace, which so shook the prince Gautama Sakyamuni that he left all and went out to join the ascetics.

In all these regions, then, as in Greece, it was in a time of stress, violence and injustice, though also in a society full of economic vitality, that the new movements arose. In Greece itself, the philosophic movement began in Ionia, among men who retained some memory of past greatness in Old Greece, preserved by the epic. It was this region, too, which had the closest contact with the technically skilful, though now intellectually stagnant, cultures of the near east; and here, conspicuously, there had been social revolutions, though we have fewer stories about Ionian tyrants than about those nearer Athens. The first recorded speculations of 'natural philosophy' take place moreover in Miletos, whose enterprises in the Black Sea had revealed lands of such startlingly different climate, geology and ways of life: where rain in summer was not surprising, but an earthquake was; and where men who did not eat bread grew corn for export (pp. 121ff). Nowhere more than in Miletos, too, had society been shaken and decent men shocked by the savageries of the class-war (pp. 214ff). Also, through the treaty with Alyattes (p. 210), renewed by Cyrus, Miletos of all Ionian cities had the closest contact with the east.

Darius, according to a famous story, once asked some Greeks at his court how much they would have to be paid to get them to eat the bodies of their parents when they died? 'And they said they would not do that for any money. Then Darius called some Indians, of the tribe called the Kallatians, ("Black Men" – aborigines) whose custom is to eat their parents, and asked them, in the presence of the Greeks, to whom an interpreter translated what was said, for what reward they would agree to cremate their parents; and they cried out, and told him not to say such horrible things. So firmly are these customs held,' comments Herodotos, 'and Pindar seems to me quite right, in the poem where he says, "Custom is king of all".'[2]

Herodotos tells the story to illustrate the thesis that all men's customs

---

[2] Hdt. iii, 38, 4; for the Pindar passage, cf. Plato, *Gorgias*, 484b; but the bearing of this qn. is different; it is not necessarily from the same poem.

are equally sacred to them, and that only a madman would laugh a other people's. But the story also illustrates the impact upon the Greeks of the discovery that customs differ. The word custom, or law, *nomos*, came to be used in the sense of 'convention', in contrast to *physis*, 'natural process', and before Herodotos was dead unscrupulous people were taking comfort from the thought that, since Law was only convention, no law is sacred. Nevertheless, the immense widening of Greek horizons by geographical discovery must have played an essential part in enabling a group of Milesians to break decisively with tradition and set out to discover, by thinking, the truth about the universe.

Thales the son of Examyes (probably a Karian name), of 'Phoenician', that is probably of Kadmeian, old Aegean, descent, lived in the Miletos of the Lydian alliance, the class-war, and the peace under the Agrarian government. He had also, it is said, like Solon, visited Egypt as a merchant. He is typical of those Greeks who knew their eastern neighbours and reflected upon what they saw.

Assyrian pharmacists, metallurgists and potters, heirs of a culture already literate for over 2000 years, had accumulated a mass of what may not unfairly be called chemical knowledge. Much of it no doubt was handed down orally and in association with practical skills, among the 'mysteries' of crafts and professions; but much even of this had been committed to writing, a step which implies some advance towards the making of general statements: the judgment 'Now I do this' must be replaced by 'When things are thus and thus, we do this or that, according to the end in view.' That any of these writings came into the hands of Greeks and could be read by them is rather improbable; they were secret, and at least in one case an Assyrian craft-recipe was committed to a kind of cypher. But the conception of matter as something which changes its form, a conception known in a fashion to every metal-smelter, potter or cook, must have been made more explicit. Now the most fundamental new concept ascribed to Thales is precisely that of a basic matter underlying all its transformations. The basic question asked by him and his successors was 'What is it?' Thales, who could observe the apparent emergence of land from water in the silt shoals at the mouth of the Maeander (a process which was presently to leave old Miletos high and dry); familiar with steam and ice (the latter well-known to Milesians north of the Black Sea); and perhaps too, as Aristotle conjectured, reflecting on the necessity of water to all life, answered, Water.[3]

It was attractively suggested by Gordon Childe that, when bronze-age metal-workers explored the western Mediterranean, they could not in the long run prevent local barbarians from observing the processes of smelting and metallurgy. What they could do was to keep secret the spells and ceremonies proper to their crafts, a secrecy which was to be the reverse of disadvantageous to the Europeans.[4] The same process may well have taken place when Greeks were learning all they could of the wisdom of the east. Its results appear conspicuously in medicine, when the unprejudiced common sense of the Krotonian Demokedes at the court of Darius proved superior to the temple-medicine of Egypt, and in the next century in the superb approach of Hippokrates to the problem of the 'Sacred Disease': 'As to the Sacred disease, as it is called ... I consider that all diseases are equally sacred, and all equally natural.'[5] We notice also Thales' attitude to the celebrated eclipse (p. 211). Babylonians and Sumerians before them had observed eclipses for thousands of years, had recorded their dates and observed regularities in their occurrence. Never doubting, as indeed few Greeks doubted, that an eclipse was an omen of evil, they had refined so far as to go to an observatory in the hills, away from the river swamps, and observe when an eclipse was due, reporting the omen or absence of an omen according to whether the eclipse took place, i.e. was visible in Mesopotamia. Thales' reaction to the approach of an eclipse during the Medo-Lydian war, on the other hand, was simply to report it due *this year*; a natural phenomenon.

That Thales was interested in the doings of craftsmen is highly probable. His legend represents him as an informal and unceremonious person, capable of sitting in the kitchen when it was cold, and inviting visitors to join him there, 'for there are gods here too'. As he is also said to have said that 'All things are full of gods', probably his views were hylozoic or pantheistic. 'The magnet has a soul; for it can move iron' is a saying ascribed to him by Aristotle.[6] Another well-known

---

[3] Ar. *Metaph.* i, 983b. Th.'s travels, D.L. i, 27.
[4] Childe, *The Prehistory of European Society* (Penguin Books, 1958).
[5] *On the Sacred Disease*, 1; cf. Hdt. iii, 33; Demokedes in Persia, *id.* iii, 131ff.
[6] Ar. *On the Soul*, i, 2, 405a; 5, 411a; D.L. i, 244 and (on Th.'s alleged visit to Egypt) 27; cf. Aetios, Proklos, Plut. (*Isis and Osiris, Mor.* 364d) *ap.* Kirk and Raven, *Presocratic Philosophers*, pp. 76f.

story represents him as an adroit man of business: he paid a deposit for priority of the use of every oil-press in Miletos and Chios (more evidence of their close association), out of season, when he could do it cheaply; and by thus cornering the means of production, made a handsome profit when the olive-crop came along.[7] Miletos was a city in which the craftsmen (the Cheiromacha, p. 214) had asserted themselves in the republic. A realistic attitude was characteristic of the Milesian school. It is sometimes denied that Greek philosophers ever experimented. This is unsound; we have a glimpse of Greeks doing so, even in Plato.[8] They did not do so systematically, but they certainly did so sometimes, and they were, as Burnet said, born observers. Miletos was a good place in which to watch industrial processes, as well as geological change; and here took place, if not the birth of modern science, the birth of that naturalistic rationalism which the Greek observational sciences of astronomy and medicine required.

Thales is also said to have made important discoveries in mathematics. The Phoenician traders are said to have introduced improvements in arithmetic; and he may well, too, have been one of the first Greeks to study the Egyptian geometry and arithmetic which interested Herodotos,[9] and of which something is now known at first hand, especially from the famous Rhind Papyrus of about 1700 B.C. The geometry, 'land-measurement', served the practical purpose of marking out again the boundaries of plots after the inundations of the Nile. The services of a surveyor were always available, for the king's taxes depended on the size of the holdings. Aahmes, the writer of the papyrus, expounds a primitive but serviceable method of multiplication, though division, done entirely by trial, remained a formidable process; and he deals with simple problems involving volume, such as how many measures of corn a granary will hold. His arithmetical sums deal with equally practical problems, such as the calculation of rations and wages. A little more elaborate are the Egyptian methods of determining what they called the *seqt* or *seqet* of a pyramid, the ratio between the height and half the side of the base; this ratio determined the angle

[7] Ar. *Politics*, 1259a. That he could foresee a good olive-crop is impossible, but he may have thought he could.

[8] e.g. *Symposion*, 175d; cf. Empedokles (fr. 100) and the 'toddy-lifter'; Burnet, *Early Gk. Philosophy*, p. 27.

[9] Hdt. ii, 109; Phoen. arithmetic, Proklos, *On Euclid*, 65, 3 (Thales, 11 DK).

of slope of the sides, and was thus of vital importance to the masons dressing the outer blocks.

The Greek achievement lay in the fact that in taking over all this they *generalised* it. Of the rules of land-measurement they made Geometry; where the Egyptians had confined themselves to practical problems, a Greek philosopher would propose a *theorema*, a proposition for contemplation, good in itself as a source of aesthetic, intellectual delight in its truths and its inevitability. Marxists have complained that Greek science was ultimately stultified by the divorce between the aristocratic, contemplative tradition of Plato and the slaves or other humble people who did the world's work.[10] But the Platonic tradition never wholly dominated the Greek field, and the divorce was not complete until Roman times. The practical Archimedes, killed by a Roman soldier in 212 B.C., was a long time after Plato. Nor does it appear how the Greeks could have laid the foundations which they did for medieval Arabic and modern European mathematics without their purely theoretical speculations.

The most famous of the early Greek generalisations was that of Pythagoras (pp. 379ff). The Egyptians had long known that a triangle with sides in the ratio of 3, 4 and 5 had a right angle between its short sides, and used this method of getting their angles 'right'. Pythagoras characteristically advanced from this point to his famous Theorem. But Thales before him is also said to have made mathematical discoveries, or at least to have devised solutions to practical problems of a geometrical character. For example he is said to have measured the height of a pyramid by measuring its shadow and the shadow of his staff – some versions said choosing a time of day when the length of the shadow and the height of the object were equal.[11] He is also said to have devised a method of calculating the distance of a ship out at sea. From this Eudemos, the mathematician and pupil of Aristotle, concluded that he had proved that if two triangles have a side and two angles equal, they are equal in all respects. He was also credited with the propositions that the angles at the base of an isosceles triangle are equal; that if two straight lines intersect, the vertically opposite angles

[10] e.g. B. Farrington, *Head and Hand in Anc. Gce.*, G. Thomson, *The First Philosophers*, esp. chap. xv (both in many respects excellent books). E. R. Dodds, Comm. on Plato, *Gorgias*, 512c, exonerates the philosophers.
[11] In Proklos, *On Euclid*, 157, 10 (DK 11 A 20).

are equal; and that the angle in a semicircle is a right angle (Euclid, i, 5, i, 15 and iii, 31).[12]

This is now usually doubted. Thales could have solved these concrete problems by applying the principle of the *seqt*; and we know too that the idea of a map, which suggests the use of simple proportion, was known in Miletos (probably introduced from Babylonia) in the time of his successor Anaximandros (p. 339). The problem of calculating a height is said to have occurred to Thales in Egypt; and the problem of calculating the distance of a ship from the shore is similar. Suppose Thales to have established two observation posts, O and P (see fig. 1), a known distance apart and in sight of each other, provided with markers (e.g. stones on the ground) showing halves and quarters of a right angle, and to have provided himself with a diagram, marked on the ground, with a base-line of, say, one foot per furlong of the distance between the posts (fig. 2). Then let an observer at O signal when a ship bears off marker A, B or C; and Thales at P, even if he could observe no more than that it bore between X and Y, but nearer to X, could measure off on his plan a serviceable approximation to its distance. This, it may be noted, is a comparatively inconvenient observation; that of a ship approaching the base-line, e.g. a harbour-mouth, from directly out at sea, would give better opportunities. Tradition is emphatic in making Pythagoras the first theoretical geometer; but it is possible that Thales did reveal additional possibilities in the application of what he learned from the Egyptians. The men who planned the tunnel at Samos in the next generation (p. 315) carried out more difficult calculations than these.

Thales, like the rest of the 'Seven Sages' was a practical man and a statesman. The story that while walking and observing the heavenly bodies he fell into a well, to the amusement of a Thracian slave-girl who had come to draw water, has the air of a popular joke at the expense of 'unpractical' scientists (the connection in which Plato quotes it[13]); the prototype of all stories about absent-minded professors. One of the earliest and best attested stories of him is that he proposed a federal union of Ionia.[14] Its capital, he proposed, should be at centrally placed Teos, where presumably a joint executive and council were to sit; while the cities should continue to conduct their own internal

---

[12] Eudemos, *ib.*; Pamphile in D.L. i, 24; cf. Burnet, *EGP* pp. 45f; Kirk, *Presocr.* 83f.
[13] *Theaitetos*, 174a.   [14] Hdt. i, 170.

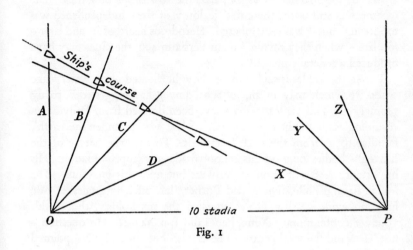

Fig. I

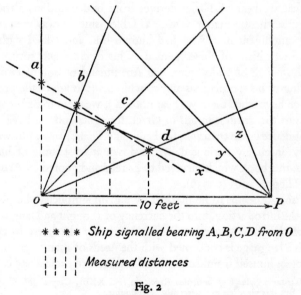

* * * * Ship signalled bearing A, B, C, D from O

| | | | | Measured distances

Fig. 2

affairs 'in the manner of *demoi*', like the townships of Attica. The scheme was still-born; the cities' jealousy of their independence was too strong; but it was remembered. Herodotos heard of it; and later – too late – when they revolted from Persia in 499, the cities may have produced a federal coinage.[15]

The earth, Thales is said to have thought, floated upon water, 'like wood'[16]; which may mean, as Schrödinger has suggested,[17] partly submerged. This view too may have been derived from Babylonian cosmologies, with their conception of 'the waters under the earth', familiar to us from the Old Testament. To the true nature of the heavenly bodies none of his school made any approximation. His importance rests not upon his answers but upon his questions. The Ionian natural philosophers, said Burnet, 'left off telling tales'.[18] We have no evidence that Thales attacked the mythology, though his younger contemporary Xenophanes did (pp. 343-4). His question – not 'How did the world come to be as it is?' but 'What is it?' – pointed the way to science.

All that we hear of Thales derives from oral tradition: a tradition including authentic matter as well as fables, since it was preserved in part by intelligent men who had known him and talked with him. The most brilliant of these, named as his disciple and successor by Greek historians of philosophy, was Anaximandros, son of Praxiades. In reading of his speculations and conclusions (though of the processes by which he reached them we hear nothing), we seem to be encountering one of the greatest minds in Greek thought; and we have reason for confidence in the tradition, for he, unlike Thales, to whom writings are only unreliably attributed, wrote down at least some of his conclusions, in a book which survived to be read and quoted by Aristotle's pupil, Theophrastos (p. 339).

His thought seems to be marked by a giant simplicity; he played a part in the introduction, into the currency of thought and language, of some of the most general concepts, inevitably the latest to appear. Primitive language is concerned with the needs of man to get his food and protect himself from dangers, and is therefore exclusively concrete

[15] P. Gardner, *Coinage of the Ionian Revolt*, in *JHS* XXIII; Caspari (M. Cary), *JHS* XXXV. But this view has more recently been doubted.
[16] DK 11 A 14, from Ar. *On the Heavens*, 294a.
[17] *Nature and the Gks.* p. 58.   [18] *EGP* p. 10.

and particular. The absence of some general words, which to us are
fundamental, is characteristic of it. The introduction of such words,
without which to think generally and to classify is a major intellectual
effort, was one of the achievements of Greek philosophy; and it is
worth while to remind ourselves of evidence that it *was* an achievement; the human race was not born possessing these concepts. Thus,
we hear of Australian native peoples who have words for every kind of
useful tree and food-plant (and pass on to their children an impressive
body of knowledge about them), but have no word for tree in general;
of north-west American Indians who use seven sets of number-words,
according to the objects being counted: one for men; one for animals
and flat objects; one for trees and other long objects; one for round
objects and time (because 'suns' and 'moons' are round?); one for
canoes, one for measures, and one for counting when no definite object
is referred to. The last, we are not surprised to hear, is believed to be a
recent development. English still uses entirely different words for
groups of different kinds of animals (flock, herd, pack, covey, shoal,
etc.), or for twos: pair, brace, couple; while 'collection', 'aggregate'
and 'number' itself are importations from Latin. Abstract nouns and
psychological terms are the last of all to be introduced; the classical
Greek words for 'mind' and 'spirit' are originally physical, except
perhaps *nous* ('thinking', *from* the verb *noeo*, and not *vice versa?*);
phren, *phrenes*, 'midriff', perhaps originally 'lungs'; *psyche*, perhaps
'marrow', 'brain', 'vital fluid', all identified; *thymos*, 'breath', like our
'ghost' and 'spirit'. Early classical Greek was indeed well supplied with
abstract nouns for such concepts as 'hardness', 'softness', 'redness', and
had facility in forming them; but for the words 'quality' and 'quantity'
themselves, language had to wait until Plato or a contemporary of his
coined them, *poiotes* and *posotes*, 'such-and-suchness' and 'so-muchness',
which must, just because of their generality and abstractness, have
seemed odd and difficult words when they were unfamiliar.[19]

It is difficult to put ourselves back into the position of those first
abstract thinkers, pushing into the jungle for the first time, where we
follow on a high-road. Without abstract terms, without optical glass,

[19] Number-words, cf. T. Dantzig, *Number, the Language of Science*, p. 6; B. Russell, qd
ib.; Sapir, *Language and Environment*, p. 239; psychological terms, R. B. Onians, *Origins
of European Thought about the Body, the Mind, the Soul, the World, Time and Fate*. ('Psyche
perhaps marrow' contradicts 'Psyche is air', below (p. 341). I think the former almost
certainly wrong; . . . it doesn't fit the earliest Greek evidence. – E.R.D.)

without algebra or a positional numerical notation, and with only the rudiments of geometry, they had, however, the elation of men conscious of a knowledge new to them, in their awareness of Egyptian mathematics, Babylonian astronomy, and Phoenician methods of calculation. They had also a confidence, magnificent if, as it proved, naive and childlike ('You Greeks are all children', as the Egyptian priest is said to have said to Solon[20]), that, to an unbiased and unflinching effort of the mind, the truth must be accessible.

Anaximandros' particular contribution was one of the most general concepts of all. Continuing the discussion where Thales had left it, he declined to posit as the 'beginning and element' of all things either water or any other observable substance; he preferred to speak of *to apeiron*, 'the boundless', connoting both the qualitatively undefined and quantitatively infinite – 'immortal and indestructible' as Aristotle says, apparently quoting his words.[21] He also postulated that 'boundless worlds', meaning apparently an infinite number of worlds, arise and pass away within the boundless. These worlds he also called 'gods'.[22] The conception of a plurality of worlds is of startling boldness; yet it may have owed something to the character of earlier Greek mythology (already under some eastern influence) in which Hesiod and probably others had described the 'Birth of the Gods' out of an original Chaos or Void. If each world, including this world, *was* to Anaximandros a god, it would follow that man, the dominant species, is a participator in a divine nature; and this too was a conception already current in the cult of Dionysos (pp. 364ff).

'The earth, he said, floated free in space, held by nothing, but abiding because of its equal distance from all things; and its shape was cylindrical, like a drum of a column, one of its flat surfaces being that on which we tread, and the other opposite to it.'[23] This equally bold, simple and original conception got rid of the problem of whether there is an Absolute Bottom, which had worried primitive cosmologists, not only in Greece. A charming piece of mythology reported from Ceylon gives a glimpse of a whole succession of persistent questioners attacking this question within the limits of a mythological framework; and what finally emerges is that the earth is supported by a giant; the giant

20 Plato, *Tim.* 22b.
21 *Physics*, 203b (DK 12 A 15).
22 Cicero, *Nature of the Gods*, i, 10/25 (DK 12 A 15).
23 Hippolytos, *Refutation of All Heresies*, i, 6, 1ff (DK 12 A 11).

stands on the back of a giant tortoise; the tortoise stands on the back of an elephant; and the elephant's legs go All The Way Down. Thales, for whom the earth floats in water, probably thought of the water (above as well as below the Firmament, as in Babylonian cosmology) as pervading all space; but he is not free from the natural postulate of an absolute Down and Up. Anaximandros had taken a long stride towards a conception of gravity.

As to how the separate worlds and various substances come into being, he said that it was by a separating out of opposites through their perpetual motion (another postulate); such opposites, Aristotle explains, were the hot and cold, moist and dry (pointing towards the Four Elements of later Greek natural philosophers). The cold and moist elements sank to the centre, and the earth was surrounded, above the atmosphere, by a sphere of fire. This broke up into circling wheels or tubes of fire, surrounded and concealed by dark mist (*aer*, not yet simply 'air'); a kind of 'Zeta' apparatus. The fire is visible through holes in the tubes, giving rise to the appearance of the heavenly bodies, and eclipses and the phases of the moon are caused by the periodic total or partial blocking of these vents.[24] The formation of a world is the local and temporary prevalence of certain opposites over the others; and 'whence is the genesis of the things that are, thence also must their destruction arise; for they render judgment and requital to each other for their injustice according to the order of time, as he says, using these rather poetic terms'. The quotation is from the Neoplatonist Simplicius, using Theophrastos' *Opinions of the Natural Philosophers*; and is seems that we have, here at least, a citation of phrases if not of a whole sentence from the great Ionian himself.[25] It shows the extent to which even he was still constrained to think of the physical world in anthropomorphic terms.

The continuing debt to Babylonia appears in the tradition that Anaximandros introduced into Greece the *gnomon*, the upright of a sundial, by which the Babylonians first measured 'the twelve parts of the day'.[26] He is also said to have made a map of the world; and a Sumerian map, of a kind, has actually been discovered.[27] But we do

[24] Ar. *Phys.* 187a; (Plut.?) *Strom.* 2, Hippol. *loc. cit.* (DK 12 A 9-11).
[25] DK 12 A 9; Burnet, *EGP* 52; Kirk, *Presocr.* 104ff.
[26] Euseb. *Praep.* x, 14 (DK 12 A 4); Hdt. ii, 109.
[27] Strabo, i, p. 7 (q. Eratosthenes), etc. (Anax. 6 DK); Sumerian map illust., e.g. in Woolley, *The Sumerians*, pl. 22.

not find in the ancient east any adumbration of the Ionian's daring hypotheses.

Equally daring were his hypotheses on the origin of man. At first, he considered, the whole earth when formed was covered by the water; then this was gradually dried up by the sun, the sea being what is left of it.[28] 'The first living creatures were marine creatures, and were covered with spiny shells; then, as time went on, they emerged on to the land and, their shells breaking, they shortly changed their manner of life.'[29] Among these were the ancestors of mankind, descended from fish, perhaps, he thought, of the shark or dogfish type, which gave some protection to their young.[30] It looks as if he may have made observations on human embryos, and also (as is recorded of his younger associate Xenophanes, p. 342) on fossils; but he may also have known of the Babylonian myth of the primaeval fish-man Oannes.

Of Anaximandros' life we hear nothing. One inferior source makes him Founder of the Black Sea colony Apollonia (p. 119); but as no one else mentions this, it was more probably a namesake. One anecdote, too good to omit, represents him too, like Thales, as a man free from pomposity. He was singing for joy; and some rude children laughed at him. The great man's attention was drawn to this. 'Well,' said Anaximandros, 'then we must sing better, because of the children.'[31] The humility attributed to him fits so well with the majestic simplicity of his thought, that it might well be true.

With Anaximenes, called 'a pupil of Anaximandros', we seem to encounter a more pedestrian mind. He wrote, we are told, in 'a simple and unpretentious Ionic"[32] *Le style, c'est l'homme*; though no doubt also, with Anaximandros behind him, he had the less need to use mythological terms. But his best-known tenet, that the primal substance is *aer*, is not so much of a recession from his master's great generalisation of *to apeiron* as it might appear. First, it is wrong to translate *aer*, as yet, as 'air'; for 'air', pure and simple, was a concept which Greeks did not yet possess. They had words for wind, *anemos*, for breath, *pneuma* (*spiritus*), and for air rendered opaque, mist; and that is *aer*. They had even a word for bright mist, such as might be seen rising 'when Zeus the Thunderer scatters the clouds'; that is *aither*,

[28] Ar. *Meteor.* 353b (DK 12 A 27). [29] Aetios, v, 19, 4 (DK 12 A 30).
[30] Plut. *Symp.* viii, 8, 4 (DK *ib.*). [31] D.L. ii, 2. [32] D.L. ii, 3.

whence 'ether'. But for air in none of these relations to our senses, early Greek had no word; it was *no thing* that anyone had yet felt to be of significance, and was ignored, as it still is when we say that there is nothing in the bucket. Anaximenes, who was interested in respiration, contributed to making men conscious of it. But his primary doctrine was that the primal substance is *a mist*, and that from this the denser substances are formed by a process of thickening; for this he used a word derived from an industrial process seen by Milesians among the Scythians: *pilosis*, literally 'felting'.[33] He considered this 'mist' to fill all space. His chief difference from Anaximandros is thus that he considers the primary matter to have definite qualities. In its simplest form, it is what we breathe; and the *psyche* also is air, as in some primitive Greek thought and language. 'When most uniform, it is invisible to the eye; but it is made perceptible by cold, heat, wetness or motion; and it is always in motion. . . . Winds arise when the *aer* is dense, and moves under pressure; and when it becomes denser still, clouds are formed, and so it changes into water. Hail occurs when the water descending from the clouds solidifies; and snow, when the same solidifies in a wetter condition.'[34] In this paraphrase we see him in the act of introducing *air* as a scientific concept into currency. He also made observations on phosphorescence at sea.[35]

Anaximenes thus regarded air as matter in its simplest form; and as Schrödinger has remarked, 'had he said "dissociated hydrogen gas" (which he could hardly be expected to say), he would not be far from our present view'.[36] From a scientific point of view, his achievement is that he reduced qualitative differences of matter to something quantitative and (though not by him) measurable. To later Greeks his work seemed the culmination of that of the Milesian school; and it was to him especially that fifth-century Ionian natural philosophers looked back as their predecessor.[37]

The invention of science is the unique thing in the Greek achievement, and for that reason has received emphasis; but in this age of the rise of the higher religions, even in Greece probably more men were

---

[33] (Plut.) *Strom.* 3, Hippol. *Ref.* i, 7 (DK 13 A 6, 7). – But '*Aither* is rather the special stuff of which the sky is made; cf. A. B. Cook, *Zeus*, I, p. 101.' – E.R.D.
[34] Hippol. *ib.*; Aetios, iii, 4, 1 (DK 13 A 7, 17).
[35] Aet. iii, 3, 2 (DK, *ib.*).   [36] *Nature and the Gks.* p. 59.
[37] So D.L. (ii, 6) makes Anaxagoras his 'pupil'; cf. Kirk, *Presocr. Philosophers*, 162.

interested in new speculations about the nature of the gods than in those about the physical world. One most interesting figure, in touch with the Milesians, but pre-eminently a religious thinker, was the poet Xenophanes of Kolophon.

Xenophanes wrote sternly of his native city as having been ruined because her citizens 'learned futile luxury from the Lydians'[38]; he could have read of this in Mimnermos. He lived to be very old; he writes, 'Already sixty-seven years have been scattering my thoughts over Grecian land; and then it was twenty-five years from my birth, if indeed I can speak exactly of these things.'[39] He is said to have lived a wandering life in the west, settling for a time at Zankle and for a time at Katane; to have mentioned an eruption of Stromboli after sixteen years' quiescence, and to have made observations of marine fossils 'in the stone-quarries at Syracuse' and at Malta; from which, in the scientific manner of the Milesians, he inferred that floods had covered what is now land, and that the impressions had been deposited when the rock was soft mud.[40] All this, though not supported by quotations, was probably derived from his poems, mostly elegiac, which reveal him as a many-sided intellectual in the best Ionian tradition. Elsewhere, in a pleasant passage on conversation over the wine on a winter evening, he depicts men questioning the new-comer about himself, as Greeks still indefatigably do: 'Who are you,a nd from where? Who were your family and parents? How old were you when the Persians came?'[41] This, with the facts that he criticised Pythagoras (p. 375) and that Herakleitos criticised him (p. 398), approximately dates him. He was probably one of the Ionians who retired to the west rather than live under the Persians, and this (*c.* 540) was what marked an epoch in his life when he was about twenty-five years old.

Probably, though no one says so, he traded, like Solon; pretty certainly also he made a living, or part of one, by reciting his own verses. In them, he helped to spread a knowledge of the speculations of the Milesians. He wrote lighter verse too; he is said to have poked fun at his younger contemporary, Simonides of Keos,[42] who was in the west before he died (if we may date Xenophanes about 565-470). He wrote famous lines attacking the excessive adulation of athletes

---

[38] Ath. xii, 526a (DK 21 B 3).   [39] D.L. ix, 19 (DK 21 B 8)

[40] D.L. ix, 18; ps.-Ar. *Marvels*, 833a; Hippol. *Ref.* i, 14 (DK 21 A, 1 and 48).

[41] Ath. ii ,54e (DK 21 B 22).   [42] Schol. on Aristoph. *Peace*, 697 (DK 21 B 21).

which were imitated by Euripides[43]; and his longest fragment shows him, received as a gentleman among gentlemen, laying down the law on how to behave at a party, *not* singing songs about faction-fighting 'in which there is no good', remembering to thank the gods for good cheer, and drinking to the point where a man can still make his own way home, 'unless he is very old'. But in the same lines he also deprecates singing poems about the wars of Titans and Giants and Centaurs, those 'fables of former times'[44]; the most exciting and unedifying portions of the mythology. And this introduces what became his chief intellectual concern.

Did he, one wonders, know of the religious thought of the Persians, who, Herodotos tells us, 'make no cult-statues . . . and think those who do so foolish . . . because they have not formed the idea that the gods are anthropomorphic, as the Greeks have'?[45] In any case, first among Greek writers, Xenophanes decided that anthropomorphism was absurd, and the old tales about the amours of the gods and about war in heaven deplorable:

> Homer and Hesiod have ascribed to the gods all the deeds that are shameful and disgraceful among men: theft and adultery and deceiving one another. . . . Men imagine the gods wearing clothes and talking like us. . . . The Ethiopians make their gods black and flat-nosed, and the Thracians theirs grey-eyed and red-haired. . . . But if animals could paint and make things like men, horses and oxen too would make the gods in their own image![46]

But what, then, are the gods like? Xenophanes has an answer to this question. To begin with, the supreme God is *One*: 'One God, greatest among gods and men, not like mortals either in body or mind.' (Xenophanes did not, we see, exclude the existence of other superhuman beings.) 'He is all sight, and all mind, and all hearing; . . . and he remains in one place, not moving at all; it is not seemly for him to be now here and now there. . . . But he sways all things without effort by the thought of his mind.'[47] Such was Xenophanes' belief; but, he admits,

> No man has clearly seen, nor shall there ever be one who *knows*

---

[43] DK 21 B 2, cf. Eur. *Autolykos*; both *ap.* Ath. x, 413c-14c.
[44] Ath. xi, 462c (DK 21 A 1).   [45] i, 131.
[46] DK 21 B 11 to 16, probably all from one poem, though from scattered sources.
[47] *ib.* fr. 23 to 26.

about the gods and the things I say about all things; for even it a man should happen to say what is exactly right – still, he himself does not know; but opinion is over all things.[48]

He speculated about the physical world, in the Milesian manner; about fossils, as we have seen; about the earth, which he imagined in naive manner, flattish on top and extending downwards to infinity; about sea and sky: 'She whom they call Iris' (the deified rainbow) is a bright-coloured cloud; about matter: 'all things are arisen from earth and water'; about our perceptions of quality, which are relative: 'If God had not made the yellow honey, men would have thought figs much sweeter.'[49]   In this, as in his audacity and his rejection of the popular religion, he has a good deal in common with his younger contemporary, Herakleitos, but it is not in the Greek manner to agree easily.   Early Greek writers rarely mention each other except to criticise, and Herakleitos despised Xenophanes as a dabbler in multi-farious studies (p, 398).

In his old age, later Greeks believed that Xenophanes settled at Elea, Hyele (Italian Velia), south of Poseidonia, lately founded by the Phokaian refugees; and that there he taught a thinker no less great and more systematic: Parmenides (pp. 391ff). The evidence for this is not good (it *may* all be derived from taking literally a remark put by Plato into the mouth of the 'Eleatic stranger' in his *Sophist*[50]), and the report that he wrote a poem of 2000 lines on the foundation of the city (a subject eminently worthy of an epic, if it included the battles with Etruscans and Carthaginians) is weak and late[51]; but it would be rash to pass on this a stronger verdict than 'not proven'. In any case, his poetry had wide influence. He was the first Greek monotheist, and few philosophers after him were anything else; and his thought, reject-ing the mythology of the mystery religions, bridges the gap between the 'physics' of Miletos and the metaphysics of Parmenides.

---

[48] DK *ib.* 34, *ap.* Sext. Emp. vii, 49.

[49] Earth, fr. 28 DK; Ar. *On the heavens*, 294a (q. Empedokles, fr. 39 DK, perhaps a criticism of X.); Iris, fr. 32 DK (*ap.* Eustath. on *Il.* xi, 27); matter, fr. 29, cf. 27; relativism, fr. 38 (from the grammarian Herodian, who q. it for the unique comparative *glysson*).

[50] *Sophist*, 242d; cf. Ar. *Metaph.* 986b, ps.-Ar. *On Melissos, Xen. and Gorgias*; D.L. ix, 21, *Suda, s.v.* Parmenides, etc.; Kirk, *Presocr.* 165f (and cf. 171f) argues that all this derives from Plato's remark, 'not necessarily intended as a serious historical judgment', but I am not convinced that he is right.

[51] Only in D.L. ix, 20 (from the forger Lobon? – so Kranz and Kirk).

Chapter XVIII

The Mystery Religions

ON the new movements in religion, since we have no contemporary religious literature except some of the Homeric
Hymns, we have to build up our views cautiously, from scraps
of evidence mostly of later date.

The religion of classical Athens, as known to us from the drama and
from Plato, includes elements unmentioned in Homer; and the 'new'
or rather non-Homeric elements (some of them were probably very
ancient) are not completely fused with the Olympian religion of the
city-state. It was scarcely possible not to participate in the city's
festivals – even supposing that anyone wanted to abstain; it was dangerous to be thought 'not to believe in the gods whom the city
worships', as Diagoras the Melian and Socrates found[1]; but only some
people were initiated into some or other of those non-Homeric rites
known as *Mysteries*, from *müo* to close the mouth; rites about which
one had to be silent.

The Mysteries were concerned with the worship of agrarian gods,
not prominent in Homer; Dionysos, who was persecuted; Persephone,
who was carried off to hell and returned; and the anomalous Dying
Zeus of Crete. The Gods who *are* prominent in Homer are important
also in tragedy; the gods of the mysteries are important only in a few
plays, most of them lost and known to us only in quotations. Nevertheless it is clear that both Aeschylus and Euripides were deeply
interested in the 'new' cults.

On the rise of Dionysos to prominence in the sixth century, our
best evidence comes from the Isthmus region in the revolutionary
period, when Arion at Corinth made the Dithyramb a literary art-
form and Solon is said to have credited him with 'Tragedy'; when

---

[1] Favorinus, *ap.* D.L. ii, 40, claiming to q. the original indictment against Socrates; on
Diagoras, D.S. xiii, 6, Ath. xiii, 611; cf. Aristoph. *Clouds*, 830 and schol.; *Birds*, 1072, cf.
186; *Frogs*, 320 and schol.

Kleisthenes of Sikyon introduced choral dances in honour of Dionysos as part of his *Kulturkampf* against Argos; when Sousarion brought comedy, the 'song of the village' into Megara under its democracy, and Thespis staged the first recorded 'tragedy' in Attica under Peisistratos (pp. 198, 251, 310, 361). All this took place when the formerly despised, 'dusty-footed', 'sheepskin-wearing' countrymen and uplanders were beginning to wear better clothes, come into town, support political leaders and in general, as Theognis notes disgustedly, claim the rights of human beings. There is therefore no difficult question as to why it happened. The vegetation gods were of more importance to the peasants than to kings or gentry. To Theognis, who mentions him once (l. 976), Dionysos' name is a periphrasis for wine; to the men who danced and sang in his honour in the 'village song' he and Demeter and her daughter were the gods on whom depended the daily works of their hands, which failing, nothing stood between them and starvation; and the tyrants, who depended on popular support, did honour to the peasants' gods. In the new age and in the cities, these cults were influenced by rites and ideas introduced from Thrace; some Greeks believed, also from Egypt[2]; but it is a mistaken question to ask, 'Was Dionysos northern or old Aegean?' He was both; and the question to ask about the northern influence (to which the answer is suggested above) is why the Greek world was ready to receive it.

J. H. Breasted[3] describes a similar development in Egypt, nearly 2000 years before: the rise of the popular religion of the beloved Osiris, 'the imperishable life of the fruitful earth, which died and rose again', under and partially in rivalry with 'the Solar faith of the state temples' – after the disintegration of the centralised Old Kingdom. He suggests a comparison with the struggle in the Roman Empire between 'the devotion of the common folk to the risen Jesus, a popular faith, and the organised state worship of... the Invincible Sun'. A closer parallel to Aurelian's state solar cult would perhaps be the state solar cult of Akhnaton, in a later Egyptian period; a foredoomed attempt to establish by law a Religion of All Sensible Men; but there is a parallelism, between Amon-Ra with his entourage and the Olympians, and between Osiris and Dionysos. Greeks, indeed, identified them, as they identified other foreign gods with their own; and they can scarcely be said to have been wrong, though Herodotos, a more careful observer

[2] e.g. Hdt. ii, 49f, 146.   [3] *The Dawn of Conscience*, esp. pp. 95, 109, 237.

than most, made reservations.[4] Their myths did show resemblances: Dionysos, like Osiris, is killed, even torn to pieces by his enemies the Titans (we have only late accounts of this story[5]), both because the vegetation dies amid the storms of winter and (perhaps this is more important) because *we* do violence to the vine when we cut the grapes and press them; his sufferings are those of John Barleycorn. But the Sorrowful Mother of Greek myth is not, like Isis, *his* mother Semele (she only came to a bad end, destroyed by the radiance of her Husband, the Sky-God), but Demeter, seeking for her daughter, carried off by the Lord Hades and only at long last restored for eight months of the year, as we read in her Eleusinian 'Homeric' Hymn. The mythology of Dionysos is wilder and more barbarous, just as the use of wine is apt to be more riotous than that of bread; but it also includes stories of the persecution of the God and his followers by human kings: by Pentheus of Thebes, as told by Euripides, and said to have been told also by Thespis and Aeschylus, and, actually in the *Iliad*, the earliest certain mention of Dionysos, by 'Lykoorgos, son of Dryas' at 'Nyse'.[6] Lykoorgos (Lykourgos) is a shadowy figure, not fitted into any early heroic pedigree. In this he resembles his namesake of Sparta (p. 269), whom the Delphic Oracle 'rather thought' to be a god (p. 268). Was he indeed, we may wonder, originally a god, and *the same* god? In any case the story, like the Pentheus story, may well recall actual persecutions of Dionysiac dancers, 'Wild Women' by night on the hill-sides, by royal worshippers of the heavenly Olympians, to whom this 'dancing madness' of the common people seemed a threat to social stability.[7] There may have been rivalry between Apollo and Dionysos even at Delphi, ending in a strange and anomalous compromise: Apollo resigned his place to Dionysos for three months in each year, the months of his *apodemia* or Going Abroad to the far north (p. 347); curious and interesting, in view of the northern influences on Greek religion at this time.[8]

---

[4] 'Osiris who, they *say* (δή), is Dionysos', ii, 42, 2.

[5] Paus. (viii, 37, 5) attributes it to Onomakritos; disbelieved by Wilamowitz, *Glaube der Hellenen*, II, 378ff; but cf. Dodds, *The Greeks and the Irrational*, 155f and nn.

[6] *Il.* vi, 130; Thespis, *Suda, s.v.*; Pollux, vii, 45 (or a forgery by Her. Pont.? – cf. D.S. v, 92). Aesch. see Aristoph. Byz. *Hypoth.* to Eur. *Bakchai.* Earlier still, Ventris and Chadwick (*Documents in Mycenaean Greek*, 127) claim to find Diwonusojo on a Pylos tablet.

[7] Rohde, *Psyche* (Eng. trn.), p. 284 cps. the persecution of the 14th-century 'mad dancers' in the Rhineland as heretics.

[8] Plut. *Mor.* 388f; though the earlier evidence of Alkaios does not make it clear that the *apodemia* was due to rivalry; cf. Parke and Wormell, *The Delphic Oracle*, I, p. 11f and nn.

Apollo's northern connections were part of a two-way traffic, in objects and probably also in ideas. While the legendary noble savages 'at the back of the North Wind' enjoyed prestige in Greece – their name appears already in the later epics – Apollo of *Delos* enjoyed prestige enough among some northern people, alleged at Delos to be the Hyperboreans themselves, for certain Sacred Objects, wrapped in straw for concealment (as in a Thracian cult of 'Artemis', Herodotos notes) to be regularly received at Delos from them. From (or via) the Adriatic, they reached Dodona, and thence through Euboia from city to city and by Tenos (omitting Andros for reasons not given, probably a quarrel), they came to the holy isle. It is a mere guess, though an attractive one, that the packages contained amber. Some people, then, believed not to be Greeks, had traffic with the Delian Apollo; presumably the Delian priests did something to make it worth while; for still in Pausanias' time similar packages, now despatched from Scythia via Sinope to Prasiai in eastern Attica, continued to be received.[9]

Early Greek 'mysteries' were not confined to the cults of Dionysos and Demeter. Of increasing prestige in classical times were those of the Kabeiroi and the Kouretes. The Kabeiroi had a revered sanctuary on the island of Samothrace; Herodotos, who had evidently taken the trouble to be initiated there, identifies them with certain dwarfish Egyptian gods, said to be sons of a similarly dwarfish Hephaistos (Ptah?).[10] Other early prose-writers, add that they were six in number, three male and three female, children of Hephaistos, the Smith-god, and Kabeiro, or of a son of Hephaistos named Kasmeilos or Kadmilos. Since the name Khasamilis occurs in the Hittite records as the name of an ancient, deified king, and Khabiriyas as that of a regiment of royal guards, the local and learned writer Demetrios of Skepsis may well have been right in deriving the cult from Phrygia, where there was a Mount Kabeiron.[11] Their genealogy, with its variations, was a product of Greek systematising; Demetrios says that there was no story included in their mysteries. He adds that the cult was found also in the

---

[9] Hdt. iv, 32ff; Hesiod and 'Homer', *Epigonoi, ib.*; cf. *H. H. to Dionysos*, 29; Paus. i, 31, 2.
[10] Hdt. ii, 51; iii, 37.
[11] Akousilaos, Pherekydes, *ap.* Str. ix, 472 (end), (from Demetrios of Skepsis?). 'Kasmeilos and Kabeiroi' addressed in a ritual inscr. of Imbros, *IG* XII, viii, 74 (2nd century B.C.?); Kadmilos in a list with Demeter, Kore and Hephaistos, D.H. ii, 22; Kamillos, Str.; cf. Kern in PW, X, 1398ff; Sayce in *JHS* XLV (on the Hittite names).

adjacent Lemnos and Imbros, and in the Troad. Herodotos calls the early historic non-Greek people of these islands, who established the cult, Pelasgoi, his general term for pre-Hellenic Aegean peoples; but archaeology enables us to be more precise, and to accept those ancient texts which make them kindred of the Etruscans, or of that element in Etruria which, as Herodotus believed, really was probably immigrant there from Asia Minor.[12]

The Kabeiroi, then, were gods of a people who were *early workers in metal*; children of Hephaistos, as the Greek systematisers said; introduced from Asia Minor, where the working of iron was probably first perfected; and dwarfish, like many other mythical patrons of early mining and metal-work: the Daktyls ('Tom Thumbs'? or 'The Clever-fingered'?) of Ida in Crete, said in a lost Hesiodic poem to have discovered iron-working[13]; the Telchines of Rhodes, credited with discovering both bronze and iron and several other useful arts – malicious or mischievous at times, these, like similar 'little people' in other mythologies, and, in one version, mermen, with webbed fingers[14]; or, indeed, the Nibelung dwarfs of Germany. But the Kabeiroi were not only interested in metal-working. We find them later associated, or in the Greek manner identified, with Demeter, Persephone, Hades and Hermes, the Guide of the Dead.[15] The connecting link is that all these are connected with *the earth* and the regions under earth. Their mysteries included, like most mysteries which admit to a fellowship, a sacramental meal; so much we learn from a Hellenistic inscription, in which a priest declares that he 'broke the Bread and poured the Cup for the *Mystai*'.[16] They were impressive enough to attract many great men of Greece and Rome; the parents of Alexander the Great are said to have met there.[17] One Methapos, an Athenian, apparently of the priestly Lykomidai, introduced them into Thebes. Here archaeology shows that their sanctuary dates from soon after the Athenian occupa-

[12] Hdt. i, 94; Tyrrh. equated with Pelasgoi, Hellanikos, *ap.* D.H. i, 28 (fr. 1 Müller, 4 Jac.); neighbours, nr. Kreston, Hdt. i, 57, (in Chalkidike), Thk. iv, 109. Della Seta's excavations on Lemnos discovered numerous cremation-burials, with axe and iron knife (not the Gk. sword and spear); grey and black pottery, like the Etruscan bucchero (also typical of NW Asia Minor): summary in *JHS* XLVII, p. 259.

[13] *Ap.* Pliny, *NH* vii, 56/197, Clem. Alex. *Strom.* i, 16, 75; cf. (without H.'s name), Str. ix, 473.

[14] Kallim. *H. to Delos*, 32, D.S. 55f, Eustath. *On Homer*, p. 772, etc.; Str. (ix, 466) comments on the (family?) resemblance of all these dwarfs.

[15] Schol. on Ap. Rhod. i, 917 (q. Mnaseas, a pupil of Eratosthenes).

[16] See Farnell, *Gk. Hero-Cults*, p. 373.　　　　　[17] Plut. *Alex.* 2.

tion of their islands; and here the cult became assimilated to the local and popular mysteries of Dionysos. Dedications of toys suggest that worshippers celebrated the birth of a Divine Child, an event central to other manifestations of esoteric Dionysianism; and on a vase fragment from the sanctuary we see the Child, explicitly labelled PAIS, standing before a reclining, bearded figure, cup in hand on a dinner-couch. Dionysos, one would think; but this figure also is explicitly labelled: KABEIROS.[18]

The Kouretes of Crete were not deities, but worshippers, or their heroic prototypes. They worshipped the dying and resurrected Cretan Zeus; and it was in his phase as the Divine Child that they attended upon him. Their name is Greek, meaning Young Men, *Kouroi* (cf. *gymnetes, gymnoi*). They danced in armour, with clashing of spear and shield and of cymbals; the legend said, in memory of their ancestors, who did so after the birth of Zeus at the entreaty of Rhea his mother, so that his father Kronos, who devoured his children, might not hear the lusty cries of the Divine Child and come to find him.[19]

The probable history of this rite is plain. The Cretan Zeus is almost certainly continuous with the Young God, associated with the Great Mother in Minoan art. Further back, at a less anthropomorphic level, he is the Life 'of the corn and of the people', as associated (or rather, never separated) in the Athenian Thesmophoria[20]; the son of Mother Earth. The tall young men who dance in his worship may originally have been leaping to make the crops to grow taller, a form of magic (doing something like what one wants to happen) known down to modern times in northern Europe[21]; and the object of clashing arms or other metal is to frighten away his cosmic Enemy and devourer (too much rain, too much heat, the violence of the Sky power, who is also the fertilising Father). What was important was what was *done*, not what was said about it; indeed, about holy things, perhaps the less said the better; moreover, the language of early cultivators can hardly have been capable of handling any but the most concrete concepts. Hence

[18] Guthrie, *Orpheus and Greek Religion*, fig. 12, and pp. 123ff; Paus. iv, 1, 7.

[19] *Loc. class.* Str. ix, 462-9 (a learned though sometimes bewildered excursus which seems as though destined for a modern periodical; a thorough knowledge of it may save some searching of encyclopaedias and 'collected fragments'). Cf. Eur. *Bakchai* 119ff; D.S. v, 70; illustration (coin), Guthrie, *op. cit.* fig. 11.

[20] Schol. on Lucian (*Courtesans' Dialogues*, ii, 1), ed. Rohde in *Rhein. Mus.* XXV (1870), p. 548; Farnell, *Cults of the Gk. States*, III, 89.

[21] Frazer, *GB*[3], *Spirits of the Corn and the Wild*, II, p. 330 and n.

in a later and more sophisticated age, to which the idea that the God Kronos could be frightened away by noise appeared absurd and impious, there was no impediment to an explanation of what was done by way of a story, *mythos*, the usual Greek way of accounting for rituals that had once been purely magical.

Why these Cretan rites, which were of concern to all the people and conducted in public,[22] ranked as *mysteria*, requiring initiation, is not immediately obvious; the Thesmophoria, though secret from all except the celebrant women, are *not* so called. One possible reason is that admission to the Cretan rites was (we may suppose) combined with *rites de passage* (or of 'completion', *teletai* as the Greeks said) by which the *Kouroi* were admitted to the status and duties of manhood; whereas the *Thesmophoriazousai* were the already 'completed' married women with their *teletai* behind them. But also, at Athens the word *mysteria* meant, *par excellence*, the famous Mysteries of Eleusis.

The people of Eleusis, dwelling in the most fertile plain of Attica, conducted these rites in honour of Demeter or Deo the Mother, who first revealed to men the cultivation of corn, and of Persephone her daughter: usually called not by their holy names (Persephone *never* in the context of the mysteries) but The Mother and The Maiden, or simply The Two Gods. At some other places the name of the Daughter was actually a secret.[23] When Attica was united, Athenians came to be admitted; later, other Greeks and Romans were admitted too. Within the civilised world, Demeter recognised no distinction of male or female, bond or free; a slave in a fourth-century play speaks of the kind master who introduced him to the customs of Greece, taught him to read and had him initiated.[24]

The *story* of Demeter at Eleusis was no secret; it was told in the long and lovely 'Homeric' Hymn, whose delight in flowers and fields, mountains and valleys, gives it almost a romantic character: how the Lord Hades carried off Persephone for love, as she was gathering flowers in the Plain of Nysa (that widely-travelled land); how Demeter wandered seeking her; and how when she heard the story from the all-seeing Sun, for anger she left the gods and wandered among men,

[22] D.S. v, 77, 3ff.
[23] e.g. in Arcadia, at Onkeion, Paus. viii, 25, 7, at Akakesion, 37, 9; in Stenyklaros, *id.* iv, 33, 4f, cf. Collitz, *Dialektinschr.* no. 4689.
[24] Farnell, *Cults*, III, Ref. 173 (Theophilos, in Meineke, *Fr. Com.* III, p. 626).

while crops failed because her favour was withdrawn, and Zeus himself became afraid that mankind would perish and the gods would lose their sacrifices.

But Demeter came to Eleusis and sat by the Maidens' Well, in the likeness of an old woman; and the King's daughters came to draw water and spoke kindly to her. She told them that she had escaped from pirates who had kidnapped her from Crete to sell as a slave; and they took her home to their mother, who made her nurse to her late-born baby son. They offered her wine, but she would not drink it; but she accepted 'to observe the rite' a 'posset' of meal and water flavoured with mint[25]; such a drink as her fasting worshippers were to drink thereafter. Little Demophon flourished under her care, and the goddess would even have made him immortal, had not the queen, waking at night, seen the strange nurse putting the baby in the fire, and shrieked. This apparently broke the spell, and offended Demeter, who put down the baby and, resuming her awful beauty, declared herself. So Demophon had to die like other men; for in dealing with the gods, as with nature, ignorance does not save. But Demeter retained a kindly feeling towards the house of King Keleos, and after Hades had restored Persephone (through the good offices of Zeus, who was under severe economic pressure) she taught her Works, her *Orgia*, to the princes there. Among them are named Triptolemos and Eumolpos, famous, with varieties of legend, at Eleusis for centuries. 'Happy', says the poet, 'is he among men on earth who has seen these things; but he who has not completed the holy rites, or has no part in them, has no like portion even in death, down in the misty gloom.'[26]

Persephone, we hear, might have come home for good; but crafty Hades, before letting her go, had given her a sweet pomegranate-seed and made her eat it; and having thus taken food in his house she was bound to him. (The common pre-rational idea, that by accepting a gift one is magically bound, occurs also in the *Works and Days* (85ff), in the story of Pandora.) So for eight months she is with us, and for four, each year, in the House of Hades, while the earth is barren. But Hades promised her great honour as his queen, and that 'upon men who do wrong there shall be vengeance for ever, upon men who propitiate not thy power with sacrifice'.

Several points in the myth 'prefigure' the Mysteries: the wineless

---

[25] ὁσίης ἕνεκεν, l. 211.   [26] 480ff.

drink, the holy well, and also the figure of the maiden Iambe, who at Eleusis was the first to make the sorrowful mother smile, by her pointed jests; a personification of the iambic raillery with which friends 'saw off' the initiates from Athens, to avert any jealousy of malicious Powers at their great happiness. More we do not know; but what, we may wonder, was the significance of the story that the king's child, if the queen had kept silence, would have attained immortality through fire?

The Hymn is early, perhaps seventh century; the digamma, the W-sound which the Greeks were losing, is still apparent in the metre. We cannot, however, infer anything from the fact that Eleusis has a king and there is no mention of Athens; epic poets knew well that the heroic age was not their own, and this poet, like Homer in the *Iliad*, preserves correctly the memory of the bronze-age states. The later mythology is somewhat different; there are traces of foreign, allegedly Thracian, influence, clear in classical times. Eumolpos, Eleusinian in the Hymn, is later called a Thracian, and has a son Immarados, while the old King Keleos acquires a daughter Saisara – names certainly not Greek.[27] But the most striking omission in the Hymn is that of the name of Iakchos. Iakchos, perhaps originally an Attic local deity, was certainly identified in classical Athens with Dionysos the son of Zeus and Semele.[28] His first extant appearance in connection with Eleusis is in Herodotos' story of the vision of two Greek exiles with Xerxes' army. It was autumn – the festal season. Athens lay waste, and there were only barbarian soldiers everywhere; but the exiled Damaratos, king of Sparta, and Dikaios of Athens saw a cloud of dust moving on the road to Eleusis 'as it were of thirty thousand men', and heard singing which the Spartan did not understand; but it seemed to the Athenian to be 'the mystic Iakchos' ' hymn, as sung by the pilgrims.[29]

Most of what we hear about the Mysteries naturally concerns the

[27] Paus. i, 38, 1-3; he cites as sources Homer (but no poem known to us) and Pamphôs 'an Athenian hymn-writer' (vii, 21, 3), 'earlier than Homer' (viii, 37, 6), whose hymns were preserved by the priestly house of the Lykomidai along with some ascribed to Orpheus (ix, 27, 2). The line ascribed to Empedokles by Gellius (iv, 11, 9; Emp. fr. 141 DK) expressing a taboo on beans (cf. p. 355) is assigned to Pamphos by Philostratos (*Heroika*, ii, 19), and to Orpheus by Didymos (DK *loc. cit.*). The Lykomids also claimed a *Hymn to Demeter* as written for their family by Mousaios, Paus. iv, 1, 4.

[28] Addressed as *Iakche Semeleie* at the Lenaia, schol. on Aristoph. *Frogs*, 409; cf. Soph. *Ant.* 1119. 'If Iacchus comes from *iaché* ["shout"] it may have been used independently as a title of Dionysus and as the name of an Eleusinian daemon: the equation of the two would then be evidence of fifth-century syncretism rather than "Dionysiac influence" on Eleusis.' – E.R.D.

[29] Hdt. viii, 64.

preparatory rites, which were not secret. It appears that initiation was a gruelling business and not to be lightly undertaken. First, in the spring, the time of the Return of the Maiden, all candidates had to be initiated into the Lesser Mysteries at Agrai.[30] Then in the autumn, on the thirteenth day of the month Boēdromion, the corps of the Young Warriors of Athens marched out under arms to bring home the Sacred Things.[31] On the sixteenth the candidates assembled, and the Hierophant or Revealer of the Sacred Things in his Preliminary Address solemnly warned the unworthy to depart: all who would go further without great danger must be 'of intelligible speech and clean of hands'.[32] The cleanness was largely ritual; blood-guilt, even incurred in self-defence, excluded, it is true; but Diogenes the Cynic sneered at the Mysteries as promising greater happiness in the after-life to the initiated sinner than to the uninitiated hero.[33] Then the command was heard 'Mystai, to the sea!' and thither they went, each carrying a small pig for a vicarious offering. With the salt and water of the sea they cleansed themselves, transferring any ritual uncleanness to the victims, which were afterwards sacrificed.[34] In the fourth century there then followed the two-day Epidauria, the festival of the Healer Asklepios, 'during which the Mystai stay in their houses'[35] – in 'retreat'. Finally on the nineteenth the great procession, the Exodos of Iakchos, moved out from the Sacred Gate in the early morning, bearing the image of the 'Fair Young God' and the other Sacred Things, and escorted once more by the young citizen soldiers.

The fifteen-mile march took all day, for there were halts for prayers and praises at many 'stations' along the route. The first was not far from the walls: an altar to the West Wind and a shrine of Demeter and her Daughter, together with the state gods, Athena and Poseidon, at the place where the hero Phytalos ('the Planter') had received Demeter in his house, and received for his reward the first fig-tree.[36] Then, approaching the Kephissos, the acolytes chanted, 'Pass over the bridge,

[30] Plato, *Rep.* 364e; Agra, 3rd-century inscr., Farnell, *Cults*, III, ref. 185; season, *CIA* I, 1, of 5th century.
[31] Inscr. (of Roman date), *CIA* III, 5 (Farnell, ref. 187).
[32] Libanios, *Corinthian Oration*; Origen, *Against Celsus*, iii, 59 (Farnell, ref. 217a and pp. 166f).
[33] D.L. vi, 39.
[34] Hesych. *s.v. Halade, Mystai*; cf. Aristoph. *Frogs*, 337f.
[35] *Ath. P.* 56, 4; Philostr. *Life of Apollonios*, iv, 18.
[36] Paus. i, 37, 2, q. inscr. on Ph.'s monument.

O Maiden; the earth is almost ploughed'[37]; and there by the bridge were their friends, come to speed them on their way with the iambic mockery that was to avert *nemesis*.[38] Next, was the altar of Zeus Meilichios, 'Sweet Zeus', a substitution of a euphemism for a name of dread; for this was Zeus in pre-anthropomorphic, serpent form. Here the descendants of Phytalos had purified Theseus for the slaying of Sinis the robber, who was of his mother's father's kin.[39] Then came the chapel of Kyamites, the eponymous hero of the Bean. Of him, says Pausanias, 'I cannot say for certain whether he first sowed beans, or whether they gave this name to some hero because it was impossible for them to ascribe the discovery of beans to Demeter. He who has been initiated at Eleusis or read the so-called Orphic literature knows what I mean.'[40]

This guarded language refers to an ancient sex-taboo, observed, Herodotos tells us, by priests in Egypt; it was adopted also by Empedokles and the Pythagoreans (p. 376). Aristotle explains it, on the ground that the lentoid shape is that of the testicles. (So also cowry shells owe their magical reputation to being compared to the female genitals.) They were among the many things that the Flamen Dialis at Rome might not touch or name; conversely, they were eaten at Roman funeral feasts, no doubt to strengthen the life-force, and used n the apotropaic ritual of the Lemuria ('Hallowe'en') as described by Ovid.[41]

At the top of the low pass through the ridge of Aigaleos there was another temple, 'originally of Apollo, alone'; but later, statues of Athena and Demeter and her daughter were installed here too.[42] The site is that of the monastery, with its famous mosaics, which still preserves the Apolline name of Daphní. A little further on there was a small temple of Aphrodite, 'with a wall of unhewn stones in front of it, worth seeing'.[43] Its foundations can still be seen. The towers of Eleusis came in sight in the distance, as the pilgrims passed the adjacent rock buttress, with the niches in its face holding votive figures; but

---

[37] Proklos on Hes. *WD* 389, q. 'the Eleusinian ritual'.
[38] Hesych. *s.v. gephyrismos*, Str. ix, 400. The 'iambic' satires were said in classical times to commemorate those of the maiden Iambe, who alone could make the sorrowing Demeter smile, *H.H.* 202ff.
[39] Paus. i, 37, 4.   [40] *ib.* 4.
[41] Hdt. ii, 37; Emped. fr. 141 DK (cf. n. 27 above); Ar. *On the Pythagoreians, ap.* D.L. viii, 34; Plut. *Roman Questions*, 95; Ovid, *Fasti*, v, 443ff.
[42] Paus. i, 37, 6.   [43] *ib.* 7.

there were more 'stations' yet: the Ponds, Rheitoi, on the right of the road where it comes down to the sea, 'sacred to the Maiden and to Demeter; and the fish are reserved for the priests'; the tomb of Eumolpos, said to have been of Thrace, but a descendant of Oreithyia of Athens, killed in war against King Erechtheus; Erineos, 'the very place where Pluto carried off the Maiden', by the Eleusinian Kephisos; and at last, Eleusis, and the Well of the Fair Dance, 'where first the women of Eleusis danced and sang to the Goddess'.[44]

The stars must have been shining by the time the pilgrims arrived and broke their fast. No wine was drunk, but the 'posset' of mint-scented meal and water, in memory of the Mother, whose footsteps they have been following all day; and sacred food was eaten. It was received from a box or chest, and what remained was carefully collected again. Thus the initiates could repeat afterwards the 'Password', *Synthêma*, of the Mystai: 'I have kept the fast; I have drunk of the Barley; I have taken from the sacred Chest; having tasted thereof I have placed it in theBasket, and again from the Basket into the Chest.'[45] And so, probably at once, overwrought and tense as they were, to the Initiation in the pillared Hall of the Mysteries, 'by fire-light, at night'.[46]

The great gate in the wall of the sacred place was set askew to the road, so that the profane, looking in, saw nothing but another high wall a few yards away. That, not unnaturally, is our position. 'What passes within the wall', says Pausanias, 'my dream forbade me to write; and for non-initiates, what they may not see, obviously it is unlawful to inquire.'[47] Only Christians, in late antiquity, would have no scruple in talking about what they had been taught to regard as the devil's imitation of the true Mysteries; and when they do, unfortunately they are not careful of their details, often mixing statements that demonstrably refer to the Phrygian mysteries of Kybele and Attis with their denunciations of Eleusis.[48] The tendency of late paganism itself was towards syncretism, holding, as Greeks always had, that other men's gods were often one's own under another name, even that the mysteries

---

[44] Paus. i, 38, 1–3; 5f.

[45] Clem. Alex., *Protreptikos*, p. 18 (ed. Potter); an intelligent witness, and one who had been a pagan. (But 'having tasted' (the only evidence for food) is an emendation of Lobeck's: *engeusamenos* (non-classical) for *ergasamenos* 'having done'. The mss. reading, though obscure to us, is not necessarily wrong. – E.R.D.)

[46] Hippol. *Ref. Her.* v, 7ff.

[47] Paus. i, 38, 7.

[48] Farnell (*Cults*, III pp. 177ff), whose cautious treatment of the subject is a model.

of the Kabeiroi were 'the same' as these, as some explicitly said[49]; that truth, in fact, is the same whatever the approach to it. However, some initiates did become Christians later, and through them a few details of the ritual are preserved. Even the guarded language of classical authors tells us a few things. 'No Mystery ever was celebrated without dancing', says Lucian (*On Dancing*, 15); and we may well believe that, since prehistoric times, the Initiators of youths and girls into adult 'completeness' had danced and mimed ideas and feelings that were beyond their words. It was for his parody of the dress and actions as well as words of the Hierophant that Alkibiades was arraigned.[50] In Aristotle's phrase, the worshippers 'should receive not instruction but impressions, and be brought into a certain state' of feeling.[51] An excerpt from a late rhetorician suggests what state:

The soul at the point of death, says Themistios (about A.D. 360) 'suffers the same feelings as those who are being initiated into great mysteries. First there are wanderings and weary devious hurryings to and fro; journeyings full of fears and uncompleted (*atelestoi*; which also meant 'uninitiated'); then, before the end, every sort of terror; shuddering and trembling and sweat and horror. And after that a marvellous light meets you, and pure regions and meadows receive you, and there are voices and dancing and wonderful and holy sounds and sacred sights, and he that is completed and initiated wanders free and unrestrained, and is crowned and joins in the worship, and is among pure and holy men, seeing those who live here uninitiated, a foul horde, trodden under his feet and rolled in filth and fog, abiding in their miseries through fear of death and lack of faith in the blessings there.'[52]

The hell of mud at least is an Attic idea; it is mentioned in Aristophanes' *Frogs*. The early Hall at Eleusis, its foundations now laid bare, is a simple structure, and offers little room for elaborate staging; but one must allow for the effects of fasting, tension and dim light. Presumably the beginning of the service was dark and grim; then one passed from 'hell' to 'heaven'. A door, it seems, was thrown open, and before eyes accustomed to darkness the Hierophant appeared, displaying the Sacred Things in a blaze of light.[53]

---

[49] Cf. Strabo's reasoned discussion (ix, 466-8) in the essay cited, n. 19; and, already, Hdt. ii, 50 and 144ff.

[50] Lysias vi, 51.   [51] Fr. 15 Rose (from Bishop Synesios, *Dion.* 10).

[52] Farnell, ref. 218h (from Stobaios); cf. p. 179.

[53] *Frogs*, 272ff. Inscr. from Eleusis and hints from late writers in Farnell, ref. 218j, k, l.

Some parts of the mysteries still showed their agrarian origin. At some point, the Mystai looked up to heaven and cried, 'Rain!' (it was the season for the first rains of autumn); they looked down to earth and cried, 'Conceive!'[54] There was probably a Sacred Marriage or union of Zeus and Deo. There was Wrath of Deo, hence called Brimo, the Terrible One. A Christian writer sneers, 'Is there not a descent into darkness and the solitary meeting of the Hierophant and the Priestess?'[55] There was also a Birth. The Hierophant proclaimed, 'The Queen has borne a holy child: Brimo, Brimos.' (Clement and Hippolytos, though the latter does also draw upon the Phrygian mysteries, his only concern being to show that Gnosticism is pagan, both present this formula as Eleusinian.)[56]

With the actions there was probably a commentary. Cicero says that the teaching at Eleusis was Euhemerist, presenting the Actions as a dramatic representation of the doings of ancient kings and queens; Varro that the tradition of the Mysteries was 'all concerned with the discovery of agriculture'.[57] The two accounts are not (as Farnell suggests) incompatible, and may both be true for that age. That the *interpretation* of the mysteries was not stereotyped was probably the secret of the lasting hold of Eleusis upon the minds of intelligent men. The 'things done' and 'things shown' were the heart of the matter, and for over a thousand years men interpreted them according to their lights.

Finally, the long ordeal over, the Initiated gave themselves up to joy in the companionship of Iakchos. The last scene is his midnight revel on the 'torch-lit strand' of the bay, where even old men danced, forgetting their years and fatigue.[58] And there, we may suppose, they slept.

So much of the revelation was enough for many; but some worshippers returned, after one or more years, for the further initiation called the Epopteia; and it was to them, according to Hippolytos, that there was shown as 'the great and wonderful and most perfect mystery – an

[54] Hippol. *loc. cit.* (n. 46); whence Lobeck emended Proklos on Pl. *Timaios*, 293b.
[55] Asterios, *Praise of the Martyrs*, 113b (4th century); Zeus and Deo-Brimo, Clem. *Protr.* p. 13 P.
[56] *locc. citt.*
[57] Cic. *Tusc.* i, 13/29, cf. *Nature of the Gods*, i, 42/119; Varro, *ap.* Aug. *City of God*, vii, 20; cf. Farnell ref. 202n, from the rhetorician Sopatros, on the candidate eager to hear the voice of the Hierophant.
[58] *Frogs*, 340ff; cf. Soph. *O.C.* 1048.

ear of corn, reaped in silence!' Hippolytos might perhaps have thought
less contemptuously of this if he had remembered a Christian text first
spoken *to Greeks*: 'Unless the grain of the wheat fall into the ground
and die, it abideth alone....'[59]

The Mysteries of Eleusis do seem to have produced a deepening of
religious sense in many of their devotees; even a deepened ethical
sensibility, in spite of the absence of any discernible teaching. 'You
have been initiated', says Andokides the orator to a jury specially
impanelled from among Mystai, 'and you have seen the holy things of
the Goddesses, that you may punish the impious and preserve the
innocent'; and later in the same speech he speaks of a lady whom the
Goddesses had made so sensitive to right and wrong that 'she thought
it profitable to die rather than live and see (the wickedness) that was
going on'.[60] Pindar sums up, echoing the thought of the old Hymn,
in a Dirge for an initiate, Megakles, nephew of Kleisthenes the reformer:

> Blessed is the man who has seen these things before he goes
> beneath the hollow earth. He knows the end of life, and life's
> God-given beginning.[61]

Even the dignified rites of Eleusis, then, had been influenced by the
rise of Dionysos, having taken into their system the post-epic figure of
'Semeleian Iakchos'. Eleusis in turn, through its prestige, exercised
wide influence upon the cult of Demeter in other places. In Crete and
Thera and at Ephesos, in Boiotia and Arcadia, she was worshipped as
Eleusinian[62]; and it is most improbable that this list is complete.

A similar syncretism affected other mysteries; and in some, at least,
an element of ancient savagery remained. In a famous fragment of
Euripides' *Cretans*, the chorus of initiates addresses King Minos:

> Son of . . . Tyrian Europa and great Zeus, . . . I come from the
> sanctity of temples roofed with cut beams of our native wood, its
> true joints of cypress made fast with Chalybean axe and cement from
> the Bull. Pure I have lived since I became initiate of Idaian Zeus,
> having endured the thunders of night-wandering Zagreus and his
> raw feasts; I have held aloft the torches to the Mountain Mother

---

[59] Hipp. *loc. cit.*; John xii, 24.   [60] *On the Mysteries*, §§ 31, 125.
[61] Fr. 137 Bgk. (from Clem. Alex. *Strom.* iii, p. 518, on Eleusis).
[62] Respectively: *CIG* 2554; 2448; Str. xiv, 633; Paus. ix, 4, 3 (cf. 24, 1); viii, 25, 2;
29, 5.

and been called a Bakchos of the Kouretes, sanctified. Clothed in raiment all white, I shun the births of mankind, touch not the coffins of the dead, and keep from eating food that has had life.[63]

Euripides already thus connects this Cretan worship with that of the Asian Mountain Mother, which had indeed probably spread to bronze-age Crete. The initiate is vegetarian (Porphyry's point in quoting the passage) *except* (as in a totemic ceremony) in the sacramental meal when he eats the raw flesh of the sacred Bull, whose blood is mixed with the glue of his temple rafters.

The name Zagreus, of uncertain origin, seems to have appeared in literature first in Aeschylus and in the late epic (sixth-century?) *Alkmaionis*.[64] He is always connected with the gods of earth and under earth. Aeschylus, who not infrequently introduced variations in the still not completely crystallised mythology, is said to have called him 'brother of Hades'; but usually he was identified with Dionysos. 'Bakchos and Hades are the same', said Herakleitos, an unfriendly critic of these *orgia*, in which the gods of death were worshipped or placated in the hope of rebirth.[65]

That the initiate is 'called a Bakchos' is often cited as evidence that the Dionysiac worshipper was made one with his God, a conception startlingly different from anything in Olympian religion; but here care is necessary. 'Bacchus' as a name of Dionysos is so familiar in Greco-Roman mythology that it may come as a shock to find that *as a name of the god* it appears, after Herakleitos, first in Sophocles.[66] It is not older than our evidence for *bakchoi* (and *bakchai*), first also in drama, the 'perfected' initiates in the *orgia*, as in the line from a hexameter hymn, already proverbial when Plato quoted it: 'Many are the wand-bearers, but few the *bakchoi*' ('Many are called, but few are chosen'). The deliberately sinister phrase of Euripides, 'Bakchai of Hades', is less difficult than some have found it. 'Hell-witches' or 'Maenads of death' is the sense; Hekabe and the other Trojan women having just, in an orgy of revenge, murdered two young children.[67] *Bakchoi*, 'orgiastic worshippers', like *Bakides*, 'seers', was probably the title of many before

---

[63] *Ap.* Porphyry, *On Abstaining from Flesh*, iv, 19.

[64] Both in *Et. Mag. s.v.*; with the etymology 'Mighty Hunter'. Possibly from Mount Zagros in Assyria (G. Davis, *ap.* Cook, *Zeus*, I, 651) reaching Crete from Phoenicia along with the early eastern bronzes, pp. 85f.

[65] Herakl. fr. 127 Byw., 15 DK, from Clem. Alex. *Protr.* p. 30 P; Kallim. *ap.* schol. on Lykophron, 207, and *Et. Mag.*, *Zagreus*.

[66] *O.T.* 211; called Bakcheios Theos, ib. 1105.   [67] *Hek.* 1077; cf. *Phoin.* 1489.

it was the name of one; as an epithet, *later* a name, of Dionysos it will have meant 'reveller' (like another of his names, Bromios). An intermediate stage may be found in Herodotos and in the 'Homeric' Hymn to Pan, in the phrase Bakcheios Dionysos, Dionysos the Reveller.[68]

Dionysos was also a name of terror: Man-Tearer, Raw-Meat-Eater were among his titles[69]; and his mythology is full of tales like the rending of Pentheus by his *Bakchai*, of Orpheus (p. 368), or the punishment of the daughters of Minyas, who (because they *refused* to honour him, as a late account says – but was it the original one?) were driven mad and ate the child of one of them.[70] But the survival of such legends and their fascination for a Euripides or an Aeschylus is clearly connected with the fact that Dionysos was also Lyaios, the Liberator: liberator from the inhibitions which make civilised life possible. Dionysiac tragedy was a mental purge, said Aristotle in a famous sentence[71]; and men who did not commit deeds of horror derived a sense of relief from seeing them enacted, as well as enjoying the beauty of choral lyric or being edified by examples of heroism.

And among the tales of horror, it seems, though never enacted on the Attic stage nor publicly recounted in classical literature, was that of the murder and eating of Dionysos himself. Once, said a legend, which according to Diodoros was enacted publicly in Crete, but elsewhere revealed only in Mysteries,[72] the Divine Child *was* actually caught by his enemies. The evil Titans lured him into their power by the display of toys: a spinning top, knuckle-bones and a looking-glass – such things as were dedicated to the Child at the Theban Kabeirion. They caught him and devoured him. His father Zeus blasted the Titans with his thunderbolt; and himself ate the heart of the Child, which had been preserved (our late version of the legend says) by Athene; and subsequently begat Dionysos over again, as the son of Semele. For the first or chthonian Dionysos was the child of Zeus and Persephone, sky-god and earth-goddess. When the Greek names were applied to these deities and compared with the Hesiodic genealogies, it thus appeared that the Divine Child was the son of Zeus by his own

---

[68] *H. H. to Pan*, 46; Hdt. iv, 79.

[69] Aelian, *VH* xii, 34; Plut. *Themist.* 13; cf. W. Otto, *Dionysos: Mythos und Kultus* (Frankfort-am-M., 1933), p. 104, with further refs.

[70] Apollod. iii, 5, 2, Plut. GQ 38, etc.; Otto, *op. cit.* 96ff.   [71] *Poetics*, 1449b.

[72] v, 75, 4, cf. 77, 3; Clem. *Protr.* p. 15 P; detailed (euhemerised) account, Firmicus Maternus, *Errors of Pagan Religions*, 6 (in Kern, *Orphicorum Fragm.* p. 234); cf. Linforth, *Arts of Orpheus*, ch. v.

daughter; a story shocking to Greek morality, and typical of those which, Plato's Socrates suggests, should only be revealed, if at all, to the initiates of some very *expensive* mystery.[73]

Variations and difficulties arose, it is obvious, from the comparison of myths which had arisen in different localities; that of Semele in Thebes, that of the Dying Zeus in Crete, etc. In the long run it proved impossible even for the Greeks to systematise all of them; and local devotion prevented many variations from dying out. In one version the Young God fled from his persecutors and hid himself, taking many shapes, but was caught and torn to pieces in the form of a Bull. This was a myth, presumably, that had grown out of ancient bull-slaughter-ings and bull-devourings which, since the bull was the largest and finest animal known to the Aegean world, represented the height of com-munal religious frenzy. Bull-sacrifice was still especially acceptable to Dionysos in classical times. Aristophanes speaks of the 'Bakchic rites of Kratinos' bull-devouring tongue' in a dig at his hard-drinking and vigorous old rival; and in some contexts the God, as in ancient days, still *was* the Bull. Plutarch quotes a hymn from the Eleian countryside, still in use in his time:

> Come, hero Dionysos,
> To this Eleian temple,
> To this pure shrine, with the Graces,
> Hasting on thy hoofèd foot,
> Goodly Bull, goodly Bull,

where 'hero', a word never used of the Olympians, is used, strikingly, of the Dying God. Pausanias says of this cult: 'The Eleians honour Dionysos most highly among the gods, and say that he comes among them in the Feast of Revelling' (*Thyia*). As Diodoros soundly says, after his account of the Cretan claim to have originated all the Mysteries 'they have also many other myths, which would take long to record and would be impossible for readers to take in all together'.[74]

A speaker in a dialogue of Cicero enumerates no less than five Dionysi of different parentage, and Diodoros three.[75] Modern scholar-

---

[73] *Republic*, ii, 378a.
[74] Tzetzes on Lykophron 355; Aristoph. *Frogs*, 355; hymn in Plut. *GQ* 36 (Edmonds, LG III, p. 510); Paus. vi, 26, 1; D.S. v. 77, 8. (Or *heros* here only = 'Lord' (cf. Hera), without any reference to mortality. – E.R.D.)
[75] D.S. iii, 63–64; Cic. *Nature of the Gods*, iii, 23/58 (this list is not exhaustive; it *omits* D. son of Semele).

ship has posed the question, 'Who was Dionysos?' in the form 'Where and when did the Dionysiac cult originate?' It is not really the most important question. We have seen evidence of influences, which affected classical Athens and later Greece, from ancient Crete and Thebes, from Thrace and Samothrace and Asia; yet many Mystai were no doubt content to believe, as sometimes they were told, that despite all variations these powers were one. They were quite right. For scholarship there was (and is) no single answer; for religious feeling, no problem. The interesting question for us is 'Why did these rites come into prominence when they did?' or in other words, 'Why was Greek society *then* susceptible to them?'

To this question most of the foregoing has been in some sort an answer; these primitive-looking cults, no doubt based on very ancient agricultural magic, 'come into town' and into notice in literature when the peasantry gained importance in society. But entirely consistent with this answer in social terms is the psychological answer: that Greeks, passionate, sensitive, and schooled to observe the decencies of city life and the Apolline ethics of 'Nothing Too Much', found in the Dionysiac worship relief from civilised repressions. The Dionysiac religion was almost a cult of excess, in a freedom to which wine unlocked the door. But this had a further consequence. Excess leads to a reaction, which in moral man takes the form of penitence. Contemporarily with the rise of Dionysianism, some Greeks (not all) discovered the sense of sin.

The sense of sin includes, often at least, a sense of duality: 'The good that I would, I do not; and the evil that I would not, that I do'[76]; it includes, often, ambivalent feelings towards the flesh, when the same 'dear sin' is at once hated and cherished. There may be a tendency to reject the flesh and its desires, especially sexual, at least in thinking moments, as 'not myself' – which raises a difficult question of 'What then, *is* the true self?' In Freudian terms, there is a differentiation of the *Id*, a mere 'it', the rejected flesh, and a moral super-ego. Such feelings lead, in some strong characters, to asceticism; and in fact, in the phase of increased individualism to which parts of the Greek world had now come, a movement which may fairly be called puritanical developed in, though it rarely dominated, some of the cities. Meanwhile the Olympian religion with its festivals, the older mysteries which it

[76] Paul, *To the Romans*, vii, 19, cf. 15.

controlled, and the largely secular laws of society continued to control the behaviour of most men, and to satisfy many. In classical Athens and in the circle of Socrates, the established religion could satisfy a Xenophon, but not a Plato.

To men who were both sensitive and intellectually curious, the sense of sin presented a question; the problem of evil, indeed, in a newly acute form: Why *are* we at all, if we are so foul? As a follower of Pythagoras was to put it, 'Whence came man, and whence became so evil?'[77] And to this mythology found an answer. Both men and gods, according to tradition, were descended from the old Titans, the slayers of the Divine Child.[78] The sense of sin also dovetailed with the feelings of awe and anxiety to placate divine displeasure, with which men did violence to the Body of the God when they reaped the corn and trod the fruit of the vine. Among some English harvesters within living memory there was competition *not* to be the man who cut the last corn in the field; it was called the Neck; and from it was made in some places a puppet, which was carried with honour in the homeward procession and set up in the barn.[79] This is probably one reason at least why certain new rituals, by which some Greeks sought purifications from feelings of guilt, became attached especially to the worship of Dionysos.

Plato, who most explicitly among classical writers presents us with pictures of reward and punishment and purificatory ordeals after this life (or rather between successive lives on earth), in one place refers to sinners (rebels against social discipline) as 'showing off the old Titan nature'; and a late commentator gives the most explicit account we have of our connection with the murder of Dionysos. Man arose, says Olympiodoros, from the smoke of the burning when Zeus blasted the Titans.[80] Our bodies are thus formed of the ashes of the primaeval

[77] Hippodamas, *ap.* Iambl. *Life of Pythag.* c. 82; q. by E. R. Dodds, *The Greeks and the Irrational* (a work to which the following pp. are much indebted), p. 155.
[78] Paus. (viii, 37, 5) attributes this to Onomakritos; and to believe that Pindar alludes to it in the lines qd. by Plato, *Men.* 81b–c, makes good sense of a difficult and much discussed passage (Pind. fr. 133 Bgk., Schroeder); cf. Xenokrates *ap.* Olympiod. on Plato, *Phaidon*, 84; H. J. Rose, 'The Ancient Grief', in *Greek Poetry and Life*, pp. 79ff; Dodds, *op. cit.* 155f and nn.; both justifying the acceptance of the tradition, despite the contrary argument of Wilamowitz, *Glaube der Hell.* II, 194ff, 378f.
[79] D.S. (iii, 62) cites some Gk. rationalisers as giving just this account of Dionysos, as a 'John Barleycorn' of the vine. – For some other English 'neck' ceremonies see Frazer, *Spirits of the Corn* etc., I, pp. 264ff.
[80] Pl. *Laws*, 701c; cf. Dodds, *op. cit.* pp. 176f, n. 132; Olymp., see n. 78 above.

sinners; but, because they had eaten the substance of the Divine Child, there is in every man also a seed of the divine, which must be cherished by purity and can be liberated; but not by suicide, for we are in prison in the body, and must be obedient and serve our time.[81] We have no earlier account of this myth, and there *were* other versions of the Titan origin of man; but both the crudity of the story and its materialism (where later Greek religious writers talk of the soul) look early; and we have several allusions to shocking myths which, in classical Greece, were only revealed to initiates; and the story does well explain several of Plato's more cryptic and guarded passages. Famous among these is one where Socrates refers to a doctrine, taught by 'priests and priestesses who are concerned to give a (rational) account of what they do' and also by 'Pindar and many other poets – such as are inspired by God': the doctrine that the soul is immortal and that we have all lived before. He then quotes (we may presume, from Pindar):

> For those from whom Persephone accepts the penalty of ancient grief, their souls she sends again to the sunlight above, in the ninth year; and of them shall come glorious kings and men swift in their might, and great sages; and for after time they are called holy heroes among men.[82]

Those born to greatness among men – kings, athletes and sages, says Pindar characteristically – and destined to receive heroic honours, are those, it seems, who are reborn *forgiven*. The poet, like Plato, holds a doctrine of rebirth, and something rather like a doctrine of *karma*; and much is explained if the 'ancient grief', *of* which 'Persephone accepts the penalty' (the genitive is puzzling, and has been endlessly discussed) is some 'original sin' such as the murder of Dionysos, her son.

A sense of guilt and a desire for release (in Latin, absolution) fits such a mythology; and the acceptance of the myth redoubled men's anxiety to find some rites or way of life which would procure the release. The demand was met, and the mythology fostered, by many teachers, and often by adherence to groups of devotees, practising ritual observance or mental discipline or both. Some of the teachers, we are told, were low peddlers of indulgences, promising a heaven of 'perpetual drunkenness'[83]; some were men of high seriousness and intellectual power, like

---

[81] Plato, *Phaidon*, 62b; *Kratylos*, 400c (cf. quotation of a poem of 'Orpheus', 402b).
[82] Plat. *loc. cit.* n. 78 above.
[83] Plato, *Rep.* ii, 363c-d (cf. 364e-5a).

Plato and Pythagoras, both of whom founded schools of philosophy, mental training and contemplation, which were also religious brotherhoods.

Among such groups Herodotos mentions in passing some who observed a taboo, found also in Egypt. Egyptians wore white woollen cloaks, he tells us, over their linen tunics, but these were never taken into temples, nor buried with them; there was a taboo on this (*ou gar hosion*). 'In this they agree with the so-called Orphics and the Pythagoreians; for those who partake in their rites also have a religioustban (*ou ... hosion* again) on being buried in woollen garments; and hey have an esoteric doctrine (*hieros logos*) about this.' Another group of manuscripts reads '*This* (*sc.* practice) agrees' for 'they agree', and adds, after 'Orphics', 'and Bakchic – really Egyptian' (making the reference one to 'Orphic and Bakchic *rites*'), which is very interesting, if right. In any case however, Herodotos knew of peculiar religious groups observing this taboo (groups, therefore, with recognised rules), who ascribed their doctrines to Orpheus.[84] What was this sect?

The name of Orpheus, whether a figure of myth or a real Thracian 'Shaman', first becomes known to us as that of the lyre-player and sweet singer who sailed in the *Argo*. To Ibykos of Rhegion, who worked at Samos under Polykrates, he is already 'famous Orphes'[85]; and probably earlier, in a relief from the Treasury of the Sikyonians at Delphi, he stands, lyre in hand, in a ship, with his name in Doric, ORPHAS, inscribed beside him.[86] These are his earliest appearances. The name of the *Argo* is already 'known to all' in the *Odyssey*, and Jason and his son by Hypsipyle of Lemnos are named in the *Iliad*; Orpheus is not, and in what version he first joined the crew is unknown; in the fifth century it was still possible to man an *Argo* without him.[87] But this adventure-story, not worked over by Homer, retains, especially in its background, many elements of hieratic myth. It is connected with the Athamantid family in the northern Achaia, royal in the heroic age, and still in Herodotos' time (it appears from another of his most obscure passages) in certain circumstances liable to be sacrificed. It is the story

---

[84] Hdt. ii, 81; discussed, Linforth, *Arts of Orpheus*, pp. 38ff; Dodds, *op. cit.* 169 n. 80, 171 n. 96.

[85] Fr. 10 Bgk. (Priscian, vi, 92, who q. for the form of the name).

[86] Illust., e.g. Guthrie, *O. and Gk. Religion*, Pl. 2.

[87] *Od.* xii, 70; *Il.* vii, 468f; Pherekydes (*ap.* schol. on Ap. Rhod. i, 23) named one Philammon instead of O.

of the King who married the Cloud-Nymph, and of the famine that happened when he was unfaithful to her, and the Clouds went away to a far land (Aia, which means simply Land); and of how Iason ('the Healer'?) went at last to recover the fleece of the Flying Ram (golden in most accounts, but purple in Simonides), which had rescued the children of the King and the Cloud when about to be sacrificed. Later, Herodotos says, King Athamas himself was about to be sacrificed (he must have been a very old man by that time, but fairy-tales are careless about these things), when his grandson Kytissoros, the son of Phrixos who had been rescued by the Ram, came back from the far land (identified with Kolchis by Herodotos) and rescued *him*; but the wrath of the God, Zeus Laphystios, the Devourer, rested upon Kytissoros' family thereafter.[88] The whole story transparently shows its origin in some ancient complex of rain-making magic and sacrifice of kings, which had been uneasily discontinued. Efforts to turn the story of the Quest of the Fleece (the clouds of morning?) into a pan-Hellenic heroic saga later resulted in assembling on board all the chief heroes of the generation before the Trojan War (even the huntress Atalanta).[89] Orpheus however is unknown to our records before about 550, and his presence is probably to be connected with the religious aspects of the myth. The prohibition of blood-sacrifice was one of the things with which classical tradition connected him.[90]

The other tales certainly recorded of Orpheus in the fifth century were those of how he went to the lower world to win back his wife, charming Hell by his music,[91] and failing only, as later writers tell us, because the Powers below put him off with a phantom likeness of her,[92] or because, as in the most famous version, he looked back too soon[93]; and of his death, depicted on a number of Attic vases, torn to pieces or battered to death by the Dionysiac Wild Women of Thrace.[94] His head continued to sing, or to prophesy, as vases show it, with a youth eagerly writing down its precious utterances, while Apollo stands over it with outstretched hand[95]; perhaps forbidding it, as a late writer

---

[88] Hdt. vii, 197; Simon. *ap.* schol. Ap. Rh. iv, 177.   [89] Apollod. i, 9, 16, 7ff.

[90] Aristoph. *Frogs*, 1032 ('O. taught you religious rites and to abstain from bloodshed'); cf. Plato, *Laws*, 782c.

[91] First extant ref., Eur. *Alkestis*, 357ff.

[92] First ext. ref., Plato, *Symp.* 179d.

[93] Evidence post-Alexandrian; see Guthrie, *op. cit.* (n. 86) pp. 30ff and nn.

[94] Guthrie, fig. 4; pl. 4; pp. 64f.

[95] Kern, *Orpheus*, p. 9; Guthrie, pl. 5; fig. 7(a); pp. 35ff.

records.[96] The head was also said, we do not know how early, to have been swept 'down the swift Hebrus to the Lesbian shore', and a temple of Bakchos, mentioned by Lucian, to have been built over the place where it came to rest.[97]

Aeschylus, with his strong religious interests, devoted a whole tetralogy to legends and cults of Thrace (would that we still had it, or more of it!) and in this Orpheus figured. It was called the *Lykourgeia* (apparently, like the *Oresteia*, rather loosely).[98] Its three tragedies were *The Edonians*, *The Bassarides* and *The Young Men*, with the satyr-play *Lykourgos*, including in its comic relief the invention of beer.[99]

From the *Edonians* Strabo quotes some vigorous anapaests describing the sound and fury of Thracian music: the 'instruments of Kotys', timbrels that madden, strings and 'bull-voiced drums'.[100] Swinburne, who knew the fragment, gives some of the spirit of it:

> But the fierce flute, whose notes proclaim
> Dim goddesses of fiery fame,
> Cymbal and clamorous kettle-drum,
> Timbrel and tabret, all are dumb
> That struck the high, still air to flame;
> The singing tongues of fire are numb
> That called on Cotys by her name
> Edonian, till they felt her come
> And maddened, and her mystic face
> Lightened along the streams of Thrace.[101]

Dionysos appeared in this play among his worshippers; an effeminate figure, as in Euripides. 'Whence comes this girl-man?' snarls the persecuting Thracian king at his prisoner; and some of his followers were represented as eunuchs.[102]

In the *Bassarides*, Orpheus himself fell a victim to the women votaries. The writer who tells us this adds that he 'did not honour Dionysos, but deemed the Sun the greatest of the gods, whom he also called Apollo; and he used to rise by night, and at dawn on the Mount Pangaion he awaited his rising'. (The identification of Apollo with the sun, not otherwise heard of in literature until very much later, *might* be

---

[96] Philostr. *Life of Apollonios*, iv, 14 (Kern, *Orph. Fr.* T. 134).
[97] Lucian, *Against the Unlearned*, 109ff (Kern, *op. cit.* T. 118).
[98] Aesch. frags. 55ff Dindorf.   [99] Ath. x, 447c.   [100] x, 470.
[101] *Prelude* (in *Songs Before Sunrise*), stanza 12.
[102] Schol. on Aristoph. *Thesm.* 135; Eustath. (on *Il.* ix, 535, 539) p. 772.

one of Aeschylus' variations on the mythology, derived from local cults (cf. p. 360 above); but neither it nor Orpheus' devotion to Apollo is explicitly said to be from the same source.)[103]

Orpheus was thus associated with a journey to the world of the dead, and with another to 'the place where the sunbeams are stored, by the lip of Ocean, where divine Jason went'[104]; this in a legend which dealt with the prevention of a human sacrifice and its consequences. These voyages, it has lately been pointed out, are such as are said to be made 'in the spirit' by the northern Shamans (p. 125 above). He was also associated, but as an enemy rather than a devotee, with Dionysos. He might thus well be considered a religious reformer and an authority on the world of the dead. This is the context in which, by about 520, we find that poems were circulating, attributed to him and his disciple or son Mousaios, giving teaching on these matters. 'Oracles of Mousaios', Herodotos tells us, were among the books collected by Hipparchos at Athens, where the 'expert' on them, Onomakritos, was caught forging additions to them.[105] A considerable corpus of Orphic poems is extant, some of them addressed to Mousaios, and including an *Argonautika*, hexameter Hymns, in imitation of the 'Homeric', and some magic lore, as in the *Lithika*, on the protective properties of precious stones. None of these forgeries, however, is demonstrably early, many are certainly Hellenistic or later, and their chief interest is as evidence on the sub-rational underworld of later Greek paganism.

If Orpheus lived in the heroic age, it followed that his alleged works were much older than Homer's, and the numerous Homeric lines and phrases that occurred in them were supposed to have been borrowed *by* Homer. The more rationalist orthodox had their doubts about this from the first. Herodotos in a famous passage declares, 'I believe that Hesiod and Homer flourished four hundred years before my time at most; and it is they who described in poetry the generations of the gods for the Greeks and gave them their names and prerogatives and distinguished their functions and told us what they look like; and the poets said to have lived earlier than these were, in my opinion, later.'[106] Egyptian mythology and rites were, he says, much older, and he

---

[103] (Ps.?)-Eratosthenes, *Katasterismoi* (on the myths of the constellations), c. 24 (T. 113 Kern). Linforth in *TAPA* LXII (1931), pp. 11ff., points out that the same writer, *ib.* 29, cites Eur. *Alkestis* in a passage quoting much matter *not* from that play; we cannot therefore attribute the whole of this passage to Aeschylus.

[104] Mimnermos, *ap.* Str. i, 46 (*not* naming O.).   [105] Hdt. vii, 6.   [106] ii, 53.

believed that Greek religion had borrowed from them. Ion of Chios, the friend of Sophocles, and one Epigenes, (probably an Alexandrian), attributed some Orphic poems by name to sundry Pythagoreans; and it was a well-known theory, though probably a mere guess, that some, or even most of the corpus, were the work of the attested forger Onomakritos.[107] Others suggested that the poems were the work of a later Orpheus, of Kroton, giving Aristotle occasion to lay down that 'Orpheus the poet' had never existed.[108]

But the books met a felt want, and against this the 'higher criticism' strove in vain. There were, it appears, enough people even in classical Greece weighed down by guilt and fearful of hell (a fear on which the poets did not omit to play) to keep in business a considerable number of practitioners in absolution. Not all of these necessarily used the name of Orpheus, but many did, along with that of his son Mousaios and *his* son[109] (Eumolpos?). From Theophrastos we hear their name, the Orpheotelestai, to whom his Superstitious Man runs off on the slightest provocation.[110] And it was their *books*, with their affectation of an august antiquity, that these 'Orphic initiators' paraded in support of their claim to privileged knowledge. While the Olympian religion and the established Mysteries, like Catholicism, were carried on by the tradition of a church (the city-state), the Orphic purifiers, like Protestant 'Lollards', in an age of writing, preached a 'religion of the Book'. Not all probably used the same books, nor did the great classical writers think much of them. Herodotos rejects their claims; Sophocles ignores them; Theseus in Euripides speaks of 'vapourings of many books', and Plato in the *Republic* of a 'hubbub of books', which sounds as if (like the extant Orphic poems) not all were consistent.[111] But they 'met a felt want', and something which may loosely be called Orphism survived, influencing and influenced by other mystery cults, to the end of antiquity. Most striking of all, the figure of Orpheus was regarded not unkindly by early Christians, and before the figure of Christ

---

[107] D.L. viii, 8; Clem. *Strom.* i, 21; *Suda, s.v.* O. (Kern, TT. 183, 222, 223, 248); Linforth *Arts of O.* 110-118. (Ep. an Alexandrian grammarian, cf. Clem. *Strom.* v, 8, 49, 3, Ath. 468c – E.R.D.)

[108] *Suda, s.v.*; Ar. *ap.* Cic. *Nature of the Gods*, i, 38/107; Ar. *On Philosophy, ap.* Philopon. on Ar. *On the Soul*, 1410b (Ar. fr. 7 Rose).

[109] Plato, *Rep.* ii, 363c.

[110] *Characters*, 16.

[111] Eur. *Hippol.* 954; Plato, *Rep.* ii, 364e; Dodds, *Gks. and the Irrational*, p. 149 and n. 92 (p. 170).

received artistic representation, the Good Shepherd was frequently represented by the allegorical figure of Orpheus.[112]

Of the teaching of the Orpheotelestai we can form no complete picture; nor, in the absence of any organised church or hierarchy, of which there is no trace,[113] was there anything to prevent as many variations, fortified by new forgeries to taste, as in the wilder cults of the modern west. Late Orphism certainly based a doctrine of original sin upon the myth of the Rending of Dionysos, introduced into a half-Greek and wholly barbarous Theogony[114]; but how early this began we cannot tell. A doctrine of the transmigration of souls appears, without mention of Orpheus, in Empedokles (pp. 377f); and in Plato's Myth of Er in the underworld, the soul of Orpheus himself chooses rebirth as a swan.[115] Some Orphic men at least forswore intercourse with women, one of their poems pirating a line from the *Odyssey*, 'There is nothing more shameless nor more horrible than a woman' – a sentiment worthy of the Dark Ages. (The Homeric context was 'than a woman who plans such deeds' – as Klytaimnestra![116]) Almost inevitably they were accused of homosexuality, like celibate orders in many contexts – not least, the Bulgarian Bogomiles in Orpheus' native Thrace, who also rejected the flesh, and whose enemies contributed the word *bougre* to western languages.[117] Those known to Herodotos would not be buried in wool, an animal fibre; and some, at least, were vegetarian. Virgin and also vegetarian, and an Orphic devotee, according to his enraged father, is that somewhat priggish but pure and gallant figure, Euripides' Hippolytos. As a huntsman, he

[112] Guthrie, *O. and Gk. Religion*, figs. 18 (a), (b), pp. 262-3 (catacomb paintings), pl. 15 (ivory pyxis of 6th century A.D.; showing O. with lyre and Phrygian cap among beasts); *ib.* 18c, cf. Talbot Rice, *Beginnings of Christian Art*, pl. 1 (catacomb paintings, the Good Shepherd among sheep, similar groups but without the Orphic attributes). The cylinder-seal showing a crucified figure with inscr. ORPHEOS BAKKIKOS (Guthrie, fig. 19) is now suspected of being a forgery, see G.'s comments in edn. 2.

[113] A. J. Toynbee's conception of 'the historic Orphic Church' as playing a part in Greece comparable to that of the Christian Church in western Europe (*Study of History*, V (1939), 84ff, is withdrawn in Vol. IX, p. 739 (1954), in face of Linforth's criticism.

[114] See Clem. Alex. etc. (n. 72 above); earliest evidence for the detailed theogony is in a fragmentary papyrus from Gurob (3rd century B.C.; fr. 31 Kern); it includes the names and phrases 'Save me, Brimo ... Demeter and Rhea ... armed Kouretes ... Eubouleus ... (king?) Irikepaigos' (cf. Erikepaios in other late texts) '... to place in the basket ... top, bull-roarer, knuckle-bones ... mirror'; in short, the whole apparatus of the later, syncretistic Orphicism.

[115] *Rep.* 620a.

[116] Clem. *Strom.* vi, 15, p. 738; cf. *Od.* 427.

[117] Cf. Norman Cohn, *The Pursuit of the Millennium* (London, 1957), Part i, on those mediaeval popular heresies which present many analogies to our subject.

can hardly have been a quite logical Orphic (if there were any such), and his failure to practise respect for all life has been a scandal to good scholars[118]; but it seems impossible without straining the meaning of the Greek to deny that that is what his enraged father says.

Orphic or other, the new movements in religion emphasised everything that the cities' Olympian cults did not. They were 'enthusiastic' (in the eighteenth-century sense), puritanical and other-worldly. From two lost plays of Euripides characters are quoted as saying, in almost the same words

> Who knows if that be life which we call death
> And life be dying?

And one continues

>   – save alone that men
> Living bear grief, but when they yield their breath
> They grieve no more and have no sorrow then.[119]

It is all very un-Homeric.

---

[118] *Hipp.* 948ff on which cf. Linforth, *Arts of O.* pp. 50ff; Dodds, *op. cit.* p. 148.
[119] Eur. *Phrixos* (Argonautic!) fr. 833 Nauck, tr. J. A. Symonds; cf. *Polyeidos* (fr. 638 N).

CHAPTER XIX

Pythagoras and Western Greek Thought

THE next movement in the history of Greek thought takes place in the West; but the protagonists are still Ionians. From Kolophon, in face of the Persians, emigrated the young Xenophanes, who had known or at least known about Thales; from Samos, to escape the despotism of Polykrates as men later said, Pythagoras, son of Mnesarchos, said to have been a gem-cutter[1]; and Parmenides of Elea, if he 'flourished' about 504 as tradition says,[2] was probably the child of a pair of those stout-hearted Phokaians who abandoned their city to keep their freedom.

The west was following, with a certain time-lag, the same course of development as the mother-country; the colonies, though founded as communities of small-holders, had not been slow to produce classes of rich and poor farmers and landless men. The first western Tyrant recorded is Panaitios of Leontinoi (615 or 608 tr.), general in a war against Megara, with the support of his troops.[3] After 550, powerful tyrannies also arose at Akragas and Gela, and finally at Syracuse; but their history belongs not to that of the growth of Greek civilisation, but to that of its struggle for existence against Persia and Carthage. South Italy, meanwhile, was rent by a series of savage internal wars, in which Siris and Sybaris were destroyed.

The fierceness and insecurity of western Greek life affected its thought. The philosophies that arose there are religious, in contrast to the scientific bent of the Ionians. Pythagoras was under the influence

[1] D.L. viii, 1. Early refs. (Hdt. ii, 123, iv, 95; Ar. *Metaph.* 986a) give only the name Mnesarchos; numerous variations appear in later accounts, cf. D.L. *ib.*, Clem. Alex. *Strom.* i, 62, Porphyry, *Life of P.* 9 (*Leben*, 8 DK).

[2] D.L. ix, 23. Plato, *Parmenides*, 127a, (cf. *Sophist*, 217c) makes him as an old man meet the 'very young' Socrates (dramatic date about 450?), which Raven accepts (*Presocratic Philosophers*, p. 263). Personally I believe Plato's dramatic settings to be 'historical fiction'; cf. that of his *Protagoras*, where Kallias, who inherited his family property about 423, entertains among others the sons of Pericles, who died in 430; see the learned criticism of Athenaios, xi, 505-6.

[3] Polyainos, v, 47; a demagogue-tyrant, Ar. *Politics*, 1310b, cf. 1316a.

of the mystery-religions; Herodotos, we have seen, mentions a Pythagorean taboo as also 'Orphic'[4]; Ion of Chios thought that he and his followers were among the Orphic forgers.[5] Even Parmenides, influenced by the poetry of Xenophanes, is less scientist than mystic. Both are concerned in their several ways to show men how to live in a formidable and changing world, by the contemplation of an order which is unchanging.

About 550, it seems, the Achaians of South Italy renewed their efforts to exclude other Greeks from 'their' area; and the state which suffered was Ionian Siris. Why this happened just then, we can only guess; but Sybaris, rich not only in lands and native subjects but as an intermediary on trade-routes from Miletos to Etruria, may have resented Siris' opening of a rival overland route to the west coast at Pyxous; a route, the use of which we may infer from the fact that Siris and Pyxous struck 'alliance' coins with the same types.[6] Greed for more land no doubt played a part too. Siris was overwhelmed by the power of Sybaris, Kroton and Metapontion; there was much destruction; priests and refugees were slain at the altars. The 'sightless' eyes of an archaic statue were explained long after as those of the cult-statue of Athena Polias, who had closed her eyes at the sight. We hear also of a plague arising from the destruction of this war, which was considered a judgment on the victors.[7]

Long afterwards, Themistokles of Athens, putting pressure on his Peloponnesian allies against Xerxes to fight outside their all-but-island citadel, reminded them that 'Siris in Italy is ours of old', and threatened that if left unsupported the Athenians would sail away and take refuge there.[8] The claim, made as though undisputed, has never been explained; but Athenian trade, as we have seen, had long been invading the west. Was the claim perhaps based on that of fugitives from Siris, who, since their mother-city Kolophon was now prostrate under Persia, may have resorted to the 'senior land of Ionia' (as Solon called it) at the court of Peisistratos? Was not Athens 'mother' of Kolophon?

Kroton next fell upon Lokroi, which is said to have attempted some

----

[4] ii, 81.   [5] D.L. viii, 8; Clem. Alex. *Strom.* i, 131.

[6] J. Perret (*Siris: Recherches critiques sur l'histoire*, Paris, 1941, pp. 247ff) argues cogently that these coins, with the Sybarite type of a bull, were issued after the Sybarite conquest; but in any case they make it likely that the Siris-Pyxous portage was known and used. Illust. also by Hill, *Hist. Gk. Coins*, pp. 6, 7.

[7] Justin xx, 2. Statue, Str. vi, 264; cf. Dunbabin, review of Perret, *op. cit.*, in *JHS* LXV.

[8] Hdt. viii, 62.

diversionary action in support of Siris. The stroke had been long enough expected for the Lokrians to appeal for help to Sparta. Sparta was not disposed to intervene (though not many years later the Spartan prince Dorieus was active in the west); but with the typical Greek gesture of 'benevolent non-belligerency' she is said to have sent the images of the Dioskouroi. Rhegion, with good reason, sent men; but even so, the Lokrians were prodigiously outnumbered by the Krotonian host to which they gave battle on the River Sagras.[9] 'It needed a series of miracles'[10] to save them; and miracles, according to our sources, took place. Fighting for their existence, the Lokrians won a surprising victory. The Lokrian Aias of Homer, the Dioskouroi in their red Spartan riding-cloaks, were said to have been seen fighting on their side. A sixth-century temple at Lokroi, with a terracotta *akroterion* of a horseman on its gable, may perhaps have been dedicated to the Great Twin Brethren in memory of this day.[11] The details of the 'Sagra story' became proverbial in Greece as 'too good to be true'[12]; but there was no doubt about the main fact. Lokroi survived, to entertain Ionian artists and to make a distinctive contribution to early classical art (see p. 387); and Kroton, her morale severely shaken, relapsed to enjoy her wealth in undistinguished peace for some years.[13]

To this community, prosperous but listless, came Pythagoras; he was probably already a man of some reputation.[14] His teaching or preaching struck an answering chord; before long he found himself leader of a brotherhood including the élite of Krotonian society. Milon the wrestler, six times Olympic victor (532–512) was one of his disciples.[15] Pythagoras taught the immortality of the soul, and its transmigration through human and animal bodies; the earliest evidence on him that we have is from Xenophanes, who mentioned some of his alleged reincarnations, and added that he asked a man to stop beating a puppy, saying that he recognised in its howls the voice of a departed friend.[16] The corollary, bracing to the Kroton of his day, was that, as

[9] Justin, xx, 3; D.S. viii, 32; Str. vi, 261. [10] Dunbabin, *Western Gks.* 358.
[11] Justin, *ib.*; Konon (*FGH* 26, from Photios), 18; Paus. iii, 19, 11ff; Dunbabin, *WG* 295 and n. 4, citing Orsi, *Dedalo*, VI, 345ff.
[12] ἀληθέστερα τῶν ἐπὶ Σάγρᾳ, Str. *ib.*, *Suda, s.v.*
[13] Justin, xx, 4; Lokr. art, Dunbabin, *WG* 292-6.
[14] Aristoxenos, *ap.* Porph. *Life of P.* 9 (DK *Leben*, 8); already prominent in Samos, cf. Hdt. iv, 95.
[15] M.'s victories (and legend), Paus. vi, 14, 5ff; his house a Pyth. meeting-place, Iambl. *Life of P.* 249 (DK *Leben*, 16).
[16] Xen. *ap.* D.L. viii, 36.

Plato's Socrates would say, a wise man's first duty is to care for his soul
and purify it. This was to be done by righteousness and by ritual
observance – for instance, by abstaining from certain foods, such as
beans. Whether Pythagoras was also a vegetarian is disputed.[17]

The list of other Pythagorean observances makes strange reading.
Some are rules of piety: e.g. Pour a libation over the handle of the cup
(not where one drinks); Do not have the image of a god on a ring
(used as a seal for mundane purposes); Do not turn aside into a temple
when going elsewhere. Christian priests would give the opposite
advice, but in Pythagoras' world the tendency was not towards a
'Sunday religion', but to pray to the gods on all occasions, mostly for
very mundane advantages. When setting out for a temple, 'Bow
down' (make an act of worship), and thereafter do not do or speak of
any worldly matter. But others seem to be simply pre-rational taboos
or rules against 'ill-luck'; e.g. Do not stir the fire with a knife (Do not
hurt the fire?); Do not sit over a pint-measure (to have emptiness under
one, thought of as unlucky?); On rising from bed, roll the bedclothes
together and do not leave the imprint of your body. Here the magical
'sense' is clear; any malign influence that falls upon the imprint may
harm the person; Frazer compares the very widespread belief that you
may lame an enemy by stabbing hi footprints. Similarly, Do not
leave the imprint of a cooking-pot in the ashes. Do not cut your nails
at a sacrifice; in Pythagoras, probably for the sake of reverence; but
the prohibition also occurs in Hesiod, an example of the world-wide
belief that magical harm may befall one through these *bits of one's self*;
an idea not unknown, amid the current recrudescence of superstition,
at the present day! So also, Spit upon your nail-parings (to avert any
such danger by repudiating them?) Less in need of explanation is: Do
not turn back when leaving home, 'for the Erinyes follow'.[18]

After this one is not surprised to hear that Pythagoras (or the medical
school of Kroton, which had existed before his arrival and was influenced by him) 'made use also of incantations in dealing with some
ailments'; though it is also quite likely, whether or not Iamblichos had
any authentic information, that the school adhered chiefly to the dietetic
method of treatment and relied less on drugs and least of all on surgery.[19]

[17] The tradition that he was is older than the neoplatonists; cf. Str. xv, 716; but Aristotle
and Aristoxenos disbelieved it, see D.L. viii, 19f, Gellius, iv, 11 (DK *Leben*, 9).
[18] Iambl. *Protreptikos*, 21 (DK 58 C 6; 6th edn., p. 466); Porph. *Life*, 42 (*ib.*); D.L. viii,
17; cf. Frazer, *GB*³ I, *The Magic Art*, pp. 207–211.   [19] *Life*, 163f (DK 58 D 1, p. 467).

This would have been in the best tradition of early Greek medicine.

To identify certainly the doctrines of the sage himself is impossible, since he left nothing in writing and his disciples attributed all the doctrines of the school to its Founder.[20] What is clear is that to be a Pythagorean meant not only to accept certain theories, but to be a 'committed' follower of a way of life.[21] The taboos, which our neo-platonist sources are at pains to allegorise as symbolising ethical doctrines, are usually now believed, because of their primitive character, to have been quite literally held, among the earliest tenets of the school, as part of their practice of purity. The doctrine of transmigration of souls is the one point on which we have contemporary evidence, and many of the other Pythagorean practices follow naturally from that. One version, for example, had it that the soul did not pass into those animals which were acceptable for sacrifice, and that for this reason they alone might be eaten.[22] Pythagoras himself is said to have claimed to remember his past lives, as Aithalides, as Euphorbos, killed at Troy, whose shield, dedicated in a temple, he clairvoyantly identified, as one Hermotimos, also said to have identified the shield, and as Pyrrhos, a fisherman of Delos.[23] (This, in terms of the current genealogies, would imply reincarnation once in five generations.) And if the sources on Pythagoras are late, we have from Empedokles of Akragas in the next century some of his own lines, claiming to have been 'ere now a boy and a girl, and a bush and a bird and a dumb fish in the sea'.[24] Empedokles modelled himself in part on Pythagoras, teaching 'Purifications' (including the bean taboo[25]) and claiming to be ready to pass out from the cycle of rebirth. Having attained to the highest order of life, among 'prophets and poets of hymns and healers and leaders' – all of

---

[20] Josephus, *Against Apion* i, 163; Plut. *Mor.* p. 328 (DK 14, 18); D.L. viii, 6, differs – on inadequate grounds; he cites Herakleitos (fr. 129 DK, among the 'zweifelhafte'; see below, p. 398). Diels rejected this as a forgery meant to show that some later books *were* written by P., but 'as Bywater pointed out' it really 'only says that he read books' (Burnet, *EGP* 134 n. 2); cf. also D.L. viii, 15. Hence Plato and Aristotle never attribute any philosophical or mathematical doctrine to P. by name; Plato names him only once (see next n.), and probable or certain Pythagoreans who figure in the dialogues, such as Philolaos, Eche-krates, Timaios, appear only as intelligent men in their own right. Ar. refers to them rather as 'the Italian school', e.g. *Metaph.* 985b, 989b, and a lost work which he wrote *On the Pythagoreans* appears from its fragments (190-205 Rose) to have studied the legend and alleged miracles of the sage but to have ascribed doctrines to the school and very rarely (but once at least if we may trust Aelian, *VH* iv, 17, fr. 191) to P. by name.

[21] *Rep.* x, 600a.

[22] Iambl. *Life of P.* 85 (DK 58 C 4; p. 464).

[23] Herakl. Pont. *ap.* D.L. viii, 4f.

[24] Fr. 117 DK *ap.* D.L. viii, 77.

[25] Fr. 114 DK *ap.* Gell. iv, 11 *et al*

which he was[26] – he claimed to 'walk among men as a god, no longer a mortal', entering cities garlanded and beribboned (as on a high religious festival), while admiring crowds followed him in the hope of counsel or prophecy or a miracle of healing.[27]

Pythagoras is said, on the contrary, of his humility to have coined the term *philosophos*. Earlier sages had been called 'wise men', but he said that none was wise but one, that is God, and described himself only as a 'lover of wisdom'.[28] But his disciples claimed for him more than human status. Stories were told (they were known to Aristotle) that, as he got up to leave the theatre, he accidentally showed his thigh, and it was golden; that he bit a deadly snake and killed it; that he was seen at the same time in Kroton and in Metapontion; that as he was crossing the river Kosa, the river-god greeted him in human speech; that he entertained the northern shaman Abaris and 'took from him his golden arrow, without which he could not find the way, and made him to confess' (what, is not stated). Therefore they called him 'the Hyperborean Apollo', and 'the man who bought his house and dug it up dared not tell anyone what he had seen, and was arrested and put to death at Kroton as a temple-robber; for he was convicted of stealing the golden beard of the statue, which had fallen off'.[29] It was at Metapontion that Herodotos heard the story that Aristeas of Prokonnesos (of the Hyperborean Epic, p. 125) appeared there (240 years after he was last seen alive at his home, on Herodotos' calculation), and 'bade them set up an altar to Apollo, with a statue beside it of a man, Aristeas of Prokonnesos; for that Apollo had come to their country, and to no other in Greek Italy, and he, who was now Aristeas, had been with him; but then, when he followed the god, he was a crow'. And the Delphic Oracle bade them obey the vision, 'and it would be better for them. And the statue is there now, with the name of Aristeas, beside the cult-image of Apollo, and with laurel trees round it, . . . in the market-place.'[30] Some Pythagoreans are said to have taught as a secret doctrine that there were three orders of rational beings: gods, men, and 'such as Pythagoras'.[31]

[26] Fr. 146 DK, *ap*. Clem. *Strom*. iv, 150 (cf. 147, Clem. v, 122); Raven, *Presocr. Phil.* p. 35.
[27] Fr. 112 DK, *ap*. D.L. viii, 62, Clem. *Strom*. vi, 30.   [28] D.L. i, 12.
[29] Iambl. *Life of P.* 140-143; Aelian, *VH* ii, 26, and Apollonios, *Marvels*, 6, (all qd. by Rose, *Ar. Fragm*. 191) q. Ar. for some of the same details, all of which therefore *may* be from Ar. *On the Pythagoreians*.
[30] Hdt. iv, 15.   [31] Ar. fr. 192, *ap*. Iambl. *Life of P.*, 30.

We hear of two kinds of Pythagoreans: the Mathematicians and the Akousmatics, or Hearers, whom the Mathematicians denied to be real Pythagoreans at all.[32] (One of the meanings of *akousmata* was, in fact, 'tall stories'.) For the sage, despite all the cycle of 'shamanistic' stories attached to him, keeps his place among the great thinkers. He was, in a real sense, the first European mathematician.

Two major discoveries are ascribed to him; and it is quite certain that *someone* made them in the circles that revered his name. One of these is that there is a connection between number and music.[33] Probably by stopping a lyre-string at $\frac{3}{4}$, $\frac{2}{3}$ and $\frac{1}{2}$ of its length, he noted that one obtained the fourth, fifth and octave of the note of the whole string. The other is the famous theorem (though hardly in the form in which it stands in Euclid, I, 47), That the square on the hypotenuse of a right-angled triangle equals the sum of the squares on the other two sides. The earliest extant author to ascribe this explicitly to him seems to be the architect Vitruvius.[34] But Egyptian 'land-measurers', as we have seen, had long known the fact that, by constructing a triangle with its sides in the ratio of 3, 4 and 5, one could obtain a right-angle. Pythagoras is said to have discovered a method of finding an infinite series of numbers which give the same result; probably that of 'setting out from the odd numbers'[35] (since every square of an odd number equals the difference between the squares of the two consecutive numbers that add up to the first square: $3^2 = 9 = 5^2 - 4^2$; $5^2 = 25 = 13^2 - 12^2$; $7^2 = 49 = 25^2 - 24^2$; etc.). Perhaps it was for this 'revelation' that the sage (without compunction, it appears) is said to have sacrificed an ox.[36]

Pythagoras had thus discovered that both what we see and touch and what we hear, shapes and sounds, in their purest manifestations, the geometric and the musical, are capable of description in terms of simple numerical relations. From this he seems to have leapt to the intuition that this was the secret of the universe, and that 'the elements of num-

---

[32] Iambl. *Life of P.* 81 (DK 18, 2, under Hippasos; the excommunicated Pythagorean whose disciples the Akousmatic 'heretics' were said to be: see *ib.* 88, DK 18, 4).

[33] Ar. *Metaph.* 985b (in general terms); details (but garbled) in Iambl. *Life*, 115; music as a purgative 'medicine for the soul', Aristoxenos (the best of evidence here) in DK 58 D 1 (p. 468, ll. 19ff); cf. Raven, *Presocr. Phil.* 229ff, 236ff; Schrödinger, *Nature and the Gks.* 33f.

[34] Vitruv. ix, Preface, 5ff; cf. Proklos on Euclid, p. 426 Friedl. *ap.* Raven, *op. cit.* 231 n. 3.

[35] Attrib. to P. by Heron, *Geometry and Stereometry*, pp. 56, 146, ed. Hultsch.

[36] Apollodoros, *ap.* D.L. viii, 12.

bers are the elements of all things', 'rather than fire and earth and water';
'for mathematical facts are of the things that ARE, without movement'.
So says Aristotle,[37] cautiously attributing the doctrines always to 'the
so-called Pythagoreans'. Since however they were not in a position to
anticipate mathematical physics, in which Pythagoras would have
delighted, many of their identifications of numbers with things or
concepts were fanciful; unity being male and two female, three was
marriage; or (as Aristotle adds, *loc. cit.*) that '*This* modification of
number was Justice, *that* was Soul and Reason, another Opportunity
(*kairos*) and so on'. Ten was Number itself, Pythagoras having noted
that all nations 'count up to ten and then start from one again' (it did
not occur to him, apparently, that this had anything to do with our
having ten fingers), and also that $10 = 1 + 2 + 3 + 4$; the first four integers,
which are also the numbers that appeared in the observations on the
musical string. This number, represented (for lack of any better
notation) by a pattern of $1 + 2 + 3 + 4$ points (or pebbles on the ground)
in the form of an isosceles right-angled triangle, was called by Pythagoreans the *Tetraktys*, and by it, or by its revered Inventor, they swore
the most solemn oaths. [38]Tangible objects were also thought to be or
to consist of numbers, thus conceived as patterns of points; we even
hear of a certain Eurytos of Taranto (*c.* 450?) who used to pick out
with pebbles, green, red, black or of other colours, an outline drawing
of a horse, man or plant, thinking thus to shed light on what was the
'number' of each species.[39] (One wonders if this was the origin of the
art of mosaic, first certainly known to us in fourth-century Olynthos?)
So easily can the ideas of a visionary become superstitions. But it
followed from the original theory, as Aristotle points out,[40] that the
'points' had magnitude, the minimum magnitude, as it were. The
early Pythagoreans had perhaps not consciously drawn this inference,
but rather never arrived at the conception of number as completely
abstract; and it may be that the theory had a more important consequence also: was it, perhaps, the point of departure for the materialist
atomism of the fifth-century Ionians?

Bound up with the number-theory was an elaborate doctrine of

[37] *Metaph.* 985b, 989b (DK[6] p. 452, 1ff, p. 456, 17f).
[38] Aetios, i, 3, 8 (DK 58 B 15).
[39] Ar. *Metaph.* 1092b (DK 45, 3; p. 420, 12ff); for the colours, Alexander of Aphrodisias,
Comm. on Ar. *ad loc.*; Kirk and Raven, *Presocr. Phil.* p. 314.
[40] Ar. *Metaph.* 1080b, on which cf. Raven, *op. cit.* 246ff.

Opposites. Ten pairs (in accordance with the dogma of the Decad) were regarded as fundamental: limit and unlimited (or infinity); odd and even; one and plurality; right and left; male and female; stationary and moving; straight and curved; light and darkness; good and evil; square and oblong.[41] In every case, the 'good' principle was that in the first column. It is not impossible that this emphasis on opposites, which reappears in Herakleitos, may have owed something to the dualism of the Persian religion. Later legend, which represented Pythagoras as having travelled widely in his youth – Alexandrian writers said, even to India, to learn the doctrine of metempsychosis from the Brahmans – included a tale that he visited 'Zaratas the Chaldaean', who is Zarathustra.[42]

The nature and movements of the heavenly bodies naturally interested Pythagoras; the Babylonians had already treated them arithmetically, dividing the day into twelve 'hours' as Herodotos says, by marking out their sundials.[43] Eight apparently moving heavenly bodies were visible to the eye: the sun, moon, five other 'planets' or wandering stars, and the 'sphere of the fixed stars'. Pythagoras or an early Pythagorean (Philolaos, according to Aetios) added a ninth by the bold intuition that the earth is also a star, though near the centre of the universe, revolving round a central fire and making its own day and night as it turns its inhabited surface to and from the sun; and the sacred number ten was made up by positing a 'counter-earth', *antichthon*, which revolves on the other side of the Fire, concealed from us by our earth itself.[44] Claiming moreover to have observed that 'their speeds, judged by their distances, are in the same ratio as the musical concordances', they said that the sound of their movement formed a harmony, the 'music of the spheres', which to our ears, accustomed to it from birth, is silence.[45]

But even in the mathematical field, one great disappointment awaited Pythagoras. The theorem about right-angled triangles inevitably led to attempts to find the ratio between the equal sides of an isosceles right-angled triangle and the hypotenuse, and to complete

[41] Ar. *Metaph.* 986a, referring particularly to Alkmaion of Kroton 'who was a young man when P. was old'.
[42] Hippol. *Ref. Her.* i, 2, 12 (DK 14, 11), from Aristoxenos.
[43] Hdt. ii, 109.
[44] Ar. *On the Heavens*, 293a (DK 58 B 37); *Metaph.* 986a (DK *ib.* 4, p. 452, 13ff); Aetios, ii, 7, 7 (DK 44 A 16); Raven, *Presocr. Phil.* 256ff.
[45] Ar. *op. cit.* 290b (DK 58 B 35).

failure; for as failure appeared the discovery that this hypotenuse, the diagonal of a square, is incommensurable with the side.[46] The 'inferior' rectangle with sides of 3 and 4 yielded a simple ratio; its diagonal was 5; but the square itself, which of all figures 'ought' to have behaved satisfactorily, did not. At the very heart of geometry evil itself, the irrational, the unlimited, could not be eradicated; God concealed himself and did not reveal the answer. It is said to have been for revealing to the uninitiated this terrible secret that Hippasos of Metapontion was expelled from the society, his grave dug and his burial rites celebrated in his lifetime; and that thereafter, by divine judgment, he was lost at sea.[47] Hippasos was, it seems, a free-thinking and rebel Pythagorean; he is said to have held independent and more materialistic views, akin to those of Herakleitos[48]; he stuck to and announced his views, and was not content that they should be and should be counted as those of the Founder and the Party[49]; and he is also said to have opposed Pythagoras and the majority politically, as we shall see.

Pythagoras was by nature a contemplative. Some go to the Games, he is said to have said, to sell their goods (at the great fairs), some to compete for honour, and some to look on.[50] Of these three classes, the vulgar, the active and the contemplative, he preferred the last. But circumstances had made him, willy-nilly, a political figure. His followers, serious-minded, loyal to one another and drawn, inevitably, from the leisured classes, dominated the government, a full-citizen body of 1000 it is said,[51] as in several other Greek cities. Socially as well as in the ideal sense, such a government could only be aristocratic; and morally, it might well appear to outsiders an irksome Rule of the Saints, who for reasons of their own interfered with a man beating his own dog.[52] In Greek Italy as elsewhere, widening circles of the *demos* were ceasing to be amenable to direction and demanding some share in control; very likely, it was precisely the feeling that their ascendancy was threatened that disposed some of the gentry to rally to

---

[46] Iambl. *Life*, 247 (DK 18, 4, p. 108, 22f); cf. Ar. *Anal. Pr.* 41a; Burnet, *EGP*, p. 105. One would like to know whether P. pushed his arithmetic as far as $119^2 + 120^2 = 169^2$.
[47] Iambl. 88, 246f (DK *ib.*).
[48] Ar. *Metaph.* 984a, and doxographers, DK 18, 7.   [49] Iambl. 88 (DK *ib.*).
[50] D.L. viii, 8 (from Herakl. Pont.? – cf. D.L. i, 12).   [51] Iambl. 257 (DK 18, 5).
[52] Cf. Burnet, *EGP*, p. 90, n. 1; he and G. Thomson (*The First Philosophers*, pp. 249ff) seem to go too far in denying that the P. society was politically anti-democratic. Like most of the friends of Socrates, how could they have been anything but aristocratic in the political sense?

the Pythagorean freemasonry. Politically, the brotherhood was a *hetaireia* or alliance of like-minded men, the characteristic form of oligarchic or would-be oligarchic organisation.

But, as this *hetaireia* had been founded for intellectual and religious purposes and not for political, when a major political question arose it had its weaknesses. Those who demanded a wider suffrage found leaders both without its ranks and within. The discontented found a leader in one Kylon, who though rich and of good family had been refused entry to the Society[53]; and within its ranks Hippasos and two others are said to have advocated a more democratic suffrage and the principle that outgoing magistrates should be accountable to the people.[54] For whatever reason – perhaps from dislike of political strife, and having lost some of his confidence since finding himself in a mathematical impasse – Pythagoras, a saddened man, withdrew from Kroton (the story that he was murdered in a revolution is rejected by the better ancient authorities[55]) and ended his days at Metapontion, where the ear of corn that was the badge on the city's coins suggests a quieter and more agricultural society. Without him, the conservative majority in the society closed their ranks, and were still in control of Kroton when Great Greece was shaken by the disaster of the war with Sybaris.

Sybaris, now in sole possession of the portages to the Tyrrhenian Sea, and with the lands of murdered Siris to expand into, had reached the climax of her proverbial power and luxury.

'Sybarite stories', including some that had done duty already for Siris and Kolophon, were a branch of Greek humour. The typical young Sybarite complains of the crumpled rose-leaf in his bed, or of having sustained a rupture from seeing men working in the fields, and his friend replies, 'It has given me a pain merely to hear of it.' Some 'had not seen the sun rise or set in years'. They piped their wine down to the coast for export. They planted trees for shade along their roads; they excluded crowing cocks and noisy trades from residential areas. The story that one of their luxury-inventions was that of chamber-pots gives a glimpse of the level of primitive discomfort from which these gibes were launched.[56]

---

[53] Iambl. 248ff (DK 14, 16), from Aristoxenos.   [54] See n. 51.

[55] Iambl. 251 (DK 14, 16, p. 104, 11f).

[56] Aelian, *VH* ix, 24; Ath, xii, 518c, e; 519c-e; and cf. the section, 518c to 522d (beginning, characteristically 'What need is there to speak of the Sybarites?')– The practice of

Such stories were not intended to do justice. Sybaris was formidable. The story that she had 5000 'knights' would be credible in such a territory (nearly two-thirds the area of the whole Peloponnese), were it not that the addition of '300,000 infantry' in the same sentence makes it apparent that both figures are merely a wild guess.[57] The reported perimeter of her walls, six miles round, but far from circular, between her two rivers, would give room for a city population of some 50,000.[58] Her system of alliances, attested by the characteristic coinage of south Italy, with the devices in relief on the obverse side and sunken (incuse) on the reverse, covers the whole Achaian west: Sybaris, Kroton, Kaulonia and Metapontion, Laos on the west coast, and towns, otherwise unknown, whose names began with the syllables Ami- (or Asi-), Mol- and Pal-; probably inland towns in the Sybarite territory, enjoying local self-government. The alliance-coins of Siris and Pyxous also use the Sybarite badge of a bull, which gives rise to the suggestion that these are not coins of independent Siris but of a new Siris recolonised by the Sybarite conquerors.[59] And if her cavalry-horses were trained to execute 'musical rides', modern examples remind us that this is not incompatible with their being also trained for battle.[60] Sybaris is said to have granted citizenship freely to newcomers,[61] as she might well in such a time of expansion. Her great Games (and their valuable prizes) outshone Olympia.[62]

This expanding and powerful city might indeed sound more than a little like fifth-century Athens, if Sybaris had survived to produce her own history. But a little before 510 a revolution supervened. The commons, increasing in numbers and prosperity, found a leader in one Telys; many nobles fled or were banished, and Telys ruled as tyrant or, as his supporters said, king. Telys aspired to win support also in Kroton, betrothing his daughter to a rich and powerful Krotonian

quoting the collection of stories of luxury, lechery and sadism, assembled by Ath. in Book xii (pp. 510-554), from the diverse places where they stand among the *fragmenta* of the numerous authors whom Ath. quotes, gives an exaggerated impression of the prevalence of excesses in the ancient world, which modern authors have failed to correct. These fragments *are not a chance collection*, but part of the life-work of a Man with a Muck-Rake. Dunbabin, *WG* 75-83, gives a sensible and balanced estimate of Sybarite civilisation. The regulations against noise, for example, might well be considered 'simply as good police regulations' (Lenormant, qd. by Dunbabin, p. 79).

[57] See Str. vi, 263; D.S. x, 23, xii, 9. 'Skymnos', 341, says 100,000.

[58] Str. *ib.*; Dunbabin, p. 77.   [59] Head, *Hist. Num.*[2] 70, 83; n. 6, above.

[60] Despite the story retailed about this by Ath. (xii, 520c ff); a story also told about Kardia, as Ath. notes, *ib.*, from Charon of Lampsakos.

[61] D.S. xii, 9, 2.   [62] Her. Pont. *ap.* Ath. 522a; 'Skymnos', 345ff.

named Philip, an Olympic victor; but the Krotonians banished him, and Telys (now that Philip was a political failure?) broke off the engagement. Philip thereupon, still wealthy enough to man a ship of war with 'his own men', sailed away to Cyrene.[63] Meanwhile many Sybarite exiles took refuge at Kroton, and Telys, probably regarding them with good reason as a menace to him, demanded their extradition with threats of war. The exiles took sanctuary, and the Krotonians (swayed by a speech from Pythagoras, we are told, inevitably; but he had probably left before this) refused to surrender them. They sent an embassy of thirty men to Sybaris to attempt further negotiations; but Telys (regarding the state of war as already existing?) had them massacred and their bodies cast out from the city and left unburied. Then, with a huge army (300,000, against 100,000 Krotonians, we are assured) he marched on Kroton.[64]

The Krotonians rallied grimly, appointing Milon as their general. Whatever their own political differences, the attitude of Sybaris closed all gaps; and on the frontier river Tetraeis, as before on the Sagras, the smaller army won a crushing victory. They were said to have had the useful aid of Dorieus, prince of Sparta, with an expedition which he was leading to western Sicily; but the Krotonian patriotic account said nothing of this. A charge led by Milon, equipped it was said like Herakles, with lion-skin and club, broke the Sybarite line. Of the reasons for the total Sybarite débâcle we have no evidence; perhaps they had lost, with the exiles, many of their experienced military leaders. The embittered Krotonians gave no quarter. Telys was killed, and the victors, pressing on to Sybaris, captured the town, seventy days after the beginning of the campaign. They destroyed it, turning the river Krathis across the site so that it should never again be inhabited; and for nearly sixty years the surviving Sybarites lived scattered, many of them at Laos and Skidros on the west coast.[65] The savagery of this war is the more intelligible, when we see it as a class and party conflict between kindred peoples.

Kroton succeeded to the leading position in south Italy, and her alliance-coinage in turn, continuing into the fifth century, extends over

[63] Hdt. v, 44–47 ('King' in the Sybarite, 'tyrant' in the Krotonian version, 44; Philip 47). T. a demagogue-tyrant, D.S. xii, 9, 2.

[64] D.S. xii, 9, 3f; Ath. xii, 521d, perhaps from Phylarchos (cf. *ib.* b, c).

[65] D.S. xii, 9, 5; Iambl. *Life of Pyth.* 260 (R. Tetraeis; Traeis em. Bentley, from D.S. xii, 22, 1); Str. vi, 263; Hdt. v, 44; vi, 21.

Kaulonia, 'Te-' (Temesa?) and other unidentified towns. The land of Sybaris was too valuable to be left unoccupied; and occupied it was, by some shrunken community, tolerated by Kroton and perhaps partly of colonists from thence. It also struck alliance-coins with Kroton, in which the tripod of Kroton occupies the obverse and the bull of Sybaris the reverse or less honourable side.[66]

The influence of the Pythagorean brotherhood remained strong for some time after the death of the sage; it is said to have been broken by a movement led by Kylon (p. 383), described by Iamblichos as *exarchos* of the Sybarites (governor of the conquered territory?). But the final destruction of the society at Kroton must have been long delayed if, as we are told, Lysis, a survivor of it, became the teacher of Epameinondas. The event itself, notorious and catastrophic, must be historical, however muddled and contradictory our sources. The people, suspecting the brotherhood of political conspiracy, are said to have surrounded the house of Milon, where a meeting was being held, set it on fire, and killed all the brethren except Lysis and Philolaos, who alone succeeded in breaking through the mob. The other cities where Pythagorean brotherhoods existed took no action; indeed other meeting-houses of the sect are said to have been destroyed in similar risings elsewhere.[67] But even now the political influence of the movement was not quite at an end. At Taranto, as late as the fourth century, the mathematician and philosopher Archytas rose to a position comparable to that of Pericles at Athens. Seven times elected by a democratic assembly General of the republic (a position which it was not normally permitted to hold more than once) and undefeated in battle, he befriended Plato in an hour of need, and was one of the sources of Plato's knowledge of Pythagoreanism[68]; the oral tradition of the movement having been meanwhile summarised and set down in writing by Philolaos.[69]

The promise of Achaian Italy was dead, blighted by its own faults in the same generation which saw the ruin of Ionia; but the long list of names of thinkers, eastern and western, who visited Athens or who are discussed by Plato, shows that both could still influence classical Athens. Some archaeological evidence, though of later date, helps to fill in the picture of Greek religion in the west, which had no doubt

[66] Dunbabin, *WG* 365, 366 n. 1 (q. Kahrstedt in *Hermes*, LIII).
[67] Iambl. *Life of P.* 249 (DK 14, 16); Polyb. ii, 39; Justin, xx, 4.
[68] D.L. viii, 79, 82f; Plato, *Letter* 7 (relevant portions excerpted in DK 47 A 5).
[69] D.L. viii, 15, 84f; schol. on Plato, *Phaidon*, 61e (DK 44 A 1a).

both influenced and been influenced by the thought of the school.

From Lokroi comes a famous and unique series of votive pictures – tablets, about twelve or thirteen inches square, decorated in relief with figures impressed from matrices when the clay was soft, and thereafter painted.[70] Their style is of the early fifth century, and their subjects indicate that they came from the famous Lokrian sanctuary of Persephone. They have been found piecemeal in the earth brought down by the rapid denudation of a hillside, in which the sanctuary itself has been engulfed. Some show figures of animals, among which the Dionysian bull and the cock (which Pythagoras would not sacrifice) are significantly common. Others show scenes from a story or pageant which has been interpreted as the seizure of Persephone, the solemn ceremonies of her marriage to Hades and, in a few pictures, Persephone opening a chest or basket which contains a babe: the Divine Child. In another Persephone enthroned, sometimes with her Bridegroom, receives gifts. A young god (Hermes?) brings a ram or lamb; a figure in a serpent-drawn car (Triptolemos?) brings ears of wheat. In one unique scene Dionysos (so *not* here identified with the Child, unless like some gods he grew up at once) brings a vine and a cup. The Cock appears repeatedly, perching on a basket, or forming the carved head of a staff. We are continually reminded of what we can divine or guess about the mysteries of Eleusis.

Later and more anomalous among documents on Greek religion, but of great interest, are the little gold tablets found in graves, mostly in south Italy, buried near the head or right hand of the deceased, and inscribed with fragments of hexameter verse intended to guide the deceased in the world beyond death: a Greek *Book of the Dead*. They used to be universally described as 'Orphic tablets'. The more rigorous criticism of recent years has pointed out that no text connects them with the name of that prophet; nor are the texts fragments from the late Orphic poems surviving. But they are from poems of that kind; and as we have seen, Pythagoras and his circle were suspected by some classical Greeks of ascribing to Orpheus poems of their own. There

[70] Discovered piecemeal since 1850; most, excavated by Orsi in 1908, are now on view at Reggio Calabria. The following para. is from notes on a lecture by Mme P. Zancani Montuoro at Cambridge, August, 1958, and conversation, which I gratefully acknowledge. She is preparing their publication. – On the cock, here prominent, cf. Iambl. *Protrept.* 21 (DK 58 C 6; p. 466, line 27); D.L. viii, 20 (though whether its sacrifice was practised or forbidden, they disagree).

are eleven now known: five were found near Sybaris, three of them with versions of the same text, and two, found folded together, with different texts; associated pottery has been dated about 350-250. One, with another text, the longest, comes from Petelia, in south Italy; three, with three lines each, including elements of the Petelia text, from Eleutherna in Crete; and one, with part of the same text as the three from Sybaris and with the name of its 'holder', Caecilia Secundina, is said to be from Rome. This and the Petelia tablet are in the British Museum; those from Crete in the National Museum, Athens, as is the latest discovered (1950), from Pharsalos; those from Sybaris at Naples.[71]

One of the two Sybaris tablets found together is so carelessly copied that little can be made of it; but the names of several gods can be made out: 'Kybeleian Kore' (showing some syncretism), Demeter, Zeus, the Moirai, and probably Phanes, a god important in late Orphic texts.[72] Its companion begins,

> But when the soul leaves the light of the sun, go on thy way to the right with good care. . . .

The Petelia tablet seems to give later lines from (perhaps) the same poem of directions to the soul:

'And thou shalt find in the house of Hades, on the left, a spring, and a white cypress standing by it; to this spring draw not near. But thou shalt find another, from the Pool of Memory, cold water pouring forth; but there are guards before it. Say: "I am child of earth and starry heaven; but my race is of heaven; and this ye also know yourselves; and I am parched with thirst and perishing; but give me quickly of the cold water flowing from the Pool of Memory." And they themselves shall give thee to drink of the divine spring; and then thereafter thou shalt reign with the other heroes.' The bottom of the tablet is broken, but about two more lines followed, including the words 'die' and (still in the metre) 'wrote this'. Would that we had the subject of this verb!

The three Cretan tablets have lines from a similar poem:

[71] C. Smith and D. Comparetti in *JHS* III; A. Olivieri, *Lamellae Aureae Orphicae* (*Kleine Texte*, Bonn, 1915); G. Murray, app. to J. Harrison, *Prolegomena to the Study of Gk. Religion* (with texts); Kern, *Orph. Fragmenta*, pp. 104ff DK 1, 16-21 (with texts); discussion and trn., Guthrie *Orph. and Gk. Religion*, pp. 171ff. The Pharsalos find, *Arch. Ephemeris* (Athens), 1950-51.
[72] First, in extant lit., in 'O.' hexameter *ap.* D.S. i, 11, 3.

'I am parched with thirst and perishing; but give me to drink of the unfailing fountain on the right, where the cypress is.' – 'Who art thou? Whence art thou?' – 'I am a son of earth and starry heaven.'

The other three Sybaris tablets give, with variations, the words which the soul is to address to the Powers below, and their reply; this is a conflated version:

> I come pure from among the pure, O Queen of those under earth, (and) Eukles, Eubouleus and other deities. For I too boast that I am of your blessed race; and I have paid the penalty for unrighteous deeds, when fate laid me low, and the flash of thunderbolts; but I have sped forth from the sorrowful weary wheel; I have won to the longed-for crown with my swift feet. I have gone beneath the bosom of the Mistress, the Queen of Under-Earth. And now I am come a suppliant to holy Persephone, that she may with good will bring me to the abode of the saints.

One tablet adds the reply:
'Happy and most blessed, thou shalt be a god instead of a mortal'; and it closes with the formula (not metrical): 'A kid, I am fallen into milk' – presumably meaning, 'I have attained my one desire.'
More fully, the divergent Sybaris tablet continues:

> Hail thou that hast suffered the passion that thou hadst never suffered before; from a man thou art become a god; a kid, thou art fallen into milk. Rejoice, rejoice, faring on thy rightward journey to the holy meadows and the Groves of Persephone.

Lastly, the Roman tablet seems to be in the form of a sort of passport:

> Pure from among the pure she comes, Queen of those under earth, Eukles, Eubouleus, child of Zeus, glorious; and I have this gift of Memory, songful among men. – 'Caecilia Secundina, go, lawfully become divine.'

'This gift of Memory' is probably the tablet itself. Eubouleus (like Eukles, probably originally a euphemistic name of Hades) is a name also known at Eleusis.[73]
The analogy with the Egyptian Book of the Dead is striking; so is

---

[73] Paus. i, 14, 2f.

the phrase 'the sorrowful weary wheel' with the Indian expression, the wheel of rebirth. The 'wheel' here is not quite unique in Greek literature; it recurs in the neoplatonist Proklos, in his commentary on the *Timaios*.

But it is the analogies with Plato himself which are the most striking. One recognises at once the waters of the underworld to which his souls of the dead journey 'through terrible and burning heat'.[74] (They are near the Central Fire?) The common herd in Plato drink of the Spring of Forgetfulness, Ameles, before they take their new bodies; this must be the spring on the left, under the mysterious White Cypress; but Er in the story is forbidden to drink of it, that he may remember. Remembrance of their past lives is the characteristic of the 'divine men' like Pythagoras and Empedokles, who are ready to 'pass out from the wheel'. It seems certain that this 'book of the dead' and Plato's vision of Hades have a common source, presumably Pythagorean.

The superstitious side of Pythagoreanism is typical of tendencies that might have been fatal to Greek rationalism. It is a common modern belief that classical Greece was growing irreligious. Nothing could be further from the truth. The classical period saw, along with the increase of individualism, an increase in personal religion or, at the worst, religiosity; Xenophon, aristocrat, soldier and disciple of Socrates, is in this respect also a typical Athenian of his time.

Striking evidence on the intellectual 'climate' of classical Greece is to be found in personal nomenclature; in the development of a choice of names compounded with those of gods; names calculated to place the child under the protection of a deity and to remind the adult of his religious obligations. Early Greek names, such as the names in Homer, are not of this type; they are names redolent of heroic and aristocratic prowess and self-confidence, of pride in horses, in political leadership (the names compounded with -stratos, -laos, -demos), in strength and fame, when they are not (like Achilles, Nestor, Solon, Gryllos) of origins lost in the mist of antiquity. The few names compounded with Theo – Theokles of Naxos ('Famed like a god', a Homeric notion?) or Theopompos ('Conductor of the sacred procession'?) are scarcely an exception; 'Diomedes' is connected with the Homeric epithet *dios* 'bright', rather than with the name of Zeus, and the name of Herakles,

---

[74] *Rep.* x, 621a. J. S. Morrison, in *JHS* 75, compares this soul-journey of Er to the shamanistic flight of Parmenides, *q.v.* below.

to whom Hera is hostile, may be suspected of being an adaptation of something pre-Hellenic. The Homeric repertoire continued in use in Macedonia, long enough for many of Alexander's officers to bear names known, often as those of quite obscure people, in Homer or in the mythic genealogies.

The new type of nomenclature, compounded with the names of particular deities, first appears in the sixth century, and in exactly the area which produced the first philosophers, in Ionia and on its borders. In Herodotos' history, such names are numerous, though still in a minority, in the generation active about 500: Apollophanes, Artemisia, Dionysios, Dionysophanes, Hekataios, Hermippos, Hermotimos, Hermophantos, a Herodotos of Chios, Herophantos, Metrodoros, two Pythagorai and a Pythogenes; all from Asia Minor. Of Athens, a Hermolykos and an Olympiodoros fought in 479; and a few such names – Demetrios, twice, Apollodoros, twice, three names beginning with Kephiso- and four with Dio-, (but none with Atheno-) appear among the 177 on the Erechtheid War Memorial of 459.[75] In the fourth century, they are common, and in the Hellenistic age Demetrios and Dionysios, surpassing in popularity even Apollonios and Apollodoros, are the commonest of all Greek names.

We owe it to the intellectual toughness of philosophers that the growth of religiosity did not everywhere develop into mere superstition. In the circles immediately influenced by Pythagoras, the great name in this connection is that of Parmenides.

Parmenides of Elea, said to have 'flourished' about 504 (a generation after the foundation of his city and the *floruit* of Xenophanes), knew the cosmology of the Pythagoreans; he is said to have learned about it from an otherwise unknown Pythagorean, Ameinias, to whom he built a shrine, as to a hero (no doubt this was what preserved Ameinias' name); but Aristotle emphasises his debt to Xenophanes.[76] It is evident that he had experienced the feeling which has been called 'an intense sensation that IT IS'[77]; a feeling which is implicit in all consciousness, but is not usually isolated. It was the doctrine of sheer, existent Being and of what follows from awareness of it, that he felt compelled to

[75] Hdt. ix, 21, 105; *IG* I², 929 (Tod, *GHI* 26).
[76] D.L. ix, 21, from Sotion, who denied that X. was his personal teacher; perhaps rightly; as Raven says, he must have had some reason for rejecting Ar.'s view in favour of this unknown name; cf. Ar. *Metaph.* 986b (DK 28 A 6); *Presocr. Phil.* 264f.
[77] Cf. Clare Luce in *The Road to Damascus* (London, 1949), pp. 186f.

teach, setting forth his thoughts in verse,[78] like Xenophanes and the Orphic 'ghost' writers. In religious fashion, he set forth the account of his mystic vision in a myth: he had been rapt from earth in a chariot with red-hot and screaming axle (evidently lubrication had not yet been discovered), by 'the maiden daughters of the Sun', to 'the gates of the paths of Night and Day, enclosed between a lintel and stone threshold'. The doors were shut, and 'Justice of many penalties' (*Dike*, in Homer 'the way things are') 'holds the fitting keys'; but the Maidens besought her, the gates opened wide, and the Goddess took him by the hand and addressed him: 'Youth, . . . thou must learn all things: both the rounded heart of unshaking truth, and the opinions of men, in which is no true belief.'[79]

What he sets forth thereafter in the first part of his poem, *The Way of Truth*, is difficult reading; difficult not from complication of thought, but from extreme simplicity and abstractness. He had applied reason to his intensely clarified sense of reality, and concluded that, since all that is, is, there is no such thing as the non-existent. Moreover, since that which is cannot have come to be out of non-existence, it can have had no beginning; nor can it change, for if it were to change, it would un-be what it is: 'Only this way of discourse remains, that IT IS; and on this way are many signs that it has no genesis and no destruction; for it is whole and unshaking and unending; nor ever Was it nor Shall Be, since it is all together now, one, continuous; what birth will you seek for it? How and whence did it grow? "Out of not being", I will not let you say nor think; for it is unsayable and unthinkable that IT IS NOT. And what need would have stirred it, later or sooner, starting from nothing, to grow? Thus necessarily it either IS entirely, or not. Nor will the strength of conviction admit anything to come to be, beside it; therefore nature ("the way-things-are", *Dike*, again; "Justice" is too anthropomorphic) does not permit either becoming or perishing, relaxing her bonds, but holds them.'[80]

'Moreover it is unmoved in the limits of mighty bonds, without beginning or end, since coming-to-be and perishing have been driven far away, and true belief has rejected them; but it abides the same in the same place by itself and so abides there firm. . . .'[81]

[78] Preserved in great part by Simplicius; Raven, *ib.*

[79] DK 28 B 1; Eng. trns., Burnet, *EGP*[3], pp. 172ff, Raven, 266ff, Thomson, *The First Philosophers*, 289ff, with discussions.

[80] DK 28 B 8.   [81] *ib.* lines 26ff.

'Moreover since limit is the uttermost, it is completed every way, like the bulk of a well-rounded sphere, equal all ways from the middle; for it must not be any greater or any less this way or that; for there is no not-being that should prevent it reaching alike, nor is there any being wherefore there should be this way more and this way less of being, since it is all inviolate; for as it is all ways equal to itself, so it is uniformly within limits.'[82]

Parmenides would clearly have delighted in the modern concept of a curved space, unbounded but finite. The striking and startling thing about his thought is the ruthlessness with which he follows reason. Unflinching thought, for him, must lead to truth (since we cannot think the thing that is not): 'for to think is the same as to be'; a thought that pleased Plotinos, who quotes it while appreciating the fact that Parmenides, a man of his age, could not describe his One Being as anything but corporeal.[83]

The reality of any change is thus denied, and (since there is no less Being in any place than in any other) so is the reality of motion; and if the senses tell us otherwise, so much the worse for the senses. Hence the famous proposition that Achilles can never overtake the tortoise, said by some to have been laid down by Parmenides himself, but generally agreed to have been at least sharpened as a weapon, and reinforced with other paradoxes (such as that of the arrow in flight, which has position) by his best disciple, the Eleatic Zenon.[84]

Nevertheless, even if the 'opinions of men' (their *doxai*, 'seemings') are illusory, the fact remains that we do have them, and Parmenides proceeds to give an account of the phenomenal world. He continues, still reporting the revelation made to him by 'the goddess Dike':

'There I end for thee my trustworthy discourse and thought (*noema*) concerning truth; but from this point learn thou the opinions (*doxai*) of men, hearing a deceitful order in my words.' Many readers have been puzzled, that he could feel it worth while to do this; but Simplicius, the commentator on Aristotle to whom we owe the preservation of so much of the poem, saw the point. He introduces the last quotation: 'Now passing from objects of thought to objects of sense (*noeta* to *aistheta*), he says...'[85] After his vision, he and his disciples have

[82] DK 42ff.
[83] DK 28 B 3 (Plotin. *Enneads*, v, 1, 8; also Clem. Alex. *Strom.* vi, 23).
[84] Favorinus, *ap.* D.L. ix, 29; Ar. *Physics*, 239b, cf. 219b (DK 29 A 1 and 24 ff).
[85] DK 28 B 8, 50ff; Simpl. *Physics*, 30, 13 (DK p. 234, 20ff).

still to live in the phenomenal world, and one opinion may be better than another; so he gives his account of it. In it two opposites, Light and Night, are fundamental, and the appearance of the heavenly bodies is caused by a series of *stephanai*, 'headbands', 'the narrower bands filled with unmixed flame, those following them with night, but therewith goes a share of flame; and in the midst of these is the *daimon* who steers all; for she originates all the affairs of hateful birth and sexual intercourse, sending the female to mix with male and male with female.'[86] (So, like a Pythagorean or an Orphic devotee, he regards not only phenomena with contempt, but the flesh with loathing.) The differences of men's intellect are of physical origin: 'for as each has the mixing of his wandering members, so is men's accompanying intellect; for the same is that which thinks (*phroneei*, "is spiritually active") the natural growth (*physis*) of the members for men, each and all; for the thought is the more.'[87] He writes in the spirit in which, perhaps, a modern Hindu might write of natural science, or as a psychologist may try to give the most useful account of the connections of irrational phantasies.

[86] DK 28 B 12 (from Simpl.).
[87] DK 28 B 16, cf. A 46 (from Theophrastos, *On Perception*; Ar. *Metaph.* 1009b).

CHAPTER XX

Herakleitos of Ephesos

AN outlook no less tough and sombre accompanies very different speculations in the work of the last great thinker of this generation in the east, Herakleitos of Ephesos.[1]

Herakleitos is said to have been of royal descent, and to have resigned the titular kingship, whose chief prerogative was the priesthood of Demeter Eleusinia, in favour of his brother.[2] He was out of humour with a rising democracy, which had exiled the legislator Hermodoros; on which Strabo quotes him as saying, 'The Ephesians might as well go hang themselves, every man, and leave the city to boys, since they have driven out Hermodoros, the best man among them, saying, "Of us let no one man be best – and if one is, let him be best somewhere else and among other men!"'[3] He is dated about 500[4]; but no details were known of his life, except what could be deduced from the book or collection of oracular dicta which he left, dedicated, it is said, in the Temple of Artemis.[5] The book was much studied, not only its real profundity but its proverbially obscure style constituting a challenge to scholars; and from it some of the little men of antiquity endeavoured with childish ingenuity to extract a biography, preserved for us by the good Diogenes.

Herakleitos is the last of the great Ionian primitives of philosophy. His approach to the question 'What is the stuff of the world?' is as direct and naive as that of the Milesians; but if Anaximenes, as Schrödinger says (p. 341), deserved credit for saying 'a mist', or matter in its simplest form, then so does Herakleitos for saying, 'Fire'; for thus to him matter, animate and inanimate, and the energies of men, all are

---

[1] The fragments of Herakleitos, much more numerous than those of his predecessors, are cited here according to the numeration of Bywater and Diels-Kranz; e.g. in n. 6, 20/30 signifies fr. 20 Byw., 30 DK (part 22 B); sources follow; citations of other passages from ancient authors are introduced by 'cf.'.

[2] Antisthenes, *ap.* D.L. ix, 6; Pherekydes, *ap.* Str. xiv, 632*.

[3] xiv, 642.   [4] D.L. ix, 1.

[5] *ib.* 6. – Ar. (*Rhet.* 1407b) criticises its (primitive) punctuation.

transformations of one cosmic energy. The world is eternal: 'This world, the same for all, no one made, either of gods or men; but it was always and is and shall be an everliving fire, measures kindling and measures going out.'[6] 'The same for all' takes up another of his leading doctrines, approved by scientists today, that of the real as the 'public' world: 'Men awake have one world in common, but in sleep they turn aside, each into a world of his own.'[7] 'Wherefore one must follow the common; but though the word is common, the majority live as though they had private insight (*phronesis*).'[8] 'Word' is *logos*; in Herakleitos, no doubt literally the spoken or written word, his own discourse; but inasmuch as the *logos* is thought made public, it begins already to carry the sense of 'reason'. His first sentence may have been, after the author's name: 'But though this word IS (true) for ever, men fail to understand it, both before hearing it and when they hear it for the first time; for though all things happen according to this word, they are like men of no experience when they experience such words and deeds as I relate, distinguishing each according to its nature and declaring how it is; but the rest of men are as unaware of what they do when awake as they are forgetful of what (they experience) in sleep.'[9]

The *cosmos* is eternal, but things within it are ever changing. 'All things flow' was a summary of this part of his argument: 'One cannot step into the same river twice.'[10] 'All things are exchanged for fire and fire for all things, as are goods for gold and gold for goods.'[11] 'Fire lives the death of air and air lives the death of fire, water lives the death of earth and earth of water.'[12] 'The first turning of fire is the sea; and of the sea, half is earth and half whirlwind.'[13] What prevents the eternal flux from being a chaos is Measure: 'The Sun will not overstep his measures; or the Furies, the servants of Zeus, will find him out.'[14] The anthropomorphic language is to be understood metaphorically. God to Herakleitos is not anthropomorphic: 'That one thing that alone is wise both wishes and does not wish to be called Zeus.'[15] 'God is day and night, summer and winter, war and peace, satiety and want'[16]; but, just as 'the most beautiful ape is ugly compared to the human race', so

---

[6] 20/30; Clem. *Strom.* v, 105.   [7] 95/89; Plut. (*On Superstition*) *Mor.* 166c.
[8] 92/2; Sext. Emp. vii, 133.   [9] 2/1; *Sext. ib.*
[10] 41/91; Plut. *Mor.* 392b; cf. Plato, *Kratylos*, 402a (where, as usual in Plato, it is hard to say how much is precise verbal quotation); comment, Ar. *Metaph.* 1010a.
[11] 22/90; Plut. *ib.*   [12] 25/76; M. Aurelius, iv, 46 (*et al.*, see *ad loc.*).
[13] 21/31; Clem. Al., after 20/30, see n. 5 above.   [14] 29/94; Plut. *Mor.* 604.
[15] 65/32; Clem. *Strom.* v, 116.   [16] 36/67; Hippol. *Ref. Her.* ix, 10.

'the wisest of men is an ape compared with God, both in wisdom and beauty and in everything else'.[17]

The mutual transformations of the elements in the 'flowing' world may be compared to a war: 'War is the father and king of all things, and has made some men gods, some slaves and some free'[18]; 'men must know that war is common (to all), and justice is strife, and all things happen through strife and must (do so)'.[19] Sometimes one element gets the upper hand; a doctrine which the Stoics perhaps inferred from him was that our aeon will end in a conflagration: 'Fire will come and judge and overtake all things.'[20] But Anaximandros, he seems to imply, is wrong when he calls this 'injustice'. 'They would not have known the name of justice, had not this been so.'[21] 'To God, all things are beautiful and good and just; but men reckon some things unjust and some just.'[22] The cosmos is 'a harmony (or "a structure", *harmonia*) of opposite tensions, as in the lyre and the bow'.[23] Opposites are intimately connected: 'The way up and the way down are the same'[24]; 'Sickness makes health sweet and good; hunger, satiety; weariness, rest.'[25] Our judgments are relative: 'Donkeys prefer chaff to gold.'[26] The doctrine of the unity of opposites, taken up by Hegel (he explicitly says, from Herakleitos) and from Hegel transmitted to the dialectical materialism of Marx and Lenin, has thus been among the most influential of all Ionian intuitions.

For all his brilliant pontificating about the cosmos, he is not deeply interested in scientific details; differing in this from the Milesians. The best that can be said for his guesses on astronomy is that they are original: the stars are 'cups' of fire with their open sides towards us, and there is 'a new sun every day'.[27] He is said to have referred to Thales' astronomical interests,[28] and from the tone in which he invariably refers to earlier thinkers when his words are quoted, it is likely that he censured him for his interest in detail. His own procedure is less scientific and more mystical. Wisdom is to know one thing, not many: 'One thing is the wise: to know judgment (*gnomen*): how all things are steered through all things'[29]; and the source of his own philosophy is

---

[17] 98-9/82-3; Plato, *Hippias I*, 289a.   [18] 44/53; Hippol. *ib.*
[19] 62/80; Origen *Against Celsus*, vi, 42.   [20] 26/66; Hippol. *ib.*
[21] 60/23; Clem. *Strom.* iii, 10; cf. Ar. *Eud. Eth.* 1235a (DK 22 A 22).
[22] 61/102; Porphyry, i, 69, 6 Schröder.   [23] 45/51 (cf. By. 56); Hippol. *Ref.* ix, 9.
[24] 69/60; Hippol. *Ref.* ix, 10.   [25] 104b/111; Stobaios, *Fl.* i, 177.
[26] 51/9; Ar. *N. Eth.* 1176a. [27] D.L. ix, 10 (and cf. ix, 7-11 *passim* on H.'s cosmology).
[28] D.L. i, 23.   [29] 19/41; D.L. ix, 1.

his own mind: 'I searched myself.'[30] Of almost all predecessors he is contemptuous. Homer could not solve the riddle of the fisher-boys, when he asked them what they had been catching and they said, 'What we saw and caught, we left behind, and what we did not see or catch, we bring with us'[31] (interesting as an early reference to the legendary *Life of Homer*). The answer was 'Lice'. 'Hesiod is the teacher of most; they think he knows the most – he who did not recognise night and day; for they are one.'[32] 'He said Homer ought to be chased out of the Games and beaten, and Archilochos too.'[33] 'Learning many things does not teach wisdom; else, it would have taught Hesiod and Pythagoras, and Xenophanes too, and Hekataios',[34] the Milesian statesman and geographer. 'Pythagoras the son of Mnesarchos practised enquiry (*historie*) most of all men, and having made a selection of these writings claimed a wisdom of his own: a lot of learning, a mischievous skill.'[35] The only sage for whom he has a good word is Bias, 'who had more reason than the rest'.[36] (He said, 'Most men are bad.'[37])

Herakleitos' knowledge of Pythagoras is interesting. He may have known of his reputation at Samos, though in view of the amount of coming and going (but at this time chiefly going) he *may* also have heard of him from Kroton. He was not sympathetic to the mystery-religions, though he knew something of them too; nor did he think much of popular religion in general. 'Men try to purify themselves all wrong, staining themselves with blood, as though after stepping in mud one were to wash in mud. . . . And they pray to these statues, as though one were to hold conversation with houses, not knowing what gods and heroes really are'.[38] (The evidence *from a Greek* is interesting, as showing that Greek religion really could, as the Jews alleged, become naive idolatry.) He girded at 'night-walkers, magi, *bakchoi*, wine-vat celebrants, *mystai*' (the reference to the Median magi is of interest; their dualism may have interested him); he threatens them with trouble

---

[30] 80/101; Plut. *Mor.* 1118c; cf. D.L. ix, 5.

[31] Byw., note on fr. 47; 56 DK; Hippol. *Ref.* ix, 9; cf. ps.-Plut. *Life of Homer* (*Vitae Homeri*, ed. Wilamowitz, p. 23).

[32] 35/57; Hippol. *Ref.* ix, 10.

[33] D.L. ix, 1.

[34] *ib.* Cf. Lao-tze (?), *Tao Tê Ching*, ch. 81.

[35] 17/129; D.L. viii, 6; genuineness doubted by Diels and others, but not by Kranz; cf. (in favour) Bywater *ad loc.*, Burnet *EGP* p. 134 n. 2, Kirk and Raven, *Presocr. Phil.* p. 219 n. 1.   [36] 112/39; D.L. i, 88.   [37] *ib.*

[38] 129, 130, 126 (in that order), Byw.; better as one fr. (5 DK); Origen, *Against Celsus*, vii, 62, keeping the ms. reading (*allos*).

after death, for all their esoteric lore, 'for the mysteries that are in favour among men introduce their initiates in unholy fashion'.[39] 'If it were not to Dionysos that they made their procession and sang a hymn to the shameful parts, they would have been behaving most shamelessly. But Dionysos, in whose honour they go mad and revel, is the same as Hades.'[40] Elsewhere, impressively, 'There await men after death such things as they hope not, nor expect'[41]; but, 'If a man hope not, he shall not find what he does not hope, that is beyond search and attainment.'[42] Some have also found a reference to the doctrine of the mysteries in the cryptic saying, 'Time is a child at play, playing draughts; the kingdom is a child's'; we are reminded of the playthings of the Divine Child, and also of some of the late Orphic writings, in which a personified Time is among the deities.[43]

He had no patience with magic rites, or with those with which Greeks tried to make their dead more comfortable: food and drink offerings, burial of gear and clothing. 'Corpses ought to be thrown out – more so than muck.'[44] The fiery soul was what mattered. Since water is the 'first transformation' of fire, 'it is death to souls to become water'.[45] The souls of the uncontrolled can positively be seen drowning: 'When a man is drunk, he is led by a beardless boy, stumbling and not knowing where he steps, having a wet soul.'[46] So, 'it is not best for men to obtain all they wish'.[47] 'A dry soul is wisest and best.'[48] But the souls of the wise and spirited do not thus drown, but leave the body with their fire undimmed; among these he includes specifically those killed in battle – those, it has been suggested, who die in the acme of health, not in sickness, with their 'fiery' impulses dominant. 'Gods and men honour those killed in battle'; and 'Greater deaths win greater portions.'[49] Bishop Hippolytos, who was ready to claim this sage, revered by the Stoics, as a *präexistent Christlicher* and superior to the heretics of his own day, attributes to him the doctrine that such heroes

---

[39] 124-5/14; Clem. *Protrep.* 22.
[40] 129/15; Clem. *ib.* 34.
[41] 122/27; Clem. *Strom.* ii, 312.
[42] 7/18; *id.* ii, 17.
[43] 79/52; Hippol. *Ref.* ix, 9 (though the word is different; *Aion* in Herakl., *Chronos* in the late Orphika, e.g. Kern, *Orph. Fr.* nos. 54ff).
'Neither word is known in connection with any *early* Gk. mysteries; the later Chronos is borrowed from Persian Zervanism. Nor are draughts among the toys of Dionysos. The reference is purely moonshine.' – E.R.D.
[44] 85/96; Plut. (Sympos. iv, 4) 644f.
[45] 68/36; Clem. *Strom.* vi, 16.
[46] 73/117; Stob. *Fl.* v, 7.
[47] 104a/110; *id.* i, 176.
[48] 76/118; *id.* v, 8.
[49] 102/24, 101/25; Clem. *Strom.* iv, 16 and 50; cf. Kirk, *Presocr. Phil.* p. 210.

enjoyed an after-life of service: 'to rise up again and to become waking
guardians of the living and dead'.[50] Hippolytos also quotes the typically
Herakleitan line: 'immortal mortals, mortal immortals, living the
death of those and dying their life'.[51] It is not unlike the view of the
heroic man which was to be held by Pindar and Empedokles (pp. 365,
377f).

In this, as also in his political dicta, Herakleitos echoes the current
thought of his age; he accommodates to his own philosophy ideas that
would have been familiar to a Tyrtaios or a Phokylides. His ethics are
summed up in the fine saying, 'Character is a man's *daimon*'[52] – his
tutelary spirit, and so his fate, as in the current word *eudaimon*, 'happy';
a sentence that asserts freewill and moral responsibility against popular
fatalism. So, in politics, he asserts the claims of law. '*Hybris* is to be
suppressed more than a conflagration.'[53] 'The people should fight for
its law as for its walls.'[54] The law, like truth, represents what is common or 'public'; 'for all human laws have their sustenance from one
(law?) that is divine'.[55] He seems aware of some inconsistency between
this doctrine and his contempt for the assembly which had rejected
Hermodoros, and argues, 'It is law also to obey the counsel of one
man.'[56] 'One man is ten thousand to me, if he be the best.'[57]

He was aware of the difficulty of his epigrammatic and oracular style,
the style which, beside the nickname of 'the Weeping Philosopher'
gained him in Roman times that of 'the Dark' or 'Obscure'[58]; a difficulty due, surely, less to 'aristocratic disdain' than to the inherent
difficulty of his task, tackling, as he was, highly abstract questions with
an early-iron-age language. He did not regard that style as beyond
criticism. It is to an oracle (not a poet or entertainer) that he compares
himself. Plutarch *On the Pythian Oracles* twice cites him, the first time
in paraphrase: 'The Sibyl "with raving lips", as Herakleitos says,
"speaking words unamusing, unadorned with cosmetics or perfume,
reaches through a thousand years with her speech", through the god.'

---

[50] 123/63; Hippol. *Ref.* ix, 10.   [51] 67/62; Hippol. *ib.*
[52] 121/119; Stob. *Fl.* iv, 40, 23.   [53] 103/43; D.L. ix, 2.
[54] 100/44; *ib.*   [55] 91b/114; Stob. *Fl.* i, 179.
[56] 110/33; Clem. *Strom.* v, 116.   [57] 113/49; Galen *et al.*

[58] *Ainiktes*, 'speaker in riddles', Timon of Phlious, *ap.* D.L. ix, 6; *obscurus*, Cicero, *De
Fin.* ii, 5/15, etc. On the phrase 'Weeping Philosopher', Kirk well says that this judgment
is 'entirely trivial', and founded partly on Theophrastos' reference to his *melancholia* (*ap.*
D.L. *ib.*), which did not as yet mean 'melancholy' but 'impulsiveness' (cf. Ar. *N. Eth.*
1150b): *Presocr. Philosophers*, p. 184.

It is impossible to say just how much of this is in Herakleitos' words; but a little later, Plutarch quotes verbally: 'the lord of the Delphic Oracle, neither tells nor conceals, but gives a sign.'[59]

Herakleitos was not a major influence upon the thinkers who immediately followed him; the early atomists look back rather to Anaximenes and the Pythagoreans, and take account of Parmenides. But he was not forgotten; he was used, according to their lights, by sceptical sophists; and later he came into his own. He was well known to Plato; he was honoured and interpreted, sometimes arbitrarily, by generations of Stoics, and is treated with respect by early Christian scholars. Lastly, no pre-Socratic has had so much influence upon modern thought, especially through Hegel (p. 397). The primitive epoch of the movement that began with Thales comes to a worthy close in the work of this profound and lonely genius.

[59] 11/93; 29/94; Plut. *Mor.* 397a, 404d.

On the Dates in this Book

THE ancient chronologists, on whom our predecessors were dependent for the dates in early Greek history, give some dates which are certainly and some more which are probably considerably too early. The clearest cases are some which can now be checked from contemporary oriental sources. Such are the dates of Bokkhoris (Dyn. XXIV) and the first recorded post-Homeric Greek contacts with Egypt (*acc.* 780 Jerome; 778 in the Armenian version of Eusebios, ed. Schoene, II, pp. 76-7; true date, *c.* 718, see p. 55 above); and of Gyges, according to Herodotos, 714-686, recorded by Asshurbanipal's archives to have fallen in battle after 648. Some other dates, especially of colonies which have been excavated, can be approximately checked from the evidence of Greek pottery styles. Care is necessary, since our customary dates for these still rest largely on the literary evidence, especially that of Thucydides for the Sicilian colonies (vi, 3ff). As Dunbabin pointed out (*Western Greeks*, pp. 435ff), Thucydides and the best of the other literary evidence did put the chief foundations in the right order; but the recent work of Vallet and Villard on Selinous and Marseilles (pp. 144-6, nn. 41, 50) suggests that even his dates may have to be scaled down. Some other traditional dates, again, are commonly reduced in modern books on grounds of inherent probability: e.g. Theopompos of Sparta, an epoch-making figure – the conqueror of Messene named by Tyrtaios, and the king who accepted the limitation of the monarchy according to Aristotle (*Politics*, 1313*a*) – *accessit* 785 (Apollodoros) or thereabouts (variations collected by Clinton, *F.H.* I, pp. 337f); but since he is only the eighth ancestor of Latychidas (Leotychides), *fl.* 479 (Hdt. viii, 131), he is usually dated much nearer 700 (as e.g. by Wade-Gery in *CAH* III, 537, n. 2).

Nevertheless, some dates, especially of some of the eastern colonies, which are too early, still lurk in some modern books.

Among Eusebios' sources, one at least assigned to the mid-eighth century a number of colonial foundations, for instance, which another of his sources, almost certainly quite rightly, assigned to the seventh. Repeatedly, he *quotes* widely differing dates; he was a good scholar, and it is most unlikely that he did this from mere carelessness. He thought the earlier dates of sufficient authority to deserve quotation. Unfortunately, if he discussed this difference between his sources, his discussion has not come down to us. E.g. Jerome's

Latin edition (the Armenian has a page missing) also records the fall of Assyria both in the generation of 844-818 and in 619 and 608 (Arm. concurring; probably the duration of the final war was intended), of which the later dates are approximately right. Among his Greek dates we find (sometimes with variations of a year or two among the versions, which probably arise simply from the difficulty of fitting events on to single lines in a manuscript date-chart) the following:

Foundation of Cyrene, 761, 758	(True date *c.* 630, Hdt. iv; p. 137 above)
Foundation of Trapezous, 756	(Its mother-city Sinope is founded 629, Jerome, Synkellos)
Foundation of Kyzikos, 755	(675 Arm., Synkellos; 679 Jerome)
Foundation of Naukratis, 747 (cf. Polycharmos of Naukratis, *ap.* Ath. xv, 675-6, on a Naukratite trading with Cyprus in 688)	(Under Dyn. XXVI, i.e. after 650, Hdt., Strabo; p. 129 above)
Thales *agnoscitur*, 747	(*Agnoscitur* 640 Jer., 639 Arm., 636 Synk.; foretold eclipse 585 Arm., 584 Jer.; died 547 Arm., 546 Jer.)

Similarly, the tyranny of Phalaris *apud Acragantinos* is dated 650 to 619 (before the city was founded according to Thucydides and the archaeologists!) as well as for sixteen years from 570 or 567. Eusebios' dates for the reign of Gyges (698-663) are more moderate than those of Herodotos, though still too early; and his *floruit* for Archilochos, 664 or 663 (along with 'Simonides', i.e. Semon-ides of Samos and Amorgos) is probably well within Archilochos' lifetime.

But for Archilochos too (a cardinal date for the growth of Greek civilisation) there was an earlier reckoning, recorded by Cicero (*Tusc.* i, 1): *regnante Romulo*. This would be entirely consistent with the dating of the colonisation of Thasos (not in Eusebios) in which Archilochos took part under the leadership of his father, to Olympiad 15 or 18, 720-705 B.C., according to Dionysios (Periegetes?) and Xanthos respectively (*ap.* Clem. Alex. *Stromateis*, i, 21). This date must be brought down, to accord with the true date of Gyges, whom the poet mentioned (Hdt. i, 12). (*No* ancient source speaks of Archilochos taking part in 'an early reinforcement' of this colony.) The traditional date of the foundation of Parion (708 Eus. Arm., 710 Jerome) must then also be brought down, since it was a daughter colony of Thasos (p. 108, above); just as that of its neighbour Abydos must be accommodated to that of Gyges, who authorised its founda-tion (Strabo, xiii, 590); while Priapos and Prokonnesos were founded 'about the same time', *id.* 587. Astakos, later Nikomedeia (705 Arm., 710 Jerome) must also be later, as it was a daughter-colony of Kalchadon (Chalcedon), founded 684 according to some mss. of Jerome (*anno* 1332, ed. Fotheringham) or 674/1342 (Clinton, *F.H.*; not in Arm. or Synkellos; om. Schoene); and Kal-chadon itself should probably be brought down to about 646: seventeen years

(Hdt. iv, 144) before Byzantion, which was dated 629 by a local historian (p. 114).

Of the Black Sea colonies, the eras of some are given in the poem, by an unknown local writer, formerly attributed to Skymnos of Chios, in terms of synchronisms with events in near eastern history. We have no means of checking the accuracy of the synchronisms; but if they *are* right, they too indicate that some of Eusebios' dates are too early. Thus, Istros (656/4 Eus.) is dated by 'Skymnos' 'at the time of the Scythian invasion of Asia'; i.e. towards the end of the century. Borysthenes (Olbia), founded 644 according to Jerome, is dated by 'Skymnos' 'at the time of the Median Empire', which, historically, should mean after the fall of Nineveh in 612. The earliest pottery from the site, according to current archaeological systems, suggests that Eusebios here was not far wrong; but finds of Protocorinthian ware at Selinous now suggest that some traditional 'pottery-dates' are in turn too early (see Chap. VII, n. 41). Other Eusebian dates for colonies, such as Abdera (abortive, Hdt. i, 168), Lampsakos, Akanthos and Stageira (all 655–650) cannot be checked; but it is obviously rash to treat any of them as verbally inspired.

In the sixth century, as we approach the age of historical writing, there is less room for serious error; but even here, indications in Herodotos, our only authority not separated by centuries from the events, suggest (though he does not give a systematic chronology) that the dates about 600, worked out by the chronographers, are too high. Thus, in Herodotos, Periandros' dealings with Alyattes of Lydia are said to be 'a generation before' the Spartan expedition against Polykrates about 525 (iii, 48); the Kypselidai are still important at the time of the Bridal of Agariste (*c.* 570) (vi, 128); and Aristokypros, the son of Philokypros the king of Soloi who was visited and named in his poems by Solon, was killed in battle about 498 (Hdt. v, 113). This is possible, if Solon about 580 met Philokypros when still young; but it is obviously easier if Solon's archonship (dated 594 by Sosikrates, *ap.* Diog. L. i, 62, and *vulgo* (after Clinton, vol. II, p. 298) but 592 in the *Ath. Pol.* and variously in our versions of Eusebios: 593 Jerome ed. Fotheringham, 591 Jerome ed. Schoene, 590 Arm. ed. Schoene) was really later. The variations, even ignoring those within the Eusebios ms. tradition, do not suggest that the date was recorded on a contemporary and trustworthy archon-list. In like manner but with stronger reasons, one must doubt the date for the death of Periandros, 585 (Sosikr. *ap.* D.L. i, 95), and therewith the Eusebian dates for the whole dynasty, 658–586 inclusive.

Why, it must be asked, did Greek chronographers so often get their dates too early? The methodological question, on which this depends, is why they adopted a palpable over-estimate of forty, or it seems rather, thirty-nine years, for the generations of the Spartan kings. The Spartan genealogies, which we are fortunate to have quoted by Herodotos (see above) were rightly regarded as providing a valuable framework for the chronology of our period. Authentic they almost certainly are, for some centuries back from the generation of 500-480; the most reassuring fact about them is that neither contains the name of the legislator Lykourgos, whom any 'heraldic' pedigree-faker would certainly have worked in. But the average length of their generations in the fifth-fourth centuries is, in both houses, just over thirty-one years; reigns, a little more numerous because sometimes two in a generation, average just over twenty-five years. (English sovereigns crowned since 1066 average just over twenty-three years, as do Kings of France from 840 to 1793; Kings of Scots from Malcolm Canmore (*acc.* 1057) to James VI (d. 1625), nearly twenty-six.)[1]

But the Greek chronographers also tried to synchronise the Spartan king-lists with others, such as those of Corinth, and with the lists of prehistoric kings (most of them clearly mythical) and later archons for life compiled at Athens; and it so happened that, for the period from the last Athenian king, Kodros, killed by the Dorians, to the life-archon Aischylos, synchronised with Theopompos at Sparta, Athens gave thirteen names for a period which Theopompos' pedigree was held to cover in nine generations. It would obviously be highly convenient if the period was estimated at a number of years which could be divided both by nine and thirteen and by a number of years that could be that of a generation. This, according to an attractive theory,[2] may it seems, actually have been done: the proposed total being 351 years $= 39 \times 9$, $= 27 \times 13$. If the same supposed average length for Spartan reigns was then continued for seven generations more, down to the invasion of Xerxes in 480, the beginning of the Dorian kingdom, sixteen generations before, would fall in 1104; Kodros and twelve Athenian life-archons would cover the years 1104 to 754 inclusive, and a new epoch, that of Athenian archons elected for limited terms, roughly coinciding with the beginning of the age of colonisation, would begin in the (afterwards famous) year 753. There certainly does seem to have been a view current (and quite rightly) that a new period of rapid development did begin

---

[1] Beloch (*GG* I, ii, p. 1) denies the authenticity, beyond a couple of generations, of any orally transmitted pedigrees; but his argument depends on a false analogy with modern conditions. Even private (e.g. Athenian aristocratic) pedigrees probably were preserved with some care, as being, in the age before legal documents, the sole titles to lands and citizen rights; family cults and grave-monuments were expected to be adduced as evidence in support, cf. *Ath. Pol.* lv, 3. For the transmission of a long royal pedigree in the Scottish Highlands so late as A.D. 1250, cf. John of Fordun's *Chronicle* (v, ch. 48; ed. Skene, vol. I, pp. 294f) on the *montanus* who stepped forth from the crowd at the coronation of Alexander III, and saluted the young king by name and by the names of all his ancestors back to Fergus, an historical character, the first King of Scots in Alba, and beyond him to Gathelus, the eponymous ancestor of the Gael.
[2] The theory of Dr M. Miller; see her 'Herodotus as Chronographer', in *Klio* XLVI (1965); summary by Burn in *JHS* LXIX (1949).

about the seventh and eighth generations before 480; and in the opinion of some person or persons, whose views influenced both Eusebios' and much earlier Greek chronography, every kind of movement had to begin or to be revolutionised about that time. Within the middle twenty years of the eighth century, we have reported the end of the life archonship at Athens, the first ephors at Sparta (757/6), the end of the monarchy at Corinth (ninety years before the usurpation of Kypselos or *c.* 747), and King Pheidon at Argos (at Olympia 748, Paus. vi, 22). We have reported the first colonies in the Marmara and the Black Sea, in Cyrenaica and in Egypt; as well as Syracuse, dated a little later, 735, through the authority of Thucydides, but founded by Archias, who, according to the Parian Marble, was 'tenth from Temenos', like Pheidon of Argos. In literature we have Archilochos according to some (though not to Eusebios); and finally, for good measure, Thales of Miletos. It comes to appear almost inevitable that the year 753 itself (or adjacent years according to some Roman calculations) was adopted as the era of the foundation of Rome, likewise seven reigns (the last cut short) before the generation of 480; a site on which archaeologists are, here too, now disposed to date the first scanty remains about the mid-seventh century.

As to who first adopted the thirty-nine-year generation, we are without information; but it was probably early. It is noteworthy that there seem to be traces of it even in Herodotos. Kleomenes of Sparta first appears in 519 (480 + 39; Hdt. vi, 108, cf. Thk. iii, 68, 5); Cyrus and Croesus both come to the throne in 559/8; the four earlier Mermnadai reign for 156 years (Gyges *acc.* 714 = 480 + 39 × 6), and so do the four Kings of the Medes, including the twenty-eight years of the Scythian anarchy (Hdt. i, 106, 1, cf. 130, 1, on the interpretation favoured by Meyer, *Forschungen z. Alten Gesch.* I, 153ff). A strong candidate is Hellanikos, from whom we find Plutarch quoting the statement 'Theseus was fifty years old when he' [carried off Helen]! (*Theseus*, 31). 'Herodotos . . . certainly did not invent any dating methods, and we must suppose that he took over (the above) from a predecessor, who was more of a "pure mathematician" – which means Hellanikos, the only candidate.' – M. Miller, in a letter.

It must be noted, finally, that the earliest Greek chronography did not use as an epoch the now famous date 776 B.C., the First Olympiad. The Parian Marble of 264 still does not use it, though Thucydides had begun to use Olympiads for dating for contemporary history. Its use probably first became possible after the publication of the list of victors by Hippias of Elis, who, according to Plutarch (*Numa*, 1) found no very compelling evidence to work on. Even if there had been a complete list from 776, it must be pointed out that it is most unlikely that it would have added references to contemporary historic events. In fact, it seems likely that Hippias compiled the list from names found in local legends. The list, so far as preserved in our scattered sources, can now be conveniently studied in the work of Dr Luigi Moretti, *Olympionikai* (*Acc. Naz. dei Lincei*, Serie VIII, vol. VIII, 2, 1957); where it will be found that nearly all the early names, like that of Koroibos, the first recorded victor himself, are those of locally famous legendary heroes. It was probably reserved for none other than Hippias to arrange them in order.

In these circumstances, I have thought it best often to quote dates from our sources with the appended reminder 'tr.' (traditionally). They are the work of sensible men, who did their best with what they had, fitting stories derived from oral saga, or preserved by mention in lyric and elegiac poetry, into a framework derived from genealogies or more or less reliable lists of kings or magistrates or victors, sometimes themselves, for the earlier periods, later compilations. They are seldom (I believe, never) certainly exact before the late sixth century. The Trojan War, outside our period, must, it now seems clear with the continued progress of archaeology, be dated in the great days of Mycenae, before 1200; if Eratosthenes and his predecessors were not far wrong in computing its end at 1183/2 (but Kallimachos 1127, Ephoros 1136, Sosibios 1172, the Parian Marble 1209/8), they were lucky as well as clever. I would withdraw what now seems to me my quaint suggestion of twenty-five years ago that it should be dated about 1000 on the strength of the Herakleid genealogies (*JHS* XXXV, p. 146); Wade-Gery is right: 'the end of the second millennium was a time of utter exhaustion', which 'stretched chronologies artificially bridge' (*The Poet of the Iliad*, pp. 27f and nn.). At twenty-five years per reign, the Spartan pedigrees (or king-lists?) take us back to the *eponymoi*, Agis and Eurypon, early in the ninth century, the age of the early geometric pottery which marks the beginning of the recovery. 'What is always suspect is the filiation, beyond the eponymous ancestor, to a too famous legendary name: as of the Spartan kings to Herakles' (Wade-Gery, *op. cit.* p. 66). For the period covered in this book, I find myself in general agreement with Beloch (*GG* I, ii, chaps. xx, 'Die zweite Kolonisationsperiode', and xxv, 'Die Kypseliden'); and in disagreement with Blakeway on the date of Archilochos, in *Greek Poetry and Life*, the Essays presented to Gilbert Murray; refuted by Jacoby in *CQ* LV (1935), pp. 97ff.

Index

Not every proper name occurring in this book has been indexed; e.g. not those of later writers, if mentioned only as authorities, even in the text. Individual Bakchiad kings must be sought *via* Bakchiadai, members of Sappho's circle *via* Sappho, and many *oikistai* under their colonies. 'Inseparable' pairs (*e.g.* Dipoinos and Skyllis) are indexed under their first component only. Non-Greek geographical names occurring only once or twice are indexed selectively, and allusions to matters treated elsewhere are ignored (e.g. the story of Tellos is mentioned three times, but indexed once). It is hoped that such an index may be more useful for the purpose of tracing information and (especially) references to authorities, ancient and modern, than an index compiled on mechanical principles or an exhaustive bibliography.

References of the form (e.g.) '48n14', without stops, indicate that the information indexed is in the Note.

Long vowels in Greek are indicated below by the circumflex, ^; with the exceptions of diphthongs, final -*e* and, in men's names, -*es* and -*on*, which are invariably long.